POLITICAL DICTIONARY OF THE STATE OF ISRAEL

POLITICAL DICTIONARY OF THE STATE OF ISRAEL

Susan Hattis Rolef, Editor

SECOND EDITION

SUPPLEMENT 1987 – 1993

(From Page 348)

MACMILLAN PUBLISHING COMPANY
New York

MAXWELL MACMILLAN CANADA
Toronto

MAXWELL MACMILLAN INTERNATIONAL
New York Oxford Singapore Sydney

Macmillan Publishing Company
866 Third Avenue, New York, N.Y. 10022

Maxwell Macmillan Canada
1200 Eglinton Avenue East
Suite 200
Don Mills, Ontario M3C 3N1

Library of Congress Catalog Card Number:
93–20521

Set, printed and bound by
Keter Publishing House, Jerusalem

Printed in Israel

printing number
1 2 3 4 5 6 7 8 9 10

Library of Congress Cataloging-in-Publication Data

Political dictionary of the state of Israel / Susan Hattis Rolef, editor.—2nd ed.
p. cm.
ISBN 0–02–897193–0 : $55.00
1. Israel—Politics and government—Dictionaries. I. Rolef, Susan Hattis.
DS126.5.P62 1993 93–20521
320.95694'03—dc20 CIP

FOREWORD

The *Political Dictionary of the State of Israel* is an attempt to give the reader basic, reliable information on all aspects of Israeli politics. In some 450 articles arranged alphabetically, it deals with prominent personalities and controversial political figures; parties and other political groups including all the parties which ever entered the Knesset (parliament), and most of the Jewish parties from Mandatory times; outstanding events — the Arab-Israel wars as well as the sensational affairs that have shaken the Israeli political scene from time to time; the Knesset and how it functions; the electoral system and coalition agreements; the media; Israel's economic and foreign policy; its relations with the Great Powers and other nations and with the Diaspora.

Special terms used with a particular connotation are explained in the light of their political implications, such as "status quo," "Masada complex," or "Without *Ḥerut* or *Maki*." We have also included some expressions in Hebrew which have become familiar in Israel even to people not speaking the language. Historical background is given in entries such as Mandatory Palestine, Zionism and the Arab-Israel conflict. Cross references to other relevant entries are indicated by an asterisk (*) in the text.

In the transliteration of Hebrew words and nam… n represented by *ḥ* and the
letter *kaf* by *ch*; in modern Israeli Heb… ttish *loch* or German *ach*.
Where two consecutive vo… has been used to divide
them. Parties and ins… glish or are consistently
referred to in the En… are listed under these
names. A glossary of … 351.

In 1971, the late Evy… *Political Dictionary of*
the Middle East in the 20t… the current edition
the dictionary was divid… *h World*, by Yaacov
Shimoni and the *Political* … written by Evyatar
Levine for the original ed…

The list of entries was c… jects, politicians,
civil servants and journalists … ary; their initials
appear at the end of the artic…

In addition I should like to … tries: Professor
Michel Abitbul; Uri Avneri, … r of the army
magazine *Ma'archot*; former M… rish (Labor);
Haim Kubersky, formerly Dir… Yossi Sarid
(CRM); Professor Alice Shalvi; … uel Tamir;
and last but not least, MK Moha…

Of the contributors, special me… arty who
made himself constantly available. … illel who
offered moral support for the projec… assisted
me beyond the call of duty. Needles… is book
would never have materialized.

I should like to dedicate this diction… duced
me to the fascinating world of Israeli …

Jerusalem, March 1987 … THE EDITOR

CONTRIBUTORS

A.A.	ARIEH AVNERI	Journalist, *Yediot Aḥaronot* newspaper
A.B.	AVI BECKER, PhD	Lecturer, Bar Ilan University; Dir., Jerusalem office of the World Jewish Congress
Al.B.	ALEXANDER BLEIGH, PhD	Coordinator, Biographical Dictionary of Leading Palestinians project, Truman Center, Hebrew Univ.
A.D.	AVRAHAM DISKIN, PhD	Sen. Lecturer, Dept. of Political Science, Hebrew Univ.
A.E.	ABBA EBAN	Chairman of Knesset Foreign Affairs and Security Committee; previously Foreign Minister
A.K.	AHARON KLIEMAN, Prof.	Dept. of Political Science, Tel Aviv Univ.
A.N.	AMNON NEUSTADT, PhD	Lecturer in Political Science, Tel Aviv Univ.
A.S.	AVRAHAM SELAH, PhD	Lecturer in International Relations, Hebrew Univ.
D.A.	DANNY AZRIEL	Attorney
D.B.M	DOV BEN-MEIR	Labor Member of Knesset, Deputy Mayor of Tel Aviv
D.G.R.	DIANE G. ROSENSHINE	Movement of Masorti Judaism in Israel
D.H.	DAN HOROWITZ, Prof.	Dept. of Political Science, Hebrew Univ. Entries "Yishuv" and "Mandatory Palestine" adapted from *Origins of the Israeli Polity* (Chicago Univ. Press 1978)
E.L.	EVYATAR LEVINE	Attorney and Journalist — deceased
El.L	ELIAHU LENKIN	Attorney, previously commander of the *Altalena*
G.Y.	GAD YAACOBI	Minister of Economics and Planning
H.B.	ḤAIM BARKAI, Prof.	Dept. of Economics, Hebrew Univ.
H.F.S.	HENRY FRANK SKIRBOL, PhD	Reform Rabbi, Dir. of the Union of American Hebrew Congregations in Jerusalem
H.H.	ḤAIM HERZOG	President of Israel
I.M.	ISRAEL MEDAD	Coordinator, *Teḥiyah* Knesset faction, assistant to Member of Knesset Geula Cohen
I.P.	ISRAEL PELEG, PhD	Dir., Government Press Office
I.R.	ITAMAR RABINOWITZ, Prof.	Dir., Dayan Center, Tel Aviv Univ. Entry "Lebanon and Israel" adapted from *The War for Lebanon 1970–1985* (Cornell Univ. Press 1985)
J.H.	JEFF HALPER, PhD	Lecturer in Anthropology, Hebrew Univ.
J.K.	JUDITH KARP	Deputy Attorney General
L.L.	LEOPOLD LAUFER, PhD	Researcher, Truman Center, Hebrew Univ.
M.A.	MENASHE AMIR	Journalist, *Kol Yisrael* Radio

M.B.	MERON BENVENISTI	Dir., West Bank Data Project; all entries excluding "Benvenisti Prognosis" adapted from *West Bank Handbook* (*Jerusalem Post* 1986)
M.B.Z.	MICHAEL BAR-ZOHAR, PhD	Author. Previously Labor Member of Knesset
M.B.P.	MORDECHAI BEN-PORAT	Dir., World Organization of Jews from Arab Countries. Previously Member of Knesset and Minister without Portfolio
M.L.	MOSHE LISSAK, Prof.	Dept. of Sociology, Hebrew Univ. Entries on "Yishuv" and "Mandatory Palestine" adapted from *Origins of the Israeli Polity* (Chicago Univ. Press 1978)
M.M.	MOSHE MAOZ, Prof.	Dept. of Middle East Studies, Hebrew Univ.
M.Z.	MOSHE ZAK	Editorial Board, *Ma'ariv* newspaper; completing doctorate
N.L.	NETANEL LORCH, PhD	Previously Secretary of the Knesset
P.O.	PINḤAS OFER	Orientalist
R.C.	RA'ANAN COHEN	Previously Coordinator of Arab Affairs, Israel Labor Party
Ray.C.	RAYMOND COHEN, Prof.	Dept. of International Relations, Hebrew Univ.
R.I.	RAFAEL ISRAELI, Prof.	Dept. of Islamic History, Hebrew Univ.
S.H.R.	SUSAN HATTIS ROLEF, PhD	Political scientist, writer and researcher
S.M.	SERGIO MINERBI, PhD	Ministry for Foreign Affairs
S.S.	SHLOMO SLONIM, Prof.	Dept. of American Studies, Hebrew Univ.
S.T.	SHMUEL TAMIR	Attorney. Previously Member of Knesset and Minister of Justice
Sh.C.	SHAUL P. COLBI	Previously, Ministry of Religions
Sh.M.	SHAUL MEYZLISH	Journalist; editor, *Encyclopaedia of Judaism*
U.D.	URI DROMY	Editor, *Ma'archot* (army magazine)
V.N.	VICTOR NAHMIAS	Journalist, Israel Television
Y.A.	YITZḤAK ARBIT	Previously, Ministry for Foreign Affairs
Yo.A.	YOSSI AMITAI	Orientalist
Y.B.R.	YOEL BAR-ROMI, PhD	Ministry for Foreign Affairs
Y.D.	YEHUDA DOMINITZ	Previously Dir., Aliyah Dept., Jewish Agency
Y.M.	YOHANAN MANOR, PhD	Information Dept., World Zionist Organization
Y.R.	YAACOV ROI, Prof.	Dept. of Russian History, Tel Aviv Univ.
Y.S.	YAACOV SHIMONI	Editor, *Political Dictionary of the Arab World*
Z.A.	ZEIDAN ATSHI	*Shinui* party Member of Knesset
Z.E.	ZEEV EITAN, PhD	Sen. Researcher, Institute of Strategic Research, Tel Aviv Univ.

A

Abuḥatzeira, Aharon Member of *Knesset. Born 1938 in Morocco. Abuḥatzeira immigrated to Palestine in 1946. He served in the *Naḥal* and was a high-school teacher until 1972 when he was elected Mayor of Ramleh on the *National Religious Party (NRP) ticket. Abuḥatzeira represented the NRP in the 8th Knesset (1974) and the 9th (1977) and **Tami*, of which he is Chairman, in the 10th Knesset (1981) and the 11th (1984).

He was appointed Minister of Religious Affairs in the first *Begin government in 1977. In August 1980 he was charged with corruption during his tenure as mayor of Ramleh. The case became an ethnic issue when the Moroccan community argued that Abuḥatzeira had acted no differently than other public figures do and was being singled out because he was a Moroccan. On January 13, 1981, the Knesset revoked Abuḥatzeira's immunity and on the 25th he requested leave of absence from the government to stand trial. There were two trials on various charges, the first opening in February, the second in August, 1981.

Abuḥatzeira left the NRP and in May 1981 established *Tami* (an acronym for the Hebrew phrase meaning Movement for Jewish Tradition), a predominantly Moroccan party. He claimed that the NRP did not give the **Edot Mizraḥ* sufficient representation and had not offered him moral support through his trials.

Running on a purely ethnic platform that called for closing the social and economic gaps between Sephardim and Ashkenazim, Tami gained three seats in the 10th Knesset, and Abuḥatzeira was appointed Minister of Labor, Social Affairs and Immigrant Absorption. On April 19, 1982, the second trial ended, and Abuḥatzeira became the first minister in Israel to be found guilty of a felony. The following day he resigned from the Cabinet but retained his Knesset seat. On August 17, 1982, he began a three-month sentence which he served by reporting daily to the prison. In March 1984 Abuḥatzeira surprised the Knesset by presenting a bill calling for early elections, on grounds of *Tami*'s dissatisfaction with government allocations of welfare funds. The bill was passed in a secret vote — by a majority of one. Abuḥatzeira was the only member of *Tami* in the 11th Knesset.

administered territories One of the terms frequently used to refer to the territories occupied by Israel in the course of the *Six-Day War which were not returned to Egypt, Jordan (or Syria) and in which Israeli law has not been applied.

Up until 1981 these territories were administered by a Military Administration; since then by a Civil Administration subject to the *IDF and the Ministry of Defense.

The legal system in the administered territories in the *West Bank is based on Jordanian law as modified by Israeli military legislation, the Mandatory *Emergency Regulations of 1945 and Israeli interpretations of international law. Application of all these laws is subject to the scrunity of the Israeli High Court of Justice to which the local inhabitants have the right of appeal. In the *Gaza Strip which had been ruled by but never annexed to Egypt, only the mandatory law, military legislation, and international law apply.

The Jewish settlements established in the administered territories and the settlers living in them are subject to Israeli law, regulations of the Ministry of the Interior and force of orders by the Israeli commander of the relevant region. (See also: *Occupied Territories)

Africa and Israel Zionist interest in Africa was expressed by Theodor *Herzl in his book *Altneuland*: "Once I have witnessed the redemption of the Jews, my people, I also wish to assist in the redemption of the Africans." In the beginning of the century the Zionist organization considered and rejected a proposal to establish the Jewish National Home in Uganda. However, the history of practical relations between Israel and the Black African states began only in the late 1950s and may be divided into three periods: 1956–73 marked by enthusiastic and successful establishment of formal relations; 1973–82, characterized by the sudden severance of diplomatic relations and the maintenance of semi-clandestine contacts; and since 1982, a slow and cautious renewal of relations with some African states.

In the late 1950s and early 1960s, soon after the first Black African states gained independence from colonial rule, Israel, under the guidance of then Foreign Minister Golda *Meir, established diplomatic relations with 32 African states. The State of Israel, which was isolated in the Middle East, and surrounded by hostile Arab neighbors, endeavored to establish diplomatic ties among the nations abutting the Arab states. Meir first visited Africa in 1958, where she expressed the belief that Israel could and should play a significant role in fighting Black Africa's grave problems of disease, ignorance, unemployment, hunger and lack of housing. Some of the best men in the Israeli diplomatic service were sent to Africa, including Ehud Avriel, posted to Ghana, and Shlomo *Hillel, to Guinea and later to the Ivory Coast. For example, Israel's cooperation with Ghana was widely acclaimed throughout the African continent. Furthermore, a wide program of technical cooperation was established under the dynamic direction of Aharon Remez, and hundreds of Israeli experts were sent to African states in order to develop local skills, mainly in agriculture, in which Israel had gained special expertise, particularly in the irrigation of arid zones.

The **Histadrut* was active in establishing cooperatives and trade unions and the first Afro-Asian seminar on Cooperation was organized in Israel in 1958. An Afro-Asian Institute was established by the *Histadrut*, and is still functioning as the International Institute for Development, Cooperation and Labor Studies. Israeli experts differed from their European colleagues in that they were ready to go out to the field and speak to the local farmers, and they were able to improvise alternative solutions and raise the standard of living of the peasants rapidly and at low cost.

In 1972, at the peak of its activity in Africa, Israel was involved in 67 development projects, 23 of them agricultural, in 28 African countries. During the years 1958–71, 2,763 Israeli experts were sent to Africa, more than half the Israeli experts sent to the Third World. Many economic links of mutual benefit were established in that period. Joint ventures were set up, such as the Black Star Shipping Line, with Ghana, and the Sonitra building company in the Ivory Coast, in which the *Histadrut* construction company Solel Boneh was involved. Commercial ties were also developed.

The major benefit of this activity besides the positive voting patterns of the African states in the *United Nations and other international forums at this time, was the creation of a general atmosphere of goodwill toward Israel in these states.

Until the *Six-Day War Israel had diplomatic relations with 32 Black African states: there were 23 permanent embassies and 9 non-resident representatives. After the Six-Day War, *Egypt, a member of the *Organization of African Unity (OAU) pressured the African states to sever diplomatic relations with Israel. A few of them, such as Guinea, did so at that time.

Cooperation continued, although the new situation was uncomfortable for some African leaders. In the words of President Houphouët-Boigny of the Ivory Coast: "Israel is a friend, but the Arabs [of North Africa] belong to our own family."

In November 1971 the OAU sent a delegation of four Heads of State, Senghor of Senegal, Mobutu of Zaïre, Ahidjo of Cameroun and the head of the Nigerian Military Government, General Gowon, to Israel and Egypt, with the purpose of finding ways to start a peace process between the two states. During a second visit Senghor presented to Prime Minister Golda Meir a proposal to post UN troops in Sharm-e-Sheikh. However, this plan was premature. When the *Yom Kippur War broke out almost all the African states accepted the decision of the OAU, taken under strong pressure of its Arab members, to sever diplomatic ties with Israel — despite the fact that Israel had been attacked simultaneously by Egypt and Syria. Twenty-nine African states broke their diplomatic relations with Israel. Lesotho, Malawi and Swaziland did not. In some countries, like the Ivory Coast, the commercial and economic ties previously established were so strong that they survived the breach.

When Israel carried out the *Entebbe Operation on July 4, 1976, in which Israeli and Jewish hostages were rescued and flown from Uganda to Israel with a stop in Kenya, the OAU Assembly of Heads of State and Government was in session in Mauritius. On July 5 the organization passed a resolution which "strongly condemned Israeli aggression against Ugandan sovereignty," the killing of people and wanton destruction of property. It subsequently called for an urgent session of the UN Security Countil. An African draft resolution which made no mention of the hijacking or of terrorism but denounced "Israel's brazen and naked aggression" and demanded that Israel compensate Uganda for damage caused during the raid, was not even put to a vote. Mauritius, which had not broken relations with Israel in 1973, did so on July 6, 1976.

Limited contacts were maintained at different levels in the period after 1973. African ministers occasionaly met with Israeli diplomats and ministers at the UN, special Israeli emissaries were sent to Africa, and in some countries offices representing Israeli interests were allowed to act within the framework of foreign embassies. Belgium, Switzerland and Denmark provided services of this kind.

The disappointment of the African leaders with the unfulfilled promises of huge financial aid and cheap oil by the Arab oil-producing countries, as well as the radical change in the international standing of Israel following the *Egyptian-Israeli Peace Treaty, caused a slow process of renewal of diplomatic relations with Israel.

In 1982 Zaïre was the first African country to resume diplomatic relations with Israel. Liberia followed in 1983 and the Ivory Coast on February 12, 1986. By September 1986 seven African states had full diplomatic relations with Israel: Cameroun, the Ivory Coast, Lesotho, Liberia, Malawi, Swaziland and Zaïre, and interest officers represented Israel in five more states: Gabon, Ghana, Guinea, Kenya and Togo. In the fall of 1986 Israel was negotiating with eight African states regarding the reestablishment of diplomatic relations.

In 1985, at the UN Conference on the Emergency Situation in Africa, the Director-General of the Israeli Ministry for Foreign Affairs, David Kimche, stated that Israel was engaged in a number of projects in several African countries and was prepared to enter into immediate discussions with any country on problems of drought and food production, stressing that Israel could assist the African states to move from subsistence agriculture to market-oriented agriculture.

On the issue of apartheid in *South Africa, which is of special concern to all Black African states, Israel, while condemning it on moral grounds, is concerned about the 120,000-strong Jewish community in South Africa. Although Israel has maintained close relations with the South African government, it voted at the UN in 1961 in favor of an African resolution condemning apartheid and calling for sanctions against South Africa, and has subsequently repeated condemnations of the system. Though Israel's relations with South Africa are much more limited than those of most Western states, Arab oil-producing countries and many African states, under Arab pressure it has been singled out by the Black African states for special condemnation.

(S.M.)

Agranat Commission A commission of inquiry set up on November 21, 1973, under the 1968 Commissions of Inquiry Law to prepare a report on the *Yom Kippur War **Mehdal*. The commission members — President of the Supreme Court Dr. Simon Agranat, chairman, Supreme Court Judge Moshe Landau, *State Comptroller Dr. Yitzḥak Nebenzahl, ex-Chief of Staff Professor Yigael *Yadin and ex-Chief of Staff Army Ombudsman Ḥaim Laskov — were to prepare a report on the information which had been available before the war regarding Egypt's and Syria's movements and intentions; on the evaluations and assessments by the authorized military and civilian authorities of this information; and on the preparedness of the *IDF for war in general and on the day before the outbreak of war on October 6, 1973, in particular.

The commission heard 90 witnesses and received evidence from an additional 188 military personnel. On April 1, 1974, it published a 40-page interim report which outlined the reasons for the surprise: the IDF had held the "conception" that Egypt would not attack without superior air power, i.e., sufficient to attack Israel in-depth and dislocate its Air Force, and that Syria would not attack without Egypt. "Nasser's signals" from Egypt and Syria noted by Israeli intelligence before the war should have served as a warning but, due to the "conception", were evaluated incorrectly. Egyptian maneuvers were not recognized as preparations for war and therefore the Head of Intelligence Branch had not given the IDF sufficient warning. Consequently, appropriate measures, such as general mobilization of the reserves, were not taken by the IDF on time.

The commission recommended the establishment of a ministerial committee on security; the evaluation of intelligence by several bodies; the appointment of an intelligence advisor to the

Prime Minister; a clear distribution of powers, duties and responsibilities among the government, Prime Minister, Minister of Defense and Chief of Staff. It also recommended the dismissal of the Head of *Aman (army intelligence branch), Eliahu Za'ira, and other intelligence officers; the removal of Chief of Staff David Elazar for not having his own intelligence evaluations, for failing to prepare a detailed defense plan and for being overconfident of the IDF's ability to push back the enemy with regular forces only. The Commander of the Southern Command, Shmuel Gonen, was criticized and it was recommended that he be removed from active duty until the commission completed its work.

The commission stated that it felt free to reach conclusions regarding the direct responsibility of individual ministers but not regarding their ministerial responsibility. Surprisingly, the commission found no fault with the conduct of Minister of Defense Moshe *Dayan and praised that of Prime Minister Golda *Meir. Nevertheless, Meir decided to resign, and the new government which was formed by Yitzḥak *Rabin on June 3, 1974, did not include Dayan or Foreign Minister Abba *Eban. On July 10, 1974 the commission presented a second 400-page interim report of which only the introduction was published. This report provided detailed evidence for the commission's findings and supplements to the previous report. The final report was presented on January 30, 1975. It contained more than 1,500 pages, but once again only the 40-page introduction was published. This report dealt in great detail with the events of October 8, 1973 in the Sinai and with the first day of fighting on the *Golan Heights. In both cases the army's lack of preparedness and poor coordination were severely criticized. It also dealt with other subjects as well, among them instruction, discipline and emergency stores. However, the commission did not deal with the lack of sufficient air-support during the fighting as many felt it should have. Gonen was exonerated and declared fit for active service.

Among the practical results of the commission's report were the strengthening of the evaluation tools of the **Mossad* and the Ministry for Foreign Affairs Research Department to complement those of the Intelligence Branch; the appointment of an intelligence advisor and general defense advisor to the Prime Minister (Ariel *Sharon was appointed by Rabin to this post); the dismissal of the Chief of Staff and the Head of the Intelligence Branch, while other commanding officers were shifted to different posts.

Agudat Yisrael Established in 1912 by extreme Orthodox German Jews, *Agudat Yisrael*, Association of Israel, is an ultra-religious party with an anti-Zionist orientation. Commonly referred to as "the *Agudah*," the party later spread to Eastern Europe. It opposed ideas that were "new and not of the Torah," and reforms which threaten to introduce value changes in individual conduct and socio-national patterns of behavior which are not based on the Torah and the *Halacha* (Jewish law).

According to the *Agudah*, national redemption can be realized only through an act of Providence, and therefore no attempt should be made to hasten the establishment of a state, particularly one which is not based on the *Halacha*. Thus, the *Agudah* strongly opposed Zionism. It also opposed the everyday use of Hebrew — the holy language.

In order to prevent public objection to the establishment of a Jewish state in 1947, the *Jewish Agency Executive sent the *Agudah* a formal letter, signed by David *Ben Gurion, Rabbi Judah Leib *Maimon and Yitzḥak Gruenbaum, in which undertakings were given that the Jewish state would observe certain religious practices. This document is commonly regarded as the first religious *status quo agreement.

Since the establishment of the state the *Agudah* has objected to the celebration of Independence Day, to service in the *IDF, to the use of a national flag and other national emblems, and to the enactment of a "secular" *Constitution. The *Agudah* gives de facto recognition to the state in order to receive government allocations for its educational institutions. However, this recognition does not imply acceptance of the state's institutions, which are not *Halacha*-based.

The supreme authority in the party in Israel is *Mo'etzet G'dolei Hatorah*, the Council of Great Torah Scholars, made up of the heads of 15 major *yeshivot* (centers of religious learning), most of them Lithuanian, and the heads of the Hassidic "courts," who are referred to as *Admorim*. The spiritual leader of the Council is the *Admor* of Gur (Rabbi Alter). This Council must officially approve any proposal, decision or act taken by the *Agudah* MKs though in practice they have a good deal of freedom of action. On religious grounds the *Agudah* MKs have struggled to amend the Pathology (autopsies) Law, the Abortion Law, the Archaeology Law (in an effort to prevent digs in areas which might have been Jewish cemeteries in the past), and the definition of a Jew in the *Law of Return. They also fought against El-Al flights on the Sabbath and other acts by public institutions which they deem to be a desecration of the Sabbath. The *Agudah* is dovish on foreign affairs and security matters, in contrast to the nationalist religious parties. The *Agudah* has participated in governments led by **Mapai* and the **Likud* and is a member of the *National Unity Government, but, with the exception of a Minister of Welfare, Rabbi Y. M. Levine, in the years 1949–52, it has refrained from accepting cabinet posts. Since 1977 and *Agudah* MK, carpet manufacturer Avraham Shapira, has been chairman of the Knesset Finance Committee, commonly regarded as the most powerful and influential of Knesset committes. The *Agudah* ran on a joint list with **Poalei Agudat Yisrael* for the 3rd, 4th and 8th Knessets. Before the election to the 11th Knesset (1984), the *Agudah*'s Sephardi supporters broke away and joined **Shass*. Against the background of friction between the Hassidic and Lithuanian streams in the party Rabbi Eliezer Shach, leader of the latter, instructed his supporters to vote for *Shass*, leaving the *Agudah* with only two seats in the 11th Knesset.

Agudat Yisrael has an extensive educational network for both boys and girls and publishes a daily, *Hamodi'a*. There are powerful branches of the party in the US and Europe, representatives of which participate in the "Great Assembly", the party's highest institution.

Knesset Seats: 2nd Knesset (1951) — 3; 5th Knesset (1961) — 4; 6th Knesset (1965) — 4; 7th Knesset (1969) — 4; 8th Knesset (1973) — 4; 9th Knesset (1981) — 4; 10th Knesset (1981) — 4; 11th Knesset (1984) — 2. The *Agudah* ran together with **Po'alei Agudat Yisrael* as the *Religious Torah Front for the 3rd, 4th and 8th Knessets. (Sh.M.)

Aḥad Ha'am (1856–1927) Hebrew essayist, thinker and leader of *Ḥibat Zion*. Born Asher Hirsch Ginsberg in Kiev, Aḥad Ha'am came from a well-to-do Hassidic family and spent his childhood and youth in the study of the Bible and Talmud. Later in Berlin, Breslau, Vienna and Odessa he studied Rabbinic and general literature and philosophy. He settled in Palestine in 1922 where he became the spiritual father of cultural *Zionism.

He had reservations about political Zionism and the immediate settlement of **Eretz Yisrael* (the Land of Israel), fearing that the national consciousness of the Jews was not sufficiently strong to withstand the attending despair should Zionism end in disaster. Furthermore, he did not believe that the Zionist program could solve the Jewish problem and argued for an alternative program — the establishment of a Jewish cultural center in Palestine.

He argued that Zionism should aim to resolve not the problem of the Jews as individuals, but the problem of Judaism as an historical national culture. The object of Zionism was moral — the emancipation of the Jews from the inner slavery and the spiritual degradation which assimilation had produced, and the creation of a sense of national unity and a life of dignity and freedom in the land of their original civilization where Jews could again become culturally and spiritually creative. Zionism required a revival of spirit among the Jewish people at large. The means of this revival would be the renascense of the Hebrew language, Hebrew literature and thought. However, the establishment of the Jewish center in Palestine was not a substitute for Jewish life in other parts of the world, but a means of strengthening it.

Aḥdut Ha'avodah A socialist party set up in 1919 by volunteers who served in the *Jewish Legion, several members of the **Po'alei Zion* party in Palestine and a large group of non-aligned persons. *Aḥdut Ha'avodah* means the unity of labor and is a shortened form for *Hitaḥdut Zionit-Sozialistit shel Po'alei Eretz Yisrael*. In 1930 *Aḥdut Ha'avodah* joined with **Hapo'el Hatzair* to found **Mapai*. The party advocated the unification of the Jewish labor movement in Palestine and developed concepts concerning forms for settlement units and labor units which were implemented by the movement. The party advocated an activist **Yishuv* defense policy and a maximalist approach in the political sphere which rejected compromise. It favored social democracy and did not accept the Marxist doctrines of class warfare and the dictatorship of the proletariat.

The central figures in the party were David *Ben Gurion, Berl *Katznelson, Yitzḥak *Ben Zvi, David Remez and Yitzḥak *Tabenkin. The party was active in organization and settlement work and political, security and cultural activities within the labor movement. The **Histadrut*, established in 1920, eventually took over some of these functions. (D.B.M.)

Aḥdut Ha'avodah-Po'alei Zion Commonly called *Aḥdut Ha'avodah*, this workers' party was established in 1946 following a split in **Mapai* in 1944. The section which broke off from *Mapai (Si'a Bet)* was made up of a group of members who objected to the policy of the **Histadrut* leadership, and got together with a group of members from **Hakibbutz Hame'uḥad* to set up a faction called *Hatnu'ah Le'aḥdut Ha'avodah*. Politically the new faction was pro-Soviet and more radical than *Mapai*. In 1946 it united with **Po'alei Zion Smol* to form the new party. In 1948 the party united with **Mifleget Po'alim-Hashomer Hatza'ir* and set up **Mapam*.

Following the anti-Semitic Prague and Moscow trials of the early 1950s most of the original members of *Aḥdut Ha'avodah-Po'alei Zion* left *Mapam* and reestablished their own independent party and published a daily paper *Lamerḥav*.

The party ran independently for the 3rd and 4th *Knessets and was represented in the Alignment in the 7th to 12th governments. After **Rafi* broke off from *Mapai* in 1965, *Mapai* and *Aḥdut Ha'avodah* created the first *Alignment which stood for election to the 6th Knesset. The party continued its separate existence until the establishment of the *Israel Labor Party in 1969. Politically, the party's policy was one of activism in settlement and defense. Its members objected to the idea of the partition of Palestine in 1947/48 and during the *War of Independence it favored the occupation of Judea and Samaria by the *IDF. After the *Six-Day War most of its members, including the party's spiritual leader Yitzḥak *Tabenkin supported the idea of *Greater Israel. However, another of the party's leaders, Yigal *Allon, advocated the return of some of the occupied territories which would not threaten Israel's security (See *Allon Plan). On internal issues the party adopted a strong anti-bourgeois line and advocated predominance for labor settlements and the workers.

Knesset Seats: 3rd Knesset (1955) — 10; 4th Knesset (1959) — 7; 5th Knesset (1961) — 8.

(D.B.M.)

Aḥvah A Knesset faction established in 1980 by three members who had been elected to the 9th Knesset (1977) on the list of the *Democratic Movement for Change: Shlomo Eliahu, Akiva Nof and Shafik Assad. By the end of the 9th Knesset only one member, Eliahu, remained in *Aḥvah* (meaning fraternity).

Al-Ard Arabic for the earth. A political group formed in 1959 with the intention of creating a non-Communist Arab political body which would manifest the national yearnings of the *Arabs of Israel. Most of the leaders of the group were intellectuals such as Mansour Kardush and Sabri Jeris. In its efforts to gain ground the new group had to fight the Israeli authorities — since it did not accept the legitimacy of the State of Israel, the traditional structure of the Arab society which it viewed as helping the Israeli authorities rule over Arab society, and **Maki*, with which it competed for the support of the Arab voter. *Al-Ard* called on the Arab voter to boycott the elections to the 4th Knesset (1959), which was in fact a call to refrain from voting for *Maki*.

During the years 1960–65 *al-Ard* was occupied with legal battles. In 1960 it sought to establish a company but the registrar of companies refused to register it for reasons of "security and public safety." The Supreme Court approved the registration in July 1964, but when the group wished to establish an Ottoman association as the basis for the establishment of a party to run in the elections to the 6th Knesset (1965) its request was denied since the principles and goals of the association "did not correspond with the Israeli democracy." At the end of 1964 the Minister of Defense signed an order prohibiting *al-Ard* activities. Despite this order some of the group's leaders tried to present a list for the 1965 elections but the Central Elections Committee denied it permission to run. When an appeal to the Supreme Court failed, the group began to disintegrate. Several of *al-Ard*'s leaders were among the founders of the *Progressive List for Peace which, unlike *al-Ard*, is a party in which Arabs and Jews are equally represented. (R.C.)

Alignment A left-of-center political bloc, *Hama'arach Le'aḥdut Po'alei Yisrael* — the Alignment for the Unity of Israeli Workers — popularly known as the *Ma'arach*, was formed in 1965 between **Mapai* and **Aḥdut Ha'avodah-Po'alei Zion*. In 1968 the bloc, together with **Rafi*, formed the *Israel Labor Party. In preparation for the elections to the 7th *Knesset a new Alignment was set up between the Israel Labor Party and **Mapam*. The Alignment led all of Israel's coalition governments from 1965 to 1977 when it lost the elections and joined the Opposition. Since September 1984 it has been a member of the *National Unity Government on the basis of equal representation with the **Likud*.

In the 1981 elections to the 10th Knesset, the Alignment gained 47 seats to the *Likud*'s 48. In order to ensure equality in the distribution of posts in the 10th Knesset Shulamit *Aloni of the *Civil Rights Movement (CRM) joined the Alignment. However, despite the parity which was established between the Alignment and the *Likud* it was the latter which was able to form the coalition government in 1981. The CRM withdrew from the Alignment before the elections to the 11th Knesset in order to run independently.

The *Independent Liberals, who decided not to run for the 11th Knesset as an independent list, joined the Alignment just before the 1984 elections. The Alignment gained 44 seats in the 11th Knesset to the *Likud*'s 41, but neither bloc was able to form a coalition which would enjoy the support of the majority of the Knesset members. As a result the two blocs formed the National Unity Government based on parity between them. However, as a result of the concessions which the Alignment had to make, *Mapam* and MK Yossi *Sarid from the Labor Party withdrew from it. The loss of their seven seats was only partially compensated by Ezer *Weizman's *Yaḥad* party, which joined the Alignment with its three seats.

Though the mainstream of the Alignment has retained its social-democratic orientation, the departure of the socialist *Mapam* and the inclusion of the Independent Liberals and *Yaḥad* have moved the bloc further towards the center.

Knesset Seats: 6th Knesset (1965) — 45; 7th Knesset (1969) — 56; 8th Knesset (1973) — 51; 9th Knesset (1977) — 32; 10th Knesset (1981) — 47; 11th Knesset (1984) — 44.

aliyah The Hebrew word *aliyah*, meaning ascent, has been used to describe the migration of Jews to *Eretz Yisrael* (the Land of Israel). It is a synonym for the term *Shivat Zion* (the return to Zion) which has existed as long as the Jewish Diaspora. The term *aliyah* expresses the ideological motive — both religious and Zionist — for Jewish migration to *Eretz Yisrael*, and distinguishes it from other migrant movements motivated by overpopulation, the discovery of new lands, the search for riches, etc. It expresses the Jewish striving to return to the land of the forefathers, the Holy Land, and the termination of the punishment of exile. In recent generations it has been an expression of renewed Jewish nationalism and the main goal of the Zionist movement (See: *Zionism).

Throughout the ages, until 1881, there was a sporadic *aliyah* of individuals and groups to *Eretz Yisrael*. However, as of 1881, when the Jewish population of Palestine was approximately 24,000 (almost exclusively pious Jews living off charity), the nature and volume of the *aliyah* changed, arriving in waves, each with its own characteristics and impact.

The first groups of *olim* (ascenders or immigrants) arrived in 1881–82 from Russia (the Biluyim) and Yemen. From this time until the outbreak of World War II the various waves of *aliyah* were numbered. The First *Aliyah* took place between 1881 and 1904. In the years 1882–84 pogroms in Eastern Europe were the main cause of *aliyah* from *Romania and Russia, many of the arrivals having been members of the *Ḥovevei Zion* (lovers of Zion) movement. A second wave came in 1890–91 and a third in 1900–03. The number of *olim* who arrived in this period is estimated at 30,000–40,000. They established the towns of Rishon Letzion, Rosh Pinah, Zichron Ya'acov, Gedera, Ekron and Yesod Hama'alah on lands belonging to the Baron Edmond de Rothschild (1845–1934) and with his support.

The Second *Aliyah*, which began in 1904, was also motivated by the outburst of pogroms. It continued until the outbreak of World War I. Many members of this *aliyah* were pioneers, influenced by the revolutionary movements in Russia and other East European states, combining social ideals with the idea of Jewish national revival. In this period the foundations of the Jewish workers' movement in *Eretz Yisrael* and of the cooperative labor settlements (*kvutzot*, **kibbutzim* and **moshavim*) were laid.

During the First and Second *aliyot*, Palestine was under Ottoman rule, which was hostile to, and strictly limited, Jewish immigration. At the outbreak of World War I there were approximately 85,000 Jews in Palestine. At the end of the war their number was down to less than 60,000 as a result of the expulsion of over 20,000 Jews by the Turks.

The *aliyah* was resumed and accelerated at the end of the war, following the *Balfour Declaration and the British occupation of Palestine. The Third *Aliyah* arrived in the years 1919–23 and numbered over 35,000, some of them returnees who had been exiled by the Turks. Eighty-five percent of the *olim* in these years arrived from Russia and Poland, the remainder coming from other European states, as well as Turkey, Yemen and Iraq.

The Fourth *Aliyah* arrived in the years 1924–28, and was called the "Grabatsky *Aliyah*," named after the Polish Prime Minister who was responsible for harsh economic decrees against the Jews of Poland. Since the *United States placed severe restrictions on immigration in 1924, 62,000 Jews arrived in Palestine in the years 1924–25, which were years of prosperity in the country. There followed three years of economic depression which resulted in a net *yeridah* (descent or emigration) of Jews from Palestine.

By 1928 the number of Jews in Palestine was 155,000. The next wave, the Fifth *Aliyah*, lasted from 1929 to 1939, reaching a peak in the years 1933–36. This *aliyah* brought to Palestine close to a quarter of a million Jews, with the Jewish population reaching approximately 400,000 in 1936. This wave runs partially parallel with the rise of National Socialism in Germany, and it was the 36,000 *olim* from Germany who left the strongest mark on the country, even though 75,000 *olim* arrived from Poland at the same time. In this period a special effort was made to enable the German Jews to leave Germany with their assets (See: *Transfer) and the first groups of *Youth Aliyah (children coming to Israel without parents) arrived.

Throughout the period of the British Mandate, from the first White Paper of 1920 until the British departure in 1948, laws were implemented which limited the immigration of Jews into Palestine and divided the immigrants into categories (capitalists, workers, students, etc.). A constant struggle was waged between the Jewish **Yishuv* and its institutions (the *Jewish Agency and **Va'ad Le'umi*) and the British administration on the volume of *aliyah*, which was based on schedules and certificates in accordance with the arbitrary evaluation of Palestine's "economic absorptive capacity." After 1936 politically motivated limitations were introduced as well.

In the late 1930s, as the persecution of the Jews in Europe intensified and Britain further limited the inflow of Jewish immigration into Palestine, "illegal" immigration — popularly known as *Aliyah Bet* — developed. In the years 1933–39, 25,000 *ma'apilim* (Hebrew for defiers — the "illegal" immigrants) are estimated to have entered Palestine — 22,000 on board 49 boats, the remainder infiltrating the country as tourists.

During World War II, 50,000 *olim* came to the country legally (within the framework of the 1939 White Paper policy) and 12,000 arrived as *ma'apilim*. Five boats sank with 2,800 *ma'apilim* on board.

After World War II, when there were 100,000 Jews in displaced persons camps and many more refugees, the British allowed only 1,500 Jews to enter Palestine every month — among them *ma'apilim* who had been caught trying to enter illegally and expelled to camps in Cyprus. Consequently, *Aliyah Bet* increased from 1946 to the first half of 1948 when 17,000 legal and 39,000 "illegal" immigrants arrived. The British policy merely strengthened the Jewish resolve to expel the British from Palestine and establish an independent sovereign Jewish state.

With the establishment of the State of Israel the gates of the country were opened. The *Proclamation of Independence on May 14, 1948, announced that "The State of Israel shall be open to Jewish immigration and the ingathering of the dispersions," and "We call upon the Jewish People in all the dispersions to rally to the *Yishuv* through immigration and construction."

The first legislative act of the Provisional State Council was to cancel the laws based on the 1939 White Paper which had limited Jewish *aliyah* and land purchase. The *Law of Return of July 6, 1950, declared that "Every Jew has the right to immigrate to the country."

From May 1948 until 1951, 685,000 *olim* arrived in Israel, thus doubling the Jewish population of the country, drastically changing the demographic make-up of Israel, and further altering the map of Jewish dispersions in the world. Whole Jewish communities moved to Israel, including 45,000 Jews from Yemen, 122,000 from Iraq, 38,000 from Bulgaria, 32,000 from Libya and 7,700 from Yugoslavia. Large sections of the remnants of the Jewish communities of Poland and *Romania, as well as a high percentage of the Jews of *Morocco, Tunis, Algeria and *Iran also arrived. And in the mid-80s the clandestine Operation Moses brought approximately 15,000 *Ethiopian Jews to Israel. *Aliyah* from the *Soviet Union had stopped almost completely in the 1920s after the consolidation of the revolutionary regime and the prohibition of Zionist activities. In the 1960s the world struggle to allow Soviet Jewry to leave the USSR intensified, and the first indications were given to the Soviets regarding "family reunions" or "repatriation." Following the *Six-Day War there was a national reawakening of Soviet Jewry which resulted in a struggle for the right to emigrate to Israel. The combined effort inside and outside the Soviet Union succeeded — the gates opened in 1971. Of 270,000 Jews allowed to leave the Soviet Union in the years 1971–81, 165,000 came to Israel, most of the remainder settling in North America. After the peak year of 1979 when 51,000 Jews left the Soviet Union, *aliyah* from the Soviet Union turned into a trickle.

In sum, in the years 1948–86, 1,800,000 immigrants entered Israel. The volume of *aliyah* has fluctuated widely from year to year, and from period to period. The peak year was 1949 with 240,000 *olim* — the nadir came in 1953, with 10,347. The volume is determined both by the opportunities of Jews to leave countries which limit emigration and the desire of Jews in the free world to move to Israel. Though the principle of selective *aliyah* in accordance with the absorptive capacity of the economy was discussed by the Israeli government, the Jewish Agency and the coordinating institution for both, it was never applied. Special efforts have been made to initiate the *aliyah* of Jews from communities in distress, while encouraging *aliyah* from the West.

While the State of Israel and its institutions bear the main brunt of absorbing the immigrants, the *World Zionist Organization and Jewish Agency are partners in the *aliyah* process. The distribution of functions was defined in the 1952 Status of the Zionist Organization Law as amended in 1975 and the covenant signed by the Government of Israel, the World Zionist Organization and the Jewish Agency which granted the Jewish Agency the tasks of organizing and encouraging *aliyah*, transporting the *olim* to Israel and dealing with their primary absorption (absorption centers and *ulpanim* — schools for the study of the Hebrew language). All these tasks are financed by funds from the United Jewish Appeal in North America and the *Keren Hayesod* (Foundation Fund) in the rest of the world.

Until 1968 there were two departments within the Jewish Agency dealing with *aliyah* and absorption, as well as an economic department to deal with individual immigrants with a separate section to deal with professionals. In 1968 the Zionist Congress decided to unite these functions in a single department.

The permanent absorption in Israel of *olim* is the responsibility of the Government of Israel and solutions to problems of housing, health, education, welfare, etc., are financed by the government budget. In 1968, as a result of a wave of *aliyah* which followed the Six-Day War, the government established a Ministry of Immigrant Absorption.

This distribution of functions between the Jewish Agency and the Government of Israel has frequently been criticized as being inefficient and over-bureaucratic. However, it represents an important part of the partnership between the State of Israel and world Jewry. (Y.D.)

Aliyah Ḥadashah Hebrew for New Immigration. A party established in 1942 by immigrants from Germany and Austria against the background of the absorption difficulties of the central European immigrants. *Aliyah Ḥadashah* viewed its mission in the early years of its existence as increasing the influence of the new arrivals in the **Yishuv*'s institutions which, they claimed, were controlled by earlier immigrants of East European origin — primarily from Russia and Poland. Such *Landsmann* (immigrants from the same country or region) parties are relatively rare in Israel and *Aliyah Ḥadashah* was alone to emerge from among European immigrants.

Once established *Aliyah Ḥadashah* also dealt with general issues relating to Zionist policy and the *Yishuv*. It rejected the *Biltmore Program and some of its leaders supported the continuation of a reformed British mandate over Palestine, or, alternatively, the establishment of a *binational state. However, once the *UN voted in favor of the establishment of a Jewish state, *Aliyah Ḥadashah* became active in the official Jewish institutions which prepared the establishment of the state, and joined the Provisional Government.

Socially it was progressive in its outlook. In 1948 *Aliyah Ḥadashah*, together with *Ha'oved Hatzioni* (the Zionist Worker — a centrist faction within the **Histadrut*) and some *General Zionists, established the *Progressive Party.

(D.B.M.)

Aliyat Hano'ar See: *Youth Aliyah

Allon Plan A plan developed over several years following the *Six-Day War by Yigal *Allon as the basis for peace with Israel's neighbors. The plan called for the return of the densely populated areas in the *West Bank and *Gaza Strip to a Jordanian-Palestinian state, and the return of most of the *Sinai to *Egypt. According to this plan Israel is to remain in control of the Jordan Valley Rift and the first mountain ridge west of it, where it would maintain settlements and early warning systems against a possible attack from the east. *Jerusalem, the Gush Etzion area and Kiryat Arbah (See: *Hebron) are to remain under Israeli sovereignty and a few minor border changes are to be introduced, i.e., around Latrun. The area in the West Bank to be returned to Arab sovereignty is to be connected to *Jordan by means of a wide corridor around Jericho, and the Gaza Strip is to be connected to it by means of a highway. In the Sinai, Israel would retain control over the *Rafa Salient, the west bank of the Red Sea leading south from Eilat to Sharm-e-Sheikh and two military airfields constructed close to the old international border. The rest of the Sinai peninsula is to return to Egypt. Most of the *Golan Heights is also to remain in Israeli hands.

The plan was based on the premise that for Israel to remain a Jewish, democratic state, in which the principle of Jewish labor is considered a basic value, it cannot continue to rule over the 1.2 million Palestinian Arabs who live in the territories occupied by Israel in 1967. On the other hand, Israel has genuine security concerns which must be catered to, which call for the demilitarization of all Arab territories west of the Jordan River and Israel's maintaining a military and civilian presence in the Golan Heights, along the Jordan Valley and along the Red Sea.

The Allon Plan as such was never adopted as the official policy of the government of Israel, but during the Labor-led governments until 1977 all the Jewish settlement activities in the West Bank, the Gaza Strip, the Golan Heights and the Sinai were within the parameters of the plan. In 1973 the principles of the Allon Plan were included in the Labor party platform as the "*territorial compromise." Except for the section dealing with the Sinai, which was superseded by the peace treaty with Egypt, the plan still constitutes part of this platform.

The plan was never accepted by any of the Arab states, but in 1974 there were prospects for the beginning of its implementation in the form of the *Jericho Plan which was thwarted by the *Rabbat Arab Summit Conference.

Yigal Allon never drew an exact map to go with his plan, and a map published in *Foreign Affairs* in 1976 was disclaimed by him.

Allon (formerly Paicowitch), **Yigal** (1918–1980) Military commander, statesman and one of the leaders of the Labor movement.

Allon was born in Kfar Tavor and educated at the Kedourie Agricultural School. In 1931 he joined the **Haganah* and in 1936 was a member of Yizḥak Sadeh's Field Troops. In 1937 he was one of the founders of Kibbutz Ginossar of which he was a member until his death. Allon served with the British army in **Syria* and **Lebanon* in 1941–42 and was one of the founders of the **Palmaḥ*, serving as its commander from 1945 to 1948. He joined the **Aḥdut Ha'avodah-Po'alei Zion* party when it was founded in 1946.

During the *War of Independence Allon commanded a series of campaigns for the liberation of the Upper Galilee and Safad in the north; the Onno Valley, Lod, Ramleh and the Jerusalem Corridor on the central front; the southern coastal plain, as well as the Negev including Beersheba and Eilat in the south. He was also the commander of troops who carried out a deep penetration raid into the *Sinai Peninsula, reaching as far as El Arish, but was ordered by David *Ben

Gurion to withdraw because of US pressure. Ben Gurion also refused to give him permission to try to conquer the whole of the *West Bank from the Arab Legion.

In 1950 Allon retired from active military service after the disbandment of the *Palmaḥ*. He became a member of the Executive Committee of **Hakibbutz Hame'uḥad*, and within the framework of *Aḥdut Ha'avodah-Po'alei Zion* became a member of **Mapam*. After the split from *Mapam* in 1954 Allon became one of the leaders of *Aḥdut Ha'avodah*, entering the Knesset in 1955. In the late 1950s Allon interrupted his political career to study at St. Antony's College, Oxford. Between 1961–67 he served, first under Ben-Gurion and then under Levi *Eshkol as Minister of Labor, in which capacity he furthered a more liberal social security system. In the first *National Unity Government, 1967–69, he served as Minister of Immigrant Absorption and Deputy Prime Minister. Under Prime Minister Golda *Meir, 1969–74, he was Minister of Education and Culture and Deputy Prime Minister, after which, under Yitzḥak *Rabin he served as Minister for Foreign Affairs and Deputy Prime Minister. As Minister for Foreign Affairs he tried to balance Israel's foreign policy between the United States and Western Europe, to contend with the anti-Israel wave which followed the *Yom Kippur War and to further the *Allon Plan for resolving the *Arab-Israel conflict which he had developed following the *Six-Day War.

Allon played a major role in the formation of the first *Alignment between *Mapai* and *Aḥdut Ha'avodah* in 1965, and of the *Israel Labor Party in which *Mapai, Aḥdut Ha'avodah* and **Rafi* united. It was frequently said that Allon had always missed being appointed to central leadership positions. In 1949 his disagreements with Ben Gurion prevented him from becoming Chief of Staff. In May 1967 he was on a mission in Leningrad and lost out to Moshe *Dayan who was chosen Minister of Defense on the eve of the Six-Day War. He was proposed as candidate for Prime Minister after Levi Eshkol's death but Golda Meir was selected. In 1980 Allon planned to contend for the leadership of the Labor party against Shimon *Peres, but died before the party conference took place. Allon abstained during the Knesset vote on the *Camp David Accords because they called for Israel's withdrawal from the Rafa Salient and the two Air Force bases in Sinai. However, he believed that the *Autonomy Plan could lead to the implementation of the Allon Plan.

Allon was elected chairman of the *World Labor Zionist Movement in 1978, and was instrumental in getting a resolution through the Zionist Congress calling for equal status for all streams in Judaism. Just before his death he realized his dream of reuniting two kibbutz movements — *Hakibbutz Hame'uḥad* and **Iḥud Hakvutzot Vehakibbutzim* — within the United Kibbutz Movement (*Takam).

Aloni, Shulamit Member of Knesset, attorney and teacher. Born 1929, Tel Aviv. Graduated from the Teachers' Seminary in Jerusalem and the Faculty of Law at the Hebrew University. Before the establishment of the State Aloni served in the **Palmaḥ*, and during the *War of Independence was in the besieged Old City of *Jerusalem. After her release by the Jordanians she worked with new-immigrant children.

Aloni joined **Mapai* in 1959. Between 1961 and 1965 she produced several radio programs which dealt with legislation and legal procedures. In the wake of one of these programs, the Office of the Ombudsman was set up in the government of Levi *Eshkol in 1965.

Aloni was first elected MK in 1965 for the *Alignment. She was not elected in 1969 and in 1973, after disagreements with Golda *Meir, she formed her own party — the *Civil Rights Movement. For a short while, 1975–76, she formed **Ya'ad* together with Lova *Eliav, and in 1981–84 she joined the Alignment. Aloni was, briefly, Minister without Portfolio in 1974 under Yitzḥak *Rabin but resigned when the *National Religious Party joined the coalition.

Since 1965 she has been a member of the Knesset Constitution, Law and Justice Committee. Aloni's parliamentary and legal work is concentrated in the field of human rights, prevention of religious coercion and the enactment of *Basic Laws. In the 6th Knesset she initiated the establishment of the statutory subcommittee for the preparation of Basic Laws. In 1966 Aloni established the Israel Consumers' Council and served as its chairperson until 1970. Aloni also draws up marriage contracts for couples who are unable or unwilling to be married by an Orthodox rabbi — the only official way for Jews to marry in Israel.

She has helped establish shelters for battered women and welfare centers for rape victims. Aloni was one of the founders of the *International Center for Peace in the Middle East and is a member of its board. (Y.A.)

Altalena An arms ship brought by the **Irgun Zva'i Le'umi* (IZL) to Israel soon after the establishment of the state. The arrival of the ship was made known to the government in advance. It carried arms, most of which had been donated by authorities in the French government, and an unknown number of passengers estimated between 853 and 940, most of them *Holocaust survivors. The *Altalena* arrived off the shores of Kfar Vitkin on June 19, 1948, during the first truce in the fighting of the *War of Independence. On June 22 it was blown up off the shores of Tel Aviv by the *IDF after a controversy broke out between the Israeli government and IZL headquarters regarding the future of the arms on board the ship and their distribution. Prime Minister David *Ben Gurion claimed that the arms should be handed over immediately to the official government of Israel and believed that the IZL, which was in the process of integrating into the IDF, was planning a revolt. Menaḥem *Begin claimed that all he wanted for his organization and men was the appreciation and recognition due them.

The details of the episode, in which several men were killed and most of the arms on board lost, are still the subject of controversy between Israel's Right and Left.

Aman Acronym for *Agaf Modi'in*, Hebrew for Intelligence Branch, which is a branch of the *IDF General Staff. Among its many tasks is the provision of intelligence evaluation for Israel's *Defense Policy for the planning of war and security policy, and the dissemination of intelligence information to the IDF and appropriate government bodies.

The Head of Intelligence is an extremely difficult office which, more often than not, as a result of criticism of the performance of the Intelligence Branch, has ended in resignation. *Aman*'s first head (1948–49), Isar Be'eri, was dismissed for having an innocent man executed. Ḥaim *Herzog headed *Aman* twice: in 1940–50 and again in 1959–62. Binyamin Gibli (1950–55) resigned because of his part in the *Lavon Affair. Yehoshafat Harkabi (1955–59) was forced to resign following the Mobilization Broadcast canard. Meir *Amit headed *Aman* in 1962–64, and was replaced by Aharon *Yariv (1964–72). Eliahu Za'ira (1972–74) was forced to resign as a result of the *Agranat Commission report on the outbreak of the *Yom Kippur War. Shlomo Gazit served in 1974–78 and was replaced by Yehoshua Saguy, who was forced to resign in 1983 following the publication of the *Kahan Commission report regarding the *Sabra and Shatilla massacre. Saguy was followed by Ehud Barak (1983–85), who was followed by Amnon Reshef.

Amana The settlement movement of **Gush Emunim* founded in 1976 when that organization switched its priorities from protest activity to the establishment of settlements in territories administered by Israel after 1967.

Amana created new forms of settlement — the Community Settlement, and the Community Village which, unlike the *kibbutz or **moshav*, are not engaged in agriculture.

Since 1977 *Amana* has become a central factor in the settlement of the *West Bank and the *Gaza Strip, and its activists have become leading personalities in the administrative structures of the settlements and the regional councils in the *occupied territories.

Amana views the settlement of the entire Land of Israel as its primary goal, placing special emphasis on the founding of settlements on the highlands running south from Nablus to Hebron and within areas densely populated by Arabs. In the years 1977–84 it enjoyed the full backing of the **Likud* governments, receiving generous financial allocations both from the government and the Settlement Department headed by the *Likud* in the *World Zionist Organization. (M.B.)

Amit (formerly Slutzky), **Me'ir** Military commander, ex-Knesset Member and company manager. Born 1921, Tiberias. In 1936 Amit joined the **Haganah* and was a member of Kibbutz Alonim between 1939 and 1952. Amit served in the *War of Independence and was appointed Commander of the Golani Brigade in 1950. The following year he was head of the Instruction Command and head of the Operations Branch in the General Staff. In 1954 he attended an officer's course in the U.K. and in 1955 was appointed Commander of the Southern Command. He was head of the Operations Branch once again in 1956 and two years later was appointed Commander of the Northern Command. In 1959 he studied Business Administration at Columbia University, New York. Amit was head of the *Mossad* between 1963 and 1968, after which he was Managing Director of Koor (See: **Histadrut*) until 1977. Amit was one of the founders of the *Democratic Movement for Change and served in the Knesset on its list. He was Minister of Transport in the first **Likud* government headed by Menaḥem *Begin, until 1978 when he left the government and joined **Shinui*. In 1980 he joined the *Israel Labor Party. Since 1978 Amit has held senior managerial posts in high-tech corporations.

anti-Zionism The concept of anti-Zionism is somewhat ambiguous. It expresses opposition to *Zionism, but not always to the same features of Zionism or for the same reasons. Another source of ambiguity results from the proximity between some types of anti-Zionism, especially the variety prevalent today, and anti-Semitism.

Initially anti-Zionism was an internal Jewish affair, one side in a religious and metaphysical debate. With the appearance of political Zionism it became a side in the ideological and political debate. In the early years the followers of Zionism were very few in number. Many Jews were attracted by other ideologies, such as Bundism (See: *Bund), Social Democracy or Communism which rejected either the territorialism or nationalism of Zionism. Most of the Orthodox camp rejected Zionism because of its secular character, while the *Reform Movement rejected it for two reasons — for professing that the Jews are not only a religious community but a nation as well, and for its advocacy of a return to Zion. All of these opponents of Zionism defined themselves as anti-Zionist.

From the start there was, however, external, non-Jewish, opposition to Zionism as well. Some of it was ideological, such as that of the *Soviet Union soon after the Bolshevik revolution, which objected to all nationalism. There was also political opposition, such as that of groups in *Great Britain and elsewhere, which viewed Zionism as a force obstructing their states' interests in the Middle East and not representing the views of all Jews. Finally there was opposition based on a clash of national interests, as in the case of Arab nationalism which claimed full rights over Palestine and became progressively more anti-Zionist as the idea of a Jewish national home developed. Since the establishment of the State of Israel, Jewish anti-Zionism has more or less vanished. The *Holocaust and continued manifestations of anti-Semitism are, in a large part, responsible. The acceptance of pluralism and concurrent loyalties in the US, where the majority of diaspora Jewry resides today, and Israel's political and military successes, have been further contributors to this phenomenon.

In 1968 the *World Zionist Organization placed new emphasis on the definition of Zionism and its goals — the unity of the Jewish people and the centrality of the State of Israel rather than **aliyah* and personal fulfilment — that facilitated the support of Zionism by most Jews. While Jewish anti-Zionism almost disappeared, Soviet and Arab opposition to Zionism mounted, reaching extreme dimensions in the campaign to defame and demonize it as of the mid-70s.

The Arabs who, after 1949, wished to rationalize their continuous military defeats, were tempted to use Zionist conspiracy theories. At first Zionism was described as an "agent and stooge of imperialism and Bolshevism." Later it was denounced as an "imperialist conspiracy against the unity of the Arab world," and as colonialist and racist by nature. This emphasis on racism appeared in article 19 of the original 1964 version of the *Palestine National Covenant which stated that Zionism is "racist and separationist in its structure and fascist in its objectives and means."

From the beginning, the Soviet regime has utilized attacks on Zionism as a means to attain goals which frequently have no connection to the Jews or Jewish national rights. Zionism was first attacked as "chauvinist, bourgeois and reactionary." Although the Soviet Union supported partition and the establishment of a Jewish state in 1947–48, partially as a means of pushing Britain out of Palestine, the campaign against Zionism was renewed in 1949. Zionism was now denounced as an international conspiracy against the Soviet Union and other Communist regimes and was under attack in a campaign against cosmopolitanism in the 1952 Prague Trials, and in the 1953 Moscow Doctors' Trials. Zionism was also blamed for the liberalization pressures in

Poland in 1956 and in Czechoslovakia in 1968. After 1970 it was denounced not only as an accomplice of the Nazis and even "the twin brother of Nazism and Fascism," but as basically evil and a movement asserting racial superiority through the theory of the chosen people.

In 1965 the Soviet Union made its first attempt to have Zionism condemned by the *United Nations as a form of racism. This happened when the *United States and Brazil tried to include mention of anti-Semitism in the international convention on racial discrimination, and the Soviet Union conditioned its consent on the inclusion of Zionism as a form of racial discrimination. Neither anti-Semitism nor Zionism were mentioned in the convention.

It was only in 1975 that the Soviet Union finally succeeded in its efforts to get the UN to equate Zionism and racism (see below). Between 1968 and 1978 more than 150 anti-Zionist books were published in the Soviet Union. In 1974 the Central Committee of the Communist Party of the Soviet Union adopted a program of measures to strengthen the propaganda against Zionism, and a special committee of the Presidium of the Soviet Academy of Sciences was set up to fight Zionism. In 1983, an anti-Zionist Committee of the Soviet Public (AKSO) was created, with national as well as international objectives.

For over 60 years the Soviet Union has used anti-Zionism as a remarkably effective tool of international subversion, through which it has been able to pursue a wide variety of domestic and foreign policy goals. It has ruthlessly promoted this instrument of subversion and disinformation to suppress dissent, intimidate its opponents, cement its satellite system in East Europe, sow confusion in the Third World and encourage destabilization of the Western democracies. In the Middle East it has used anti-Zionism to isolate and weaken the only democratic, militarily dependable American ally in the region, while penetrating the Arab world. At the same time, more than a quarter of a million Jews were allowed to leave the Soviet Union between 1965 and 1979 — 160,000 of them settling in Israel.

The Arab and Soviet attacks on Zionism until the *Yom Kippur War, had only a limited international impact, with the exception, perhaps, of the Zionism-Colonialism equation which has had some effect in New Left circles.

A watershed in the development of anti-Zionism came with passing of UN General Assembly Resolution 3379 on November 10, 1975, by a majority of 72 to 35 with 32 abstentions, which declared Zionism to be a form of racism and racial discrimination. This resolution, passed by the automatic anti-Israel voting majority, has been instrumental in institutionalizing anti-Zionism — turning it into an international concept, with a credible public, legal basis, and providing a focus for all forms of anti-Zionism — thereby starting a process which some hoped would lead to the delegitimization of the State of Israel and its subsequent exclusion from the family of nations.

In the following decade the Zionism-Racism resolution was quoted extensively and referred to in other resolutions. Attempts have have been made to have it passed in other UN agencies and international organizations. Among the successful attempts have been the 1980 Copenhagen International Conference of Women, the 1984 71st session of the Inter-Parliamentary Union and in the 1984 preamble of the Organization of African Unity (OAU) Charter on Human Rights.

Resolution 3379 has played a role in increasing Israel's international isolation, giving it the status of a quasi-pariah state in the UN and many of its specialized agencies; in the revival of anti-Semitism, since it legitimized the attack on the Jewish people as a whole and on Jews as individuals after about 30 years in which anti-Semitism had been a latent and repressed phenomenon; and in weakening the position of the West, now a minority in the UN, by ridiculing the whole system of ideals and values on which it has based the organization of the international system after World War II.

Since 1948 the campaign against Zionism seems to have been relaxed, especially in the UN, and has lost some of its effectiveness. For example, despite overt Soviet and Arab efforts, Zionism was not included in the final document of the Nairobi Women's Conference in July 1985 which listed the evils to be eradicated in order to achieve freedom, development and equality for women. Nonetheless, the Soviet Union has not relinquished its resort to anti-Zionism as a means for subversion, while as long as the *Arab-Israel conflict remains unresolved, there is little chance of the Arab states and the *Palestine Liberation Organization (PLO) giving it up in their total war against Israel. (Y.M.)

Arab Boycott The Arab economic boycott was first applied by the *Arab League against the *_Yishuv_ in *mandatory Palestine in 1946, and has been implemented against the State of Israel since its establishment in 1948.

The boycott, which is the economic manifestation of the Arab struggle against Israel, is organized by the boycott office in Damascus and is actively though flexibly implemented by 17 of the Arab states. The boycott operates on three levels: the "primary boycott" which involves the refusal of most of the Arab states openly to trade and do business with Israel; the "secondary boycott" which involves the blacklisting of companies in third countries which have economic ties with Israel beyond ordinary exports and imports of non-strategic goods; the "tertiary boycott" which pressures companies in third countries to boycott blacklisted companies. There also exists a "voluntary boycott" which involves companies in third countries boycotting Israel without being approached by the Arabs, because they are afraid that they might lose lucrative trade with the Arab states if they were known to have any contacts with Israel. While the primary boycott is regarded as legitimate, given the nature of the Arab-Israel conflict, Israel has argued that the implementation of the secondary and tertiary boycotts in countries with which it has friendly relations constitutes a breach of the non-discrimination clauses in the General Agreement on Tariffs and Trade and other international trade agreements. Furthermore, they constitute intervention by the Arab states and the Arab boycott authorities in the internal affairs of foreign countries, frequently in the form of blackmail.

Israel's anti-boycott campaign, which is run by the Economic Warfare Authority in the Ministry of Finance, in cooperation with the Ministry for Foreign Affairs, is directed at friendly states whose governments are asked to condemn the secondary and tertiary boycotts, to avoid indirect cooperation with them (for example, by refusing to authenticate signatures on negative certificates of origin) and to pass anti-boycott legislation.

Various organization in North America and Western Europe, such as the Anti-Defamation League of Bnai Brith, the American Jewish Committee and the American Jewish Congress in the *US; the Anti-Boycott Committee in *Great Britain, the Mouvement pour la Liberté du Commerce (MLC) in *France, and the Centrum voor Informatie en Documentatie Israel (CIDI) in the Netherlands assist Israel in its efforts.

The US has passed anti-boycott legislation in the form of the 1976 Ribicoff amendment to the Internal Revenue Act and the 1977 and 1979 boycott amendments to the Export Administration Act. Under the first piece of legislation, companies which have given in to boycott demands lose certain tax benefits in the foreign transactions, while under the second, companies found to have given in to boycott demands are fined. More modest anti-boycott legislation was passed by France in 1977 (but implemented only in 1984) and by the Netherlands in 1984.

It is not known what economic damage the boycott has caused Israel in terms of lost or diverted trade, the need to camouflage some trade, the decision of foreign companies not to invest in Israel, etc.

*Egypt is the only Arab state which openly trades with Israel, since 1979. Some trade also takes place with *Jordan over the *open bridges across the *Jordan River and some trade used to take place with *Lebanon through the "good fence," but none of this trade is formal.

Arab-Israel conflict

INTRODUCTION. From its very inception, toward the close of the 19th century, the Zionist settlement enterprise in Palestine awakened the opposition of the Arab inhabitants of the country. After World War I, Palestinian Arab antagonism (See: *Palestinians) to *_aliyah_, i.e., immigration, purchase of land and settlement on it by Jews became a central factor in the crystallization of a separate Palestinian collective identity.

The manifestations of political opposition by the Palestinian Arabs to the Zionist enterprise did not remain within the boundaries of the country. They were echoed among the leaders of the Arab national awakening in neighboring countries. Indeed, the Arab-Zionist conflict in Palestine was seen by leaders in the Arab countries as an inseparable part of their struggle for national liberation. The identification of *Zionism with foreign colonial rule, and the combination of Islam and nationalism in the development of the Pan-

Arab collective consciousness, sharpened the opposition to Zionism. Zionist goals, according to the leaders of the Palestinian Arab national movement, were to change the Arab and Moslem character of the country, and gain control over the Moslem Holy Places in *Jerusalem, thus the struggle against Zionism became enmeshed with religious obligation, and a central value in the Arab national ideology. In addition, the desire for national liberation from the foreign yoke, and the realization of the vision of Pan-Arab unity were nourished. The efforts of the Palestinian Arab leadership to mobilize the support of the Arab and Moslem world for its national struggle against Zionism, and the intensification of the conflict between the Arab and Jewish communities in Palestine from the early 1920s onward, led to a change in the dimensions of the problem which assumed a Pan-Moslem and Pan-Arab character. However, the deeper the sense of the Zionist danger which entered the consciousness of the public in the Arab states, the stronger grew the identification with the national struggle of the Palestinian Arabs and the temptation among the governments and political organizations in the Arab countries to make use of the "Palestine problem" for both internal and external needs. Furthermore, the identification with the struggle against Zionism became a unifying feature in the internally fragmented inter-Arab political scene, fraught with the absence of a tradition of strong central government, the lack of political stability and large social and economic gaps among segments of the population. Palestinian leaders worked for the inclusion of the Palestinian problem in the official agenda of the Arab countries by mobilizing the sympathy and practical support of their public and political circles, frequently even "over the heads" of the Arab governments and contrary to their explicit wishes. Often, Arab rulers were forced to adopt a position in conjunction with the political expectations of their subjects. Thus, identification with the Palestinian Arabs became a source of legitimization for the Arab rulers, and opposition to the Zionist enterprise became a Pan-Moslem and Pan-Arab consensus issue, which in the 1930s played a central role in the establishment of the movement for Arab unity.

However, at the same time, the Palestine problem was also a source of division in the Arab world, intensifying conflicts and disputes which had existed among the Arab rulers since the mid-1920s in the struggle for regional leadership in the Fertile Crescent. The mere existence of an unresolved Palestine problem constituted a threat to the Arab status quo, for the ascendancy of one party or another over part or all of Palestine could undermine the inter-Arab internal balance. Thus, each Arab government determined its practical policy on Palestine according to its own interests, which frequently clashed with that of other Arab governments. This tension between the collective Arab position toward Zionism, which draws from Pan-Arab and Pan-Islamic romantic sources, and political pragmatism stemming from the various existential interests of the Arab countries and their leaders, has been a permanent feature in the conflict. It has dictated the force and intensity of the political and military manifestations throughout, and has worked to the benefit of the Zionists and Israel and to the detriment of the Palestinian Arabs.

The origins of the conflict are to be found in the 35 years which preceded the Balfour Declaration. At first Arab opposition to Zionist activities was on the local, non-political level, evolving around disputes over land ownership, grazing rights, and neighborly relations. After 1908 and the Young Turk revolution, the Arab reaction assumed a political dimension which expressed itself in anti-Zionist rhetoric by Palestinian delegates to the parliament in Constantinople. However, it was not until after Palestine was occupied by Allenby's forces in 1917–18 that the conflict was institutionalized.

1917–48 The advent of World War I changed the political situation of the Zionist organization with regard to the creation "for the Jewish people" of "a home in Palestine secured by public law." Even before Allenby's forces had entered Palestine the British government published the Balfour Declaration which promised to facilitate the foundation of a Jewish National Home for the Jewish people in Palestine, on condition that this would not prejudice the civil and religious rights of the non-Jewish communities in the country. When the war ended this declaration was recognized by all the allies and was incorporated into the text of the *Mandate for Palestine granted to Britain in 1922 on behalf of the League of Nations.

The Balfour Declaration alarmed the Arab population in Palestine while the Zionists' reaction made it quite clear that they intended to convert the country into a Jewish state. In those days the Arab community in Palestine lacked countrywide political leadership, and lacked the consciousness of political uniqueness. The Balfour Declaration and the conquest of the country by the British were to bring about a fairly rapid change in these two spheres, which reflected the political reaction of the urban Arab elite. The desire to prevent the realization of Zionism served as a driving force in the political organization of the Palestinian Arabs and the crystallization of an ideology which rejected Zionism and emphasized that the country belonged to its Arab inhabitants only and could not be granted by a foreign ruler to anyone against their wishes. From this time onward the Palestinian Arab national movement placed at the center of its political platform opposition to *aliyah* and land purchases by Jews, while demanding Palestinian independence and full Arab control in a sovereign state.

In this period, the Arab national movement, still in its infancy, was led by the heads of the Hashemite family — King Hussein of the Hedjaz (who was ousted in 1925) and his sons, among whom was Feisal. The Hashemites had made contact with Britain during the war, hoping to inherit the Arab provinces which had been under Ottoman rule, despite the fact that they had no formal mandate from the Arabs of the Fertile Crescent to represent them. Feisal, who represented the Arab national movement at the Versailles Peace Conference, was prepared to support the Balfour Declaration in order to enlist the support of the Zionists for Arab demands for a state. In January 1919, he actually reached an agreement with Chaim *Weizmann by which the two nationalities recognized each other and promised to cooperate and support each other's demands. Feisal's condition for this agreement was that the Arab people should realize their national demands. The assumption that the Zionist organization had the power to assist in the realization of Arab ambitions led to the adoption of a relatively moderate position vis-à-vis Zionism by the Syrian Arab leaders, Shehib Arslan and Aḥsan el-Jabari, in the 1920s, when they were struggling against the French. However, their position rapidly changed both because of the objection of Palestinian leaders and their failure to attain their national goals with or without Zionist assistance.

The struggle of the Palestinian Arabs against Zionism in the 1920s was ineffective and made little headway. The Palestinian political leadership refused to cooperate with the mandatory authorities in the establishment of self-governing institutions but did not actually obstruct the activities of the institutions of government, even cooperating with them on a daily basis. And Palestinian Arabs did not effectively interfere with the continuation of *aliyah* and the purchase of land from Arabs. Furthermore, already in 1923 there were serious political divisions within the leadership of the Palestinian national movement, which represented a limited stratum of urban dignitaries and intellectuals. Various families and groups began to struggle for positions of leadership and influence. This internal division continued throughout most of the years of the mandate and had a decisive negative influence on the effectiveness of the Arab struggle against the Zionists. The momentum of development introduced by the Jewish immigrants also weakened the motivation of the urban elite to demonstrate practical opposition to the Zionists, even though opposition on the political-declaratory level continued.

The manifestations of violent opposition to Zionism were sporadic, short-lived and local. In April 1920 and May 1921 local disturbances, accompanied by some bloodshed, occurred as a result of incitement, but had an only marginal effect on British policy. However, a new focus of power in the Arab community picked up the leadership of the Palestinian Arab struggle by the end of the 1920s. The Mufti of Jerusalem and Head of the Supreme Moslem Council which had been established by the mandatory government in 1922, el-Hadj Amin el-Husseini, began energetically to promote Jerusalem as a center holy to Islam, and to win over popular Moslem support against the danger of Jewish domination of the Mosque of el-Aqsa and the Dome of the Rock. By means of prolonged fund-raising drives which he initiated and carried out throughout the Moslem and Arab world to repair the mosques, el-Hadj Amin consolidated his political power and prepared the ground for his rise, in the early 1930s, to a position of leadership in the Palestinian Arab national movement. In August 1929 a wave of violent disturbances by Arabs against Jews broke out against the background of a prolonged conflict regarding the rights of Jews to pray by the Wailing Wall, and systematic incitement carried out by the Supreme Moslem Council which claimed to be protecting Moslem rights at this site. These were the most serious disturbances to date in the country, and the violence reached a peak in *Hebron and Safad where ultra-Orthodox non-Zionist Jews were the main victims.

The 1929 disturbances constituted a turning point in the development of the Palestinian problem from a local issue to a Pan-Moslem and Pan-Arab one which was manifested by expressions of solidarity and material support in Moslem and Arab countries. In 1930, when a committee of inquiry was sent by the League of Nations to investigate the question of Jewish and Arab rights at the Wailing Wall, the Arab spokesmen presented the affair as one which affected all Moslems throughout the world, and representatives from several Moslem countries appeared before the committee. A further step in this process was the convening of a Pan-Islamic Congress in Jerusalem in December 1931 to deal with the defense of the places holy to Islam in Palestine, on the initiative and under the leadership of el-Hadj Amin el-Husseini.

The 1929 disturbances, like those of 1921, led to a temporary halting of *aliyah*, and to a reinterpretation of the Balfour Declaration and the Mandate, and the issuing of the 1930 Passfield White Paper. Despite the MacDonald letter of February 1931, the Zionist leaders could not disregard the negative effect of the Arab public opposition. The 17th Zionist Congress of 1931, therefore, adopted a resolution to act for the re-establishment of good relations and peace between the Jews and Arabs of Palestine, which was doomed to failure because of the absolute objection of the Arabs to the Jews being granted any political rights in Palestine. In addition, the 17th Zionist Congress assigned to the Zionist Executive the task of maintaining the principle that neither side should dominate the other, irrespective of the numerical relation between them. This formula was designed to prevent the supremacy of 800,000 Arabs over 175,000 Jews (in 1917 there were 56,000 Jews in Palestine and 600,000 Arabs) in return for a promise that when the Jews constituted the majority they would not dominate the Arabs. However, this idea, like that of political parity and *bi-nationalism raised by various Jewish personalities and groups, did not placate the Arabs, whose main immediate goal was to put an end to the numerical increase of the Jews in the country. Toward the mid-1930s the heads of the *Yishuv* and the *Jewish Agency, under the leadership of David *Ben Gurion, contacted Palestinian Arab and Syrian national leaders, in an effort to reach an agreement that Palestine would become a state with a Jewish majority but would form part of a Pan-Arab federation. In this way the ambitions of both nations would be realized without either side endangering the rights of the other, and though the Palestinian Arabs would become a minority in Palestine they would form part of the majority in an Arab federation. However, the Arab representatives in the country and outside rejected the Zionists' proposals.

Subsequently, as long as the Arab national opposition to Zionism did not raise any serious obstacles to the continuation of *aliyah* and Jewish settlement, the Zionists concentrated on increasing and strengthening the *Yishuv* in Palestine, believing that only after it constituted a serious force to be reckoned with, would there be any chance of reaching a comprehensive agreement with the Arabs. In face of the uncompromising fundamental opposition of the Arabs to Zionism on the one hand, and their political weakness on the other, the Zionist leaders accepted continued British commitment to the text of the Mandate and the Balfour Declaration. For understandable reasons the Zionist leaders were unwilling to tie the fate of the Zionist enterprise to an agreement with the Arabs.

The second half of the 1930s was marked by the intensification of extreme trends in the Palestinian Arab community which further diminished the chances for a settlement. The growing extremism was fed by the realization that the methods heretofore used had been ineffective, together with the continued decline of the traditional leadership and the growth of a new generation of young intellectuals with an extreme nationalist approach, who demanded the launching of an immediate struggle not only against the

Yishuv but against Britain as well. Above all, the extremism stemmed from the sharp increase in the numbers of Jewish immigrants to Palestine as the Nazis rose to power in Germany, and a new wave of anti-Semitism broke out in Poland. The Palestinian leadership now tried to prevent the sale of land to Jews, with limited success as many of the Arab sellers were absentee landowners. In this period land disputes between Jews and Arabs, and cases of tenants being evicted from land purchased legally by Jews, were frequent.

The violent national struggle for independence taking place in Syria and Egypt, and the existence of an organized and armed Jewish force, also contributed toward preparing the conditions for the outbreak of the Arab Revolt and General Strike in April 1936. It was led by the Higher Arab Committee under the leadership of el-Hadj Amin el-Husseini, and was directed against both the British and the Zionists. The Royal Commission, headed by Lord Peel, which arrived in the country in the summer of 1937, examined the causes of the disturbances and concluded that the mandate could not be implemented without constant and extreme use of military power; it therefore recommended that the country be partitioned between the Jews and Arabs. Most of the country would be united with Transjordan, while in the coastal plain and valleys a Jewish state would be established. The conclusions of the Peel Commission reflected the impasse which the mandatory government in Palestine had reached. Any attempt to abrogate the Jewish National Home idea would meet with an armed Jewish revolt which would be at least as difficult to suppress as an armed Arab revolt. These conclusions were based upon the numerical importance of the *Yishuv*, which by now numbered 400,000, the momentum of its economic activity, and the level of its national organization and military potential.

The Zionist organization accepted with reservations the principle of partition, with the intention of bargaining over the boundaries of the Jewish section. The Palestinian leadership rejected it out of hand, and reacted by resuming and intensifying the revolt against Britain after a pause which had lasted less than one year. Although the Emir Abdullah of Transjordan was willing to accept the plan since its implementation would extend the area under his rule, this would not be expressed publicly because of the general opposition which swept through Palestine and the Arab countries, some of which granted the Mufti material aid to support the revolt.

Furthermore, a bloody internal struggle ensued between rival factions in the Arab community in Palestine between 1937–39. In the summer and autumn of 1937 the Palestinian leadership, under the Mufti, was forced to escape, after the British had outlawed the Higher Arab Committee and arrested some of its members. Arab opposition to partition, however, had achieved its goal in forcing Britain to abandon the Peel Commission recommendations and to seek an alternative solution which would prevent the alienation of the Arab governments.

With the massive disturbances and the prolonged Arab strike came the start of official involvement of the neighboring Arab governments in the Palestine question, with the consent and later the encouragement of the British government. In October 1936, after six months of the general strike, the Arab leaders in the country agreed to stop the strike on the basis of a formal appeal by the leaders of Iraq, Transjordan, Saudi Arabia and Yemen. The involvement of the Arab governments in the Palestine issue reached a peak with their informal participation, together with the Palestinian Arabs, in the St. James Conference. It was convened in London at the beginning of 1939 in an effort to find a solution agreeable to all the parties to the conflict. The Arabs refused to hold direct talks with the Jewish representatives, and the conference ended in deadlock, after all British proposals had been rejected by the Palestinian Arabs. In the meantime the need to appease Arab opinion grew as Britain became involved in preparations for war. Arab support and friendship were now seen as vital to the British war effort, Jewish support being assured. In May 1939 the British government published a White Paper, whereby Palestine would become an independent state with an Arab majority after a transition period of ten years and *aliyah* (immigration) in the next five years was limited to 75,000 so that the proportion of the Jews in the general population would not change. In addition, limitations were imposed on land purchases by Jews.

The White Paper was the greatest political

achievement of the Arabs in Palestine, but they nevertheless rejected it, despite the efforts of the Governments of Egypt and Iraq to convince the Mufti and his colleagues otherwise.

Despite their growing involvement in the Palestine question, the Arab governments supported the Higher Arab Committee which reflected the dominant position of the Palestinian leadership, under the Mufti, in the running of the national affairs of Palestine. Arab governments' support of Palestinian leadership was reversed during World War II as a result of the political, moral and organizational weakness of the Palestinian Arabs which stemmed from the suppression of the revolt and the mutual terror carried out between the Husseini camp and its opponents. After the Mufti and most of the prominent personalities in the Husseini camp had been exiled, the Palestinian Arabs' dependence on the political support and material assistance of the Arab League established in 1945, increased.

At the same time Arab states' interest in Palestine grew against the background of religious and national factors as well as inter-Arab rivalry for power and influence. Furthermore, the Arab governments were called upon to answer the growing political and moral influence of the Zionist organization in the United States, and the growing military and economic strength of the *Yishuv*, which was viewed as a threat not only to the status and rights of the Palestinian Arabs, but to themselves as well.

In 1942 the Zionist Executive adopted the *Biltmore Program, which called for the establishment of Palestine as a Jewish commonwealth, and an immediate opening of the gates of the country to unrestricted *aliyah* — a plan which gained increasing support in political circles in the US and Britain. As the war approached its end the inclination grew — first in the dissident organizations and later also in the organized *Yishuv* — to start an armed struggle against the British. For the **Haganah* the armed struggle included bringing in "illegal" immigrants and settling the land — while for *IZL and **Lehi* it meant terrorist activities designed to get the British to leave the country.

The Arab revolt and the publication of the White Paper ended the chances of finding some sort of Arab-Jewish agreement over Palestine. Although the Arabs had officially rejected the White Paper, the new British policy offered them much more than they could have attained in any agreement with the Jews, and at the end of the war they demanded that the British comply with every word. The period of the Arab revolt had left a vast gulf between the Jews and Arabs which was deepened by the Arab economic boycott on the Jewish economy and the violent struggle which limited the positive areas of contact between them. In the meantime, the pressure on Britain mounted to allow entrance to the remnant of European Jewry which had survived the *Holocaust. In Palestine itself the Jewish armed struggle and terror against Britain intensified. The British, while trying to suppress the revolt, wished to mobilize US backing for a settlement agreeable to both sides — which would also preserve the British strategic hold in Palestine. But the gap between the two camps was too deep to be bridged by Britain.

The Arab governments insisted that Palestine be granted independence as an Arab state in which the Jews would enjoy cultural and religious rights and would be represented in the government and parliamentary institutions in proportion to their current ratio — 30 percent — of the population. The position of the Hashemite leaders of Iraq and Jordan, who were interested in settling the Palestine problem and in Palestine's integration within the framework of an Arab union under their leadership, was somewhat more conciliatory. They were willing to support extensive Jewish autonomy in those areas of Palestine in which the Jews constituted a majority — a position unacceptable to the other Arab governments which were either under the influence of the Mufti, or wished to block Hashemite control over Palestine. The Higher Arab Committee was most extreme in its position, demanding that the political weight of the Jews in the future Palestinian state be limited to around 15 percent, and that only the Jews who had arrived in Palestine before 1917 should have the right to citizenship. The gulf between the two rival communities did not close even after the Zionist Executive decided, in August 1946, to support a solution based on the principle of partition. This change did, however, open the way for an understanding between the Jewish Agency and King Abdullah in 1946 based on support for partition, the establishment of a Jewish state in part of Palestine and the annexation of the Arab part to the Kingdom of Transjordan. Abdullah was the only Arab ruler to support such a settlement.

When Britain's efforts to achieve an agreed solution to the Palestine problem failed, it decided in February 1947 to appeal to the UN for a decision. The UN Special Committee on Palestine (UNSCOP) investigated the issue in the summer of 1947 when a considerable escalation occurred in anti-British activities by Jewish terrorists as well as in "illegal" immigration. Most of the committee's members recommended the partition of Palestine into two states, while the minority proposed a federal state made up of autonomous districts — some Jewish and some Arab. The Arabs rejected both the majority and minority recommendations. In face of the declared intention of the British government in September 1947, to end the mandate, the Arab governments and the Higher Arab Committee began to make military preparations for the armed uprising of the Palestinian Arabs. However, despite the decision of the Arab League in its meetings of September-October 1947 to provide military and financial assistance to the Palestinian Arabs, to establish a joint military committee and to coordinate inter-Arab military efforts, very little was done. After November 29, 1947, when the decision was taken in the UN General Assembly regarding the partition of Palestine, the Arab governments adopted a policy of unofficial war. This approach was designed to prevent a clash between the Arab states and the UN and was considered to be the lesser evil from a British point of view. Under it, the Arab governments promised assistance in the form of arms, money and volunteers to the Palestine Arabs. However, the six months of unofficial war were marked by serious inter-Arab disputes concerning control and direction of the war and the Arab governments' failure to fulfull their obligations in terms of military assistance, plus a serious internal split within the Palestinian Arab community, most of whom were indifferent, and the absence of sufficient organization and military preparedness for an armed conflict.

Most of the Palestinian leaders were absent from the country, some through forced exile (like the Mufti), others by choice. While the organized *Yishuv* acted under a national leadership and operated an armed militia (the **Haganah*, which assumed control in the areas evacuated by the British authorities), the Arabs lacked similar institutions and level of organization. Finally, the unofficial Arab war effort totally failed. Even before the end of the mandate the Jewish state had become an established fact and the only way to eliminate it was by the armed intervention of regular armies. This decision was made close to the termination of the mandate, and resulted from the collapse of the Arab forces, the Arab volunteers and the Mufti's gangs in face of the attack by the Jewish forces; the torrent of Palestinian refugees who escaped to the capitals of the neighboring states; and growing internal public pressure on the Arab governments to act speedily in order to stop what appeared to be the massacre of helpless Arabs by Jews.

The invasion of the country by Arab armies was marked from the very beginning by competition and rivalry between the rulers of the Arab states, lack of preparedness, the smallness of the Arab armed forces, and an extreme lack of coordination among the Arab armies. In fact, each of the Arab armies carried out its war separately, a fact of which Israel took advantage by concentrating its forces and alternately striking at each of the Arab

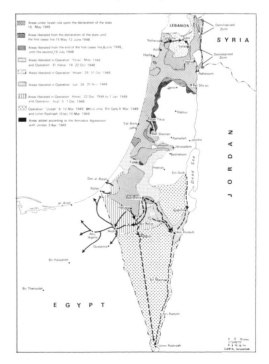

Map of the War of Independence, 1948.

Map of Armistice Lines, 1949.

armies separately. The ending of the war with separate *Armistice Agreements with *Lebanon, *Syria, *Jordan and *Egypt emphasized the divisions and lack of unity in the Arab camp.

1948–67 After the Armistice Agreements were signed, Israel, the international arena and even a few Arab statesmen felt that there would eventually be peace agreements. This did not occur. On the contrary, with the passing of time the roots of the Arab-Israel conflict deepened and became more complex and the polarization of the parties sharpened.

The 1948 War had two basic results: territorial changes and a movement of population. Aside from the consolidation and international recognition of the State of Israel, its territory was 6,200 square kilometers more than the original 14,400 square kilometers assigned to it in the UN partition plan. The Government of Israel viewed the new territory as an inseparable part of its sovereignty and argued that the partition borders had been designed for a state of peace between the Jews and Arabs. Since the Arabs had tried to prevent the establishment of the Jewish state by force, this addition was vital for its defense and security. In 1950 Jordan officially annexed what came to be called the *West Bank (approximately 5,600 square kilometers) while the Egyptians were in control of the 340 square kilometers which was to become the *Gaza Strip. Israel's borders with Syria and Lebanon were the international boundaries which had existed during mandatory times. Jerusalem, which according to the UN partition plan was to have come under a separate international regime, was divided, in fact, between Israel and Jordan. Several demilitarized zones were created along the borders with Syria and Jordan, which later became a source of tension and armed incidents.

The war led to the departure of close to 600,000 Palestinian Arabs from their homes in the area which became Israel. (Arab estimates placed their number at over 700,000.) The overwhelming majority of *refugees, about 60 percent, became Jordanian residents, about 20 percent remained in the Gaza Strip while the remainder dispersed in Syria and Lebanon. This problem was to become one of the most painful and complicated issues in Israel-Arab relations, and a constant cause for mutual accusations. The Arabs stuck to their argument that Israel is responsible for the creation of the problem and demanded that the refugees be allowed to return to their homes. Israel argued that the Palestinian refugees had voluntarily left their homes, many because of panic introduced by the Arab governments' broadcasts, and that Israel's security needs, and the need to maintain the state's Jewish character, precluded the return of the refugees to their homes.

The UN, through an international mediator, Count Folke Bernadotte, had been instrumental in bringing about short truces and had tried to present a comprehensive plan to the two sides to resolve the conflict. On December 11, 1948, the UN General Assembly decided to appoint a conciliation committee to act on its behalf with the goal of helping the parties reach a final settlement. In concrete terms the conciliation committee was to prepare proposals for a permanent international regime for the Jerusalem area, and to arrange for the return of those of the refugees who wished to come back to their homes and live in peace with their neighbors. Those refugees who preferred not to return would be resettled and rehabilitated with compensation. The conciliation committee was made up of the representatives of the US, France and Turkey and, in May 1949, it met with the representatives of Israel and the Arab states for talks in Lausanne. In the meantime the Armistice Agreements had been signed but the Arab representatives at Lausanne were willing to negotiate only on the basis of the UN partition plan, with the precondition that the return of the refugees be discussed on the basis of the UN Resolution of December 11, 1948. Israel, on the other hand, demanded that Egypt and Jordan evacuate the territories which they held in western Palestine and announced that the refugee problem would be resolved within the framework of a permanent peace settlement. It refused to consider any territorial concessions to the Arabs, and even expressed willingness to annex the Gaza Strip, with its 200,000 refugees and permanent inhabitants, on condition that it would not be required to give up any territories in return. Alternatively, Israel offered to pay compensation to the refugees and to absorb 100,000 more as its contribution to resolving the problem. In November 1949 the Lausanne talks ended. Israel announced that it would no longer take part, and that henceforth it would carry out separate negotiations with each interested Arab state. The policy of trying to reach separate peace treaties with the Arab states led Israel to renew political contacts with King Abdullah, this time with both sides eager to reach a separate peace treaty. The negotiations led to the initialing, in February 1950, of an economic cooperation and nonaggression agreement for five years. Strong opposition in Jordan and other Arab states nullified it. The crushing defeat suffered by the Arabs in the war undermined the status and stability of the old regimes in the Arab states, accelerating political and social processes of change and increasing the tendency to revolution and the destruction of the traditional ruling frameworks.

In the talks with Jordan in the years 1949–50, as well as in the contacts with the Egyptians in 1952–54, Israel was called upon to make far-reaching territorial concessions as a condition for peace, which it was unwilling to do for security reasons. The leaders of the state felt that as important as peace was, even in its absence Israel could continue to absorb *aliyah* and develop, especially since the immediate danger of an overall Arab military attack on Israel seemed remote.

Indeed, the Arab states which had just emerged from a painful defeat, suffered from military weakness, and in the course of the 1950s were forced to contend with serious internal political and military problems. But even though they were in no condition to start a new war against Israel they insisted that a state of war still prevailed, though for the time being no active military measures were being taken.

The Arab states now adopted a strategy of comprehensive struggle against Israel using every possible means, except regular armies. They were adamant in not recognizing Israel, and within the UN they carried out a persistent political struggle aimed at undermining Israel's legitimacy in the international arena. The refugee problem became the main means of accusing Israel of disregarding UN resolutions calling for the return of the refugees to their homes.

In the economic sphere, the Arab states imposed a naval, air and land blockade on Israel; a direct and indirect economic boycott (See: *Arab Boycott); and closed their borders to the passage of goods and persons.

Egypt closed the *Suez Canal to Israel vessels, or those carrying cargoes to or from it, and stuck to its policy despite a resolution by the Security Council in 1951 to the effect that this act was contrary to international law. At the same time Egypt imposed a blockade on shipping to Eilat by threatening to attack ships sailing through the Straits of Tiran in the direction of Eilat. However, the factor which contributed the most to the escalation of the conflict were acts of infiltration and murder carried out by groups of Palestinian Arabs from the Gaza Strip and the West Bank. The Arab governments were unable or unwilling to prevent these acts.

The State of Israel viewed the complex of Arab political, economic and armed acts of warfare against it as a single phenomenon to which it had to react forcefully in order to preserve its image as a state capable of defending its citizens. In October 1953, Israel began retaliatory operations to the acts of murder and sabotage, most of which were carried out against military targets in the territory of the states from which the infiltrators had come. Israel held the governments of these states responsible for the infiltrations.

These retaliatory operations were pointed to by the Arabs to prove Israel's aggressive and expansionary nature, which required them to increase their military power. Israel experienced increasing difficulty in defending the justice of its acts in the various international forums. It was using regular army units while the identity of the infiltrators was difficult to discern. The *feda'iyin* activities against Israel reached a peak in 1955–56 and led to a serious escalation in the dimensions of Israel's retaliatory acts, of which the Gaza Operation in February 1955 and the Kalkilya Operation of October 1956 were the most prominent. Finally, these frequent conflagrations, together with the closing of the Straits of Tiran and the progressively growing military power of Egypt, now receiving Soviet arms, pushed Israel to embark on an extensive military operation in cooperation with Britain and France (See: *Sinai Campaign). From Israel's point of view the campaign achieved its two main goals — ensuring quiet along its border with Egypt and the Gaza Strip, and freedom of navigation in the Gulf of Aqaba. Both lasted until 1967.

In the early 1950s the collective Arab stand emphasized total rejection of Israel's existence. Zionism and Israel were looked upon as an integral part of Western imperialism (of which the Sinai Campaign was proof). The goal of the Arabs was thus defined as liquidating Israel as a state (sometimes the liquidation of its inhabitants was also mentioned) for the sake of historical justice and the return of the country to its legal owners; the restoration of homogeneity in the region and the destruction of the danger of Israeli expansionism.

During the era of rising Pan-Arab nationalism under Nasser, it was clear that more attention would be devoted to an operational plan for vanquishing Israel. The approach which developed from the late 1950s onward, and persisted until the *Six-Day War was total: the total liquidation of Israel in the course of one glorious event. The operation would be so quick that the Powers and the UN would not have an opportunity to intervene. Because of the single nature of the liquidating operation it was necessary to delay the war until the Arab forces were absolutely ready. Nasser demanded a thorough preparation of the political, military, social and economic tools — first and foremost being the achievement of Arab unity. In the name of the holiness of the war against Israel, Nasser demanded that fundamental changes take place in the Arab states, including the overthrow of the traditional regimes. Nasser strongly rejected the approach of President Bourguiba of Tunisia in 1965 which advocated Arab recognition of the 1947 partition borders as a first stage in the process of weakening Israel, following which additional Arab demands would be raised until Israel was extinguished.

In 1963 tension mounted between Israel and Syria on the issues of the Jordan waters and the cultivation of the demilitarized areas in the Huleh Valley which Israel had drained. The Jordan waters had been the subject of conflict since the beginning of the 1950s. In the years 1953–55 efforts were made, with American mediation, to settle the dispute on the basis of the Johnston Plan for the full utilization of the river to the benefit of all the riparian states. That plan was rejected by Syria.

In the beginning of the 1960s Israel started to construct its national water carrier designed to bring water from the Sea of Galilee to the center and south of the country. Syria called upon the Arab states to stop Israel from using the Jordan waters and thereby consolidating its economic existence.

Toward the end of 1963 inter-Arab relations reached an ebb. Nasser's revolutionary course involved Egyptian participation in an expensive and hopeless war in Yemen in an attempt to challenge the traditional regime of Saudi Arabia. No less serious was the struggle which was going on between Nasser and the "revolutionary" regimes in Damascus (since the breakup of the United Arab Republic) and Baghdad, neither of which accepted his Pan-Arab leadership.

The Syrian call to deny Israel the Jordan waters was accompanied — for ideological and internal-political reasons — by a demand that a popular guerilla war be started against Israel: in other words, a limited war which would gradually build up into a full-scale war. Syria gave this practical expression by encouraging the armed organization of Palestinians in its territory and terrorist operations into Israel. Nasser, who was forced to answer the Syrian challenge, called for the convening of a Pan-Arab summit in order to work out ways to prevent Israel's utilization of the Jordan waters.

In subsequent summits during 1964–65 plans for diverting the Jordan waters in the territories of Syria, Lebanon and Jordan were discussed, as well as the establishment of a joint Arab command which would coordinate the military plans for war against Israel.

At the same time the strength of the Palestinian *feda'iyin* organizations in the Arab states grew: these organizations favored an immediate armed popular struggle against Israel. From 1963 onward the *feda'iyin* gained the material and moral support of Syria which viewed them as a political and military tool, both in the inter-Arab and the Syrian-Israeli contexts. In May 1964 the *Palestine Liberation Organization (PLO) was established under the leadership of Ahmed el-Shukeiri, in pursuance of a resolution adopted by the first Arab Summit Conference which had dealt with the need to "organize the Palestine people so that it will be able to fulfill its task in the liberation of its homeland and its self-determination." This organization was designed, first of all, as a political tool to serve Nasser's goals. But it could not block the activist goals nurtured by Syria. On January 1, 1965, the *Fatah* organization which was not part of the PLO, encouraged by Syria, began acts of sabotage within Israel. The number and severity of military incidents rose with the rise in the scope of terrorist activities, the Syrian preparations to divert the Jordan waters and the exchange of fire between Syrian and Israeli forces around the cultivation of plots in the demilitarized zones.

In November 1964 Israel aircraft together with tanks, hit the sources of Syrian fire and eliminated their earth-removing equipment. In May 1967, against mounting tension along the Israeli-Syrian border, and information concerning the alleged amassment of Israeli forces along that border, Nasser began to concentrate military forces in the Sinai in order to implement the joint defense agreement which he had signed with Syria in 1966. This was the first in a series of moves which brought about the crisis — apparently without any a priori intention of full-scale war: the removal of the UN Emergency Forces; the closing of the Straits of Tiran; war declarations and incitement to a holy war; and finally the signing of a mutual defense pact between Egypt and Jordan on May 30, which Iraq joined several days later.

1967–73 The Six-Day War awakened among the Arabs some serious self-examination about their defeat and the chances for future success. The lack of a clear and defined operational plan was pointed out as one of the major reasons for the failure. Until the Six-Day War the collective activity of the Arab states concentrated on finding a solution to disputes among them, with the Palestinian problem used as a tool by each Arab state despite the fact that it was supposed to be at the top of the scale of priorities of the Arab world. The results of the war did not do away with the Arab disputes, but there was a fundamental change in the Arab attitude towards Israel. The return of the territories which Israel had occupied during the war became paramount. The "liberation of Palestine" was now pushed into second place. This was well reflected in the formula which crystallized in the aftermath of the war, much to the PLO's chagrin; it spoke of "the removal of the vestiges of aggression, and the return of the rights of the Palestinian people."

Indeed, from now on the political activity of the Arab world regarding the conflict evolved around two main questions: what means could effect the return of the territories conquered by Israel and how to mobilize the necessary resources and distribute the military and economic burden among the Arab states.

The defeat of the Egyptian army in the war, the occupation of the Sinai and the blocking of the Suez Canal forced Nasser to reexamine his approach to resolve the conflict. Now, more than ever, Egypt had to depend on financial assistance from the wealthy Arab oil-producing states, headed by Saudi Arabia. It was thus necessary to give up the revolutionary slogans and the striving for Arab unity under Egyptian hegemony, and make do with inter-Arab coordination. One of the important lessons of the war had been the realization of the damage which the Arabs had caused themselves when they advocated the liquidation of Israel, which had brought about the alienation of the international community from the Arab cause. The need to gain the support of the international system in general, and that of the West in particular, increased especially against the background of the military defeat, and turned into a *sine qua non* for attaining a settlement favorable to the Arabs without their having to make any substantial concessions.

These constraints led Nasser to a certain change in his approach. He did not give up his basic goal but instead adopted a plan whereby Israel would be eliminated only as a result of a process and not in one thrust. Since the attainment of military superiority over Israel seemed unrealistic in the forseeable future, and the inter-Arab disputes remained, Nasser had to be satisfied with a limited war by means of which he hoped to bring about a gradual Israeli withdrawal and to deflate Israel's successful image.

The hope was that after Israel was forced to withdraw to the June 4, 1967 borders, the Arabs would raise the Palestinian demands for return and self-determination, while the withdrawal would lead to a process of disintegration and internal self-destruction in Israel. This approach served as the basis for Nasser's decision to embark on the *War of Attrition against Israel along the Suez Canal, by means of which he hoped to draw the other confrontation states into a similar effort — all this without risking an additional military defeat or a confrontation with the international arena.

From a practical point of view Nasser's new approach was reflected in the acceptance of Security Council Resolution 242 of November 1967. This resolution, accepted by Jordan's King Hussein as well, called for "a just and lasting peace" based on "respect for and acknowledgement of the sovereignty, territorial integrity and political independence of every state in the area, and their right to live in peace within secure and recognized boundaries," as well as Israel's withdrawal from territories occupied by it in the war. It also called for freedom of navigation in international waterways in the region, and a just settlement of the refugee problem.

The extremist states, headed by Syria and Iraq, rejected the resolution, because it required that Israel be recognized. However, even Nasser and Hussein were far from total acceptance of resolution 242; they demanded full Israeli withdrawal to the June 4, 1967 boundaries as a precondition to any arrangement. Furthermore, once this was done it would be necessary to turn to resolving the Palestinian problem — in other words, returning the political and civil rights of the Palestinians.

The change in Nasser's position did not help to bring the two sides closer together. Israel's brilliant military victory created a sense of invincibility which bordered on intoxication. The assumption that the Arabs would now be willing to make full peace with Israel in return for the territories was widespread among statesmen and public personalities in Israel. However, the annexation of East Jerusalem and its environs right after the war, and the declarations regarding the *Golan Heights and Sharm-e-Sheikh — were detrimental. The future of the West Bank remained open to negotiation but Israel government policy favored settlement activities in Gush Etzion, the Jordan Valley Rift and *Hebron.

The fundamental gulf between the approaches of the two sides was reflected in the failure of the international mediation efforts which the special UN representative, Gunnar Jarring, made from the end of 1967 until the summer of 1971 (See: *Jarring Mission). The only success of all the mediation efforts in this period was the cease-fire between Egypt and Israel in July 1970, which ended the War of Attrition.

Nasser's death in September 1970 enabled his successor, Anwar Sadat, to complete the Arab operational plan. Sadat sought inter-Arab cooperation and solidarity which would unite the political, military and economic power factors of the Arab world and turn them into a lever for pressing Israel into withdrawing from the territories which it had occupied since 1967.

In the beginning of February 1971 Sadat proposed an interim agreement to prolong the cease-fire for a limited period in which the dredging of the Suez Canal and its preparation for navigation would begin, on condition that Israel would withdraw partially from the east bank of the Canal. In the middle of that month Sadat took an even more far-reaching step and proposed, in reply to a note from Jarring, to sign a peace agreement with Israel which would include mutual recognition of the "sovereignty, territorial integrity and political independence" of the states in the region in return for full Israeli withdrawal from the territories occupied in June 1967. The Palestinian issue was not mentioned except in the demand for a "just settlement of the refugee problem in accordance with UN resolutions." Israel's refusal to consider complete withdrawal from all the territories was interpreted by Sadat as a desire to preserve the status quo with US support. The cool Israeli reaction, the worsening of the political and moral situation within Egypt due to the continued state of "no war and no peace," the deterioration of Egypt's status in the Arab world and the fear that the detente between the US and Soviet Union would lead to superpower acceptance of the political stalemate in the Middle East — all influenced Sadat's decision, in 1971–72, to resort once again to military means within the framework of a clear and comprehensive political strategy. In the first stage — a wide-scale military attack with limited goals which would be sufficient to break the political stalemate in the region. In the second stage there would be a diplomatic attack which would utilize the full force of Arab pressure on the West, including the use of the oil weapon.

Sadat's intention to go to war led to a military coalition with Syria whose goal was to recapture the Golan Heights. The decision was taken to initiate simultaneously a war against Israel on two fronts. These two states did not inform the other Arab states of their plans, although Egypt coordinated the oil embargo against the West with Saudi Arabia. In this period the prestige of the Palestinian organizations rose. Activities within the Palestinian population now under Israeli rule increased but hoped-for guerilla warfare modeled on that of Algeria, Vietnam and Cuba failed to be realized. They were unable to create an armed underground infrastructure in the territories under Israel's control, and were, therefore, obliged to act from Jordan and Lebanon where the PLO set up bases for organization and training. These organizations became active in harassing Israel's security system which was forced to contend with the phenomenon of urban guerillas, explosives in public places and other terrorist activity. A few Israeli Arabs (See: *Arabs of Israel) joined these organizations. In the first two years after the Six-Day War it was, in fact, the Palestinian organizations which alone bore the burden of the armed struggle against Israel, drawing it into extensive retaliatory operations across the border, among them the Karameh operation in the Jordan Valley in April 1968 and the "clean up" operation in southern Lebanon in May 1970. In 1968, after a reorganization of the PLO, the arena of operations abroad was expanded, with Israeli civilian planes serving as the main target for hijacking and random killing.

The mounting weight of the armed struggle in the Palestinian political community was reflected in the *feda'iyin* organizations gaining control over the PLO in 1968 and the removal of the old leadership headed by Shukeiri.

The rise in the prestige of these organizations was due to three reasons: the disinclination of Syria, Jordan and Iraq to use their regular forces against Israel and their preference for supporting the Palestinian organizations materially and politically; the PLO's having turned from a purely political organization into a national roof framework under which all the organized Palestinian bodies throughout the Arab world and the diaspora, were organized; and the new focus on the Palestinian problem which Israel's occupation of the West Bank and Gaza Strip created. This also brought about legitimacy in the international arena and recognition from various states and international organizations in the Arab and Moslem world, as well as in the Third World.

1973–79 The results of the *Yom Kippur War opened a new era in the history of the Arab-Israel conflict — an era of political arrangements. The successful military initiative taken by Egypt and Syria had a far-reaching moral and political influence on the whole Arab world. Enthusiasm and a sense of partnership was manifested when Iraq, Algeria, Sudan and even *Morocco sent expeditionary forces to participate in the war, and when Saudi Arabia and Kuwait imposed an embargo on the US and the Netherlands and limited the supply of oil to the West in general. Egypt secured an important political achievement when, as a result of the crossing of the Suez Canal by the *IDF during the war, most of the Black African states responded to its appeal and broke off their relations with Israel as a sign of solidarity with a fellow African state (See: *Africa and Israel).

Despite the fact that Israel managed to stop the coordinated Syrian-Egyptian attack and had penetrated deep into the territories of both states, the war appeared to the Arabs as a death blow to the myth of Israel's military superiority and proof of the recovery of the Arab camp which had assumed the political and military initiative in the conflict.

On the other hand, in Israel there was a state of shock and depression. The surprise, the sense that the political and military leaders had bungled, and the high cost in lives lost in the war, led to public ferment, protest, and deep soul-searching.

At the peak of the military confrontation the governments of the US and the Soviet Union reached an agreement regarding the formula of a resolution which was approved by the Security Council on October 21, 1973 (Resolution 338), which called upon all the parties involved in the war, to stop all military operations immediately and to start implementing all sections of Security Council Resolution 242. The resolution stated that "immediately and concurrently with the cease-fire, negotiations [will] start between the parties concerned under appropriate auspices, aimed at establishing a just and durable peace in the Middle East." This agreement between the two superpowers laid the foundation for the opening of a process of political negotiations between the parties. On December 21, 1973, a peace conference convened in Geneva with the participation of the Foreign Ministers of Israel, Egypt, Jordan, the Soviet Union and the US, and in the presence of the UN Secretary General. (Syria refused to participate in the conference.) This was the first time in the history of the conflict that a meeting of such a high political level took place among the parties, and it raised hopes for a breakthrough in the relations between Israel and its neighbors. Though the *Geneva Conference broke up after the opening session and never met again, the mere existence of the forum served as an umbrella for reaching *disengagement agreements between Israel and Egypt and Israel and Syria aided by the energetic mediation of Secretary of State Henry Kissinger.

The involvement of the American administration in the attainment of these agreements reflected the rapprochement which had occurred between Sadat's Egypt and the US following the war. The US sought to reconstruct its status in the region by means of furthering an agreement based on Israeli withdrawal. Sadat, who was aware of the low bargaining power of the Soviet Union vis-à-vis Israel, the dead end to which the prolonged dependence on the Soviet Union had led Egypt, and the power of the American influence on Israel, decided to allow the US to fulfill an active role in furthering the process of negotiations.

Already during the contacts toward the convening of the Geneva Conference, the Arabs demanded representation for the Palestinians, but rescinded when Israel and the US objected. Once the two Disengagement Agreements were signed, focus turned to Jordan. Since that country had not been directly involved in the Yom Kippur War, the negotiations with Israel would be concerned with the future of the West Bank, i.e., the Palestinian issue.

However, the new government formed in Israel in June 1974 under Yitzḥak *Rabin sought to refrain from discussing the Palestinian issue, either with Jordan or within the framework of a reconvened Geneva Conference. In addition, the Rabat Arab Summit meeting decided, in October 1974, that "the PLO is the only legal representative of the Palestinian people," and thus King Hussein lost his status as being responsible for the fate of the West Bank and Gaza Strip. No agreement was signed between Israel and Jordan and the PLO emerged with its status and prestige much advanced. In November 1974 Arafat was invited to address the UN General Asembly and the PLO was granted observer status in the organization. The Palestinian issue now turned into the spearhead of the Arabs' political efforts to weaken Israel's status and to call its legitimacy into question. The peak of this effort was the resolution adopted by the UN General Assembly in 1975 defining Zionism as racism (See: *Anti-Zionism). The substantial progress made by the Arabs in this sphere reflected, among other things, their enhanced economic power resulting from the rise in the price of oil.

Israel and the US continued to object to any PLO participation in the process of searching for a political settlement. Terrorist activities abroad continued (for example, the hijacking of the Air France plane to Entebbe in June 1976. See: *Entebbe Operation) but were limited to small extremist dissident organizations. Both *Fatah* (in the beginning of 1974) and George Habash's PFLP (in 1975) gave up direct participation in such acts. Since 1970 and Black September, Jordan was no longer a territory from which the PLO could operate and Lebanon had become its main base for attacks against Israel. In the years 1974–75 the terrorists concentrated their attacks on Israeli settlements along Israel's northern border, causing many casualties. A series of operations, the climax of which was the hijacking of a bus on the Haifa-Tel Aviv highway in March 1978, led to the *Litani Operation, in the course of which the IDF occupied the area up to the Litani River and cleared it of terrorists.

The lack of progress toward a settlement in the West Bank and the Gaza Strip did not stop the political process. In September 1975 Kissinger arranged an *Interim Agreement between Egypt and Israel, which extended and deepened the Disengagement Agreement of January 1974. The IDF now withdrew eastward from the passes in the Sinai, and the Abu Rudeis oil fields were returned to Egypt — with Egypt still officially in a state of war with Israel. Nevertheless, there were some political components in the new agreement which were not to be found in the earlier one. At this point strong and widespread objections to Sadat's policy throughout the Arab world led Egypt to enter a state of political isolation faced by a broad Arab coalition headed by Syria.

The Syrians sought to prevent Egypt from making progress toward separate agreements and to bind it to a joint Arab position in the political process, which Syria viewed as a guarantee for a settlement on its own front. Egypt did not, in fact, give up its efforts to integrate the PLO in the political process. Sadat used his influence on Arafat and his colleagues to moderate their position; give up their maximalist demands regarding the destruction of Israel; accept Security Council Resolution 242; and even establish a government-in-exile, so that they would be able to participate in the Geneva Conference.

After the 1973 war a change did occur in the approach of the PLO. In June 1974 the Palestine National Council (PNC) decided that the PLO would set up a "fighting Palestinian national government" in any part of Palestine evacuated by Israel. Two years later the PLO proclaimed that it would set up an "independent state on its national land" without determing its borders. However, this greater flexibility related only to the definition of the goal in the first stage, and was not accompanied by any significant concessions by the organization regarding its attitude toward Israel. Furthermore, the mere willingness of the PLO to become part of the political process raised strong international opposition from the radical rejectionist organizations, which gained the support of Syria, Libya, Iraq and South Yemen. The *Fatah*'s inclination to respond positively to Sadat's demands and modify its positions, endangered the continued participation of the radical organizations in the PLO, and was even accompanied by threats of murder and terrorist acts which were meant to prevent the *Fatah*'s leadership, headed by Arafat, from demonstrating excessive moderation. Consequently the PLO continued to oppose Security Council Resolutions 242 and 338 and avoided introducing changes in the *Palestine National Covenant, while demanding full backing from the Arab governments.

In the autumn of 1976 the Syrian policy in civil war-torn Lebanon reached a dead end, after its army had become involved in a confrontation with the Palestinian organizations and was forced to maintain a massive presence there. The difficulties of the Syrian regime in Lebanon, the stalemate in the political process and the isolation of Egypt laid the foundations for a renewed Syrian-Egyptian rapprochement at the end of 1976 under Saudi sponsorship, and the renewal of the political momentum at the time that Jimmy Carter was entering the White House as the new US President.

The efforts of the American administration and the Arab governments concentrated on trying to reconvene the Geneva Conference, though difficulties arose regarding the inclusion of the PLO. Syria sought to strengthen Egypt's commitment to a comprehensive agreement and demanded that the PLO be represented at the conference within the framework of an overall Arab delegation. The Egyptians, on the other hand, preferred Arab representation in separate national delegations and that the problem of Palestinian representation be resolved within the framework of the Jordanian delegation or some other delegation. However, the PLO, under Syrian encouragement and pressure, insisted on choosing its own representation. Finally, the new deadlock in the political process, the victory of the **Likud* in the 1977 Israeli general elections and the formation of a government headed by Menaḥem *Begin in July; the fear of a deterioration in the military situation in the Sinai; and the accumulation of serious internal problems in Egypt — led to Sadat's decision to try and reach a direct political agreement with Israel. On November 19, 1977, President Anwar Sadat came for an official visit to Jerusalem, after early coordination and secret preparatory talks. Sadat's move was in direct breach of the Arab consensus against direct negotiations with Israel.

The visit to Jerusalem constituted an historic breakthrough in the relations of Israel and its neighbors. However, 16 more months were to pass, attended by crises and disappointments on both sides, until the peace treaty was finally signed, aided by the personal and energetic involvement of President Carter.

Once the original enthusiasm which had accompanied Sadat's visit to Jerusalem passed, it became apparent that there was still a deep gulf in the positions of the two sides. From the Egyptian point of view the visit was evidence that Egypt no longer disputed Israel's right to exist within the June 4, 1967 boundaries, though it insisted that Israel must withdraw from all the territories which it had occupied in 1967. Israel, on the other hand, did not view the pre-Six-Day War borders as something requiring recognition, and sought to discuss the future of the territories held by it as part of the negotiations for a comprehensive peace. Furthermore, Israel wanted full peace and normal relations, something which the Egyptians were wary of accepting.

From the very beginning Sadat's initiative was strongly criticized by the "rejectionist front" states, the PLO and opposition circles in Egypt. Though Sadat rejected the criticism with disdain, he could not disregard it in face of the difficulties entailed in the negotiations with Israel and tried to ensure some tangible gains for the Palestinians. In September 1978 the leaders of Israel and Egypt and their aides were invited to closed summit talks with President Carter and his team at Camp David, where the two sides finally signed two framework agreements: "A framework for peace in the Middle East" dealing with the comprehensive settlement between Israel and its neighbors based, first and foremost, on the principle of land for peace, including the Palestinian questions and the future of the West Bank and Gaza Strip, but without mentioning the PLO; and "A framework for the conclusion of a peace treaty between Egypt and Israel," according to which the Sinai Peninsula would be returned to full Egyptian sovereignty, with part of it demilitarized, and full diplomatic relations would be established between the two states. In October 1978 the representatives of Israel and Egypt started to discuss a detailed and final draft of the peace agreement in Washington. Once again the negotiations entered difficulties which necessitated Carter's personal intervention.

The *Camp David Accords united most of the Arab states — including Saudi Arabia and its satellites and Jordan — against Sadat's policy. The Arab summit which met in Baghdad in the beginning of November, without Egyptian representatives, decided to impose a series of punitive measures on Egypt, such as expulsion from the Arab League and the breaking of diplomatic and economic relations, should it implement the agreements which it had signed at Camp David. And, indeed, once the Israeli-Egyptian peace treaty was signed, all the Arab states — except Somalia, Oman and Sudan — broke diplomatic relations, and cut back economic ties with Egypt. Furthermore, the seat of the Arab League secretariat was moved from Cairo to Tunis.

1979–85 The extreme reaction of the Arab world against the peace treaty was designed to isolate Egypt and prevent Jordan, the PLO or Palestinians from the *occupied territories from entering negotiations on the West Bank and the Gaza Strip on the basis of the Camp David Accords. The fact that Iraq and Syria stood at the head of the Arab camp emphasized the weakening of the traditional Arab states and the advantage gained by the extremists. Nevertheless, Egypt's abandonment of the military campaign against Israel caused the "eastern front" states to lose their military option. Once the punitive measures against Egypt were exhausted the Arab struggle against the peace treaty lost much of its vitality and began to die down. The anti-Egyptian front disintegrated due to internal disputes, the peak being the outbreak of the Iran-Iraq war in September 1980. The war led to the creation of an Iraqi-Saudi-Jordanian coalition against the extremist bloc led by Syria and Libya, which sympathized with the Islamic revolutionary regime in Iran.

In the meantime autonomy talks between Israel and Egypt bogged down into a complex of administrative and concrete differences of opinion, while Jordan and the PLO both acted against any Palestinian factor joining in the talks. It soon became apparent that Israeli and Egyptian interpretations of "full autonomy" were very far from one another. The Egyptians sought an effective self-administration which would eventually serve as a basis for a Palestinian state — while Israel aimed at creating administrative bodies lacking any legislative authority which would leave the de facto control of these areas in Israeli hands, thus preventing the establishment of a Palestinian state. Furthermore, contrary to American and Egyptian understanding of Begin's promises at Camp David, Israel did not cease its settlement activities in the territories.

In face of the stalemate Sadat announced, in August 1980, that as long as Israel did not bring new proposals which would enable progress to be made, he was suspending the autonomy talks.

The cessation of the talks awakened the *European Economic Community members and the new American administration under Ronald Reagan, to examine alternatives for the autonomy framework agreement. This trend served as a source of encouragement and inspiration for a similar effort by Jordan and Saudi Arabia. The most conspicuous expression of this development was the presentation in August 1981 of an eight-point plan by the Saudi Crown Prince, the Emir Fahd (See: *Fahd Plan) for a comprehensive solution to the conflict based on Israeli withdrawal to the June 4, 1967 borders, the establishment of a Palestinian state in the West Bank and Gaza Strip and implicit Arab recognition of Israel. The proposal of the Saudi plan — vehemently opposed by Syria and Libya — was the result of the growing danger of a war between Syria and Israel over the situation in Lebanon.

In April 1981 the "missile crisis" erupted when Syria introduced anti-aircraft missile batteries into the Beka'a area and in July 1981 a serious military confrontation broke out between Israel and the Palestinian organizations in southern Lebanon. Israel carried out massive air and sea bombardments of the organizations' bases, and they reacted by firing missiles and artillery at the Galilee settlements. A reprieve was attained by means of an indirect agreement between Israel and the PLO through American mediation, which granted the PLO an important political achievement in its struggle for international recognition. The difficult situation in the northern settlements and the reluctance of the Israeli government to renew the political process with PLO participation led Israel to prepare a large-scale military operation to liquidate the armed Palestinian presence in southern Lebanon, to begin in June 1982. (See: *Lebanese War.)

However, if at the outset the plan was designed to bring peace to the Galilee settlements, later it took on a totally different character — collusion with the Christians in the Beirut area, striking a blow at the Syrian force in the Beka'a and the mountains, and an attempt to do away with the PLO as a political and military factor.

In this war the weakness of the Arab world and its internal divisions were fully revealed. The Arab states appeared impotent and indifferent in face of the almost total liquidation of the Palestinian hold in Lebanon, the occupation of a large part of this country by Israel, the pushing of the Syrian forces northward and a forced evacuation of the PLO establishment, its command posts, institutions and armed forces from Beirut. However, the war also led to an undermining of Israel's political and moral status in world public opinion, and a marked decline in its support, as well as to a stalemate in the normalization process of Egyptian-Israeli relations. In the course of the war Egypt, under President Mubarak, who replaced Sadat after the assassination in October 1981, applied pressure on Israel through the US and the UN, in an attempt to bring about a cease-fire.

In the beginning of September 1982 President Reagan presented a Middle East peace plan on the basis of the principles of withdrawal in return for peace, and the linkage between Jordan, the West Bank and the Gaza Strip. Publication of the *Reagan Plan encouraged Arab leaders at the summit conference in Fez, Morocco. This conference once again dealt with the eight-point Fahd Plan, and approved an amended one which unanimously adopted the principle of a political settlement on the basis of negotiations, full Israeli withdrawal from the territories, including Jerusalem, the removal of the Israeli settlements established in the territories and the establishment of an independent Palestinian state with

Jerusalem as its capital. As opposed to the Reagan Plan the *Fez Plan emphasized the territories' links to the PLO and not to Jordan. Under Syrian pressure the original article in the Saudi plan which hinted at de facto recognition of Israel, was changed and it now stated that the Security Council would give guarantees for the peace would will exist among the states of the region, including a Palestinian state. The peace formula adopted at Fez reflected the desire of the Arab states to broaden the talks with the Reagan administration and encourage it to fulfill a role in the furthering of a process of political agreements as an alternative to the Camp David Accords. The Saudi plan did not attract the US government nor the members of the EEC. Furthermore, the war in Lebanon, while not leading to the political or military destruction of the PLO, did weaken the organization's status — especially that of Arafat — in the inter-Arab and international arenas.

The war brought about the PLO's most serious split since its establishment. Encouraged by Syria and the breach between Assad's regime and Arafat, this split reached its peak in the battles carried out by the Syrians and the Palestinian organizations and Arafat and his supporters in Tripoli, Lebanon at the end of 1983. Arafat tried to reinstate his leadership and the status of his organization through a rapproachement with King Hussein, in February 1985, with an agreement regarding political coordination on the basis of the principle of "land for peace," the establishment of a Jordanian-Palestinian confederation, and joint representation at a peace conference under UN auspices. This political coordination broke up in March 1986 without leading to any concrete results. From the outset the agreement started a serious debate in the *Fatah* leadership which placed reservations and limitations on Arafat and limited King Hussein's maneuverability vis-à-vis the US. In March 1986 Hussein announced the end of the coordination with the PLO later expelling the *Fatah* offices and its operational activists from Amman, while signalling a desire for a rapproachement with Assad — leaving Arafat in a political wilderness.

The question of the future of the political settlement continues to be influenced by the sterility of the PLO's position on the one hand, and a lack of any real change in the Israeli position regarding the future of the territories, on the other hand. There is growing evidence of a serious split in Israeli public opinion regarding the right of Israelis to settle in the territories and their permanent annexation by Israel and opposition to the continued Israeli occupation of the territories. So far, neither Israeli society nor its government institutions show any willingness to confront this problem and reach a decision. Meanwhile the process of "creeping annexation" and the integration of the economy of the territories with that of Israel may make the situation irreversible. (See: *Benvenisti Prognosis.)

(A.S.)

Arabs of Israel There were 1.3 million Arabs living in *mandatory Palestine in 1947, about 700,000 of them in the area subsequently delineated by the 1949 *Armistice Agreements as the State of Israel. By the end of *War of Independence only 156,000 Arabs remained in this territory. The remainder, having fled or been expelled to neighboring Arab states, became *refugees. The wave of Jewish immigration in the first years of the State reduced the percentage of Arabs in the population from about 14 percent in 1949 to about 11 percent in 1955. The percentage has since gone up again to about 17 percent (including the Arabs of East Jerusalem annexed in June 1967), and due to the high birth rate, their numbers are approximately 700,000.

The Arabs who remained in Israel were primarily villagers and Bedouins divided into three religious communities — Moslems (over 75 percent), Christians and *Druze.

The *Military Administration which was imposed on the Arab population by virtue of the *Emergency Regulations of 1948 and lifted only in 1966, caused many problems for them resulting in an ambivalent attitude towards the state.

Previously subsisting on agriculture most of the Arab labor force became menial workers in the Jewish economy. This change in employment was accompanied by the confiscation of a large part of Arab-owned agricultural lands, and their redesignation as state lands by the Military Administration. These developments, in addition to the direct encounter with the Western culture prevalent in Jewish society, shook the traditional Arab society, and led to its gradual disintegration. Despite the advance of the Arab minority in many fields, most notably in education where the number of high school graduates and university students has risen considerably, its social and economic integration and its political influence have remained marginal, the main reason being the security of the state. Israel has been in a constant state of military and political confrontation with the Arab states and the Palestinians outside of Israel. In addition, Zionist ideology posits a Jewish state based on *aliyah* of Diaspora Jewry, and consequently there is a clear preference being shown toward Jews in all spheres of the state's life.

The Arab population does not, and cannot, share the ideology and national ambitions of the Jewish majority, but it claims the equal rights granted by the Proclamation of Independence.

Within the Jewish population there is no unanimity of opinion regarding the nature of the Jewish state and the status of the Arabs in it. Not everyone accepts the principle of equality as stated in the *Proclamation of Independence. The extent of the political support gained by Rabbi Meir *Kahane, who advocates either expelling the Arabs from the territory of Israel or allowing them to remain as alien residents, has placed this problem high on the state's agenda.

Finally, the State of Israel has not managed to develop the tools for integrating the Arab population in the state's life, while maintaining its separate identity. The Arabs are segregated because of legitimate differences of language, religion, culture, school curriculum and also because of the neglect displayed in bringing about its integration. The Arab population, which identifies itself as part of the Palestinian people even though it has also developed an Israeli identity separate from that of other *Palestinians, feels discriminated against in terms of distribution of resources, quality of development, employment opportunities, land ownership and civil rights. Events such as the *Kafr Kassem massacre in 1956 and the expropriation that led to *Land Day in 1976, contribute to the negative feelings of the Arabs in Israel toward the state. Nevertheless, violent demonstrations, participation in terrorist acts and incitement against the state are rare, and when they do occur involve a minute percentage of the Arab population. The political struggle of the Arabs of Israel has focussed on achieving the equality promised them in the Proclamation of Independence while supporting the establishment of a Palestinian state living side by side with Israel. The identification of the Arabs of Israel with the Palestinian people is seen by most Israeli Jews as identification with the *Palestine Liberation Organization (PLO) in general and its terrorist activities in particular. However most of the spokesmen for the Israeli Arabs are careful to distinguish between the PLO as the legitimate representative of the Palestinian people in their struggle for a state, and the violent means used by the PLO to realize this goal, together with the refusal of some of its factions to accommodate themselves to the existence of the State of Israel. Even though the majority of them express support for the PLO, only a small number of Israeli Arabs have joined its ranks. This is not only because of the efficiency of the Israeli security forces but also because of the distinction made between legitimacy and violence.

In the years 1948–67 the Israeli Arabs had no contact with the Palestinian Arabs in the *West Bank, the *Gaza Strip and the neighboring countries all of which continued to struggle against Israel. These Arab states treated Israeli Arabs with suspicion and, on occasion, denounced their leaders. Following the *Six-Day War, the Arab states rediscovered the Israeli Arabs and learned to appreciate their delicate position within the Jewish state. In the aftermath of the war contact was also resumed between the Israeli Arabs and their brethren in the *occupied territories who had a much more developed national consciousness. This exposure created a new element of tension in the self-identity of the Israeli Arabs as citizens of Israel on the one hand and part of the Palestinian entity on the other.

The *Yom Kippur War brought about a further change; since Israel's invincibility had been called into question, the economic power of the Arab oil producers rose and with it the political influence of the Arab world as a whole; the PLO was recognized as the sole legitimate representative of the Palestinian people both by the Arab states (See: *Rabat Conference) and by many other states in the world.

All this strengthened the pride and national consciousness of the Israeli Arabs. At the same time the PLO changed its attitude towards the Israeli Arabs, and gave its blessing to **Rakah* whose leaders met PLO representatives in eastern Europe in 1977.

The *Progressive List for Peace, which

emerged in 1984, also received the PLO's blessing; its leaders, both Arab and Jewish, held several meetings with PLO Chairman Yasser Arafat.

In the years 1974–75 Arab Action Committees mushroomed all over Israel, representing specific interests, groups and issues. Direct contacts between individuals and groups with representatives of the PLO became more common. The events of Land Day in 1976 created a new focus of national identification for the Israeli Arabs which was shared by the Palestinians in the occupied territories and by the PLO. The 1978 *Camp David Accords and the *Egyptian-Israeli Peace Treaty were accepted by the Israeli Arabs with mixed feelings. On the one hand, it was believed that progress in the peace process would improve the status of the Arabs in the State of Israel; on the other hand, the process did not seem to be leading to an acceptable solution of the Palestinian problem.

Although Israeli Arabs constitute approximately 17% of the overall population of Israel, they constitute only 10% of the electorate because of the disproportionately large size of the 0–18 age group.

Electorally, this population has the potential to gain 12 *Knesset seats, but due to the split in the Arab vote, there have never been more than 5 Arab members of Knesset. The size of the Arab population makes it a target for the attention of Israeli parties, especially those of the Left and Center. One may distinguish four groups within the Arab population in terms of electoral behavior. One group has voted, since the establishment of the state, for the Communist Party in all its metamorphoses, not so much because of belief in Communist ideology but rather because the Party is non-Zionist and actively supports equality and the Palestinian right to self-determination.

In the elections to the 6th Knesset (1965) the *Socialist List, made up primarily of members of **al-Ard* (which had been declared illegal), tried to run for the Knesset, hoping to draw some of the Arab national vote away from **Maki*. However, the party was disqualified on the grounds that it rejected the legitimacy of the State of Israel as a Jewish state. It was only in the elections to the 11th Knesset (1984) that a new Arab-Jewish party, the *Progressive List for Peace (PLP), with a platform calling for complete Israeli withdrawal from the territories conquered in 1967, the establishment of a Palestinian state in the West Bank and the Gaza Strip, and equal rights for the Arabs in Israel, entered the Knesset with two seats. Even though the party's list was made up of an equal number of Jews and Arabs most of its voters were Arab.

The second group supported, and continues to support Zionist parties, especially the *Alignment the two main components of which — the *Israel Labor Party and **Mapam* (which accepted Arab members as far back as 1954) — have included Arabs in their lists of candidates to the Knesset in realistic places. Though it may seem anomalous that Arabs should support Zionist parties, there are several reasons for such support. Many Arabs believe that the best means of furthering Arab interests is through moderate Jewish parties which have a chance of either forming a government or being members of a coalition. Others support Jewish parties in order to serve public or private interests. There are also some who believe that only through a common Jewish-Arab struggle can the peace process be furthered.

A third group, traditional *hamulot* (extended family groups) used to support the so-called *Minority Lists associated with **Mapai* and later the Labor Party. These lists disappeared after the 9th Knesset, their disappearance expressing, to a large extent, the social changes which had occurred in Israeli Arab society, the decline of the traditional leaders and the emergence of a new, more independent leadership from among the generation which grew up in Israel.

A fourth category includes marginal groups, such as the *Village Sons and *Telem* (See **Telem* 1) which argue that the Arabs of Israel should not participate in the Israeli political game as long as the Palestinian problem is not resolved. The groups do, however, participate in the political process on the municipal level and in other non-national frameworks.

Within the framework of the *National Committee of Arab Local Council Heads municipalities and the 5 Arab Members of Knesset (in the 11th Knesset — 2 from *Hadash, 1 from PLP, 1 from Mapam, and 1 from the Israel Labor Party) work together to further Arab interests. However, unity is still an ideal rather than a reality.

area of Israel The area of the territory covered

by the Mandate for Palestine was approximately 91,000 square kilometers (35,126 square miles), of which the area west of the *Jordan River was 27,011 square kilometers (10,426 square miles). The 1947 *United Nations *partition plan allocated to the Jewish state approximately 16,000 square kilometers (6,176 square miles). The 1949 Armistice Agreement lines left Israel with 20,255 square kilometers (7,818 square miles).

After the annexation of East *Jerusalem in 1967 the area of Israel increased to 20,770 square kilometers (8,017 square miles), and after the annexation of the *Golan Heights in 1981 to 21,500 square kilometers (8,299 square miles).

The area of the *West Bank is 5,878 square kilometers (2,269 square miles) and of the *Gaza Strip 363 square kilometers (140 square miles).

Arens, Moshe Professor of Aeronautical Engineering and politician. Born in 1925 in Kovna, Lithuania, Arens grew up in Riga, Latvia and immigrated to the United States in 1939. He served in the US Army in 1944–46 and in 1947 earned a BSc in Engineering at MIT. He was **Betar* Commissioner in the US in 1947–48 and immigrated to Israel in 1948 where he became a member of Moshav Mevo'oth Betar.

From 1951–54 Arens continued his engineering studies in the California Institute of Technology, and from 1954–57 he led the development work on jet engines at the Curtis Wright Corporation. In 1958–61 he returned to Israel to be professor of Aeronautical Engineering at the Technion in Haifa until 1961 and from 1962–71 was Vice President of the Israel Aircraft Industries. In 1972–77 he was the Manager of the Cybernetics Company.

Arens was elected to the 9th Knesset (1977) as member of **Ḥerut* and was Chairman of its Central Committee in 1977–78. During the 9th and the beginning of the 10th Knessets Arens was Chairman of the Foreign Affairs and Security Committee. He served as Ambassador to Washington in 1982–83, during the active phase of the *Lebanese War.

He was appointed Minister of Defense after Ariel *Sharon resigned in 1983 and Minister without Portfolio in the National Unity Government in September 1984. After the *rotation in October 1986 Arens was put in charge of Arab Affairs in place of Ezer *Weizman. He is considered a hard-liner regarding Israel's relations with the Arab states. He also deals with the issue of Soviet Jewry.

Argentina and Israel Despite extensive lobbying by the well-organized Jewish community of Argentina after World War II, which generated widespread pro-Zionist sentiments, Argentina, under Juan Perón, abstained during the November 1947 UN General Assembly vote on the partition of Palestine. This policy resulted largely from Perón's wish not to offend the large Arab community in Argentina, and to preserve Arab good will. Nevertheless, Argentina recognized Israel on February 14, 1949, and voted in favor of its acceptance as a member of the *United Nations on May 11, 1949. In August an Israeli diplomatic mission was established in Buenos Aires — the second in *Latin America. In September an Argentinian diplomatic representation was opened in Tel-Aviv and an embassy opened there in 1956. Argentina was one of four Latin American countries which maintained their diplomatic representation in Tel-Aviv while the rest were in *Jerusalem until 1980.

Relations developed smoothly until the abduction of Adolf Eichmann (See: *Eichmann Trial) by the **Mossad* on Argentinian soil in May 1960. Argentina filed a complaint with the UN Security Council. The Council passed a resolution condemning the capture, but the dispute was settled only after Israel expressed its regret for having violated Argentinian sovereignty and law in the interest of historical justice.

Anti-Semitic tendencies and agitation had been inspired by Nazi propaganda and spread in Argentina during the 1930s and the war and *inter alia* resulted in a restrictive policy on Jewish immigration to Argentina, despite the fact that in general immigration was encouraged. Some anti-Semitism still persists. Since the 1950s there has also been a certain amount of "anti-Zionist" agitation (See: *Anti-Zionism) with more anti-Jewish than anti-Israeli components. Perón spoke of Zionism as a component of a curious conspiracy, the *Sinarquia*, the "regime of princes," consisting of the Catholic Church, Free Masons and International Jewry. In 1964 there was an attempt to launch a parliamentary investigation into "Zionist activities." However, despite the efforts of Arab officials, *Palestine Liberation Organization (PLO) agents and extreme right-wing and left-wing groups,

Argentina abstained in the November 1975 vote in the UN General Assembly equating *Zionism with racism, after having been absent from the Third Committee which dealt with the issue beforehand. Argentina has, however, consistently voted for other anti-Israeli UN resolutions.

In the 1970s the Jews were accused of planning the takeover of part of Argentina, and under the military junta which ruled the country in the years 1976–1983 Jews were among the victims of the massive violation of human rights, with many suffering brutal treatment.

In order to avoid a worse fate for the Argentinian community (there is no accurate information about the size of this community, though it is estimated that in 1960 there were 292,000 Jews in Argentina and that their number was down to about 242,000 in 1980) Israel allowed its relations with Argentina to continue with as little friction as possible.

Argentina became Israel's largest Latin American customer for arms (See: *Arms Sales) and during the Malvinas (Falkland) War in 1982, Israel continued to sell it war material, including missile systems, planes and spare parts, much to *Great Britain's displeasure. These weapons transfers were reportedly linked to the fate of Argentina's Jews by Foreign Minister Yitzḥak *Shamir in discussions held in Buenos Aires in December 1982.

The current Argentinian government has ceased its predecessor's anti-Semitic policy and relations between the two states since 1983 have been much more relaxed. In 1984 Israel exported to Argentina $15 million worth of goods, excluding arms) and imported $41 million worth of goods — mostly cereals and meat.

There are bilateral chambers of commerce in both countries.

Over the years approximately 42,500 Jews have immigrated from Argentina to Israel, 29,500 since the *Six-Day War.

Aridor (formerly Lieberman), **Yoram** Born 1933, Tel-Aviv. Member of Knesset and former Minister of Finance. Aridor holds a BA in Economics and Political Science and a MA in Law from the Hebrew University. He became a member of the **Ḥerut* Movement in 1961 and was elected to the 7th Knesset in 1969. He was Chairman of the *Ḥerut* faction in the **Histadrut* (1972–77) and when was appointed Deputy Minister in the Prime Minister's Office in the first *Begin government (June 1977) and temporarily assigned the portfolios which Menaḥem Begin was holding for the *Democratic Movement for Change which joined the government in October. In 1978 Aridor was the Likud's candidate to be Treasurer of the *Jewish Agency, but a Labor candidate, Akiva Levinsky, was chosen. In the same year he was a candidate to replace Yigal *Hurwitz as the Minister of Industry, Trade and Tourism, but the job was given to a Liberal, Gideon Patt. In 1979 he became Chairman of the *Ḥerut* Movement Secretariat. In January 1981 Aridor was briefly Minister of Communications, after Yitzḥak *Moda'i resigned, before being appointed Minister of Finance to replace Hurwitz. He announced the introduction of the "correct economics" and unlike Hurwitz's response *"Ein li"* (I haven't got any) to requests for financial support, Aridor's slogan was *"*leheitiv im ha'am*" (enhearten the people). He attempted to deal with the inflation by introducing attractive savings plans that would absorb funds from the public, and by lowering taxes on consumer goods and imports in order to reduce prices. The *Alignment referred to these measures as "election economics". Aridor planned to reduce taxes and improve the tax system while gradually reducing subsidies on basic commodities and services. Acting on Article 46 of the Broadcasting Authority Law which enables the government to make announcements on TV, Aridor made a seven-minute economic statement before the 9 p.m. news on February 14, 1981. In it he argued that the TV economic reporters were opposed to his policies and did not give him a fair chance to explain his views. The Opposition argued that he was merely trying to circumvent the law which prohibits party propaganda on TV 150 days before elections, which were scheduled for June 30, 1981.

In October 1983 Aridor's dollarization plan was leaked to the press. The details were never clarified but they were intended to remedy Israel's deteriorating balance of payments and soaring inflation by introducing the US dollar in Israel, or some kind of a shekel/dollar direct link. Its premature revelation led to Aridor's resignation and his replacement by Yigal Cohen-Orgad. Aridor was not given a ministerial post in the

*National Unity Government and is a member of the Knesset Finance Committee.

The *Bejski Commission Report of April 1986 criticized Aridor for not having acted to stop the regulation of bank shares when he was Minister of Finance even after he had become fully aware of the gravity of the situation.

Arlosoroff, Ḥaim (Victor) (1899–1933) Zionist and Labor movement leader. Born in the Ukraine Arlosoroff was taken to Germany in 1905. He joined **Hapoel Hatzair* in 1918 and in 1919 he published a pamphlet entitled "Jewish Popular Socialism" which advocated non-Marxist socialism with a practical approach to the problems of Jewish settlement in Palestine.

After studying economics in Berlin, Arlosoroff immigrated to Palestine in 1924, and in 1926 he was the **Yishuv* delegate to the League of Nations Permanent Mandates Commission. In 1930 he was one of the founders and leaders of **Mapai* and in 1931 he was appointed Head of the *Jewish Agency Executive Political Department. He was soon to become skeptical of both the durability of the British commitment to Zionism and the feasibility of a Jewish-Arab understanding in the foreseeable future. He supported Chaim *Weizmann's moderate policies but foresaw trouble for the Zionist cause among enlightened circles in Europe once the Arab national movement crystallized.

He tried to encourage the emigration of Jews from Nazi Germany in 1933 and to arrange the *transfer of Jewish property to Palestine.

Arlosoroff was assassinated by unknown assailants on June 16, 1933. The chief suspects in the murder, Zvi Rosenblatt and Avraham Stavsky, were members of *Brit Habiryonim*, (a right-wing nationalist group known to oppose Arlosoroff's moderate positions). They were tried by the British authorities and acquitted for lack of evidence. The Labor movement continued to claim that the two were guilty. On March 14, 1982 the *Begin government appointed a commission of inquiry to investigate the 49-year-old murder. The commission published its report on June 4, 1985, declaring that the suspects were innocent but also stating that the suspicions of the Labor movement were not unfounded. The Commission, however, could not determine who actually murdered Arlosoroff.

armistice agreements The agreements signed between Israel and each of its neighbors following the *War of Independence regulated the relations between them in the absence of peace and defined the international borders with *Lebanon and *Egypt (except along the *Gaza Strip) and the *Green Line elsewhere, no-man's land, demilitarized zones and limited zones. Mixed armistice commissions, with *United Nations chairmen, were set up to deal with problems arising from and related to the agreements.

The agreements were negotiated mostly in Rhodes under the auspices of UN mediator Ralph Bunche. The agreement with Egypt was signed on February 24, 1949, with Lebanon on March 23, 1949, with *Jordan on April 3, 1949, and with *Syria on July 20, 1949. No separate agreement was signed with Iraq even though Iraqi troops had been directly involved in the war.

Only on the Lebanese front did the borders drawn in the Armistice Agreements survive the *Six-Day War. Over the years there were infringements of the agreements, especially along the Egyptian and Syrian frontiers and in *Jerusalem, with Israel no longer recognizing their validity. Relations with Egypt are regulated by the *Egyptian-Israeli Peace Treaty of March 1979. Since the abrogation of the 1983 Peace Agreement that concluded the Lebanon War there is no formal agreement with Lebanon. Relations with Jordan are based on informal arrangements and with Syria on the basis of the 1974 *Disengagement Agreement and tacit understanding of areas of influence in Lebanon.

arms purchases Israel's arms purchases have been influenced by its perceptions of the threats it faces, the arms acquired by its enemies, the resources available for arms purchases, and the availability of the arms abroad.

Before the establishment of the State, the **Haganah*, *IZL and **Leḥi* devoted much effort and ingenuity to the purchase of arms, at first randomly depending on availability. However, even before 1948, arms purchasing became institutionalized.

An early deal was one between the *Haganah* and the Polish government in 1938–39, which included rifles, light machine guns and ammunition. During World War II the *Haganah* acquired clandestinely, through Jewish soldiers in the British forces, arms and ammunition from the

British stocks, and arms taken from defeated Italian and German forces. In the mid-1940s the *Haganah* acquired machine tools in the US for the production of submachine guns, mortars, hand grenades and ammunition. IZL made similar acquisitions during this period. Following the November 1947 UN General Assembly Resolution on the Partition of Palestine, the purchase of arms from countries in the Soviet bloc, especially Czechoslovakia became feasible, with Soviet approval. The arms bought in Czechoslovakia, which started to arrive in April 1948 and continued until 1950, included tens of thousands of old-fashioned rifles, and light and medium machine guns, many of which had been produced for the Germans during World War II. The deal also included 12 German Messerschmitt 109 planes, which were flown to Israel in parts, assembled and used against the invading Egyptian forces after May 15, 1948, and 20 British made Spitfires which arrived later on. Israeli personnel were trained by the Czechs to fly and maintain the aircraft. The Czech arms were brought to Israel in Israeli transport planes, flown by Israeli and foreign volunteer pilots (See: **Maḥal*).

During the *War of Independence some obsolete arms were bought also from *France including ten light Hotchkiss-35 tanks, some artillery pieces, small arms and World War II US-produced half-tracks smuggled into the country as agricultural equipment before the establishment of the State. Most of the arms on board the **Altalena* were also of French origin.

Artillery pieces, mostly obsolete, were purchased during the 1948 war from various sources. About 50 French 65-mm-guns produced in the 1890s, 50 75-mm German guns of World War I vintage, 32 75-mm guns from Mexico, and a few 105-mm guns. All these guns were phased out in the 1950s.

Israel also acquired some arms from the US by devious means, since the US had officially placed an embargo on arms sales to the Middle East. Using dummy companies, and in one case under the guise of a World War II movie, Israel bought three B-17 bombers, a few private and sports aircraft, and C-46 transport aircraft.

Two Cromwell tanks were acquired from some British soldiers who deserted from the British forces and fought on the Israeli side during the War of Independence.

The *Tripartite Agreement caused greater hardship to Israel than to the Arab states. Though *Great Britain sold Israel some arms these sales were always balanced by equal or larger sales to the Arabs. In 1953 it sold Israel a squadron of Meteor jet fighters which entered service in 1954. Israel failed to obtain additional aircraft from the three western powers, and Centurion tanks from Britain, allegedly because of Britain's displeasure with Israel's reprisal raids against the Egyptians in the *Gaza Strip. Britain did sell Israel two obsolete Z-class destroyers and three World War II submarines, which reached Israel in 1958 and were used in the *Six-Day War.

During the years 1950–55 Israel also managed to purchase from various sources some World War II surplus items which were reconditioned in Israel and put into service, such as Mustang fighters, purchased from Sweden, a few score of World War II Mosquito fighter bombers purchased in France and used in the 1956 *Sinai Campaign, obsolete British 25 pound guns purchased from a number of countries, and Sherman tanks purchased from Italy, France and the Philippines. Some of these Sherman tanks were kept in the Israeli order of battle, after further modification, until the early 1980s when they were passed on to the Lebanese Christian forces.

In 1954 Israel bought several 1949-designed Ouragan jet fighters from France. Its purchases from France increased in quantity and quality after Egypt's 1955 Czech arms deal and was accelerated before the Sinai Campaign when Israel ordered about 150 Ouragan and 4 jet Mystère fighters. The Middle East arms race now assumed a qualitative dimension.

Until soon after the Six-Day War, when President Charles de Gaulle imposed an arms embargo on Israel, Israel was able to concentrate most of its arms purchases in France, and thus standardize its arsenal of weapons.

In the years 1955–67 Israel flew about 70 Mirage III aircraft, Super Mystère 4Bs, Vautour fighter-bombers as well as Nord transport aircraft and helicopters. Fouga Magister trainers were assembled in Israel. Israel also purchased from France about 200 AMX-13 light tanks and guns to be mounted on its obsolete Sherman tanks, SS-10 and SS-11 anti-tank missiles, 155-mm artillery pieces, and 12 missile boats built according to Israeli specifications. The last five of these were smuggled out of Cherbourg in 1969. An order of 50 Mirage-5 fighters, adapted to Israel's specifications and fully paid for, was cancelled by France. As a result Israel started to assemble Mirage fighters, with parts acquired through intermediaries, and developed the Kfir which it started to produce in 1974. From 1968 onward the US, which had tried to stay out of the Israeli-Arab arms race, became Israel's main arms supplier.

In 1963 the US had sold Israel Hawk surface-to-air missiles — a defensive weapons system — after the Soviet Union had sold SAM batteries to the Arabs. In 1964 the US approved the sale to Israel by the *Federal Republic of Germany of American manufactured helicopters and obsolete M-48 tanks. After the Federal Republic cancelled its deal with Israel in 1965, similar tanks were sold directly by the US, which then helped Israel upgrade them.

In 1966 Israel concluded a deal to purchase A-4 Skyhawk subsonic fighter aircraft which entered service after the Six-Day War. After 1967 Israel increased its own arms production which had started many years earlier with the manufacture of small arms, mortars and ammunition. New production lines started from the refurbishing and improvement of foreign weapons systems. Most of Israel's more sophisticated self-produced arms included foreign components and systems. The Nesher, the first Israeli aircraft, was a Mirage 5 assembled from components acquired abroad from intermediaries. In 1974 Israel completed production of the Kfir, a modified version of the Mirage 5, with an American engine, and in 1986 the prototype of the Lavi was first flown.

The French embargo also led Israel to produce its own missile boat — the Reshef — a modification of the Saar.

In 1969 Britain cancelled a deal to sell Israel Chieftain tanks, which led to Israel's decision to produce its own tank, the Merkava, which entered service in 1979.

In the years 1970–79, as the Arab-Israeli arms race involved state-of-the-art weapons, Israel became almost totally dependent on the US for its arms. While Israel enjoyed extremely favorable payment arrangements, and received many grants (since 1985 US military aid to Israel has been completely in the form of grants) it has paid a certain political price which included acceptance of *Security Council Resolution 242, collaboration with the *Jarring Mission, acceptance of the August 1970 Rogers initiative to stop the *War of Attrition (See: *Rogers Plan), and a promise to refrain from renewing the fighting in 1970 after the Egyptians violated the standstill clause of the cease-fire agreement. In 1976 arms deliveries were briefly stopped during the US "reappraisal" which resulted from a disagreement over the 1975 *Interim Agreement. Again, in 1982, the US briefly suspended the supply of F-16 fighters, due to its disapproval of Israel's bombardment and siege of Beirut.

The American arms supplied to Israel began with the A-4 fighters, followed, in 1969–70, by the F-4 Phantoms. In 1977 the F-15s arrived, and in 1981–82 the F-16s. Israel also bought the C-130 Hercules transport plane and ARW aircraft. Helicopters included Bell 205, Bell 212, CH-53 Bell 206, AH-1 Cobra and 500 MD Defender. Israel's navy acquired Harpoon missiles. Its ground forces acquired M-48 and M-60 tanks, and finally the M-60 A3. Self-propelled artillery was armed with 155-mm M-109 and 175-mm M-107 SP pieces while the mechanized infantry acquired thousands of M-113 APCs.

Though the almost total dependence on purchases from the US could prove hazardous in the future, it has enabled Israel to standardize its arsenal. In terms of quality the American weapons supplied to Israel are as good, and frequently better than those which the Arab states have been able to purchase in the West and the Soviet bloc. (Z.E.)

arms sales Arms production began before the establishment of the state when in the years 1946–48 efforts were made to provide the **Haganah* with locally manufactured small arms and explosives. After 1948 Israel's first Prime Minister and Minister of Defense David *Ben-Gurion decided to combine the existing small, scattered and primitive factories and to turn them into the base for a modern arms industry. In the first years this new complex specialized in refurbishing old arms by grafting and improvisation. By the late 1950s the Israel Military Industries, the Israel Aircraft Industries, Ltd. and the National Weapons Development Authority (Rafael) were in existence, and Shimon *Peres, first as Director-General of the Ministry of Defense and later as Deputy Minister of Defense from 1953 to 1965, was directly responsible for programs of applied science and technology. From these early beginnings Israel's arms industry grew increasingly sophisticated, and gradually developed original items and systems, from the Uzi submachine gun in 1952 to the Lavi fighter in the 1980s. The main motivation for Israel's development of an arms industry was both the scarcity of supplies and the unreliability of suppliers. The unresolved *Arab-Israel Conflict has, throughout, made military preparedness and the constant upgrading of arms systems an imperative.

In order to make the production lines more economical and to earn foreign currency for the purchase of new materials an arms manufacturing country must find markets abroad for its products. Israeli governments have never formulated or rigorously enforced a well defined arms sales policy. Instead, decisions were taken as opportunities presented themselves and gradually the arms industry captured a significant share of Israel's industrial exports, attended by predictable economic advantages and diplomatic hazards. Most operative decisions — such as what items to sell whom, and on what terms — are taken at sub-Cabinet level, with the Ministry of Defense playing the major direct-intermediary role and the Ministry for Foreign Affairs expressing its approval or objection.

Israel's earliest weapon transfers were concluded in 1954, involving both refurbished items, such as Spitfires sold to Burma, and items, manufactured in Israel such as artillery shells sold to the Netherlands. Certainly the most controversial arms deal made in the first decade was Ben Gurion's decision to sell mortar bombs to the Federal Republic of Germany in 1959.

In the years 1960–73 arms diplomacy was used in attempts to prevent the Arab states from isolating Israel among the Third World states. Ethiopia, for example, during part of the reign of Emperor Haile Selassie, became the recipient of the largest amount of Israeli economic aid and military assistance, primarily in the form of training and advice rather than transfers of conventional arms. In the 1960s Israel established relations with over 60 countries in Africa, Asia and Latin America, giving military aid to many of them. Following the *Six-Day War and the French arms embargo, Israel's arms industry expanded and became more sophisticated. In the aftermath of the *Yom Kippur War Israel elevated arms diplomacy from a peripheral to a major activity. Until then Israeli sales, with only a few exceptions, were based on servicing and repairs, reconverting older generations of foreign-made products, and the export of small arms such as the Uzi submachine gun.

Statistics show a sharp rise after 1973, in both the allocation of resources to the Ministry of Defense and in the transfer of more sophisticated arms. According to conservative estimates Israel was, by 1979, exporting over $300 million worth of arms.

The existence of the three preconditions for military export caused this dramatic increase in the flow of arms from Israel in the decade 1975–85. First, necessity. The erosion of Israel's international standing, caused by the need to counteract Arab pressure and the Arab oil embargo made it necessary to achieve a higher degree of selective self-sufficiency in weapons-systems stocks and manufacturing capabilities and encouraged the use of foreign defense assistance as an instrument of security and diplomacy. Second, capacity. The growing sophistication of the IDF weapons modernization programs, made its products attractive on the world markets. By 1975 Israel had added aircraft engines, warships, armored fighting vehicles and missiles to its list of electronics, small arms and aircraft and its products were being tested under actual battle conditions. Third, opportunity. The 1970s was a time of international opportunities for arms sales, whether to established clients like the Shah of Iran, who as a result of the oil crisis had money to spend on armaments, or to new purchasers like Argentina, South Korea and South Africa who were canvassing the world market for supplies for their own defense needs. Arms sales came to exceed in importance the dispatch of advisors and technicians and the paramilitary and training courses offered in Israel itself. Israeli emissaries had relatively little difficulty in finding prospective clients in every region, including those loath to have formal diplomatic ties with the Jewish state and those who opposed Israel in such forums as the *United Nations.

Supportive Israeli governments — the Labor government of 1974–77 in which ex-Chief of Staff Yitzḥak *Rabin was Prime Minister,

Shimon Peres Minister of Defense and Yigal *Allon Minister for Foreign Affairs and the *Likud* governments which followed — ensured a wide consensus for an arms export program. Given their influence on national security, Israel's arms sales are conducted in secrecy. One unfortunate result are the many myths and unconfirmed rumors of Israeli global arms activities as, for example, a reported arms sale to the People's Republic of China. Military relationships with countries like South Africa, the former military regime in Argentina and Iran in the first phase of the Iran-Iraq war, partially motivated by Israel's concern for the welfare of the Jewish communities in these states, may have contributed to Israel's negative image in certain sections of world public opinion. On the other hand, given its international isolation, defense aid by Israel has also created foreign relations opportunities, as in Liberia and Zaire.

Especially complex are Israel's relations with the *United States, which, since the late 1960s, has been its main source of weapons. In terms of the prospects for Israeli defense exports the US exercises a multiple role: as indirect promoter but also critic of some Israeli arms sales practices; as co-partner in joint production efforts; as a potential market for sophisticated, high-technology subsystems; and even as a possible competitor with Israel for lucrative arms contracts in the Third World.

Israel now exports technological know-how, data packages and sophisticated electronics, computer programs and optical components of direct or indirect military application, some of which were used during the *Lebanese War. Sales of such scientific items are less conspicuous and therefore politically less sensitive than are sales of military hardware. (A.K.)

Assefat Hanivḥarim The assembly of representatives of the Jewish **Yishuv* in *mandatory Palestine, first elected in 1920, and officially recognized by the British authorities in 1928 on the basis of the Religious Communities Organization Ordinance of 1926. *Assefat Hanivḥarim* was made up of 71 members elected by a general franchise in which all Jews registered with the community could vote. Elections were based on proportional representation by political parties as are those to the *Knesset today. The assembly held one session a year at which the **Va'ad Le'umi* was elected. It could pass resolutions regarding the policy of the *Va'ad Le'umi* and had the authority to vote the budgets of the *Va'ad Le'umi* and the Rabbinical Council (See: *Chief Rabbinate). **Agudat Yisrael* refused to join the system and tried to induce other Jews not to join. After 1944 the *Revisionists and several other political groups boycotted the system.

Ata strike A strike occurred in Israel's largest textile factory in the Haifa Bay area on May 10, 1957, with full **Histadrut* backing. The strike broke out against the background of the refusal of the factory's owner, Czech-born industrialist Hans Moller, to accept salary agreements reached by the *Histadrut* and the Association of Owners of Industry. Moller insisted that he be able to fire workers for lack of efficiency and wished to maintain his paternalistic approach to manager-worker relations.

The strike, which turned violent despite explicit instructions by the Haifa Workers' Council to refrain from the use of force, did not enjoy the support of the government, which accused the workers of sabotaging the national economy. Minister of Finance Levi *Eshkol went so far as to express doubts about the wisdom of being overprotective of workers against layoffs which might be economically justified. Neither did the strike have the full support of **Mapai* and the *Histadrut*, (which had originally approved) because it was seen as a power struggle between the Secretary of the Haifa Worker's Council, Yosef Almogi, and his opponents.

The strike ended in August after an agreement was worked out by the *Histadrut* Executive with Hans Moller under which all the workers but one would return to work, the workers would receive certain pay rises and accompanying rights and the enterprise would adopt the customary rules for laying off workers. The agreement, which was attacked by **Mapam* and **Aḥdut Ha'avodah-Po'alei Zion* as a sellout, was generally viewed as a victory for the institution of job tenure over arbitrary layoffs.

In 1985, after its ownership had changed several times, and its new owners, more interested in the company's assets than in textiles, failed to replace old equipment and modernize the enterprise, Ata closed down despite efforts by the government (especially Minister of Industry and Trade Ariel *Sharon and Minister of Energy

Moshe Shaḥal) to find a new investor to take the factory over.

Attorney General The Attorney General in Israel has three functions: he is legal advisor to the government; he represents the state in civil and criminal cases, in which capacity he heads the public prosecution and is responsible for bringing offenders to justice; and he advises the government on legislation.

Part of the Attorney General's powers are derived from the law — especially those regarding the representation of the state in court cases. Other powers stem from custom. Unlike some European and North American countries, in Israel, the Attorney General is not the Head of the Ministry of Justice, is not a member of the government and his appointment is non-political. The Attorney General is appointed by the government on the advice of the Minister of Justice, and may be dismissed only by the government. However, no Attorney General has ever been dismissed and, by tradition, he continues to serve even after a government resigns.

Though the Attorney General's office is attached to the Ministry of Justice, he is not subject to the Minister of Justice or to the government and does not receive instructions from them, though he must consult the Minister of Justice or the whole government on issues involving public security. As far as the government is concerned, the Attorney General's opinion reflects the legal situation unless a court of law has decided otherwise. As legal advisor to the government he is in charge of upholding the legality of the administration, in which capacity he represents the public's interest in the preservation of the rule of law. His task is to give correct legal advice — not to serve as the government's attorney.

As head of the public prosecution, the Attorney General may delay criminal procedures and deal with appeals against refusal to investigate or prosecute.

The Attorney General is subject to the control of the High Court of Justice, and that of the Knesset, whether in the form of a report requested by the *Knesset, or a reply to a parliamentary question or motion for the agenda through the Minister of Justice and related to the spheres of his activity.

On several occasions the Attorney General has refused to uphold the government's position, as in the case of Helen Zeideman who had been converted to Judaism by a Reform rabbi and whose conversion was not recognized by the authorities, in 1970 (See: *Law of Return).

In 1955 Prime Minister Moshe *Sharett resigned over the public prosecutor's position in the *Kastzner case, and in 1964 Prime Minister Levi *Eshkol resigned over the Attorney General's opinion connected with the "committee of seven" in the *Lavon Affair.

In June 1986 Attorney General Yitzḥak Zamir terminated his term in office against the background of fundamental differences of opinion regarding the means of action in the *Shabak Affair.

Attorney Generals of Israel:

1948–50	Ya'acov Shimshon Shapira
1950–60	Ḥaim Cohen
1960–63	Gideon *Hausner (See: *Eichmann Trial)
1963–68	Moshe Ben Ze'ev
1968–75	Me'ir Shamgar
1975–78	Aharon Barak
1978–86	Yitzḥak Zamir
1986–	Yosef Ḥarish

(J.K.)

autonomy plan A plan first officially presented by Prime Minister Menaḥem *Begin on December 13, 1977 for the self-administration of the Arab population in the *West Bank and *Gaza Strip.

The plan for self-administration was prepared by Avraham (Avrasha) Tamir, then Head of the joint General Staff-Ministry of Defense Planning Division, and was presented to Begin on December 9 by Minister of Defense Ezer *Weizman. Four days later Begin brought his own plan to the Ministerial Committee on Security: it was called "Home Rule, Administrative Autonomy for Palestine Arab Residents of Judea, Samaria and Gaza."

The 19-point plan suggested the cancellation of the Military Government in the above areas, and the establishment of an elected 11-member Administrative Council for two years, with its seat in Bethlehem. The Administrative Council would deal with all the administrative affairs of the area and secondary legislation. It would include departments of education, religion, finance, transportation, construction and housing, energy, industry, trade and tourism, health, labor and welfare, refugee rehabilitation, and it would supervised a local police force. Internal and external security would remain under Israeli control. All inhabitants of Judea, Samaria and Gaza could choose either Israeli or Jordanian citizenship. Jews with Israeli citizenship would be able to buy land and settle in Judea, Samaria and Gaza and the Israeli Arabs of these areas would be able to purchase land in Israel. Freedom of movement and economic activity for Jews and Arabs would be guaranteed.

After the plan had been discussed in the Israeli cabinet and also with President Carter (who objected to the autonomy's authority deriving exclusively from Israel), Begin presented a revised version of his plan to the *Knesset on December 28, 1977. The new plan included 26 parts. It spoke of the cancellation of the administration of the Military Government. The Administrative Council was to serve for four years. To the list of the autonomy's departments was added a department of agriculture, but the energy department was removed.

According to the renewed plan Jordan was to be brought into the arrangement, one member of the Administrative Council would be appointed as representative to the Israeli government and one to the Jordanian government. The plan set out Israel's claim to sovereignty over Judea, Samaria and Gaza but proposed that the issue be left open "for the agreement and peace." There was a special proposal regarding the holy places and a provision for reexamination of the plan after five years.

In Israel many objected to the plan both among those who viewed it as a way of perpetuating Israeli control and among those who believed it would inevitably lead to the establishment of a Palestinian state.

The autonomy plan underwent further transformation in the *Camp David Accords signed on September 17, 1978. The agreement regarding the West Bank and Gaza referred to a transitional five-year period after which full autonomy would be provided for the inhabitants of these areas. The Israeli Military Government would be replaced by a freely elected self-governing authority (Administrative Council), while Jordan would be involved together with Israel and the local inhabitants in security arrangements. The details of the transitional arrangement, including the powers and responsibilities of the Administrative Council, were to be negotiated by Egypt, Israel and Jordan, with Palestinian representatives included in the Egyptian and Jordanian delegations.

At Camp David the details of the arrangements were not set out but provisions were made for the next stage on the final status of the West Bank and Gaza, as well as for negotiations for a peace treaty between Israel and Jordan. On the basis of this agreement negotiations began between Israel and Egypt regarding autonomy implementation. The Israeli negotiating team was headed by Yosef *Burg (one of the reasons for Moshe *Dayan's decision to resign from the government). Jordan did not join the negotiations, and the *PLO rejected the idea of autonomy on principle. As a result no Palestinians in the West Bank or Gaza dared to come out in favor of the idea.

On May 3, 1979, Begin presented the Israeli government with a new autonomy document which in fact made it clear that the Prime Minister had personal autonomy and not territorial autonomy in mind i.e., autonomy for the people but not for the territory. On December 24, 1980 Moshe Dayan, by now outside the government, brought a motion for the Knesset's agenda regarding the unilateral implementation of the autonomy in the West Bank. At the end of 1985 and beginning of 1986 Minister of Economics and Planning Gad *Ya'acobi again raised the issue of the unilateral implementation of an autonomy plan if the PLO failed to change its positions and Jordan refused to enter negotiations with Israel, arguing that the status quo was detrimental to Israel's interests. Prime Minister Shimon *Peres supported the idea in principle though called it a plan for "expanding the self-administration of the local inhabitants." Most of the **Likud* opposed the idea in principle, while Minister of Defense Yitzḥak *Rabin and Minister of Police Ḥaim *Bar Lev did not view the implementation of such a plan to be a practical proposition. Most of the Arabs in the West Bank and Gaza object to the plan which they believe would turn into a permanent arrangement perpetuating Israeli control and preventing their attainment of independence.

Avneri (formerly Ostermann), **Uri** Publisher and editor-in-chief of *Ha'olam Hazeh*, political activist, former member of Knesset. Born 1923 in

Germany. Avneri immigrated to Palestine in 1933. From 1938–42 he was a member of *IZL, but left on ideological grounds before Menaḥem *Begin took over the leadership. He served in the *IDF in the *War of Independence as member of a jeep-mounted commando unit on the southern front and was seriously wounded in December 1948.

In 1946 he formed *Eretz Yisrael Hatze'ira* (Young Palestine), a group which argued that the new **Yishuv* in Palestine constituted a new Hebrew nation. In 1940–50 he worked for *Ha'aretz*, writing editorials and in 1950 he bought *Ha'olam Hazeh*, a family magazine established in 1937. Avneri uses this medium to express aggressive political opposition and to uncover alleged scandals. *Inter alia, Ha'olam Hazeh* published many of the facts related to the *Lavon Affair, Moshe *Dayan's illegal archaeological activities, the *Yadlin Affair, the suspicions which led to the Ofer Affair, and the *Levinson Affair. Since the early 1950s it has advocated the establishment of a Palestinian state alongside Israel.

In 1956 Avneri established a political group named *Semitic Action which advocated the formation of an Arab-Israel federation in the Middle East. Nine years later he formed a political party — **Ha'olam Hazeh-Ko'aḥ Ḥadash* — after the government had enacted a press law which he considered restrictive to the freedom of *Ha'olam Hazeh*. The new party won a single seat in the 6th Knesset (1965). Since that time Avneri has declared that his was the first "Green Party". The party gained two seats in the 7th Knesset (1969), but subsequently split. Avneri's faction assumed the name **Meri* and ran for the 8th Knesset (1973) but did not pass the 1 percent qualifying threshold. *Meri* was one of the political groups which made up **Maḥaneh Sheli* in the elections for the 9th Knesset. Avneri served in the Knesset on behalf of the new party from 1979–81. After *Maḥaneh Sheli* split in 1983 Avneri took part in the establishment of a new progressive party, Alternative. The following year it joined in the formation of the *Progressive List for Peace (PLP) of which he is Co-chairman.

Avneri first established contact with *PLO officials in 1974 when he perceived a change in that organization's policy. At the end of 1975 he participated in the establishment of the *Israeli Council for Israeli-Palestinian Peace. Two of Avneri's PLO interlocutors — Sa'id Hammani and Dr. Issam Sartawi — were murdered by Palestinian extremists. In July 1982, in the midst of the *Lebanese War, Avneri met Yasser Arafat in Beirut. He did so once again in January 1983, in Tunis, together with Matityahu *Peled and Dr. Ya'acov Arnon. All three later joined the PLP. A third meeting took place in September 1983.

B

Bader-Ofer Law See: *Electoral System.

Bader, Yoḥanan Ex-Member of Knesset and attorney. Born 1901 in Cracow, Poland. Between 1919–24 Bader studied at the University of Cracow where he received a Ph.D. in Law. He was a member of the **Bund* and **Hashomer Hatza'ir* and joined the *Revisionists in 1925. In 1940 he was arrested by the Russians, but was released under the 1941 Soviet-Polish agreement. In August 1942 Bader left the Soviet Union with the Free Polish Army and reached Palestine in December 1943, joining the *IZL. Between 1945–48 he was held by the British in Latrun.

Bader was the founder and editor of the **Ḥerut* Movement's daily *Ḥerut* until 1966. He was a *Ḥerut* Member of Knesset from 1949 until 1977, usually speaking about economic affairs. Bader was generally acclaimed as an exemplary parliamentarian.

Baha'is Baha'ism is an eclectic religion founded in Persia in 1862, by Mirza Hussein 'Ali, "Baha'ullah." It originally grew out of Babism, one of the sectarian deviations of Shi'ite Islam, whose founder, 'Ali Muhammad of Shiraz, Bab-ul-Din or The Gate (or forerunner) of the Faith foretold its mission in 1843. The principles of Baha'ism stress the "unity of all religions, world peace and universal education."

The Baha'i faith and community were sometimes banned and persecuted in Persia and other Islamic countries. Their spiritual leadership is composed of a body of nine "Hands," called the Universal House of Justice. The main holy places are in Haifa (Tomb of the Bab) and in Bahji, near Acre (site of the Tomb of Baha'ullah). The Baha'is throughout the world are reported to number approximately 2 million. Few of them reside in the Middle East, where only Persia has a significant number.

The Baha'is are now banned in Morocco, Syria, Egypt and, since 1970, Iraq.

(Sh.C.)

Balfour Declaration A statement of British policy conveyed by Foreign Secretary Arthur J. Balfour on November 2, 1917 to Lord Rothschild. The statement, which was made largely through the efforts of Zionist leader Chaim *Weizmann, went through several drafts, the final version of which read: "His Majesty's Government view with favour the establishment in Palestine of a national home for the Jewish people, and will use their best endeavours to facilitate the achievement of this object, it being clearly understood that nothing shall be done which may prejudice the civil and religious rights of existing non-Jewish communities in Palestine, or the rights and political status enjoyed by Jews in any other country."

The statement deliberately spoke of a "national home" rather than a state, and contrary to the earlier drafts mentioned the "existing non-Jewish communities in Palestine." The last sentence of the declaration was introduced upon the insistence of *anti-Zionist Jews. The British issued the declaration in the hope that it would win over American Jewish support for *US entry into World War I, convince Russian Jews to support Bolshevik Russia's continued participation in the war, and forestall any German effort to gain Jewish support by issuing a similar declaration (the Germans did, in fact, issue a lukewarm declaration on January 5, 1918). However, *Great Britain's main consideration was that this declaration, issued several weeks before British troops began their successful conquest of Palestine, might contribute to its retention after the war. Palestine was considered an important strategic asset due to its proximity to the Suez Canal and Britain did not wish to relinquish it to any other European power. The declaration, which, at the time, was considered a great Zionist victory, was opposed by anti-Zionist Jews, pro-Arab British politicians and soldiers, and by the Arabs themselves who claimed that Britain had promised the Jews a land which did not belong to it, and this in contradiction to the McMahon-Hussein correspondence of July 1915–March 1916 which, according to the Arabs, included a British promise that Palestine would be included in an Arab state. Though the wording of the declaration was included in the text of the Mandate for Palestine, it was never recognized by the Arabs.

While the Balfour Declaration did not fulfill all the Zionist expectations, since Britain did not interpret it as a promise to help in the establishment of a Jewish state, it did open the way for extensive Jewish settlement and development in Palestine, without which a Jewish state might never have been established.

Bana'i Acronym for *Brit Ne'emanei Eretz Yisrael* (the alliance of **Eretz Yisrael* faithful). A Knesset faction founded by MKs Geula *Cohen and Moshe Shamir who broke away in the course of the 9th Knesset (1977–1981) from the *Likud* over Israel's compromises in the peace process with Egypt. In October 1979 *Bana'i* assumed the name **Teḥiyah*.

Bar Kochba syndrome A controversial theory developed by Professor Yehoshafat Harkabi of the Hebrew University in the early 1980s regarding realism in Israel's foreign and security policy. The syndrome is defined as "the admiration of rebelliousness and heroism detached from responsibility for their consequences." According to Harkabi the Bar Kochba rebellion against the Romans (132–135 C.E.), which led to the death of hundreds of thousands and to the second banishment of the Jewish people from *Eretz Yisrael*, resulted from an unrealistic assessment of historical and political circumstances, involving unreasonable risk-taking which jeopardized the Jewish national existence. Harkabi argues that by adopting the Bar Kochba rebellion and Bar Kochba himself as national symbols, the Israelis have distorted their view of the past, thus reducing the significance of the catastrophe brought on by the rebellion: "The problem is not how Bar Kochba committed a mistake — that can be explained — but rather how we have come to admire his mistake, and how it influences our national thinking. By admiring the Bar Kochba rebellion we Israelis enmesh ourselves in the predicament of revering our peole's destruction and rejoicing at an act of national suicide."

Bar Lev (formerly Zaslavsky), **Ḥaim** Military commander and politician. Born 1924 in Vienna, Austria. Bar Lev immigrated to Palestine from Yugoslavia in 1939, and served in the **Palmaḥ* from 1942–48. He commanded an armored battalion on the Egyptian front during the *War of Independence. In 1956 after completing a senior officers' course in Great Britain, he commanded an armored brigade which reached the Suez Canal in the *Sinai Campaign. Bar Lev was Commander of the Armored Corps between 1958–61 after which he studied for an MBA in economics and business administration at Columbia University in the US, receiving his degree in 1963. The following year he was Head of the Operations Branch in the General Headquarters of the *IDF until 1966 when he went to Paris to study political science. In May 1967 Bar Lev was appointed Deputy Chief of Staff. He served as Israel's eighth Chief of Staff between 1968–72 when the *Bar Lev Line was constructed along the east bank of the Suez Canal. In 1973 he was mobilized to active military service as Commander of the Egyptian front in the *Yom Kippur War. Since 1973 Bar Lev has been a Member of Knesset for the *Alignment. He was Minister of Commerce, Industry and Development in the governments of Golda *Meir and Yitzḥak *Rabin between 1972 and 1977 as well as Chairman of the Ministerial Committee for Development Areas. In 1978 he was elected Secretary-General of the *Israel Labor Party (in which capacity he started to introduce reforms into the defeated party). In 1984 he was appointed Minister of Police in the *National Unity Government where he acted to raise standards and morale in the police force.

Bar Lev Line The Bar Lev Line was a defense system built along the *Suez Canal and modified in the period when Ḥaim *Bar Lev was Chief of Staff (1968–72). The line was made up of 30 strongholds *(ma'uzim)* constructed along the canal and 11 strongholds *(te'ozim)* constructed after the *War of Attrition 8–12 kilometers inland. The *ma'uzim* were originally planned by General Avraham Eden, based on the structure of the foreward posts at Kibbutz Nirim during the *War of Independence, and were to act as the "eyes and ears" of the defense system. They were to play a vital role both in a static war, and in combatting an Egyptian attempt to cross the canal.

The *te'ozim* were the brainchild of Ariel *Sharon who argued that the *ma'uzim* were only good for shelter and hiding but not for war. *Te'ozim* were constructed outside the range of the Egyptian mortars and light weapons and included space for keeping tanks.

The line was fortified at irregular intervals — there were stretches of 15 kilometers without a stronghold — and was not fully manned when the *Yom Kippur War broke out. Only 16 strongholds were still in use and neither plan regarding the true defense function of the Bar Lev Line could be fully implemented at the time. As a result the defenders of the line were taken by surprise when the Egyptians started to cross the canal on the morning of October 6, 1973. All but one of the *ma'uzim* — the 'Budapest' stronghold — fell in battle. There were a large number of casualties among the soldiers from a Jerusalem reserve unit which happened to be manning the line. Many viewed the Bar Lev Line as a symbol of Israeli complacency during the years 1971–73, others a proof that Israel is weak in defensive strategies.

Basic Laws On June, 1950, the *Knesset adopted a resolution which stated: "The first Knesset assigns the Constitution, Law and Justice Committee with the task of preparing a constitution for the country. The *constitution will be made up of chapters, each of which will constitute a separate Basic Law. The chapters will be brought to the Knesset after the committee has completed its work. The chapters will together form the Constitution of the State."

Following the passing of this resolution, known as the Harari Resolution, the Constitution, Law and Justice Committee appointed a subcommittee on the constitution. Each subsequent Knesset has reappointed such a committee to further the enactment of the Basic Laws. The first Basic Law (the Basic Law: the Knesset) was passed by the 3rd Knesset.

There are differences of opinion as to whether the 1950 resolution binds any but the 1st Knesset. So far all the Knessets have accepted this resolution as reflecting the accepted policy regarding the constitution, even though it left many fundamental questions unanswered. Among these: Are the Basic Laws superior to ordinary laws or will they be superior only at such time as they are included in a constitution? Has the Knesset been empowered to entrench the Basic Laws by means of articles which limit the possibility of amending or cancelling them? Is a Basic Law only one which has explicitly been called a Basic Law?

There are those who argue that the Basic Laws will not be superior to an ordinary law until such time as their superiority is stated explicitly. They base their argument on the fact that Basic Laws are passed by an ordinary majority, and that such a majority cannot grant a law superior status.

On the other hand, there are those who claim that the superiority of the Basic Laws stems from the Knesset's authority as a Constituent Assembly, and that the name Basic Laws indicates the legislators' intention of granting them constitutional superiority.

There still remains the question what this superiority, if it exists, means. Two of the Basic Laws, the Basic Law: the Knesset and the Basic Law: the Government, include entrenched clauses, in other words, clauses which can only be amended by a special majority, and the High Court of Justice decided that regarding these clauses the Basic Laws are superior. On the other hand, the ordinary articles of the Basic Laws can be amended or cancelled by an ordinary majority without any special procedure, so that with respect to these articles the Basic Laws are not superior. In fact, several of the Basic Laws have been amended by ordinary majorities, both by the initiative of the government and by private members' bills. Article 5 of the Basic Law: Legislation (which has not yet been enacted) proposes that a Basic Law, or a law which contradicts, amends or changes a Basic Law, will be valid only if two-thirds of the Knesset members have voted for it.

The question arises as to the significance and identifying characteristics of the Basic Laws. The difficulty stems trom the fact that besides their name and exclusion of the year of enactment from the name of the law, most of the Basic Laws have no other essential characteristics which distinguish them from other laws. One may, however, remark that the Basic Laws are usually worded briefly and generally, while the details of their subject matter are dealt with in ordinary laws and regulations. In other words, it is the principles which are dealt with in the Basic Law, and once the Basic Laws are united into a constitution, these principles will be difficult to amend and their status will be superior.

To date, all the Basic Laws, except the Basic Law: the Knesset which was initiated by the Knesset Constitution, Law and Justice Committee, have been initiated by the government.

THE BASIC LAW: THE KNESSET was adopted by the 3rd Knesset on February 12, 1958. It does not define the powers of the Knesset, but declares that the Knesset is the House of Representatives of the state, that its seat is Jerusalem, and that it shall be made up of 120 elected members. It goes on to deal with the *electoral system, the right to vote and be elected, the term of office in a Knesset, laying down principles regarding the elections to the Knesset, the service of the Members of Knesset (MKs), their immunity and that of the Knesset premises, the Knesset's work and its committees. The law prescribes that the electoral system can be amended only by an absolute majority (Article 4), and that Article 44, which prevents the law's amendment by means of emergency regulations, can only be amended by a majority of 80 MKs (article 45).

The Basic Law: the Knesset has been amended eight times.

THE BASIC LAW: ISRAEL LANDS was adopted by the 4th Knesset on July 25, 1960. The law deals with the special relationship between the people of Israel and the land of Israel and its redemption. The law is meant to ensure that state lands (which constitute over 90 percent of the land in the state) will remain national property. The law prohibits the transfer of land owned by the state, the Development Authority or the Jewish National Fund except as prescribed by law. (See: *Land Policy).

THE BASIC LAW: THE PRESIDENT OF THE STATE was adopted by the 5th Knesset on June 16, 1964. It reenacted previous provisions which were dispersed in other laws. The law defines the President's status and his powers (see: *President). The Basic Law: the President of the State was amended twice in 1969.

THE BASIC LAW: THE GOVERNMENT (See: *Government) was adopted by the 6th Knesset on August 13, 1968. The law reenacted, with only minor changes, previous instructions which were contained in other laws.

The subject of the law is the government. It lays down that the government is the Executive of the State and its seat is Jerusalem. Next the law deals with the principles of its office by virtue of the Knesset's confidence, its collective responsibility to the Knesset and the responsibility of each Minister to the Prime Minister. The law deals with the government's make-up, the eligibility of Ministers, the procedures for forming a government, the formation of a government, the distribution of tasks among the Ministers, the government's *modus operandi*, the Ministers' service and salary, the continuity of government, its resignation and the resignation of the Prime Minister. Article 42 of the law, which prohibits its being altered, temporarily suspended or made subject to conditions by force of emergency regulations, can be amended only by a majority of the Knesset members. The Basic Law: the Government has been amended four times.

THE BASIC LAW: THE STATE ECONOMY was adopted by the 7th Knesset on July 21, 1971. The law lays down the framework for the budget laws, and the basic rule that taxes, obligatory loans, other obligatory payments and levies can only be imposed or their rates changed by law or according to the law. Regulations which impose obligatory payments are subject to the approval of the Knesset or one of its committees. In addition, the law deals with the right to carry out deals related to the state's assets, the acquisition of rights or undertaking of obligations, with the state budget and the procedures for its adoption, the printing of currency bills and the minting of coins. It also decrees that "the State Economy is subject to the supervision of the State Comptroller." The law has been amended twice to define arrangements connected with the state budget.

THE BASIC LAW: THE ARMY was adopted by the 8th Knesset on March 31, 1976. Until this law was enacted the legislative and legal basis of the *IDF was in the Israel Defense Forces Ordinance of 1948. The law follows the said ordinance, but adds instructions regarding the army's subordination to the government, the status of the Chief of Staff, and other instructions (the absence of which was pointed out by the *Agranat Commission after the *Yom Kippur War.) The law states that the IDF is the army of the state, and thus a national institution. It also decrees that the army is subject to civilian authority. The law deals with the Chief of Staff, his appointment and subjection to the Minister of Defense; the duty to serve and enlistment; and the army instructions and orders. It states that "one is not to form or maintain an armed force outside the Israel Defense Forces except by law."

THE BASIC LAW: JERUSALEM THE CAPITAL OF ISRAEL was adopted by the 9th Knesset on July 30, 1980. On December 13, 1949, Prime Minister David *Ben Gurion stated that "the State of Israel has had and will have only one capital — the eternal Jerusalem." However, a bill presented by MK Menaḥem *Begin at that time, regarding the status of Jerusalem, was not accepted.

The goal of the law, passed while Begin was Prime Minister, was to settle Jerusalem's status as Israel's capital in a Basic Law, to ensure its integrity and unity, and concentrate all the instructions contained in various laws concerning the seat of the national institutions. The law also deals with the holy places, guarantees the rights of members of all religions, and declares a policy of preference regarding the city's development.

THE BASIC LAW: THE JUDICIARY was passed by the 10th Knesset on February 28, 1984. The law deals with the judicial authority, the judicial institutions, the principle of judicial independence, the publicity of proceedings, the appointment of judges, their eligibility and service, the powers of the Supreme Court, the right of appeal, further hearings and retrial, and the principle of judicial precedent.

The law does not deal with the power of the courts to examine the legality of laws. This will be dealt with by the proposed Basic Law: the Legislature. Like the Basic Law: the Knesset and the Basic Law: the Government so the Basic Law: the Judiciary cannot be changed by means of emergency regulations, but it does not include an entrenched clause as do the other two laws. Additional Basic Laws to be enacted are the Basic Law: the Legislature, the Basic Law: the State Comptroller and the Basic Law: Human Rights.

(J.K.)

Begin, Menaḥem Zionist resistance leader, parliamentarian and former prime minister. Born 1913 in Brest-Litovsk, Russia.

Begin attended the University of Warsaw, graduating in 1935 as *magister juri*. He was active in Jewish affairs during his student years, including violent confrontations with anti-Semites.

Begin was a member of the socialist **Hashomer Hatza'ir* youth movement as a child and, at the age of 16, joined the right-wing **Betar* movement. In 1932 he became a member of *Betar*'s national executive in Poland, and headed its organizational department. He travelled across Poland and became known for his oratorical talents. In 1937 he was arrested for participating in an anti-British demonstration. During the *Betar* World Convention in 1938, Begin clashed with Ze'ev *Jabotinsky, his mentor, in demanding a radical policy reorientation with the goal of "conquest of the homeland" by force. He subsequently became involved in illegal immigration to Palestine and supported the activities of the **Irgun Zva'i Le'umi* (IZL).

On the eve of World War II, Begin was Head of Polish *Betar*. After an unsuccessful attempt to cross over into Romania, he arrived in Vilna and established a framework for the *Betar* refugees. He was arrested in September 1940 by the Soviet authorities and charged with espionage. After he was released from jail following the German invasion of Russia, he enlisted in General Ander's Polish army, and went to Palestine within its framework in May 1942. In late 1943 Begin was appointed commander of IZL. He composed the IZL's "Proclamation of Revolt" in February 1944, announcing the opening of the organization's underground campaign against the British mandatory authorities. A reward of £10,000 was offered for his capture. Living in various places and under different disguises, Begin eluded arrest and continued to direct IZL's operations until the establishment of the state in 1948. In June of that year Begin was nearly killed while on the deck of the **Altalena*. In August 1948, Begin and fellow IZL High Command members formed the **Ḥerut* party. He led *Ḥerut* and later the **Gaḥal* bloc in opposition to the Labor-led government coalitions until 1967, and then from 1970 to the 1977 political *upheaval when a *Likud*-led coalition was set up with Begin as Prime Minister.

Begin's parliamentary career was marked by numerous, frequently quoted speeches on political and legal issues, acrimonious debates with David *Ben Gurion who refused to consider forming a coalition with *Ḥerut* (See: *"Without *Ḥerut* and *Maki*"), and by active membership in the Knesset Foreign Affairs and Security Committee. In his many speeches before 1967, Begin expressed his rejection of the *partition of **Eretz Yisrael* and referred to Jordan as "the so-called Hashemite Kingdom of Jordan." In 1952 he was suspended from the Knesset for three months during the stormy protests over the *Restitution Agreement with the *Federal Republic of Germany.

By 1955 Begin had initiated talks with the *General Zionists in an effort to form a non-socialist political bloc. Ten years later an agreement was finally reached when *Gaḥal* was established by *Ḥerut* and the *Liberal Party of Israel.

On the eve of the *Six-Day War Begin joined the *National Unity Government as Minister without Protfolio. He played a significant part in the decision to order the *IDF to enter the Old City of *Jerusalem. In 1970, with the government's acceptance of the *Rogers Proposals for peace negotiations based on *Security Council Resolution 242, *Gaḥal* left the coalition and Begin resigned his posts.

Toward the 1973 elections the *Likud* bloc was set up to include additional political parties besides *Ḥerut* and the Liberals. The *Likud* won its first major electoral victory in May 1977, and on June 20, Begin was sworn in as Prime Minister. He appointed Moshe *Dayan, who left the *Alignment, as Foreign Minister — to the disappointment of some members of his own bloc.

After much preparation, including visits to the United States and Romania, Begin hosted Egyptian President Anwar Sadat in Jerusalem in November 1977. Thereafter, he devoted a great deal of his time and effort to negotiating a peace treaty with *Egypt. As a result there were several defections from his *Ḥerut* Party by members who felt that he had conceded too much in the *Camp David Accords and the subsequent peace treaty, even though he had steadfastly refused to give up any part of historical *Eretz Yisrael*. Together with President Sadat Begin was awarded the Nobel Prize for Peace in Oslo on December 10, 1979.

Following the resignation of Ezer *Weizman as Minister of Defense, Begin assumed the post in May 1980 and obtained cabinet approval for the bombing of the Iraqi nuclear reactor *Osiraq, on June 7, 1981. In the elections to the 10th Knesset the *Likud* had a second electoral victory, and Begin set up his second government, in which Ariel *Sharon was appointed Minister of Defense. Begin supported Sharon's plan for a major Israeli operation in the Lebanon which was implemented in June 1982, following the attempted assassination of Israel's Ambassador to the United Kingdom (See: *Lebanese War).

The intense internal debate over that war, the mounting casualties, and the *Sabra and Shatilla massacre carried out by the Phalange, all pressed heavily upon Begin, while the delay in establishing a commission of inquiry to investigate the Sabra and Shatilla affair sharpened public criticism against him. Having suffered three heart attacks, a mild stroke and a broken hip since becoming Prime Minister, and following the death of his wife Aliza in November 1982, Begin became depressed, and finally, on September 15, 1983, tendered his letter of resignation to the President. Since then he has lived in seclusion, only rarely appearing in public. (I.M.)

Bejski Commission Commission of inquiry appointed on January 17, 1985, under the 1968 Commissions of Inquiry Law, upon the advice of the Knesset State Control Committee, to investigate all the facts and factors which had led to the regulation of the bank shares from the beginning of this regulation until the collapse in the market for these shares in October 1983.

The commission, chaired by Supreme Court Justice Moshe Bejski, with the participation of District Court Judge Vardimus Zyler, Professors Ze'ev Hirsch, Daniel Friedman, and Marshal Sarnat, published its report on April 20, 1986. The report, which severely criticized the banks (and found them to be in breach of the law), the supervisory mechanisms and the political level, recommended the removal by resignation or dismissal, of the managing directors and general managers of five of Israel's major banks and of the Governor of the Bank of Israel; the overhauling of the capital market; and major changes in the activities of the banks, especially regarding the running of mutual and pension funds. The report placed responsiblity on several other persons who were no longer in office, but made no operative recommendations regarding them. These included two ex-Ministers of finance Yigal *Hurwitz and Yoram *Aridor. Hurwitz was criticized for not familiarizing himself with the details of the banks' activities, and Aridor for not acting to stop the banks even after he became aware of the gravity of the situation.

On May 4, 1986, the government set up a ministerial committee consisting of four members of the *Alignment, and four of the *Likud* to examine the Bejski Commission Report, especially the recommended changes in the capital market and *modus operandi* of the banks, and to examine new legislation as well.

Ben Aharon, Yitzḥak Labor leader. Born 1906 in Bukovina in the Austro-Hungarian Empire.

Ben Aharon attended university in Berlin but did not complete his studies. He was one of the founders of **Hashomer Hatza'ir*, the Jewish pioneering scouts youth, and **Heḥalutz* in Romania. Ben Aharon immigrated to Palestine in 1928 and joined **Hakibbutz Hame'uḥad*. He has been a member of Kibbutz Givat Ḥaim since 1933. From 1932–38 he was Secretary of the Tel Aviv Workers' Council and thereafter Secretary of **Mapai* for one year. In 1940 he enlisted in the British army and was taken prisoner by the Germans in 1941, where he remained until the end of the war. After the war Ben Aharon joined **Aḥdut Ha'avodah-Po'alei Zion*. He was one of the **Yishuv* leaders arrested by the British authorities on Black Saturday on June 29, 1946 in an attempt to break the power of the **Haganah* and bring about a change in the leadership of the *Jewish Agency Executive. Ben Aharon was one of the founders and leaders of **Mapam* until *Aḥdut Ha'avodah-Po'alei Zion* left *Mapam* in 1954. He was a Member of Knesset from 1949–77 and served as Minister of Transport from 1959–62, resigning in 1962 because he disagreed with the government's social and economic policies. Ben Aharon advocated uniting the Labor movement and was instrumental in the formation of the first *Alignment in 1965 and of the *Israel Labor Party in 1968. Between 1969–73 he served as Secretary-General of the **Histadrut*. Ben Aharon withdrew from politics in 1977 but remained active behind the scenes within *Hakibbutz Hame'uḥad* and **Takam* and the Labor Party Bureau.

Ben Gurion (formerly Green), **David** (1886–1973) Israeli statesman and first Prime Minister of Israel. Born in Plonsk, Poland. He regarded *Zionism as a practical doctrine to be implemented through immigration to Palestine and conquest of the land by Jewish labor. Ben Gurion arrived in Palestine in 1906, spent several years as an agricultural worker, and was active in the Socialist-Zionist **Po'alei Zion* party. His approach to socialism was pragmatic, maintaining that the realization of political Zionism had precedence over Marxist dialectics. Accordingly, at the party convention of 1907, he advocated successfully the plank in its platform stating: "The party will strive for an independent state for the Jewish people in this country."

From 1910 he served as editor of the *Po'alei Zion*'s organ, *Aḥdut*, where he signed his first article with his new name Ben Gurion (BG), which had been the name of one of the last defenders of Jerusalem against the Roman legions. He studied law in Istanbul and after the Young Turk revolt (1908), he advocated (with Yitzḥak *Ben Zvi) an Ottoman orientation for Palestinian Jewry. He hoped he would become a member of parliament and possibly even a Turkish minister. But Ben Zvi and BG were expelled from Palestine at the beginning of World War I. A year later, in New York, they established the **Heḥalutz* movement in the US. On publication of the *Balfour Declaration, in November 1917, BG wrote: "...a land is only acquired through the pains of work and creation, through the efforts of building and settling." A few months later he arrived in Palestine as a *Jewish Legion volunteer. His aim was the creation of an independent center of Jewish power in Palestine, which would become the bastion of Jewish settlement and the nucleus of the "state on the way." This nucleus was the General Federation of Labor in Palestine, the **Histadrut*, which was founded in 1920, with BG as its first Secretary-General. He was also active in the unification in 1930 of **Aḥdut Ha'avodah* and **Hapo'el Hatza'ir* in **Mapai*. In 1935 he was elected chairman of the Zionist Executive and the *Jewish Agency.

In 1937, together with Chaim *Weizmann and Moshe *Sharett, he supported the Peel Commission's plan for the establishment of a Jewish state in a small part of Palestine. After the plan was shelved, and the British followed a pro-Arab policy, BG was one of the Jewish representatives at the St. James Arab-Jewish Round Table Conference held in London in February 1939. It was followed by the White Paper of 1939, which limited Jewish immigration to Palestine and land purchases there, and aimed at ensuring permanent minority status for the Jews. BG formulated the following policy at the beginning of World War II: "Fight the war as if there were no White Paper and the White Paper as if there were no war." He now looked to the United States for support. He was the driving force behing the May 12, 1942 *Biltmore Program of the American Zionist Emergency Committee, on the establishment of a Jewish Commonwealth in Palestine. On the internal front, BG fought the *dissident groups, who used terror against the British, and at the same time worked for the creation of a Jewish defense force.

On the establishment of the state in May 1948, BG became Prime Minister and Minister of Defense. He led the decisive struggle, the *War of Independence, which accompanied the birth of the state. He built up the Israel Defense Forces (*IDF) through a successful struggle with groups attempting to maintain separate organizations within the army. During his years in office he directed the absorption of large numbers of immigrants, the development of the wilderness, and the "ingathering of the exiles." He set up a uniform national education system. He took forceful positions on foreign policy and security, and called for self-realization and pioneering settlement, particularly in the Negev. In 1953 he left the government, "for a year or two," joined Kibbutz Sde Boker in the Negev, and transferred the premiership to Moshe Sharett. Pinhas Lavon was appointed Minister of Defense. In February 1955, when Lavon resigned because of the *Lavon Affair, BG returned to the government as Defense Minister, again becoming Prime Minister in June. He was the main architect of the Franco-Israel pact and against bitter opposition supported the establishment of relations with West Germany (which commenced with the *Restitution Agreement). He was Prime Minister at the time of the *Sinai Campaign, in October 1956 which was a reaction to armed infiltration and Egyptian threats following the Egyptian-Czech arms deal of 1955. In the years 1955–63 he initiated a number of secret and unsuccessful attempts at rapprochement with Arab leaders.

In June 1963 BG suddenly resigned from all his posts for "personal reasons." Levi *Eshkol became Prime Minister and Minister of Defense at his recommendation. But tension grew between the two men because of the Lavon Affair. The "Affair" also provided the background for the struggle between the younger elements in *Mapai*, supported by BG, and the veteran leadership. In June 1965, this struggle resulted in a split in *Mapai*. BG established **Rafi* which won ten seats in the 6th Knesset. After the

*Six-Day War, *Rafi* joined *Mapai* and *Ahdut Ha'avodah*, to form *Israel Labor Party, but BG held aloof. In the October 1969 elections he headed the *State List, which won only four seats in the Knesset. In June 1970, at the age of 84, BG retired from the Knesset and political life, and returned to Sde Boker.

Many regard David Ben Gurion as the symbol of Israeli independence and the father of the country. His life in politics did not prevent him from enjoying a wide range of intellectual activities. He published a large number of books.

(M.B.Z.)

Ben Porat, Mordechai Ex-Member of Knesset and Minister. Born 1923 in Baghdad.

Ben Porat joined the *Hehalutz* movement in 1942 and immigrated to Palestine in 1945. In 1947 he joined the *Haganah* and fought in the *War of Independence. Ben Porat returned to Iraq in 1949 in order to organize the immigration of over 120,000 Jews to Israel. He was there for two years and was caught four times, but managed to escape — the last time after being tortured.

In 1955 he studied political science and was elected to head the local council of Or Yehuda, a position he held until 1969. He was one of the founders of *Rafi* and was elected to the 6th Knesset (1965). Between 1970–72 Ben Porat was deputy Secretary-General of the *Israel Labor Party while studying business administration. In 1975 he was one of the founders and served as Co-Chairman of the World Executive of the World Organization of Jews from Arab Countries (WOJAC). He was a member of the Israel Mission to the *United Nations in 1977 where he raised the issue of the Jewish refugees from Moslem countries. In 1979, after the advent of the Ayatollah Khomeini in Iran, Ben Porat was sent by the *Jewish Agency to Teheran to help Jews leave Iran. He was elected to the 10th Knesset (1981) as a member of *Telem* and was appointed Minister without Portfolio the following year. In January 1984 he resigned his cabinet post, demanding the establishment of a *National Unity Government.

Benvenisti prognosis A geopolitical analysis offered by Meron Benvenisti, initiator and Director of the West Bank Data Project, who in 1981 was number two on the *Civil Rights Movement list to the Knesset, according to which the occupation of the *West Bank and the *Gaza Strip and the Israeli control of the western part of *mandatory Palestine, have created a new geopolitical historical reality, with such significant dynamics that there is no way back to the pre-1967 status quo. The State of Israel, according to this analysis, has turned from a Jewish nation-state with a relatively small Arab minority, to a bi-ethnic state, and the *Arab-Israel conflict has in fact ceased to be an inter-state conflict as it was in the years 1948–67, and has reverted into an inter-community conflict as it had been under the British mandate.

In this inter-communal conflict each of the sides views itself as the only legitimate collective in **Eretz Yisrael*/Palestine, and sees the ambitions of the rival community as being illegitimate. The propects for the repartition of the country into an Israeli and a Palestinian state do not enjoy much support. While the majority of Palestinians are not willing to foresake the "right of return" to their pre-1948 homes, most Israelis are not willing to accept the establishment of a separate Palestinian state.

In the meantime the economic, legal, and physical integration of the West Bank and Gaza Strip with Israel has turned into Israeli control with permanent characteristics. The Benvenisti prognosis argues that this control will continue by force of inertia, since there seems little chance for a change in the perceptions of either side regarding the essence of the conflict between them, and because the interest of the Arab states (and other outside factors) in a resolution of the problem is diminishing. Thus, the Israeli control will continue within the framework of a warfare approach (i.e., *Military Administration), and in the foreseeable future will not become institutionalized by means of declared annexation.

Since Israeli withdrawal, according to this prognosis, is unlikely, the three Israeli options for the future are to maintain its Jewish character by ceasing to be democratic (with the Jewish community maintaining a complete monopoly over all instruments of power); to find some arrangement based on integrating the Arab population of the West Bank and Gaza Strip into the Israeli system of government; or to grant the Palestinian minority national autonomy.

Ben Zvi, Yitzḥak (1884–1963) Labor leader, historian and ethnographer of Jewish tribes and communities. Second President of Israel, 1952–63.

Ben Zvi was born in the Ukraine, where together with *Borochov, he founded the Zionist Socialist *Po'alei Zion* party in 1905. Ben Zvi immigrated to Palestine in 1907 and was one of the founders of **Hashomer*, the Jewish Watchmen's Association and of its predecessor *Bar Giora*. He was on the editorial board of the first Hebrew socialist magazine in Palestine *Ha'aḥdut*. Throughout the years, Ben Zvi worked closely with David *Ben Gurion. Together they studied law in Istanbul and tried to establish contacts with the Young Turk leaders before World War I. At the beginning of the war they advocated a pro-Ottoman policy, but soon both were expelled from Palestine and were active in the United States in organizing a local **Heḥalutz* pioneering movement and the American Battalion of the *Jewish Legion.

In 1920 Ben Zvi was among the founders of the **Histadrut*, of **Aḥdut Ha'avodah* in 1919, and **Mapai* in 1930. He was a member of the **Va'ad Le'umi* (the Jewish National Council), becoming its Chairman in 1931 and its President in 1944. Ben Zvi also filled important posts in the *Histadrut* and the Jerusalem municipality. He was a member of *Knesset for *Mapai* until elected President in 1952.

Betar Acronym for *Brit Yosef Trumpeldor* (the Joseph *Trumpeldor pact). A Zionist youth movement affiliated originally with the *Revisionist Movement, it was founded in 1923. Its main centers, prior to World War II, were Poland, the Baltic States and Palestine. On the eve of the *Holocaust, *Betar* numbered over 80,000 members. The movement's ideological mentor was Ze'ev *Jabotinsky. *Betar*'s principles were immediate Jewish statehood, a monistic approach to nationalism, military preparedness, national service and *Hadar* — a code of honor and strict personal behavior.

Betar established training centers abroad for its members preparing for immigration to Palestine. Unlike the socialist-oriented groups, *Betar* included courses in military instruction, in addition to agricultural training. Naval schools were located in Latvia and Italy and aviation courses were held in Palestine and New York. The strong anti-socialist stance of *Betar* led to clashes with **Histadrut*-affiliated groups in the early 1930s. *Betar* was implicated in the 1933 murder of Ḥaim *Arlosoroff, and although nothing was ever proved conclusively, the episode resulted in inter-Zionist strife. With the formation of the **IZL* and later **Leḥi*, *Betar* became a recruiting source for the undergrounds, and was eventually proscribed as an illegal organization by the mandatory authorities. It aided the pre-World War II efforts to bring illegal immigrants into Palestine. During the war *Betar* members played prominent roles in anti-Nazi actions in ghetto revolts and partisan sabotage in Europe.

Following the establishment of Israel, *Betar* founded over 20 agricultural and rural settlements. It maintains branches in 20 countries and its activities, like those of other recognized youth movements, are sponsored through the *Jewish Agency's Youth and Heḥalutz department.

(I.M.)

Beta Yisrael See: *Ethiopian Jews.

Biltmore Program Resolution adopted by an extraordinary Zionist conference which took place at Hotel Biltmore in New York in May 1942, after the actual dimensions of the *Holocaust become apparent, urging "that Palestine be established as a Jewish Commonwealth integrated in the structure of the new democratic world [after World War II]." This was the first time that the Zionist organization officially demanded a Jewish state in Palestine — henceforth its declared aim. Since it was generally recognized that the demand for a state would lead to the partition of Western Palestine, many Zionists objected to the Biltmore Program.

Bi-nationalism The establishment of a bi-national state in Palestine was one of the solutions to the Jewish-Arab conflict proposed during mandatory times. Submitting that both Jews and Arabs had a right to live in Palestine, and that neither nation should dominate the other, the idea of a bi-national state was proposed as a solution to the conflict between the two nations within an undivided Palestine. Most plans for a bi-national state were based on the principle of parity in government, irrespective of the numerical strength of either side, and the right of each nation to autonomy in its internal affairs. The bi-national state was envisaged as made up of cantons, federal or unitary. It was never the official policy of the Arabs, Zionists or British, though the idea was considered by the latter two. Official

Arab policy negated the Jews' right to free immigration and settlement in Palestine and insisted upon the establishment of an Arab state in which the Jews could enjoy minority rights. Among official Zionist leadership, Ze'ev *Jabotinsky proposed in 1922 a Jewish-Arab state based on parity in all institutions (at a time when the Jews constituted 10 percent of the population) while David *Ben Gurion proposed a canton-like system for Palestine in 1929. Both proposals should be viewed as tactical. In the early 1930s the idea of perpetual political parity was seriously considered by the Zionists, provided that it did not entail foregoing the right to free immigration and the eventual creation of a Jewish majority in Palestine. In February 1947 the British put forth proposals which contained some elements similar to the bi-national philosophy. Bi-nationalism was primarily advocated by Jewish groups, such as *Brit Shalom* (1925–33), **Hashomer Hatza'ir, Kedmah Mizraḥah* (1936–38), the League for Jewish-Arab Rapprochement and Cooperation (1939–48) and *Iḥud* (1942–48), and individuals such as Judah L. Magnes (1877–1948), Ḥaim Kalvarisky (1868–1947), Martin Buber (1878–1965) and Samuel Hugo Bergman (1883–1975). Bi-nationalism was also advocated by Viscount Samuel (1870–1963), who was the first British High Commissioner for Palestine. Since 1967, bi-nationalism has once again been considered by unorganized individuals as a possible solution to the Arab-Israel conflict but the idea is generally rejected on principle. The *Israel Labor Party insists that there is no escape from *territorial compromise because otherwise Israel will turn into a bi-national state or a non-democratic Jewish state, while the goal of Labor Zionism is that Israel should be a Jewish democratic state. When members of the *Palestine Liberation Organization (PLO) speak of a secular-democratic state they are not referring to bi-nationalism since they do not recognize the Jews as a nation.

The Arab nationalist group *Village Sons professed bi-nationalism, though in their bi-national state the Jews would be a minority.

Black Panthers A radical ethnic protest movement of second-generation Israelis of **Edot Mizraḥ* origin which developed in the early 1970s against the background of a growing feeling of deprivation within this section of the population. The Black Panthers, named after the Black protest movement in the US, demanded solutions to the social problems of their constituents and equal opportunities for the non-Ashkenazi population of Israel. Before the 8th Knesset elections (1973), the Black Panthers united with one section of **Ha'olam Hazeh-Ko'aḥ Ḥadash* which advocated moderation toward the Arab world and recognition of the Palestinian national movement. The new political list did not manage to pass the 1 percent threshold in the Knesset elections, but did enter the **Histadrut* and several local councils. One ex-Panther, Charlie Bitton, joined **Ḥadash* and has represented it in the Knesset since the 9th Knesset elections (1977). Another ex-Panther, Se'adiah Marziano, entered the 9th Knesset during the second half of its term as a member for **Maḥaneh Sheli*. Before the 11th Knesset elections Marziano and several of his colleagues joined the *Israel Labor Party.

(D.B.M.)

B'nei Akivah Youth movement of **Hapo'el Hamizraḥi*, founded in Jerusalem in 1929, with Chief Rabbi Avraham Yitzḥak Hacohen *Kook serving as its spiritual leader. The movement's first *kvutzah* (See: *Kibbutz) was founded in 1931 but was disbanded in 1934. It has since established a large number of settlements of various types, including kibbutzim. The movement also embraces *yeshivot* (Talmudical colleges) the first of which was founded in 1940 in Kfar Haro'eh. In 1954 a world framework of *B'nei Akivah* was founded.

B'nei Akivah is affiliated with the *National Religious Party. Many of the founders of **Gush Emunim* were among its graduates.

B'nei Yisrael A Jewish community in India whose origins are shrouded in mystery. In 1947 there were 24,000 members of the community living in India. Over 12,000 have immigrated to Israel.

In 1954 a controversy erupted in Israel as to whether the *B'nei Israel* were Jews according to the *Halacha* and in 1961 the Council of the *Chief Rabbinate decided that they were, but that a special investigation would have to be carried out regarding three generations of the maternal ancestry of each member of the community seeking to marry. Opposition to this decision culminated in a strike in Jerusalem in 1964, as a result of which Prime Minister Levi

*Eshkol declared that *B'nei Yisrael* are Jews in ever respect. The integration of the community in Israel has not always been effective and in the early years quite a few of its members returned to India.

"Boiling point of Israeli democracy" An expression coined by the late Binyamin Akzin, Professor of Political Science in the late 1950s in relation to the behavior of Labor movement leaders should the Labor party lose its political predominance. Akzin feared if Labor lost an election, the various power centers of the movement would try to prevent the smooth transfer of government by force. In 1977, Akzin had to admit that Israeli democracy had passed the "boiling point" test successfully.

Borochov, Ber (1881–1919) One of the fathers of Labor Zionist thought who propagated a synthesis between Zionism and socialism. In his youth Borochov joined the Russian social-democratic movement, and later became one of the founders of **Po'alei Zion*. He was convinced that the liberation of the world proletariat would neither solve the Jewish problem nor eradicate anti-Semitism, arguing that it was the extra-territorialism of the Jewish people which was the cause of the anomalies of Jewish life. Borochov's main conclusion was that the Jewish problem should be solved in an undeveloped, half-inhabited land where Jewish workers could overcome competition by the local inhabitants and international capital, develop a Jewish working class and establish an independent national economy. **Eretz Yisrael* was to be this land. Though it is commonly believed that Borochov compared the social structure of the Jewish people to an upside-down pyramid, lacking a broad working-class base, he himself apparently never used this simile.

Brezhnev Plan On February 23, 1981, Soviet leader Leonid Brezhnev stated that the *Soviet Union was willing to participate in the achievement of a Middle East settlement together with all the other interested parties, "naturally including the *Palestine Liberation Organization (PLO)". The basis for peace in the Middle East, Brezhnev declared, must be an end to the Israeli occupation of all Arab territories captured in 1967; the realization of "the inalienable rights of the Arab people of Palestine," including "the establishment of their own state"; and guarantees for "the security and sovereignty of all the states in the region, including those of Israel."

This statement is referred to as the Brezhnev Plan, and has been accepted by the Arab states and the PLO as a basis for a peace settlement. They have claimed that such acceptance implies recognition of Israel. Israel rejected the plan out of hand. (M.B.)

Brookings Report A report drafted by a panel of diplomats and academicians under the auspices of the Brookings Institute in Washington D.C. and endorsed by presidential candidate Jimmy Carter in December 1975.

The report stated that a fair and enduring settlement should contain the following elements: security, sovereignty and territorial integrity, peaceful relations, withdrawal of Israel to the June 4, 1967, boundaries, Palestinian self-determination subject to Palestinian acceptance of the sovereignty of Israel, and UN Security Council endorsement of the settlement.

The report was rejected by Israel as unfair and hostile, primarily because of its advocacy of complete Israeli withdrawal from the *occupied territories and the establishment of an additional state between Israel and *Jordan. (M.B.)

Bund Abreviation for the Yiddish Algemeiner Yiddischer Arbeiter Bund in Lite, Polen und Rusland (General Jewish Workers' Union in Lithuania, Poland and Russia). The Bund was a Russian-Jewish socialist party founded in Russia in 1897 and based on the concepts of Yiddish culture, autonomism and secular Jewish nationalism. It was strongly opposed to Zionism and the rebirth of the Hebrew language. In the Soviet Union the Bund survived until the mid-20s. The Polish branch, however, survived the *Holocaust, and participated in the Jewish resistance, but was liquidated in 1948 by the Communist regime. A world organization — the International Jewish Labor Bund — still exists, with branches in the United States, Israel and other countries. It is affiliated to the *Socialist International and does not recognize the special importance of the State of Israel in the life of the Jewish people. The Bund demands that the Jewish population of Israel recognize the supremacy of world Jewry and claims neutrality in the *Arab-Israel conflict.

Burg, Yosef National Religious Party leader. Born 1909, Dresden, Germany. Burg received comprehensive religious education and was ordained as a rabbi in Berlin. He studied at universities in Leipzig and Berlin where he received a PhD. Burg immigrated to Palestine in 1939 and became a teacher — being active within the religious Zionist community. He lived in Paris between 1946–49, caring for Holocaust survivors. When he returned to Israel he became active in **Hamizraḥi-*Hapo'el Hamizraḥi*, leading the *Lamifneh* faction which called for cooperation with the Labor movement, moderation in the political sphere, and the development of settlement activities under the slogan "*Torah Va'avodah*" (Torah and Labor). In 1956 he was one of the founders of the *National Relgious Party (NRP). Burg has been a member of Knesset since 1949 and a minister under all the Prime Ministers of Israel since 1951. In the 1st Knesset (1949) Burg was Deputy Speaker. In 1951 he was appointed Minister of Health, 1952–58 Minister of Posts, 1959–70 Minister of Social Welfare. From 1970–76 Burg was Minister of the Interior (with a four-month break in 1974). He resigned from the government in 1976 after a crisis developed in the *Rabin government over a vote of no-confidence in which the NRP abstained. Burg's party joined the coalition under Begin in 1977 and he served as Minister of the Interior, Religions and Police from 1977–81. In 1979 he was appointed Chairman of the ministerial committee for negotiations with Egypt on *autonomy for the inhabitants of Judea, Samaria and the Gaza Strip following the *Camp David Accords. Since 1977 Burg has been leader of the NRP but under his relatively moderate leadership the party lost eight of its 12 seats between the 9th Knesset (1977) and the 11th Knesset (1984).

In the *National Unity Government Burg was appointed Minister of Religions only — the Ministry of the Interior going to **Shass*. Burg had on several occasions promised to step aside and make way for the younger leadership, and in October 1986 he finally resigned his posts, being replaced in the National Unity Government under Yitzḥak Shamir's premiership, by Zvulun *Hammer. (Sh.M.)

C

Camp David Accords A framework for peace in the Middle East signed by President Jimmy Carter, President Anwar Sadat and Prime Minister Menaḥem *Begin on September 17, 1978, after a 13-day meeting at Camp David. Among the Israeli participants were also Minister for Foreign Affairs Moshe *Dayan and Minister of Defense Ezer *Weizman. The meeting at Camp David followed several months of stalemate in the peace process.

Two accords were concluded. One, a framework for peace in the Middle East, which declared *Security Council Resolution 242 to be the basis for such a peace, was divided into a section on the *West Bank and the *Gaza Strip which called for the implementation of an *autonomy plan to be followed after five years by a permanent settlement; and a section on Egyptian- Israeli relations which dealt with the process of normalization in the relations between the two states to be followed by similar agreements between Israel with Jordan, Syria and Lebanon (See: *Jordan and Israel, *Syria and Israel, and *Lebanon and Israel). The second accord was a framework for the conclusion of a peace treaty between *Egypt and Israel, based on a complete withdrawal of Israel from the Sinai "up to the international recognized border between Egypt and mandatory Palestine," (See: *Taba) to be followed by the establishment of normal relations involving full recognition, including diplomatic, economic and cultural relations; "the termination of economic boycotts [See: *Arab Boycott] and barriers to the free movement of goods and people; and the mutual protection of citizens by the due process of law."

For Egypt it was important to link the agreements regarding the West Bank and the Gaza Strip with the peace process between itself and Israel to avoid accusations that Egypt was willing to conclude a separate peace treaty which would "sell out" the Palestinians. Israel's main concern was not to appear to be giving up its claim for control over Judea, Samaria and the Gaza Strip.

However, while Egypt did in fact embark on the course of a separate peace with Israel, Israel conceded that the negotiations regarding the permanent status of the West Bank and the Gaza

Strip "must also recognize the legitimate rights of the Palestinian people and their just requirements," and that Jordan would be actively involved in the area in which the autonomy was to be implemented during the interim period.

The accords were accompanied by an exchange of letters regarding *Jerusalem in which Begin declared Jerusalem to be indivisible and the capital of Israel, while Sadat declared Arab Jerusalem to be an indivisible part of the West Bank which should be returned to Arab sovereignty. Carter also verified that Begin had informed him that Israel took the terms "Palestinians" and "Palestinian People" to mean "the Arabs of *Eretz Yisrael*."

The *Knesset approved the Camp David Accords on September 27. Voting in favor were 84 MKs, including most of the *Alignment; voting against were 19 MKs, including Moshe *Arens and Shlomo *Hillel, because of the undertaking to withdraw from all of the Sinai; 17 MKs, including Yigal *Allon and Yitzḥak *Shamir, abstained.

Canaanites The name given to a small group of Jewish poets and artists in 1942 which crystallized its ideas in the Committee for the Formation of the Hebrew Youth. At the end of the mandatory period and in the early years of the state the Canaanites developed an ideology aimed at evolving a new Hebrew nation — as opposed to a Jewish one — made up of native-born Jews and Arabs, as well as immigrants who cared to join them. The historical-philosophical basis of the concept was a return to a consciousness preceding the emergence of Judaism, Christianity and Islam. The initiator and leader of the movement was the poet Yonatan Ratosh. The movement published a weekly *Alef* from 1948–53.

Following the *Six-Day War the group resumed its activities advocating the establishment of a network of Hebrew language schools for the entire non-Jewish population of the Israeli-held territories, as well as their conscription into the *IDF. It also called for the formation of a federation of Israel, the Jabal Druze and Maronite Lebanon.

Chief Rabbinate Established in 1921 under the auspices of the mandatory government as the supreme religious authority of the **Yishuv* in Palestine. The Chief Rabbinate was a continuation of the institution of the *Ḥacham Bashi* who had been the chief Jewish religious authority during the Ottoman rule.

The new institution developed in the spirit of its first head, Chief Rabbi Avraham Yitzḥak Hacohen *Kook.

The powers of the Chief Rabbinate were redefined in the 1928 regulations of **Knesset Yisrael*, which divided its authority between an Ashkenazi Chief Rabbi and a Sephardi Chief Rabbi who bore the title *Rishon Letzion*. Membership in the Chief Rabbinate Council was also equally divided between the Ashkenazi and Sephardi communities. The system of elections to the Chief Rabbinate was first established in 1935.

The ultra-Orthodox community objected to the institution which explicitly accepted its authority from the Zionist establishment whose heads were secular. Part of the secular community also objected to the institution for fear of religious intervention in non-religious affairs.

The institution of the Chief Rabbinate has continued to exist after the establishment of the state, and it deals with all matters connected with matrimony and burial among the Jews of Israel and regulates the public observance of the kashrut (dietary laws) and Sabbath. The two Chief Rabbis are also Presidents of the Supreme Rabbinical Court.

Occasionally the Chief Rabbinate has dealt with matters outside its direct responsibility. For example, the Third Rabbinical Council (1945–55) was involved in helping Jews who had survived the *Holocaust and in finding and relocating Jewish children from Christian institutions.

The two Chief Rabbis at the time of the Sixth Council (1973–83), Rabbi Shlomo Goren (previously Chief Rabbi of the *IDF) and Rabbi Ovadia Yosef (who in 1984 became the spiritual authority of **Shass*), besides being in frequent conflict with each other also dabbled in politics. Both were officially, although separately, received by the President of the United States.

In 1985 the Chief Rabbinate became actively involved in the issue of the *Ethiopian Jews who were recognised as Jews by the Chief Rabbinate in 1973. However the question about their Jewishness erupted again and the Rabbis ruled that no Ethiopian Jew can marry without first undergoing the *tvilah* (immersion in the ritual bath).

Some of the Ethiopian leaders refused to agree to a ruling which called into question their Jewishness according to Halacha. They have been supported by various non-Orthodox circles and the issue has turned into a political one.

The *Conservative Movement and *Progressive Judaism are not represented in the Chief Rabbinate and their rabbis are not recognized for purposes of performing various rituals governed by law such as marriages and conversions.

(Sh.M.)

Chiefs of Staff (See also: *IDF: Israel Defense Forces.)

1. 1948–49 Ya'acov Dori
2. 1949–52 Yiga'el *Yadin
3. 1952–53 Mordechai Makleff
4. 1953–58 Moshe *Dayan
5. 1958–61 Ḥaim Laskov
6. 1961–64 Zvi Zur
7. 1964–68 Yitzḥak *Rabin
8. 1968–72 Ḥaim *Bar Lev
9. 1972–74 David Elazar
10. 1974–78 Mordechai *Gur
11. 1978–83 Rafa'el *Eitan
12. 1983–87 Moshe Levy
13. 1987– Dan Shomron

Civil Rights Movement (CRM) A radical social-liberal political party established by Shulamit *Aloni in August 1973 after the *Israel Labor Party refused to give up their leadership of the appointments committee for fixing the party's list for the Knesset. Aloni was a member of the 6th Knesset but was left out of the list in the elections to the 7th Knesset (1969) because of her strained relations with Golda *Meir.

The CRM calls for *electoral reform, the introduction of a *Basic Law protecting human rights, recognition of a Palestinian entity and the Palestinian right to self-determination, the separation of religion and state and equal rights for women.

In the elections to the 8th Knesset which took place on December 31, 1973, the CRM won three seats, presumably garnering the protest vote that could not find any other expression since all the parties running in the elections had registered before the *Yom Kippur War. Briefly a member of the government established by Yitzḥak *Rabin, the CRM left when the *National Religious Party joined the government. In 1975 negotiations for a merger were held with **Shinui*, a party which was not yet in the Knesset, but the agreement was not concluded due to *Shinui*'s insistence that the united party should not carry out negotiations with left-wingers from the Labor party and with **Moked*. Following this abortive attempt, the CRM united in the Knesset with Arie Lova *Eliav who had broken away from the *Israel Labor Party and, with several members who had left *Shinui*, founded **Ya'ad*, which had four Members of Knesset. However, *Ya'ad* broke up over the issue of contacts with the *Palestine Liberation Organization (PLO) after Eliav and several other members founded the *Israel Council for Israeli-Palestinian Peace. The CRM gained only one seat in the elections to both the 9th Knesset (1977) and 10th Knesset (1981), but following the 1981 elections Aloni joined the **Alignment* so that it would have the same number of seats (48) as did the **Likud*.

The CRM broke away from the Alignment just before the elections to the 11th Knesset and ran on a platform which *inter alia* called for complete equality for all citizens, irrespective of religion, nationality, race or sex; freedom of religion, conscience, language, education and culture; opposition to religious coercion; recognition of the right of the Palestinian people to self-determination; negotiations with any representative of the Palestinian factor on the basis of mutual recognition; rejection of wars of choice and the use of the *IDF for political purposes outside the state.

The CRM gained three seats in the 1984 elections. It refused on principle to join the *National Unity Government and was soon joined by Yossi *Sarid who had left the Israel Labor Party because of the coalition agreement.

Shulamit Aloni believes that the CRM will eventually replace the Labor Party which has betrayed the social-democratic heritage of the Israeli labor movement.

Knesset seats: 8th Knesset (1973)–3; 9th Knesset (1977)–1; 10th Knesset (1981)–1; 11th Knesset (1984)–3, increasing to 4.

coalition agreements No party in Israel has even had the electoral power needed to establish a government by itself. Thus, all of Israel's governments have been coalition governments, formed by the head of the list which won the largest number of Knesset seats, even though the law does not insist that the coalition be formed by the largest party.

The coalition is based on an agreement which expresses the common denominator among the parties forming the coalition. It defines the proposed government's policies, the principles on which its activities will be based and mutual undertakings among its members. It usually includes also the distribution of portfolios in the government among the various partners. A coalition agreement is not a legal document; it is a political agreement, a sort of written gentlemen's agreement, and if it is broken the sanctions are political.

It may allow any of its partners freedom of voting on certain issues, determining the circumstances under which collective responsibility may be disregarded.

There may be a single coalition agreement for all members of the coalition, or the party forming the government may sign separate agreements with each of the partners, particularly when not all members join the coalition at the same time.

In addition to the coalition agreement the partners to the coalition also draft basic guidelines which define the principles on which the government's policy will be based.

The religious *status quo and its adaptations have been rooted in coalition agreements since the establishment of the state. For example, 32 out of the 43 articles of the coalition agreement signed by the **Likud* with the *National Religious Party and **Agudat Yisrael* in June 1977 dealt with the demands of the religious parties, including a promise by the *Likud* to amend the *Law of Return.

One of the most intricate coalition agreements in the history of Israel was that signed in September 1984 between the *Alignment and the Likud, which based the government on parity between the two blocs and prevented it from taking any decisions which only one of the partners supported. The agreement also included rotation provisions which stated that for the first 25 months of the government's existence Shimon *Peres would be Prime Minister and that Yitzḥak *Shamir would be Prime Minister for the following 25 months, and that, despite the provisions of the Basic Law: the Government (See: Appendix IV), the Prime Minister could not dismiss a minister from the other bloc unless the Vice-Prime Minister agreed. Thus, Peres was unable to dismiss Ariel *Sharon in 1985 when Sharon spoke against government policy and against the Prime Minister personally, and was unable to dismiss Yitzḥak *Moda'i in April 1986 when the Minister of Finance spoke disrespectfully of the Prime Minister (Moda'i resigned several months later). (G.Y.)

Cohen, Ge'ula Member of Knesset representing the **Teḥiyah*. Born 1925, Tel Aviv.

Cohen's father immigrated to Palestine from Yemen and her mother was a third-generation Israeli whose family originated in Morocco.

As a youngster Geu'la Cohen was a member of **Betar* and was inducted into the **IZL*. In 1943 she joined the **Leḥi* and became its radio broadcaster. Due to her involvement in *Leḥi* she was forced to leave her studies in a teachers' seminary. Arrested and sentenced by the British to nine-years' imprisonment, she escaped from the Jerusalem prison hospital and returned to broadcasting.

Ge'ula Cohen graduated from the Hebrew University in 1952 with an MA in Philosophy and Biblical Literature.

During the 1950s she was on the editorial staff of *Sulam*, a nationalist political monthly edited by Israel *Eldad. Later she wrote a socio-political column for *Ma'ariv*. After the *Six-Day War Cohen became involved in the campaign for Soviet Jewry, and in 1970 joined the **Ḥerut* movement. Under its auspices she established an educational institute, *Hamidrashah Hale'umit*, and in 1973 was elected to the 8th Knesset.

During the 9th Knesset (1977–81) Cohen was Chairman of the Immigration and Absorption Committee.

Following the publication of the *Begin peace proposals, she formed an internal opposition within the *Likud* bloc, and finally left *Ḥerut* in June 1979. Together with Moshe Shamir she set up the **Bana'i* parliamentary faction.

The founding conference of *Teḥiyah*, a new party based on the cooperation of three main groups — *Ḥerut* breakaways, the *Land of Israel Movement and **Gush Emunim* — was held in October 1979. In June 1980 the Knesset passed Ge'ula Cohen's "Jerusalem Bill" (See: *Basic Laws). Cohen is active in supporting settlement throughout Judea and Samaria (See: *YOSH) and the *Gaza Strip, and has tabled a law to extend Israeli sovereignty to those areas. In recent years her speeches in the Knesset have contained unyielding nationalist stances. She has, on several occasions, been ordered to leave the plenary by the Speaker due to her interjections.

In the 10th and 11th Knessets Cohen has been *Teḥiyah*'s faction chairman. In the 11th Knesset she was a member of the Constitution Law and Justice Committee, and the Knesset delegation to the Inter-Parliamentary Union.

Cohen who is generally respected for her sincerity and integrity, even by her political opponents, was widely criticized in November 1986 when she called for the purging of the security services of left-wingers as a result of the Vanunu Affair. (I.M.)

Conservative Movement The Conservative Movement developed in the middle of the 19th century in reaction to the divergent Jewish philosophies rapidly developing at the time in Germany. Large numbers of Jews were abandoning the rigid rules of Orthodoxy for the more modern ideas of the newly formed Reform Movement (See: *Progressive Judaism). Their wish to break out of the ghettos and merge into the world around them, prompted them to change certain elements within their religion.

For some, however, the Reform Movement went too far. There were a number of traditionalists who believed it was possible to become absorbed into the general community without compromising the basic precepts of the *Halacha*, while preserving certain traditions, such as Sabbath observance, *kashrut*, and the use of the Hebrew language in the liturgy.

In the 1880s the center of the fledgling Conservative Movement moved to the *United States and in 1887 the Jewish Theological Seminary of America was dedicated to "the preservation in America of the knowledge and practice of historical Judaism as ordained in the law of Moses expounded by the prophets and sages of Israel in Biblical and Talmudic writings." Solomon Shechter became chancellor in 1902 and influenced the Seminary's support of *Zionism.

Graduates of the Seminary automatically became members of the Rabbinical Assembly, an international association of Conservative Rabbis. In 1913, the American Conservative synagogues were joined under one umbrella organization called the United Synagogue of America.

There are well over one million members affiliated with some 850 Conservative synagogues throughout North America, and the Conservative Movement is the largest single Jewish religious movement in the world.

Israel's first Conservative synagogue, *Emet Ve'emunah*, was established in 1936 by a community of German Jews living in Jerusalem. Since then 40 more congregations have been established in all the country's major cities and in some *kibbutzim and **moshavim*. Most Conservative communities began with a core group of immigrants from English-speaking countries but members now consist of native-born and veteran Israelis, as well.

In 1979 the *Masorti* (Traditional) Movement was established as an organized, centrally administered movement of Conservative synagogues and rabbis in Israel. Its ideology is based on three primary principles: Torah and *mitzvot* (religious commands); tolerance and pluralism; Zionism.

Relations between Conservative Rabbis and the Chief Rabbis of their locality were unregulated but the right to perform wedding ceremonies depended on permission from the Chief Rabbis. Until the early 1970s Jerusalem provided a liberal climate for Conservative Rabbis; since then permission has been withdrawn from all Conservative Rabbis to perform weddings. The Orthodox religious establishment in Israel voices virulent objections to the Conservative interpretation of the *Halacha* and has prevented *Masorti mohalim* from performing ritual circumcisions. Each year before the High Holidays it distributes leaflets warning the public that attendance at *Masorti* services does not constitute the fulfillment of one's religious obligations. Since the religious establishment controls funding for religious institutions, *Masorti* congregations, not officially recognized by the municipalities, receive no public financial support. The *Masorti* Movement and its synagogues depend on membership dues and donations from abroad. Nevertheless, the *Masorti* youth movement, *No'am*, is officially recognized by the city of Jerusalem, and several municipalities have agreed to provide land for *Masorti* synagogues.

The *Masorti* Movement comprises two organizations: the United Synagogue of Israel, made up of congregational leaders; and the Rabbinical Assembly of Israel, including over 100 Conservative Rabbis. There are presently some 10,000 members of the *Masorti* Movement in Israel. The movement established its first kibbutz, Ḥanaton, in the Galilee in August 1984.

Other Israeli institutions connected to the *Masorti* Movement include: the Seminary of Judaic Studies which trains Conservative Rabbis; Neve Schechter, the Israel campus of the Jewish Theological Seminary; and the Center for Conservative Judaism — the Israeli headquarters for Conservative institutions; United Synagogue Youth and Ramah programs in Israel for youth and adults from abroad.

The *Masorti* Movement is active in trying to prevent passage of the amendment to the *Law of Return, and to gain official recognition by the state. (D.G.R.)

Constitution Israel does not have a formal written constitution but it does have laws and basic rules which lay down the foundations of government administration and the rights of the individual. Some of these rules are to be found in the *Basic Laws, others are passed by the Knesset in various laws while still others, especially those dealing with civil rights, were defined in a succession of Supreme Court decisions.

Among the first laws which dealt with constitutional questions were the Law and Administration Ordinance of 1948 which laid down the powers of the legislative and executive authorities; the Constituent Assembly Transition Ordinance of 1949, which dealt with the functions of the Constituent Assembly; the Transition Law of 1949 — commonly known as the "little constitution" — which established the principle of continuity in the powers of the executive authority, and the basic principles associated with the Knesset, legislation, the President and the functioning of the government; and the Constituent Assembly Elections Ordinance of 1951, which dealt with the arrangements for the Constituent Assembly and the Second Knesset. These laws were meant to be temporary laws, a bridge between the administration of the provisional institutions and the permanent institutions, and not fixed constitutional laws. However, they more or less constituted a temporary constitution.

Some were inclined to view the *Proclamation of Independence as a constitution, since it dealt with the foundations for the establishment of the state, the state's nature, institutions (the legislature and executive), the principles for its *modus operandi* and the rights of its citizens.

However, the Supreme Court stated in several decisions that the Proclamation of Independence does not have the authority of a constitutional law and is not a supreme law which can cancel laws and regulations which contradict it.

Nevertheless, the Proclamation of Independence does have primary legal validity and is frequently used by Israeli courts for purposes of interpretation, as in the case of the definition of a Jew in the *Law of Return, until the law was amended in 1970.

Even before the establishment of the state, the executive of the **Va'ad Le'umi* appointed, in 1947, a committee, chaired by Zeraḥ Warhaftig, to deal with matters relating to the constitution of the Jewish state. In December 1947, after the November 29 UN General Assembly resolution regarding the partition of Palestine called for the preparation of democratic constitutions for the two new states (Chapter B, Article 10), Judah Pinḥas Cohen was asked to prepare a draft constitution. It was this draft which served as the basis of the deliberations of the eight-member constitutional committee selected on July 8, 1948, by the Provisional State Council to gather all the relevant material on the subject.

The Proclamation of Independence had stated that the Provisional State Council and the Provisional Government would function as the state's main authorities "pending the setting up of the duly elected bodies of the State in accordance with the Constitution to be drawn up by the Constituent Assembly not later than October 1, 1948."

The Constituent Assembly, which was elected on January 23, 1949, turned itself into Israel's first *Knesset while its function as author of the Constitution was somewhat blurred. A debate ensured as to whether by turning itself into an ordinary legislature the Constituent Assembly lost its constituent powers, or whether these powers were passed on to the 1st Knesset and subsequent Knessets. The 1st Knesset held several debates on the need for a constitution.

The main arguments in favor of the constitution were: the declarations of the state's founders and the Proclamation of Independence regarding the preparation of a written constitution; the need for a document which will bind all the state's institutions, including the legislature, and act as a basis for the conduct of the state's life; the need to respect the provisions of the UN resolution of November 29, 1947; the fact that most of the states in the world have a constitution; the educational and cultural value of having a constitution in the light of which the younger generation may be educated, and which can serve as the state's "visiting card" vis-à-vis the world; the value of a constitution as a symbol of unity which would further the "melting pot" process; the value of the constitution as a manifestation of the revolution which had occurred in the existence of the Jewish nation.

The main arguments brought by those opposed to the constitution, including Prime Minister David *Ben Gurion and the *United Religious Front were: that the idea of a constitution had developed in previous centuries at times of social and economic struggles which were no longer current; the absence of a written constitution in Great Britain which was said to have strengthened the rule of law and democracy there, while civil liberties were upheld to no lesser extent than in other countries; the fact that the Proclamation of Independence included the basic principles of any progressive constitution and professed the Jewish nature of the state; that the Transition Law of 1949 passed by the Constituent Assembly was a fulfillment of the state's obligations vis-à-vis the UN, since the Transition Law was a constitution in the material sense (this was Ben Gurion's argument); that only a minority of the Jewish people was in Israel and the state did not have the right to adopt a constitution which would bind the millions who had not yet immigrated to it; that the unique nature of problems of the state would make it difficult to reach an agreement and common language regarding the spiritual principles which should formulate the image and essence of the Jewish People. The debate regarding the constitution would thus lead to a *kulturkampf* (this argument gained special force in light of the insistence of certain religious circles that the *Halacha* should be the supreme law of the Jewish State); that the State of Israel was still in a state of constant change and the process of re-evaluation would be hampered by a rigid constitution.

At the end of the debate three draft proposals were brought to a vote: a proposal of the United Religious Front that "the foundations of the administration and the distribution of its powers, and the guaranteeing of the citizens' rights and obligations will be laid down in Basic Laws"; a proposal supported by **Mapam* the *General Zionists, the **Ḥerut* Movement and **Maki* that "the Knesset assigns the Constitution, Law and Justice Committee with the task of preparing the state's constitution and presenting it to the first Knesset"; and the proposal of MK Yizhar Harari of the *Progressive Party, supported by **Mapai*, the Progressives, the *Sephardim and *Wizo which stated: "the first Knesset assigns the Constitution, Law and Justice Committee with the task of preparing a constitution for the country. The constitution will be made up of chapters, each of which will constitute a separate Basic Law. The chapters will be brought to the Knesset after the committee has completed its work. The chapters will be incorporated into the state's constitution."

On January 13, 1950, the Knesset decided to accept the Harari proposal. The Knesset decision did not deal with the question of an introduction to the constitution, its supremacy over other laws, its flexibility or rigidity, and the date for its completion. In 1986 the task was not yet completed. All of Israel's liberal parties, and those concerned with civil rights, have incorporated a plank in their platforms, advocating the completion of the writing of the constitution.

(J.K.)

CRM See: *Civil Rights Movement.

D

Dash Acronym for *(Tnu'ah) Demokratit Leshinui*. See *Democratic Movement for Change (DMC).

Dayan, Moshe (1915–1981). Military commander and political leader. Dayan was born in Kibbutz Deganiah, and grew up in Moshav Nahalal. He served in the Jewish police force — Captain Orde Wingate's Special Night Squads —

between 1936–39. In 1940 he was tried by the British mandatory authorities for underground activities in the *Haganah* and sentenced to imprisonment. A year later he lost his left eye in an Allied operation against French Vichy forces in Lebanon. After returning to Palestine he joined the **Palmah* and in the *War of Independence commanded Battalion 89. In July 1948 he was appointed Commander of the Jerusalem District, in which capacity he negotiated with King Abdullah and his representatives. In the spring of 1949 he was a member of the Israeli delegation to the armistice talks in Rhodes. In October of that year Dayan was appointed Commander of the Southern Command; in June 1952 Commander of the Northern Command. He was Head of the Operations Branch in General Headquarters in December 1952. One year later he became Chief of Staff of the *IDF, in which capacity he directed the *Sinai Campaign in 1956, becoming a national hero. Dayan played a decisive role in the development of new military tactics in the IDF. In January 1958 he left military service and spent a year doing university studies. He was elected to the 4th Knesset (1959) on the **Mapai* list, serving as Member of Knesset until his death immediately after the 10th Knesset (1981) elections.

In 1959–64 he served as Minister of Agriculture and was one of the founders of **Rafi* in 1965. He visited Vietnam as a journalist in 1966.

On the eve of the *Six-Day War Dayan was appointed Minister of Defense after strong public pressure, and was responsible for the *open bridges policy. He served in that capacity until after the publication of the *Agranat Commission Report in 1974. Dayan emerged as a national hero from the Six-Day War but lost his popularity as a result of the *Yom Kippur War. He was one of the founders of the *Israel Labor Party. Following the elections to the 9th Knesset (1977) Dayan defected to join the first *Begin government as Minister for Foreign Affairs, in which capacity he was instrumental in arranging Anwar Sadat's visit to Jerusalem in November 1977, playing a major role in the various stages of the peace process with Egypt. Dayan resigned from the government later in 1979 when Yosef *Burg was appointed as the negotiator in the *autonomy talks with Egypt.

In 1981 Dayan ran for the Knesset as head of a new list, **Telem*, which gained only three seats despite expectations of much better results. Throughout his military and political career Dayan was known as one who appreciated the Arab point of view and yet advocated firmness in confrontations with them.

Dead Sea Inland lake into which the *Jordan River flows, with no outlet. It is the most saline body of water on earth (27 percent salinity) and is situated at the lowest point on earth (396 meters below sea level). The Dead Sea contains potash and other minerals.

The whole of the Dead Sea was included in *mandatory Palestine. When Transjordan was separated administratively from western Palestine the border between the two regions was drawn along the median line of the Dead Sea. Following the *War of Independence the southwestern part of the Dead Sea up to Ein Gedi was within the boundaries of Israel. During the *Six-Day War the remainder of the western Dead Sea was also occupied by Israel.

A plant to extract potash and other minerals by evaporation was constructed by Moses Novomeyski (1873–1961) in 1934 at Kaliah, at the northern tip of the Dead Sea, after many years of negotiations regarding the granting of the concession. A branch was opened at Sdom, at the southern end, in 1937. It was the Sdom plant which remained in Israeli hands after the War of Independence and was reactivated in 1953 after the construction of a road linking it to Beersheba. The Dead Sea Works is a government-owned enterprise, and its produce constitutes an important Israeli export. The Jordanians opened their own potash plant at the south of the Dead Sea in 1982. Israel has constructed several solar pools along the banks of the Dead Sea to generate electricity, and hotels for tourists coming for cures at the sulphur-rich springs which flow into it.

The idea of constructing a canal connecting the Mediterranean to the Dead Sea which would generate electricity by taking advantage of the difference in elevation was first raised by Theodor *Herzl. The idea was advanced by Yigal *Allon in the late 1970s and in 1980 the Israel government adopted the plan to construct such a canal and tunnel from the *Gaza Strip to the Dead Sea. Besides generating electricity such a canal would help replenish the depleted water level of the Dead Sea. The original plan also proposed the construction of nuclear power stations in the Negev along the canal's course, utilizing the flowing water. The Arabs strongly objected to the project because its starting point would be in the Gaza Strip. Jordan also argued that the canal would ruin its own potash works. The project was finally scrapped in 1985 due to budgetary cuts, technical difficulties, doubts regarding its profitability, and fears that water from the Mediterranean would damage the natural deposits of the Dead Sea.

Declaration of Independence See: *Proclamation of Independence

Defense policy There have been certain constants in Israel's defense policy since the establishment of the state: the belief of the policy-makers in the inalienable right of Jews to return to **Eretz Yisrael* and establish a state there; the persistent and real external threat to the state's existence; the existence of given geographical facts; and the constraints stemming from Israel's relatively small population, limited resources and dependence on external sources of arms. However, Israel's policy-makers have differed not only in their personality and party-ideological affiliations, but also in their perceptions of *Zionism (especially regarding the importance of territories and the nature of the Jewish state), their basic approach toward the use of military force, and their evaluation of the likely behavior of external forces in given situations.

Israel was forced to form a defense policy when the Arabs threatened to prevent the establishment of the Jewish state and then declared their intention to destroy it (See: *Arab-Israel Conflict). After the *Six-Day War the scope of the threat changed as two of the confrontation states — *Egypt and *Jordan — officially adopted the position that their goal was not to destroy Israel but to regain the territories they had lost in 1967. Egypt signed a peace treaty with Israel in 1979, and Jordan has maintained indirect contacts with Israel. Since 1980 the extent of the threat has been temporarily reduced by Iraq's deep involvement in a prolonged war with Iran. However, the Iran-Iraq war will eventually come to an end, and should there be another war between Israel and any of its neighbors, Jordan and even Egypt could become involved under certain circumstances.

As early as the mid-1930s David *Ben Gurion reached the conclusion that the Arabs would accept a Jewish state only when they realized that the Jewish community or that state was so strong that they had no chance of destroying it by force. Thus Israel has always believed that it needs a military edge not only for self-defense but also to improve the prospects of peace. The example of Egypt appeared to confirm this belief.

Though the claim that Israel's aim is to establish a Jewish state "from the Nile to the Euphrates" is a product of Arab propaganda, it cannot be denied that in all the wars, except the *War of Attrition, Israel occupied territories which had not previously been in its possession.

While strong sentiments have always existed toward territories which formed part of historical *Eretz Yisrael*, and a debate has ensued as to whether such territories should or may be given up once occupied, Israel never planned a war to "liberate" territories, and the occupation of territories has been the consequence of wars which broke out for other reasons.

Israel's defense policy views territories primarily in terms of their strategic value to Israel or its neighbors. The major constraint against the annexation of strategically valuable occupied territories has been their indigenous Arab population which would upset the demographic balance in the State of Israel, though in the case of the *Sinai Peninsula Israel opted for withdrawal in 1949 and 1957 due to international pressure, and in 1975–82 in return for peace.

The *Golan Heights were annexed (Israeli jurisdiction was formally applied to them) because of their strategic importance and Syria's refusal to acquiesce to Israel's existence.

In the *War of Independence the main reason for Ben Gurion's refusal to allow the *IDF (Israel Defense Forces) to occupy the *West Bank was demographic. Only on rare occasions has Israel deliberately expelled a local population, for example, from Lydda (Lod) and Ramleh during the War of Independence. Officially, Israel does not accept the concept of population *transfer. In the debate on whether or not Israel should give up the West Bank and *Gaza Strip in return for peace, the arguments of those opposing Israeli withdrawal are strategic and/or religious, while those advocating the *territorial compromise or complete withdrawal do so because of the demographic problem and/or on moral grounds.

Until 1938 the **Haganah*, the predecessor of

the IDF, had a purely defensive military policy. As the 1936–39 disturbances intensified, the *Haganah*, though still adhering to a defensive strategy, established field companies in which men were trained for offensive operations.

When the War of Independence began at the end of 1947 the ideology of the Jewish leadership was still defensive, though the tactics adopted by the Jewish forces were both defensive and offensive. During the first phase of the war battles carried out on the basis of a defensive strategy resulted in high Jewish casualities and showed poor results. At the tactical level the Israeli forces soon began to engage in raids against Arab settlements, intended either as acts of reprisal or to tie up the Arab forces in defense. As of April 1948 (one month before independence) Israeli forces started to take the initiative whenever possible.

From 1948–67 it was official Israeli policy to support a defensive strategy involving offensive tactics, which evolved into a policy of preemptive strikes in order to avoid having to fight a war on Israeli soil. This policy, which was designed to solve the problem of the absence of strategic depth, the existence of major population centers very close to the borders, and the Arab strategic advantage on all fronts, developed into the concept of "artificial strategic depth," i.e., viewing enemy soil as Israel's strategic depth. This strategy implied that Israel should do everything to avoid an Arab first strike and meant that the IDF must be in a constant state of alert, especially its intelligence services (See: **Aman*) and mobile forces (air and armor). Israel's preemptive attack on June 5, 1967, after a period of three weeks of waiting, was viewed in Israel as a defensive act, though outside of Israel questions were raised as to whether the Arabs had really planned to attack.

The acquisition of strategic depth along all fronts as a result of the *Six-Day War led to a return to a purely defensive strategy, typified by the *Bar-Lev Line along the *Suez Canal, which was, however, not accepted by all the Israeli commanders at the time, especially Ariel *Sharon. Nevertheless, even in the *War of Attrition, which was a purely defensive war, Israel used its Air Force for deep penetration raids into Egyptian territory, and in the *Yom Kippur War, in which Israel was simultaneously attacked on the Suez Canal and the Golan Heights, after absorbing the initial attacks of the Egyptian and Syrian armies, the IDF went into an offensive which took it west of the Suez Canal and east of the previous line held on the Golan Heights. It was the strategic depth acquired in 1967 which prevented the surprise attack from touching Israel proper, though it was the strategic depth which was also responsible for the atmosphere of complacency. Israel's first, and so far only, purely offensive war was the *Lebanese War, which was planned and carried out by Defense Minister Ariel Sharon, who does not accept the defensive military doctrine.

However, the distinction between defensive and offensive wars, especially within a strategy of preemptive attacks, is not absolutely clear. While there was no question that Israel had been attacked in 1948 and 1973, and that the War of Independence and the Yom Kippur War were defensive wars, the Israeli government had the option of deciding whether or not to go to war not only in 1982 but also in 1956 and 1967. On these occasions Israel's *casus belli* involved: a concentration of Arab forces, the blocking of shipping routes to Eilat, the shelling of Israeli settlements, major terrorist acts against Israeli civilians, and massive arms acquisitions by the Arab states. However, on other occasions the existence of similar factors did not lead to war. In other words, there is no event that automatically triggers a war, other than being attacked, and it is up to the government of the day to decide whether or not to respond to a security crisis with a full-scale war.

Israel's war aims have also varied from war to war. In 1948 the initial aim was to defend the existence of the newly established state, and once this was secured, to improve the borders laid down for the Jewish state by the 1947 UN partition plan. In 1956 Israel wished to open the Straits of Tiran for Israel bound shipping, stop **feda'iyin* attacks from the Gaza Strip and forestall Egypt's amassment of Soviet-made weapons. In 1967 the original war aims were purely defensive: to reopen the Straits of Tiran and destroy the concentration of Egyptian, Syrian, Jordanian and Iraqi forces threatening Israel. The actual results were quite different: a major defeat suffered by the military forces of the Arab states, and Israeli control of the West Bank, the Gaza Strip, the Golan Heights and the Sinai Peninsula, most of which Israel was initially willing to relinquish (with the exception of *Jerusalem), in return for peace. It was only later that the ideological debate about a possible Israeli withdrawal — a debate which continues to the present day — developed and intensified.

In 1969–70 the aim was to stop Egyptian attacks on Israel's forces east of the Suez Canal. In 1973 Israel initially wanted to push back the invading Egyptian and Syrian forces and end the war with lines that would strengthen Israel's bargaining position.

And in 1982 the proclaimed war aim was to relieve the Galilee from the threat of enemy artillery and terrorist raids. However, in the latter war there was a secret agenda also, including the installation of Bashir Jemayel as President of Lebanon, the destruction of the *Palestine Liberation Organization (PLO) infrastructure, the removal of the Syrians from Lebanon, and the attainment of a peace treaty with Lebanon. The ultimate goal of all the wars has been to bring about the reconciliation of the Arab states to the existence of the State of Israel, and subsequently to achieve peace.

Though Israel has always been prepared for war, and has been involved in six wars since its establishment, to deter war has been a major element in its defense policy. Deterrence involves trying to maintain a military superiority over the combined strength of the Arab states directly or indirectly involved in the conflict, even in the face of extreme demographic imbalance and major economic constraints. However, in 1967, even though Egypt was apparently aware of the military odds, certain dynamics within the Arab camp prevailed and the Egyptians were not deterred. Israel's high state of alertness and preparedness failed in 1973 to deter a war because it also bred complacency and reliance on a single concept regarding Arab options.

On the tactical level the greatest possible freedom is given to the commanders in the field. This policy stresses initiative, flexibility, improvisation and the freedom of local commanders to exploit unexpected developments and to change operational plans. This policy requires special efforts to ensure that the middle and lower echelons of command are of the highest quality. In the actual conduct of war Israel has tried (not always successfully) to keep the fighting as short in duration as possible, a policy dictated by economic constraints, the possibility of pressure by the Great Powers and the UN, the limits of arms and ammunitions stockpiles, and the fact that the IDF is a citizens' army. Israel has also tried to avoid operations likely to lead to a considerable number of civilian casualties on the enemy side or to heavy casualities among Israeli forces. One of the major criticisms in Israel of the Lebanese War was the excessive number of casualities.

Israel has usually depended exlusively on its own forces in its armed confrontations with the Arabs. The two exceptions — the *Sinai Campaign in 1956 when Israel coordinated its operation with *France and *Great-Britain, and the Lebanese War in 1982 when some moves were coordinated with the Christian Phalange forces, were major disappointments.

Israel has never been a member of any military alliance. NATO does not include the Middle East in its frame of reference, while Middle East alliances have either been directed against Israel or, as in the case of the Baghdad Pact (1955) and CENTO (1959), have included states which were in a state of war with Israel.

Israel's defense policy is concerned not only with its confrontation with the Arab states. From the very beginning of its existence one of Israel's major defense preoccupations has been infiltration by *feda'iyin* and terrorist attacks carried out by irregular forces, mostly Palestinians, against Israel and Israeli and Jewish targets outside of Israel.

Israel's policy has been, since 1954, retaliatory attacks against the instigators of these activities or those harboring them, such retaliatory attacks taking place across the borders or even as far as PLO headquarters in Tunis (1985). Occasionally, operations have been carried out to clear a certain territory of terrorist groups, either within the territories occupied by Israel (as in the case of the Gaza Strip in 1970–71) or outside of Israel (as in the case of the *Litani Operation in 1978 and certain stages of the Lebanese War in 1982). It is impossible to evaluate the exact effect of the policy of reprisals. In 1956 it was the perceived failure of this policy which was the major cause for Israel's embarking on the Sinai Campaign. Generally speaking, it is assumed that even though the reprisals have not stopped terrorist acts, they have helped contain them.

Until the mid-1950s Israel did not have a single source of arms, and *arms purchases depended on availability. In the years 1955–67 France was Israel's main source of arms, but these supplies were stopped due to De Gaulle's increasingly pro-Arab policy and his disapproval of Israel's preemptive attack in June 1967. Since 1968 the *United States has been Israel's almost exclusive source of arms, and has occasionally tried to use its leverage with Israel, with greater or lesser success, to influence its policy regarding elements in the peace process (for example, *Security Council Resolution 242, the *Rogers Plan, the *Interim Agreement) or the conduct of war (for example, the cease-fire in the Yom Kippur War or the attack on West Beirut). A major element of Israel's defense policy has been to become as self-sufficient as possible in the manufacture of arms. The attempt to develop an arms industry which is also economically viable has encouraged Israeli *arms sales abroad. It is widely believed that Israel has a nuclear capability. Israel has so far refused to join the non-proliferation treaty or to admit that it actually has nuclear warheads (rather than just nuclear know-how). However, Israel's strategy is based exclusively on conventional forces, and it has followed a policy of acting to prevent its neighbors from developing nuclear capabilities (See: *Osiraq Operation).

De Haan assassination Considered to be the first political assassination in the *Yishuv*. Jacob Israel de Haan (1881–1924), political spokesman of **Agudat Yisrael* and the ultra-religious community in Palestine, was shot to death on June 30, 1924, as he was leaving the synagogue of the Sha'arei Zedek Hospital on Jaffa Street in Jerusalem. De Haan was born in the Netherlands, the son of a cantor. He was a poet and advocate, and was active in the leadership of the Dutch Socialist Party. After suffering a nervous breakdown he became religious, became a Zionist, and came to Palestine in 1919. De Haan published two books, sensational for their homosexual eroticism. In Palestine he was soon disappointed with the Zionist establishment and turned to the old established *Yishuv* whose head, Rabbi Joseph Ḥaim Sonnenfeld, made him the leader of the political and public struggle against the secular new *Yishuv*. When de Haan's activities began taking place outside of Palestine, holding meetings with the Emir Abdullah of Transjordan (1922) and arranging a mission to the Colonial Office in London, the **Haganah* started to view him as a dangerous enemy. *Haganah* member Avraham Tehomi was instructed to assassinate de Haan. Several *Haganah* leaders, including Yitzḥak *Ben Zvi (second President of Israel) and his wife Rachel Yana'it, were rumored to have been connected with the affair. (Sh.M.)

Deir Yassin A former Arab village on the western outskirts of Jerusalem where *IZL and **Leḥi* launched an attack on April 9, 1948, during the *War of Independence. The local **Haganah* commander, David Shaltiel (1903–1969) approved the attack even though capture of this village was low on the *Haganah*'s list of priorities. IZL and *Leḥi* insisted on carrying out the operation, arguing that the inhabitants of Deir Yassin had participated in the 1929 riots and the 1936–39 disturbances. An attempt was made by the attacking forces to warn the inhabitants to leave, but this effort merely lost the attackers the element of suprise.

In the course of the fighting a **Palmaḥ* unit arrived to aid the IZL and *Leḥi*. Following the withdrawal of this force a massacre took place in which 120–250 civilians, including women and children, were killed (the number was never verified). This development was strongly condemned by the *Jewish Agency and the majority of the **Yishuv*. Rumors of the massacre spurred the Arab exodus from the territories to be included within the Jewish state.

The Arabs point to the Deir Yassin case, as well as the Israeli attack on Kibyeh (1953) and the shooting of civilians in *Kafr Kassem (1956), as examples of Israel's maltreatment of the Arabs. Israel argues that, while the facts of the cases cannot be denied, they are regrettable exceptions and that Israeli soldiers are instructed not to kill civilians unless in self-defence and are instructed in the principles of *tohar haneshek* ("purity of arms").

Democratic Front for Peace and Equality See: **Hadash*.

Democratic Movement One of the splinters of the *Democratic Movement for Change formed after it disintegrated in 1978. The Democratic Movement was led by *Yiga'el Yadin and remained in the coalition. In 1980, Minister of Justice Shmuel *Tamir, its representative, resigned from the government and party, arguing that it was absurd that a party with four Knesset members should have three cabinet posts. By March 1981, the party had ceased to exist.

Democratic Movement for Change (DMC) A party established in 1976 as a sequel to the protest movements which emerged in Israel in the aftermath of the *Yom Kippur War. The core of the new party was Yiga'el *Yadin, **Shinui*, headed by Amnon *Rubinstein, a group of defectors from the *Israel Labor Party, headed by Meir *Amit, members of the *Free Center, headed by Shmu'el *Tamir, and groups which were active in the slum areas and on issues related to **Edot Mizraḥ*, headed by **Oded*. The members of all these groups joined as individuals since the new party insisted that only individuals and not groups could join.

The DMC ran for the 9th Knesset (1977) on a platform which included a call for *electoral reform to a system of single-member constituences; the enactment of a parties law; reduction of government bureaucracy; decentralization of government power and the strengthening of regional administrations; preparation of a *constitution; the establishment of a Ministry of Welfare in order to concentrate all the authority in this sphere within a single framework; reorganization of the education system to accelerate social integration and the closing of social gaps; a new housing policy based on rental housing; enforcement of the law in all spheres; the priority of production and exports over services; a fair distribution of the tax burden; war against "black capital" (undeclared taxable income); the preservation of the Jewish character of the State of Israel and its united capital *Jerusalem; willingness for *territorial compromise in return for true peace; opposition to the establishment of *third state west of the *Jordan River; delineation of Israel's security boundary as the Jordan River with Israeli control of areas vital for its security (See also: *Allon Plan).

Most of the party leaders hoped to enter a coalition with the *Alignment. Though the DMC gained 15 seats in the 9th Knesset (1977) the **Likud* was able to form a coalition without it. Nonetheless, it decided to join the new government and by so doing lost all its bargaining power. It had to give up some of its basic demands such as for electoral reform, and for stopping concessions to the religious parties.

The decision of the majority in the DMC to join the government, with Yadin serving as Deputy Prime Minister, Israel Katz as Minister of Welfare, Amit as Minister of Transport and Communications and Tamir as Minister of Justice led to a split in the party. In 1978 the group led by Yadin decided to remain in the government, and assumed the name *Democratic Movement, while a second group led by Rubinstein left the coalition and broke away from the party, taking on the name *Shinui Veyozmah* (Change and Initiative), and Amit returned to the Labor Party. The DMC did not run in the elections to the 10th Knesset (1981). The fate of the party, following the great hopes and enthusiasm which had accompanied its formation, has built a psychological barrier to the establishment of a new centrist-reform bloc in Israel. (D.B.M.)

Development and Peace *Pitu'aḥ Veshalom*. The name assumed by Member of Knesset Shmuel *Flatto-Sharon in 1978 for his Knesset faction of one. The name was chosen because the acronym for *Pitu'aḥ-Shalom* is the same as for Flatto-Sharon.

Disengagement Agreements Agreements reached following the *Yom Kippur War between *Egypt and Israel and *Syria and Israel, on the disposition and reduction of military forces on both sides of the cease-fire lines, and Israeli withdrawal from certain areas. Both agreements were reached through the mediatory efforts of US Secretary of State Henry Kissinger (See: *Kissinger Shuttle Diplomacy).

The Israeli-Egyptian Disengagement Agreement, concluded on January 18, 1974, provided for the withdrawal of Israeli forces from Egypt west of the Suez Canal, accepted the presence of Egyptian forces in Sinai up to the October cease-fire line, and lifted the Israeli siege of the Egyptian Third Army. It also established a 10-kilometer buffer zone under the UN Emergency Forces (UNEF), with the reduction of Israeli and Egyptian forces on either side of this line and the limitation of their equipment. Through further US mediation an *Interim Agreement was concluded between Israel and Egypt in September 1975.

The Israeli-Syrian Disengagement Agreement was concluded on May 31, 1974. It provided for Israeli withdrawal from some of the Syrian territories captured in October 1973, and from the town of Kuneitra and an adjacent area held since 1967 which was to be reinhabited by the Syrians. A buffer zone was set up, manned by a UN Disengagement Observer Force (UNDOF), while limitations were imposed on the strength and equipment of forces within 10 kilometers, and a further 25 kilometers, on either side of the cease-fire line. Efforts to negotiate a disengagement agreement with Jordan were disrupted by the Rabat Conference of October 1974 (See: *Jericho Plan). (Y.S.-S.H.R.)

Dissidents In Hebrew *porshim*. A term commonly used in the latter years of the mandatory period in Palestine to refer to the **Irgun Zva'i Le'umi* and **Leḥi* which did not accept the authority and discipline of the elected institutions of the *World Zionist Organization and the **Yishuv*—the *Jewish Agency and the **Va'ad Le'umi*, respectively.

DMC See: *Democratic Movement for Change.

Druze An independent religious community which has existed since the beginning of the 11th century when it broke away from Islam. The original members of the new sect migrated from *Egypt to *Lebanon, and after one generation of proselytization settled along the western slopes of Mount Hermon, spreading westward into the Shouf Mountains, southward into the Galilee and Mount Carmel, and eastward into what is today Syria.

The Druze religion is monotheistic, and includes the belief in reincarnation. Most of its beliefs and practices are shrouded in secrecy. No religious conversions or intermarriages are allowed, thus helping to preserve Druze exclusivity.

The Druze are village and mountain dwellers, attached to their individual plots of land and property, while harboring no separatist national aspirations. They are completely loyal to the states in which they reside, including service in the army. This basic principle, within the context of the *Arab-Israel conflict, has meant that Druze frequently find themselves serving in armies which are in open confrontation with one another.

There are about 70,000 Druze in Israel (including the Druze population of the *Golan Heights), about 600,000 in Syria, 300,000 in Lebanon, with small communities living in the United States, Canada, Latin America and Australia. In 1948 there were approximately 13,000 living within the boundaries of the State of Israel. Through natural growth and the de facto annexation of the Golan Heights their number had risen to 65,861 in May 1983, of whom 46,134 lived within the Green Line in 17 villages, 15 in the Galilee and two on Mount Carmel. Of these, nine are entirely Druze and the rest mixed mainly with Christian Arabs.

As of the late 1920s many of the Palestinian Druze cooperated with the **Yishuv*. Even before the establishment of the state there were some Druze serving in the **Haganah*, and upon the proclamation of the state the majority sided with Israel, with many Druze voluntarily fighting in the *IDF during the *War of Independence. Since 1955 Druze men have served in the IDF on equal terms with Jewish conscripts, some opting for a professional military career. About 175 Druze have been killed in action, including a large number in the *Lebanese War.

The Israeli government's decision in December 1981 to apply Israeli law to the Golan Heights caused major controversy among the Druze in that region — whether or not to accept Israeli identity cards. Syrian pressure influenced the Druze religious authorities in the Golan to take a strong negative position. It was regretted by the Israeli Druze, who favored the addition of 15,000 Druze to their community, but the Israeli authorities did not force the issue. In the first phase of the Lebanese War Israel's allies, the Phalange, conspired against the Druze in the Shouf Mountains. The Israeli Druze were instrumental in influencing Israel's decision-makers to act with restraint toward the Lebanese Druze while persuading their Lebanese brethren to do likewise regarding the IDF.

Theoretically the Druze have been full citizens since the establishment of the state, however in practice the situation is somewhat different. They were under the *Military Administration until 1962 and maintain they were discriminated against with regard to welfare services, development assistance, and appointment to senior official positions. Economically the Druze population is among the least affluent in Israel and the number of youngsters receiving higher education is relatively low, consequently, even in the private sector, few Druze have reached the top professional levels. Until the 9th Knesset (1977) elections all the Druze in the *Knesset represented *minority lists. Since 1977 there has been one Druze member in the *Likud*, and two in the *Democratic Movement for Change, one of whom was elected to the 11th Knesset on the *Shinui* ticket.

Unlike the Arab population few Druze vote for the communists, most of them voting for the minority lists and Zionist parties.

(Z.A.)

E

Eban, Abba (Aubrey Solomon) Diplomat and Member of Knesset. Born in 1915, Cape Town, South Africa. Eban was educated at Queens College, Cambridge. In 1942 he served as Allied Headquarters' Liaison Officer with the Jewish population in Jerusalem for training volunteers, and in 1944 was Chief Instructor at the Middle East Arab Center in Jerusalem. He entered the *Jewish Agency in 1946 and was Liaison Officer with the UN Special Committee on Palestine (UNSCOP) in 1947. Eban was appointed representative of the Provisional Government of Israel to the UN in 1948 and between 1949–59 was Israel's Permanent Representative to the UN, serving as Vice-President of the General Assembly in 1952. Concurrently, he was Ambassador to the US (1950–59). From 1958–66 he was President of the Weizmann Institute in Rehovot. Eban was elected to the 4th Knesset (1959) as a member of *Mapai*. From 1959–60 he served as Minister without Portfolio; 1960–63 as Minister of Education and Culture; 1963–66 as Deputy Prime Minister. As Minister for Foreign Affairs from 1966–74, he served during both the *Six-Day War, which he tried to avert, and the *Yom Kippur War. Eban resigned from the government in March 1974 together with Prime Minister Golda *Meir and Minister of Defense Moshe *Dayan as a result of the growing public criticism of the government's functioning before the Yom Kippur War, and became guest professor at Columbia University in the US. Since then he has held no cabinet post but was appointed Chairman of the Knesset Foreign Affairs and Security Committee in 1984.

Chief consultant and narrator of the nine-part TV program "Heritage" on the history of the Jewish People, Eban is considered one of Israel's most brillant orators, and speaks many languages fluently. Eban has always been known for his moderation and willingness to compromise.

economic policy Balance-of-payment deficits and inflation have been the twin problems plaguing the Israeli economy since the state's establishment. The economy has continuously operated in an environment influenced by successive waves of *aliyah* (immigration), the need for a high level of military preparedness and the occasional outbreak of hostilities.

The importance of providing employment for a rapidly growing labor force, a high percentage of it, especially in the early years, new immigrants, many of whom arrived without means and frequently without relevant professional skills, has dictated a policy of intensive economic development and growth. For a country poor in natural resources with defense needs that absorb an exceptionally high percentage of the country's resources, economic development could at no time be fully met from current production. Foreign aid and contributions by world Jewry have thus always been vital to foster economic growth.

From 1948–51, as Israel's population doubled through immigration, a policy of overall price control and rationing was introduced by Dov *Yosef, Minister of Supply and Rationing in Israel's first government. In view of the bulging budget deficits and monetary expansion, this policy created suppressed inflation which led to the development of a black market. It also involved the penalization of exports and subsidization of imports resulting in Israel's meager foreign reserves rapidly dwindling to zero. By the end of 1951 the policy, commonly known in Hebrew as the *tzenah* (austerity), collapsed.

THE NEW ECONOMIC POLICY (1952). The NEP, introduced by Israel's Minister of Finance Eliezer Kaplan, and later carried out by his successor Levi *Eshkol, involved a rapid devaluation of the Israeli pound (by about 600 percent between January 1952 and January 1954) accompanied by the abolition of price controls. This policy offered substantial incentives to exports while releasing the inflationary pressures. Tight fiscal and monetary policies supported these moves.

This overall effort to put the economy on an

even keel assumed that Israel would be able to finance a substantial import surplus — more than 10 percent of its GNP. This was achieved through the institution of the Independence Loan Organization which together with the *United Israel Appeal nearly doubled the flow of contributions and concessionary finance from Jewish sources; a request for US economic aid (See: *Foreign Aid to Israel) which was granted in 1952; and the highly controversial decision to request financial compensation from the *Federal Republic of Germany which led to the 1952 *Restitution Agreement.

By 1953 the economy entered a 20-year period of rapid growth in which the average annual rate of growth was about 10 percent.

DEVALUATION AND SLOWDOWN IN THE 1960S. Rapid growth accompanied by an annual inflation rate of around 7 percent resulted in Israel's trade gap reaching $500 million by the early 1960s. The import surplus would have been even greater had it not been for a maze of import duties and a highly complicated system of export subsidies. Though the trade deficit was more than covered by the inflow of capital, and Israel's reserves were still rising, Levi Eshkol convinced the government in February 1962 to devalue the Israeli pound by 66 percent (the effective devaluation was 40 percent for imports and 15 percent for exports). This enabled the government to do away with most of the system of export subsidization while streamlining import duties. The initial improvement in the balance of trade was, however, soon eroded by continued inflationary pressures and the government's full employment policy, and by 1964 the economy regressed in terms of inflation and the import surplus.

Pinḥas *Sapir who replaced Eshkol as minister of finance when the latter became prime minister in 1963, tried an alternative strategy, a "Slowdown Policy." This involved a brake on investment — both direct government investment and subsidies for private investment. The completion at this time of several major investment projects — including the Jordan-Negev National Water Carrier and the port at Ashdod — and the peaking of a private construction boom toward the end of 1965, rapidly stalled the momentum of the economic growth. Inflation and the deficit in the current account were both contained by the end of 1966 but at the cost of unemployment which, by the beginning of 1967, reached a level of approximately 10 percent. This economic depression, much deeper than planned, created an atmosphere of depression and unrest.

POST *SIX-DAY WAR BOOM. Developments in the aftermath of the June 1967 War undoubtedly helped the Israeli economy to move rapidly from slump to boom. However, even before the outbreak of the war fiscal expansion, focusing on public works, was high on the agenda. The unexpected war made a "public works" policy, financed by budget deficits, a foregone conclusion. The post-war boom was initiated by major projects, such as the construction of an elaborate military infrastructure in the Sinai and along the *Jordan River, a substantial rise in domestic defense expenditure, which boosted, among others, Israel's armaments industries and an ambitious housing project, designed to help absorb a new wave of immigration (primarily from the *Soviet Union and *Latin America) and to improve the living conditions of the immigrant families who had arrived from Moslem countries in the 1950s. Finally, an extremely expansive and expensive welfare policy was introduced, which led to a 100 percent leap in welfare payments between 1970 and 1976.

Government deficits, supported by an expansionary monetary policy and an improving trade balance, induced by a 16 percent devaluation in November 1967, propelled the economy into its all-time high rate of growth in the closing years of the 1960s. GNP grew by an annual average of 13 percent in 1968 and 1969, and by close to 10 percent from 1970 through October 1973. Full employment was reached by the middle of 1969 despite continuous rapid growth of Israel's labor force through 1973, which was brought about by the substantial wave of immigration, the very high birth rates in the 1950s and the availability of manual labor from the *West Bank and the *Gaza Strip. It was also largely due to this boom that the economies of the *occupied territories could be so rapidly and smoothly integrated into the expanding Israeli economy.

Until the beginning of 1970 this production and employment boom took place in an environment of stable prices. However, inflation soon started to rise again, and by the third quarter of 1973 the rate of inflation was up to 20 percent.

The eternal twin problems of the Israeli economy — the current-account deficit and inflation, once again emerged. To reduce the import surplus the Israeli pound was once again devalued by 20 percent in August 1971. However, because government demand was not correspondingly reduced, and the budgetary deficit was allowed to continue to grow, inflationary pressures mounted and the rate of inflation continued to rise.

RETRENCHMENT IN THE AFTERMATH OF THE *YOM KIPPUR WAR. The 1973–74 oil crisis, which raised the price of oil almost five-fold, followed by a commodities price boom, propelled inflation to an annual rate of close to 50 percent. The need to increase the *IDF's Order of Battle, forced on the country by the surprise attack on Yom Kippur, and to replenish its arms arsenal imposed a rapidly growing strain on government finances and the balance of payments. The petrodollar-financed build-up of Arab arms arsenals and military establishments in the immediate aftermath of the war and in the following decade, forced Israel to respond with a rapid build-up of the IDF.

The immediate Israeli response to the economic consequences of the Yom Kippur War was a determined drive to bring about a major increase in American aid. In 1974 aid from the US was four times larger than in 1972, and continued to rise over the next decade. The maintenance of American aid at an annual level of $1.5–2 billion became a major factor in the *modus operandi* of Israel's economy, affecting the attitudes of both politicians and the electorate. However, in spite of the major increase in American aid, the balance-of-payments deficit continued to rise, and with it Israel's indebtedness. Yehoshu'a Rabinowitz, who became minister of finance in Yitzḥak *Rabin's government in 1974, had to cope simultaneously with inflation and the balance of payments, as did his predecessors. Growing defense requirements and the liberal welfare policy adopted in the early 1970s, which could not be reversed for political reasons, left little room for substantial budgetary cuts. Instead, Rabinowitz was forced to raise gross taxation to around 45 percent of GNP. This resulted in an immediate decrease in the government deficit, which reduced the pressure on aggregate demand. In addition, the government reached an agreement on "Prices, Wages and Profits" with the **Histadrut* and the Industrialists' Association, which had a further dampening effect and resulted in a substantial reduction in real wages through 1976 and consequently in the lowering of production costs and demand. To cope with the balance of payments another major devaluation of the Israeli pound, followed by a "crawling peg" (which provided for continuous and small devaluations of the currency) were introduced. A slowdown in the economy, accompanied by rising unemployment, was the inevitable consequence of this effort at a comprehensive policy. However, by the end of 1976 inflation was down to less than 30 percent and the civilian import surplus was reduced by more than $500 million to $1.7 billion in 1976.

This was an impressive achievement economically, but politically the squeeze on incomes and employment contributed to the failure of the *Alignment in the 1977 elections. Forty years of predominance by the labor movement, its economic concepts and priorities, came to an end.

LIBERAL AND POPULIST ECONOMIC POLICIES. The **Likud*, which emerged victorious from the elections to the 9th Knesset (1977) was traditionally a grouping of right-of-center parties which had for years advocated a drastic reduction in government involvement in the economy, and a lessening of the economic power of the *Histadrut*, one of the labor movement's power bases, and, as they maintained, a major impediment to a free economy. A retrospective survey of the structural characteristics of the Israeli economy shows that in fact government involvement had been on the decline since 1952. In the 1960s, especially under the economic tutelage of Sapir, this process, initiated by Eshkol, had been accelerated, much to the chagrin of many socialists. Yet, even by the mid-1970s government, was still playing a much greater role in the economy than it does in other western democracies.

The "controlling heights" of government involvement, as in all countries, has been in fiscal policy, but the uniqueness of the Israeli case has been one of magnitude. Gross tax revenue which was above 40 percent of GNP, was pushed to close to 50 percent by 1976. Government expenditure on goods, services and transfer payments was correspondingly high. The direct access of the government to the Central Bank, and its control of the comparatively large flow of unilateral receipts and Independent Loan funds, gave it stronger than usual influence on monetary policy. Its effective monopoly over the domestic capital market was maintained by the obligation on pension funds and insurance companies to purchase government securities, by tax privileges on government bonds, the Law for the Promotion of Capital Investment, and the absolute control of the minister of finance of the administration of securities. Finally, foreign currency controls, imposed by the mandatory authorities in the 1940s and never revoked, ensured government dominance in the field of external economic transactions, though by the 1970s this control was practically though not formally restricted to travel abroad and the capital account of the balance of payments.

The philosophy of the economic turnabout (See: *Upheaval) initiated by the first *Likud* minister of finance, Simḥa *Ehrlich in October 1977, was to reduce government involvement in the economy. Such a policy should have involved a drastic reform in all aspects of the Israeli economy, both in terms of structure and operations. However, Ehrlich tackled only one aspect of the multi-dimensional economic structure which had developed over the past three decades — currency control, which focused on the monetary and financial facets of the system through several steps: a close to 60 percent devaluation of the formal exchange rate, and, correspondingly, a 15–20 percent devaluation of *effective* exchange rates on imports and on exports; a far-reaching relaxation of exchange controls on capital account; a substantial increase in foreign currency allocations for Israelis travelling abroad which in practical terms meant a virtual abolition of control in this sphere; and finally the right of Israeli legal entities to hold foreign currency-linked deposits. These steps were introduced at a time of full employment, with inflation accelerating from an annual rate of about 25 percent in the first two quarters of 1977 to an annual rate of 40 percent, while the civilian import deficit rose from $1.5 billion in 1977 to $1.7 billion in 1978. The inevitable rise of import prices in the wake of the devaluation accelerated the rate of inflation. Only a slight attempt to reduce government expenditure, a prerequisite for curing inflation and preventing a deterioration in the balance of payments, was made. Monetary policy, which should have been restrictive to help implement the devaluation policy, was instead highly expansionary, largely due to the full freedom of capital flows inherent in the economic turnabout, and the option — which had never before been available — to hold dollar bank accounts.

The constantly rising two-digit inflation and the corresponding build-up of inflationary expectations induced a substantial shift into dollar accounts and a reduction in the demand for Israeli currency, both of which had further expansionary effects.

This development was reinforced on the supply side of the money market by a flood of short-term capital imports, which temporarily increased reserves and ipso facto the supply of money. These monetary developments generated an immediate pressure on prices, and by the end of 1978 inflation was running at an annual rate of 70 percent. In 1979 inflation passed the 100-percent mark while the balance of payments situation deteriorated rapidly. The foreign debt, already vast due to borrowing connected with the Yom Kippur War, grew by leaps and bounds, endangering Israel's credit standing in world financial markets. At the same time the government deficit was large and did not show any sign of falling, resulting in a rapidly rising domestic debt.

In 1979 the Central Bank succeeded in reducing the size of capital imports, mostly "hot money," by imposing a prohibitive interest equalization tax of foreign credits. Thus, much of the effort of the 1977 policy regarding capital flows was nullified.

Various attempts were made to cope with the three-digit inflation and growing balance-of-payments deficit. These were, however, constrained by Prime Minister Menaḥem *Begin's populist policy (**Leheitiv im ha'am* — to benefit the people), which prevented any attempt to deal with government expenditure and its mounting deficits.

The rapid succession of ministers of finance who served the *Likud* governments between 1977–85 was an indicator of Israel's economic woes in these years. Ehrlich resigned in 1979 as a result of the adamant refusal of Begin and his government to set economic priorities and allow him to implement a tight fiscal policy. Next, Yigael *Hurwitz, during whose term the Israeli pound was replaced by the shekel (at a rate of 10 to 1), tried in vain to cut the government budget using the slogan "*ein li*" (I haven't any [money]). But when asked to provide funds for government projects he, like Ehrlich, did not receive government backing. Hurwitz was replaced by Yoram *Aridor who, following the most extreme populist policy of any of the *Likud* ministers of finance, allowed subsidies on basic foods and transportation to rise to unprecedented heights. The two- and later three-digit inflation at the turn of the decade led to wild speculation on the Tel-Aviv stock market, leading inevitably to a crash in January 1983. Aridor was forced to resign in October 1983 when the bank-share market, which had got out of hand, collapsed, and a plan to "dollarize" the Israeli economy prematurely became public knowlege. Aridor was succeeded by Yigal Cohen-Orgad who turned the clock back on the liberalization of currency control, reduced foreign currency allocations and reintroduced price and wage controls.

His term in the Ministry of Finance was cut short by the 1984 general elections.

*NATIONAL UNITY GOVERNMENT AND THE POLICY OF STABILIZATION. By the beginning of 1984 inflation passed the 400 percent mark and the current-account deficit rose to $5 billion. Thus the economic situation was the major cause for the calling of early elections, and the major issue of the election campaign. The *Alignment argued that the *Likud*, with its currency liberalization, "free gifts" to the public, the breaking up of many of the government's economic planning mechanisms (e.g., in agriculture which by 1984 was in a major crisis), the *Lebanese War, unbridled settlement and development activities in the *West Bank and the *Gaza Strip had led the Israeli economy close to ruin. The *Likud* replied that it had inherited a distorted economic system from the Alignment, that the **Histadrut* had obstructed all efforts to cure the economy, that the system of linking salaries to the cost of living index tied the government's hands, and that the balance of payments difficulties were primarily due to the maturation of foreign debts from 1973 and thus had nothing to do with *Likud* policies. It also pointed out that since 1977 Israel's high-tech industries had thrived. As a result of the political deadlock induced by the 1984 election results, a national unity government was established, which set among its primary goals withdrawal from Lebanon and putting the economy on a sounder footing. The distribution of portfolios gave the *Likud* the two major economic ministries — Finance, and Industry and Trade, assumed by Yitzḥak *Moda'i and Ari'el *Sharon, respectively. However, contrary to most of Israel's prime ministers (except Levi Eshkol) Israel's new prime minister, Shimon *Peres took an interest in and became directly involved in the management of the country's economy. While a general economic policy was being worked out a first attempt to face the issues was made through legislation and the signing of two "package deals" among the government, *Histadrut* and employers. These involved the administrative freezing of prices and of real wages, but after a two-months pause inflation was up again to over 400 percent in May and June. In July 1985 a new policy was introduced, involving small cuts in budgetary expenditures and a major tax hike, carried out by very substantial cuts in food subsidies and export subsidies. Exporters were compensated by a substantial devaluation and the effective though not formal freeze of the dollar exchange rate. A temporary breaking of the link between wages and the cost of living index was another important feature of this policy involving a planned, though temporary, substantial erosion of wages. A tight monetary policy, leading to skyrocketing real rates of interest was a major part of this policy which did, in fact, reduce the rate of inflation to a two-digit figure by December 1985. It also offered some relief to the balance of payments. On January 1, 1986, the shekel was replaced by the new shekel at a rate of 1,000 to one and kept stable at around 1.5 shekels per dollar. While the rate of inflation was brought down in 1986 to a monthly average of less than 2 percent (in July the rate was down to zero), the balance of payments showed some improvement primarily due to the fall in energy prices, and the structure of Israel's foreign debt of $24 billion was somewhat improved due to American aid in 1985 and 1986 given in the form of grants. The government had difficulties in cutting its budget and bringing about a structural change in the Israel economy at a time when many industries and the construction branch were suffering from cutbacks. While unemployment did not go above 8 percent (though geographically unevenly distributed), by the end of 1986 renewed economic growth had not yet begun and there was concern about the continuation of stability in the economy.

In April 1986, dissension between Moda'i and Prime Minister Shimon *Peres led to his replacement as Minister of Finance by Moshe Nissim. Following the *rotation the second stage of the government's economic plan, aiming at maintaining stability and encouraging growth, was presented. The main features of the plan as finally approved were: cuts in taxation rates for both individuals and companies, a temporary wage freeze, a ten percent devaluation of the shekel, liberalization of the capital market, a further 400 million shekel cut in the budget affecting all ministries except Defense, a cut in subsidies and the decrease of direct government involvement in the economy. (H.B.)

Economic Upheaval See *Upheaval.

Edot Mizraḥ Hebrew for "Oriental communities," a term which refers to the Jews who came to Israel from the Moslem countries. The terms *Edot Mizraḥ* and Sephardim are frequently used interchangeably, but this is inaccurate. The Oriental Jews are those who settled in the Middle East and North Africa after the destruction of the Second Temple, and continued to live there after the rise of Islam. The Sephardim were the Jews who lived in *Spain and were expelled in 1492. After the expulsion many Sephardi Jews settled in Moslem countries among the Oriental Jews. The Sephardi and Oriental Jews share a religious style and religious *corpus juris*. On the whole both Sephardim and Oriental Jews share social, cultural and physiognomic characteristics with the non-Jewish inhabitants of North Africa, the Middle East and Asia Minor. However, while the former spoke Ladino (a Spanish dialect mixed with Hebrew words) the latter spoke Judeo-Arabic and Judeo-Persian. Furthermore, there was more of a tradition of elitism and self-esteem among the Sephardim.

At the beginning of the Zionist endeavor in 1881–82 the Oriental and Sephardi Jews constituted about 60 percent of the Jewish population in Palestine. By 1948 they were down to 23 percent. These Jews had always believed in the return to Zion, largely for religious reasons, but they were not part of the modern Zionist movement and *World Zionist Organization (WZO), which, until 1945, were almost totally inactive in the Moslem countries. This was principally because Zionism was a movement which emerged as a response to the problems of Ashkenazi Jews in Europe who knew very little about non-Ashkenazi Jews (Sephardi and Oriental Jews constituted only 10 percent of world Jewry at the turn of the century) and because the Zionist movement was banned in many Moslem countries in the 1930s and 40s.

In the years 1919–48 only 29,518 Oriental Jews officially made **aliyah* to *mandatory Palestine, of whom 15,838 came from Yemen and Aden (there had been waves of Yemenite immigration to Palestine previously in 1881 and 1907). Massive immigration from the Moslem countries started after the establishment of the state — with 491,555 arrivals in the years 1948–60, of whom 168,313 came from North Africa and 126,360 from Iraq. The new state was hard-pressed to cope with the flow of immigrants. The absorption facilities were meager, with many of the new arrivals being housed in tents and shacks in transit camps or taken immediately on arrival to new settlements far from the existing population centers. In fact, the majority of the population that was settled in over 300 agricultural communities established in 1948–54, and 33 medium to small new towns, mainly in the Galilee and Negev established in 1948–57, were from *Edot Mizraḥ*. In these homogeneous settlements the national policy of *mizug galuyot* (the intermingling of the exiles) was not often implemented. Since the Ashkenazi majority was inclined to view the Oriental Jews as primitive and ignorant, the ideal of *mizug galuyot*, where it was implemented, manifested itself in an attempt to break down the traditional structures and enforce western values and ways. The immigrants had not expected to shed their historical diaspora-related distinct ethnic identities. In the 1950s and 1960s there was some discrimination — both institutional and attitudinal — against the Oriental Jews, some of whom came to regard the period after their immigration as one of humiliation. The dire economic circumstances of that period added to their sufferings while the social changes enforced on them precipitated a reaction against the Israeli establishment in the 1970s and particularly against the institutions of the dominant labor movement

(*Mapai;* **Histadrut*, *kibbutzim, etc.). These were held responsible for what was termed a deliberate policy of discrimination intended to preserve social, economic, and educational gaps and to keep the Oriental Jews away from central power positions. This resentment was particularly felt among the North African Jews who had arrived in Israel without their religious, intellectual and political leadership.

In the early years of the state few Oriental Jews supported the ethnic parties (the Sephardi and Yemenite lists disappeared by the 3rd Knesset). Most supported **Mapai*, less for ideological reasons than in the hope of material gain.

Since a high percentage of the immigrants from Moslem countries were religious, the Ashkenazi-led religious parties hoped to build up their electoral power with the passive support of the Oriental Jews. However, dissatisfied with the role assigned to them, the Oriental community established new religious parties: in 1981 much of the Oriental support of the *National Religious Party switched to **Tami*, a predominantly Moroccan party, and in 1984 to **Shass*, an ultra-religious non-Zionist Sephardi party, which drew away all Oriental support from **Agudat Yisrael* and many of *Tami*'s voters.

The **Ḥerut* Movement was from the start ideologically attractive to many Oriental Jews who were made to feel at home in the party. The membership of Oriental Jews in **IZL* and **Leḥi* was disproportionately high. After 1977 the **Likud* reaped the fruit of Oriental desire for revenge against the Labor establishment: support for *Gaḥal/Likud* in the development towns went up from 29.1 percent in 1965 to 48.9 percent in 1981, while support for Labor declined from 53.8 percent to 29.2 percent, and that for the NRP from 13.1 percent to 3.4 percent. A similar, though slightly weaker swing occurred in lower-class urban neighborhoods.

Lack of experience and weak organization made it difficult for the *Edot Mizraḥ* to form separate political organizations in the early years of the state but as they grew into a majority they were able to work for their fair share of the existing political cake.

Despite dissatisfaction and frustration, violent outbreaks against the establishment were very rare. The *Wadi Salib riots in 1959 and the *Black Panther demonstrations, especially in the years 1971–73, were the exceptions. Nevertheless they played an important role in increasing public awareness of the problem, and motivated the existing parties to recruit potential Oriental leaders. *Mapai*, and later the *Israel Labor Party, were, however, slow to read the writing on the wall. Prime Minister Golda *Meir actually said that the Black Panthers (many of them school dropouts with criminal records and IDF rejects) were "not nice boys." After 1964 **Oded*, made up of recently arrived students and intellectuals of Moroccan origin, tried to change the image of the Oriental Jews, and to bring about an improvement in conditions, but the movement had no clear political direction and had only a marginal effect.

Until the 1970s the *Edot Mizraḥ* had very little representation in the centers of power. For example, no representative of the development towns was given a seat in the Knesset until 1962 when one delegate was elected and served until 1965. In 1969 two representatives were elected to the Knesset. In 1971 Yisrael Yeshayahu, a Yemenite, became Secretary-General of the Israel Labor Party, and was later elected Speaker of the Knesset. In 1972 the *World Federation of Sephardi Communities, which had been denied recognition since 1925, was officially recognized as the representative body of Orientals and Sephardim, and was granted representation in the World Zionist Organization; and a department for Sephardi communities was established in the Jewish Agency. The Knesset representation of *Edot Mizraḥ* also started to rise, reaching 24 percent in the 11th Knesset, a substantial gain, although their proportion in the population is well over 50 percent.

The Oriental Jews did, however, penetrate the *Histadrut* power structure and the local authorities much more rapidly than the national power structure, with representation in the Zionist establishment top echelons remaining especially low. In 1983 Israel *Kessar (a Yemenite) was elected Secretary-General of the *Histadrut*. In the same year Moshe Levy (an Iraqi) was chosen as Israel's 12th Chief of Staff.

It was only in Begin's first government (1977) that an authentic *Edot Mizraḥ* leader David Levy (a Moroccan) was finally appointed to a senior ministerial post. The *Likud* victory in that year unleashed a wave of anti-Labor invective among the Oriental Jews which reached an unprecedented level of violence during the 1981 election campaign. A cultural struggle also ensued. The media were accused of denying a hearing to popular Oriental music, which was referred to derogatorily as "central bus station cassette music." A comment by Libyan-born Labor MK Ra'anan Na'im in 1981 to the effect that he could not stand *gefilte fisch* (an eastern and central European Jewish dish) became the culinary expression of the new *Kulturkampf*. Outward manifestations of "ethnicity" are now highly acceptable in Israel, and "affirmative action" is a norm — particularly in education — in the public sector.

It is impossible to predict what political direction these developments will take in the future. Although the *Likud* encourages the feeling among the *Edot Mizraḥ* that at last they are getting a "fair deal," in fact the economic, social and educational gaps between *Edot Mizraḥ* and Ashkenazis remain. In the undercurrent of the power struggle within the *Ḥerut* Movement anti-Ashkenazi rhetoric has appeared. *Tami*, as a party which concentrates on the ethnic issue, will, apparently, cease to exist after the 11th Knesset. The future of *Shass* is not clear. A new protest movement, *Tnu'at Ha'ohalim* (the Tents Movement), emerged in the early 1980s, *inter alia*, protesting against the pouring of resources into new settlements in the *occupied territories rather than into solving the housing problems of the poorer sections of the population within the *Green Line.

The movement ran in the elections to the 11th Knesset but did not pass the qualifying threshold.

The Israel Labor Party has been making efforts to regain some of the Oriental vote by opening its ranks to new forces, but the party must overcome existing major psychological barriers.

Egypt and Israel Egypt first became actively involved in the Palestine question in 1939 when it was invited to participate in the February/March London Round Table Conference on the future of Palestine at which the British held separate sessions with the Jews and Arabs who refused to sit formally around the same table with the Jews. However, informal direct meetings did take place between the two sides. Egypt's involvement both in the Palestine issue and regional Arab affairs increased when it became the major and decisive force within the Arab League which had been established in 1945. It was this growing involvement which pulled Egypt into the war with Israel in 1948 (See: *War of Independence),contrary to an explicit Egyptian decision not to engage regular forces in the fighting, and against the specific advice of its army commanders.

The Egyptian forces which fought against Israel in the south were finally defeated, but remained in control of what came to be known as the *Gaza Strip area which had been intended to form part of the Arab state in Palestine. The debacle of the Egyptian army in the 1948/49 war increased the political instability in that country and was a major factor in the fall of the regime of King Farouk and the assumption of power by the "Free Officers" junta led by General Mohammad Naguib and Colonel Gamal Abdel Nasser after a coup d'état on July 23, 1952.

In mid-April 1954, Nasser assumed full control in Egypt, putting the more moderate Naguib under house arrest. The new regime was highly radical, and from the very beginning made it clear that the 1948/49 war was not over, and that a second round with "the state of the Zionist gangs" was imminent.

In the years 1953–55 the activities against Israeli targets of armed Palestinian **feda'iyin* from the Gaza Strip increased. These Palestinian irregular forces were armed and trained by Egypt. In February 1955 Israel retaliated with a massive attack against an Egyptian army base in Gaza, killing 38 Egyptian soldiers. Nasser viewed this attack as a harsh blow to his army's prestige, and it was one of the factors leading to the start of a major rearmament effort. Failing to find arms in the West he signed a large arms deal with Czechoslovakia in October 1955 — a deal which had the full blessing of the *Soviet Union and marked the beginning of Soviet penetration into the Middle East. The Czech arms deal caused great concern in Israel, and the idea gained ground that Israel should strike against Egypt before it became too strong. This inclination intensified as a result of Egypt's closing of the straits of Tiran to Eilat-bound shipping in 1954 and the continued raids from the Gaza Strip. Nevertheless, in the first four months of 1956 an American mediator, Robert Anderson, a personal friend of President Dwight Eisenhower, made four trips between

Tel Aviv and Cairo in an attempt to bring about some agreement between the two states. According to David *Ben Gurion the mediating efforts came to an end when Nasser told Anderson that these contacts were endangering his life. The formation in October 1956 of a Unified Military Command by Egypt, *Syria and *Jordan was the development which finally convinced Israel to act in coordination with *France and *Great Britain who wished to protect their own interests after Nasser's nationalization of the *Suez Canal in July 1956. Despite Israel's forced withdrawal because of American and Soviet pressure from the *Sinai Peninsula and *Gaza Strip following the *Sinai Campaign, the campaign succeeded in creating new circumstances. Firstly, a United Nations Emergency Force (UNEF) was stationed along the Egyptian side of the 1949 Egyptian-Israeli Armistice lines. UNEF's task was to patrol the border and to prevent — by its presence rather than by direct action — clashes, particularly those caused by the penetration of the *feda'iyin* into Israeli territory. A UNEF detachment was also stationed at Sharm-e-Sheikh on the Straits of Tiran to ensure the free passage of Israel-bound ships. Secondly, Nasser realized that the physical annihilation of Israel would require prolonged and careful preparation, and that it was not simply the ineptitude of the Farouk regime which had caused the 1949 defeat.

As the leading force within the Arab League — until 1977 its headquarters were in Cairo and its Secretary-General was an Egyptian — Egypt initiated the establishment of the *Palestine Liberation Organization (PLO) in 1964. It directed the attempts in the early 1960s to divert the flow of the Jordan River in order to cut Israel off from one of its most important sources of water, and was instrumental in the establishment of the United Arab Command in 1967. It was also Egypt which led the Arab states to break their diplomatic relations with the *Federal Republic of Germany after it established diplomatic relations with Israel in 1965.

In May 1967, under the false impression that Israel was planning an attack against Syria, Nasser, to prove his leading position in the Arab world, mobilized his armed forces. Despite Israeli efforts to convince him that it had no intention of attacking Syria, Nasser requested the withdrawal of the UNEF from the Sinai Peninsula on May 16th. The following day local Egyptian commanders requested the immediate evacuation of all UNEF positions, including that at Sharm-e-Sheikh, as Egyptian forces took up positions along the border and reimposed a blockade on the Gulf of Aqaba. These acts constituted for Israel a *casus belli* (See: *Defense Policy) and after diplomatic efforts to bring about a reversal of the Egyptian moves failed, the *IDF (Israel Defense Forces) which had been in a state of full alert and preparedness for several weeks, attacked Egypt early on the morning of June 5th. Later it was argued that Nasser had had no plan to attack Israel and that he had simply been carried away by his own rhetoric and pressures stemming from the complicated and disturbed inter-Arab relations. However, there is no doubt that Israel had felt genuinely threatened and had acted accordingly.

In the course of the *Six-Day War Egypt once more lost the Gaza Strip and Sinai Peninsula, while the Suez Canal was blocked and closed for the next nine years. The crushing Israeli victory finally convinced Egypt that it could not uproot Israel from the Middle East by force, and it set for itself a short term objective — to regain the Sinai.

The closure of the Suez Canal and the presence of Israeli troops along its East Bank, caused Egypt a major loss of income, as did the loss of its oil fields at Abu-Rudeis. In addition, hundreds of thousands of Egyptian inhabitants of the towns along the canal fled into the Egyptian interior, both in the aftermath of the Six-Day War and during the *War of Attrition which followed, spreading a war consciousness throughout Egypt which had not previously existed.

The Six-Day War also resulted in greater research in Egypt regarding Israel. The study of Hebrew and Jewish culture was intensified in several Egyptian universities, while an Institute of Strategic Studies was established by the daily *Al-Ahram*, concentrating most of its efforts on the study of Israel — all this under the slogan "know your enemy."

The War of Attrition was initiated by Egypt in the middle of 1968 to try to force Israel to withdraw from the canal without becoming involved in another full-scale war. On June 23, 1969 Nasser declared: "I cannot conquer the Sinai but I can wear Israel out and break its spirit by attrition." The fighting came to an end through American mediation in August 1970, when both Israel and Egypt accepted the second *Rogers Plan and the resumption of the *Jarring Mission which had been initiated in 1968 following *Security Council Resolution 242 but had been suspended in the Spring of 1969.

Nevertheless, Nasser continued to speak of a military solution and very soon after the cease-fire agreement was signed, violated the standstill along the Suez Canal. President Nasser died the following month. An unresolved debate continues as to whether Nasser had been seeking an accommodation with Israel and peaceful coexistence, or whether he sought to gain time while preparing for another round of fighting at some future date.

Nasser's successor, Anwar Sadat extended the cease-fire several times, and showed interest in the Jarring Mission until Israel rejected an Egyptian proposal for an additional prolongation of the cease-fire in return for a limited Israeli withdrawal along the canal. When Sadat was convinced that Israel could not be persuaded to move he started to prepare for another war, with the limited objective of crossing the Suez Canal and breaking the political stalemate. This war, the *Yom Kippur War, proved to be, *ex post facto*, a necessary station on the road toward new relations between Egypt and Israel.

On October 6, 1973, Egypt succeeded, in coordination with Syria, to surprise Israel completely. The Egyptian army crossed the Suez Canal and occupied the *Bar Lev Line. Knowing full well Israel's superiority in its balance of military forces with Egypt, Sadat had no intention of regaining control of whole of the Sinai Peninsula. After recovering from the initial shock, the IDF managed to cross the canal into Egypt, occupy a wide territory on its west bank, encircle the Egyptian Third Army which had operated in the southern part of the canal, and reach Kilometer 101 on the Suez-Cairo road. At the time of the cease-fire the forces of both sides were scattered in various locations, and active US mediation was required to bring about a *Disengagement Agreement. Though the Yom Kippur War was hardly a glorious victory for the Egyptian forces, the mere fact that Egypt had managed to surprise Israel and cross the canal was viewed as a sufficient victory to give the Egyptian army back its lost honor.

Israel, on the other hand, was no longer contemptuous of Egypt as it had previously been, and a good deal of soul-searching began as to how the war happened and whether it could have been averted.

The Egyptians were determined not to let a new status quo take root, knowing that the old situation had served Israel's interests and that a new one was likely to act to Israel's benefit as well.

After the 1974 Disengagement Agreement and the 1975 *Interim Agreement Sadat concluded that a renewed effort would be needed to uproot Israel from the remainder of the Sinai and hoped that the US would exert sufficient pressure on Israel to bring this about. However, when he determined that these hopes were unlikely to be realized he opted for direct action — the visit to *Jerusalem.

The continued economic and social crisis in Egypt was the major driving force behind the new move. After preliminary discussions between Moshe *Dayan and Hassan el-Tohami in Morocco, President Sadat decided to address the *Knesset in Jerusalem, thus lowering the wall of fear and suspicion which divided the two countries. This visit led, 15 months later, to the *Egyptian-Israeli Peace Treaty signed in Washington on March 26, 1979. (It also cost Sadat his life at the hands of an assassin on October 6, 1981, eight years after the outbreak of the Yom Kippur War.)

Soon after the visit to Jerusalem it became apparent that the gap between the basic positions of both parties was large. Sadat insisted that the peace with Israel would not be a separate peace but a step toward a comprehensive peace which would include a solution to the Palestinian problem acceptable to the Palestinians themselves. Menaḥem *Begin, on the other hand, hoped that he could trade off the return of the whole of the Sinai Peninsula for a free hand in the West Bank and Gaza Strip and that some form of autonomy for the Palestinians within the territories under Israeli control would be sufficient (See: *Autonomy Plan). In addition, the support which Sadat hoped to gain from the more moderate Arab states failed to materialize, and Egypt was ousted from the Arab League whose headquarters were moved from Cairo to Tunis. All the Arab states broke off their political, economic and cultural relations with Egypt, and a "rejectionist front," led by Syria, was established in Baghdad. Despite the difficulties with Israel and the ostracization in the Arab world Sadat persisted in the peace process, with the *United States acting as a vital mediator and prodder. The *Camp David Accords of September 1978 were a face-saving framework for both Egypt and Israel, on the basis of which Sadat could claim that he had not neglected the Palestinian question, while Begin could claim that the same agreement conformed to his own point of view. Six months after the Camp David Agreements were concluded the Peace Treaty was signed, the two states exchanged ambassadors and a slow process of normalization began.

Sadat's assassination by a Moslem extremist in 1981 during a military parade celebrating the outbreak of the 1973 War, did not, at first, put a stop to the peace process, as Israel fulfilled its obligation to complete the withdrawal from the Sinai by April 1982. Nevertheless, Sadat's successor, Hosni Mubarak, did not have the same vision as his predecessor and following the outbreak of the *Lebanese War in June 1982 and the *Sabra and Shatilla massacre, the Egyptian Ambassador was recalled from Tel Aviv. The normalization process virtually ceased, and while Israeli tourists continued to travel to Egypt, very few Egyptians visited Israel. The Egyptian press resumed its attacks on Israel and the dispute over *Tab'a (600 sq. meters near Eilat) became Egypt's major formal excuse for not resuming diplomatic relations with Israel, even after Israel completed its withdrawal from Lebanon in 1985. Egypt also demanded progress in the resolution of the Palestinian problem. When Israel finally agreed to go to arbitration over Tab'a, and a compromise was signed regarding its terms, a meeting between the Prime Minister Shimon *Peres and President Mubarak took place in September 1986. This summit meeting which was held six years after the previous Egyptian-Israeli summit, resulted in the return of an Egyptian Ambassador to Israel and new hope for the resumption of the process of normalization in the relations between the two states.

Though indirect relations and cooperation in the West Bank have developed between Israel and Jordan, and cordial, though not formal diplomatic relations, have been established with *Morocco, Egypt, the largest Arab state, remain the only one of the 23 Arabs states to maintain diplomatic relations with Israel. (V.N.)

Egyptian-Israeli Peace Treaty The first peace treaty to be signed between an Arab state and Israel. The process which led to the signing of the treaty started with the signing of the *Disengagement Agreement of 1974, the *Interim Agreement of 1975 and the *Camp David Accords of September 1978.

The treaty was signed in Washington D.C. on March 26, 1979, by Israel's Prime Minister Menaḥem *Begin, Egyptian President Anwar Sadat and American President Jimmy Carter, following a visit by Carter to the Middle East earlier in the month to overcome last-minute difficulties, especially in Israel where Begin was under pressure from his own party not to sign a treaty by which Israel would undertake to withdraw from the whole of the *Sinai Peninsula.

The treaty brought about an immediate termination of the state of war between the parties, provided for a gradual withdrawal of Israel from the remainder of the Sinai (the withdrawal ended in April 1982), and for the establishment of "normal and friendly relations" between the two states, including full recognition, diplomatic, economic and cultural relations, termination of boycotts (See: *Arab Boycott) and discriminatory barriers to the free movement of people and goods, and a guarantee for the full mutual enjoyment by each other's citizens of the due process of law. Egypt and Israel undertook to recognize and respect each other's right to live in peace within secure and recognized boundaries, and to "refrain from the threat or use of force, directly or indirectly, against each other" and to "settle disputes between them by peaceful means," and those arising out of the treaty itself by means of negotiations. "Any such disputes which cannot be settled by negotiations shall be resolved by conciliation or submitting to arbitration," as in the *Tab'a dispute. The treaty also provided for limited free zones on both sides of the international boundary, and the presence of UN forces and observers, and for unimpeded passage of Israeli ships through the *Suez Canal and the Straits of Tiran. The process of normalization of relations did not proceed as anticipated by the treaty, and though ambassadors were exchanged between the two countries the Egyptian Ambassador was recalled as a result of the *Lebanese War and was returned only in September 1986. The Tab'a dispute, another cause of tension between the two countries, was finally sent to arbitration at the end of 1986. However it was the assassination of Anwar Sadat on October 6, 1981 and domestic difficulties in Egypt which were the main cause of the "cold peace". Nevertheless, Egypt has shown no inclination to retreat from the treaty.

Ehrlich, Simḥa (1915–1983). Parliamentarian, Minister of Finance, leader of the *Liberal Party of Israel.

Born in Poland, Ehrlich studied at the Hebrew Gymnasium in Lublin and was active in the *General Zionist youth in Poland. He immigrated to Palestine in 1938, worked as a farm laborer in Nes-Zionah, studied a trade and entered the optical business, opening his own firm to produce tinted lenses in 1961. Ehrlich became involved in General Zionist politics on the municipal level, entering the municipal council of Tel Aviv in 1955 and becoming Deputy Mayor from 1962–65. In 1965 Ehrlich was elected for a third term to the Tel Aviv municipal council as Head of the newly-formed **Gaḥal* list. In 1969 Ehrlich left the Tel Aviv municipal council and was elected to the 7th Knesset, playing an active role in the Finance and Interior Committees. He was elected Chairman of the Liberal Party of Israel in 1976, and following the 1977 political *upheaval was appointed Minister of Finance. As Minister of Finance Ehrlich created the economic upheaval involving the cancellation of foreign exchange control, travel tax and service import tax. During his term as Minister of Finance there was a serious deterioration in the balance of payments, a massive increase in the import of consumer goods and a rapid rise in the rate of inflation. Due to public pressure Ehrlich resigned from his post as Minister of Finance, but continued to serve in the government as second Deputy Prime Minister. In this capacity he was in charge of the development of the Galilee, the Arab sector and the reabsorption of *yordim* (emigrants returning to Israel). In the second *Likud* Government (1981) Ehrlich served as Deputy Prime Minister and Minister of Agriculture. When Yitzḥak *Moda'i was appointed Chairman of the Liberal Party Presidium Ehrlich remained final arbiter in the party. (Y.A.)

Eichmann Trial Trial held in the Jerusalem District Court from April to December 1961, against Nazi war criminal, Adolf Otto Eichmann (1906–1962). Eichmann had been the SS Chief of Operations in the implementation of the Nazi scheme to exterminate the whole of European Jewry. When the *Einsatzgruppen* (Nazi murder units) began their slaughter of Soviet Jewry, Eichmann organized the deportation of Jews from Central Europe to the extermination centers in the East. At the beginning of 1942, after the Wansee Conference, which he prepared and organized, Eichmann was given extensive powers to direct the deportations of European Jews to the death camps. Eichmann was abducted by the **Mossad* from *Argentina where he had lived as Ricardo Klement. Argentina loged a complaint with the *United Nations Security Council which condemned the abduction, though it took cognizance of the need to bring Eichmann to trial.

Eichmann was charged with "crimes against the Jewish people... crimes against humanity... war crimes and membership in an 'enemy organization'," an offence under the Nazi and Nazi Collaborators (Punishment) Law of 1950.

The Chief Prosecutor was Attorney General Gideon *Hausner. The court heard over 100 witnesses, and studied more than 1,600 documents. Eichmann, who argued that he had only followed orders, had said in an interview in 1957, that "had we killed all of them... I would have been happy."

Eichmann was found guilty and sentenced to death - the first and only death sentence to be passed in Israel. He appealed to the Supreme Court which dismissed his appeal in May 1962.

The trial was viewed in Israel as extremely important not only in terms of bringing a major Nazi criminal to justice, but for its educational value, for in the course of the trial the whole story of the *Holocaust, was retold.

Israel had also hoped to find and bring to trial Dr. Joseph Mengele, infamous for his medical "experiments" performed on Jews, primarily on twins, at Auschwitz. However, Mengele was never caught and apparently died in the 1970s in Brazil.

Eitan (formerly Kaminsky), **Rafael** Military commander and politician. Born in 1929, Moshav Tel Adashim.

Eitan, popularly known as Raful, took courses

in Middle East studies at the University of Tel Aviv and graduated from the *IDF National Security College. He joined the *Palmaḥ in 1946 and in the *War of Independence was in the Harel Brigade which played an important role during the battles to open the road to Jerusalem. He also fought in the San Simon battle in Jerusalem during which he was wounded. He was Commander of a paratroop company in 1954 and participated in most of the retaliatory operations of the 1950s. Eitan was appointed commander of a paratroop battalion in 1965 and later served as Deputy Commander of a paratroop brigade and Head of the Operations Branch of the General Staff. He served as the Commander of a paratroop brigade during the *Six-Day War in which he was severely wounded. In 1969 he became Commander of the paratroopers and infantry and served in the *Yom Kippur War. In 1974 Eitan was appointed Head of the Northern Command; 1977–78 he was Head of the Operations Branch, and in 1978–83 he was Chief of Staff. He was criticized by the *Kahan Commission for his failure to try to prevent the *Sabra and Shatilla massacre, but since his term as Chief of Staff was almost over, he was not dismissed. While serving as Chief of Staff Eitan was reponsible for bringing in underprivileged marginal youth into the army — an act which was highly controversial for while it gave these youths another chance to integrate in the society, it also increased criminal activities in the IDF.

In 1983 he founded the poltical party *Tzomet* which united with **Teḥiyah* before the elections to the 11th Knesset (1984). Eitan has been a MK since 1984 and a member of the Foreign Affairs and Security Committee and the State Control Committee. At the end of 1986 there was growing tension between Eitan and Geula *Cohen in the *Teḥiyah* over the balance of control in the party.

Eldad (formerly Scheib), **Israel** Educator, publicist and underground leader. Born in 1910, East Galicia.

Eldad's family moved to Vienna in 1914 then to Lvov. He received his PhD from the University of Vienna with a dissertation on Schopenhauer, and a year later graduated from the city's Rabbinical seminary. He taught in the *Tarbut* Jewish education system in Vilna and Warsaw and contributed to the Yiddish press. He joined **Betar* and became a member of its Polish executive. In 1938 Eldad met Avraham Stern (See: **Leḥi*) at the *Betar* World Conference at which he clashed with *Jabotinsky during the debate over the proposal of Menaḥem *Begin for the armed uprising against the British in Palestine.

Fleeing the German invasion, Eldad and his wife resettled in Vilna and shared an apartment with the Begins. In 1941 they were among 2,500 Zionists allowed by the Soviet authorities to move to Turkey, from which they immigrated to Palestine. Eldad taught Bible at a Tel Aviv high school and assumed a leading role in *Leḥi* as ideologue and editor of the movement's publications. Most of *Leḥi*'s broadsides and posters were authored by him. After Stern was murdered, Eldad became one of *Leḥi*'s three leaders. Arrested by the British in 1944, he escaped two years later.

At the conference of *Leḥi* veterans in February 1949 a split occurred between the supporters of *Yellin-Mor who sought to establsh a political party with a neo-socialist platform, and those who followed Eldad's line of concentrating on education and extra-parliamentary activity. *Sulam* (ladder) became the organ of Eldad's group, espousing a maximalist Revisionist stance which defined the goals of Zionism as the establishment of *Malchut Yisrael* (The Kingdom of Israel), the eventual borders of which would extend to the Nile and the Euphrates. *Sulam*, which ceased publication in 1964, strongly attacked the **Mapai*-led governments.

Eldad was accused of inciting various acts of violence and anti-state underground activities, most notably in the 1957 murder of *Kasztner, but no proof was ever found to link him to these acts.

On orders of *Ben Gurion, acting in his capacity as Defense Minister, Eldad was banned from teaching. Even after winning a Supreme Court injunction he could not find a teaching assignment. He worked as a translator and was awarded the Tschernichovsky Prize for his Hebrew rendition of the works of Nietzsche. Eventually Eldad joined the academic staff of the Haifa Technion, and Beersheba University. The 1967 military victory brought Eldad to the forefront of the Zionist nationalist Right. He founded a student society, the National Cells, and became a columnist for *Ha'aretz* and *Yediot Aḥaronot.*

Elections to the Knesset Due to the *War of Independence Israel's first general elections were held only on January 25, 1949, eight months after the establishment of the state and before the signing of the *Armistice Agreements which formally brought the war to an end.

Both new and old parties participated in the 1949 elections (See: **Yishuv*). Some indication regarding the relative power of the pre-state parties existed based on the results of elections held in mandatory times. However, the effect of the war and other developments which had taken place since the last elections for **Assefat Hanivḥarim* were held in 1944, could not be predicted. **Mapai*, which had ruled in the *Yishuv* institutions since the beginning of the 1930s, gained 46 seats out of the 120 seats of the Constitutent Assembly, which later became the 1st Knesset. Even though *Mapai* did not gain an absolute majority its relative power was substantial for the following reasons: a) no other party even got close to its electoral achievement (**Mapam* was second with 19 seats); b) *Mapai* was a pivotal party in the center of the political spectrum — all the parties further to the right won only 48 seats while the parties to its left together won 26; c) several parties, especially the *Minority Lists connected with *Mapai* (two seats), the *Progressive Party (five seats), and to a lesser extent the *United Religious Front, which for the first and last time included all the religious parties (16 seats) and some of the *Sephardi List (four seats) preferred, or at least agreed to join a coalition led by *Mapai*.

David *Ben Gurion had made it clear before setting up his first government that the **Ḥerut* Movement and the Communist **Maki* were not potential coalition partners (See: *"Without *Ḥerut* and *Maki*"). *Mapam*, which at this time still advocated a pro-Moscow policy, did not join the coalition because of its own preference not to cooperate with parties to its right, and because Ben Gurion was not happy about its sectarian attitude (See: **Mamlachtiut*). *Ḥerut*, which had emerged from the *IZL and was viewed as the extreme nationalist Right, won 14 seats. This meant that *Ḥerut*'s relative power vis-à-vis *Mapai* and the centrist parties was much more substantial than the relative power of the IZL had been vis-à-vis the **Haganah*. Yet, until 1967 *Ḥerut* was the Opposition, and only in 1977 did it gain sufficient support from other parties to form a government.

The *General Zionists, who until the early 1930s had constituted the largest Zionist political party and had then joined *Mapai* in the leadership of the *Yishuv* as the second largest party, suffered a major defeat, obtaining only seven seats. The new Progressive Party, which appealed to the traditional voters of the General Zionists, was partly responsible for this dismal result. Two ethnic parties — the *Sephardi List (four seats), and the *Yemenite Association (one seat) were to survive only through the second Knesset, while the party which emerged from the **Leḥi*, the *Fighters List (one seat), never participated in elections again.

The 1st Knesset did not survive a full term due to persistent crises on issues of religion and state, and the prolonged economic crisis (See: *Economic Policy). New elections were held on July 30, 1951.

The electorate in the elections to the 2nd Knesset grew by almost one third due to the massive immigration of the two previous years. The major change in the results of these elections compared to the previous elections was the meteoric rise of the General Zionists (20 seats) and the fall of *Ḥerut* (eight seats). *Mapai* lost one seat, *Mapam* lost four, the Sephardim lost two, while the religious parties, which ran separately, lost one seat, as did the Progressive Party. Other parties which gained seats were *Maki* (one seat) and the Minority Lists (three seats). The makeup of the Knesset remained more or less stable through the three following elections: the 3rd Knesset, held on July 26, 1955, against the background of the removal of the General Zionists from the coalition after its members had abstained on a vote of no-confidence connected with the *Kastzner case and the return of Ben Gurion to the government as Minister of Defence after Lavon's dismissal; the 4th Knesset (November 3, 1959) at the time of the *Wadi Salib riots and the issue of arms deals with the *Federal Republic of Germany; and the 5th Knesset, held on August 15, 1961 with the reverberations of the *Lavon Affair. In all three *Mapai* held its strength at 40–47 seats. Its future partners in the *Alignment: *Mapam* and **Aḥdut Ha'avodah — Po'alei Zion* (which broke away from *Mapam* just before the elections to the 3rd Knesset) together held

16–19 seats. The religious parties received 17–18 seats. The three center-to-right parties (*Ḥerut*, General Zionists and the Progressives) which had together received 26 seats in the 1st Knesset and went up to 32 in the 2nd, kept their strength to 31–34 seats (the General Zionists and Progressives united into the *Liberal Party in 1961). The Minority Lists had together four-five seats, while the Communists fluctuated between three and six seats.

Thus, one may observe a noteworthy stability in the relative strength of the various political blocs, even though changes took place in the power of the individual parties within each bloc. For example, in the 1951 elections the strength of the General Zionists trebled and that of *Ḥerut* declined dramatically. However, in subsequent elections *Ḥerut* reemerged as the largest right-wing party while the General Zionists declined.

This stability, which is a rare phenomenon in a multi-party political system with proportional representation, is especially marked if we recall that during this period mass immigration continued, and between 1949 and 1961 the electorate trebled.

Many theories regarding the nature of the Israeli voter and Israeli politics were developed to explain it. One argument was that the parties' control over financial resources and their allocation according to the *party key enabled them to maintain their relative strength despite the rapid growth of the electorate. Another theory, which is not substantiated by aggregate figures, claimed that votes floated among parties belonging to the same political camp rather than between them.

In the elections to the 6th Knesset, on November 2, 1965, *Ḥerut* and the *Liberal Party ran in a single bloc — **Gaḥal* — initiated by Menaḥem *Begin who sought legitimization for his party in return for a generous allocation of seats to the Liberals. *Gaḥal*, which did not do as well as expected (26 seats) nevertheless turned into the second largest list in the Knesset. The first *Alignment, made up of *Mapai* and *Aḥdut Ha'avodah*, under the leadership of Levi *Eshkol, gained 45 seats despite the fact that *Mapai*'s erstwhile leader, Ben Gurion, had broken away over the Lavon Affair and together with some of *Mapai*'s younger leaders (including Moshe *Dayan and Shimon *Peres) set up **Rafi*, which gained ten seats. From the point of view of the Israeli voter this was a test case for the influence of personalities in the determination of voting patterns. Undoubtedly, many voters remained loyal to Ben Gurion — but the majority of *Mapai* supporters continued to support the party despite the departure of its leader of over 30 years.

Mapam appeared independently for the last time in these elections, obtaining eight seats. The minority lists received four seats, while the Communists split into two parties — *Maki* and **Rakaḥ* — which together received four. The religious camp maintained its strength with 17 seats. For the first time since the elections to the 2nd Knesset a new party entered the Knesset — Uri *Avneri's **Ha-olam Hazeh — Ko'aḥ Ḥadash*, which gained a single seat.

By the elections to the 7th Knesset, which took place on October 28, 1969, the Israeli political system had undergone an extreme transformation, the effects of which are still evident today. On the eve of the *Six-Day War *Gaḥal* joined the government and Menaḥem Begin from *Ḥerut* and Yosef Sapir from the Liberals became Ministers (without Portfolio) — marking the first time in Israel's history that *Ḥerut* and Begin were included in the government, while Moshe Dayan returned to the government as Minister of Defense on behalf of *Rafi*. The military victory drastically changed the political debate in Israel: the future of the territories captured in the war form a major part of the platforms of most of the political parties, whereas until 1967 only *Ḥerut* spoke of the extension of Israel's borders.

Towards the end of 1968 *Mapai, Aḥdut Ha'avodah* and most of *Rafi* (without Ben Gurion) formed the *Israel Labor Party and set up the new Alignment with *Mapam* before the 1969 elections.

The new Alignment, under the leadership of Golda *Meir, won 56 seats in the elections to the 7th Knesset. Ben Gurion's new party, the *State List, received only four seats. The parties to the left of the Alignment obtained six seats, the religious parties 18 seats, and *Gaḥal* 26 seats. The *Independent Liberals, who had broken away from the Liberals in 1965 when *Gaḥal* was formed, obtained four seats while the *Free Center, which broke away from *Gaḥal* received two. This was the zenith of the Alignment's power. In subsequent elections the Alignment progressively lost seats and the right-wing bloc increased its power. In the aftermath of the 1969 elections a new *National Unity Government was formed, this time with much wider representation for the *Gaḥal* members who were given six cabinet seats. However, *Gaḥal* withdrew in protest when the government accepted the second *Rogers Plan in 1970.

From the end of the *War of Attrition in August 1970 until the *Yom Kippur War in October 1973, the atmosphere in Israel was one of confidence and security. Elections to the 8th Knesset were to have taken place in the month of the outbreak of the Yom Kippur War and were postponed for two months, during which the foundations of the whole Israeli political system were shaken. The results of the elections, which took place on December 31, 1973, did not fully reflect the public's reaction to the **Meḥdal* (fiasco), and its protest. *Ḥerut* appeared in the 1973 elections at the head of a much wider camp than in the past. *Gaḥal* was broadened and the **Likud* was established, largely through the manipulations of Ariel *Sharon who had joined the Liberal Party, and included factors which had broken away from the Labor movement. In addition to *Ḥerut* and the Liberals the *Likud* included the Free Center, the State List and the Labor Movement for Greater Israel (See: *Land of Israel Movement). The focus of public criticism was Minister of Defense Moshe Dayan, hero of the *Sinai Campaign and the Six-Day War who was now held responsible for the *Meḥdal*. Though the Alignment barely managed to retain power after losing five seats, the *Likud* achieved impressive results, topping *Gaḥal*'s mandates by 13.

Since the Knesset had decided not to reopen the list of candidates for the elections after the Yom Kippur War, no protest lists emerged at this stage, though Shulamit *Aloni's *Civil Rights Movement, an anti-clerical dovish party which had been formed largely because Aloni was dissatisfied with the place alotted her in the Alignment list of candidates, enjoyed the support of Labor voters who wished to protest against the government's *Meḥdal*. Surprisingly, the CRM gained three seats, while the Independent Liberals managed to hold on to their four. Together with the Minority Lists the Alignment could build a camp of 61 Knesset seats and was clearly the preferred party for the leadership of the new government. But this meager majority was strengthened by the addition of five MKs further to the left who preferred an Alignment-led government to one led by the *Likud*. The Alignment was once again able to form a government, which was joined by the *National Religious Party (NRP) with its ten seats. The *Likud*, despite its impressive electoral achievement, was disappointed.

The religious parties together lost two seats, and were now down to 15. The NRP, the traditional partner of the Labor camp in government coalitions, had, as of the 1969 elections, adopted a very hawkish platform on foreign affairs and security issues, comparable to those of *Gaḥal* and later of the *Likud*. **Agudat Yisrael* whose position regarding the territories occupied in 1967 was dovish had vowed, upon withdrawing from the coalition in 1952, that it would not join any government until the arrangements regarding the enlistment of women into the army were changed.

In trying to form a new coalition the Alignment was thus caught between potential partners who were either doves or hawks and either religious or anticlerical. The situation was further complicated by the appointment of the *Agranat Commission to investigate the background and first stages of the Yom Kippur War. Eventually a government was set up by Golda Meir with the Independent Liberals and the NRP, but upon the publication of the interim report of the Agranat Commission it resigned, having served for less than three months. Thus the rule of the *Mapai* old-timers came to an end, and the Alignment sought a new leader. The new leader could be identified neither with *Aḥdut Ha'avodah* nor with *Rafi*, and could not be connected to the *Meḥdal*. When *Mapai*'s "strongman" Pinḥas *Sapir refused to replace Meir, a new political figure, a former Chief of Staff and Ambassador to the US, Yitzḥak *Rabin, who had occupied the 21st place on the Alignment List in the 1973 elections, was selected. At first Rabin set up a government with the CRM and without the NRP. Later on the NRP joined and the CRM withdrew. Shimon Peres was appointed Minister of Defense and Yigal *Allon Minister for Foreign Affairs. Moshe Dayan and Abba *Eban were left out of the government, thus completing the mini-upheaval within the Alignment.

The Rabin Government ended its days in a state of crisis. An official ceremony celebrating the arrival of F-15 planes from the US was held in an air force base on a Friday afternoon. *Po'alei Agudat Yisrael*, alleging a desecration of the Sabbath, brought before the Knesset a motion of no confidence in the government. Several NRP ministers failed to support the government and were dismissed.

Rabin resigned and the government became a transition government until new elections could be held, thus preventing the resignation of the ministers from the Independent Liberal Party (in accordance with Article 25(c) of the Basic Law: the Government). To complicate matters further, not long before the new elections were to be held on May 17, 1977, it was discovered that Rabin's wife owned an illegal bank account in the US and Rabin, accepting full responsibility, ceased to function as Prime Minister, being replaced by Shimon Peres. The *Yadlin Affair and Ofer Affair, as well as the unproved suspicion that Abba Eban too held money in foreign banks in contravention of the law, were additional blows to the Alignment. Against this background a new centrist party, the *Democratic Movement for Change (DMC) emerged, made up of figures from academia (Yiga'el *Yadin and Amnon *Rubinstein) and "defectors" from the Alignment (Meir *Amit) and the *Likud* (Shmuel *Tamir).

The *Likud*'s election campaign was run by Ezer *Weizman, a relatively new member of *Ḥerut* who was viewed by many as a potential heir to Menaḥem Begin. The gradual legitimization of *Ḥerut* in the eyes of the Israeli public, which began with the establishment of *Gaḥal*, and the gradual delegitimization of the Labor camp which started with the Lavon Affair and intensified with the Yom Kippur War *Meḥdal*, the various scandals mentioned above and the natural process of corruption which accompanies retention of power for too long by any one political movement, as well as the emergence of the DMC, led to the 1977 *upheaval. The DMC emerged from the 1977 elections with 15 Knesset seats but this success nevertheless failed to be translated into a political victory due to the fact that the *Likud*, up from 39 seats to 43 seats (largely due to massive support from the **Edot Mizraḥ*) was able to form a government without the DMC, supported by 62 MKs. The new government consisted of: the *Likud*'s 43, *Shlomzion*'s two, the NRP's 12, *Agudat Yisrael*'s four, and Moshe Dayan who joined Begin's government as an independent and became Minister for Foreign Affairs.

The religious parties managed to increase their combined strength to 17, and on the extreme Left **Maḥaneh Sheli*, a new party, gained two seats. The Communists, now called **Ḥadash*, increased their power from four to five. The Minority Lists, the Independent Liberals and the CRM which had together held ten seats in the 8th Knesset now had only one seat each.

Begin's first government went through several transformations. It was originally set up on June 20, 1977. The DMC joined on October 24. In September 1978, while the Camp David negotiations were in progress, the members of **Shinui* and several other members of the DMC left the coalition. Several other groups and individuals broke away later from what was left of the DMC. While the government's main achievement was the signing of the *Camp David Accords in September 1978 and the peace treaty with Egypt in March 1979, it also scored some failures.

The government's *economic policy seemed to falter as one Minister of Finance replaced the next (See: *Ministers of Finance); the normalization with Egypt did not materialize since the autonomy talks did not progress; a succession of ministers resigned from the government: Minister of Transport and Communication Amit on September 15, 1978; Minister for Foreign Affairs Moshe Dayan on October 23, 1979; Minister of Defense Ezer Weizman in May 1980; Minister of Justice Shmuel Tamir on August 13, 1980; Minister of Finance Yigael *Hurwitz on January 21, 1981; and Minister of Religions Aharon *Abuḥatzeira, who was accused of various acts of corruption.

As a result of this situation elections to the 10th Knesset were moved forward from November to June 30, 1981. The *Likud*'s situation seemed hopeless as opinion polls at the end of 1980 and the beginning of 1981 showed the Alignment to be way ahead. However, the picture had changed by polling day. The reduction of taxes on imported consumer goods by the new Minister of Finance Yoram *Aridor — who argued that in this way the rate of inflation would be brought down — led to an immediate rise in the standard of living of the individual, which reassured many voters. Menaḥem Begin, whose health had deteriorated and who appeared to be losing his grip, seemed to have returned to himself. Several security-related events, among them the destruction by the Israel Air Force of Iraq's nuclear plant *Osiraq, in June, boosted the *Likud*'s popularity in certain circles. After the *Likud* had made extensive propaganda use of the animosity between Shimon Peres and Yitzḥak Rabin the Alignment tried at the last moment to improve its prospects by announcing that Rabin was Peres's candidate for Minister of Defense although his name had not appeared on the original list of senior ministerial candidates. The election campaign was the most violent (both verbally and physically) that Israel had ever known. The *Likud* unexpectedly emerged the winner with 48 seats to the Alignment's 47, though Shulamit Aloni subsequently joining the Alignment to balance the two blocs. The unusual outcome of the elections was that the two major blocs together had 96 out of the Knesset's 120 seats, seemingly indicating a movement toward a two-party system.

On the whole the small parties suffered defeat. Three of the small parties which had been represented in all the previous Knessets — the Independent Liberals, **Po'alei Agudat Yisrael* and the Minority Lists — did not manage to pass the one percent qualifying threshold. The NRP suffered the greatest blow — going down to six seats from the 10–12 it had received in each of the previous elections. Many of the NRP's traditional voters moved to two new lists: **Teḥiyah* and **Tami*, which received three seats each. *Agudat Yisrael* kept its four seats.

It was thanks to these four parties that Begin was able to form his second government. The only parties which would have rather had a government headed by the Alignment were **Ḥadash* with its four seats, *Shinui* (the only remaining splinter of the DMC) with two seats and the CRM with one, which joined the Alignment. Moshe Dayan's new party, **Telem* obtained only two seats and was in no position to play a pivotal role between the two blocs, as it had hoped to do.

The two main issues in the election campaign to the 11th Knesset in 1984 were the same two issues which occupied the government and public opinion throughout the 10th Knesset: the economic situation and the *Lebanese War. Aridor's policy merely aggravated the economic situation, and the premature leaking to the press of his dollarization plan led him to resign toward the end of 1983, with another *Ḥerut* member, Yigal Cohen-Orgad replacing him at the Ministry of Finance. The new elections were held before Cohen-Orgad could bring about any real change in the economy.

In the beginning of June 1982 the *IDF invaded Lebanon according to a plan long considered by Ariel Sharon, now Minister of Defense. The official reason for the war was the attempted assassination of Israel's Ambassador to London, Shlomo Argov, and its official goal was to bring peace to the Galilee. The war was also intended to liquidate the *Palestine Liberation Organization (PLO), introduce a new government in Lebanon willing to sign a peace treaty with Israel, and to get the Syrians out of Lebanon.

This war, more than any other event, sharpened the cleavages in Israeli society and its body politic. The differences of opinion concerned the need for the war, its aims and methods. Sharon's plans were seriously disrupted by the assassination of Lebanon's President-elect Bashir Jemayel, followed by the massacre at *Sabra and Shatilla which resulted in the appointment of the *Kahan Commission to investigate the responsibility for the massacre. The commission's report resulted in the removal of Sharon from the Ministry of Defense and the appointment of Moshe *Arens in his place. The IDF remained in Lebanon, increasingly acting as a policeman between feuding Lebanese camps, and its casualities eventually rose to over 600. Undoubtedly, the deteriorating situation in Lebanon was one of the factors which contributed to Begin's resignation in October 1983, though some claimed that his deteriorating health and depression were the primary reasons for his resignation.

Early elections were called for July 23, 1984, as a result of a move by *Tami* leader Abuḥatzeira (who had completed a three month prison sentence) to change labor and welfare laws. As in 1981, so in 1984 public opinion polls showed the Alignment with a large lead over the *Likud*, and as before the outcome of the elections was different from the polls. It was argued once again that the opinion polls themselves influenced voting patterns. Many *Likud* voters who had considered voting for parties other than the *Likud*, changed their minds after learning of the low ratings which the *Likud* received in the polls. Many voters decided to opt for the smaller parties. The Alignment, hoping to avoid the harmful effects of the polarization of the previous elections, carried out a non-controversial campaign, and lost three seats. The *Likud* lost seven seats, but did much better than predicted. The remainder of the Knesset's 45 seats were divided among smaller old and new parties. The extreme Right was greatly strengthened: *Teḥiyah* increased its strength to five seats and Rabbi Meir *Kahane, who had failed to pass the qualifying threshold in previous elections, won a seat. On the extreme Left, *Ḥadash* kept its strength to four seats, and the new Arab-Jewish party the *Progressive List for Peace gained two seats. The two parties viewed as the Alignment's satellites — the CRM and *Shinui* — won three seats each. Ezer Weizman, who had left the political arena in 1980, tried to achieve what Moshe Dayan had not been able to do, but his new list, **Yaḥad* won three seats only, while Yigael Hurwitz's list **Ometz* received only one. *Tami* also went down to a single seat, while the remaining 12 seats were divided among the four religious parties: NRP — four, *Agudat Yisrael* — two, **Shass* — four and **Morasha* — two. This distribution of seats, which totally dispelled the theory that the Israeli political system was moving toward a two-party system, resulted in a stalemate, with neither of the two major political blocs able to form a government without the other. This led to the establishment of a National Unity Government, after *Mapam* and MK Yossi *Sarid left the Alignment and *Yaḥad* joined it. Among the new government's main goals were pulling the IDF out of Lebanon and curing the economy. (See also: *Government of Israel; *Knesset; *Electoral System.) (A.D.)

electoral reform Since the first elections to the Constituent Assembly (1st Knesset) in January 1949 many changes have been introduced into the Electoral Law. These changes have dealt with the administration of elections, restrictions on election propaganda, the financial support which the state grants the contesting lists, etc. But no substantial change has been introduced in the manner in which candidates are elected by the voters or the allocation of seats to competing lists. The only change relating to these issues was the reintroduction in 1969 of the Hagenbach-Bischoff (de'Hondt) method — known in Israel as the Bader-Ofer Law — regarding the distribution of surplus votes according to the largest average cost method (See: *Electoral System).

In theory the electoral system could be substantially changed without the absolute majority required to change Article 4 of the Basic Law: the Knesset (See: *Basic Laws), but this fact is not generally understood by the politicians. Various personalities and many parties have brought proposals over the years for every conceivable type of electoral reform. All the proposals were designed to reduce artificially the number of parties in Israel, and/or to increase the voters' ability to select individual candidates. Among the proposals raised have been the institution of single-member constituencies as is customary in Britain (the first one to propose this was David *Ben Gurion, and among later ones was Yiga'el *Hurwitz); a drastic raising of the qualifying threshold (proposed, among others, by the *General Zionists); the institution of multi-member constituencies (proposed by Attorney David Bar Rav Ḥai); the introduction of multi-member constituencies with pools of votes in order to preserve a semblance to the national proportional representation of the parties (proposed by MK Bo'az Mo'av from the *Civil Rights Movement); the introduction of the single transferable vote as is customary in Ireland (proposed by various members of the *Democratic Movement for Change); and the introduction of preferential voting of other types.

The best-known reform proposal would introduce the additional member system, or as it is frequently referred to — the mixed system. According to this proposal most of the representatives (about 90 out of the 120) would be elected in multi-member constituencies (one of the proposals calls for 18 five-member regions) and the rest in national lists. According to most of those who support these proposals the national representatives will be so elected as to compensate the small lists for the disproportionality of the regional elections, as is customary in several West European countries, such as the *Federal Republic of Germany. Such a proposal was adopted by the Knesset plenary in preliminary readings in 1972 and 1974, but was not enacted. In both cases 61 MKs supported the proposal. One of the prominent initiators of these proposals was Minister of Economics and Planning Gad *Ya'acobi, who continues to lobby strenuously for their adoption.

In August 1986 an amendment to the Basic Law: the Knesset, tabled as a private member's bill by MK Mordechai Virshubski of **Shinui* with the signatures of 42 MKs from most factions of the Knesset, was passed in preliminary reading. The bill calls for a mixed constituency/proportional representation system according to which 80 of the Knesset's 120 members will be elected in 20 constituencies, each of which will elect four MKs on a proportional representation basis. The other 40 Knesset members will be elected proportionally on a national level. The bill was sent to the Knesset Constitution, Law and Justice Committee for further deliberation.

In the *Coalition Agreement which led to the establishment of the *National Unity Government in 1984 it was stated that there will be no change in the electoral system without prior agreement between the *Alignment and the **Likud*. It was also decided to set up a committee in which both blocs would be equally represented to deal with the issue. Such a committee was set up with Gad Ya'acobi as chairman. Though the committee reached an agreement to raise the qualifying threshold, the proposed change was approved by the institutions of the Alignment but not of the *Likud*. On all other questions the committee was unable to make any progress, primarily because of the *Likud*'s commitments to the religious parties, which oppose change.

(A.D.)

electoral system Like most western parliamentary democracies Israel elects its parliament, the *Knesset by a system of proportional representation. However, unlike most other systems, the principle of proportionality is strictly adhered to in Israel (as in the Netherlands) and the Israeli voter is unable to influence directly the election of individual candidates. One of the reasons for the adoption of a rigid proportional list system is to be found in the traditions which crystallized in the **Yishuv* during mandatory times. At that time resources were proportionally distributed by the parties which held absolute control in preparing the lists of candidates (See: *party key).

When the State of Israel was established many features of the British legal and administrative system were adopted. However, the British electoral system was not adopted, due to the vested interests of the existing parties in the old system and the obvious disadvantages of the plurality (first-past-the post) system whereby the candidate with the most votes in a constituency gets elected even if he or she does not have the support of the majority. The electoral system in Israel is based primarily on two laws: The Basic Law: the Knesset and the Knesset Elections Law, combined version of 1969. Among the other laws which deal with related subjects the most important is the Financing of Parties Law of 1973.

The general framework for the elections was set down in Article 4 of the Basic Law: the Knesset: "The Knesset shall be elected by general, national, direct, equal, secret and proportional elections, in accordance with the Knesset Elections Law. The section shall not be amended save by a majority of the Members of the Knesset." This article is one of the few in Israeli legislation which requires such a majority. The principle of generality ensures the active right of every Israeli citizen who is at least 18 years old to vote, and the right to be elected of any Israeli citizen who is at least 21 years old. Even though the Basic Law: the Knesset gave the legislator the authority to disqualfy anyone from voting, the Knesset has never made use of this authority. The holders of certain official positions may not stand for election, such as the President of the State, the State Comptroller, religious and civil judges, officers in the *IDF and senior civil servants.

The principle of national elections holds that the whole of Israel is a single voting constituency insofar as the distribution of mandates is concerned. Thus, contrary to what is customary in most parliamentary democracies, election candidates do not represent geographical constituencies, and the final calculation of the distribution of Knesset seats is done exclusively on a national basis.

Direct elections mean that the voter elects the Knesset directly — not through some body of electors.

Equal elections mean equality among the votes cast. A Supreme Court decision broadened the equality principle to include equality of opportunity among all the contesting lists.

The principle of secrecy ensures the integrity of the elections. The elections law lists the punishments for the violation of secrecy. *Flatto-Sharon elected to the 9th Knesset (1977) was convicted of a related offense (bribing voters) and imprisoned.

The principle of proportionality is expressed in the fact that each list of candidates is represented in the Knesset by the number of members which is proportional to its electoral strength. In other words, the percentage of seats which a list receives of the total number of Knesset seats (120) is very similar to the percentage of the valid votes which the list received of the total votes cast. Elections to the Knesset take place very four years unless the Knesset has decided on its own early dissolution or the deferment of elections by means of a special law. Early dissolutions took place in 1951, 1961, 1981 and 1984. Due to the *Yom Kippur War the 1973 elections were delayed by almost two months. The contest in the elections is among lists of candidates. In other words, the voter supports a list with a recognizable symbol but cannot express his preference for any particular individual candidate. Any faction in the outgoing Knesset, or group of no less than 750 eligible voters, may present a list of candidates. Occasionally several factions in the outgoing Knesset present a common list of candidates for the elections to the next Knesset. Thus **Agudat Yisrael* and **Po'alei Agudat Yisrael* appeared together as the *Religious Torah Front in the elections to the 3rd Knessest (1955) and *Mapai* and *Aḥdut Ha'avodah — Po'alei Zion* appeared together in the first *Alignment in the elections to the 6th Knesset (1965).

A recent amendment to the Basic Law: the Knesset prohibits lists which act, directly or indirectly, against the existence of the State of Israel as the state of the Jewish people, against the democratic character of the state, or which incite to racism.

A list of candidates which has obtained less than one percent of the valid votes cast does not participate in the distribution of seats. The lists which have passed this qualifying threshold will receive a number of seats which is proportional to the electoral strength of each. This is done by dividing the total number of votes cast for all lists which have crossed the one percent threshold by 120; the result is the number of votes a list must win in order to qualify for a single seat. Surplus votes for a party which are insufficient for an additional seat were distributed, until 1969, according to the Hare method, to the list with the largest number of surplus votes. In 1949 and again since 1973 the Hagenbach-Bischoff (de Hondt) method, known in Israel as the Bader-Ofer method has been used as is customary in most parliamentary democracies. According to this system the extra seats are distributed to the lists with the highest average vote per seat. Any two lists may reach a surplus-votes agreement before the election, whereby the number of seats which the two received are calculated together, and only then are the number of seats to be allocated to each determined, according to the Bader-Ofer method.

Candidates enter the new Knesset if their position on the party's list corresponds to the number of seats gained by their party. However after the elections a Member of Knesset may defect from his own faction and join another faction (e.g., MK Yossi *Sarid left the Alignment and joined the *Civil Rights Movement after the elections to the 11th Knesset in 1984); remain in the Knesset as an independent (e.g., Moshe *Dayan left the Alignment to join the first *Begin government in 1977); or join with other Knesset members to form a new faction (e.g., the Civil Rights Movement and Arie Lova *Eliav from the Alignment set up *Ya'ad*, with 4 Knesset seats in 1975).

There are no by-elections in the Israeli system. When a Member of Knesset dies or resigns from the Knesset the next candidate on his party's list enters in his or her place.

The Israeli electoral system has been criticized mainly on two grounds: 1) that the rigid adherence to proportionality is responsible for the great fragmentation in the Knesset (there have been as many as 15 lists represented in the Knesset, and never fewer than ten), and for the distortions and fragility of Israel's coalition governments; 2) that a system which does not afford the electorate an opportunity to vote for a specific candidate creates a Knesset whose individual members are not directly responsible to their voters. Many proposals for reforming the electoral system have concentrated on these two criticisms (See *Electoral Reform). (A.D.)

Eliav, Arie Lova Educator and ex-Member of Knesset. Born 1921, Moscow. Eliav immigrated to Palestine with his parents in 1924 and was educated at the Herzlya Gymnasium in Tel Aviv. He served in the *Haganah 1936–40 and with Jewish units in the British army in the Middle East and Europe from 1940–45. During the following three years he was active in *Aliyah Bet* (illegal immigration) and served in the *IDF in the *War of Independence in 1948–49. From 1949–53 Eliav was Assistant Director of the Jewish Agency Settlement Department. In 1953 he studied agricultural economics and aid in Britain on a UN grant and from 1954–57 headed the Lachish Regional Development Project in southern Israel, within the framework of which one urban center and 50 rural settlements were established. During the *Sinai Campaign he commanded a combined air and sea operation to save the Jews of the city of Port Said. From 1958–60 Eliav was First Secretary at the Israel Embassy in Moscow and from 1960–62 headed the Arab Regional Development Project in the Negev. He headed the Israeli aid and rehabilitation mission to the earthquake-stricken Ghazvin region of Iran, planning and supervising the reconstruction of that region from 1962–64. Elected to the 6th Knesset in 1965, he was Deputy Minister in charge of industrialization of development areas in Israel from 1966–67 and Deputy Minister in charge of Immigration and Absorption from 1968–70. He served as Secretary-General of the *Israel Labor Party from 1970–72. He objected to the *Galili Document (1973) primarily because of the opening it gave to private land purchases in the *West Bank and the *Gaza Strip and shortly thereafter headed an Israeli aid mission to earthquake-stricken Managua in Nicaragua, to organize temporary living quarters. By 1975 he had left the Israel Labor Party and, together with the *Civil Rights Movement, established a new party, **Ya'ad*, which broke up soon thereafter over the issue of recognition of the Palestinian national movement. In the years 1976–77 he participated in talks with Palestinian leaders in Paris and was one of the founders, and chairman of **Maḥaneh Sheli* party, serving in the Knesset in 1977 as one of its two representatives. He initiated a rotation system in the party and left both the Knesset and the party in 1979, and from 1979–80 was lecturer and fellow at the Center for International Affairs at Harvard University.

A teacher in the adult-education program in the town of Or Akivah from 1980–81, in the following year he taught at the Regional College of Tel Ḥai in the Upper Galilee. During 1982–85 he negotiated the exchange of Israeli prisoners of war in the *Lebanese War, including the controversial exchange of four Israeli soldiers captured by Aḥmed Jibril's organization (See: *Palestine Liberation Organization) for over 1,000 Palestinian and other terrorists. Eliav was chairman of the Board of Trustees of the International Center for Peace in the Middle East from 1982 and then tried to return to the Israel Labor Party and be placed on its list for the elections to the 11th Knesset. When his attempt failed he decided to run for the Knesset on a personal ticket, letting his supporters know that if elected he would rejoin the Labor Party. He did not pass the one percent qualifying threshold. From 1984–85 he was a teacher at the Regional College of the Negev, working primarily with new immigrants from Ethiopia. Since 1985 he has been a teacher in the adult education project of the Israeli Prison Authority. In April 1986 Eliav rejoined the Israel Labor Party.

Emergency Regulations Emergency regulations in Israel are based on the Defense (Emergency) Regulations issued by the British High Commissioner in Palestine on September 22, 1945. The British regulations were based on the 1937 Palestine (Defense) Order in Council which stated in Article 6(1) "The High Commissioner may make such regulations as appear to him in his unfettered discretion to be necessary or expedient for securing the public safety, the defense of Palestine, the maintenance of public order and the suppression of mutiny, rebellion and riot, and for maintaining supplies and services essential to the life of the community." The Emergency Regulations are also based in the Israeli legal system: the 1948 Law and Administration Ordinance, in Article 9(a), decrees that "should it appear to the Provisional State Council necessary, it may declare that there is a state of emergency in the country and upon the publication of the declaration in the official Gazette the Provisional Government may authorize the Prime Minister or any other minister to make emergency regulations as appear to him to serve the defense of the State, the public's security and the maintenance of vital supplies and services." On May 21, 1948, the Provisional State Council announced a state of emergency in the country, and this state of emergency is in force to the present day.

Of the original Emergency Regulations, those dealing with prohibited immigration and requisitions were abolished in 1948, while the 1979 Emergency Authority Law (Detentions) replaced part of the section dealing with detentions. Parts of the remainder have been amended and new temporary regulations have been added from time to time dealing with security and economic matters. Until 1966 the *Military Administration was based on the Emergency Regulations. Most recently the regulations were used to introduce a price freeze and other economic measures within the framework of the economic stabilization policy pursued by the *National Unity Government.

Many efforts have been made over the years to abolish the Emergency Regulations, which are viewed as anti-democratic because they give the government powers to introduce extreme measures without the scrutiny of the Knesset or the courts.

Two of the most persistent fighters against the Emergency Regulations in the early years of the state were MKs Menaḥem *Begin and Tawfiq *Toubi. Begin argued that the regulations were a shameful vestige of "alien rule," and that they were anti-democratic. He also objected to the military administration arguing that an alert civil administration could take care of Israel's internal security problems.

Toubi argued that the Emergency Regulations were contrary to the principle of democratic freedom and human rights, and that they were used to oppress the Arab population of Israel. However, none of the private member bills introduced to abolish the regulations was ever passed by the *Knesset. A recent private member bill on the subject has been proposed by Elazar Granot from *Mapam* and was placed on the Knesset table on July 8, 1985. It seeks to limit the period to 12 months for which an emergency situation may be declared. He also argues that there must be a direct connection between issuing and implementing the regulations and the state of emergency.

Several of the *Basic Laws contain articles which cannot be changed by means of Emergency Regulations.

energy policy No coal and only very small quantities of oil have ever been found within the territory of Israel; thus, about 97 percent of Israel's energy supplies must be imported. This dependence superimposed on the continued *Arab-Israel conflict makes Israel extremely vulnerable not only economically but in terms of security as well. Consequently one of the major considerations for Israel's decision to sign the *Restitution Agreement with the *Federal Republic of Germany in 1952 was the concern that Israel might otherwise be unable within a matter of months to pay for its oil imports.

Throughout its existence most of Israel's potential oil sources were in unfriendly states or states with unstable regimes. The situation worsened in 1979 when the regime in *Iran, which for years had been Israel's main source of crude, was overturned by the Ayatolla Khoumeini, and when Israel returned the remainder of the Sinai oil fields as stipulated in the *Egyptian-Israeli Peace Treaty (the Abu Rudeis field had been returned in 1975 within the framework of the *Interim Agreement). Though in the *Memorandum of Understanding of 1975 the *United States undertook to supply Israel's energy requirements in a time of crisis (subject to Congressional approval), in recent years Israel has tried to secure regular supplies of crude by means of long-term contracts with Mexico, Norway and *Egypt. (*Great Britain has refused to sell Israel oil for fear of the *Arab boycott). These contracts cover about 70 percent of Israel's purchases of crude, the remainder being purchased as available on the spot market.

While continuing to prospect for oil in its own territory and on its continental shelf, Israel has tried to reduce its reliance on oil by constructing new power stations to operate with either coal or oil. In 1985 45 percent of Israel's electricity was produced from oil and 55 percent from coal. Of its total energy consumption 76 percent was supplied by oil and 22 percent by coal. The construction of nuclear power stations was considered and rejected toward the end of 1986 due to economic constraints.

Besides trying to diversify its sources of imported energy and reduce its dependence on oil, the Government of Israel has invested substantial resources in research and the development of locally available alternative sources of energy: solar, wind, shale oil, hydroelectric and the recycling of urban, industrial and agricultural wastes. Of these, solar energy has the greatest potential. Solar ponds for the generation of electricity have been constructed on the *Dead Sea, using Israeli developed technologies. The quantity of electricity generated by this method is as yet small. Solar energy is widely utilized for heating water and for creating steam at low pressure. About 2 percent of Israel's energy consumption is from solar energy.

A major hydroelectric project, the Mediterranean-Dead Sea canal project which was planned to take advantage of the differences in height between the two seas, was shelved in 1985 for economic reasons. The Arab states had objected to the project because its western section was to have run through the *Gaza Strip. *Jordan objected, claiming that the canal would ruin Jordanian potash works on the Dead Sea.

Experiments are being undertaken in the production of oil and electricity from shale oil of which Israel's reserves in the Negev, although of low quality, are estimated at over 10 billion tons. In recent years Israel has implemented energy saving plans resulting in an annual saving of about 2.5 percent, and it is estimated that the potential for saving is much greater. The government is trying to introduce saving through legislation, regulations and information.

Entebbe Operation Operation carried out by the Israel Air Force in Uganda — at a distance of 4,000 kilometers from Israel — on July 4, 1976, to rescue the 98 Israeli and Jewish hostages who were travelling in an Air France Airbus hijacked by Palestinian and German terrorists on June 27, 1976.

The hijackers, who first landed the plane in Benghazi, Libya, finally landed in Entebbe, Uganda, where the non-Jewish passengers were separated from Jews and eventually released. Israel attempted negotiations with Idi Amin, the Uganda ruler, who fully cooperated with the hijackers, while simultaneously making preparations for a military operation, based on intelligence information on the situation at Entebbe airport and careful planning of the operation's logistics. After the plan was approved by the cabinet, four large carrier aircraft departed from Sharm-e-Sheikh, flying directly to Entebbe. In the course of the successful operation three Israelis were killed, including Yonatan Netanyahu. Dora Bloch, an elderly woman left behind because she had been hospitalized, was later murdered. (Her body was returned to Israel in June 1979). On the return trip to Israel the aircraft landed in Nairobi, Kenya, to refuel and to give medical attention to several of the badly wounded. Though Israeli Chief of Staff Mordechai *Gur announced that Israel had force-landed in Kenya, it had apparently been coordinated with Kenya's leader Jomo Kenyatta.

While the Arabs, many African states and the Communist bloc condemned Israel's operation as an act of piracy, it was lauded in the West. In Israel the success of the operation raised morale in the *IDF which had been at a low ebb since the *Yom Kippur War. The *United Nations Security Council was unable to reach agreement on a resolution on the issue.

This operation conformed to Israel's declared policy at the time that it would refuse to negotiate with terrorists or concede to their demands, no matter how great the risks. The first major breach of this policy was the Israeli decision in 1984 to negotiate with Aḥmed Jibril's PFLP and its agreement to release over 1,000 terrorists held in Israel in return for four Israeli prisoners held by Jibril's organization.

Eretz Yisrael Hebrew for Land of Israel. The Hebrew term covers the territories which at one time or another constituted a part of the Jewish Kingdom(s) at the time of the First and Second Temples. *Eretz Yisrael* extends to the east of the *Jordan River. While certain sections of the Zionist Movement insisted that the modern Jewish state should be established in the whole of *Eretz Yisrael*, the majority accepted the reality that the State of Israel would be established in only part of *Eretz Yisrael*.

During the British mandate the Zionists insisted on Palestine being referred to officially also as *Eretz Yisrael*, but the most the mandatory authorities were willing to concede was the use of the Hebrew acronym for *Eretz Yisrael* after the name Palestine on all official documents, the currency, stamps, etc.

None of the parties in Israel today (not even **Kach*) demand that Israel should seek to occupy the whole of *Eretz Yisrael*, though the right-wing parties reject Israeli withdrawal from any territories of *Eretz Yisrael* occupied by Israel in the course of wars imposed on it. Since the *Sinai Peninsula is not part of *Eretz Yisrael*, the Israeli withdrawal was not resisted as strongly as might a possible future withdrawal from the *West Bank and *Gaza Strip.

Eshkol (formerly Shkolnik), **Levi**(1895–1969) Zionist Labor leader, Israeli statesman, Prime Minister 1963–69.

Born in the Ukraine, Eshkol immigrated to Palestine in 1913, where he worked in agriculture and as a guard. He was a co-founder of Kibbutz Deganiah Bet and volunteered for service in the Jewish Legion from 1918–20. He was active in the Labor movement as promoter and director of several **Histadrut* institutions and corporations. He also served on the **Haganah* High Command, and as Secretary-General of the Tel Aviv Workers' Council from 1944–48.

After the establishment of Israel, Eshkol became Director-General of the Ministry of Defense, under David *Ben Gurion, and in this capacity founded and promoted Israel's arms industry. A member of the Knesset from 1951 until his death. He was Minister of Agriculture, 1951–52, and Minister of Finance, 1952–63, and exerted considerable influence on the growth of Israel's economy. He served simultaneously as Treasurer of the *Jewish Agency, 1950–52 and Director of its Settlement Department, 1949–63, in which capacity he was responsible for the development of agricultural settlement in Israel and the absorption of many thousands of immigrants.

In 1963, Eshkol succeeded Ben Gurion as Prime Minister. Though Ben Gurion had himself recommended him, he soon turned against Eshkol, accusing him of mishandling state business in general and the *Lavon Affair in particular. In the 1965 general elections **Mapai* beat **Rafi*. From 1963–67 Eshkol served also as Minister of Defense — a post he handed over, on the eve of the *Six-Day War, to Moshe *Dayan, because of public pressure. In 1967 his government was broadened into a *National Unity Government which continued after the elections to the 6th Knesset (1969) but came to an end in 1970 when **Gaḥal* broke away. (Y.R.)

essek bish Hebrew expression with the connotation of "scandal" used to describe the first stage of the *Lavon Affair and the *Pollard Affair.

Ethiopian Jews The Ethiopian Jews (*Beta Yisrael* as they call themselves, *Falashas as they are called by others) have roots in the northwest of Ethiopia that probably go back to ancient times. Though their exact origins are shrouded in obscurity, the fact that Ethiopia was traditionally a part of the Semitic Middle East and that Judaism has had such a fundamental impact on Ethiopia's national legends and culture, makes the presence of Jews in that country highly plausible. A Falasha Kingdom is mentioned in the chronicles of the Ethiopian kings from the 15th century, but it was conquered and dismantled by combined Ethiopian-Portuguese forces in the 17th and the 18th centuries. "Falasha" derives, it is thought, from the Amharic word *filasi,* meaning a landless group or person, a reference to the defeat of the Jews and their loss of sovereignty and with it their transformation into an outcast group. (Today the term Falasha is considered derogatory). The status of the Ethiopian Jews was formally decided by the Israeli *Chief Rabbinate in 1973 when Sephardi Chief Rabbi Ovadia Yosef determined that they were descendants of the tribe of Dan and as Jews entitled to immigrate to Israel under the *Law of Return. Ethiopian policies of assimilation, however, delayed their emigration, and prevented many from coming altogether. Fifteen thousand Ethiopian Jews live in Israel (1986) following immigration movements which began in the early 1970s, and increased in the early 80s. The culmination was the mass immigration of the 1984–85 "Operation Moses" at the time of the famine in Ethiopia. Estimates of those remaining in Ethiopia vary from 5,000 to 20,000.

The absorption of the Ethiopian Jews into Israeli society is positively affected by a highly favorable stereotype, their own motivation to integrate into the wider society, and their capacity to adapt to new social situations. They have also benefited from material support from various absorption bodies far in excess of that received by previous waves of non-Western immigrants.

Though a biological racism is not prevalent in Israel the Ethiopian Jews must cope with a certain amount of anti-black prejudice, as well as with resistance to full acceptance as Jews by some Orthodox (primarily Ashkenazi) rabbis. The most bitter confrontation has been with the Chief Rabbinate which insists on a "symbolic conversion" for the whole community because of doubts as to whether many of its members are Jews according to the *Halacha* (Jewish law). However, many of the Ethiopian Jews have adamantly refused to undergo the symbolic conversion on the grounds that their Jewishness is beyond question. Attempts by the Rabbinate to prevent marriages of those who refuse the ritual bath required for the symbolic conversion is being challenged in the Supreme Court.

A further problem has been the smothering absorption bureaucracy which has arisen around the immigrants and which threatens to isolate them from the general population. Immigrants often spend up to five years in homogeneous absorption centers, partly due to a shortage of housing, or their refusal to leave, and then are frequently given apartments in economically and socially weaker areas of the country. High unemployment, inadequate educational facilities and the scattering of families constitute serious problems. Most of the Ethiopian children have been assigned to religious schools.

Unlike the other non-Western communities in Israel the Ethiopians quickly organized themselves into pressure groups. The Union for Saving Ethiopian Jewish Families, established in 1979, lobbies in the areas of *aliyah* (immigration) and absorption. *Beta Yisrael* held a long and bitter demonstration opposite the headquarters of the Chief Rabbinate at the height of the conversion struggle. The Association of Ethiopian Immigrants concentrates on the preservation of the Ethiopian culture through dance and handicrafts. Support groups in Israel and North America provide important financial and advisory assistance. These groups include the National Committee for Ethiopian Jews established by the Knesset.

(J.H.)

European Economic Community The EEC was established in 1957 by *France, the *Federal Republic of Germany, Italy, and the Benelux states, under the terms of the Treaty of Rome. By 1986 six additional states had joined: *Great Britain, Ireland, Denmark, Greece, *Spain and Portugal.

After 1958 Israel approached the EEC in order to establish special economic relations with this group of states. On June 4, 1964, a first agreement was signed between Israel and the EEC. This agreement was of limited economic value but included a clause linking future EEC concessions on citrus to other Mediterranean countries to renegotiation of the agreement with Israel.

On October 4, 1966 Israel applied for association status, but was turned down. Following the *Six-Day War the EEC recommended that negotiations start for a preferential agreement with Israel. A new agreement was signed in Luxembourg on June 29, 1970, simultaneously with an agreement with Spain. Most of Israel's industrial exports received a reduction in tariffs of 50 percent — an important economic advantage for the Israeli industry.

The first enlargement of the Community, in 1973, led to the signature of a new comprehensive agreement in May 1975, establishing a free trade area for industrial products, and providing concessions for Israeli agricultural products. While non-tariff barriers continue to exist, there are no European custom duties on Israeli industrial goods and Israel is progressively lowering its own tariffs on imports from Europe until they end entirely by 1989.

The agreement for a parallel free trade area with the *United States signed in 1985, puts about two thirds of Israel's international trade in the unique position of having privileged relations with both the EEC and the US.

The competition of industrialized countries because of the full reciprocity of the actual agreement with the EEC, obliges Israeli industry to improve its productivity and quality standards so that it can successfully open extensive new market of hundreds of millions of customers for its products.

The entry of Spain and Portugal to the EEC posed new problems for Israel's agricultural exports to the Community, since Spain, which is already a major producer of the same Mediterranean products which Israel produces, especially citrus, will have a real competitive edge over Israel after the transition period. Following a decision by the Council of Ministers of the EEC on November 25, 1985, negotiations have begun between Israel and the EEC in order to find suitable solutions to the problem of safeguarding Israel's traditional exports to Europe.

In 1985 the 12 states of the EEC exported $8,379 million worth of products to Israel, while Israel exported $6,268 million worth to them. Although economic relations are by far the most important aspect of Israel's relations with the EEC (30 percent of total Israeli exports go to the Community and 43 percent of its total imports come from the 12 states) there is also a political dimension to these relations. In 1970 the EEC introduced a policy of political cooperation among themselves, and since that year have coordinated their Middle East policies. Following the *Yom Kippur War, and as a consequence of the first oil crisis, the EEC states, then nine in number, issued the first of a succession of statements on the *Arab-Israel conflict. This statement, published on November 6, 1973, included the following four principles: 1) the inadmissibility of the acquisition of territory by force; 2) the need for Israel to end the territorial occupation which it has maintained since the war in 1967; 3) respect for the sovereignty, territorial integrity and independence of every state in the region and its right to live in peace within secure and recognized boundaries; 4) recognition that in the establishment of a just and lasting peace, account must be taken of the legitimate rights of the *Palestinians.

Since 1973 several additional declarations have been issued. The most well known of them is the Venice Declaration of June 30, 1980, which supported the Palestinians' right to self-determination and stated, *inter alia*, that the *Palestine Liberation Organization (PLO) must be associated with peace negotiations. Several statements were also issued by the Community in connection with Israel's military involvement in Lebanon in 1982, and the Community even suspended the signature of a cooperation protocol because of the *Lebanese War.

While the Community has argued that its statements express a balanced policy regarding the Arab-Israel conflict, Israel considers these declarations to have a pro-Arab bias, caused largely by economic interests, and points out that they contribute nothing to the improvement of the prospects of a peace settlement in the Middle East. Furthermore, Israel believes that since the PLO has so far refused to accept *Security Council Resolutions 242 and 338, to give up the use of terror and to recognize Israel's right to exist, its participation in negotiations would be an obstacle to peace.

Since 1974 the EEC has also been engaged in a Euro-Arab dialogue which it has been unable to conduct on a declared non-political level. Israel views this dialogue with suspicion because only one side to the controversy participates. A German proposal in 1974 that a simultaneous Euro-Israeli dialogue begin was not implemented.

In its fight against the *Arab boycott Israel has attempted to persuade the EEC to coordinate the legislation of its 12 members in an attempt to stop the boycott's implementation in Europe. With the same purpose in mind Israel has also invoked anti-discrimination clauses in the Treaty of Rome and in the EEC's agreements with the Maghreb and Mashreq states (Egypt, Jordan, Lebanon and Syria), but so far with no results.

(S.M.)

F

Fahd Plan Proposed by Crown Prince Fahd (later King) of Saudi Arabia on August 7, 1981. The plan's main points were: 1) Israeli withdrawal from all Arab territory occupied in 1967, including East Jerusalem; 2) the removal of Israeli settlements established on Arab lands since 1967; 3) guaranteed freedom of worship in the holy places for all religions; 4) affirmation of the right of the Palestinian people to return to their homes, and compensation to those who decide not to do so; 5) *UN control of the *West Bank and *Gaza Strip for a transition period not exceeding a few months; 6) the establishment of an independent Palestinian state with *Jerusalem as its capital; 7) affirmation of the right of all states in the region to live in peace; 8) the UN or some of its members to guarantee and implement these principles.

Prince Fahd issued his plan in the conviction that Sadat had only obtained a separate peace for Egypt, and that the *Camp David Accords would lead nowhere. Those Arab states which accepted the Fahd Plan asserted that point 7 included and implied recognition of the State of Israel. Israel rejected the plan and also questioned whether the Saudis were really willing to recognize Israel. *PLO chairman Yasser Arafat at first welcomed the plan as a basis for negotiations, but when it became apparent that neither Iraq nor Syria supported it, renounced it, and the November 25, 1981 Arab Summit at Fez, which was to have approved the plan, was adjourned so that the Saudis would not lose face.

Falashas Name in common usage for the *Ethiopian Jews, which is, however, considered by them to be derogatory.

Feda'iyin Arabic word meaning suicide squads or commandos. A term based on medieval Islamic concepts, associated with the Shi'ite-Isma'ilis and the *Hashashiyin* (the assassins). Within the context of the *Arab-Israel conflict the term was used to refer to Palestinian infiltrators who carried out acts of terror and sabotage in Israel up to the *Six-Day War.

Federal Republic of Germany and Israel The system of relations with the Federal Republic of Germany (FRG, West Germany) is one of the most complex in Israeli foreign relations.

At the outset it must be pointed out that the "other" German state, the German Democratic Republic (GDR, East Germany), views itself as a new state established after World War II and not as the successor state of the Third Reich, thereby denying all responsibility for what occurred in Germany before its partition. This fact and the one-sided acceptance by the GDR of the Soviet policy insofar as the *Arab-Israel conflict is concerned, prevented the establishment of any formal contacts between Israel and East Germany.

In contrast the FRG expressed its willingness to undertake the responsibility stemming from the past. The relations between Israel and West Germany involve difficult and complex relations between two peoples: the German and Jewish peoples. In light of the crimes committed by the Germans against the Jews, it seemed that any formal contact between the two would be unthinkable.

On September 15, 1949, the first elections to the Bundestag, the West German Parliament, were held, and Konrad Adenauer was elected Chancellor. Adenauer understood the need and urgency for reconciliation and rapprochement with the Jewish people, and on November 11, stated in an interview to a Jewish newspaper that he recognized in the name of the German people the crimes committed against the Jewish people and expressed his wish to aid in the rehabilitation of the Jews through moral and material reparations — *Wiedergutmachung*. At the same time Adenauer recognized the legitimate right of Israel as a Jewish state to receive material restitution from the FRG. In that interview Adenauer mentioned the sum of 10 million DM which would be granted in the form of goods.

The first formal meeting between Israelis and Germans took place in 1950 within the framework of the Inter-Parliamentary Union in Istanbul. This unplanned meeting was the first step toward future contacts. The Israeli delegation, headed by Yitzḥak *Ben Zvi (who would become Israel's second President), expressed its willingness to raise the German suggestions regarding reparations in the *Knesset. At first, contacts on the reparations issue were between the Germans, and primarily, Nahum *Goldmann of the World Jewish Congress — and Israel was not directly involved. On March 12, 1951, the Government of Israel approached the four Great Powers (France, UK, US and USSR) with a demand for reparations by the Germans. The Powers pressed Israel to approach Germany directly.

Adenauer's declaration to the Bundestag of September 27, 1951, in which he formally and clearly recognized the obligation of the Germans toward the Jewish people and the State of Israel brought about a change, even though there were many individuals and groups in Israel, especially on the Right, who objected to any contact with the Germans.

On January 7, 1952, a violent demonstration was organized by Menaḥem *Begin against Israel's accepting any reparations from Germany. Begin stated then that "there will never be dealings with Germany," but two months later, in March 1952, direct talks began in Wassenar, in the Netherlands on the *Restitution Agreement. The agreement was finally signed on September 10, 1952. The uniqueness of the agreement was that it was signed by two countries which did not maintain diplomatic or any other relations, and that one of the parties to the agreement, the Jewish Claims Conference, headed by Naḥum Goldmann, had no international legal status.

From the beginning the Arabs pressured the FRG not to reach an agreement with Israel. They argued that reparations in the form of goods would increase Israel's military capability and pose a threat to them. In October 1952 the Arab League informed the Federal Republic that ratification of the agreement would harm Germany's economic interests in the Arab states which at this time stood at about 3 billion DM. Nevertheless, the Bundestag ratified the agreement on May 4, 1953.

The agreement was of vital importance to both sides. For Germany willingness to repent was an important step toward its integration in the Western Alliance. In this way Adenauer hoped to further the reunification of Germany which would be placed at the center of East-West relations. For Israel the agreement was a mini-Marshall Plan of the greatest economic importance. Nevertheless, it was received in Israel with mixed feelings, since many felt that mixing reparations and Germany's moral obligation was objectionable. At this time Israel would not consider the establishment of diplomatic relations. For a decade from the mid-50s West German considerations concerning diplomatic relations with Israel were complicated by its demand to be recognized as the sole representative of the German people, expressed in the Hallstein Doctrine under which West Germany reserved the right to break off relations with any state recognizing East Germany. While this demand did not affect Israel the Arabs referred to the doctrine in bargaining with the FRG. In May 1956, at a conference of West German ambassadors convened in Istanbul, the possibility was raised that the Arabs might recognize the GDR if diplomatic relations were established between the Federal Republic and Israel. This fear delayed the establishment of diplomatic relations between Israel and the FRG until 1965.

Nevertheless, Israeli relations with West Germany existed in terms of arms sales. In a secret agreement, the foundations of which were laid in discussions between Shimon *Peres and Franz Joseph Strauss which began in 1957, mutual arms deliveries were agreed upon. Keeping the military connection secret proved extremely difficult and details began to leak out.

The question of arms deliveries was also discussed in the historic meeting between Prime Minister David *Ben Gurion and Adenauer in March 1960 in New York where talks centered on economic questions connected with the development of Israel, and especially the Negev — Ben Gurion's pet project. The meeting was of great symbolic value, and opened the way for direct contacts between the two states at all levels. However a high degree of sensitivity remained. In 1959 swastikas and abusive inscriptions against the Jewish people were painted on synagogues and in Jewish cemeteries in Germany. Soon after this, in May 1960, the **Mossad* captured Adolf *Eichmann in *Argentina and brought him to Israel to stand trial for crimes committed against the Jewish people. The trial opened on April 11, 1961. These two events, particularly the latter, served to remind the world of the Nazi atrocities, and the Jews in Israel of the not-so-distant past.

Two additional issues disturbed the development of relations between the FRG and Israel in the first half of the sixties. The first was the activities of German scientists in *Egypt, the second the question of the Statute of Limitations with regard to Nazi crimes. In the early 1960s German experts on rocket development began helping Egypt develop missiles which would be used against Israel. All Israeli appeals and demands to the German government were ignored. The German government, using legal-administrative reasoning, argued that there was nothing it could do to stop its citizens from working in Egypt. The problem was finally resolved toward the mid-60s when the *Mossad* took measures against individual German scientists and their activity in Egypt, causing the project to become less attractive.

The Statute of Limitations for the prosecution of Nazi criminals was scheduled to run out May 20, 1965. Not only had there been a delay in starting Nazi trials so that many witnesses and criminals had died or disappeared, but also an avenue was about to open which would grant legal immunity for all those who had so far managed to escape justice. Israel was not alone to protest. Countries such as Poland, the Netherlands and France, which had suffered at the hands of the Nazis, were actively concerned. The argument that the war criminals were not ordinary criminals was finally accepted in 1979, when it was decided that the Statute of Limitations would not apply to Nazi criminals.

Relations between West Germany and Israel were established in 1965 against the background of a crisis in the FRG's foreign policy. Information regarding arms sales to Israel was revealed and Egyptian President Nasser insisted that they be stopped immediately. The FRG, under Chancellor Ludwig Erhard, had difficulty reaching a decision, and a major debate ensued among the parties. On January 24, 1965, Nasser announced the forthcoming visit of East German leader Walter Ulbricht to Egypt. According to the Hallstein Doctrine this should have automatically led to West Germany's breaking off diplomatic relations with Egypt. But, on February 12, 1965, the West German government announced its unwillingness to continue supplying arms to countries in regions of international tension. It was, however, too late to prevent Ulbricht's visit. West Germany reacted by withdrawing economic aid to Egypt. The decision not to sever relations with Egypt was taken primarily because of US fear that it would increase Soviet influence in the region. At the same time, contacts with Israel on the establishment of diplomatic relations were begun. On May 12, 1965, relations were established. Rolf Pauls was Germany's first Ambassador to Israel, and Asher Ben Nathan was Israel's first Ambassador to Bonn.

The normalization of relations on the diplomatic level symbolized the introduction of extensive contacts on the political, social, economic and cultural levels. Even though there was strong sympathy and even identification in West Germany with Israel's position in the *Six-Day War, the consequences of the overwhelming Israeli victory marked a turning point in the relations between the two states. The first signs became apparent in 1968 with the growing strength of left-wing movements in the Federal Republic, which viewed support of the Arab-Palestinian position as part of their struggle against the Establishment, and Israel as an imperialist power. At that time all the East European countries except Romania had broken relations with Israel, and the golden age of Franco-Israeli relations had come to an end.

In the course of the seventies West Germany stopped viewing its relations with Israel on purely bilateral terms but multilaterally, as part of the *European Economic Community (EEC) efforts to formulate a common policy vis-à-vis the Arab-Israel conflict. Though the past has continued to play a role in West Germany's policy toward Israel, its significance has progressively diminished. On November 6, 1973, the nine community members published their first statement referring to the "legitimate rights of the Palestinians," rather than the Palestinian "refugee problem."

In 1980, in the Venice Declaration, the EEC called for the participation of the *Palestine Liberation Organization (PLO) in peace negotiations. The first official visit of a member of the Israeli government to the FRG was by Foreign Minister Abba *Eban in February 1970. This visit was followed by a series of mutual visits, the most noteworthy being that of Chancellor Willy Brandt to Israel in June 1973. Nevertheless, the progressive change in German policy toward Israel was subtly expressed by Brandt — Germany and Israel no longer enjoyed "special relations" but "normal relations with a special character." This innuendo was even more marked within the framework of Chancellor Kohl's visit to Israel in 1984.

During Menaḥem Begin's premiership (1977–83) personal relations were markedly cooler. Begin had always taken a non-compromising and aggressive position toward West Germany, which manifested itself most strongly in his unprecedented personal attack on Chancellor Helmut Schmidt. Relations were further aggravated during the *Lebanese War. The deterioration on the German side was especially marked among the younger generation, and the word "anti-Semitism" gave way to a new expression — *anti-Zionism.

The Begin-Schmidt crisis and Chancellor Kohl's statement during his visit to Israel regarding his having been but a boy during the Third Reich and thus personally "clean" of any Nazi past, were counterbalanced by the successful visit of West German President Richard von Weizsäcker to Israel in 1985. Although the atmosphere between the two states improved, in fact Germany's commitment to Israel can no longer be measured in moral terms. The approach is much more pragmatic and critical, influenced by the passage of time and by developments in the Middle East. Nonetheless, a planned return visit to the FRG by President Ḥaim *Herzog in April 1987 raised a furore in Israel.

One of the central features of German-Israeli relations is economic. FRG is Israel's second largest trading partner after the US, and in 1986, Germany took first place in terms of numbers of tourists visiting Israel. Israel is second only to France in terms of numbers of youth exchanges with Germany. Cultural relations have also thrived. For many years German was not spoken over the Israeli media and the first German Cultural Week in Israel, in 1971, was accompanied by demonstrations and disturbances. Even though Wagner's and Strauss' music is still not played German cultural activities in Israel are widespread, and the Goethe Institute is active in Tel Aviv.

At the end of 1986 military cooperation was reported to have reached new heights. Scientific cooperation is also highly developed. The three largest funds associated with the major political parties in Germany are at work in Israel for the furtherance of social and cultural cooperation. Nevertheless, for Israel the past continues to play a major role in its relations with West Germany. This was recognized by German President von Weizsäcker in a speech to the Bundestag on May 8, 1985, on the 40th anniversary of the end of World War II. He said: "Whoever criticizes the situation in the Middle East should think of the fate to which Germans condemned their Jewish fellow human beings, a fate that led to the establishment of the State of Israel under conditions which continue to burden people in that region even today." (A.N.)

Fez Plan A set of points adopted at the Arab summit meeting in Fez, Morocco on September 8, 1982, in reaction to the *Reagan Plan of the previous week. The Fez Plan was essentially a modified version of the *Fahd Plan, and called for:

1) Israeli withdrawal from all occupied Arab territories including East Jerusalem; 2) dismantling the Israeli settlements in the Arab territories; 3) guarantees of freedom of worship for all religions and rites; 4) affirmation of the Palestinian right of self-determination, and the exercise of that right under their sole representative, the *Palestine Liberation Organization (PLO); 5) a transition period of a few months during which the *West Bank and the *Gaza Strip would be supervised by the *UN; 6) the establishment of a Palestinian state with *Jerusalem as its capital; 7) a UN Security Council guarantee for the peace and security of all states in the region including a Palestinian state; 8) a UN Security Council guarantee for the implementation of the above principles.

The changes from the Fahd Plan were significant. Articles 1 and 2, which spoke of Israeli withdrawal and the dismantling of settlements, no longer referred to 1967, implying the possibility that these two articles may also refer to settlements within the *Green Line. Article 4 spoke of the Palestinian right to self-determination and of the PLO as being the sole representative of the Palestinians while the Fahd Plan spoke merely of the right of the Palestinians to return to their homes and did not mention the PLO. Article 7 of the Fez Plan spoke of a UN Security Council guarantee for the peace and security of all states in the region, and not of an affirmation of the right of all states in the region to live in peace, as mentioned in the Fahd Plan. Finally, in Article 8, the Fez Plan called for a Security Council guarantee for the plan's implementation, whereas the Fahd plan left an option open for guarantees by some of the UN members, i.e., the Western powers only. Israel rejected the Fez Plan, but it was raised again by King Hassan of Morocco in his talks with Prime Minister Shimon *Peres in July 1986.

Fighters List Hebrew name: *Reshimat Haloḥamim*. Party of ex-**Leḥi* members which ran for the 1st *Knesset (1949) and gained a single seat which was occupied by Nathan *Yellin-Mor.

As Yellin-Mor started moving to the Left, several prominent ex-*Leḥi* members, including Israel *Eldad and Geula *Cohen, left the party.

Fighting Family A term coined by Menaḥem *Begin in the early 1950s to describe the close ties of ex-**IZL* members, many of whom formed the core of the **Ḥerut* movement.

Final Solution A term used to describe the policy of genocide implemented by Nazi Germany against the Jewish people. Due to this use of the term Israeli politicians are extremely careful not to use it in connection with the search for a settlement of the *Arab-Israel conflict where the terms "permanent solution" or "permanent settlement" are used. (See: *Holocaust)

Flatto-Sharon (formerly Szeyjewicz), **Shmuel** Businessman and former Knesset member, born 1930 in Lodz, Poland.

Flatto-Sharon immigrated as a child to France where he later became a successful businessman. He established residence in Israel in 1972. Three years later charges were brought against him in France, in his absence, for allegedly embezzling hundreds of millions of francs from French investors. He was also accused of real estate fraud.

The French government called for his extradition from Israel. In order to gain immunity Flatto-Sharon ran in the elections for the 9th Knesset (1977). Despite the fact that he did not speak Hebrew he won enough votes for two Knesset seats. However, since he did not have two people on his list he entered the Knesset on his own, naming his party **Pitu'aḥ Veshalom*. While he was an MK in 1979-80, he was found guilty and sentenced in absentia. As MK, Flatto-Sharon became involved in various attempts to release Jewish hostages, prisoners and *"Prisoners of Zion". In 1979 he financed a squad which tried to track down Idi Amin. In 1980 he contributed funds to slum-area activists who established a squatters' tent "settlement" outside Rishon Letzion, which they called *Ohel- Moreh*.

On August 1, 1979 the Knesset lifted Flatto-Sharon's immunity after it decided to charge him for bribing voters in the 1977 elections. He was convicted and sentenced to nine months' imprisonment in May, 1981. As a result the Knesset House Committee decided to suspend his Knesset membership, but the suspension was overruled by the High Court of Justice. Flatto-Sharon ran again for the 10th Knesset (1981) but failed to pass the one percent qualifying threshold. In 1983 he was involved in a private effort to free Israel's prisoners of war in the *Lebanese War. He ran a third time for the 11th Knesset (1984) but failed once more. He served his prison sentence from October 1984 as a "day" prisoner (he went home at night). He was the first person in Israel ever convicted of election bribery. On October 28, 1985, Flatto-Sharon was arrested in Milano by request of the French government. In April 1986 Flatto-Sharon escaped Italy in disguise and returned to Israel.

foreign aid (from Israel) As part of its *foreign policy Israel has operated a program of technical assistance to developing countries since 1958. Within the framework of this program over 55,000 persons from developing countries have received training in Israel or abroad under Israeli auspices, and close to 10,000 Israeli advisors have assisted with projects throughout the developing world. Despite the benefits which the program has undoubtedly brought to the developing countries involved, it has brought Israel few direct political or economic benefits in return. Indirect benefits have included keeping communication lines open, utilizing economic opportunities and countering Arab attempts to isolate Israel.

While in the 1950s Israel shared the experience of new statehood with many of the newly-independent African and Asian states, together with the urgent need for economic development and social progress, Israel emerged into statehood with a relatively sophisticated economic and social infrastructure and an experience with self-government from its pre-state days (See: **Yishuv*), as well as a national ethos for pioneering and nation-building. But, unlike most of the newly independent countries, Israel started its independent national existence surrounded by hostile states intent on its destruction, or at least on keeping it isolated.

These features and circumstances inspired Israel's leaders in the late 1950s to respond to specific requests for help, and gradually to develop a varied program of training and expertise which it offered to any developing country seeking such assistance. David *Ben Gurion as Prime Minister and Golda *Meir as Minister for Foreign Affairs, both viewed Israel's commitment to the developing world as not only politically logical but also as a moral obligation.

The first developing country to enjoy Israel's assistance was Burma, whose Prime Minister, U Nu visited Israel in 1955. Newly independent Ghana was second, in 1957. In both cases earlier contacts through **Histadrut* circles paved the way, as did the participation of David Hacohen, Israel's dynamic first ambassador to Burma and a former director of the *Histadrut*-owned Solel Boneh construction company.

In 1958 Meir visited Africa, and moved by the monumental challenges facing the young African countries, became a strong advocate of Israeli assistance. Later that year, *Mashov* (Hebrew acronym for *Maḥlakah Leshituf Pe'ulah Beinle'umi* — Department of International Cooperation) was set up in the Ministry for Foreign Affairs, and the assistance program became an official aspect of Israeli foreign policy. At the peak of its operations in the mid-sixties the department employed a staff of 80 and had an annual budget of approximately $10 million. In 1964, 2,446 participants from developing countries trained in Israel and 698 expert assignments were carried out in these countries.

The early period of the program was marked by rapid growth, a good deal of enthusiasm and improvisation. In retrospect it is clear that both Israel's capacities and possibilities of transferring technology and knowhow in the absence of concomitant capital assistance and a suitable social environment, were overestimated. Israel's attractiveness in the eyes of developing countries lay in its non-imperialist past, not yet marred by its post-1967 image; its image as a successful, rapidly developing society which could empathize with the challenges of development and nation-building; its impressive economic growth, despite poverty in natural resources and shortage of capital; its social orientation which, in the early years, placed great emphasis on cooperative and socialist development.

In line with its own achievements, Israel developed institutions for training and project development in various fields: the Center for International Agricultural Development Cooperation (CINADCO) in agriculture; the (*Histadrut*) International Institute for Development, Cooperation and Labor Studies (formerly the Afro-Asian Institute) and the Center of Cooperative and Labor Studies for *Latin America in cooperative enterprises; the Mount Carmel International Training Centre for Community Services in community development and the involvement of women; the Settlement Study Centre in integrated regional planning and development; the Hebrew University Hadassah Medical School Special Program in Public Health; and Volcani Institute for Agriculture Research, special course in Irrigation and Management of Water Resources.

Additional programs in many fields were added on an ad hoc basis, as Israel sought to project the image of a "development supermarket." Especially interesting, but potentially sensitive, were projects managed by Israel's Ministry of Defense. These included military training programs as well as various military pioneering service programs for youth, patterned after Israel's Naḥal and Gadna (pre-army paramilitary training for youth). In 1966 Israeli advisors were working in these types of programs in 17 countries — 13 of them in Africa.

Aside from the government a number of quasi-public companies became active, with government encouragement and support, and established joint-venture partnerships in developing countries. These included Solel Boneh (construction), Agridev (agriculture); Mekorot (water works construction), Zim (shipping), Amiran (export) and Tahal (water planning). Unlike the official government programs which involved primarily training and project advisory services, such joint ventures had more of a commercial character, and were intended to develop major indigenous institutions. Amiran Ltd., for example, took a 20 percent share in Cossata, a new government-supported cooperative marketing organization in Tanzania; Zim helped establish and invested in Ghana's Black Star Shipping Line; and Solel Boneh established and managed among other projects, the Nigersol Construction Company, a public corporation operating in western Nigeria.

Many training programs and in-country projects succeeded beyond expectations, and have left behind a heritage of good will and notable accomplishment. Thus, Israeli opthalmologists working in Liberia, Ethiopia, Tanzania and other African countries since the early 1960s are estimated to have performed about 12,000 eye operations and examined 300,000 outpatients, in addition to training local nurses and physicians. Again, in 1974, in the semi-arid Azua region of the Dominican Republic, some 3,000 families were resettled and trained in diversified irrigated agriculture under the direction of three Israeli advisors supplemented by specialists; an arid-zone research center and applied research stations were set up, while new food processing plants provide employment for hundreds of people.

However, the chronic dependence on financing from non-Israeli sources has often been a major constraint to success, while involvement in politically- or militarily-sensitive areas has occasionally implicated Israel in the domestic affairs of partner countries. For example, domestic politics and charges of corruption paralyzed the operations of two joint-venture companies in western Nigeria for over a year in 1962. In Uganda charges of Israeli support for Idi Amin's overthrow of Milton Obote in 1971 marred Israel's image. A year later Amin himself denounced Israel in the harshest terms, broke off diplomatic relations, cancelled military training and millions of dollars' worth of other contracts, and expelled 149 Israeli advisors and their families.

In addition to Uganda, which broke off relations in order to gain Libyan support, four other African countries — Chad, Niger, Mali and Congo-Brazzaville — responded to persistent Arab pressure and promises of aid, as well as to Israel's deteriorating image, and severed relations in 1972. The following year, within a month after the outbreak of the *Yom Kippur War and the imposition of the Organization of Petroleum Exporting Countries (OPEC) oil embargo, 20 African countries broke off relations with Israel. Only four small states — Malawi, Swaziland, Lesotho and Mauritius — maintained official ties.

Israel's policymakers had to decide whether to close the doors of the assistance program to those countries which had broken off relations, as Israeli public opinion and national pride demanded, or to continue the assistance program and in this way maintain contacts, as often unofficially desired by many of the countries concerned. The Government of Israel opted for pragmatism — and continued to accept participants to its training programs from countries with which it had no official relations, but officially discontinued sponsoring in-country projects — though private Israeli commercial operations were still allowed, and in some cases even unofficially encouraged.

Nevertheless, the diplomatic situation had a significant effect on Israel's technical cooperation program. The number of African training participants — the largest group until 1972, fell sharply, and African in-country projects, officially serviced by Israeli experts, virtually ceased. Among these were settlement projects in Zambia and Madagascar, youth training programs in 10 West African countries, and an afforestation program in Chad.

The focus of the assistance program now shifted toward *Latin America, Asia and Oceania. Since 1974 half of the trainees coming to Israel, and more than two-thirds of those attending Israeli-sponsored local courses, have been from Latin America and the Caribbeans while over two-thirds of the Israeli expert-assignments abroad have also been to the same areas.

The African experience did, however, dampen public enthusiasm in Israel for aid to other nations, and Israeli government financial support for the cooperation program (which amounted to almost $7 million — not including overhead expenses of the Department for International Cooperation — in 1971) was drastically cut. The early 1980s saw a further sharp decline in numbers of participants in training courses, as well as expert-assignments abroad (trainees from Israel: from 1,230 in 1980 to 654 in 1985; expert-assignments: from 334 in 1980 to 97 in 1985). Moreover, restrictive conditions required by the various third-party financiers have deprived the program of some of its flexibility. There has also been an erosion in the nation- building ingredient and pioneering enthusiasm which had given Israeli aid its special character in the earlier period.

New opportunities for normalization of ties with Black Africa have been encountered at the beginning of the second half of the 1980s. By mid-1986, four Black African countries had restored full diplomatic relations with Israel, and others were expected to do so in the near future. Aid will undoubtedly play a major role in these resumed relations but, to be fully effective, its national priority must be upgraded. Moreover, Israel will have to move cautiously to avoid becoming entangled in the internal affairs of receiving countries. It will have to recultivate a nation-building, field-orientated operational style and concentrate on selected sectors of demonstrated capability where need and interest are high. (L.L.)

foreign aid (to Israel) Long before the establishment of the State of Israel the **Yishuv* received funds from abroad, almost exclusively from Jews who supported the Zionist enterprise. With the *Proclamation of Independence and the mass influx of Jewish *refugees from Europe and the Arab countries, both need and access to resources increased significantly. As a sovereign political entity, Israel no longer had to rely solely on the financial resources of world Jewry, though for the first two decades of the state's existence this flow of capital exceeded all others.

Like other newly independent countries in the post-World War II era, Israel began to receive assistance on a government-to- government basis, as well as from international assistance agencies. As a result of the complex political developments related to the *Arab-Israel conflict, foreign economic and military assistance was of special importance to Israel, and though it is not one of the world's neediest countries, both in per capita and in absolute terms, Israel receives more foreign aid than any other country in the world.

Israel's largest single supplier of economic and military assistance has been the *United States. At a meeting that took place ten days after the proclamation of independence between Israel's first president Chaim *Weizmann and US president Harry Truman, the latter expressed "special interest" in providing economic development loans and ensuring Israel's defensive capacity. American concern for Israel's economy and defense remained a fixed feature of the US-Israel relationship (See: *Foreign Policy). Until 1967 Israel acquired most of its military assistance (sometimes with tacit US approval) from *France and the *Federal Republic of Germany (See: *Arms Purchases).

Total official US assistance to Israel in the years 1950–85 amounted to $31.3 billion, more than that given to any other country.

While US military aid to Israel began only in 1959 with a $0.4 million loan, US economic aid began soon after the establishment of the state with two loans amounting to $135 million from the Export/Import Bank in 1949 and 1951. Half the funds were used for agricultural development, and the rest for industrial development and essential infrastructure. In 1952, as hundreds of thousands of Jewish refugees poured into Israel, the US inaugurated a program of economic development support and food relief, designed to help Israel expand its economy, train manpower and finance commodity imports, thus alleviating the country's balance-of-payments deficit (See: *Economic Policy). Under the Food for Peace program inaugurated at the same time the US provided Israel with $638 million worth of wheat, dairy products, fats, oils and feed in the years 1952–80 — ten percent in the form of grants, the rest as long-term loans repayable partly in local currency, which in turn was reinvested in productive projects jointly approved by both countries.

As Israel became economically stronger during the later 1950s and in the 1960s, economic aid became relatively less important to the economy's development, though more than 20 percent of Israel's import surplus continued to be financed by US aid.

The composition and terms of the assistance did, however change significantly. Technical assistance was terminated in 1962, other grant programs were gradually phased out, and development loans were progressively reduced and finally discontinued in 1968. In 1967 US assistance dropped to a low of $13.1 million reflecting two popular policy tenets — the belief that the US could stay out of the Middle East arms race, and the notion that Israel's economy no longer required large amounts of foreign aid. Both assumptions were soon proved wrong. Another important source of aid to Israel in these difficult formative years was the *Federal Republic of Germany (FRG), motivated on the German side by a sense of moral obligation, but also by the need to gain international respectability. While formally the 1952 *Restitution Agreement represented compensation for Jewish property confiscated by the Third Reich (not reparations), to all intents and purposes it was an aid program.

Under the terms of the agreement Israel received grants totalling $757 million over a 12-year period, 1953–65, almost equal to total US aid (grants and concessional loans) for the same period. In addition, the Israeli economy benefited indirectly from the restitution payments made to thousands of individual *Holocaust survivors. These payments (which, unlike the restitution paid to the State of Israel, continue to the present day) amounted to almost $1 billion in the years 1953–65, thus exceeding government-to-government transfers. Total German transfers from both sources exceeded those of world Jewry for this period.

In the late 1950s and early 1960s the FRG also became an important, though low-profile arms supplier to Israel. The US, still reluctant to enter the arena with direct military aid, encouraged this relationship, at least in its later stages, and in 1964 authorized the sale of US M-48 tanks by West Germany to Israel.

In 1960 the FRG initiated a program of economic assistance to developing countries of which Israel was one of the first beneficiaries. The assistance, largely in the form of credits on easy terms, has fluctuated since 1962 between 130 and 160 million DM per year.

If foreign governmental assistance to Israel in the early formative years was of crucial importance, its significance has increased manifold in the 1970s and 1980s. Once the euphoria of the

*Six-Day War had been dissipated together with the hopes for a quick settlement, all expectations for a reduction in Israel's dependence, and a phasedown of external aid, evaporated. The major consequence of this situation was that the US abandoned the policy of limiting its role as arms supplier to Israel and what it termed the moderate Arab states. The size of the US aid program to Israel increased almost nine-fold, from $71.1 million in 1970 to $600.8 million in 1971. Since then the level has never declined below $400 million per annum, and in 1979 reached a high of $4.81 billion. Until the *Yom Kippur War the bulk of the assistance was in the form of military credits. Following the war, the growing pace and cost of the arms race together with economic slowdown resulted in demands for increased US economic assistance.

Since 1974, not only has the quantity of US economic aid grown substantially, but its character has gradually changed from food and project-related assistance to generalized support of Israel's chronically negative balance of payments, and from largely loans to exclusively grants. On the military side, similarly, credits have been replaced by grants. The latter and other technical measures were designed to ease Israel's long-term foreign indebtedness and strengthen its position on the international financial markets.

Consequently Israel's economic dependency on the US has grown and had it not been for yearly US injections of between $2–3 billion in recent years, Israel would have faced the threat of financial collapse.

American generosity is based on a unique combination of moral, political and strategic precepts and perceptions: US acceptance of a moral commitment, dating back to the days of President Truman, to the continued existence and welfare of Israel; recognition of Israel's democratic character as a political asset which supports US foreign policy objectives; appreciation of Israel's acceptance and support of US policy goals around the world, and the absence of any overt anti-American feelings in Israel; growing acceptance of Israel as a strategic asset in countering possible Soviet expansionism; recognition that the peace process may be influenced positively by making Israel feel economically and militarily secure, and by signalling to the Arab states that the US is committed to Israel's existence.

Like other factors influencing inter-state relations, these are not static but depend on the general political atmosphere between the two countries, and support by the US Administration, Congress and public opinion.

Domestic conditions in the United States, Arab influence, US- Soviet superpower considerations and irritants such as the *Pollard Affair, could influence US policy in the future. Within Israel there is concern that the heavy dependence on US economic, military and diplomatic aid will limit Israel's freedom of action, and increase US ability to use its leverage, directly or indirectly, to influence Israel's foreign and even domestic policies. It must be pointed out, however, that the US has seldom made full use of its leverage, and that Israel does not coordinate all its policy moves in advance with Washington. (L.L.)

foreign policy Israeli foreign policy since 1948 has been dominated by the continuing *Arab-Israel conflict and by memories of the *Holocaust and the centuries of Jewish persecution which preceded it.

While Israel's main foreign policy goal is to achieve peace with its neighbors, the refusal of the Arab states to reach a settlement and their declared intention to weaken and even to destroy the Jewish state, have forced Israel to devote its main efforts to the maintenance of security, and the avoidance of international isolation.

Until 1952 Israel was inclined to avoid conspicuous alignment with either of the major blocs involved in the Great Power rivalry. However, due to the increasingly pro-Arab policy of the *Soviet Union, Israel grew progressively closer to the western countries whose values it shared and which provided it with crucial military and economic aid. Despite the growing ties with the western countries, Israel's formal accession to the Atlantic Alliance or the *European Economic Community (EEC) never became a practical proposition.

Until the *Six-Day War Israel's main allies in the military sphere were in Western Europe. The *Sinai Campaign was fought in alliance with *Great Britain and *France. In the years 1955–67 France was Israel's primary source of arms, while West Germany was an additional important source in the years 1959–65 (See: *Arms Purchases).

Though the *US refused direct arms sales to

Israel in the first decade of the state's existence, it offered Israel vital backing in the diplomatic and economic spheres. It was the US which was instrumental in getting the 1947 UN partition resolution through the General Assembly, initiated the recognition of Israel in May 1948 and sponsored Israel's admission into the UN in 1949. Thus, the movement for Israel's legitimization in the international community was largely inspired and pioneered by the US.

Furthermore, the US has been the main and crucial supporter of the Israeli economy since 1950–51, helping Israel avert economic destruction throughout the 1950s when mass immigration might have made it impossible for Israel to provide essential services for its population.

After 1967, when France, under President Charles de Gaulle, ceased its arms supplies to Israel, and especially during and after the *Yom Kippur War the US became Israel's main supplier of arms, as well as of diplomatic support and economic aid. The intimacy of the American-Israeli relationship is quite remarkable. Economic aid has become prodigious, while military aid runs into billions, and the US frequently uses its veto power in the Security Council to defend Israel's legitimacy.

However, Israel does not always confide in the US before taking major foreign policy or military decisions and US support of Israel is not automatic. The American-Israel Public Affairs Committee (*Aipac*) as well as various Jewish organizations are constantly on the alert in Washington. Western Europe continues to be Israel's main trading partner, and bilateral relations with most West European states are friendly, though since the *Six-Day War Europe has been less supportive of Israel due primarily to the rising economic power of the Arab oil-producing countries, and the growing European criticism of Israel's response to the Palestine problem.

As a parliamentary democracy Israel feels great affinity with other democratic states. However, throughout its existence Israel has tried to develop formal relations with all states irrespective of their social regimes and ideologies. At the outbreak of the Six-Day War Israel had diplomatic relations with over 90 states — including those of the East bloc (excluding the German Democratic Republic) and most of the non-Moslem Third World states.

With the outbreak of the Six-Day War all the East European countries, except Romania, broke off diplomatic relations with Israel. It was only in the mid-1980s that first steps were taken toward the renewal of these relations. Israel had invested special efforts in the late 1950s and 1960s in nurturing close relations with the newly independent Black African states and the newly independent states in Southeast Asia, such as Burma, Thailand, Cambodia and Singapore, granting them economic, technical and occasionally military aid. However, in the course and aftermath of the Yom Kippur War the African states broke their diplomatic relations with Israel because its forces had entered Egyptian territory to repel the Egyptian attack. Fear of the Arab oil embargo also contributed to the tendency of Third World states to constitute an automatic anti-Israel voting bloc in the UN and other international organizations. Informally, however, relations have been maintained with some of these states, usually on an economic and technical basis. Since the early 1980s several African states have resumed diplomatic relations with Israel, partially as a result of their disillusionment with Arab promises of aid.

Even though Israel's de facto existence has been recognized by most non-Moslem states, very few have recognized *Jerusalem as Israel's capital, and of those who have diplomatic relations with it, only a handful established embassies in West Jerusalem. This policy preceded the Six-Day War when Israel reunited the city, and is connected with the UN decision in November 1947 to internationalize the city. Most of the states which did keep their embassies in Jerusalem, including most of the Latin American countries and the Netherlands, moved them to Tel Aviv after Israel passed the *Basic Law: Jerusalem, in 1981. Israel has tried to convince the US to move its embassy to Jerusalem, but so far to no avail. Despite the almost total lack of international support, Israel refuses to consider the repartitioning of Jerusalem. The most it is willing to concede is that there should be a special status for the Moslem and Christian holy places. In the meantime, all countries conduct their business with Israel de facto by contacts with government and parliamentary agencies in Jerusalem.

Israel's attitude toward the UN, which had sanctioned Israel's emergence to statehood, has grown increasingly cool over the years, both as a result of disappointing experiences with various UN peace-keeping forces, and because as the membership of the organization grew its voting system came under almost total control by the Arab and Moslem states. The General Assembly and UN agencies have adopted unbalanced anti-Israel resolutions, the most virulent of which was the resolution of November 10, 1975, equating *Zionism with racism (See: *Anti-Zionism). The latter resolution put the seal on the general Israeli feeling that the UN was not an arena in which Israeli diplomacy had any hope of success.

Israel's declared aim has been and remains the advancement of a permanent peace settlement with its neighbors, but for years this appeared to be a unilateral Israeli dream since after the assassination of King Abdullah of *Jordan there was no Arab leader willing to openly recognize Israel's sovereingty.

Anwar Sadat's visit to Jerusalem in November 1977, which was the culmination of a process which began with the 1973 *Geneva Peace Conference, followed by the 1974 *Disengagement Agreements and the 1975 *Interim Agreement, marked a clear breakthrough. However, Sadat's assassination on October 6, 1981, disappointment with the cold peace with Egypt, and the absence of simultaneous progress on other fronts, have discouraged hopes of further breakthroughs. While the *Israel Labor Party and the *Alignment have been willing, since the late 1960s, to make *territorial compromises on all fronts in return for a true peace (See: *Allon Plan), the **Herut* Movement, *Gaḥal and later the **Likud* though willing to accept total withdrawal from the *Sinai have been unwilling to give up any part of Judea, Samaria and the *Gaza Strip. Despite this difference, both major political blocs condition peace on effective security arrangements for Israel, neither is willing to accept the establishment of an additional Arab state between Israel and Jordan and both believe that there should be only two states in the territory of *Mandatory Palestine on both sides of the Jordan River. However, while the *Likud* believes that the border between these two states should run along the Jordan River and argues that *"Jordan is Palestine," the Alignment is willing to include most of the *West Bank and Gaza Strip in a Jordanian-Palestinian state. Israel does not believe that there is any substitute for its own force of deterrence, and is suspicious of proposals that its independent power be replaced by international guarantees. As a result of Jewish history and Israel's experience as a soveriegn state, it has based its *defense policy on the "worst case assumption," and has been much more aware of dangers than of opportunities.

Within the *National Unity Government, formed in September 1984, differences of opinion exist on the issue of peace negotiations within the framework of an international conference, though there is a consensus that no official representatives of the *Palestine Liberation Organization should participate in such negotiations. This rejection is based on the PLO refusal to accept the basic rules of the international community, to abstain from terrorism or to articulate its recognition of Israel's right to exist. Israel's policy vis-à-vis the PLO has been to try and prevent its recognition by states friendly to Israel and to strike at those responsible for planning and carrying out acts of terror against Israelis and Jews in Israel and abroad.

Major Israeli diplomatic efforts are also invested in trying to stop arms sales to the Arab confrontation states, and in trying to prevent friendly states from tacitly supporting the implementation of the *Arab boycott in their territories. On the commercial level Israel's foreign policy is actively engaged in promoting Israel's trade abroad, including *arms sales. The range and scope of Israel's trade patterns, as well as its volume indicates that the Arab effort to isolate Israel economically has been unsuccessful.

An important part of Israel's relations with other countries is through world Jewry. However, these relations are only partially in the domain of the Ministry for Foreign Affairs, and are primarily the concern of the *World Zionist Organization and the *Jewish Agency. Concern for the welfare of Jewish communities abroad, especially communities in distress, such as Soviet Jewry, the Jews of *Iran the *Ethiopian Jews and the Jews of *Syria, have dictated Israeli policy moves to try to get these Jews out of the said countries, or to persuade governments to prevent the persecution of Jews in their respective countries. (A.E.)

France and Israel France's interest in the Middle East, an interest related to its status as "the senior daughter of the Church," as a "Muslim power" ruling over a major Muslim population in North Africa, and as a Great Power competing with other great powers for influence and control, goes back for many centuries.

France's special interest in the Middle East was recognized in the aftermath of World War I when it was granted mandates over Syria and Lebanon. As a mandatory power it remained in the Middle East until right after World War II.

France's attitude towards *Zionism shifted from indifference and skepticism regarding its political viability at the beginning of the movement's existence, to a growing hostility after 1904. Nevertheless, several declarations of sympathy for Zionism were elicited from French officials in the course of World War I, and after World War II France granted the Zionists discrete though effective support in the organization of immigration (mostly "illegal") to Palestine, the provision of arms (See for example: **Altalena*) and the setting up of training camps.

Though France voted in favor of the UN Partition Plan of November, 1947, it played an active role in the inclusion of a special provision regarding the internationalization of *Jerusalem in this plan. France also failed to support Israel's first abortive attempt to gain admission as a member of the *UN in November 1948, and granted it de facto recognition only in January 1949 (de jure recognition was granted in May 1949). However, it was the French chairman of the UN Trusteeship Council who in 1950 proposed that the division of Jerusalem between Israel and *Jordan be internationally recognized and that only the Wailing (Western) Wall and the Christian *Holy Places be internationlized.

In November 1950, following the *Tripartite Declaration by which the *United States, *Great Britain and France expressed their decision to strengthen the status quo, and to stabilize the situation in the Near East by strictly limiting arms sales to the states in the region, a trade agreement was first signed between France and Israel.

France was one of the initiators of the Security Council resolution of September 1, 1951, which stated that neither party to the *Arab-Israel conflict could reasonably assert that it was actively a belligerent, and called upon *Egypt "to terminate the restrictions on the passage of international commercial shipping through the Suez canal."

In subsequent years a gradual rapprochment took place between the two states, resulting primarily from the efforts of Shimon *Peres, then Director-General of the Ministry of Defense, and the French ambassador to Israel, Pierre Gilbert. By the end of 1954, several arms procurement agreements were signed between France and Israel, involving aircraft (Nord Atlas and Mystère II), tanks (AMX13) and artillery (155-mm guns), and an agreement for technical cooperation in the nuclear field, which paved the way for a further agreement in 1955, enabling France to make use of an Israel-developed process for the production of heavy water.

The outbreak of the revolt against French rule in Algeria in November 1954, the cumulative evidence of Egypt's active involvement and support for it, and its direct confrontation with France over the nationalization of the *Suez Canal strengthened the rapprochment between France and Israel into a de facto alliance.

In 1956 France became Israel's main source of arms and military equipment, including heavy tanks and Mystère IV jet fighters, a position it was to maintain until the *Six-Day War.

After its users had failed to prevent Egyptian President Gamal Abdel Nasser's nationalization of the Suez Canal, the French leadership started considering military action to regain control, and in August 1956 approached Israel with a plan for action. Israel's initial agreement in principle was, however, jeopardized by Britain's demand that it launch a general war against Egypt, which would then justify a Franco-British intervention to protect the freedom of international navigation and save Egypt. Nevertheless, on October 24, 1956, two agreements were concluded. One, between France, Britain and Israel, described the precise scenario of Israel's strike against the Egyptian forces in the Sinai, followed by an Anglo-French ultimatum to Egypt and Israel to withdraw their forces from the canal zone. The second agreement included a French promise of naval and air protection for Israel's cities in the event of an Egyptian air strike.

The political failure of the *Sinai Campaign and the Suez War did not disturb the close relationship that developed between the two countries in the military, economic and cultural spheres. In 1957 France started to help Israel construct a nuclear reactor at Dimona in the Negev

(See: *Nuclear Policy), and despite its own financial difficulties granted Israel a $45 million loan. A cultural agreement signed in 1959 resulted in the encouragement of the teaching of French as a third language (after Hebrew and English) in Israeli schools, and the establishment of chairs for Hebrew in several French universities.

De Gaulle's assumption of power in 1958, and his subsequent efforts to extricate France from Algeria, caused concern among the Israeli leadership. And indeed, after 1959, relations between the two countries began to decline. In 1959 Renault, a national corporation, submitted to the *Arab boycott and cancelled a major contract with an Israeli car manufacturer.

*Ben Gurion's official visit to France and warm reception by de Gaulle in June, 1960, temporarily dispelled Israeli apprehensions. However, in a meeting between the two leaders the following year de Gaulle seemed reserved and stiff, expressing reservations regarding Israeli arms sales to Africa. He nevertheless toasted Israel as "our friend, our ally."

The major change in French policy toward Israel started after Algeria gained independence in 1962, and de Gaulle embarked on a new independent global policy. He now sought a more balanced policy vis-à-vis Israel and the Arab world. Nevertheless, Israel continued to receive French arms and France granted it political support on such issues as the formalization of its relations with the *European Economic Community, and the diversion of water from the *Jordan River for its national water carrier, a project opposed by the Arab states, especially *Syria.

At the same time France reestablished diplomatic relations with all of the Arab states, began showing greater sympathy for their grievances against Israel, and became increasingly more critical of Israel at the United Nations. In this period Ben Gurion was greatly disturbed by the prospects of a federation being established by Egypt, Syria and Iraq, and asked the Great Powers to issue a joint declaration regarding the territorial integrity and the security of all the states of the Middle East. To de Gaulle Ben Gurion proposed that a formal military alliance be signed between Israel and France. However, de Gaulle turned the proposal down in 1963, arguing that the existing relationship between the two countries (and their military establishments) was sufficient.

During a private visit to France by Prime Minister Levi *Eshkol at the end of June 1964, de Gaulle again referred to Israel as France's "friend and ally," and some new projects of cooperation in the field of oceanography and arid-zone research were considered, but the gradual deterioration in the relations between the two countries continued.

At the beginning of the crisis which preceded the *Six-Day War de Gaulle made his position clear to Israel's Minister for Foreign Affairs Abba *Eban. Eban was made to understand that de Gaulle refused to accept Israel's position that Egypt's obstruction of the free passage of Israeli or Israel-bound ships in the Gulf of Aqaba could be a cause for Israel to exercise its right of self-defense under article 51 of the UN Charter. Neither was de Gaulle willing to join any international initiative to ensure Israel's freedom of passage. He strongly urged Israel not to resort to force: "...if Israel is attacked, we shall not allow her to be destroyed — but if you attack we shall denounce your initiative," he said. He had no doubt that Israel was militarily stronger than the Arabs, and was concerned about the increased international tensions which a new Middle East war would create. De Gaulle hoped to use his good relations with both Israel and the Arab states to play a central role in defusing the crisis, and to set in motion a process which would lead to some Great Power decision regarding the resolution of the various problems of the Arab-Israel conflict.

On June 3, 1967 France announced its embargo on arms shipments to all states in the Middle East. Since most of France's arms sales to the Middle East were to Israel and France was Israel's main source of arms, the embargo was effectively an embargo on Israel, and increased Israel's sense of isolation.

The outcome of the Six-Day War thwarted all of de Gaulle's hopes regarding a prominent role for France in the Middle East, and subsequently he started to view Israel as a rising regional power whose wings it was in France's interest to clip. De Gaulle's growing opposition to Israel's policies was best manifested in his famous press conference of November 27, 1967, at which he called the Jews "...an elite people, self-assured and domineering," and claimed that after doubling its population by the absorption of new elements it was now bent on expansion. "That," de Gaulle explained, "is why the Fifth Republic disengaged itself from the special and very close bonds that the previous regime had forged [with Israel]."

Under President Georges Pompidou France gave up its self- proclaimed neutrality, associating itself increasingly with the Arab point of view. France also managed to exert great influence on the EEC's Middle East policy though due to the neutralizing effect of states like *West Germany the EEC policy remained more balanced than that of France.

After the Six-Day War the general arms embargo was changed into a selective one affecting primarily the delivery of 50 Mirage V jet fighters which had been adapted to Israel's special requirements, and for which Israel had paid in full. However, following Israel's raid on Beirut airport on December 29, 1968, in response to a Palestinian terrorist attack on an El Al plane in Athens, France reintroducted a total embargo on arms deliveries to Israel.

It was against this background that on December 24, 1969, Israel smuggled out of Cherbourg five gunboats built and paid for by Israel. Several days later the French Government officially announced its decision to sell 110 Mirage jet fighters to the new officers' regime in Libya.

The murder of 11 Israeli athletes during the 1972 Olympic games in Munich was condemned by President Pompidou. However, he added that "Palestinian terrorism will not be suppressed unless there is a political solution to the Palestinian problem, which is fundamentally a human problem."

Following the outbreak of the *Yom Kippur War French Foreign Minister Michel Jobert was reluctant to define the war launched by Egypt and Syria against Israel on October 6, 1973, as an act of aggression — since they were merely trying to obtain the return of their own territories. Furthermore, in 1973 more than 70 percent of France's energy consumption was from oil, and most of this came from Arab oil-producing states. Thus, France's reaction to the energy crisis and Arab political pressure, besides a rush to conclude bilateral agreements with individual Arab oil producers, was to influence the EEC nine to issue, on November 6, a conciliatory joint declaration on the conflict — the first, though not the last of its kind.

In contrast to the United States' efforts to organize the oil users and to confront the oil producers, France turned to the United Nations, asking for the convening of a world conference on energy, and was instrumental in initiating a dialogue between Europe and the Arab countries in 1974.

Its dependence on Arab oil, and its hopes to win new markets in the Arab oil-producing countries were responsible for the intensification of the pro-Arab French policy. In 1975 the *Palestine Liberation Organization (PLO) was authorized to open an official representation in Paris, and the following year France refused to extradite PLO leader Abu Daud to Israel for his part in the Munich massacre. In 1976 the government virtually neutralized anti-boycott legislation passed by the National Assembly.

French reservations regarding the peace process initiated by President Anwar Sadat's visit to Jerusalem in November 1977, and the *Camp David Accords in 1978 were to a large extent responsible for the reserved reaction of the EEC. In 1980, again largely due to French efforts, the EEC issued the Venice Declaration, which besides speaking of the Palestinian right to self-determination also called for PLO participation in the negotiations for peace.

Under the presidency of François Mitterand French policy toward Israel has undergone a notable change, although some observers argue that much of the change is in style and tone rather than in essence. Mitterand, who had visited Israel several times in his capacity as a socialist leader, paid a state visit to Israel in March 1982. Not only was this the first official visit to Israel of a French Head of State, but it officially took place in Jerusalem, despite the vigorous opposition of the Quai d'Orsay. During this visit Mitterand addressed the *Knesset, saluting the extraordinary history of "the noble and proud Jewish people."

France's policy regarding the Arab-Israel conflict has changed in two respects: firstly, while France still advocates the right of the Palestinian people to self-determination Mitterand hinted that this right might be realized within the framework of a Jordanian-Palestinian state; secondly, Mitterand expressed approval for the Camp David Accords and for the principle of direct negotiations between Israel and its neighbors. In addition he seemed to rule out the PLO as a partner in such negotiations as long as it refuses to recognize Israel's right to exist.

The *Lebanese War slowed down the rapprochement, and France, which until the middle of 1986 held forces in Lebanon within the framework of UNIFIL, expressed its objection to Israel's activities in Lebanon, including its treatment of the PLO. However, since 1983 relations have improved.

In the economic sphere, there has been a steady and substantial expansion (20–25 percent per annum) of the trade between the two countries. In June 1983, an agreement was signed to promote and protect mutual investments — and this despite the Arab boycott which blacklists foreign companies which invest in Israel. France also played an active role in the approval of a new financial protocol between Israel and the EEC, after negotiations had been suspended during the Lebanese War.

Scientific and technological exchanges have also increased impressively, after many years of stagnation. In 1983 about one- third of all the foreign scientists visiting Israel came from France. In April 1984 the Association Franco-Israelienne pour la Recherche Scientifique et Technologique was set up to promote joint scientific and technological research and development ventures.

On the cultural level the first Alliance Française institution to be opened in Israel was inaugurated in Jerusalem in January 1986. (Y.M.)

Free Center Rightist party led by Shmuel *Tamir during the years 1967–76. Hebrew name: *Hamerkaz Haḥofshi*. The background to the establishment of the party was the attempt by a group of members of the **Ḥerut* Movement during its 8th Conference in June 1966 to bring about changes in the organizational and administrative system of the party. Menaḥem *Begin viewed this effort as a rebellion against himself and the team around him, and reacted by launching an attack against the "rebels." The debate turned into a struggle over the democratic character of the party that ended with Tamir and his colleages being ousted from the *Ḥerut* Movement. They subsequently set up the Free Center. Two additional *Ḥerut* MKs joined Tamir, Eliezer Shostak and Avraham Ti'ar, as well as some of *Ḥerut*'s young guard, leaders of the National Workers Federation (**Histadrut Ha'ovdim Hale'umiyim*), the Blue-White (*Ḥerut*) **Histadrut* faction (*Tchelet Lavan*), and some ex-senior commanders from the *IZL, students and representatives of the development towns.

Following the *Six-Day War the Free Center called for a policy which would enable massive Jewish civilian settlement in Judea, Samaria and the *Gaza Strip, the application of Israeli law in these territories, the rehabilitation of the Arab *refugees who remained in the territories under Israeli control, and the taking of steps toward true coexistence with the Arab population as a bridgehead to peace in the region.

In the economic sphere the Free Center supported free enterprise, cutting down the public bureaucracies and making them more efficient, the prevention of economic centralization, the cancellation of foreign exchange controls, the encouragement of rental housing, the separation of the trade unions from the productive sector of the *Histadrut*, obligatory arbitration in vital services, national health insurance, etc. The Free Center also called for major changes in the system of government, and *electoral reform.

In the elections to the 7th Knesset (1969) the Free Center gained two seats. While serving in the Knesset it concentrated on uncovering corruption in the public sector, initiating the extension of the municipal area of *Jerusalem, initiatives for peace with *Lebanon, and a just solution for the Arab inhabitants of Bir'am and Iqrit who had been expelled from their villages during the *War of Independence.

In the elections for the 8th Knesset the Free Center joined in the initiative to establish the **Likud* with **Gaḥal* and the *State List. However, in 1975 there was a split within the Free Center, when Tamir, who supported the idea of an Arab- Israeli settlement based on compromise, left the *Likud*, and together with Akiva Nof left the Knesset in January 1977. The leaders of the National Workers Federation, under Eliezer Shostak, decided to remain in the *Likud* within the framework of a new faction **Hamerkaz Ha'atzma'i* (Independent Center). The members of the Free Center joined the *Democratic Movement for Change when it was established in 1976.

Knesset seats: 7th Knesset (1969) — 2; 8th Knesset (1973) — 4, within the *Likud*.

functional compromise A concept regarding the political future of the *West Bank and *Gaza Strip which advocates an Israeli-Jordanian condominium in the territories.

It envisages a situation in which Israel is in physical control of the territories, and in charge of security, land and water resources and Jewish settlement, while *Jordan supervises the actual administration of the Arab population, and the provision of services to them.

The common Israeli-Jordanian interest in such an arrangement is to reverse the trend of growing support for Palestinian separatism, and to reduce the power and influence of the *Palestine Liberation Organization (PLO) in the *occupied territories.

The Israeli-Jordanian secret collaboration on the territories since the breach between King Hussein and PLO Chairman Yasser Arafat — as manifested by the appointment of Arab Mayors in Ramallah, Hebron and el-Bireh, and the opening of a branch of the Jordanian Cairo-Amman Bank in the autumn of 1986 — is viewed as falling within this concept.

G

Gaḥal (political bloc) Acronym for *Gush Ḥerut-Liberalim* (*Ḥerut*-Liberal Bloc), a parliamentary bloc which existed from 1965–73, made up of the two main non-socialist parties, the *Ḥerut* Movement and the *Liberal Party. First proposed by Menaḥem *Begin in 1955, the *Gaḥal* agreement was signed just before the 1965 elections to the 6th Knesset.

Under the agreement the two political organizations would continue to exist separately but would run jointly for the Knesset and would together direct a united opposition to the **Mapai*-led government. In the beginning of 1967 three MKs, led by Shmuel *Tamir, broke off from *Gaḥal* to form the *Free Center which rejoined *Ḥerut* and the Liberals when the **Likud* was formed in 1973.

Gaḥal was coopted into the *National Unity Government formed on the eve of the *Six-Day War, with Menaḥem Begin and Yosef Sapir (Liberal) becoming Ministers without Portfolio. After the 1969 elections to the 7th Knesset *Gaḥal* received six ministerial posts.

In August 1970, following the government's adoption in principle of the *Rogers Plan, which called for a withdrawal from territories occupied by Israel in 1967 *Gaḥal* resigned from the coalition and once again became the major opposition group.

Gaḥal was seen as a major development in the legitimization of the *Ḥerut* Movement and its entrance into the mainstream of Israeli politics. *Ḥerut*'s strident nationalism was somewhat muted and the Liberal economic program provided the bloc with a broader base of appeal to larger sections of Israel's populace. In 1973 *Gaḥal* was replaced by the **Likud*.

Knesset seats: 6th Knesset (1965) — 26; 7th Knesset (1969) — 26. (I.M.)

Gaḥal (volunteer fighters) Acronym for *Giyus Ḥutz-La'aretz* (mobilization abroad), the Hebrew name given to immigrant volunteers, mostly survivors of the *Holocaust who had been interned in Cyprus by the British or gone through Displaced Persons camps in Europe and who came to Israel to fight in the *War of Independence. Unlike the members of **Maḥal*, most of the members of *Gaḥal* remained in Israel after the war.

Galili document Drafted by Israel *Galili and approved by the secretariat of the *Israel Labor Party on September 3, 1973, the document dealt with the government's proposed policy in the *occupied territories (the *Sinai peninsula, the *West Bank and *Gaza) for four years, until 1977.

The document called for the development of the economy, infrastructure and social services for the Arabs in the territories; the development of economic ties between Israel and the territories; encouragement of local government and a rejuvenation of the municipal representation in the territories (in 1976 free elections were held for the first time in the West Bank and Gaza returning several of the elected mayors identified with the *Palestine Liberation Organization); the continuation of the *"open bridges" policy with Jordan; control over the employment of Arabs from the territories in Israel, under terms of equal pay and working conditions; the permanent resettlement of refugees in the Gaza Strip; the encouragement of Jewish settlement and the development of rural and urban settlements in the *Rafa Salient, the Jordan Valley Rift (See: *Jordan River) and the *Golan Heights; the continued development of Jerusalem and its environs and the increase of its Jewish population; the examination of the possibility of constructing a deep-water port south of Gaza for the development of the Rafa Salient; the development of an industrial center for Kfar Saba across the *Green Line and the development of Israeli industry in the region of Kalkilya and Tulkarem; the concentration of most land purchases in the territories in the hands of the Israel Land Administration but also permitting private land purchases where necessary, as long as the land was purchased for constructive enterprises within the framework of the government's policy and not for speculative purposes.

The main purpose of the document was to pacify some members of the Labor Party, especially Moshe *Dayan, before the 1973 general elections, while remaining more or less within the framework of the *Allon Plan. However, the document was seriously criticized in the *Alignment by *Mapam*.

Galili (formerly Berczenko), **Israel** (1911--1986) Military and political leader. Galili was born in Russia and immigrated to Palestine in 1914. He was a founder of **Hano'ar Ha'oved Vehalomed* youth movement and of Kibbutz Na'an, of which he remained a member until his death. He was one of the leaders of the **Haganah* prior to the establishment of the State. After the split of **Mapai* in 1944 Galili was one of the leaders of **Aḥdut Ha'avodah — Po'alei Zion*, and when that party joined **Mifleget Po'alim-Hashomer Hatza'ir* in 1948 to form **Mapam* he was one of its leading figures. When *Mapam* split from the party in 1954 Galili became Secretary-General of *Aḥdut Ha'avodah-Po'alei Zion*.

Galili was a member of Knesset from 1949–77. He was not a candidate for the 9th Knesset (1977) because he did not obtain the required support of 60 percent of the *Israel Labor Party Central Committee.

In 1966 Galili joined the Cabinet as Minister without Portfolio, and was generally considered to be one of the personalities determining Israel's foreign and defense policies, especially in the government of Golda *Meir where he was the *éminence grise* throughout her leadership. He remained Minister without Portfolio until 1977. In the summer of 1973, before the elections to the 8th Knesset, Galili drafted a proposal for Labor Party policy in the *West Bank and the *Gaza Strip (See: *Galili Document) which was adopted as the party's official policy. The document was viewed as an attempt to pacify the maximalists in the party.

After 1977 Galili was one of the "Party Elders", frequently being consulted on questions of policy and tactics. He encouraged Yigal *Allon to contest the party leadership in 1980.

Gaza Strip Region surrounding and including the town of Gaza along the Mediterranean coast in the south of the territory of *Mandatory Palestine. No administrative unit by this name existed before the *War of Independence when the area was occupied by Egyptian troops. The region is 40 kilometers (25 miles) long and 6.5–14.5 kilometers (4–9miles) wide, with an area of 350 square kilometers (135 square miles). In 1948 the population of the Gaza Strip was about 70,000, but due to the influx of refugees after the war, it grew considerably. In 1967, when the region was occupied by Israel in the course of the *Six-Day War the population was over 360,000 and in the mid-1980s it rose to over 500,000 of whom over 60 percent are refugees and their descendants.

The main town in the region is Gaza, an ancient settlement, named in the Old Testament as one of the five cities of the Philistines, and the site of Samson's death. Under the British Mandate it was a district capital and the largest exclusively Arab town in Palestine, with a population which was mostly Muslim. There was also a small Christian-Arab community in Gaza. A medieval Jewish community which had declined in the 18th century and was revived in 1882 had departed after the 1929 disturbances. In 1948 the population of the town of Gaza numbered 40,000; after the *War of Independence it grew to over 100,000 through the influx of refugees. By the mid-eighties the population had risen to 130–140,000.

From 1948 to 1967, when the region was under Egyptian occupation, a large proportion of the population was unemployed and dependent on the rations distributed by the United Nations Relief and Welfare Association (UNRWA).

Since 1967 about 50% of the labor force of the Gaza Strip has found employment in Israel, and material conditions have much improved. However, a large part of the population still lives in refugee camps and social conditions are far from satisfactory.

The 1949 Israel-Egypt Armistice Agreement confirmed Egypt's occupation of the region which had taken place in the course of the war. Egypt though claiming special responsibility for the Gaza Strip never annexed it or claimed it as part of its territory. In September 1948 Egypt permitted an attempt to form a "Palestine government" in Gaza which claimed authority in the whole of Palestine — but it failed to gain overall Palestinian support. Its formal dissolution was declared by the Arab League in 1952 (See: *Palestinians). However, even while it existed the "Palestine government" had no governance authorities in the Gaza Strip itself which was administered by a military governor appointed by the Egyptian minister of war. Only in 1958 was a local executive council appointed, made up of local notables, and a legislative council partially elected by indirect elections. In fact, the new institutions did very little.

Prior to the 1956 *Sinai Campaign the Gaza Strip served as a base for raids into Israel by Palestinian saboteurs (See: **Feda'iyin*) whom Israel believed to have been aided and even dispatched by the Egyptians. Israel retaliated by carrying out counter raids, including the brutal February 1955 raid on Gaza later cited by President Gamal Abdel Nasser as proving that no peace settlement with Israel was possible. These *feda'iyin* incursions from the Gaza Strip were one of the main factors leading to the 1956 Sinai Campaign, in the course of which Israel occupied the region. Early in 1957 Israel was compelled to withdraw and the Gaza Strip reverted to Egyptian military administration. Despite the establishment of the UN Emergency Force (UNEF) which was stationed in the region saboteurs' attacks continued. Just before the *Six-Day War Nasser concentrated large Egyptian forces along the border with Israel and requested the withdrawal of UNEF. In the first stages of the war Israel once again occupied the Gaza Strip, and this time retained control. Egypt did not demand its return in the peace treaty with Israel.

Since 1967 Israel has administered the Gaza Strip through a military governor, aided by a civil administrator. In the first years of the Israeli occupation the Gaza Strip was a center of sabotage and terrorist activity by the various branches of the *Palestine Liberation Organization (PLO), some of it directed against the Palestinians themselves. By 1972, Israel had suppressed these activities, primarily through the policy of Ariel *Sharon who headed the Southern Command in this period. Simultaneously, Israel attempted to deal with the social unrest in the Gaza Strip by thinning out the overcrowded refugee camps and re-housing some of their inhabitants. This was resisted by some of the refugees who feared that through resettlement they would lose their claim to their old homes in the territory of Israel.

Since 1967 Israel has constructed 11 Jewish settlements in the Gaza Strip. While municipal elections were held in the West Bank under Jordanian law, in 1976, no such elections have been held in the Gaza Strip. The mayor of Gaza was dismissed in January 1971, due to his uncooperative policy. His replacement, Rashad el-Shawa, a local notable, was dismissed for the same reason in October 1972, reappointed in 1975 and dismissed again in 1982.

While economic conditions in the Gaza Strip have improved through the employment of many of its inhabitants in Israel, economic development in the area is hindered by restrictions imposed by the military government and the limited outlet for Gaza-made products which do not have the same free access into Jordan that products manufactured in the West Bank have.

While supporters of "Greater Israel" refuse to consider the return of the Gaza Strip to Arab sovereignty, those who favor *territorial compromise envision the inclusion of at least part of the region in the Jordanian-Palestinian state to which Israel would be willing to concede territories in return for peace (See: *Jordanian Option, *Allon Plan), with connections to it by means of a highway. Those who advocate the "*Third State" option argue that the whole of the Gaza Strip, like the whole of the West Bank should constitute this state. After the *Camp David Accords were concluded Egypt informally suggested that the autonomy arrangement be first applied to the Gaza Strip.

General Zionists Zionist Party. The name

which was first given to non-socialist, non-religious, non-partisan Zionist groups which got together in 1929 during the Zionist Congress in Zurich, following which the World Association of General Zionists was established. In 1931 the association became a party with a fixed platform and apparatus called the World Alliance of General Zionists, the main principles of which were: preference for Zionist rather than party, religious or social interests; development of private initiative in settlement and trade in *Eretz Yisrael* and care for the interests of the middle class; international control over **Heḥalutz* and *Hachshara* (training for settlement). Before long the General Zionists split into two groups — the General Zionist Association (Faction A) headed by Chaim *Weizmann, which was closer to the labor movement and the General Zionist Alliance (Faction B) headed by Menaḥem Ussishkin, which was more right wing.

The first major confrontation between them was in 1931 when Faction B voted against Weizmann's candidacy as Chairman of the Zionist Congress. In 1935 it demanded that a separate workers' organization be established outside the **Histadrut*. As a result Faction A broke off and established a faction within the *Histadrut* called *Ha'oved Hatzioni* (the Zionist worker). The factions reunited in the early 1940s under the leadership of Moshe *Sneh, but only temporarily. A new controversy broke out when Faction B proposed to accept *Ha'iḥud Ha'ezraḥi* (the civil union — an organization of private employers) as members, to which Faction A objected. In 1948 Faction A together with *Ha'oved Hatzioni* and **Aliyah Hadashah* set up the *Progressive Party while Faction B united with *Ha'iḥud Ha'ezraḥi* to establish the Federation of General Zionists — the Center Party. This party's platform included: the development of a welfare state and the construction of a society based on personal freedom and social justice; the right of every person to an appropriate standard of living; the ensuring of the liberal-democratic character of the regime; the enactment of a constitution; increasing the civil control over election campaigns; electoral reform; a state-run education system; releasing the economy from the division into political-economic sections.

Before the elections to the 5th Knesset (1961) he General Zionist Federation reunited with the Progressive Party, setting up the *Liberal Party of Israel, but this union lasted only until 1965 when the ex-General Zionists in the Liberal Party decided to set up a political bloc (**Gaḥal*) with the **Ḥerut* Movement, and the ex-Progressives established the *Independent Liberal Party. As a result of this split the World Conference of General Zionists split as well.

Knesset Seats: 1st Knesset (1949) — 7; 2nd Knesset (1951) — 20; 3rd Knesset (1955) — 13; 4th Knesset (1959) — 8. (D.B.M.)

Geneva Peace Conference UN *Security Council Resolution 338 called for, *inter alia*, negotiations "between the parties concerned under appropriate auspices aimed at establishing a just and durable peace in the Middle East." Subsequently, in December 1973, the *US and the *Soviet Union convened a conference which met in Geneva under the auspices of the UN. *Egypt and *Jordan agreed to participate on condition that other states would be present and they would not have to negotiate directly with Israel. Their official excuse for participating in the conference, the first of its kind in the history of the *Arab- Israel conflict, was that it was a means to obtain Israeli withdrawal from the territories it had occupied in 1967. *Syria refused to participate, while Israel declared that it would not sit with the Syrians unless the latter published lists of Israeli prisoners captured during the *Yom Kippur War and allowed the Red Cross to visit them. The participating Arab states wanted *France and *Great Britain to be present at the negotiating table, but Israel and the Superpowers did not agree. Neither the *Palestine Liberation Organization (PLO) nor any other Palestinian representatives were invited to the opening session, though the participation of Palestinian representatives in later meetings was to have been on the agenda.

The opening session of the Geneva Conference took place at the Council Chamber of the Palais des Nations in Geneva on December 21, 1973. The Secretary-General of the UN, Kurt Waldheim, took the chair with the Foreign Ministers of the two Superpowers acting as co-chairmen. Due to the Arab refusal to sit with Israel at a round table, the participating delegations sat at separate tables arranged as a hexagon, with one table left empty for the Syrian delegation. Under the full blaze of TV cameras and the press, the six participants gave their opening speeches. Following this ceremony, the conference was adjourned until after the *Knesset elections in Israel on December 31. An Egyptian-Israeli military committee began meeting in Geneva on December 26, 1973 to discuss a separation of forces, but final agreement was reached through the diplomatic efforts of Secretary of State Henry Kissinger (See: *Kissinger Shuttle Diplomacy; *Disengagement Agreements).

The Geneva Conference has not reconvened since December 1973 although the Arabs, the Soviet Union and various West European countries consider it to be the desired framework for arriving at a comprehensive peace settlement in the Middle East.

Israel has always expressed its preference for bilateral negotiations with the Arab states over international conferences. The subject of the Geneva Conference was raised in the *Memorandum of Understanding signed by the US and Israel in September 1975, wherein the US gave Israel assurances as to the conditions under which the conference might be reconvened. These included that the timing of the reconvention of the conference would be coordinated with Israel; that the PLO would not be a partner as long as it did not recognize Israel and Security Council Resolutions 242 and 338; that the US would consult Israel regarding its positions and strategy regarding the Geneva Conference; that the US would make every effort to ensure that all substantive negotiations at the conference would be on a bilateral basis; that the US would oppose any attempt by the Security Council to adversely change the terms of reference of the conference; and that the US would together with Israel ensure that the conference be conducted with the purpose of advancing "a negotiated peace between Israel and its neighbors."

The conference was not reconvened, and even though the Israeli government under Menaḥem *Begin approved the idea of an international conference in September 1977, the Egyptian-Israeli peace process proceded through different channels. However, the idea of convening an international conference came up again in 1985, at the initiative of King Hussein of Jordan, who viewed it as an umbrella for direct negotiations with Israel. Prime Minister Shimon *Peres expressed Israel's acceptance of the idea during his United Nations appearance in October 1985, and agreed to the participation of authentic non-PLO representatives in the Jordanian delegation to the conference. The idea lost momentum in February 1986 when the breach between King Hussein and PLO chairman Yasser Arafat occurred, and suffered a further reverse after the *rotation in Israel, when **Likud* leader Yitzḥak *Shamir became Prime Minister. The *Likud* objects to the international conference on principle since most of the participants would not be partial to Israel's point of view, and insists on direct negotiations between Israel and its neighbors. The *Alignment, on the other hand believes that the conference is the only way to promote negotiations with Jordan.

Golan Heights Part of the province of Kuneitra and Fiq in Syria, occupied by Israel during the *Six-Day War. A volcanic plateau at the southern foot of Mount Hermon, the Golan Heights contain many archaeological remains of Jewish settlements from the time of the Second Temple until the 4th century AD — including sites of close to 30 synagogues.

The Golan Heights was one of Syria's most economically backward regions. After the *War of Independence the Syrians converted the Heights into a military fortress which commanded the Sea of Galilee, the Ḥuleh Valley and the fertile northern Jordan Valley, and was frequently used for artillery shelling of Israeli settlements and traffic, the Ḥuleh Drainage Project and the National Water Carrier (through which Israel moves water from the *Jordan River to the Negev).

During the Six-Day War the Golan Heights were captured by the *IDF after intense fighting and only 6,000 (mostly *Druze) remained from a population of around 40,000 (mostly of the town of Kuneitra).

During the *Yom Kippur War the Syrians launched a surprise attack on the Golan Heights overruning part of it, but were repulsed during the second stage of the fighting when Israel expanded the territory under its control by some 20 kilometers, to the peak of Mount Hermon in the north.

According to the *disengagement agreement signed between Israel and Syria on May 31, 1974, Israel returned to the Syrians an area which included part of the ghost town of Kuneitra, but retained two of the three strategic hills surrounding the town. Buffer and thinned-out zones were established on both sides of the cease-fire line and a UN Disengagement Observation Force was installed. An exchange of prisoners of war also took place.

On December 14, 1981, the *Knesset passed the Golan Heights Law, proposed by the *Teḥiyah's Ge'ula *Cohen which applied Israeli law, jurisdiction and administration to the area. As a result the US delayed certain arms deliveries to Israel. Unrest developed among the Druze inhabitants of the Golan Heights when Israel issued identity cards to them; divided loyalties among the Druze caused further tension during the 1982 *Lebanese War.

Since 1967 Israel has established 35 rural settlements and one urban center (Katzrin) in the Golan Heights. There is almost complete consensus in Israel that the Golan Heights must never be returned to the Syrians because of its strategic position and the Syrians' use of it before 1967. In international forums there is greater understanding for Israel's position regarding the Golan Heights than its position regarding the *West Bank and the *Gaza Strip.

Goldmann, Nahum (1895–1982) Jewish and Zionist leader. Born in Lithuania, Goldmann moved to Frankfurt-am-Main in 1901. In 1913 he visited Palestine while a student at Heidelberg University. During World War I he was employed in the propaganda section of the German Foreign Ministry, and supported a pro-German Zionist orientation. At the end of the war Goldmann obtained a PhD. He was co-founder of a German-language Zionist periodical in 1921 and four years later was co-founder of a publishing house established to produce the German language *Encyclopaedia Judaica* until 1933. In the early 1920s Goldmann joined *Hapo'el Hatza'ir*, and in 1926 he joined the Zionist radical faction which he represented in the Zionist Actions Committee. As chairman of the political committee of the 17th Zionist Congress in 1931 he helped to remove Chaim *Weizmann from the leadership of the *World Zionist Organization (WZO). The new president, Naḥum Sokolow, invited him to join the Foundation Fund fund-raising campaign in the US. There Goldmann met Stephen Wise, and in 1936 they founded the World Jewish Congress, with Wise as President and Goldmann as Chairman of the executive.

Between 1935–39 Goldmann was in Geneva acting as representative of the *Jewish Agency, as well as of the Comité des Délégations Juives (he had become Chairman in 1933) to the League of Nations. In 1940 he considered settling in Palestine but moved to New York at the request of David *Ben Gurion. He became a member of the Zionist Emergency Committee, and during and after World War II he tried to get the American government to admit more Jews from Europe.

Together with Moshe *Sharett, Goldmann solicited international support for the *partition plan. He was offered a seat in the Provisional Government after the establishment of the state — but declined. Eliezer Kaplan urged him to join *Mapai* but he declined, unable to accept the principle of party discipline. From 1948–56 Goldmann was co-Chairman of the Zionist Organization Executive. He was the chief architect of the *Restitution Agreement signed with Germany in 1952. From 1953–77 he was President of the World Jewish Congress (WJC). He was elected President of the WZO in 1956 and officially settled in Jerusalem in 1962, becoming a citizen in 1964. Though never directly involved in Israeli politics, Goldmann helped the *Liberal Party in its election campaign for the 5th Knesset (1961).

After 1967 Goldmann became increasingly critical of the Israeli government on the peace issue. Goldmann was not reelected President of the WZO in 1968 and subsequently became a Swiss citizen. Golda *Meir, at the time Secretary-General of the newly formed *Israel Labor Party, was one of the main forces in the campaign against his reelection.

In 1969 Goldmann planned to go to Cairo to meet President Gamal Abdel Nasser who was apparently willing to see him, but Prime Minister Golda Meir vetoed the initiative. In 1972 he proposed that "random payments" be made to the Soviet Union to enable Jewish professionals to emigrate — but this was opposed in the Israeli government. Goldmann called on the Carter Administration to "break the pro-Israel lobby" in 1977. *Beit Hatfutzot*, the Museum of the Diaspora, which Goldmann had started to plan in 1970, was inaugurated in 1978, and his name added to its official title in 1979.

In 1979, in an interview to the Hamburg weekly *Die Zeit* Goldmann referred to Israel as "the failure of an historical experiment — a greater disaster than Auschwitz." Later in the year he wrote in *New Outlook* that to survive in the Middle East Israel must be neutralized under international guarantee. He also expressed willingness to meet *Palestine Liberation Organization (PLO) Chairman Yasser Arafat. German Chancellor Helmut Schmidt viewed Goldmann as a personal friend and much to Israel's chagrin valued his opinions on the Middle East. One month before his death Goldmann published an advertisement in Le Monde calling for an Israeli-Palestinian initiative based on mutual recognition between Israel and the PLO.

Gordon, Aharon David (1856–1922) Spiritual leader and philosopher of Labor Zionism, and in particular of **Hapo'el Hatza'ir*. Born in Russia, Gordon received a religious education and studied Russian and secular subjects on his own. He was the financial manager of Baron Guenzburg's estate for 23 years. After the estate was sold Gordon immigrated to Palestine in 1904 where he insisted on doing manual labor in the vineyards and orange groves of Petaḥ Tikva and Rishon Letzion, and later in the Galilee. Toward the end of his life he and his family joined Kibbutz Degania. Gordon idealized physical labor (especially farming), cooperation and mutual aid as the base of the Jewish national revival and as a major means for improving the individual and achieving self-realization. He opposed socialism in its Marxist form, and was not interested in political affairs. Gordon viewed the cosmos as a unity of which man is a part, though he develops his individuality through personal experience. Man has to return to the soil in order to return to the source of his rejuvenation and must base his relations with other men on a higher level than the purely utilitarian. People unite into national communities embodying a living cosmic relationship. He developed the concept of "*Am-Adam*," translated as "people-humanity," meaning people incarnating humanity. The Jews had to recreate themselves as a national people working the soil, but this nation would be an integral part of humanity which, *inter alia*, dictated his approach on Jewish-Arab relations. "Their hostility," he said of the Arabs, "is all the more reason for our humanity."

government Israel is a parliamentary democracy in which the government, which is the executive authority of the state, is subject to the *Knesset's confidence and to its supervision.

Israel's first de facto government was the Provisional Government which took over at midnight on May 14, 1948 from *Minhelet Ha'am* (the People's Executive) established two months earlier to prepare for the takeover of authority within the territory of the Jewish state. The Provisional Government, headed by David *Ben Gurion, was made up of 13 members — four from **Mapai*, two from **Mapam*, two from the *General Zionists, one from the *Sephardi List, three from the religious parties (one each from **Hamizraḥi*, **Hapo'el Hamizraḥi* and **Agudat Yisrael*). Ben Gurion deliberately excluded the *Revisionists and **Maki* from the coalition (See: *"Without *Ḥerut* and *Maki*").

The work procedures of the government were formulated in the following months as the *War of Independence raged.

Following the elections to the Constituent Assembly/First Knesset (1949) the first government of Israel was formed by Ben Gurion on March 8, 1949 (See: *Governments of Israel). By 1986 Israel had 22 governments in the course of 11 Knesset terms.

Following elections, or following the resignation of the government in the middle of a Knesset term when new elections will not be called, the president assigns the task of forming a new government to a Member of Knesset whose chances of doing so are considered best. Customarily, he is the leader of the largest faction in the Knesset. He has 21 days to complete the task and should he fail the president may turn to another Member of Knesset and may repeat the process as many times as necessary to form a government.

Since the government requires the Knesset's confidence to function, it must enjoy the support of at least 61 of its 120 members. So far, no single list which ran for the Knesset has ever received 61 mandates, so that all of Israel's governments have been coalitions.

The coalition is based on an agreement, or contract between the parties making up the government which defines common government policy goals and the principles which are to guide its activities and determines which special requests made by particular members will be accepted by the others (e.g., the right not to vote with the government on certain topics or issues connected with the religious *status quo). The *coalition agreement is not a legally binding document.

Coalition governments in general and that of Israel in particular have several marked weaknesses: because of their heterogeneity they reduce the government's ability to act firmly; decisions are frequently taken on a pragmatic basis rather than on the basis of a plan or program; because of coalition obligations, the number of ministers and deputy ministers is bloated (e.g., in the *National Unity Government there are 25 ministers and six deputy ministers); the power of tiny parties whose support is needed is enhanced far beyond what is warranted.

The government's status, formation, composition and duties are regulated by the Basic Law: the Government (See: *Basic Laws) passed on August 6, 1968. The original legal basis of the government was Article 2 of the 1948 Law and Administration Ordinance, to which additional instructions and regulations were added. The 1949 Transition Law, nicknamed "the Little *Constitution," replaced the 1948 Ordinance and served as the government's legal basis until the 1968 law was passed. Since 1968 the *Attorney General has expressed his opinion on matters relating to the government's authority, limitations and duties.

According to Article 29 of the Basic Law: The Government "the Government is competent to perform in the name of the state, subject to any law, any act the performance of which is not assigned by law to another authority." In other words, under Israeli law the government has absolutely unlimited powers, as long as it is not limited by the Knesset.

The government's regulations and procedures were enacted over the years. Under Article 26 the government itself has full authority in this sphere. Customarily regular government meetings are held on Sundays.

The prime minister is *primus inter pares* (first among equals). In fact the powers bestowed by the law upon the prime minister do not express the full scope of his influence and authority. These are determined, to a large extent, by his personality, his authority, and the specific political circumstances. The prime minister has a say in the appointment of ministers from his own party, but has only limited say with regard to the choice of ministers representing other parties in the coalition. Thus, in the National Unity Government Shimon *Peres had no say in the choice of Ariel *Sharon as Minister of Commerce and Industry who had been vehemently attacked by the *Alignment for his role in the *Lebanese War when he was Minister of Defense on behalf of the *Likud*. The cabinet's agenda and the way its meetings are conducted are largely determined by the prime minister. Frequently, disputes between ministers or ministries are brought to him for mediation. He may dismiss a minister from his cabinet though the political conjuncture may limit this right. The prime minister has a major say in the composition of ministerial committees and appointments to senior government posts. He is in charge of all the branches of the intelligence service, including the **Mossad* and the **Shabak*. The prime minister is the final authority regarding the publication of information concerning the government's work and policy. Finally, he represents the government in national and international events. The state, however, is officially represented by the *President.

During the premierships of David Ben Gurion, Levi *Eshkol (until the eve of the *Six-Day War) and Menaḥem *Begin (following Ezer *Weizmann's resignation from the government), the Prime Minister also held the Defense portfolio, while during the premierships of Moshe *Sharett and Yitzḥak *Shamir (1983–84) the Prime Minister also held the Foreign Affairs portfolio.

The resignation or death of the prime minister leads to the resignation of the whole government.

While the prime minister must be a member of Knesset other ministers need not be. However, members of Knesset who have been appointed as cabinet members may not resign their Knesset seats after their appointment (See: *Norwegian Law). Ministers are usually responsible for ministries, but there can be ministers- without-portfolio and ministers (two) who serve as deputy prime ministers.

The number of ministries and the distribution of functions among them is not fixed by law. Frequently, this distribution is based on political rather than practical considerations. Several different functions may be included in a single ministry in one government, and be distributed among several ministries in another. For example, in the *Likud*-led governments, the ministries of the Interior, Religions and Police were all united in a single ministry under Yosef *Burg of the *National Religious Party (NRP). They were divided once again into three separate ministries in the National Unity Government with Yitzḥak Peretz (**Shass*) in charge of the Ministry of the Interior, Yosef Burg (NRP) in charge of the Ministry of Religions and Ḥaim *Bar Lev (Alignment) in charge of the Ministry of Police.

The government is collectively responsible to the Knesset. This means that the whole government is responsible for the actions of each of its members, and each minister is responsible for the actions of the government as a whole. Following the *Kahan Commission Report on the *Sabra and Shatilla massacre, which placed indirect responsibility for the event on Minister of Defense Ariel Sharon there were calls for the resignation of the whole cabinet under the principle of collective responsibility. The responsibility of each minister for the actions of the government as a whole implies that a minister who is unwilling to support the government on an issue, unless he has been exempted in the coalition agreement from such support, should resign. In fact, the principle of collective responsibility has been greatly eroded, especially in periods in which national unity governments have served.

In the National Unity Government formed in 1984 various ministers took the liberty of openly criticizing or expressing public opposition to various aspects of the government's policy without being called upon to resign. In December 1985 **Agudat Yisrael*, which is a member of the coalition though not in the cabinet, actually proposed a motion of no-confidence in the government and was allowed to remain in the coalition in spite of this.

Another principle which is not upheld by the Israeli government is the secrecy of government deliberations. Leaks to the press are a common phenomenon for which no practical remedy has been found. As a last resort the prime minister may dismiss an offending minister under Article 21A of the Basic Law: the Government.

The government resigns not only upon the resignation or death of the prime minister but also following the election of a new Knesset. However, it continues to serve until a new government is formed. A vote of no-confidence by the Knesset, passed by a majority of the members voting, also results in the government's resignation.

The government is also dependent on the Knesset for the passage of all primary legislation, most of which is of government origin. Nevertheless, subsidiary legislation, unless involving expenditure, may be introduced by the government without Knesset approval. The Knesset plenary supervises the government's work by means of motions for the agenda, questions and reports by the ministers regarding the activities of their ministries. The various Knesset committees may initiate investigations into issues related to the work and responsibility of the ministries within their domain. Clearly, the broader the coalition the less effective the Knesset's supervision of the government (G.Y.)

Governments of Israel

PROVISIONAL GOVERNMENT:
May 14, 1948–March 7, 1949.
Prime Minister: David *Ben Gurion.
Coalition members: **Mapai*, **Mapam*, *General Zionists, **Aliyah Ḥadashah*, **Hamizraḥi* and **Hapo'el Hamizraḥi*, **Agudat Yisrael*. 13 ministers.
Resigned on February 16, 1949, when Chaim *Weizmann was elected President. The President then began consultations for the formation of a new government.

FIRST GOVERNMENT (1ST KNESSET):
March 7, 1949–October 30, 1950.
Prime Minister: David Ben Gurion.
Coalition members: *Mapai*, *United Religious Front, *Progressives, *Sephardim, *Minority Lists. 12 ministers.
The Prime Minister resigned on October 15, 1950, against the background of demands by the United Religious Front regarding education in the new immigrant camps and religious education system.

SECOND GOVERNMENT (1ST KNESSET):
October 30, 1950–October 8, 1951.
Prime Minister: David Ben Gurion.
Coalition members: *Mapai*, United Religious Front, Progressives, Sephardim, Minority Lists 13 ministers.
The government resigned on February 14, 1951

against the background of the Knesset's rejection of proposals by the Minister of Education and Culture regarding the registration of children in schools.

THIRD GOVERNMENT (2ND KNESSET):
October 8, 1951–December 23, 1952.
Prime Minister: David Ben Gurion.
Coalition members: *Mapai*, *Hamizraḥi* and *Hapo'el Hamizraḥi*, *Agudat Yisrael*, **Po'alei Agudat Yisrael*, Minority Lists. 13 ministers.
The government resigned on December 19, 1952, against the background of a controversy with *Hamizraḥi* regarding the intensification of religious education.

FOURTH GOVERNMENT (2ND KNESSET):
December 23, 1952–January 26, 1954.
Prime Minister: David Ben Gurion.
Coalition members: *Mapai*, General Zionists, *Hamizraḥi* and *Hapo'el Hamizraḥi*, Progressives, Minority Lists. 16 ministers.
The Prime Minister resigned December 6, 1953, expressing his wish to settle in Kibbutz Sde Boker.

FIFTH GOVERNMENT (2ND KNESSET):
January 26, 1954–June 29, 1955.
Prime Minister: Moshe *Sharett.
Coalition members: same as Fourth Government. 16 ministers.
The Prime Minister resigned on June 29, 1955, against the background of the decision of the General Zionists to abstain during a vote on a motion of no-confidence brought by **Herut* and **Maki* regarding the government's position in the Grunwald trial (See: *Kasztner Affair), and their subsequent refusal to resign from the government.

SIXTH GOVERNMENT (2ND KNESSET):
June 29, 1955–November 3, 1955.
Prime Minister: Moshe Sharett.
Coalition members: *Mapai*, *Hamizraḥi* and *Hapo'el Hamizraḥi*, Progressives, Minority Lists. 12 ministers.
Served as a transition government.

SEVENTH GOVERNMENT (3RD KNESSET):
November 3, 1955–January 7, 1958.
Prime Minister: David Ben Gurion.
Coalition members: *Mapai*, *Hamizraḥi* and *Hapo'el Hamizraḥi*, *Mapam*, **Aḥdut Ha'avodah-Po'alei Zion*, Progressives, Minority Lists. 16 ministers.
The Prime Minister resigned on December 31, 1957, after making efforts to establish rules to prevent leaks from cabinet deliberations.

EIGHTH GOVERNMENT (3RD KNESSET):
January 7, 1958–December 17, 1959.
Prime Minister: David Ben Gurion.
Coalition members: *Mapai*, *National Religious Party (NRP), *Mapam*, *Aḥdut Ha'avodah-Po'alei Zion*, Progressives, Minority Lists. 16 ministers.
The Prime Minister resigned on July 5, 1959, when *Aḥdut Ha'avodah-Po'alei Zion* and *Mapam* decided to vote against the government concerning arms sales to the *Federal Republic of Germany and subsequently refused to resign.

NINTH GOVERNMENT (4TH KNESSET):
December 17, 1959–November 2, 1961.
Prime Minister: David Ben Gurion.
Coalition members: *Mapai*, NRP, *Aḥdut Ha'avodah-Po'alei Zion*, *Mapam*, Progressives, Minority Lists, one non-partisan member. 16 ministers.
The Prime Minister resigned on January 31, 1961, after a motion of no-confidence was proposed by **Ḥerut* and the General Zionists regarding the *Lavon Affair, despite the fact that the motion was rejected by the Knesset.

TENTH GOVERNMENT (5TH KNESSET):
November 2, 1961–June 26, 1963.
Prime Minister: David Ben Gurion.
Coalition members: *Mapai, Aḥdut Ha'avodah-Po'alei Zion*, NRP, *Po'alei Agudat Yisrael*, Minority Lists. 15 ministers.
The Prime Minister resigned on June 16, 1963, for personal reasons. In fact, he felt that he did not enjoy sufficient support from his colleagues.

ELEVENTH GOVERNMENT (5TH KNESSET):
June 26, 1963–December 23, 1964.
Prime Minister: Levi *Eshkol.
Coalition members: same as Tenth Government. 16 ministers.
The government resigned on December 15, 1964, due to Ben Gurion's demand that the Lavon Affair be investigated by a commission of inquiry made up of members of the Supreme Court.

TWELFTH GOVERNMENT (5TH KNESSET):
December 23, 1964–January 12, 1966.
Prime Minister: Levi Eshkol.
Coalition members: same as Tenth Government. 16 ministers.
The government resigned on the election of the 6th Knesset.

THIRTEENTH GOVERNMENT (6TH KNESSET):
January 12, 1966–March 17, 1969.
Prime Minister: Levi Eshkol.
Original coalition members: *Alignment, NRP, *Mapam*, *Independent Liberals, *Po'alei Agudat Yisrael*, Minority Lists. 18 ministers.
On June 5, 1967 **Gaḥal* and **Rafi* joined the government: it was called the *National Unity Government. The government resigned as a result of the Prime Minister's death on February 26, 1969. 21 ministers.

FOURTEENTH GOVERNMENT (6TH KNESSET):
March 17, 1969–December 15, 1969.
Prime Minister: Golda *Meir.
Coalition members: Alignment, *Gaḥal*, NRP, Independent Liberals, Minority Lists. 21 ministers.
Served as a transition government.

FIFTEENTH GOVERNMENT (7TH KNESSET):
December 15,1969–March 10, 1974.
Prime Minister: Golda Meir.
Coalition members: same as Fifteenth Government. 24 ministers. *Gaḥal* left on August 6, 1970. After August 1970, 22 ministers.
The government resigned on the election of the 8th Knesset.

SIXTEENTH GOVERNMENT (8TH KNESSET):
March 10, 1974–June 3, 1974.
Prime Minister: Golda Meir.
Coalition members: Alignment, NRP, Independent Liberals. 22 ministers.
The Prime Minister resigned on April 11, 1974, against the background of public criticism in the aftermath of the *Yom Kippur War and the absence of sufficient support among the coalition members.

SEVENTEENTH GOVERNMENT (8TH KNESSET):
June 3, 1974–June 20, 1977.
Prime Minister: Yitzḥak *Rabin.
Coalition members: Alignment, Independent Liberals, Minority Lists, *Civil Rights Movement (replaced in October 1974 by the NRP). 21 ministers.
The government resigned on December 22, 1976, against the background of the abstention of the NRP in a vote of no-confidence over the desecration of the Sabbath, following which the NRP ministers were dismissed.

EIGHTEENTH GOVERNMENT (9TH KNESSET):
June 20, 1977–August 5, 1981.
Prime Minister: Menaḥem *Begin.
Coalition members: **Likud* (including **Shlomzion*), *Democratic Movement for Change (joined the government on October 24, 1977), NRP, *Agudat Yisrael*, one independent member (Moshe *Dayan). 19 ministers.
The government resigned upon the election of the 10th Knesset.

NINETEENTH GOVERNMENT (10TH KNESSET):
August 5, 1981–October 10, 1983.
Prime Minister: Menaḥem Begin.
Coalition members: *Likud*, NRP, *Agudat Yisrael*, **Tami*, **Teḥiyah* (joined the government in September, 1982), **Telem*. 20 ministers. The Prime Minister resigned because of poor health.

TWENTIETH GOVERNMENT (10TH KNESSET):
October 10, 1983–September 13, 1984.
Prime Minister: Yitzḥak *Shamir.
Coalition members: *Likud*, NRP, *Agudat Yisrael*, *Tami*, *Teḥiyah*, *Telem*. 20 ministers.
The government resigned following a vote by the Knesset on April 4, 1984, to dissolve the Knesset and call for early elections.

TWENTY-FIRST GOVERNMENT (11TH KNESSET):
September 13, 1984–October 20, 1986.
Prime Minister: Shimon *Peres.
Coalition members: Alignment (including **Yaḥad*), *Likud*, NRP, *Agudat Yisrael*, **Shass*, **Morasha*, **Shinui*, **Ometz*. 25 ministers.

TWENTY-SECOND GOVERNMENT (11TH KNESSET):
October 20, 1986–
Prime Minister: Yitzḥak Shamir.
Coalition members: same as Twenty-first Government. 25 ministers.

Great Britain and Israel On May 14, 1948, the British mandate in Palestine ended. Britain, foreseeing an Arab victory in the *War of Independence, declined to recognize Israel and, while supplying arms to its Middle East allies — *Egypt, Iraq and *Transjordan — imposed a blockade on arms to the Jewish state. British officers were seconded to Arab armies, though they were under strict instructions from London to honor the 1947 partition boundaries.

At the *UN, Britain, one of the five Permanent Members of the Security Council, openly supported the Arab cause. Only when the Arab armies encountered difficulties did the British delegate press for a truce. He also revealed interest in a settlement that would transfer the Negev below the 31st parallel to Transjordan and Egypt.

At the end of 1948, during the War of Independence, Israel advanced into the Sinai Peninsula and came into direct military confrontation with Britain. On December 31 Israel was informed by the *United States that Britain would enter the war against Israel under its 1936 treaty with Egypt unless Israeli forces withdrew from Egyptian soil. In fact, the ultimatum was an American idea. But at the time Prime Minister David *Ben Gurion was seriously concerned that Britain was seeking a pretext to reestablish its position in Palestine. On January 7, 1949, the Israel Air Force, engaged in reconnaissance flights over Egyptian lines, shot down five British Spitfires. The next day British troops landed at Aqaba, Jordan. The crisis was resolved when Ben Gurion gave the order to withdraw from the Sinai and Egypt expressed its willingness to enter armistice negotiations.

The Spitfire incident marked a turning point in Anglo-Israeli relations. In Britain the Labor Government was severely criticized for its actions. On January 18, as a conciliatory act, Britain announced the release of Jewish internees being held in Cyprus. Then on January 26 in a debate in Parliament Winston Churchill attacked Ernest Bevin for his continuing refusal to recognize the State of Israel, accusing the Foreign Secretary of a very strong streak of bias and prejudice. Four days later His Majesty's government granted Israel de facto recognition. Anglo-Israeli relations were normalized. A financial agreement was concluded clearing up the various mutual claims left over from the mandate, and long-standing trade links were restored. Nevertheless, Britain was still an Imperial Power and her wider interests and commitments in the Middle East had ultimate priority. She had bases throughout the area and a special relationship with *Jordan. It was on British advice that King Abdullah backed out of a formal peace treaty with Israel. On April 24, 1950, Abdullah announced the annexation of the *West Bank. Promptly recognizing this act the British government simultaneously accorded de jure recognition to Israel. On May 25, 1950, Britain together with the United States and *France issued a *Tripartite Declaration to support the status quo. The need to maintain a certain level of armed forces was recognized, the use of force was opposed, and action was promised to prevent violation of frontiers or armistice lines.

The declaration was never enforced. Britain continued to adhere to the UN arms embargo against Israel, nor did she conceal her pro-Arab sympathies. In November 1955 Prime Minister Anthony Eden fueled Israeli suspicions by expressing the traditional foreign office view that there should be a compromise between the existing armistice lines and the borders laid down by the 1947 partition plan. Israeli reprisals against Jordan for Palestinian infiltration also caused contention. After Israel's retaliatory attack at Kalkilya in October 1956 Britain even threatened to come to Jordan's assistance.

Yet within weeks Britain and Israel were fighting together against Egypt as the result of a unique and momentary convergence of interests. Anglo-Egyptian relations were in crisis, despite Britain's final withdrawal from its Suez bases. Throughout the Middle East Nasser's agents worked to undermine and displace British influence. When the United States retracted the offer of loans to build the Aswan Dam, President Gamal Abdel Nasser of Egypt nationalized the *Suez Canal on July 26, 1956. Considering the canal a vital strategic and economic artery, Eden determined to restore it to international control and dispose of Nasser in the process.

France and Britain weighed the possibility of military action. France saw Israel as a crucial ally in any campaign against Egypt, but Eden who had always been pro-Arab, at first strongly opposed the idea. He eventually recognized, however, that only Israel had the land forces available on the spot, and only an Israeli attack on Egypt could provide the pretext for Great Power intervention. Ben Gurion was suspicious of Britain, but wishing to settle accounts with Nasser, he needed the UK in order to destroy the Egyptian Air Force, whose bombers would threaten Israeli cities in the event of war. He was also concerned that Jordan might intervene and Britain would feel compelled to join her. On October 24, at Sèvres, British, French and Israeli delegations secretly concluded a plan involving an initial Israeli attack, an Anglo-French ultimatum and subsequent intervention to "separate" the combatants. On October 29, the operation was launched by Israel and on October 31, 12 hours later than promised, British and French planes began bombing Egyptian airfields (See: *Sinai Campaign). The tissue of self-interest binding Israel and Britain soon tore apart. Forced to call off the invasion due to heavy American pressure Britain emerged humiliated from the Suez affair. The order of the day was to restore ties with the United States and the Arab world; the secret understanding with Israel was seen as an aberration. However, there were some positive aspects to the relations between the two countries: Israel had acquired the image of a gallant combatant, and Britain agreed to sell her naval vessels and tanks. Britain also pledged in 1957 to join with others to protect freedom of passage through the Straits of Tiran. Nevertheless, old habits soon reappeared. In July 1958 King Hussein's throne came under threat and Britain was obliged to airlift troops to Jordan from Cyprus, flying through Israeli air space. Much to Ben Gurion's chagrin, Britain did not approach Israel directly for clearance, preferring to use the good offices of the Americans.

The Mancroft affair also reflected the state of relations. Britain had always turned a blind eye to companies complying with the *Arab boycott. Indeed, until 1986 the Foreign Office verified the signature on chamber of commerce documents certifying that a given company did not trade with Israel. In December 1963 the Norwich Union Insurance Company gave in to Arab pressure and discharged Lord Mancroft, a Jewish businessman, from its London board. When a public outcry ensued the British government condemned the action but did nothing to outlaw the boycott itself. Meanwhile Britain's power in the Middle East was draining away. Hussein survived but Britain's Iraqi friend, Nuri es-Said, was murdered. By May 1963 Harold Macmillan's government had recognized the United Nations as being primarily responsible for the maintenance of peace in the area. In February 1966 a Defense White Paper announced Britain's final withdrawal from Aden and military-force cuts against a background of financial constraints.

Despite Britain's straitened circumstances she still had vital interests in the Middle East. Another Arab-Israel war might interrupt the flow of oil and the closure of the canal would greatly add to shipping costs. Her policy in the crisis of May 1967 therefore reflected dual necessities: to deflect Israel from going to war while encouraging a negotiated settlement, to avoid making a commitment of British forces that could harm relations with the Arabs while working closely with the United States. Britain supported the proposal of a joint declaration reaffirming the right of free passage through the Straits of Tiran, closed by Nasser on May 23, and the dispatch of a multinational flotilla to assert the principle. By the eve of war Britain was reconciled to Egyptian rights of control and inspection over cargoes, including oil. But public sympathy for Israel was strong and so the supply of spare parts for Israel's Centurion tanks was expedited (See: *Six-Day War).

Although *Security Council Resolution 242, which Britain played a leading role in drafting, did not directly refer to the *Palestinians, the issue soon moved to the forefront of British concerns. Edward Heath's government, which came to power in June 1970, was less well-disposed than its Labor predecessor toward Israel. In September 1970 a British Airways plane was seized and held against the release of Palestinian prisoners in Israeli jails as well as the release of a hijacker held in British custody. Britain abruptly demanded Israeli cooperation and only Hussein's expulsion of the *PLO from Jordan avoided a clash. A few weeks later British policy was definitively laid down in a speech at Harrogate: a final Middle East settlement should entail Israeli withdrawal to the June 4, 1967, boundaries, subject to minor changes, the establishment of a formal state of peace and the fulfillment of the legitimate aspirations of the Palestinians.

Britain's entry into the *European Economic Community on January 1, 1973, strengthened this position, since Heath sought to align Britain with France's foreign policy rather than with that of the United States. In the October 1973 *Yom Kippur War Britain adopted a pro-Arab posture: an embargo was placed on the shipment of spare parts and ammunition to Israel; landing permission was refused to American transport aircraft en route to Israel; the use of Royal Air Force bases in Cyprus was denied to US reconnaissance planes; on October 13 Britain opposed a cease-fire at the UN, despite Israeli willingness, because of Egyptian reluctance.

With Heath's fall in February 1974 Anglo-Israeli relations began to improve: Labor Prime Minister Harold Wilson, and James Callaghan after him, were old friends of Israel's Labor leaders; their ties with Washington were closer; and the flow of North Sea oil made them less dependent. The arms embargo was lifted and submarines were built for Israel. Less sympathy was manifested toward the Palestinian cause: Britain would not recognize the *Palestine Liberation Organization (PLO) until it changed its policies and in November 1974 Britain voted against inviting Arafat to address the UN General Assembly. Wilson was particularly helpful concerning Soviet Jewry. He planned to visit Israel in 1976 but retirement intervened.

The replacement of Yitzḥak *Rabin by Menaḥem *Begin as Prime Minister of Israel at the head of a **Likud* government in 1977, had little effect on relations despite the history of Britain's contacts with Begin before 1948. The peace negotiations with Egypt, which began in November 1977, increased British interest in Israel and when Begin made the first official visit by an Israeli prime minister to Britain in December 1977, he received a warm welcome. Increasingly, though, British diplomacy evolved within the European political community. Once the peace treaty with Egypt was signed in 1979 disagreements resurfaced.

The Venice Declaration of June 1980, which called for negotiations with the PLO and recognized the Palestinian right to self-determination — which was rejected in Jerusalem — became the new basis of British policy. In turn, Israel's settlements policy was unpopular, as were the Golan Heights and Jerusalem laws. A nadir was reached in 1982 when Israel invaded Lebanon (See: *Lebanese War), and supplied arms to Argentina in the Falkland War. Britain joined her Community partners in embargoing arms to Israel.

Following Shimon *Peres's appointment as prime minister in 1984 Anglo-Israeli relations quickly improved. Israel's withdrawal from Lebanon, a settlements freeze and overtures to King Hussein were appreciated. Britain sought to include the PLO in negotiations but suffered a setback when Palestinian representatives, invited to London in October 1985, failed to endorse UN Resolution 242.

There was a successful exchange of official visits by Peres and Prime Minister Margaret Thatcher in 1986. Differences of principle remained but were outweighed by common interests: opposition to terrorism and the search for a Middle East settlement. In November 1986 Britain broke off diplomatic relations with Syria when conclusive proof was presented that the Syrian Embassy in London had been directly involved in an attempt to blow up an El Al plane en route from London to Tel Aviv. (See also: *Balfour Declaration; *Mandatory Palestine.)

(Ray.C.)

Greater Israel Term customarily used for *Eretz Yisrael Hashlemah*, the exact translation of which is "the Integral Land of Israel." The term refers to the indivisibility of *Eretz Yisrael* including the territories west of the *Jordan River in Israeli hands since 1967. There are many in Israel who object to the term Greater Israel because of its historic German connotation.

Green Line Israel's pre-June 5, 1967 eastern border delineated in the *armistice agreements with Syria and Jordan and its southern border with the *Gaza Strip in the armistice agreement with Egypt in the aftermath of the *War of Independence. The border line was colored green on the original maps drawn up at Rhodes. Israel's border with Lebanon since 1948 and its border with Egypt since 1982 are referred to as "International Boundaries" since these are internationally recognized as fixed boundaries. There is a broad consensus in Israel today that the existing disengagement lines in the *Golan Heights and the *Jordan River should be Israel's "security borders" even if certain territories will eventually be returned to Arab sovereignty. Only **Ḥadash* and the *Progressive List for Peace call for Israel's withdrawal to the Green Line.

Gur (formerly Gurban), **Mordechai** Labor politician and former Chief of Staff. Born 1930, Jerusalem.

Gur received a BA in Middle East Studies from the Hebrew University of Jerusalem. He enlisted in the *IDF in 1948, serving in operational and policy-making positions. In 1959–60 he attended the École Militaire-École de Guerre in Paris. He was Commander of the division which liberated *Jerusalem in 1967 and in 1972–73 was Military Attaché in the Israel Embassy in Washington DC. After the *Yom Kippur War, Gur returned to his post as Commander of the Northern Command. He was Chief of Staff between 1974–78, during which period he was responsible for the *Entebbe Operation in 1976 and the *Litani Operation in 1978.

Gur attended Harvard School of Business in

1979, after which he served as Director of Koor Mechanics until 1984. He was elected to the 10th Knesset (1981) as member of the *Israel Labor Party and served as Minister of Health in the *National Unity Government, in which capacity he dealt with the serious financial difficulties of the Israeli health system against the background of major budgetary cuts and strikes. Gur has on several occasions expressed his intention of eventually contesting for the Labor party leadership. He resigned his cabinet post when the *rotation agreement was implemented in October 1986 due to his objection to serving under Yitzḥak *Shamir who he claimed was implicated in the *Shabak Affair. Since resigning from the government Gur has served as chairman of the board of directors of Solel Boneh, the **Histadrut* construction company.

Gush Hebrew for "the bloc," a political group set up in the mid-1950s in **Mapai*, against the background of the emergence of the younger generation (*tze'irim*) in the party. The *Gush* which was based on the Tel-Aviv party branch, was made up of second rank leaders who held undivided loyalty to David *Ben Gurion, and viewed themselves as protectors of the party and guardians of its honor. They were less interested in the substance of the party's policy than in its personal make-up, and tried to perpetuate the system by which political appointments were made by cooption rather than elections. During its heyday (1955–1965) the *Gush* held most of the key middle-level organizational posts in *Mapai*.

Gush Emunim Hebrew for "Bloc of the Faithful," an extra- parliamentary religious Zionist movement which advocates the extension of Israeli sovereignty over Judea, Samaria (See: **Yosh*) and the *Gaza Strip as a vital goal of Zionist fulfillment. This is to be achieved through the creation of a massive Jewish civilian presence throughout these areas. In pursuit of this goal *Gush Emunim* is engaged not only in settlement activities but in education, social projects, information programs and **aliyah* (immigration) promotion.

Gush Emunim advocates coexistence with the Arab population and is strongly opposed to Meir *Kahane and *Kach.

Gush Emunim draws its ideological inspiration from the teachings of the late Rabbi Zvi Yehuda *Kook who taught that the main purpose of the Jewish people is to attain both physical and spiritual redemption by living in and building up an integral **Eretz Yisrael*. The territory of *Eretz Yisrael* is assigned a sanctity which obligates its retention once liberated from foreign rule, as well as its settlement even in defiance of government authority. *Gush Emunim* views itself as independent of regular Zionist party politics. Its outlook has been described as "political theology."

Gush Emunim was founded in February 1974. The two leading figures were Ḥanan Porath and Rabbi Moshe *Levinger. Initially the movement was affiliated to the *National Religious Party but within several months it severed all party links.

The first phase of *Gush Emunim*'s activities was characterized by repeated attempts to establish Jewish settlements in areas outside the parameters of the *Allon Plan upon which the settlement policy of the *Rabin government was based. These were marked by mass marches, demonstrations and sit-ins at proposed settlement sites, which were occasionally accompanied by clashes with the armed forces. The group which sought to settle in Eilon Moreh was forcibly removed seven times from the area near ancient Sebastia before it was granted permission to move temporarily into the Kaddum army camp from which it later transferred to Mount Kabir, east of Nablus. Those in Israel who oppose *Gush Emunim* argue that the government should never have given in in this case. For *Gush Emunim* this episode constituted a breakthrough.

Gush Emunim gradually broadened its public support base to include non-religious groups such as the *Land of Israel Movement, the *Ein Vered* Circle which is associated with the Labor movement, **Likud* members as well as recent arrivals from the *Soviet Union.

Following the 1977 political *upheaval *Gush Emunim* entered a second phase. Principally through government initiative, dozens of rural communities were established and the Jewish population beyond the *Green Line significantly increased to over 40,000 by 1984 (including non-*Gush Emunim* settlements). Though *Gush Emunim* found the new *Likud*-led government and *World Zionist Organization much more conducive to its activities and goals, a measure of tension developed due to the *autonomy proposals included in the *Camp David Accords and the withdrawal from the whole of the *Sinai as agreed in the peace treaty with *Egypt.

In 1978 **Amana* was established as *Gush Emunim*'s settlement arm. *Bema'aleh* was later set up as its new immigrant branch, and an English language periodical, *Counterpoint*, was started.

In the spring of 1982 *Gush Emunim* activists formed the Movement to Halt the Withdrawal from Sinai which spearheaded the resistance in the *Rafa Salient. Though *Gush Emunim* has developed a bureaucracy, its organizational diffusion has somewhat muted its influence. Most of the Jewish inhabitants in *Gush Emunim* settlements in Judea, Samaria and the Gaza Strip are not hard-core *Gush Emunim* followers, and many are attracted to living in them less for ideological reasons than from economic and quality of life considerations.

The movement was initially embarrassed when it was discovered that the members of the so-called *Jewish Underground were members of *Gush Emunim*. Under the leadership of its new Secretary-General, Daniella Weiss, a ten-member executive, selected in late 1984, has carried on a struggle to release from prison the members of the Jewish underground whose motives, but not whose means, *Gush Emunim* justifies.

Since the formation of the *National Unity Government in 1984 and the de facto freeze of new settlement activities, followed by the renewal of terrorist activities in Judea, Samaria and the Gaza Strip, *Gush Emunim* has entered a third phase. Its leaders call for a greater assertion of authority by the armed forces and civilian authorities, and for a renewed settlement drive, especially in the towns of *Hebron and Nablus.

Attempts to maintain civilian armed patrols in Judea, Samaria and the Gaza Strip following terrorist attacks were stopped by the authorities.

The Council of Jewish Communities, which represents both *Gush Emunim* and non-*Gush* settlements, has evolved as a political lobby. It publishes a journal, *Nekudah*, which is regarded as a *Gush Emunim* ideological organ. Though *Gush Emunim* itself is not a political party, many of its leaders have joined the **Teḥiyah* and **Morasha*. In the 11th Knesset *Gush Emunim* members Rabbi Eliezer Waldman and Gershon Shafat are members for the *Teḥiyah*, while Rabbi Ḥaim Druckman was a member for *Morasha* until he returned to the NRP in April 1986. (I.M.)

H

Ḥadash Acronym for *Ḥazit Demokratit Leshalom Ulshivyon* (democratic front for peace and equality), the name **Rakaḥ* adopted before the elections to the 9th Knesset (1977) after it was joined by a section of the *Black Panthers and other leftist circles. In its platform *Ḥadash* demanded Israeli withdrawal from all the territories occupied in the *Six-Day War, including East *Jerusalem; the establishment of an independent Palestinian state in all the territories west of the *Jordan River which would be evacuated by Israel; Israeli recognition of the *Palestine Liberation Organization (PLO) as the official representative of the Palestinian people; the reduction of resource allocations for security and armaments; the nationalization of property; the raising of tax rates on the rich; a war against "black capital"; the development and expansion of welfare services for the masses, including cheap housing for young couples from the slum areas.

In the elections to the 11th Knesset (1984) the main rival of *Ḥadash* was the newly formed *Progressive List for Peace which offered the Arab electorate an alternative non-Zionist party.

President Ḥaim *Herzog was invited to address the *Ḥadash* conference in December 1985 and accepted the invitation despite protests from the right-wing parties. This acceptance was partially explained as a gesture of good will toward the *Soviet Union, and constituted a departure from the traditional attitude of Israeli governments toward the communists in Israel since David *Ben Gurion (See: *"Without *Ḥerut* and *Maki*").

Knesset Seats: 9th Knesset (1977) — 5; 10th Knesset (1981) — 4; 11th Knesset (1984) — 4. (D.B.M.)

Hadassah Women's Zionist Organization of America.

A voluntary organization which until 1983

functioned in the US and Israel only. Hadassah was established in the US in 1912 by Henrietta Szold (1860–1945) for the purpose of teaching *Zionism to the Jewish women of America and encouraging their active participation in the provision of medical care and public health services in Palestine. In the late 1960s Hadassah turned over most of its hospitals, dispensaries, special programs (including school lunches, child health and welfare centers and playgrounds) to the central and local government authorities in Israel. It still runs two large medical centers in Jerusalem with a nursing school, supports *Youth Aliyah and vocational training schools. Hadassah is an active member of the *World Zionist Organization within the framework of the confederation and a major fund-raiser.

In 1983 the Hadassah Medical Relief Association was established within the framework of Hadassah with both women and men members of all creeds and branches in 17 countries to support and publicize the medical work of Hadassah in Israel.

Haderech Leshalom See: *Way to Peace.

Haganah Hebrew for "defense." Jewish underground organization established in 1920 — upon a resolution passed by the *Aḥdut Ha'avodah* party convention — "to defend Jewish life, property and honor." Its establishment followed Arab riots, particularly in the Jewish quarter of Jerusalem, and the British failure to defend the Jews there, which was compounded by severe measures taken against the Jewish Legion, which did intervene, under its commander Ze'ev (Vladimir) *Jabotinsky.

Organized Jewish self-defense began early in the 20th century with the founding of **Hashomer* to defend settlers against hostile Arabs, whose hope of plunder was later reinforced by awakening Arab nationalism.

The *Haganah* was closely linked with the **Histadrut*. In 1931 seceding members of the *Histadrut* founded a rival body, later known as the **Irgun Zva'i Le'umi* (IZL). The two organizations merged in 1937, under the authority of the Jewish national institutions. However, Zionist-*Revisionist members of IZL maintained their separate organization (from which **Leḥi* seceded). During the Arab riots of the 1930s, the *Haganah* and the IZL disagreed on methods of defense. The *Haganah* followed a policy of restraint and opposed retaliation against the bases of Arab guerrilla bands, in order to avoid harming innocent people and to safeguard prospects of agreement with the Arabs; the IZL advocated retaliation. There was later a similar disagreement when the *Haganah* argued that the Jews of Palestine could not defeat the British Empire by force of arms, which the IZL advocated. In addition, the *Haganah* strongly opposed individual acts of terrorism carried out by the IZL and *Leḥi*.

Each Jewish settlement was responsible for its own defense under the general supervision of the *Haganah* High Command. However, after the massacre of the Jews of Hebron in 1929, its organization was more centralized. It organized smuggling and storing of arms; later, it manufactured weapons. During the 1936–39 disturbances, the emphasis was on defense of settlements. Members of the *Haganah* joined the supernumerary Jewish police set up by the government. Gradually, a more active policy was adopted, and Arab guerrillas were attacked in their own bases ("Field Units," 1937; "Special Night Squads" under Orde Wingate, 1938).

In World War II the *Haganah* ordered its members to join the British Army. Meanwhile the **Palmaḥ* — permanently mobilized commando units — was formed and assisted in operations against Vichy-French Syria and Lebanon. Several *Haganah* members parachuted behind enemy lines in Europe to conduct various operations and also to help the Jews in Occupied Europe. At the end of the war, *Haganah* members serving in the British Army in Europe smuggled Jews to the coast. From there the *Palmaḥ* transported them to Palestine, running the gauntlet of the British blockade of Jewish immigrants. In 1946–48, when the struggle in Palestine intensified, the *Haganah*, despite repressive British measures, became more active in the armed resistance (mainly smuggling in Jews and related activities), sometimes in cooperation with the IZL and *Leḥi*. This struggle was one of the factors that led to the establishment of Israel in 1948.

By the end of 1947, the *Haganah* comprised the following units: — a) a permanent cadre of about 400 men; b) about 2,000 supernumerary police; c) three *Palmaḥ* battalions (11 armed companies, four reserve companies; air and naval and special reconnaissance units) of about 3,000 men; d) about 10,000 men in the infantry *(Ḥish)* between the ages of 18 and 25, who underwent intensive week-end training; e) reserve units of guards *(Ḥim)* comprising men aged over 25; f) youth brigades *(Gadna)* whose members, aged 15–18, had undergone premilitary training. The *Haganah* formed the nucleus of the armed forces which fought during the initial stages of the *War of Independence and from it evolved the *IDF. It was dissolved in 1948 upon the establishment of independent Israel. (E.L.)

Ha'iḥud Hebrew for "the Unity," *Ha'iḥud* was a Knesset faction established in the 9th Knesset (1977–81) by MK Se'adia Marziano who broke away from **Maḥaneh Sheli* and MK Mordechai Elgrably who had been elected to the Knesset as a member of the *Democratic Movement for Change.

Hakibbutz Ha'artzi-Hashomer Hatza'ir A *kibbutz movement founded in 1927, it is affiliated with **Mapam* and includes 85 kibbutzim. In almost all *Kibbutz Ha'artzi* kibbutzim children live in children's houses, and the collective principles are adhered to more strictly than in most other kibbutzim.

The movement objects on principle to Jewish settlement in Judea, Samaria and the Gaza Strip, but has several settlements in the Jordan Valley Rift (See: *Jordan River) and the *Golan Heights.

Hakibbutz Hadati Hebrew for "the religious kibbutz," *Hakibbutz Hadati* is an association of kibbutzim which originally belonged to **Hapo'el Hamizraḥi* and are today affiliated with the *National Religious Party. *Hakibbutz Hadati* was founded in 1935 and its ideology is based on that of **Torah Va'avodah* (Torah and Labor).

The movement has 16 kibbutzim of which three are in the Gush Etzion area and one in the Jordan Valley.

Hakibbutz Hame'uḥad Hebrew for "the united kibbutz," this kibbutz movement was founded in 1927. Most of its members belonged to the left-wing maximalist part of **Mapai* after 1930. After the split in *Mapai* in 1944 members of *Hakibbutz Hame'uḥad* founded the core of *Si'ah Bet* and in 1946 were among the founders of **Aḥdut Ha'avodah-Po'alei Zion*.

In 1951 most of the kibbutzim in *Hakibbutz Hame'uḥad* whose membership was predominantly *Mapai* broke away to form **Iḥud Hakvutzot Vehakibbutzim*. The remainder of the kibbutzim in *Hakibbutz Hame'uḥad* supported **Mapam* until 1954, *Aḥdut Ha'avodah-Po'alei Zion* from 1954 to 1968, and the **Israel Labor Party* since then.

Even though *Hakibbutz Hame'uḥad* adopted a resolution in 1955 in favor of Jewish settlement throughout **Eretz Yisrael*, after 1967 all of its new kibbutzim were within the parameters of the *Allon Plan.

In 1979, when *Hakibbutz Hame'uḥad* and *Iḥud Hakvutzot Vehakibbutzim* reunited in the **Takam*, it had 57 kibbutzim.

Hamaḥanot Ha'olim Hebrew for "the rising camps," a scouting youth movement established in 1931 to encourage youth in the city schools to go out and work in agricultural settlements. In 1945 a group affiliated with **Mapai* left the movement. In 1950 certain groups from the Scouts, especially in the Haifa area, joined *Hamaḥanot Ha'olim*.

The movement is affiliated with the world youth movement *Dror* which was connected with **Hakibbutz Hame'uḥad* until the latter joined the **Takam* in 1979.

Hamerkaz Ha'atzma'i Hebrew for Independent Center. Rightist party set up in 1975 following a split in the *Free Center *Hamerkaz Haḥofshi*, because of ideological differences between Shmuel *Tamir and Eliezer Shostak who continued to support a rigid and extremist policy regarding *"Greater Israel." Underlying the ideological aspect was Tamir's struggle for leadership of the **Likud*.

Following the split, both parties remained within the *Likud* with two Knesset seats each. In 1976 the *State List together with the *Tnu'at Ha'avodah Lema'an *Eretz Yisrael Hashlemah* and *Hamerkaz Ha'atzma'i* established the **La'am* faction within the *Likud*. The members of *Hamerkaz Haḥofshi* joined the *Democratic Movement for Change. (D.B.M.)

Hamerkaz Haḥofshi See: *Free Center.

Hamerkaz Haliberali See: *Liberal Center.

Hamishtar Haḥadash Hebrew for "the New Regime," a political movement founded in 1957 by persons of various political backgrounds with the goal of changing the political system in Israel.

Among the initiators of the movement were Shmuel *Tamir, Eliezer Livneh, Erie Jabotinsky (son of Ze'ev *Jabotinsky, who had been member of the 1st Knesset on behalf of the **Ḥerut* Movement), Professor Yeshayahu Leibowitch and Eliakim Ha'etzni (See: *Shurat Hamitnadvim*).

Hamishtar Haḥadash called for the enactment of a *Basic Law which would ensure the separation of authorities in the state; the strengthening of the judicial system; guarantees for the basic rights of citizens and personal freedom; a change in the system of elections to a personal regional one (See: *Electoral Reform); full freedom of speech, organization and movement; a national health system; the formalization of military service; releasing the individual from party "enslavement" and dependence on parties; equality for all citizens irrespective of religion and origin; and the full integration of the Arab population in all spheres of life and society. In the economic sphere the movement called for the encouragement of personal initiative and the cancellation of all types of controls. It also called for the separation of the Trade Unions from *Ḥevrat Ha'ovdim* (the **Histadrut* holding company) and worker participation in *Histadrut* enterprises. In foreign policy it called for the reunification of **Eretz Yisrael* by peaceful means, within the framework of an Israeli-Jordanian federation, which would then form a confederation with *Lebanon; positive initiatives for peace; cooperation with the neighboring states and full Israeli integration in the region. Resolving the refugee problem was called for both on moral grounds and as a political necessity. The movement existed until 1959, but after deciding to concentrate on ideological activities and not to run in the elections to the 4th Knesset (1959), it disintegrated. (S.T.)

Hamizraḥi Hebrew for "the Oriental" or "the easterner," *Hamizraḥi* is a world-wide religious federation in the *World Zionist Organization and was a separate religious party in Israel until it united with **Hapo'el Hamizraḥi* in 1956 to form the *National Religious Party (NRP). It was set up as the Zionist movement of religious Jewry in Eastern Europe in 1902. *Hamizraḥi*'s spiritual father was Rabbi Yitzḥak Ya'acov Reines (1839–1915). The movement's origins are to be found in the 19th century when Rabbi Shmuel Mohaliver (1824–1898) set up the "Mizraḥi Bureau" in Bialystok to nurture the spirit of Judaism. In 1918 such a bureau was set up in Palestine as well by Rabbi Y. L. *Maimon. The three basic principles on which *Hamizraḥi* was based were: the redemption of Israel may progress gradually and be started by man through the settlement of the country, i.e., one should not sit idly and wait for the Messiah; the redemption is meant for the whole of the Jewish people, thus everyone must join forces and work together in order to approach it i.e., the religious forces should cooperate with the secular forces in the Zionist movement; each and every Jew has a part in Israel and its Torah, therefore an effort must be made to bring everyone closer to the Torah through spiritual influence.

In 1925 the Zionist Organization recognized *Hamizraḥi*'s schools as an autonomous stream in the educational system of the **Yishuv* — in 1953 this stream became the religious section of the national education system of Israel.

Since the *Chief Rabbinate was established in 1921 *Hamizraḥi* has had great influence over it and has participated in almost all the Zionist Executives. Despite the fact that a section in the movement was close to the *Revisionists *Hamizraḥi* joined the **Mapai*-led coalition in the Zionist Executive which was set up in 1935 — thus beginning the *"historic coalition" which lasted until 1976. *Hamizraḥi* always struggled for the Sabbath rest and *kashrut* (dietary laws) in all national institutions and in settlements and organizations supported by the Zionist Organization and State of Israel. It insisted that if Israel is to have a constitution it should be based on the *Halacha* (Jewish religious law).

Among its institutions *Hamizraḥi* set up Bank Hamizraḥi and the sports club Elitzur. In 1937 it founded, with *Hapo'el Hamizraḥi*, the daily paper *Hatzofeh*. *Hamizraḥi* won two seats in the 2nd Knesset. (D.B.M.)

Hamizraḥ Leshalom Hebrew for "the East for Peace," *Hamizraḥ Leshalom* is a non-parliamentary movement, founded on May 29 1983, by a group of Israeli Jewish intellectuals educators and community activists from **Edot Mizraḥ*. It is essentially an ideological forum seeking to change the right-wing image of the Oriental Jews regarding peace, and to air ideas about the integration of Israel within the Middle East. The movement's goal is to encourage the peace process in the region. It perceives of settlements across the *Green Line as a danger to this process, and opposes all activities which could harm the achievement of a settlement, including acts of terror and incitement committed by either side. It supports a dialogue between Jews and Arabs to find a solution to the Palestinian problem. Most of the movement's activities are in the sphere of information, publications and research. (M.B.)

Hammer, Zvulun National religious leader. Born 1936 in Haifa.

Hammer is regarded as a typical product of the generation of *kipot srugot* (knitted skull-caps — the head dress of modern religious Jews which replaced hats and black cloth skull-caps). He was educated in the national religious school system and served in the *IDF within the framework of the **Naḥal* (military service associated with work on a kibbutz), and was an instructor in the *B'nei Akivah* religious youth movement. Hammer studied at the religious Bar Ilan University and served as chairman of its student union. Later he became leader of the *National Religious Party (NRP) young guard.

Hammer was instrumental in turning the NRP from a party whose main concern was religious affairs into a movement with deep involvement in foreign affairs and security issues, while actively assisting **Gush Emunim* and those in favor of settling Judea, Samaria and the Gaza Strip.

In the political sphere Hammer emerged as a brilliant tactician who managed to remove Dr. Yitzḥak Raphael from the NRP leadership and become number two man to Dr. Yosef *Burg.

He was first elected to the 7th Knesset (1969). In 1975–76 he served as Minister of Welfare in the *Rabin government. Together with his colleague Dr. Yehuda Ben Meir, Hammer was instrumental in breaking up the *historic coalition between the NRP and the *Israel Labor Party, when the NRP joined the **Likud*-led coalition formed after the elections to the 9th Knesset (1977). He served as Minister of Education (1977–84), in which capacity he introduced free secondary education and pre-kindergarten classes, and acted to advance the status of the teachers.

The *Lebanese War and the major loss of power by the NRP in the elections to the 11th Knesset (1984) resulted in Hammer adopting a more moderate position in an effort to reunite and revive the national religious camp. He argued that pluralism, freedom of opinion and the establishment of a bridge between the secular and religious sections of the population must take precedence over the issue of *Greater Israel and its settlement.

Following Burg's resignation from the government in October 1986 Hammer replaced him as Minister of Religions in the *National Unity Government under Yitzḥak *Shamir. (Sh.M.)

Hano'ar Ha'oved Vehalomed Hebrew for "youth that work and study," *Hano'ar Ha'oved Vehalomed* is an Israeli youth movement founded in 1926 as an integral part of the **Histadrut*, to sponsor educational activities among working youth.

In 1933 a group of its members founded the movement's first *kibbutz — Na'an. In 1959 it merged with *Habonim-Hatnu'ah Hame'uḥedet.*

Though it is not officially affiliated to any party, most of its leaders belong to the *Israel Labor Party.

Ha'olam Hazeh-Ko'aḥ Ḥadash Hebrew for "This World — New Force," this extreme anti-establishment movement was organized before the elections to the 6th Knesset (1965) by Uri *Avneri, editor of the weekly *Ha'olam Hazeh*. It fought for civil rights, the revelation of economic and political scandals and corruption, and the rights of the *Arabs of Israel and against the *Military Administration and the security services. In the 1965 elections *Ha'olam Hazeh-Ko'aḥ Ḥadash* gained one Knesset seat and Uri Avneri became active in a wide range of parliamentary issues including foreign affairs and security where his position was extremely moderate. He advocated understanding with the Arabs, territorial compromise (after 1967), recognition of the Palestinian national entity and seeking ways for peaceful coexistence. In the elections to the 7th Knesset (1969) *Ha'olam Hazeh-Ko'aḥ Ḥadash* gained two seats, but in the course of the Knesset term the party split into two movements, one called *Demokratim Yisraelim* (Israeli democrats) which included the *Black Panthers, the other *Meri Veḥazit Hasmol* (rebellion and the left front) which included the intellectual group Si'aḥ (*Smol Yisraeli Ḥadash* — new Israeli Left). Neither movement passed the one percent threshold in the elections to the 8th Knesset (1973).

After the emergence of the Green party in the *Federal Republic of Germany Avneri argued that *Ha'olam Hazeh-Ko'aḥ Ḥadash* had been the first "Green" party. (D.B.M.)

Hapo'el Hamizraḥi Hebrew for "the Eastern worker," *Hapo'el Hamizraḥi* is a national-religious labor federation established in Jerusalem in 1922 as part of the *Torah Va'avodah* (Torah and Labor) movement. Its goal was to unite all workers who wished to labor in accordance with the *Halacha*. Its members believed that **Eretz Yisrael* could be built only through labor. Over the years *Hapo'el Hamizraḥi* established many settlements, *kibbutzim organized within the Religious Kibbutz Movement (See: **Hakibbutz Hadati*), and **moshavim* organized within the association of *moshavim* of the agricultural center of *Hapo'el Hamizraḥi*.

The federation established many economic organizations. In 1929 it founded the youth movement *B'nei Akivah*, and was a partner with *Hamizraḥi* in the foundation of the daily *Hatzofeh* and the sports club Elitzur in 1937. In 1929 *Hapo'el Hamizraḥi* also organized a council for working women known today as *Emunah*. Over the years it set up a network of yeshivot (schools of religious studies) associated with the *B'nei Akivah* movement, and after the establishment of the state many of these turned into *Yeshivot Hesder* — yeshivot whose students study and at the same time serve in the *IDF.

Members of *Hapo'el Hamizraḥi* joined the *Histadrut health fund, *Kupat Ḥolim*, in the 1920s after *Kupat Ḥolim* undertook to maintain strict *kashrut* in its kitchens. *Hapo'el Hamizraḥi* joined the *Histadrut* in 1953. In 1956 it merged with *Hamizraḥi* to set up the National Religious Party.

Hapo'el Hamizraḥi ran for the 2nd Knesset (1951), gaining eight seats. (D.B.M.)

Hapo'el Hatza'ir Hebrew for "the young worker," *Hapo'el Hatza'ir* is a Zionist socialist party established in 1905 by pioneers from the East European *Tze'irei Tzion* (youth of Zion). The small workers' camp in Palestine was split between *Hapo'el Hatza'ir* and **Po'alei Zion* which was also established in the same year.

Hapo'el Hatza'ir's ideological starting point was the uniqueness of the Jewish workers' movement in Palestine. It therefore rejected most of the socialist doctrines developed in Europe and adopted by *Po'alei Zion*, the *Bund* and others. *Hapo'el Hatza'ir* did not celebrate the 1st of May and had no ties with the international workers' movement. It supported constructive work, i.e., pioneering labor, and activities which fortified the economic, political and social status of the Jewish community in general and the workers in particular.

Hapo'el Hatza'ir established the first *kibbutz — Deganiah — and was one of the initiators of the **Moshav* Nahalal. However, it objected to the idea of the "enlarged kibbutz." Under the leadership of Ḥaim *Arlosoroff the movement's attitude to socialism and the international workers movement changed. In 1923 the party sent observers to the Congress of the Second International in Hamburg. It gradually drew closer to **Aḥdut Ha'avodah* which had been founded in 1919, but united with it only in 1930 when the two founded **Mapai*. Among its founders and leaders were Yosef Sprinzak, A. D. *Gordon and Levi *Eshkol. The party was active in the struggle for Jewish labor, enhancing the value of manual labor and creating a Jewish working class. Though *Hapo'el Hatza'ir* developed as a party in Palestine, branches were established in Europe as well — in Germany, Austria and Poland. In 1920 the world association of *Hapo'el Hatza'ir* and *Tze'irei Tzion* was established. The party's organ was *Hapo'el Hatza'ir* which appeared from 1907 to 1970. (D.B.M.)

Harari resolution See: *Constitution and *Basic Laws

Hashomer Hebrew for "guard," the association of Jewish watchmen in **Eretz Yisrael* was active between 1909–20. The origins of the association go back to 1907 when Yitzḥak *Ben Zvi, Alexander Zeid (1886–1938) and Israel Shoḥat (1886–1961) founded a similar group called Bar Giora. *Hashomer* was founded by pioneers of the Second **Aliyah* some of whom had been active in revolutionary movements and Jewish self-defense groups in Russia, and most of whom were members or sympathizers of **Po'alei Zion*. The object was to protect Jewish settlements against Arab attacks. The slogan of *Hashomer* was: *"bedam va'esh Yehudah naflah — bedam va'esh Yehudah takum"* ("in blood and fire Judea fell — in blood and fire Judea will arise"). By 1912 *Hashomer* was responsible for the protection of seven major Jewish settlements. The *shomrim* (watchmen) spoke Arabic, wore a mixture of Arab and Circassian garb and carried rifles. Candidates had to undergo a year's trial and could become members only after two thirds of the members voted in their favor. In 1914 there were 40 full members of *Hashomer*. During World War I the association's leaders were exiled. *Hashomer* was disbanded upon the decision of *Aḥdut Ha'avodah* in 1920 when the *Haganah* was established.

Hashomer Hatza'ir Hebrew for "young guard." *Hashomer Hatza'ir* is a Zionist socialist pioneering youth movement, whose aim is to educate Jewish youth in Israel and abroad for *kibbutz life. The movement was founded in Vienna in 1916 when two groups *Tze'irei Tzion* (the youth of Zion) and *Hashomer* (the guard) united.

**Hakibbutz Ha'artzi-Hashomer Hatza'ir* was founded in 1927 and served as a permanent framework for kibbutzim which absorbed *Hashomer Hatza'ir* members who had started to arrive in Palestine after World War I. The Palestine federation of *Hashomer Hatza'ir* was established in 1930. Its first kibbutz was Nir David, founded in 1936.

During World War II some East European members of *Hashomer Hatza'ir* fought in the ranks of the Red Army, some reached **Eretz Yisrael* while others became members of the Jewish resistance, Jewish partisans and ghetto fighters. The commander of the revolt in the Warsaw ghetto, Mordechai Anielewicz was a member of *Hashomer Hatza'ir*.

The movement played an active role in settlement, defense and "illegal" immigration activities before the establishment of the state. It developed a strict ideology which sought a synthesis between Zionism and a Socialism which leaned toward Marxism — between pioneering construction and class warfare. Heavy emphasis was placed on the pure conduct of individual members. In recent decades ideological issues have become more flexible. Since 1948 *Hashomer Hatza'ir* has been politically affiliated with **Mapam*.

Hatnu'ah Hame'uḥedet Hebrew for "the united movement." *Hatnu'ah Hame'uḥedet* is a youth movement established in 1945 when a group affiliated with **Mapai* broke off from **Hamaḥanot Ha'olim* and joined the *Gordonia-Maccabi Hatza'ir* movement.

When the principle of **mamlachtiut* (state system) was applied, *Hatnu'ah Hame'uḥedet*, like all other politically affiliated youth movements (in fact, all youth movements except the Scouts) had to stop functioning within the school system. In 1954 the movement merged with world *Habonim*.

Until the establishment of the **Takam* in 1979 *Hatnu'ah Hame'uḥedet* was affiliated with **Iḥud Hakvutzot Vehakibbutzim*.

Hatnu'ah Lema'an Eretz Yisrael Hashlemah Ideological Movement. Hebrew for "The Movement for Greater Israel." See: *Land of Israel Movement.

Hausner, Gideon Politician and attorney. Born 1915, Poland.

Hausner immigrated to Palestine in 1927 and studied at the Herzliya Gymnasium in Tel Aviv, after which he graduated with a degree in law from the Government of Palestine Higher School of Law. Hausner was a member of the **Hamaḥanot Ha'olim* youth movement, and the **Haganah*. During the *War of Independence he served in the Jerusalem Brigade and later served as military prosecutor and as President of the Military Court.

Hausner was active in the *Progressive Party and lectured at the Hebrew University in Jerusalem. In 1960–63 he served as Attorney General and appeared as General Staff Prosecutor in the *Eichmann trial. He first entered the 6th Knesset as an Independent Liberal in 1965 and served as Minister without Portfolio in the *Rabin government, 1974–77. In the 9th Knesset he was the only Member of Knesset representing the Independent Liberal Party. Hausner has been Chairman of Yad Vashem (the Holocaust memorial complex in Jerusalem) since 1969.

Ḥavereinu A Hebrew word meaning "our comrades" or "our colleagues," *Ḥavereinu* is an institution set up in 1954 by Prime Minister Moshe *Sharett which included the **Mapai* Ministers, the Secretary-General of the **Histadrut* and the Secretary of *Mapai*. This ad hoc group came to be regarded as the main decision-making body in *Mapai* even though it had not been authorized as such, and was thus resented by the official party institutions. *Ḥavereinu* continued to exist in various forms until 1977.

Ḥazan, Ya'acov Party leader, former MK. Born 1899 in Brest Litovsk, Russia.

Ḥazan attented the Politechnion in Warsaw and was one of the founders of the Hebrew Scout Movement in 1915. He was also one of the founders and leaders of *_Hashomer Hatza'ir_ in Poland and a member of *_Heḥalutz_ there.

Ḥazan immigrated to Palestine in 1922 and worked in the groves near Ḥadera, and the draining of swamps in the Beit She'an area. He was one of the founders of Kibbutz Mishmar Ha'emek, of which he is still a member, and of *_Hakibbutz Ha'artzi_ in 1927. He was also member of the central bodies of the *_Histadrut._

Ḥazan founded *_Mapam_ with others, in 1948 — becoming a Member of the 1st Knesset in 1949, and he remained as MK until 1973. Ḥazan, together with Me'ir *Ya'ari, was party leader in those years and its main spokesman. He strongly favored the establishment of the *Alignment in 1969 and in 1982 put his full weight behind _Mapam_'s remaining in the Alignment at a time when nearly half the Central Committee called for _Mapam_'s leaving it.

Hebron City in Judea south of Jerusalem, one of the four major Jewish religious centers in _Eretz Yisrael._ Population in 1985 approximately 75,000. Since ancient times when it served as King David's first capital there has almost always been a Jewish presence in Hebron. It is the site of the Machpelah burial cave of the Patriarchs and their wives, purchased by Abraham. In 1929 a massacre perpetrated by Arab rioters put an end to Jewish communal life in Hebron. After the *Six-Day War a group of Jews under the leadership of Rabbi Moshe *Levinger returned to the city. In April 1968 they rented a small hotel for 70 guests and then refused to vacate. The group rapidly gained the support of Ministers Yigal *Allon, Menaḥem *Begin and Zeraḥ Warhaftig (NRP) for a renewed civilian Jewish presence in Hebron, and after a month of negotiations were transferred to the military government compound. The settlement attempt met with much opposition from both Jews and Arabs and has proved to be the most problematic center of controversy over Jewish settlement in *_Yosh_ (Judea and Samaria).

Permission to establish a Yeshiva came in August and on October 19, 1968, after a grenade attack at the Machpelah cave, the government approved the construction of Kiryat Arba, a Jewish suburb on the town outskirts.

Originally planned for 250 housing units, by 1986 there were over 800 Jewish families in Kiryat Arba and other neighborhoods which expanded on to nearby hills. It was a group of settlers from Kiryat Arba who, in 1973, formed the _Elon Moreh_ nucleus which was the forerunner of *_Gush Emunim._

On April 19, 1979, two dozen women with their children surreptitiously broke into the Jewish-owned Beit Hadassah building in the heart of the former Jewish quarter in Hebron proper and established living quarters. Again, after protracted negotiations, demonstrations and the murder of a yeshiva student in the Hebron market, in February 1980 they were granted official permission to remain there.

In 1984 half a dozen families moved into temporary units at Tel Rumeida, another former Jewish quarter of Hebron. However, all further development was halted by Minister of Defense Yitzḥak *Rabin.

Rabbi Levinger, who became a prominent leader of _Gush Emunim_, has over the years managed to obtain the support of political personalities from various parties on the Israeli political Right. Opposition to the renewed Jewish presence within the city of Hebron, comes from the Israeli Left which considers it unnecessarily provocative and politically unnecessary. This presence has been termed "abrasive" by Minister of Police Ḥaim *Bar Lev. And there are those who argue that too great a military force is tied down protecting the Jewish inhabitants of Hebron.

In 1985, a *_Kach_ member was elected to the municipal council of Kiryat Arba and joined the municipal coalition. He resigned in September 1986 over disagreements regarding the presence of Arabs in the town.

In April 1986 the *_Teḥiyah_ held its second conference in Kiryat Arba, an act which led to a protest meeting organized by the *Peace Now movement, with the participation of several members of the *Civil Rights Movement, the *Progressive List for Peace and Palestinians in Hebron. There was an attempt to obstruct the protest meeting by a group of Jewish settlers by blocking the main road from Jerusalem to Hebron. (I.M.)

Heḥalutz Hebrew for "the Pioneer." This is the name given to various federations of Jewish youth as of the 1880s, which encouraged their members to immigrate to *_Eretz Yisrael_, preparing them for manual labor and settlement and teaching them the Hebrew language. After the

First World War, when the *World Zionist Organization started to finance the activities of the movement, members had to belong to it. The world organization of *Heḥalutz* was set up in 1921 at a conference at Karlsbad. The Movement's center was established in Warsaw where its organ, *He'atid* (the future), was published.

Heḥalutz as such was non-partisan, though some of its federations were associated with specific parties. The movement reached its zenith in 1935 when it had some 90,000 members. The *Holocaust virtually annihilated *Heḥalutz* which had been especially strong in Eastern Europe. Since the establishment of the state, various youth movements, the World Zionist Organization and the State of Israel have fulfilled some of the functions previously filled in the Diaspora by *Heḥalutz*.

Ḥerut Hebrew word meaning "freedom". See: **Ḥerut* Movement.

Ḥerut Movement Political party founded in 1948. Until 1965 *Ḥerut* ran for the *Knesset independently, and thereafter together with other parties within the framework of **Gaḥal* and after 1973 within the **Likud*. Since 1955 *Ḥerut* has been the second largest party in the Knesset, but only in 1977 was it able, as head of the *Likud* to establish a government without the Labor Movement.

Ḥerut was founded in June 1948 by the High Command of **IZL*. Its undisputed leader, until his retirement from public life in 1983, was Menaḥem *Begin. Even though an ideological descendant of Revisionism, *Ḥerut* ran independently of the *Revisionist Movement in the elections for the 1st Knesset (1949). Unity was achieved the following year, but internal party squabbles led to the departure of several veteran Revisionist leaders from *Ḥerut* in 1951. In 1965 *Ḥerut* formed the *Gaḥal* bloc together with the *Liberal Party of Israel. At the 1966 party convention, a dispute over the question of leadership broke out. Begin was accused by Shmuel *Tamir of being responsible for the electoral defeats. The result was the breakaway of three *Ḥerut* Knesset members and their setting up of a new party, the *Free Center.

In 1973 the *Likud* bloc was formed, again with *Ḥerut* as the main political component. **La'am* which had been a member of the *Likud* since 1976 merged with *Ḥerut* in 1985, and in 1986 negotiations began to merge the Liberal Party with *Ḥerut* into a single party.

Ḥerut was the principal opposition party in Israeli politics until 1977. Its political platform, faithful to the outlook of Ze'ev *Jabotinsky, stressed the integrity of the Jewish homeland. The earlier demand for a state on both banks of the Jordan River was much muted after 1965, and to all intents and purposes has been given up. Begin frequently pointed out, when asked about the *"territorial compromise" that by giving up *Transjordan the Jews had already compromised 74 percent of their land.

Ḥerut has always promoted an activist defense policy, a national economy based primarily on private enterprise, advocating the abolition of the system of economic sectorialism (the main goal being the reduction of the government and **Histadrut*-owned sectors), and calling for compulsory arbitration to settle labor disputes. It also emphasizes respect for Jewish religious values. *Ḥerut* has been characterized as a party of protest, capitalizing on the dissatisfactions of the **Edot Mizraḥ*, the lower economic classes and the nationalists. The core leadership for over three decades came from among former *IZL* veterans (See: the *Fighting Family). The current leader, Yitzḥak *Shamir, Prime Minister after Begin's resignation in 1983, and again in 1986, emerged from **Leḥi*.

In 1963 *Ḥerut* sponsored a faction within the **Histadrut, Tchelet Lavan* (blue-white), which gradually increased its power to up to 29 percent in the 1977 *Histadrut* elections. Affiliated with *Ḥerut* are the **Betar* youth movement and sports clubs, the *Brit Nashim* women's association, settlement and agricultural centers. Until 1966 a daily newspaper, *Ḥerut*, was published. Today *Ḥerut* issues a monthly, *Be'eretz Yisrael*. Until 1979 *Ḥerut* convened biennially to elect its leaders, review party institutions and pass resolutions affecting the movement's ideological orientation. Between conferences the supreme representative body is the Central Committee with more than 1,000 members. After the 1979 Conference, there were repeated postponements, and when the conference finally met in March 1986, it broke up inconclusively due to factional strife. While Begin was movement chairman no factionalism developed, and all claimants to power were thwarted or forced to leave the party. Since Begin's retirement in 1983 *Herut* has divided into rival camps headed by Yitzḥak Shamir, Ariel *Sharon (who joined the party after the 1977 elections), and David *Levy, a leader who emerged from the Moroccan community.

Until 1967 *Herut* was excluded from all government coalitions following *Ben Gurion's axiom *"Without *Herut* and *Maki*." The political climate in Israel in the 1950s sought the delegitimization of *Herut*. It was portrayed by **Mapai* as trumpeting strident nationalism, adventurism, being violent and potentially undemocratic. The street riots organized by *Herut* outside the Knesset in 1952 to protest the *Restitution Agreement with the *Federal Republic of Germany, was referred to as the true expression of *Herut*'s nature.

During the emergency period prior to the *Six-Day War two *Gaḥal* representatives were coopted into the government, with Begin becoming Minister without Portfolio. In the second *National Unity Government established in 1969 *Gaḥal* had six ministers, of whom three — Menaḥem *Begin, Ezer *Weizman, and Ḥaim Landau were members of *Herut*. *Gaḥal* left the government in 1970 in protest over the acceptance of the *Rogers Plan.

Herut, as the largest partner in the *Likud* bloc, came to power in 1977, was returned in 1981 and continues to serve as part of the coalition in the National Unity Government formed after the 1984 elections. Since October 1986 *Herut* leader Yitzḥak Shamir has stood at the head of the national unity government.

Knesset Seats: 1st Knesset (1949) — 14; 2nd Knesset (1951) — 8; 3rd Knesset (1955) — 15; 4th Knesset (1959) — 17; 5th Knesset (1961) — 17; 6th Knesset (1965) — 15 (out of *Gaḥal*'s 26); 7th Knesset (1969) — 15 (out of *Gaḥal*'s 26); 8th Knesset (1973) — 17 (out of the *Likud*'s 39); 9th Knesset (1977) — 19 (out of the *Likud*'s 43); 10th Knesset (1981) — 26 (out of the *Likud*'s 48); 11th Knesset (1984) — 26 (out of the *Likud*'s 41).

(I.M.)

Herzl, Theodor (Binyamin Ze'ev) (1860–1904) Prophet of the Jewish State, father of political *Zionism and founder of the *World Zionist Organization.

Herzl was born in Budapest to a half-assimilated family, and moved to Vienna at 18 where he studied law. Restricted professionally because of his Jewishness Herzl turned to journalism and writing. He published hundreds of feuilletons and many plays. In 1892 Herzl suggested that the Jewish problem might be solved by baptizing all the Jewish children. However, the Dreyfus Affair (1894–95), which he observed as the Paris correspondent of the *Neue Freie Presse*, impressed on him the power of anti-Semitism even in an enlightened democratic state such as France. He concluded that the only solution was the exodus of the Jews from their Diaspora and their ingathering in a sovereign state. He first considered *Argentina where Baron Hersch had attempted to settle Jews but later decided on Palestine. Herzl published his *Judenstaat* (The Jewish State) in 1896 and founded the Zionist organization at the first Zionist Congress which he organized in Basle in 1897 — the Basle Program stated that "the aim of Zionism is to create for the Jewish people a home in Palestine secured by public law." Until his death in 1904 Herzl attempted to obtain a charter from the Ottoman Sultan for Jewish settlement in Palestine, and carried on an extensive diplomatic effort among all sovereigns who might be useful. He was, however, willing to consider establishing the Jewish state in Uganda when the possibility was raised in 1903 by British Colonial Secretary Joseph Chamberlain. The plan was finally rejected by the Zionist Congress of 1905, a year after Herzl's premature death.

Herzog, Ḥaim President of the State of Israel, politician, military officer, attorney. Born 1918, Ireland.

The son of Rabbi Isaac Herzog, Chief Rabbi of Ireland (1921–36), then of Palestine and Israel (1936–48), Herzog studied at the Merkaz Harav and Hebron yeshivas and Law at the Government of Palestine Higher School of Law. He continued his studies at London and Cambridge, becoming a barrister at Law in Britain. Herzog served in the **Haganah* during the Arab Revolt of 1936–39, and in the British army in Europe during World War II. He was Head of British Intelligence in northern Germany at the end of World War II. In 1948 he headed the security branch of the *Jewish Agency and after the establishment of the state was operations officer in the 7th Brigade of the *IDF in the battle of Latrun. He was Director of Military Intelligence in 1948–50 and

1959–62 and Military Attaché in Washington DC in 1950–54 and after that served as Commanding Officer of the Jerusalem district and Commander of the Southern Command from 1957 to 1959. He retired from active military service in 1962 with the rank of *aluf* (major general).

In 1962–72 Herzog was Managing Director of GUS Industries, and in 1972–83 he was a senior partner in a law firm, specializing in representing major corporations. In 1965 he became Secretary of the Tel Aviv branch of **Rafi*, and from 1967 the leading military commentator for the Israel Broadcasting Services. After the Six-Day War he was appointed Military Governor of the *West Bank and *Jerusalem. In 1973 Herzog gave daily commentaries on the *Yom Kippur War on the radio, becoming famous for his balanced and credible presentations.

Herzog was Permanent Israeli Representative to the UN between 1975 and 1978 and upon the adoption by the General Assembly of Resolution 3379 in November 1975 equating *Zionism with racism, demonstratively tore the text of the resolution. Herzog also explained the *Entebbe Operation to the UN General Assembly. Upon his return from New York Herzog became a member of the Bureau of the *Israel Labor Party.

In 1981–83 he was a Member of the 10th Knesset and of the Knesset Foreign Affairs and Security Committee as well as the Constitution, Law and Justice Committee.

In 1983 he was elected Israel's 6th President, defeating the **Likud*'s candidate in a secret vote of the Knesset.

In 1986 President Herzog pardoned eleven of the senior officers implicated in the *Shabak Affair, a decision which raised questions regarding the President's power to pardon.

In November 1986 Herzog paid an official visit to several countries in Oceania, the Far East and Southeast Asia, a visit which was to constitute a breakthrough in Israel's relations with that part of the world.

In April 1987 President Herzog paid an official visit to West Germany. This was the first visit by a president of the State of Israel and it aroused much comment in Israel.

Hillel, Shlomo Diplomat, politician and Knesset Speaker, born 1923 in Iraq.

Hillel immigrated to Palestine in 1934 and was a member of *Kibbutz Ma'agan Micha'el from 1941–58. He studied economics, political science and public administration at the Hebrew University of Jerusalem. During 1946–51 he was engaged in arranging illegal immigration of Iraqi Jewry to Israel. He was a Member of the 2nd Knesset (1951–55) and 3rd Knesset (1955–59) as member of **Mapai*. He was Ambassador in several African states from 1959–63 and following that was Director of the African Department in the Ministry for Foreign Affairs. In 1964–67 Hillel was a member of the Israeli delegation to the *United Nations. He was Deputy Director-General in the Ministry for Foreign Affairs on Middle Eastern Affairs until 1969 when he once more entered the Knesset. From 1969–73 he served as Minister of Police and was Minister of the Interior and Police from 1973 to 1977. During the 9th Knesset (1977–81) he was Chairman of the Knesset Committee of the Interior and the Environment. In the 10th Knesset (1981–84) he was member of the Foreign Affairs and Security Committee, and Knesset observer at the Council of Europe. And in the 11th Knesset (1984) Hillel was elected Speaker of the House. Since his election Hillel has concentrated on improving the work of the Knesset, educating youth and the public for democracy and blocking the presentation of racist legislation.

Histadrut Founded in 1920 as the federation of Jewish labor, *Hahistadrut Haklalit shel Ha'ovdim Be'eretz Yisrael* (The General Federation of Workers in *Eretz Yisrael*) has accepted Arab workers as full members since 1969. In 1920 the *Histadrut* had 4,500 members — in the 1985 *Histadrut* elections there were close to 1.5 million registered members.

The *Histadrut* is at one and the same time a trade union, a mutual aid society, a productive economic system and a center of cultural activities, sports and learning. The reason for its having developed in this unique way is connected with the development of the **Yishuv* in mandatory Palestine, when the rapidly developing labor movement, made up primarily of new immigrants, not only sought to defend the Jewish worker but to develop a socialist Zionist society and economy.

The structure of the *Histadrut* is as follows: the *Histadrut*'s Conference, which is the federation's supreme institution, is elected once every four years by proportional representation. Its decisions are binding on all *Histadrut* members, branches, institutions and enterprises. The *Histadrut* Council, which is selected by the Conference according to the balance of forces in it, is the body which in between meetings of the Conference acts as the *Histadrut*'s supreme institution, meeting once every six to eight months.

The Executive Committee is elected by the Council and runs the *Histadrut*'s affairs through its departments. Only the institutions dealing with control and adjudication are independent of it. The Executive Committee meets once every four to eight weeks.

The Central Committee is selected by the Executive Committee for the everyday running of the *Histadrut*, and meets once a week.

The trade union section of the *Histadrut* is responsible for negotiating, usually on an annual basis, framework agreements concerning wages, working conditions and labor contracts with the Industrialists' Association and the government. The affiliated trade unions are then responsible for the agreements in each separate economic branch. Though wildcat strikes are not uncommon, most strikes are sanctioned and supported by the *Histadrut*. The so-called "labor economy" is run by *Ḥevrat Ha'ovdim* (the *Histadrut*'s holding company) which was founded in 1923. *Ḥevrat Ha'ovdim* is almost identical in its personal make-up to the *Histadrut*, but is run separately. It embraces about 25 percent of the national economy. Its construction and industrial activities are carried out mainly through six conglomerates of which Koor is the largest industrial complex, employing 34,000 workers, and Solel Boneh is the largest construction company in the country. It has been involved in extensive development projects abroad, and at its peak employed about 14,000 workers. In 1986 Solel Boneh, like the rest of Israel's construction industry, sank into financial difficulties.

Ḥevrat Ha'ovdim also embraces production, service and consumer cooperatives, the *kibbutz (collective settlements) and **moshav* (semi-collective settlements) movements, and a number of joint enterprises with the government, the *Jewish Agency and other public and private factors. The labor economy is responsible for approximately 75 percent of Israel's agricultural production and 20 percent of its industrial production. Its financial institutions include *Bank Hapo'alim* (the Worker's Bank), which is the second largest bank in Israel, and *Hasneh*, Israel's largest insurance company.

It is frequently argued that the *Histadrut* has a built-in contradiction because it is both a major employer (it is the second largest employer after the government) and a representative of the workers. However, as an employer the *Histadrut* has always been a leader in terms of wages and working conditions, and in times of economic difficulties has been most cautions about firing workers.

Formally *Kupat Ḥolim*, the largest health fund in Israel with an extensive system of clinics and hospitals to which 83 percent of the Israeli population belong — is part of *Ḥevrat Ha'ovdim*, as are the various *Histadrut* pension funds which are responsible for 93 percent of the pensions paid out in the country. But in fact these institutions are independently coordinated by the *Histadrut*. The *Histadrut* provides adult and youth education, runs one of the major sports clubs in Israel, *Hapo'el*, with over 600 branches, publishes a daily paper, *Davar*, and operates one of the largest Hebrew publishing houses, *Am Oved*, as well as an Arabic publishing house.

The *Histadrut* maintains strong links with foreign labor organizations. Until the end of World War II it was a member of the Amsterdam International and the World Federation of Trade Unions. In 1950 it joined the International Confederation of Free Trade Unions. It represents Israel's workers in the International Labor Organization. It maintains an Afro-Asian Institute for labor Studies and Cooperation which since 1960 has trained over 15,000 students from 97 developing countries, many of which broke off diplomatic relations with Israel following the *Yom Kippur War.

Membership in the *Histadrut* is personal and non-political, but its governing bodies and those of the constituent unions are organized on party lines. While the various labor parties have always constituted a majority in the *Histadrut*, in recent years non-socialist parties have gained strength.

The *Histadrut* is considered one of the power centers of the Labor Movement in Israel, even though a large percentage of its members vote for non-socialist parties in the general elections. Especially since 1977 the **Likud* has tried to increase its own representation in the *Histadrut*'s institutions even though it has its own labor union, *Histadrut Ha'ovdim Hale'umiyim* (the union of national workers) and health fund, *Kupat Ḥolim Le'umit* (the national sick fund). In the 1977 *Histadrut* elections the *Likud* gained close to 29 percent of the votes compared to the *Alignment's 56 percent, but in 1985 the *Likud*'s strength fell to 24 percent while the Alignment's went up again to 69 percent.

During the *Likud*-led coalitions in 1977–84 efforts were made to pass a National Health Act in the *Knesset so that the *Histadrut* would lose control of *Kupat Ḥolim*, one of its main attractions to the public.

Since the establishment of the state the Secretary-General of the *Histadrut*, always a member of **Mapai* or the *Israel Labor Party, has been a Member of Knesset. Relations between the government and the *Histadrut*, even when Labor was in power, have never been smooth, due to inevitable clashes of interest regarding the government's economic policy. Nevertheless, the *Histadrut* has always been consulted and closely associated with the government's *economic policy and is essential for the success of any government endeavor in economics. It was a partner, together with the employers and the government, to the two package deals introduced by the *National Unity Government at the end of 1984 and the beginning of 1985 for stabilizing the economy. It was also an active partner in the stabilization plan introduced by the government in July 1985 to bring down inflation, and reduce the balance of payments deficit and in the second stage of the plan introduced in January 1987 to maintain stability and growth. In this capacity the *Histadrut*'s main concern has been to avoid the erosion of salaries and to prevent mass unemployment. Due to the financial difficulties which several of *Ḥevrat Ha'ovdim*'s enterprises experienced in 1986, the *Histadrut* has had to contend with the apparent contradiction between its roles as manager and representative of labor.

Secretaries-General of the *Ḥistadrut*:

1921–35	David *Ben Gurion
1935–44	David Remez
1944–49	Yosef Sprinzak
1949–50	Pinḥas Lavon
1950–56	Mordechai Namir
1956–61	Pinḥas Lavon
1961–69	Aharon Becker
1969–73	Yitzḥak *Ben Aharon
1973–84	Yeruḥam Meshel
1984–	Israel *Kessar

Histadrut Ha'ovdim Hale'umiyim The "National Workers Federation" was founded in 1934 after the withdrawal of the *Revisionists from the *World Zionist Organization (WZO), in competition with the **Histadrut*. Originally it tried to compete with the *Histadrut* by its willingness to accept lower wages for its workers and breaking strikes. It rejected the socialist ideology and did not celebrate the 1st of May, choosing instead to commemorate the birth date of Theodor *Herzl. In 1964 it objected to the decision of the **Ḥerut* Movement to join the *Histadrut* with its own faction — *Tchelet Lavan*. Its leaders were among the founders of the *Free Center and later broke off as the Independent Center *(*Hamerkaz Ha'atzmai)* and joined **La'am*. Today *La'am* is once again an integral part of *Ḥerut*.

Histadrut Ha'ovdim Hale'umiyim has over 80,000 members, runs a health fund — *Kupat Ḥolim Le'umit* — maintains over a dozen agricultural settlements as well as a youth movement, a housing company and other institutions.

"historic coalition" Popular name for the political coalition between **Mapai* and **Hamizraḥi* which was first established in 1935 within the framework of the Zionist Executive and which survived until 1976 between the *Israel Labor Party and the *National Religious Party (NRP). The coalition was based on the Labor Movement's acquiescence to a religious *status quo which included public observance of the Sabbath, *kashrut* in public kitchens, the maintenance of a religious education system and the monopoly of the religious establishment over questions of the personal status of Jews in Israel. In return, the religious Zionists supported Labor's economic, social and security policies. Labor also felt that it was important to have the religious parties inside the coalition both because they represented a significant section of the population and because they would be an obstructive force in opposition.

The coalition collapsed after the NRP gradually became more extreme in its policy regarding the future of the territories occupied by Israel in the *Six-Day War. In 1977 when the **Likud* was in a position to form a government, it was willing to make much greater concessions on religious issues. The immediate issue over which the historic coalition broke up was the abstention of some members of the NRP in a vote on a motion of no-confidence brought by *Agudat Yisrael* in 1976 over the alleged public desecration of the Sabbath in connection with a ceremony at an Air Force Base.

The Labor Party hopes to renew the historic coalition, which is viewed with some nostalgia, since that is its only hope of returning to power without a coalition with the *Likud* in the foreseeable future. The religious camp, on the other hand, viewed the coalition as a somewhat degrading arrangement that came into being when there was no alternative.

Holocaust The word holocaust means "wholesale destruction and loss of life, especially by fire." It is used to describe either the whole Jewish experience in the Third Reich from 1933 to 1945 — starting with loss of rights and personal humiliation and ending with the gas chambers — or the actual systematic extermination of European Jewry by Nazi Germany during the Second World War, but especially after the Wannsee Conference of January 20, 1942, where the *final solution and the methods to be used to execute it were discussed. All in all close to 6 million Jews were murdered in the Holocaust by the *Einsatzgruppen* and in specially-constructed death camps, of which Auschwitz was the best known.

The killing of the Jews was different from all other crimes committed by the Nazis against humanity. It was based on an ideology and involved a policy of genocide — an attempt to liquidate the whole Jewish race. This was to be carried out immediately, as a first priority, frequently contrary to all economic or military reason, and with a total absence of any inhibitions or moral scruples by the perpetrators. Many of Germany's satellites, and individuals from occupied countries took an active part in the policy's implementation.

It is frequently argued that the State of Israel was established as a result of the Holocaust. There is no doubt that the catastrophe which befell the Jews, and the total inability of the Jews outside Nazi occupied Europe to save their brethen, convinced many who had previously been *anti-Zionists that the establishment of Jewish state was the only safeguard against another Holocaust. The Holocaust also influenced many states to vote in favor of the UN partition plan in the General Assembly on November 29, 1947, though it did not cause any of them to take measures to ensure the state's survival after May 15, 1948, when Israel was invaded by the Arab armies (See: *War of Independence). However, the embryo of the Jewish state existed before the Holocaust, and sooner or later a Jewish state was bound to emerge, even though the timing of its actual establishment and the Jewish determination to establish it without further delay, were affected by the Holocaust.

The Holocaust is responsible for Israel's extreme sensitivity in all that concerns its security and continued existence, which occasionally seems to go beyond the real threat posed by the *Arab-Israel conflict. This sensitivity also manifests itself in the rhetoric of many Israeli leaders and politicians, most notably in that of Menaḥem *Begin who lost his parents in the inferno and barely escaped himself. In the 11th *Knesset there are four Holocaust survivors, Dov Shilansky and Eliahu Ben Elissar (*Likud*), Shevaḥ Weiss (*Alignment) and Ḥaike Grossman (**Mapam*), all of whom mention the Holocaust frequently in their speeches and writings. The Holocaust also manifests itself in political slogans such as "never again." It is officially commemorated in Israel on Holocaust Day, one week before Independence Day.

In 1961 Adolf Eichmann, one of the principal war criminals who escaped justice in 1945, was kidnapped by Israeli agents in *Argentina and brought to trial in Israel. Efforts were made to capture Dr. Joseph Mengele in Paraguay, but without success. In February 1986 Ivan Demjanjuk was extradited from the *United States to Israel to stand trial for war crimes of "Ivan the Terrible" committed at the concentration camp of Treblinka.

In the early days of the state many Israelis refused to purchase German goods or travel to Germany. During the debate regarding the *restitution agreement with the *Federal Republic of Germany in the early 1950s, Menaḥem Begin led the struggle against Israel's acceptance of German money for Jewish property confiscated during the Nazi era. Today such feelings are much weaker, but even though relations between Israel and the Federal Republic, established in 1965, are friendly, Israel resists referring to them as "normal."

The Federal Republic, while recognizing its moral debt to Israel and the Jewish people, stemming from the Holocaust, refuses to offer Israel automatic international support because of this debt, or to refrain from criticism of Israel. The German Democratic Republic refuses to accept any responsibility for the Holocaust.

Holy Places

JEWISH All the Land of Israel is holy for Jews, but the Temple Mount in Jerusalem is especially sacred. The Western (or Wailing) Wall, a retaining wall which borders the Temple Mount is today the only part of that site at which Jews worship. The Wall is the last remnant of the Second Temple, and according to Jewish tradition the Divine Immanence *(Shechinah)* still abides there even though the Temple was destroyed in 70 CE. After the *Six-Day War the Israeli government forbade Jews to pray on the Temple Mount in order to prevent tension with the Muslims, for whom the site of the al-Aqsa and Omar Mosques is holy. Most of the Jewish religious authorities have supported this ban for religious reasons. Under Muslim rule, access to the Wall by Jews was severely curtailed owing to Muslim veneration of their own religious sites on the Mount. Under the British Mandate, the authorities tried to settle the conflicting claims and rights to the Wall on the basis of the status quo. But there was much dispute over the Wall — culminating in the disturbances of 1928 and 1929 (See: *Mandatory Palestine). When the Old City of Jerusalem was occupied in 1948 by Jordan, a Jordan-Israel agreement provided for free passage for Jews to the Wall. However, this agreement was not honored by Jordan and Israelis were barred from access between 1948 and 1967. Since June 1967, all Holy Places under Israeli rule are freely accessible to all.

There are other sites, mainly tombs of patriarchs, matriarchs and sages, which are objects of veneration and the goal of devout pilgrimages, mostly during the major festivals. These, however, do not really merit the name of Holy Places, and if such terminology is employed it is the result of the influence of other religions. These include the cemetery on the Mount of Olives; the Tomb of the Patriarchs (Cave of Machpelah) in *Hebron, the Tomb of Rachel on the outskirts of Bethlehem; the Tomb of Shimon Bar Yoḥai in Meron; the alleged Tomb of King David on Mount Zion; the tombs of Rabbi Me'ir Ba'al Haness and of Maimonides in Tiberias; the Synagogue of Rabbi Yitzḥak Luria (the "Holy Ari") in Safed, and many others of lesser importance.

CHRISTIAN The Christian Holy Places are sites associated with events related in the Christian Scriptures. Churches were generally built at these sacred spots to mark the locality and make it a center of worship. There are about 100 Christian Holy Places in Israel belonging to the Catholic, Orthodox and Monophysite churches. (The Protestants do not single out specific sites for veneration.)

The most important sanctuaries in *Jerusalem are the Church of the Holy Sepulchre at the traditional site of the Crucifixion and the Tomb of Jesus; the Via Dolorosa, with its Stations; the Cenacle (the Room of the Last Supper); the Mount of Olives, with the Tomb of St. Mary, the Garden of Gethsemane and the Church of the Ascension. In Bethlehem, the most important Holy Places are the Church of the Nativity and the nearby Shepherds' Field. In Nazareth, the most important sanctuaries are the Catholic Basilica of the Annunciation and the Church of St. Gabriel, which the Orthodox believe to be the site of the Annunciation. Holy Places in Galilee include the Church of Cana, the place of the first miracle, and Mount Tabor, the site of the Transfiguration. The Sea of Galilee is venerated for its association with many miracles performed by Jesus. Many churches and chapels near its shores mark scriptural episodes such as the Sermon on the Mount and multiplication of loaves and fishes. The *Jordan River, the traditional site of the baptism of Jesus, is considered as especially holy.

In many Holy Places there are both Catholic and Orthodox churches. Several very important sanctuaries are jointly owned by several denominations and are the objects of conflicting claims. Typical examples are the Church of the Holy Sepulchre, the Church of the Nativity, the Tomb of Mary and the site of the Ascension. The ownership of and worship at such sites are regulated by the rules of the status quo, which were defined by a Firman of the Ottoman Sultan in 1852.

MUSLIM The holiest city of Islam is Mecca, the birthplace of the Prophet Muhammad, and the site of the Mosque of the Ka'ba, the venerated black stone. One of the five central precepts of Islam is to make a pilgrimage to Mecca *(Hajj)* at least once in one's lifetime. The most venerated city after Mecca is Medina *(al-Madina)*, where the Prophet took refuge and where, according to Muslim tradition, his tomb stands. Third in order of holiness is Jerusalem. There, on the Temple Mount area, called by Muslims *al-Haram al-Sharif*, the Noble Sanctuary, stand the mosques of *al-Aqsa* (the Farthest One) and the Dome of the Rock (also called the Mosque of Omar). According to Muslim tradition, Muhammad ascended to heaven from this place, while his horse, al-Buraq, remained tied at the Western Wall. By choosing the site of the Temple as one of its Holy Places Islam emphasized its ties with Judaism and with Christianity. In September 1969 a mentally disturbed foreigner entered the al-Aqsa Mosque and set fire to it, even though the area is guarded by the Muslims themselves. A plan by the *Jewish Underground to blow up the mosques on the Temple Mount in 1984 was foiled.

The Tomb of the Patriarchs in Hebron, mentioned above as sacred to Jews, is also deeply venerated by Muslims — particularly that of Abraham ("God's Friend," *Khalil Allah*, in Muslim tradition). A mosque, *Haram al-Khalil*, built in the 7th century on earlier, ancient foundations, enshrines the burial cave. Since 1967 the Israeli authorities have maintained a certain status quo to enable Jews and Muslims to pray and hold services in this site without interfering or clashing with each other.

The *Druze sect venerates the tomb of Shu'aib, the legendary ancestor of the community, identified with Jethro the Midianite, Moses' father-in-law. The tomb is situated at Hittin in Israel. (See also: Baha'is.)

The *Proclamation of Independence states that "the State of Israel shall safeguard the Holy Places of all religions" while the 1980 Basic Law: Jerusalem (See: *Basic Laws) ensures the sanctity of all the Holy Places in Jerusalem and provides a guarantee against attacks on them.

Hurwitz, Yiga'el Minister, Knesset Member, farmer and manager of enterprises. Born 1918, Naḥlat-Yehudah.

Hurwitz grew up in Nahalal which he left in 1940. He joined the *Jewish Brigade during World War II. After the war Hurwitz settled in Kfar Warburg. He participated in the attempt to set up an underground movement *Am Loḥem* (fighting people) to mediate between the **Haganah* and **IZL*. In 1946 he set up a short-lived party *Tnu'at Ha'am* which sought a middle road between **Mapai* and the *Revisionists. During the *War of Independence he continued to work his two farms and was not called up for active service in the *IDF. After the war, Hurwitz became Head of the Southern *Moshavim Corporation, setting up and managing dairy and meat processing enterprises until 1966. He joined *Mapai* in 1961 and was a member of its Central Committee from 1961–65 when he joined **Rafi*, remaining with David *Ben Gurion in 1968 when the rump of *Rafi* joined the *Israel Labor Party. He entered the 7th Knesset in 1969 on the *State List.

By the end of the 7th Knesset both Ben Gurion and Meir Avizohar (number two in the State List) left the Knesset, and Hurwitz remained the head of the four-man faction.

In 1968 he purchased two dairy product enterprises belonging to Rasco — the United Dairies and Tene-Nogah. In 1972 he purchased a third dairy firm — Adanir. In 1973 Hurwitz joined the **Likud*, thus securing four seats for the State List. Hurwitz, who gained all his economic experience in business and industry, had long given up on the Labor movement's socialist ideology, feeling that the structure of the Israeli economy was distorted, with industry and agriculture too dependent on the establishment. He viewed *Begin as the incarnation of the idea of "Greater Israel."

In 1976 Hurwitz was one of the founders of **La'am* in which capacity he ran with the *Likud* in the elections to the 9th Knesset (1977). He was appointed Minister of Industry, Trade and Tourism in Begin's first government. He soon threatened to resign unless $3 billion were cut from the budget, and finally did so in 1978 over the *Camp David Accords to which he objected. In 1979 Hurwitz also objected to the *Egyptian-Israeli Peace Treaty since he did not trust Sadat, and objected to the withdrawal from the oil fields and air bases in the Sinai. In 1979 he warned against an economic catastrophe within three years, and claimed that the Israeli political situation was being undermined, partially due to the helplessness of its economic leadership. He was uneasy about the massive *economic aid Israel had begun to receive from the *US.

In 1980 Hurwitz was appointed Minister of Finance after the resignation of Simḥa *Ehrlich, when his best-known motto, *"ein li"* (I haven't any), became famous. However, he did not receive government backing for his policy of severe budgetary cuts and resigned from the Ministry of Finance several months before the 1981 elections. In the elections to the 10th Knesset Hurwitz was third on **Telem*'s list of candidates, entering the Knesset in October 1981 after Dayan's death. However in 1983 he broke away from *Telem*, reestablishing his own faction — *Rafi* — the State List. Hurwitz ran for the 1984 elections on his own list **Ometz* which gained a single seat in the 11th Knesset. He ran on a purely economic platform which called for "Hurwitz for Minister of Finance," and was widely quoted on his warning against "an economic Yom Kippur" and on his slogan *meshuga'im — terdu mehagag* (Madmen — get off the roof). Hurwitz is a Minister without Portfolio in the *National Unity Government.

The *Bejski Commission on the regulation of bank shares found Hurwitz responsible for being insufficiently informed about the scope and severity of the problem during his tenure as Minister of Finance.

I

IDF: Israel Defense Forces The IDF was formally founded on June 27, 1948, despite the fact that, as of November 30, 1947, the armed forces of the **Yishuv* were already engaged in a war against the unorganized forces of the Arab community of Palestine, supported by weapons and volunteers from the neighboring Arab states.

The origins of the IDF are to be found in its precursors, **Hashomer*, the *Jewish Legion, the **Haganah*, the **Palmaḥ*, the *Jewish Brigade, **IZL* and **Leḥi*.

Since its establishment the IDF has fought six wars: the *War of Independence (1948–49), the *Sinai Campaign (1956), the *Six-Day War (1967), the *War of Attrition (1969–70), the *Yom Kippur War (1973) and the *Lebanese War (1982). In between wars it has almost constantly been involved in border skirmishes and major or minor operations across the border.

Over the years the IDF has changed considerably, in terms of size, organization and weaponry, as have the armed forces of Israel's enemies.

In the six wars, as well as the various engagements and border skirmishes between the wars, Israel suffered some 17,000 fatalities. The majority of them occurred in two wars: the War of Independence (7,000 killed), and the Yom Kippur War (2,800 killed). The number of soldiers wounded in battle was much higher. As a result of these wars the IDF acquired vast combat experience.

REGULAR AND RESERVE COMPONENTS OF THE IDF: After the War of Independence the IDF was organized as a force comprising regular and reserve forces. The ratio of regular to reserve forces is one to two (i.e., one-third regular and two-third reserves). The Air Force and the Navy have a larger component of regular personnel than the Army.

The reserves are organized in separate units, though some reserve soldiers are assigned to regular units. The reserve units have a nucleus of regular officers and men who keep the unit running and the weapon systems in combat condition. The reserve units usually train regularly once a year, and perform guard and security duties as well.

Normally men are called up for 30 to 45 days of reserve duty per annum. Following the Yom Kippur War some reserve units were mobilized for 6 months. The call-up system is intended to ensure that the reserves are available for combat in minimal time, some being ready for action within 24 hours from call-up. To this end call-up exercises are held from time to time.

In the past the mobilization of the whole of the IDF with all its reserves has required several days, but this time-gap is constantly being reduced.

The regular units comprise career soldiers (NCOs and officers) and conscripts. Conscription is general. Permission not to serve in the army is granted for two reasons only: health and religion. Men serve for three years, and women for two years. Women over 24, married women, and women with religious objections to military service are exempt from service. Among the men most yeshiva students are exempt. Men who are new immigrants and over the age of 26 serve for a year and a half, and older new immigrants are exempt from regular military service though they are usually coopted into the reserves.

The *Arabs of Israel are exempt from military service for security reasons, and the issue of alternative national service (as for religious women) has not yet been resolved. Some Christian Arabs and Bedouins, and all the *Druze and Circassians serve in the army, on the basis of the Draft Law. Some of them join the career military service.

REGULAR ARMY SERVICE: Most of the senior command and staff positions are filled by career officers. Senior NCOs in regular units and in the skeleton units of the reserve forces are also career soldiers. The exact number of men and women serving a career service is unknown, but is estimated at several tens of thousands. Normally they serve 20 to 30 years, and many begin a second career upon retirement from the IDF. Some retired generals have gone into politics (See: *Military and Politics).

The existing setup allows the career component of the IDF to become highly competent professionally, which is especially important in the age of sophisticated weaponry.

TRAINING: All IDF forces undergo thorough and intensive training which is based mostly on an indigenous Israeli doctrine. Nevertheless, Israel's military doctrine and its national security perceptions were greatly influenced by what the founding fathers of the IDF learned during World War II in the British Army, the Red Army and in the *Palmaḥ*.

The doctrine and training have undergone several changes resulting from the experience gained by the IDF in the wars it has fought since 1948.

Another factor influencing training in the IDF is budgetary constraints. As the IDF has grown in size, and its weapons systems have become increasingly more sophisticated, training has taken up an ever growing portion of the defense budget. Thus, on occasion, training has been less intensive than desirable as a result of the rising prices of tank and artillery shells, combat aircraft flight hours, and sailing costs of naval combat vessels. Nevertheless, the IDF tries to train its units under conditions as similar as possible to battlefield conditions, with as much live ammunition exercises as budget permits. The means of electronic warfare and new training aids (such as videotapes for analyzing combat aircraft training sorties) have become an integral part of training.

At various times officers and NCOs have been sent to study abroad in military schools in the *US, *Great Britain, *France and the *Federal Republic of Germany. The knowhow acquired at these schools has been integrated into the IDF's training programs.

CIVILIAN CONTROL OVER THE IDF: The highest ranking officer in the IDF is the Chief of the General Staff who holds the rank of *Rav Aluf* (Lieutenant General). In accordance with the Basic Law: the IDF (See: *Basic Laws) he is subject to the civilian authorities in the person of the Minister of Defense, who is subject to the Prime Minister and the Cabinet. The government deals with defense issues within the forum of the Ministerial Committee for Defense which is chaired by the Prime Minister, and consists among others of the Ministers of Defense, Finance, and Foreign Affairs. No single major move has ever been taken by the IDF without the authorization of the Government, a Minister, or the Ministerial Committee.

The activities of the IDF are supervised by the *State Comptroller, the Knesset Foreign Affairs and Security Committee and the Knesset Financial Committee.

Though at the field level the IDF has a good deal of freedom of action, and has on occasion taken measures not fully foreseen and approved as such by the government level (e.g., as in the case of the Lebanese War), all decisions regarding war and peace have been taken by the government. In such cases the IDF serves in a professional advisory capacity, and, as decided by the *Agranat Commission, may be held responsible for providing erroneous advice.

CIVILIAN LEADERSHIP AND MILITARY COMMAND: The Minister of Defense, who heads the defense hierarchy, is a politician and a civilian. Of the ten persons who have held the position since the establishment of the state (See: *Ministers of Defense) six had no military career, while four (Moshe *Dayan, Ezer *Weizman, Ariel *Sharon and Yitzḥak *Rabin) were former *Chiefs of Staff or senior officers. David *Ben Gurion, Levi *Eshkol and Menaḥem *Begin served, at least for a while, as both Prime Minister and Minister of Defense.

Until 1986 Israel has had 12 Chiefs of Staff, none of whom were involved in politics while serving in the army, though each was agreeable to the party in government. All the Chiefs of Staff came from either the paratroopers, armor or infantry, and most of them had a distinguished career as combat soldier before rising to the highest level of command. Six of the 12 served in the *Palmaḥ*, two served in the Jewish Brigade, three served in the *Haganah*, and the twelfth Chief of Staff served his entire military career in the IDF. He is also the first non-Ashkenazi to serve in this post. One Chief of Staff, Yiga'el *Yadin, resigned over disagreements with the Prime Minister; one, David Elazar, was forced to resign as a result of the conclusions of the Agranat Commission which investigated certain issues regarding the Yom Kippur War; and another, Rafael *Eitan, was reprimanded by the *Kahan Commission following the *Sabra and Shatilla massacre. All 11 former Chiefs of Staff left the army after completing their tour of duty.

THE GENERAL STAFF: The Israeli General Staff is a unified staff commanding the whole of the IDF. The General Staff is headed by the Chief of the General Staff. It does not include staff officers who are permanently posted to it. High officers alternate between the General Staff and field and staff service at unit or regional command level.

The organization of the General Staff, which has undergone changes over the years, is currently made up of: Operations, Intelligence, Logistics, Manpower, and Planning branches, each headed by an officer holding the rank of *Aluf* (Major General). The commanding officers of the regional commands hold the same rank. Training is a department within the framework of the Operations Branch but is also headed by an *Aluf*. The Chief Commanders of the Air Force, Navy and Ground Forces are also *Alufim* and members of the General Staff. Other services such as the Armored Corps, the Infantry, Artillery and Engineer Corps have their own professional staffs but have no operational command function, and are headed by officers holding the rank of *Tat Aluf* (Brigadier General) who are subordinate to the Ground Forces Command. The Medical Corps, the Ordnance Corps, etc., are also headed by *Tat Alufim*, and are subordinate to the Head of the Logistics Branch.

In the past Intelligence and Planning were departments within the Operations Branch, and there was no Ground Forces Command.

ORGANIZATION, SIZE AND WEAPONS OF THE GROUND FORCES: The Ground Forces Command is in charge of training doctrine, central schools and placement of officers, NCOs and personnel. The operational command of the units is in the hands of three regional commands: Northern, Central and Southern, each headed by an *Aluf*.

The regional commands control divisions and independent brigades. The number of divisions and/or brigades subordinate to any regional command is more or less equal in peace time, but divisions or brigades may be transferred from one regional command to another, depending on the tactical and strategic needs. Normally all regional commands have control of regular and reserve divisions and brigades.

In 1986 the IDF had 12 armored divisions and 20 independent infantry/paratroop brigades including both regular and reserve units. The number of men and women in the ground forces is about 440,000, of whom 130,000 are in regular service. In 1986 the major weapons systems included 3,800 tanks (Merkava, improved Centurion, M-60, improved M-48, Improved (Russian) T-54/55 and T-62). The artillery comprises 1,000 pieces (155mm M-109 SP Howitzer, 175mm M-107 SP, 155mm towed Howitzers, 130mm guns, 122mm D-30, and several models of heavy mortars). Rocket launchers include 290mm and 122mm multiple rocket launchers. Ground-to-ground rockets include lance rockets. There is also bridging equipment, anti-tank missiles (TOW, Dragon and AT-3 Sagger) and anti-aircraft guns and missiles (Chapparal and Redeye).

ORGANIZATION, SIZE AND WEAPONS OF THE AIR FORCE: The number of men and women in the Air Force is 80,000 of whom 30,000 are in regular service. The Air Force is deployed mainly in 11 air bases, two of which were moved to the Negev after the withdrawal from the *Sinai Peninsula.

The organization of the Air Force is in squadrons and wings. A squadron comprises aircraft of the same model, while a wing may comprise different models. The operational control over the activity of the Air Force is central, i.e., control by the Air Force command post, which is part of the command post of the IDF. It comprises also units of command and control, early warning, radar, SAMs, electronic warfare and service and maintenance units.

In 1986 the number of combat aircraft was 645. The spearhead of these aircraft are 50 F-15 and 75 F-16 fighter aircraft. Other models in service are the Israeli produced Kfir, F-4 Phantoms and A-4 Skyhawks. The IAF also flies 88 transport aircraft, the most important of which are 24 C-130 Hercules aircraft and 10 Boeing 707 aircraft. It has in service 188 helicopters, of the models AH-1G/AH-1S Cobra, 500 MD Defender, CH-53, SA-321, AB-212 and AB-206, and 170 training and liaison aircraft. It also flies electronic warfare aircraft and four aerial early warning aircraft, Model E-2C. On order are 75 additional F-16 aircraft. Some older models will be withdrawn from service. The fate of the new Israeli-developed aircraft the Lavi is still uncertain.

ORGANIZATION, SIZE AND WEAPONS OF THE NAVY: The Navy personnel is 20,000, half of whom are regular sailors. The Navy is deployed mainly in three naval bases, in Haifa, Ashdod and Eilat. The units are organized in squadrons, according to the type of vessel. The control is central, by the command post of the Navy, which is part of the command post of the IDF.

The principal vessels in service are three IKL/Vicers Type 206. These are boats of German design, produced for Israel in Britain in 1977. There are 24 fast-patrol missile boats, of three models: Sa'ar 2 and 3, almost identical, produced in France in the 1960s, Sa'ar 4 (Reshef) produced in Israel in the early 1970s and Sa'ar 4.5 (Aliyah) produced in Israel in the late 1970s and early 1980s. The missile boats are armed with Israeli Gabriel missiles and US-made RGM-84 Harpoon missiles. The navy also operates two Flagstaff type missile-carrying hydrofoils. It has in service 47 small patrol boats for coastal defense, 13 landing craft of various models and two small hovercraft. The navy has on order Dvorah, a small fast-patrol missile boat. It is also planning to construct several more modern submarines and several Sa'ar 5 missile frigates.

HIGH TECHNOLOGY: The numerical inferiority of the IDF compared to the combined forces of its adverseries has forced Israel to try and keep a costly qualitative edge. In the spheres of electronic warfare, counter-electronic warfare, electronic surveillance, command and control and related fields Israel produces much of its own requirements.

High technology is to be found in all branches of the IDF. The ground forces have improved command and control techniques, while constantly improving the tanks and artillery pieces in service. The intelligence service has concentrated on improving its acquisition and processing capabilities. Since the Arab Air Forces have the same or similar models of aircraft to those flown by the Israel Air Force, Israel has introduced technological improvements into its own planes. The same applies to missile boats and missiles.

NAḤAL: The *Naḥal* (Hebrew acronym for *No'ar Ḥalutzi Loḥem* — fighting pioneering youth) compromises about 5,000 men and women, most of them graduates of youth movements, whose objective is to join existing *kibbutzim or establish new ones. These groups serve part of their service working in existing kibbutzim and the rest training in regular military combat units — infantry, tank or paratroop — in which they serve. Later on they are sent to a new (temporary or permanent) settlement, normally along the borders. The force is commanded by an officer holding the rank of *Tat Aluf*.

WOMEN'S SERVICE: Women have served in the IDF since its inception. During the War of Independence women soldiers participated occasionally in combat action. Since 1949 no women have been allowed to participate in combat.

Ḥen (Hebrew acronym for *Ḥeil Nashim*, Women's Corps), is responsible for placement, conditions of service, wellbeing of women, etc.

Women serve as clerks, drivers, radar operators, nurses, MDs, social workers, teachers, instructors at the various service branch schools, in various intelligence duties, in the legal service of the IDF and in administrative capacities.

THE MILITARY RABBINATE: The Military Rabbinate is led by a Chief Military Rabbi holding the rank of *Aluf*, with Rabbis (all Orthodox) in every regional command and division. The Military Rabbinate carries out duties similar to those of military chaplains in the American and European armies. They maintain synagogues at the unit level, supervise the *kashrut* of the kitchens, oversee observance of the Sabbath and Jewish holidays. In wartime they are responsible for evacuating the dead, identifying and burying them in military cemeteries.

The *Yeshivot Hesder* have similar service arrangements to those of the *Naḥal.*

TERRITORIAL DEFENSE: During the 1936–39 disturbances defense of the Jewish settlements was a major part of the activities of the *Haganah.* During the early phases of the War of Independence some of the decisive early battles were fought by agricultural settlements such as Tirat Tzvi and Kfar Szold. In April 1948 Mishmar Ha'emek repulsed a massive attack by the Palestine Liberation Army under Fawzi al-Qawuqji.

Sixteen Jewish settlements were taken by the Arab forces during the War of Independence of which six, Be'erot Yitzḥak, Yad Mordechai, Nitsanim, Sha'ar Hagolan, Masada and Mishmar Hayarden were retaken during the later stages of the war. As the war progressed regular forces of the IDF started to participate in the defense of settlements.

In the 1956, 1967 and 1973 Wars territorial defense played no role on the Israeli side. In the 1973 War the IDF ordered the evacuation of the civilian population from the settlements on the *Golan Heights, orders which were only grudgingly obeyed.

In the current security measures against terrorist activities, the territorial defense of the settlements plays an important role in collaboration with the IDF. Currently the IDF comprises units designed to support the Jewish settlements in war but this territorial defense is not expected to fight a war on its own, or, with few examples, defend itself unaided against a major attack. A realistic distribution of labor between the IDF and the settlers releases the IDF from many territorial defense duties.

BUDGETARY CONSTRAINTS: Due to the IDF's relatively large size (close to 12 percent of the population, including reserves), and its sophisticated weapons systems, Israel has been forced to spend an exceptionally high proportion of its GNP on defense.

While most NATO members spend around 3 percent of their GNP on defense (Japan spends less than 1 percent), Israel, due to its frequent wars and the arms race imposed on it by its neighbors, has spent as much as 32 percent of its GNP in the peak years 1973 and 1974. In the years 1964–66 the figure was a "low" 10 percent, and in 1986, around 16 percent (4 billion out of a GNP of 25 billion). American military aid in the form of loans and grants has helped Israel carry the burden (See: *Foreign Aid to Israel). In 1970 this aid amounted to $30 million. In 1971 it rose to $545 million. In 1974, as a result of the Yom Kippur War it shot up to $2.5 billion of which $1.5 billion were in the form of a grant. In 1984 the US military aid to Israel was $1.7 billion of which half was given as a grant. In 1985 it was a grant of $1.4 billion. In 1986 it amounted to about $1.8 billion. Similar sums have been requested for 1987 and 1988. The foreign aid component is included in the defense expenditure figures.

While Israel spent in 1985 $4 billion on defense, *Syria spend $3.3 billion, Egypt $3.7 billion, Jordan $526 million, Saudi Arabia about $17.5 billion, Iraq $12 billion and Libya an unknown yet vast sum as well. Compared to these figures the Israeli defense expenditure is relatively low. The cut in defense expenditure to 16 percent of GNP resulted from the severe budget cuts required by the economic stabilization plan of 1985, and has had an impact on both the training and the rate of renewal and upgrading of weapons systems. The cut was made possible without jeopardizing Israel's security because of the continued Iran-Iraq war and the *Egyptian-Israeli Peace Treaty which leaves Syria alone as an immediate direct threat.

In the second stage of the government's economic plan introduced in January 1987, the budget of the Ministry of Defense was the only one not reduced. (Z.E.)

Iḥud Hakvutzot Vehakibbutzim The Union of the *Kvutzot* and the Kibbutzim (See: *Kibbutz) is a movement which split from **Hakibbutz Hame'uḥad* in 1951 over ideological issues, a split which led to similar divisions in several kibbutzim and in families as well. The *Iḥud* reunited with *Hakibbutz Hame'uḥad* in 1979 to form the **Takam* (United Kibbutz Movement). Politically the *Iḥud* was close to **Mapai* but membership in the movement was not conditional on party membership. In 1979 the movement had 87 kibbutzim. One of the movement's most talented leaders, Moshe (Mussa) Ḥarif, who entered the Knesset in 1981, and was viewed as a potential future leader of the *Israel Labor Party, was killed in a car crash several months after his election.

Immigration See: **Aliyah*

Independent Liberal Party of Israel A successor to the *Progressive Party (1949–61), the Independent Liberal Party (*Liberalim Atzma'im*) was established in 1965. In 1961 the Progressive Party had united with the *General Zionists and established the *Liberal Party of Israel. In 1965 the Liberal Party split when the majority decided to establish a political bloc with **Ḥerut* to form **Gaḥal*. Most of the ex-Progressives decided to establish their own party, the Independent Liberal Party, objecting to the sharp shift to the right which the merger with *Ḥerut* implied.

The Independent Liberal Party ran for the Knesset on a platform advocating a social-democratic system in which private, national and cooperative initiatives all contribute to the common goal. It supports a policy of salary scales based on educational and professional qualifications, supports compulsory arbitration in labor disputes in the public sector, the nationalization of the health services, the enactment of a *constitution. On foreign affairs and security matters it follows a moderate line. The independent Liberals were members of all the Labor-led governments from 1965 to 1977. After losing their only seat in the 9th Knesset (1977) (held by Gideon *Hausner) the Independent Liberals joined the *Alignment before the elections to the 11th Knesset (1984) and are represented by one MK (Yitzḥak Artzi).

Knesset Seats: 6th Knesset (1965) — 5; 7th Knesset (1969) — 4; 8th Knesset (1973) — 4; 9th Knesset (1977) — 1; 11th Knesset (within the Alignment) — 1. (D.B.M.)

Interim Agreement The second *Disengagement Agreement between *Egypt and Israel reached through the mediation of US Secretary of State Henry Kissinger (See: *Kissinger Shuttle), signed on September 4, 1975 in Geneva. The agreement provided for: 1) an Israeli withdrawal on the Suez front to the eastern ends of the strategic Mitla and Giddi Passes, with most of the vacated territory becoming a new UN buffer zone 12 to 26 miles deep and the old buffer zone becoming part of the existing Egyptian limited-force zone; 2) an Israeli evacuation of the Abu Rudeis and Ras Sudar oil fields and of a narrow strip along the Gulf of Suez connecting the oil fields to Egyptian-controlled territory south of Suez, with joint UN-Egyptian administration and no military forces stationed within the evacuated area; 3) a joint undertaking to refrain from the use or threat of force or military blockade, to observe the cease-fire scrupulously and to renew the mandate of the UN Emergency Force annually; 4) the passage of non-military Israeli cargo through the Suez Canal; 5) American-manned electronic early-warning stations in the area of the Mitla and Giddi Passes; 6) a joint Israeli-Egyptian commission to deal with problems as they arose and to assist UNEF; 7) a military work group which would meet in Geneva to draw up a protocol establishing in detail the stages of the implementation of the agreement.

The Interim Agreement was acompanied by *Memoranda of Understanding signed by the US with Israel and with Egypt.

International Center for Peace in the Middle East An apolitical organization founded in 1982 by the monthly magazine *New Outlook* to accommodate scholars, political figures and businessmen in Israel and abroad who are involved in the quest for peace in the Middle East.

The goals of the center are to sponsor research and discussion leading to concrete conclusions and promoting general peace in the area; to encourage relations between Israel and the Palestinians based on mutual recognition; to free the Middle East from the arms race between the superpowers; to bring about cooperation between the Jewish and Arab worlds; and to promote freedom, tolerance and equal cultural and political rights for national minorities. Among the members of the center are members of *Knesset, judges and professors. The center publishes research papers in its fields of interest and holds occasional conventions and symposia in Israel and abroad. (M.B.)

Iran and Israel Iran has always demonstrated an ambivalent attitude toward Israel. On the one hand Iran is a Moslem state located close to the Arab states where the influence of religious ministrants is strong; on the other, Iran views itself as an Aryan country whose language and culture are different from those of the Arabs, and whose inhabitants still remember the Arab invasion of their homeland which destroyed their cultural infrastructure. Since the establishment of independent Arab states in the region Iran has feared their territorial demands, especially regarding the oil-rich Khuzestan region, the Persian Gulf and Shatt-el-Arab.

The first contacts between Iran and Palestine were made in 1921 when Iran assigned the treatment of the affairs of some 30,000 Iranians who lived at that time in Palestine to its consulate in Egypt. In 1934 an independent consulate was established in Jerusalem.

Iran supported the Arab policy in Palestine and voted against the UN partition plan. However, after considering both regional and global issues, Iran announced its de facto recognition of Israel on March 11, 1949, despite the massive propaganda against the establishment of the state.

The Ayatolla Kashani, an influential Iranian religious leader at that time incited the crowds and asked for volunteers to fight against Israel. However, Prime Minister Said took advantage of Kashani's exile in Lebanon, and when the parliament was in recess due to the Persian new year, quietly announced the recognition.

Even these low-profile relations were severed after the rise of Dr. Mohammad Mossadeq as Prime Minister, and his anti-western struggle, led to the closing down of the consulate in Jerusalem. However, the removal of Mossadeq in 1953 created a suitable background for the resumption of relations. The Shah began a wide-scale operation for suppressing his opponents — especially on the extreme Left. The rise of Egyptian President Gamal Abdel Nasser, which strengthened the feelings of Arab nationalism, and the renewed pressure by Iraq against Iran encouraged the development of "under the table" relations between Iran and Israel. These relations were boosted upon the arrival in Teheran of Iranian-born Me'ir Ezri, as the representative of the Israeli Ministry for Foreign Affairs. The Israeli representation had functioned until then in the Jewish Agency offices in Teheran, but now opened its own offices. On January 30, 1960, the Shah repeated his de facto recognition of Israel at a press conference. The Arab states protested and Nasser declared the severance of relations with Iran, while embarking on acts of overt subversion against the Shah. As Arab hostility mounted a more convenient climate was created for tightening the relations between Iran and Israel. Arab subversion led to intelligence cooperation, and the beginning of military cooperation between the two states.

In January 1963 the Shah announced the implementation of the White Revolution for the economic, social and cultural development of Iran, and sought to benefit from Israel's experience in these spheres. This led to a great expansion of the ties, and the increase of the Israeli representation in Teheran, whose official status was "Economic Mission." In the early 1960s Me'ir Ezri was given the status of Ambassador, a status which was also assumed by his successors: Uri Lubrani and Joseph Marmelin.

Iran turned into the main supplier of oil to Israel and trade relations were expanded, parallel with a deepening of military, intelligence and technological cooperation. In 1973–74 Israel's visible exports to Iran amounted to $33 million; four years later they were $230 million. Israel received 65 percent of its oil from Iran by 1978. Many Israeli personalities visited Iran secretly. Some say that all the Israeli Prime Ministers starting with David *Ben Gurion and ending with Menaḥem *Begin visited Teheran and met with the Shah.

However, as relations between the two states became stronger, so the propaganda of the religious and oppositon circles (Communists, the Left, the "national front") against the Shah and the State of Israel increased. Upon the declaration of the White Revolution in 1963 and the strengthening of the relations with Israel, the Ayatolla Khomeini made his first speech against the Shah, and pointing at these ties, he asked: "Does Jewish blood flow in the veins of the Shah, or perhaps his mother is Jewish?" During the days which preceded the *Six-Day War, as well as during the *Yom Kippur War, the incitement against Israel reached new peaks. Extremist groups led by Khomeini, or close to his doctrines, established contact with the *Palestine Liberation Organization (PLO) and started to train in its bases in Lebanon.

Even before the Yom Kippur War the Shah decided to distance himself somewhat from Israel and strengthen his relations with the Arab states. The death of Nasser and the rise of Sadat paved the way for a significant improvement in the relations between Iran and Egypt, and during the Yom Kippur War the Shah allowed Soviet supply planes to fly over Iran on their way to Egypt.

The struggle of the Shah's opponents, headed by the Ayatolla Khomeini, to topple his regime was accompanied by strong anti-Israel propaganda. The Shah was accused of cooperation with the Zionists to suppress the Palestinian people and prevent the spread of Islam. Accusations were spread regarding close cooperation between the **Mossad* and the *Savak* — the Iranian security service — to suppress the opposition, and against militant Arab states. Israel was also accused of participating in the mass killing of demonstrators in Teheran on September 8, 1978, several months before the fall of the Shah.

Upon his rise to power on February 10, 1979, Khomeini started to implement the anti-Israel policy which he had advocated during his long years in exile. He broke off relations, stopped the export of oil and announced the need to destroy Israel. In his declarations Israel was called a cancer in the body of the Islamic nation, the enemy of Islam, and the enemy of humanity. "The liberation of Jerusalem" was declared to be one of the main goals of the Islamic revolution, in order to renew the Caliphate (this time Shi'ite). He came out against compromise and negotiations with Israel, and supported the resolution of the Palestine problem only by military means. He even presented the long Iran-Iraq war as "a war for the liberation of Jerusalem and the liquidation of the Zionist entity," and called President Sadam Hussein of Iraq "a Zionist infidel." He also declared the last Friday of the Ramadan month as the "day for the liberation of Jerusalem" throughout the Moslem world. A week after Khomeini's rise to power PLO chairman Yasser Arafat was received in Teheran, and the following day he was granted the building of the Israel representation in Teheran which was turned into the "Embassy of Palestine." Iran started to develop relations with the Shi'ites in Lebanon, and encouraged them to carry on an armed struggle against Israel, pouring large sums of money into extremist organizations, such as *Khizbollah, Jundallah* and *Amal Islami.*

On the international scene, Khomeini's Iran has demanded Israel's expulsion from the UN, the International Labor Organization (ILO) and other organizations, and opposed Israel's retur to UNESCO (See: *United Nations). Despit this state of hostility, news was published fron time to time regarding the flow of large quanti ties of Israeli arms to Iran for the continuation o the war against Iraq.

In 1982, Minister of Defense Ariel *Sharo acknowledged that there had been certain arm deliveries to Iran. In November 1986 it wa revealed that Israel had been involved in arm deliveries to Iran at the request of the US govern ment, in connection with the release of America hostages held by extremist Shi'ite groups in Leb anon. In addition, several individual Israelis wer implicated in private arms-sales to Iran.

There is a debate in Israel regarding Israel' interests in connection with the Iraq-Iran Wa since both sides are self-declared enemies c Israel. However, the existence in Iran of a larg Jewish community has clearly affected Israel' attitude as well. (M.A.

Irgun Zva'i Le'umi (IZL) A Hebrew terr meaning "national military organization. Known commonly by its acronym, *IZL*, it was a underground defense and resistance organiza tion. It was founded before the establishment o the state in Jerusalem in 1931 following a disa greement over policy and tactics within th **Haganah* and its response to the 1929 riot Eschewing **Histadrut* supervision, *IZL* sough Revisionist support (See: *Revisionist Move ment), and that of other non-Labor groups, whil pursuing an activist orientation. Its first com mander, Avraham Tehomi, returned to the rank of the *Haganah* in 1937 and the *IZL* becam almost exclusively Revisionist, with Ze'e *Jabotinsky formally viewed as Suprem Commander.

Reacting to the disturbances which broke ou in April 1936, *IZL* adopted an activist policy contrary to the *Haganah* policy of *havlagah* (self restraint). On November 14, 1937 Arab buse were fired at, marketplaces were bombed an individual Arabs killed. An *IZL* membe Shlomo Ben-Yosef, arrested at this time, wa hanged by the mandatory authorities in Jun 1938, and became one of *IZL*'s martyrs, calle *Olei Hagardom* (those that were hanged). At th same time *IZL*, like the *Haganah,* was als engaged in bringing "illegal" immigrants fron Europe to Palestine. By 1940 many thousand ere brought in this way. Following the publication of the 1939 White Paper, *IZL* launched a series of attacks against British institutions and installations and assassinated officers of the Central Investigation Department (CID) accused of torturing *IZL* detainees.

Upon the outbreak of World War II *IZL* ceased its anti-British activities and encouraged its members to enlist in the British army and participate in the war against Nazi Germany. *IZL* Commander David Raziel (1910–1941) was killed during a British commando raid in Iraq. In November 1943 Menaḥem *Begin was appointed the new *IZL* Commander and on February 1, 1944 declared a revolt against Britain, accusing that country of betraying the Jewish people. Over the next four years, the *IZL* attacked scores of British installations, army camps, police stations, government offices, mining roads and railways and sabotaging British targets in Europe as well. Angered and concerned by *IZL*'s insubordination, part of the *Haganah* leadership and individual members cooperated with the British authorities in identifying and capturing *IZL* members in an operation termed the *Saison* ("open season"). While *IZL* was greatly weakened by this campaign, it was not destroyed. It was primarily Begin's restraint which prevented the outbreak of civil war between his supporters and the *Haganah*.

After the British Labor Government came into power in 1945, it failed to change the 1939 White Paper policy and *IZL* participated in the Hebrew Resistance Movement with the *Haganah* and *Leḥi*. On July 26, 1946, the Government Secretariat and British army headquarters were greatly damaged in an *IZL* attack on the King David Hotel in Jerusalem. The attack was to have constituted part of a coordinated operation by the *Haganah, IZL* and *Leḥi*. The operation, in fact, was cancelled at the last moment by the *Haganah*, due to Chaim *Weizmann's disapproval of the activities of the Hebrew Resistance Movement, but *IZL* proceeded with its own plan carried out during office hours, causing the deaths of 91 persons. As a result of the King David operation the brief cooperation between the *Haganah, IZL* and *Leḥi* came to an end.

IZL developed a method of retaliation against the British which involved the flogging of British military personnel following the flogging of *IZL* members by the British, and the hanging of two British sergeants after three *IZL* members had been hanged on July 29, 1947. This policy stopped both the floggings and hangings by the British.

IZL rejected the UN partition plan of 1947 and continued its operations against the British and reprisal attacks against the Arabs without any coordination with the *Haganah*. The massacre which took place after the *IZL*-led attack on *Deir Yassin became another *cause célèbre* between the organized **Yishuv* and the dissidents. *IZL*'s attack on Jaffa led to a mass exodus of Arabs.

IZL, which according to its own statistics numbered 5,000 on the eve of the establishment of the state, officially disbanded on June 1, 1948, two weeks after the declaration of independence, but maintained a separate unit in Jerusalem which was not as yet integrated into the State of Israel. Part of the arms brought on board the **Altalena* had been earmarked for this unit. However, the ship was sunk after a bitter confrontation between the *IDF and *IZL*, which was viewed by both sides as a final power struggle. On September 20, 1948, the *IZL* units in Jerusalem were forcibly disbanded, after the assassination of UN Mediator Count Bernadotte. *IZL* units abroad continued to operate until December.

On June 15, 1948, Begin founded the **Ḥerut* Movement which adopted *IZL*'s emblem — a hand grasping a rifle held over a map of **Eretz Yisrael* on both sides of the *Jordan River; *IZL* veterans still refer to each other as the *"fighting family." (I.M.)

Irreversibility Thesis See: *Benvenisti Prognosis.

Israel Communist Party See: **Ḥadash*, **Rakaḥ*, **Maki*.

Israel Council for Israeli-Palestinian Peace (ICIPP) A political association which calls for mutual recognition between the State of Israel and the Arab Palestinian people, through its authorized representative organization. Among the founders of the ICIPP were Mattityahu *Peled, Uri *Avneri and Ya'acov Arnon, who were also among the founders of the *Progressive List for Peace, Arie Lova *Eliav and the veteran Sephardi leader Eliahu Eliashar, who was its honorary president until his death in 1983. The

ICIPP was founded in Tel Aviv in December 1975, at a conference attended by Israeli peace-activists. Following its establishment the ICIPP issued a 12-Article manifesto which remains the Council's basic document. *Inter alia* the manifesto states: "We affirm that this country is a common homeland for both its peoples — the people of Israel and the Arab Palestinian people" (Article 1); "...that the core of the conflict between Jews and Arabs is the historical confrontation between the two peoples in this country which is dear to both" (Article 2); "...that the only way to peace is coexistence between two sovereign states, each possessing its distinct national identity: the State of Israel for the Jewish people, and a state for the Arab-Palestinian people, as an expression of its right to self-determination in whatever political framework it might choose" (Article 3); "...that the establishment of an Arab-Palestinian state alongside Israel will be the outcome of negotiations between the Israeli Government and authorized, recognized representatives of the Arab-Palestinian people, without negotiations with the *Palestine Liberation Organization (PLO) being ruled out, on the basis of mutual recognition" (Article 4); "...that the boundaries between the State of Israel and the Arab-Palestinian state will be based upon the pre-1967 armistice lines, with minor modifications, agreed upon between the parties concerned, and after settling the problem of *Jerusalem" (Article 5); "...that the establishment of the Arab-Palestinian state will decisively contribute to resolving the national and humanitarian refugee problem." (Article 8).

Several months after its foundation, the Council was involved in the "Paris encounters" with unofficial PLO representatives, notably with the late Dr. Issam Sartawi, who was assassinated by Palestinian rejectionists at the conference of the *Socialist International in Albojeira, Portugal on April 10, 1983. Contacts between the ICIPP delegates and Sartawi and his colleagues had many fluctuations, but established a continuous dialogue between the two sides. In the wake of the *Lebanese War Peled, Avneri and Arnon met with Arafat and other key PLO figures, and it was agreed that a permanent framework for political coordination between the two parties should be set up. The assassination of Sartawi constituted a serious setback to the plan's implementation.

The ICIPP has some 300 registered members all of them Jewish or Arab residents of Israel, wh have signed the Council's manifesto.

The Council publishes a monthly English language newsletter, *The Other Israel*, which i circulated among its friends and supporters.

(Yo.A.

Israel Defense Forces See: *IDF: Israe Defense Forces.

Israel Labor Party Social-democratic party established in 1968 following a three-way merger between **Mapai*, **Aḥdut Ha'avodah Po'alei Zion* and **Rafi*. The party never stood fo elections since a year later, in 1969, it formed th *Alignment together with **Mapam*. Within th institutions of the new party *Mapai* received 5 percent of the membership, while each of th other parties received 22.5 percent. This sectoria structure was maintained until the party's firs Conference in the spring of 1971. Since then th sectorial rule has formally ceased to exist, thoug some vestiges remain.

The formation of the Labor Party at a critica juncture in Israel's history was partially responsible for *Mapai*'s more compromising position regarding the *Arab-Israel conflict being mute in Israel's policy until 1977. The *Galili Document of 1973 was a clear manifestation of thi phenomenon. The second Labor Party Confer ence took place in the spring of 1977, in whicl Minister of Defense Shimon *Peres conteste Prime Minister Yitzḥak *Rabin's leadership o the party. Rabin won by a small majority, bu resigned the premiership soon thereafter due t his wife's bank account scandal.

The Alignment electoral defeat in May 197 found the party, under the leadership of Shimo Peres as Party Chairman and Ḥaim *Bar Lev a Secretary-General, shattered and in chronic debt A slow process of rehabilitation and the openin of the party's ranks to new members began.

Yigal *Allon was planning to run for the part leadership at its third Conference which was t be held in 1980. Following Allon's death Rabi once again contested the leadership at the Con ference which was held in December 1980, bu Peres won an impressive victory, winning ove 72 percent of the votes.

Following the second electoral defeat in 198 the Labor Party continued in the attempts t adjust to the new political reality and started t prepare for early elections. The main criticism by the Labor Party of the three *Likud-led governments was in the economic sphere where inflation and the balance of payments deficit were allowed to get out of control; in the political sphere where no progress was made in the peace process after 1979 and in the military sphere where a hopeless war was launched in Lebanon (See: *Lebanese War) (the Labor Party supported only the occupation of the 40 kilometers adjacent to Israel's northern border); in the sphere of settlement where the party objected to intensive settlement activities in the densely populated areas of the *West Bank; and for inciting parts of the population against the Labor Movement.

Despite high hopes regarding an electoral victory in the 1984 elections, the result of the election was a draw, leading to the formation of a *National Unity Government in September 1984 under the premiership of Shimon Peres in which the Labor Party and its partners in the Alignment and **Shinui* received 50 percent of the Cabinet portfolios, with an undertaking to transfer the premiership to Yitzḥak *Shamir, in October 1986.

The fourth Labor Party Conference, held in April–May 1986, decided to democratize the way in which the Party elects its institutions and the Knesset list, and to further equality for women.

The Labor Party, wishing Israel to remain a Jewish democratic state in which there is a large and stable Jewish majority and complete equality of rights for its Jewish and non-Jewish citizens; to end Israel's control over 1.3 million *Palestinian Arabs in the West Bank and *Gaza Strip; to find a solution to the Palestinian problem within the framework of a Jordanian-Palestinian State; and to secure for Israel defensible borders — is ready to enter peace negotiations without prior conditions on the basis of *Security Council Resolutions 242 and 338, though the *Palestine Liberation Organization (PLO) and any other organization which support the *Palestine National Covenant, deny Israel's right to exist and use terror, cannot be partners in negotiations. The repartition of *Jerusalem is also not negotiable. The Labor Party objects to the annexation of the West Bank and the Gaza Strip, and to an Israeli return to the May 1967 borders — calling for a *"territorial compromise" which from an Israeli point of view must cater to Israel's legitimate security needs. The Labor Party's settlement policy is based on its vision of Israel's future borders.

Since the Labor Party maintains close relations with many social-democratic and Labor parties around the world, it is more sensitive to international public opinion than is the **Ḥerut* Movement which is more isolated.

In the economic sphere the Labor Party's main goal is to achieve economic independence, growth and full employment. It supports a mixed economy with government, **Histadrut* and private sectors all playing an important role, and central economic planning and direction based on multi-year plans. It favors socio-economic experiments in the sphere of worker enterprise-ownership, and the development of urban cooperative enterprises. The Labor Party believes that intensive agricultural planning and centralized marketing both in Israel and abroad are the only bases for a viable agricultural sector in Israel.

Labor is viewed as a supreme value, and theoretically all forms of speculation and non-productive employment are frowned upon.

Though the party accepts the religious *status quo as it existed until 1977, and is inclined to dilute its policy on religion and state in view of the probability that it might form a government which will be dependent on at least some of the religious parties, it advocates respect for all religions, and Jewish religious pluralism which will ensure official status for the *Reform Movement and *Conservative Movement in Israel, while objecting to a change in the definition of "Who's a Jew" in the *Law of Return and to both religious and anti-religious coercion.

The Israel Labor Party was headed by Levi *Eshkol in 1969, Golda *Meir 1969–73, Yitzḥak *Rabin 1974–77, and Shimon *Peres since 1977. The Secretaries-General of the party have been Pinḥas *Sapir 1969–70, Arie Lova *Eliav 1970–71, Yisrael Yeshayahu 1971–72, Aharon Yadlin 1972–74, Me'ir Zarmi 1974–77, Ḥaim *Bar Lev 1978–84, and Uzi Baram since 1984.

Knesset Seats: 7th Knesset (1969) — 47 (out of the Alignment's 56); 8th Knesset (1973) — 43 (out of the Alignment's 51); 9th Knesset (1977) — 28 (out of Alignment's 32); 10th Knesset (1981) — 40 (out of the Alignment's 47); 11th Knesset (1984) — 38 (out of the Alignment's 44).

IZL See: **Irgun Zva'i Le'umi*.

J

Jabotinsky, Ze'ev (Vladimir) (1880–1940). Zionist leader, statesman and writer.

Born in Odessa, Russia, Jabotinsky was educated in the liberal tradition of emancipation with little formal Jewish content. He left school at 17 and became a newspaper correspondent, first in Berne and then in Rome. In Rome he pursued university studies. He returned to Russia in 1901 and was jailed the following year as a suspected socialist. Jabotinsky participated in the defense of Odessa Jews during the wave of pogroms following the Kishinev massacre in 1903. He graduated the University of Vienna in 1908, became a major Zionist propagandist and served as a Zionist agent in Turkey for two years. During World War I Jabotinsky initiated the idea of the participation of Jewish volunteer units to fight with the British army in Palestine. Eventually, three battalions were formed as the *Jewish Legion and Jabotinsky reached the rank of lieutenant. In 1920 he headed the **Haganah* in Jerusalem and directed the defense of the city during the Arab riots in April. He was arrested by the British authorities for carrying illegal arms and sentenced to 15-years imprisonment. Later, the sentence was quashed. Elected to the Zionist Executive in 1921, he travelled to the *United States on a fund-raising mission, but resigned in January 1923 in protest over the policies of Chaim *Weizmann toward the mandatory power, which he saw as the whittling away of political Zionism. He was especially critical of the surrender of *Transjordan and the increased links with the Zionist Labor Movement.

In 1923 Jabotinsky founded a youth movement, **Betar* in Riga, Latvia and in 1925 the World Union of Zionist *Revisionists in Paris. His Zionist Congress speeches were noted oratorical appearances and he became the main opposition spokesman. In 1928 Jabotinsky settled in Palestine but after the 1929 riots he left the country and was not allowed to return. In 1934 in London he signed three agreements with David *Ben Gurion to halt the internal feuding which had resulted from the *Arlosoroff murder and labor disputes between the **Histadrut* and other sectors of the **Yishuv*. However, the agreements were rejected by the *Histadrut* members.

Jabotinsky led the Revisionist movement ou[t] of the *World Zionist Organization in 1935 establishing the *New Zionist Organization i[n] Vienna. He pursued a policy of alliances wit[h] governments, most of them known for their anti-Semitism, which might show interest in his pla[n] to evacuate 1.5 million East European Jews t[o] Palestine. He strongly opposed the *partitio[n] plan proposed by the 1937 Peel Commission. I[n] addition he supported the **IZL* in its anti-Ara[b] terror campaign and its opposition to the polic[y] of self-restraint pursued by the organized *Yishuv*.

Upon the outbreak of World War I[I] Jabotinsky lobbied for the formation of a Jewis[h] army. He travelled to the United States in th[e] beginning of 1940 to continue his campaign, bu[t] died there without accomplishing his mission. His body was reinterred in Israel in 1964 whe[n] Levi *Eshkol reversed Ben Gurion's refusal t[o] permit the reburial. (I.M.)

Jarring Mission Swedish Ambassador Dr Gunnar Jarring (born 1907) was selected as special envoy to the Middle East by the Secretary-General of the *United Nations following th[e] 1967 *Six-Day War, on the basis of *Security Council Resolution 242, to "promote agreemen[t] and assist efforts to achieve a peaceful an[d] accepted settlement" to the *Arab-Israe[l] conflict.

Because the Arab states refused to hold direc[t] negotiations with Israel, Jarring was obliged t[o] commute between Jerusalem and the Arab capitals. His talks were suspended in the spring o[f] 1969 without results when the representatives o[f] the four Great Powers began to discuss the Middle East issue. In August 1970 the Jarring talk[s] were resumed, after an American initiativ[e] resulted in a renewal of the cease-fire and militar[y] standstill which put an end to the *War of Attrition (See: *Rogers Plan). However, Israel suspended the talks when it became apparent tha[t] Egypt had, with Soviet assistance, violated th[e] agreement by moving anti-aircraft missiles clos[e] to the *Suez Canal. The talks resumed in December 1970 and on February 8, 1971, Jarring submitted his own proposals for a peace arrangemen[t] which would involve an Israeli commitment t[o] withdraw its forces from occupied Arab territor[y] to the former international boundary between Egypt and the British Mandate of Palestine" on the understanding that satisfactory arrangements were made for: the establishment of demilitarized zones; practical security arrangements in the Sharm-e-Sheikh area for guaranteeing freedom of navigation through the Straits of Tiran; and freedom of navigation through the Suez Canal. On the other hand Egypt would give a commitment to enter into a peace agreement with Israel, and to make explicit therein to Israel, on a reciprocal basis, undertakings and acknowledgements covering the following subjects: termination of all claims of states of belligerency; respect for and acknowledgement of each other's independence; respect for and acknowledgement of each other's right to live in peace within secure and recognized boundaries; responsiblity to do all in their power to ensure that acts of belligerency or hostility did not originate from, or were not committed from, the respective territories against the population, citizens or property of the other party; non-interference in each other's internal affairs.

The proposal was accepted in principle by Egypt on February 15, but on February 26 Israel rejected the notion of its withdrawing to the 1967 borders and called for direct negotiations without preconditions. To all intents and purposes this brought the Jarring Mission to an end.

Jericho Plan A plan which was discussed in 1974 in connection with a proposed disengagement agreement between Israel and *Jordan, by which Israel would return Jericho and its environs to Jordan in return for an arrangement similar to that signed with Egypt and Syria in 1974. The plan, which was promoted by Yigal *Allon who discussed it with Secretary of State Henry Kissinger (See: *Kissinger Shuttle), was abandoned following the *Rabat Arab Summit Conference which declared the *Palestine Liberation Organization (PLO) the sole representative of the Palestinian people and the only body entitled to negotiate on its behalf.

Jerusalem Capital of Israel (population 452,500 in 1983). Holy city of the three major religions (according to a list compiled by the UN there are 15 places sacred to Christians, five to Muslims and ten to Jews — see *Holy Places). During the British mandate (1922–48) Jerusalem served as Palestine's capital. Since the establishment of the state it has been the seat of the Israeli *President, the *Knesset, the *government and the *World Zionist Organization. The Old City and the eastern part of Jerusalem were occupied in 1948 during the *War of Independence by the Jordanian Arab Legion except for Mount Scopus, which became an Israeli enclave. Since the *Six-Day War Israel has held the whole of the city.

Jerusalem is built on the Judean Hills, approximately 800 meters (2,600 feet) above sea level. It was first mentioned in Egyptian sources of the 17th and 18th centuries BCE and was a Jewish city from King David's time (1037–969 BCE) until the destruction of the Second Temple by the Romans (70 CE). During the Second Jewish Revolt, led by Bar Kochba (in 135), Jerusalem became a Jewish city once more; after the suppression of the revolt, it was renamed by the Romans Aelia Capitolina and Jewish settlement was forbidden. The Persians (614–29) allowed Jewish settlement. From the time of the Muslim conquest (638) there have always been in Jerusalem both a large Muslim, Arabic-speaking community and a Jewish community. Jerusalem was briefly under Christian rule 1099–1187 and 1229–44 when Jews were not allowed to settle in the city.

The history of West Jerusalem begins in 1860 with the building of Jewish quarters outside the walls of the Old City. Jewish settlement within the Old City was forcibly interrupted on May 28, 1948, when the Jewish Quarter (1,700 inhabitants) surrendered to the Jordanian Arab Legion.

The *United Nations Resolution of November 29, 1947, providing for the *partition of *mandatory Palestine and the establishment of a Jewish and an Arab state, recommended that Jerusalem should come under an international regime,separate from the two states and under the supervision of the UN Trusteeship Council. Nevertheless, the UN did nothing to defend the city and its inhabitants, or to secure their physical needs. Nor were steps taken toward the elaboration of a "detailed statute," as resolved, or for an administration.

The plan for internationalizing Jerusalem presented by Count Folke Bernadotte, the UN mediator, was rejected by both the Arabs and the Jews and was not approved by the UN. However,

JEWISH POPULATION OF JERUSALEM

Year	Total Population	Jews	Percentage of Jews
1860	12,000	6,000	50
1892	42,000	26,000	61.9
1922	63,000	34,000	53.9
1942	140,000	86,000	61.4
1948	165,000	100,000	60.6
1967 (July)	266,000	200,000	75.0
1983 (June)	452,500	327,300	72.3

the General Assembly reaffirmed on December 11, 1948, that the city should be "under effective UN control." The Palestine Conciliation Commission, just appointed, was instructed to prepare a "detailed proposal for a permanent international regime" for Jerusalem, while the Security Council was to ensure the demilitarization of the city (but in fact did nothing). In December 1949 the Assembly "restated its intention" to establish an "international regime" which would provide adequate protection for the Holy Places, and charged the Trusteeship Council with preparing the "Statute of Jerusalem." *Jordan stated during the debate in the Assembly that it would not discuss any plan to internationalize Jerusalem.

The Jews had accepted the 1947 Assembly Resolution but the Arabs had rejected it, claiming that it denied the Palestinians' right to self-determination. Rejecting the Jews' right to self-determination, the Arabs embarked on war. West Jerusalem was shelled by Qawuqji's "Rescue Army." Several Arab areas were conquered by the Israelis but the Old City and East Jerusalem fell to Jordan on May 28, 1948. On December 1, 1948, Jordan established its administration there, and on April 24, 1950, it officially annexed — despite the bitter opposition of all the other Arab stages — most of the *West Bank, including the eastern part of Jerusalem. Jordan again emphasized its objection to the internationalization of Jerusalem. Israel, too, withdrew its agreement, claiming that the Arab invasion restored to the Jews their historic right to the city and that it would guarantee the safety of the Holy Places.

In its report published in June 1950, the Trusteeship Council again proposed that Jerusalem be a *corpus separatum* under international administration. The *Soviet Union withdrew its support for internationalization in view of the opposition of both the Arab and Jewish inhabitants. In January 1952 the General Assembly passed a resolution placing on the governments concerned the responsibility for reaching agreement about all disputed points, in accordance with previous UN resolutions. This resolution, which practically recognized the status quo, was the last one on this subject to be passed by the UN until 1967.

The Israel-Jordan *Armistice Agreement of April 3, 1949, finalized the complete partition of Jerusalem already existing de facto. The agreement provided for a joint committee to ensure free access to the Holy Places, to the Jewish cultural institutions on Mount Scopus and to the Jewish cemetery on the Mount of Olives, and placed a limit on the amount of arms allowed into Jerusalem. This joint committee never met and the Jordanians ignored their commitment to allow Jews access to the Holy Places. The Jewish cemetery on the Mount of Olives was desecrated. Access to Mount Scopus was granted to a limited number of policemen only. (E.L.)

On January 23, 1950, the Knesset pointed out that with the establishment of the State of Israel Jerusalem became once again the capital of the Jewish people. Most of the foreign diplomatic missions accredited to Israel were nevertheless situated in Tel Aviv since most of the states which maintained diplomatic relations with Israel never recognized Israel's authority over any part of Jerusalem. The reasons for this were: (1) the status of a *corpus separatum* assigned to Jerusalem under the UN partition plan; (2) the fear of angering the Arab states; (3) the refusal on the part of some states to accept Jewish control over the Christian Holy Places. Twenty embassies were nevertheless established in West Jerusalem at the time of the outbreak of the *Six-Day War, only two of them — the Netherlands and Yugoslavia — representing European countries.

In 1965 Teddy *Kollek was elected on a *Rafi* ticket as Jerusalem's Mayor, in which capacity he was still serving (as an independent, though known to be affiliated with the *Alignment) in 1987.

In general elections the **Likud* and religious parties receive an overwhelming majority of the votes in Jerusalem. The city's community of ultra-religious Jews refuses to recognize the authority of the State of Israel and does not vote in either the municipal or national elections (See: *Neturei Karta). There is occasionally tension between ultra-religious and secular Jews.

In June, 1967, after its occupation by Israeli forces, East Jerusalem and some of its environs became subject to Israeli "law, jurisdiction and administration." Under the law local Arabs who did not choose to become Israeli citizens received Israeli identity cards as residents of Jerusalem but remained Jordanian nationals. This arrangement entitles them to travel freely in Israel and abroad, to participate in Israel's economic life as well as to elect and be elected to the Municipal Council. While several thousands have voted in municipal elections, the majority have chosen not to exercise this right as a formal protest against the annexation of East Jerusalem. No East Jerusalemite has ever stood as a candidate to the City Council.

Efforts have been made to adjust the implementation of municipal bylaws to the needs and life-style of the Arab population in order to create an atmosphere of cooperation and peaceful coexistence. Though political organization has not been permitted, the publication of a large number of daily and weekly papers, which support either various groups within the *Palestine Liberation Organization (PLO) or Jordan, have been allowed. The East Jerusalem press, while subject to censorship, nevertheless reflects the political mood of the Arab population and its objection to the current political situation.

Kollek's popularity among Jerusalem's Arabs is one of the factors that has contributed to the existence of a relatively peaceful atmosphere in the city, despite occasional outbursts of unrest between Arabs and Jews after terrorist attacks.

Before 1967 only 59 percent of the houses in East Jerusalem had running water and only 40 percent had electricity. Subsequently East Jerusalem was connected to the Israeli water system and the East Jerusalem Electric Company (which has had serious financial difficulties and has been unable to renew its equipment) supplied all of East Jerusalem and the new Jewish neighborhoods with electricity up until 1987. In December 1986 the Company agreed to relinquish its concession to supply electricity to the Jewish neighborhoods. For the Arabs the East Jerusalem Electric Company has become a symbol of Arab rights.

A major problem is the lack of a satisfactory master plan for East Jerusalem, which makes it extremely difficult for the inhabitants of that part of the city to receive building permits or even to enlarge existing buildings. Though the problem is technical the Arab population interprets it as political.

The curriculum in the East Jerusalem primary schools is that used by the *Arabs of Israel in their schools. The Jordanian curriculum is used in the municipal high schools which cater for about half of the Arab pupils in the city.

Since 1967, the Jewish Quarter in the Old City, destroyed in the war of 1948–49 has been rebuilt and resettled by Jews.

The Hebrew University campus and the Medical Center on Mount Scopus were restored, expanded and put back into active use. New Jewish neighborhoods surrounding the city were established so that it could not be divided again: Ramot and Neveh Ya'acov in the north, East Talpiot and Gilo in the south and a suburban settlement, Ma'aleh Adumim, to the east of the city.

After the Six-Day War most of the Ministries which had remained in Tel Aviv, except Defense and Agriculture, were moved to Jerusalem.

Since the reunification of the city Israel has maintained the security of the Holy Places, freedom of access and worship for all, and the rights of the various religious communities to their Holy Places. More than 100,000 citizens of all nations, including those of Arab states at war with Israel, visit the city every year. Nevertheless, the de facto annexation of East Jerusalem to Israel in 1967 aroused opposition both among the Arab states and in the UN General Assembly which resolved, on July 4 and 14, 1967, that steps taken by Israel to alter Jerusalem's status were invalid, and called on it to cease immediately all such activities. Since that time the General Assembly has consistently condemned the Israeli rule in Jerusalem. In two sharply worded resolutions the Security Council called on Israel, on May 21, 1968, and July 3, 1969, to cancel all steps taken to annex East Jerusalem. UNESCO regularly sends inspection teams to observe Israel's archaeological activities in the city, and has condemned it for "changing the character of Jerusalem through the archaeological digs," even though Israel has taken the utmost care to preserve the Old City's special character.

After the Six-Day War, some Arab leaders indicated that they would be ready to accept the internationalization of Jerusalem, though most Arab spokesmen demanded that East Jerusalem be returned to Jordan. Since the 1974 *Rabat Conference the Arab states have held that East Jerusalem should be the capital of any future Palestinian state.

Following the *Yom Kippur War, when Pan-Arab and Pan-Islamic feelings reached new heights, the Muslim states reemphasized their demand that East Jerusalem return to Arab control, with King Feisal of Saudi Arabia as the most uncompromising spokesman regarding Jerusalem's Muslim character. An official resolution to this effect was adopted by the Islamic Conference Organization at a meeting held in Pakistan in February 1974, which established the al-Quds (Jerusalem) Committee under the chairmanship of King Hassan of *Morocco. The Israeli government has forbidden Jews to pray on the Temple Mount to prevent tension with the Muslims, for whom the site of the al-Aqsa and Omar Mosques is holy. Most Jewish religious authorities have supported this ban for religious reasons. In September 1969 a mentally disturbed visitor from Australia entered the al-Aqsa Mosque past the Muslim guards and set fire to it. A plan by the *Jewish Underground to blow up the mosques on the Temple Mount in 1984 was unsuccessful. In the beginning of 1986 the Knesset Interior Committee warned that illegal construction works were being carried out on the Temple Mount by the Moslem *Waqf* (religious endowment).

In order to facilitate worship at the Western (Wailing) Wall, the most sacred of Jewish sites, houses close to the Wall were demolished soon after the Six-Day War and their occupants compensated and transferred to other houses. Since then excavations have uncovered the continuation of the Wall to the north while excavations to the south have uncovered the City of David.

On July 30, 1980, the Knesset passed the Basic Law: Jerusalem (see: *Basic Laws) which declared "integral and united Jerusalem" to be the capital of Israel and the seat of the President of the State, the Knesset, the government and the Supreme Court. The government ensures the sanctity of all the Holy Places, and provides a guarantee against attack on them or "anything liable to disturb the free acceess of members of all the religions to the places holy to them, or their feelings toward those places." Although this law merely reaffirmed old principles, it led to strong international reactions.

On August 20, 1980, UN Security Council Resolution 478 called on members of the UN to withdraw their diplomatic missions from Jerusalem. The 13 states which had maintained their embassies in Jerusalem after 1973 (when the Yugoslavian and six African embassies were closed down after their states severed diplomatic relations with Israel) moved them to Tel Aviv. Only one — Costa Rica — subsequently moved its embassy back to Jerusalem. An initiative in 1984 taken by the *United States House of Representatives to move the US Embassy in Israel to Jerusalem was rejected by the Administration because a "change in the US position on the status of Jerusalem would seriously undermine our ability to play an affective role in the Middle East peace process."

Ten countries, although they do not maintain embassies in Jerusalem nevertheless have consulates there, but their official status is ambiguous, and they are usually independent of the embassies in Tel Aviv and deal primarily with matters connected with the *occupied territories.

Despite the international opposition to Israel's policy in Jerusalem, all the parties in Israel, except for **Ḥadash* and the *Progressive List for Peace, object to the repartitioning of the city, its internationalization or the return of any part of it to Arab sovereignty. There is a consensus that there should be a special administrative status regarding the places holy to Christianity and Islam, which would be agreed upon once a comprehensive peace settlement is achieved.

(S.M.-S.H.R.)

Jewish Agency Article 4 of the Mandate for Palestine, as finally approved by the League of Nations in 1922, provided for the establishment of "an appropriate Jewish Agency" to be "recognized as a public body for the purpose of advising and cooperating with the Administration of Palestine in such economic, social and other matters as may affect the establishment of the Jewish national home and the interests of the Jewish population in Palestine, and, subject always to the control of the Administration, to assist and take part in the development of the country. The Zionist Organization, so long as its organization and constitution are in the opinion of the Mandatory appropriate, shall be recognized as such agency."

Until 1929 it was the *World Zionist Organization (WZO) which acted in the capacity of Jewish Agency. In that year a separate body was established, called the Jewish Agency, which involved, in addition to representatives of the WZO, prominent *non-Zionist Jewish personalities willing to share in the building of the national home. These included such figures as the author Scholem Asch, French socialist leader Leon Blum, nuclear scientist Albert Einstein, and American leaders Louis Marshall and Felix Warburg. However, the following year soon after the inauguration of the enlarged Jewish Agency the partnership between the Zionists and non-Zionists failed to materialize due to the outbreak of riots in Palestine and the death of Marshall. Thus, though non-Zionists continued formally to be represented in the Jewish Agency it was primarily the Zionists who were active in it. The Jewish Agency represented the Jewish community of Palestine and the Zionist organization vis-à-vis the British Government, the Palestine Admistration and the League of Nations, and dealt with the facilitation of Jewish immigration to Palestine; the advancement of the *Hebrew language and culture; the purchase of land in Palestine for the Jewish people through the Jewish National Fund (See: *Land Policy); the development of agriculture and settlement on the basis of the principle of Jewish labor; fulfillment of Jewish religious needs in Palestine without infringing on individual freedom of conscience.

Upon the establishment of the State of Israel the functions of the Jewish Agency were taken over by the government. In 1952, under the Law of Status, the Jewish Agency and the WZO, now effectively a single organization, were designated as the bodies responsible for the "ingathering of the exiles" and their absorption in Israel. In July 1954 a covenant between the Government of Israel and the WZO-Jewish Agency Executive, spelling out the *modus operandi* of cooperation between the two, was signed. After 1960, when the Jewish Agency for Israel, Inc., was established in the US, the non-Zionists started becoming active again, and were invited to sit on the Agency's Board of Governors.

In the aftermath of the *Six-Day War, which brought world Jewry and Israel closer together, a process of restructuring the Jewish Agency began. In an agreement signed in 1971 the Jewish Agency was reconstituted on the basis of a partnership among the WZO (50 percent), the *United Israel Appeal (30 percent) and the *Keren Hayesod* (Foundation Fund: 20 percent) (See: *Land Policy) — the fund-raisers thus gaining equal status with the Zionists. Though under the agreement there is a functional separation between the Jewish Agency and WZO — with the Jewish Agency concentrating on work in Israel with the financial backing of world Jewry, and the WZO on work in the Diaspora — the two organizations are managed by the same Chairman, Director-General, Treasurer, Comptroller and Board Members. Under this agreement the reconstituted Agency was put in charge of immigration and absorption from "countries in distress," educational and youth activities, particularly *Youth Aliyah, agricultural settlement within the *Green Line and immigrant housing. In 1972 the Amigur Housing Management company was established to deal with the latter task. Since 1977 the Jewish Agency has also been in charge of Project Renewal, a special program for the rehabilitation of distressed neighborhoods throughout Israel through the cooperation of the local residents and "adopting" overseas Jewish communities. In 1981 the Caesarea Conference of the Jewish Agency Board of Governors reviewed the ten-year partnership and explored its future. The fund-raisers' wish to increase their say in the partnership, and to reduce the influence of Israeli politics in the work of the Agency was emphasized on that occasion, and since then, has come into strong relief.

Jewish Brigade During World War II Palestinian Jews volunteered for service in the British Army, particularly the East Kent Regiment (the Buffs), three companies of which became the Palestine Regiment. Others served with sappers and commando units and fought in Ethiopia, on the Western Front and in Greece, and some served in the British Air Force and the Navy. Palestinian volunteers numbered some 26,000 Jews (out of a population of about 450,000) and 9,000 Arabs (out of about one million).

The Brigade was formed in Sept. 1944 under Brig. Ernest Frank Benjamin, an English Jew, after heavy Jewish pressure and years of British objection on economic and political grounds. The Brigade numbered about 5,000 men, had its own flag and emblem, and saw service in Egypt, the North Italian front, and northwest Europe. Men of the Brigade did much to aid Jewish survivors of the *Holocaust, and helped to smuggle them to Palestine.

The Brigade was disbanded in the summer of 1946. Many of the future leaders of the *IDF received their military education in its ranks.

Jewish Legion Jewish battalions in World War I consisted of the 38th (recruited in England, 1915–17), 39th (organized in America, 1917–18, by David *Ben Gurion and Yitzḥak *Ben Zvi) and 40th (mainly from Palestine, 1918) Battalions of the Royal Fusiliers, and the Zion Mule Corps (initiated and organized by Ze'ev *Jabotinsky and Yosef *Trumpeldor in Egypt in 1915 and led by the latter who was one of its captains). They totaled around 6,400 men and were collectively called the Jewish Legion.

The Jewish Legion was formed as a result of the Zionists' conviction that they should support Great Britain and her allies in order to accelerate the establishment of a Jewish National Home in Palestine. The Legion's formation had been preceded by lengthy discussion. Some Zionist leaders advocating neutrality as the correct policy for the Zionist movement since Jews lived in all the countries directly involved in the war.

It was disbanded in May 1921 because of the participation of Legion soldiers in the defense of the Jewish quarter of Jerusalem against Arab rioters and in the smuggling of arms for Jewish self-defense. Many of its members were later active in the formation of the **Haganah*.

Jewish underground A group of 25 men, most of them residents of Judea and Samaria (See: **Yosh*), convicted of crimes which include murder and terrorist activities directed against Arabs in the years 1980–84. Arrested in April 1984, they were sentenced in July 1985, after a lengthy trial, to various prison terms, three of them to life imprisonment. They were held responsible for bombing the cars and the injuring of three West Bank mayors, killing students at Hebron's Islamic College, grenade attacks, planting bombs on buses and conspiring to blow up the Dome of the Rock on the Temple Mount.

The discovery of the underground spurred the **Gush Emunim* movement into debate over failures in education and internal discipline. Harsh criticism was voiced over the group's disobedience to the state's authority in the field of security, and its elitist approach. Opponents of *Gush Emunim* pointed to the underground as an inevitable consequence of the philosophy and activities of the *Gush*. Much sympathy was nevertheless expressed for the men and their motives even by those who rejected their acts. Continuous terrorist acts against Jews in Israel and the territories gave rise to the feeling that the Israeli security authorities were not doing enough to stop them and had even sanctioned *Palestine Liberation Organization (PLO) activity through support of such bodies as the Palestinian National Guidance Committee. Consequently sympathizers raised funds for the families of the accused and for their legal defense.

After the sentencing, a movement for clemency began and amnesty legislation was tabled in the *Knesset. In June 1985, upon the release of 1150 Arab and other terrorists in exchange for four captured Israeli soldiers, the wives of the convicted men went on a hunger strike to protest their husbands' continued detention.

Other groups in Israel, especially on the Left, insisted that the members of the underground should be punished severely, both as a matter of legal principle and as a warning to other groups who might wish to take the law into their own hands.

By mid-1986 most of the convicted men were free, either through clemency or termination of their prison sentences. (I.M.)

Jordan and Israel The only comprehensive public agreement between Israel and Jordan was the *Armistice Agreement signed on April 3, 1949, which became de facto void in June 1967. Nevertheless, many non-public undertakings were reached between the two states and they have withstood the wars and crises of the past 38 years.

The mechanism laid down in the Armistice Agreement — a mixed armistice commission headed by a UN representative, and a special Israeli-Jordanian committee — has been dismantled but a channel of direct contacts at the highest level, between the King of Jordan and the Prime Minister of Israel, has remained open. These contacts, while achieving practical arrangements along the border between the two states, have not achieved the goal of an overall settlement. On the eve of the establishment of the State of Israel the leaders of the *Yishuv* were inclined to reach an agreement with King Abdullah whereby he could annex the territories allotted the Arab state in the 1947 *United Nations partition plan, in return for staying out of the approaching war. Golda Meyerson (later *Meir) met Abdullah to discuss this proposal on November 15, 1947, and Abullah reacted favorably; at a second meeting which took place on May 12, 1948, he rejected the proposal. The only arrangement which Abdullah was willing to accept was autonomy for the regions inhabited by Jews for one year, to be followed by their annexation to *Transjordan. The King informed Meir that if the Jews replied in the negative he would have to join in the invasion of Palestine. Meir's reply was: "We are willing to respect borders as long as there is peace, but in the event of war we shall fight in every place in accordance with the force we shall have."

Despite the outbreak of war on May 15, 1948, contacts continued, although at a lower level, based on the commom Israeli-Jordanian objection to the internationalization of *Jerusalem, the King's interest in an outlet to the Mediterranean and his wish to obtain Israeli acquiescence to his annexation of the Arab areas of Palestine. On July 7, 1948, a first agreement was signed on the demilitarization of Mount Scopus in Jerusalem.

The following month representatives of the two countries met in Paris to discuss Israel's attitude to the Jordanian annexation of the *West Bank. Further contacts included the signing in Jerusalem on November 30, 1948, of an agreement between Moshe *Dayan and Colonel Abdullah Tal of a "sincere truce" agreement, and the installation of a direct telephone line between the Jordanian and Israeli commanders in Jerusalem — the first-ever "hot line" to be installed between warring forces.

Jordan was the first Arab state which expressed willingness to negotiate an *armistice agreement with Israel. However, the agreement was concluded only after Israel had gained full control over the Negev down to Eilat on the Gulf of Aqaba following the signing of the Armistice Agreement with *Egypt, and Jordan had given up the Wadi Ara area (the "northern triangle") held by the Iraqi expedition force, in separate negotiations held between the two states. (The issue of Israel's advance to Eilat was dealt with in an exchange of official notes between Abdullah and Moshe *Sharett.) The Armistice Agreement was signed in Rhodes on April 3, 1949, but various questions remained unsolved. Consequently Sharett visited Abdullah on May 5, 1949, to discuss the common rejection of the internationalization of Jerusalem and the issue of an outlet to the sea for Transjordan. On the latter point differences of opinion emerged, with Israel offering an outlet in Haifa and Abdullah demanding passage through Beersheba to an outlet in Gaza in the Egyptian-occupied *Gaza Strip.

On February 24, 1950, a document laying down the principles of a five-year non-aggression agreement between Israel and Jordan was initialed. It dealt with the armistice lines, no-man's land, joint committees on economic and territorial issues, a free zone for Jordan in the harbor of Haifa, trade cooperation and financial compensation for persons who had lost their property in Jerusalem as a result of the partition of the city. However, the agreement was never concluded since on April 3, 1950, the Arab League decided to expel any Arab state which reached a separate economic, political or military agreement with Israel.

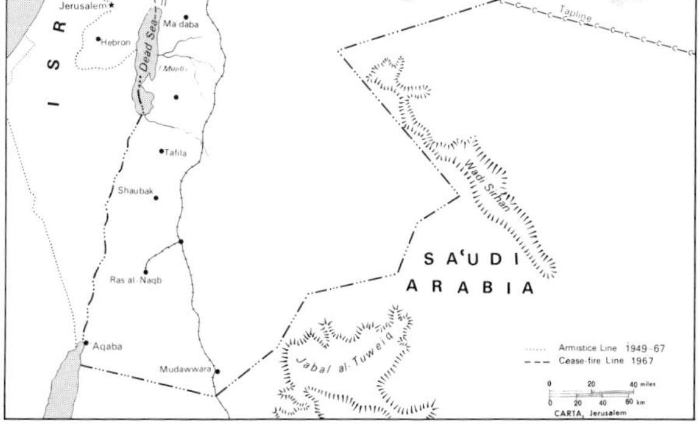

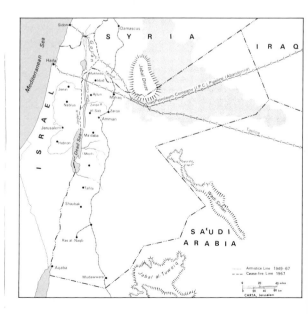

Map of Jordan.

Following King Abdullah's assassination in Jerusalem on July 20, 1951, Israeli Prime Minister David *Ben Gurion, fearing that Abdullah's opponents might gain control over the kingdom, gave the *IDF instructions to prepare for the occupation of the West Bank. However, as the situation in Jordan stabilized the plan was shelved.

Constant infiltration into Israel from Jordan and the stalemate in the efforts to reach agreements with regard to access to the *holy places, Israel's access to Mount Scopus, the opening of the Jordanian road to Bethlehem through Israeli territory, and the Tel Aviv-Jerusalem road through Jordanian-held Latrun, increased the tension between Israel and Jordan, reaching a climax in the Israeli retaliatory operation at Qibya in October 1953.

Jordan subsequently initiated a condemnation of Israel at the UN Security Council, and tried, unsuccessfully, to obtain an explicit British undertaking regarding British assistance in the event of a major military conflagration. Israel tried, also without success, to get the UN Secretary-General to convene an Israeli-Jordanian conference under Article 12 of the Armistice Agreement.

The Qibya Operation did not bring about a change in Israel-Jordan relations; it was merely a landmark in a succession of retaliatory operations: the Qalqilya Operation (1956), the Samu' Operation (1966) and the Karameh Operation (1968).

By August 1955, 2,150 complaints regarding border incidents had piled up in the Israeli-Jordanian mixed armistice commission. A war between Israel and Jordan was averted only because of the outbreak of the *Sinai Campaign and Suez War. King Hussein offered to come to Egypt's assistance, and Moshe Dayan threatened Jordan with a plan, supposedly discussed by Ben Gurion and the French, to partition Jordan, with Iraq gaining the East Bank of the *Jordan River and the West Bank becoming an autonomous area attached to Israel. However, Egyptian President Gamal Abdel Nasser dissuaded King Hussein from joining the war.

In July 1958 the western powers came to King Hussein's rescue when his throne seemed to be in danger, and Israel allowed the passage of British aircraft through its airspace (See: *Great Britain and Israel). This indirect Israeli assistance marked a turning point in Israel-Jordan relations. Five years later, in the aftermath of the establishment of the Egyptian-Iraqi-Syrian Federation, there was a wave of anti-Hashemite demonstrations in the West Bank; Ben Gurion placed the IDF on alert along the border, especially in Jerusalem, and was instrumental in getting President Kennedy to dispatch ships of the Sixth Fleet to the Eastern Mediterranean.

In September 1963 King Hussein invited a personal representative of Prime Minister Levi *Eshkol, Ya'akov Herzog, to meet him in London with the goal of gaining Israeli help to attain American aid. This meeting opened a permanent channel for Israeli-Jordanian contacts with Herzog as Special Emissary. It was through this channel that an agreement was reached for the distribution of the water of the Jordan River with American financial assistance and that Israel acquiesced to the supply of American tanks to Jordan after Hussein promised not to use the tanks in the West Bank, a promise which he broke on the eve of the *Six-Day War.

Among the causes for Hussein's entering the Six-Day War was his "Samu' syndrome": in November 1966 an IDF unit entered the West Bank town of Samu' in broad daylight and engaged Jordanian forces in retaliation for the killing of three Israeli soldiers near Arad. This was followed by violent demonstrations in *Hebron, *Jerusalem and Ramallah, which were subsequently quelled. On June 5, 1967, the first day of the war, Israel tried directly and through the use of UN, US and British channels, to dissuade Hussein from entering the war, but to no avail. However, on the night between the 6th and 7th of June requests started to reach Israel for a cease-fire. On June 7 a ministerial committee decided to expand Israel's war aims on the Jordanian front to include the liberation of Jerusalem, Judea and Samaria. This decision was unanimously approved by the cabinet the following day when the whole of the West Bank was in Israeli hands.

On June 19, the Israeli government adopted a majority decision that the Jordan River is the security border of Israel, and efforts were made to negotiate with a Palestinian representation which would agree to take over the administration of the West Bank, leaving security matters in

Israel's hands. The US encouraged Israel and Jordan to renew their dialogue.

The policy of *open bridges over the Jordan River supplanted the original policy of breaking the West Bank off from Jordan which had resulted in the blowing up of the bridges across the river at the end of the war. The open bridges led to several bilateral arrangements between Israel and Jordan: a partial return of refugees who had moved eastward across the bridges during the war and provisions for the crossing of tourists and visitors. They were also responsible for the renewal of the Israeli-Jordanian dialogue, leading to the development of alternative options by the political and military establishments in Israel regarding the future of the West Bank.

In December 1967 Abba *Eban had a meeting with Hussein in search of a quid pro quo between the two countries. Hussein spoke of an outlet to the sea at Gaza for which he was willing to "pay" with other territories in the West Bank. However, it was only in the summer of 1968, when efforts to find a "Palestinian option" failed that the *Israel Labor Party, which led the government, opted for the *Jordanian option, and in the autumn of that year Yigal *Allon first raised his proposal for a territorial settlement with Hussein (See: *Allon Plan). Hussein rejected the plan, and was not even willing to consider it as a basis for bargaining.

Nevertheless, the discussions did not end. The Chiefs of Staff of the two countries met, followed by a meeting between the Israeli Chief of Staff Ḥaim *Bar Lev and Hussein. Though no progress was made regarding a political settlement, these contacts reduced the tension and enabled the resolution of many local problems. For example, quiet was restored to the border near Aqaba and Eilat after Katyusha rockets had been fired at Israel from Jordanian territory. An agreement was also reached enabling the Jordanians to repair the Ghor Canal which had been damaged in an Israeli retaliatory operation.

During the years 1968–69 the Jordanian army allowed the Palestinian organizations to operate across the border and many clashes occurred along the Jordan River. The Karameh Operation of March 1968 was one of Israel's efforts to put military pressure on the Palestinian organizations, but it was widely publicized due to the clash between Israeli and Jordanian army units. On the same day Israel carried out another — unpublicized — military operation southeast of the *Dead Sea when Israel gained control over the As'safi area from which the Dead Sea Works at Sdom had been attacked. Both Jordan and Israel preferred to keep secret the fact that this area had on several occasions changed hands. It was only in March 1970 that an agreement was reached between Moshe Dayan and King Hussein which returned the area to Jordan on condition that it would not be used in future for attacks against Israel.

Israel enabled the development of administrative links between the West Bank and Jordan. For instance, talks on education took place between Israeli and Jordanian representatives, and Jordanian schoolbooks bearing the emblem of the Hashemite Kingdom were reintroduced into West Bank schools, after the deletion of all anti-Jewish and anti-Israel material.

In the course of 1970 the contacts between Israel and Jordan were further strengthened. In September the Jordanian government asked Israel, through the US, to take action to deter the Syrians who had invaded northern Jordan, while the Jordanian army tried to put down an uprising of armed Palestinian organizations against the Hashemite regime. Israel, with strong interests in not allowing the Kingdom to topple, put its forces on alert which served as a warning to the Syrians to back off. The subsequent expulsion of the *Palestine Liberation Organization (PLO) from Jordan as a result of Black September greatly eased the possibility of cooperation between the two countries. In the years 1971–72 Israel assisted Jordan in agricultural development in the eastern Jordan Valley Rift, and a meeting took place between Crown Prince Hassan and the Israeli Minister of Agriculture Ḥaim G'vati.

In this period Hussein also raised with Prime Minister Golda Meir the possibility of an *interim agreement being signed between the two countries, similar to that being discussed with Egypt at the time.

The *Yom Kippur War put an end to these discussions. Though Hussein did not open a third front against Israel along the Jordan River, he did send an armored brigade to the *Golan Heights to assist the Syrians who were suffering heavy losses.

Like Egypt, Jordan participated in the *Geneva

Peace Conference which opened in December 1973, and demanded that it be included as well in talks on a *disengagement agreement. Hussein raised the issue again with Golda Meir in March 1974, turning down the offer of a corridor to Ramallah and demanding a 10-kilometer Israeli withdrawal along the Jordan River. He raised the same demand during meetings which he held with Prime Minister Yitzḥak *Rabin, Minister of Defense Shimon *Peres and Minister for Foreign Affairs Yigal Allon on August 29 and October 19, 1974, the latter meeting taking place a week before the *Rabat Conference at which Hussein was stripped of his mandate to represent the West Bank and to speak in the name of the *Palestinians. In the August discussions Allon raised the *Jericho Plan but Hussein refused to discuss it or Peres' proposal for an Israeli-Jordanian condominium in the West Bank.

On May 28, 1975, Hussein once again met the Israeli team and blamed Israel for the Rabat conference resolution which put Jordan out of the picture, arguing that this could have been prevented had Israel signed a disengagement agreement with Jordan. "Now you will have to turn to the PLO," he told Yitzḥak Rabin.

Regular meetings between Israel and Jordan continued until August 23, 1977. One of the agreements reached in this period was to move the border along the Arava a little westward to enable Jordan to construct a road to Aqaba (Israel had, apparently, moved the border eastward). The meeting in August 1977 took place between Hussein and Foreign Minister Moshe Dayan who wished to find out whether the King would be willing to consider a territorial compromise in the West Bank. Hussein replied in the negative and Israel opted for the process which led to the peace treaty with Egypt.

In September 1978 Hussein contacted Sadat at Camp David offering to join the negotiations, but Sadat rejected the offer. This rejection led Hussein to denounce the *Camp David Accords, despite the fact that they allotted a major role for Jordan in a final settlement.

The 1982 *Reagan Plan tried to bring King Hussein back into the negotiations cycle but Arafat refused to approve and nothing came of it. In 1985 Hussein opened his own initiative for Jordanian-Palestinian negotiations with the US to be followed by Jordanian-Palestinian negotiations with Israel. Within the framework of this initiative King Hussein met Israeli Prime Minister Shimon Peres in October 1985, and preliminary moves toward negotiations between Israel and a Jordanian-Palestinian delegation were discussed. It was agreed that Israel would accept an international conference as an umbrella for Israeli-Jordanian negotiations, and that Jordan would convince the PLO to recognize Israel's right to exist within secure borders. However, extremist factions in the PLO prevented any softening of its attitude toward Israel, and in February 1986 Hussein, in disgust, denounced PLO conduct. In July 1986, Hussein shut down the Fatah offices in Jordan.

King Hussein knows it is thanks to Israel's refusal to negotiate with the PLO that his own importance is enhanced, and the PLO needs him in seeking US recognition. It is for this reason that he continues the meetings with Israel on the operational level regarding questions of agriculture, water, border passages and health. Trade between the two states is carried out privately, in which the Arabs of the West Bank play an active role. In October 1986 a Jordanian bank was allowed to open in Nablus and Jordanian-supported Mayors were appointed in Ramallah, Hebron and El-Bireh. (M.Z.)

Jordanian option Term used to describe the policy of seeking to reach a settlement of the Palestinian problem with Jordan rather than directly with the Palestinians. It is argued that Jordan is predominantly a Palestinian state — its territory was part of *mandatory Palestine and most of its population, many of whom live in the West Bank or abroad, are Palestinians — its only non-Palestinian feature being the Hashemite ruling family, who came from the Arabian Peninsula in the early 1920s.

Under the Jordanian option Israel would be willing to return most of the territories in the West Bank and the Gaza Stip to Jordanian sovereignty in return for a permanent peace settlement with the Jordanian-Palestinian state which could be a federation or a single state. Negotiations to attain this settlement should be conducted with a Jordanian-Palestinian negotiating team, where the Palestinian delegates would not include official members of the *Palestine Liberation Organization (PLO). The Jordanian option is associated primarily with the *Israel Labor Party.

"Jordan is Palestine" A term which was coined by Ariel *Sharon when he was Minister of Defense to describe a policy which sought to have Jordan recognized as the Palestinian state. Like the *Jordanian option this approach recognizes Jordan as a predominantly Palestinian state. Throughout the western world "Jordan is Palestine" associations have been established to promote the idea primarily by persons associated with **Ḥerut*. Sharon has on several occasions advocated Israeli contacts with the *Palestine Liberation Organization (PLO) for the purpose of helping it gain control over Jordan.

Jordan River A river running from north to south, separating Western from Eastern **Eretz Yisrael*. The river travels a length of 140 kilometers, but is more than twice that (330 kilometers) when diverging and converging channels are measured. It has three tributaries in the North: the Banias (which until the *Six-Day War was in Syrian hands in the Golan Heights), the Ḥatzbani (in *Lebanon) and the Dan (in Israel). The Yarmuk (in *Jordan) runs into the Jordan River at a point south of the Sea of Galilee, through which the river flows. The Jordan River empties into the *Dead Sea. It is mentioned frequently in the Old and New Testaments, and is considered holy by the Christians.

In the Ottoman Empire the Jordan River constituted an administrative border among various districts, and in mandatory times separated Palestine and *Transjordan which were both formally part of the Mandate for Palestine. Since the Six-Day War the Jordan River has been the cease-fire line between the territories occupied by Israel in the *West Bank in June 1967, and the Kingdom of Jordan.

In mandatory times a hydroelectric power station was constructed on the river south of the Sea of Galilee by Pinḥas Rutenberg (1897–1942). It was abandoned in the *War of Independence. After efforts to bring about cooperation among the riparian states in the use of the Jordan River waters failed in the 1950s, Israel constructed its own National Water Carrier to carry water from a point north of the Sea of Galilee to the Negev in the south of Israel. The carrier started to function in 1964. Arab efforts to sabotage the Israeli project caused much tension on the Israeli-Syrian border until the Six-Day War.

Since June 1967 traffic has been allowed to move between the West Bank and Jordan across the River Jordan on the basis of the *open bridges policy. Except for **Ḥadash* and the *Progressive List for Peace which demand complete Israeli withdrawal from all the territories occupied in 1967, there is a consensus in Israel that the Jordan River should be Israel's security border, implying that an Israeli military and civilian presence should be maintained along it and no Arab army should cross it, irrespective of who controls the interior of the West Bank.

Judea and Samaria See: **Yosh*.

Judiciary The absolute independence of the judiciary in Israel is guaranteed by law. On recommendation of a public nominations committee, judges are appointed by the *President for life. Retirement from the bench at the age of seventy is mandatory. The Supreme Court, located in Jerusalem, has nationwide jurisdiction. It is the highest court of appeal on rulings of lower tribunals. Sitting as a High Court of Justice (in Hebrew *Bagatz* — acronym for *Beit Din Gavo'ah Letzedek*) it may grant relief in the interests of justice from rulings of any other jurisdiction, including appeals from the *West Bank and the *Gaza Strip where Israeli law does not apply.

Magistrates and district courts exercise jurisdiction in civil and criminal cases, while juvenile, traffic, military, labor and municipal appeal courts each deal with matters coming under their competence. Any person may appear in his own defense in any court in Israel without legal counsel. There is no trial by jury in Israel.

In matters of personal status such as marriage, divorce, maintenance, guardianship and the adoption of minors jurisdiction is vested in the judicial institutions of the respective religious communities: the Rabbinical Court, the Moslem religious courts (*Sharia* courts), the religious courts of the *Druze and the juridical institutions of the nine recognized Christian communities in Israel: Greek-Catholic, Maronite, Syrian-Orthodox, Eastern (Orthodox), Latin (Catholic), Gregorian-Armenian, Armenian (Catholic), Syrian (Catholic), and Chaldean (Uniat).

K

Kach Name of the party established by Rabbi Meir *Kahane in 1971 as an extension of his Jewish Defense League. The name *Kach* was adopted only in 1973 when the party had to choose an acronym under which to run in the Knesset elections. The Hebrew letters pronounced "Kach" were chosen, apparently without thought; it was, however, commonly believed that Kahane had deliberately taken the name from the slogan inscribed on the **Irgun Zva'i Le'umi* (IZL) emblem which read *Rak Kach* — "only thus!"

When the party ran for the first time in the elections for the 8th Knesset in 1973, it called for Israel to be a Jewish state according to the *Halacha* (Jewish law) with an exemplary Jewish society. Arabs could become citizens after a security check, on condition that they served in the armed forces and assumed other civic responsibilities, or they could remain in the country as non-citizens, or emigrate. *Kach* did not obtain the minimum number of votes required in order to enter the Knesset either on this occasion or in 1977. In 1981 an attempt to disqualify the list in the Central Elections Committee failed; it ran on a platform which called for the expulsion (see *transfer of population) of all Arabs from *Eretz Yisrael* since there was a danger of their becoming a majority in the country and coexistence (according to *Kach*) was impossible. It also called for the abrogation of the *Camp David Accords and the *Egyptian-Israeli Peace Treaty, no withdrawal from the *Sinai and the rejection of the *Autonomy Plan, for the establishment of an anti-terrorist organization to reciprocate Arab terrorist attacks with terror, and for the removal of the mosques from the Temple Mount (Kahane claims that "removal" means moving them by 100 meters, not destroying them). *Kach* also called for outlawing the Communist party which it considers a fifth column.

In the 11th Knesset elections in 1984 the Central Elections Committee disqualified *Kach* which ran on an almost identical platform to that of the previous elections. In his letter to Rabbi Kahane High Court Justice Gavriel Bach, Chairman of the Central Elections Committee explained the disqualification on the grounds "that this list advocates racist and anti-democratic principles which are contrary to the *Proclamation of Independence of the State of Israel, openly supports acts of terror, tries to incite hatred and hostility among various parts of the population in Israel, and tends to hurt the religious feelings of some of the citizens of the State, and rejects the goals and basic foundations of the democratic political system in Israel."

Kach appealed to the High Court of Justice, which decided that the Central Elections Committee could disqualify lists only for technical reasons and not on grounds of their nature, objectionable as it may be.

Subsequently, on July 31, 1985 both the Basic Law: the Knesset (See Appendix III) and the Election Law were amended to enable the Elections Committee to disqualify lists which *inter alia* incite to racism and reject the democratic nature of the state.

Kach obtained one seat in the 11th Knesset, and under the protective mantle of his immunity as MK Kahane became more active than ever in advocating the expulsion of the Arabs from *Eretz Yisrael*, and harassing Jewish women married to Arabs. An amendment to the Penal Code which makes racial incitement a punishable offence, was passed by the Knesset in August 1986. Though *Kach* was the main target of this amendment, MK Kahane voted for it.

Kach has attempted to introduce bills resembling the Nuremberg Laws in their content, but the Knesset Speaker has refused to table any of them. *Kach*'s popularity rises after every terrorist attack, especially among the youth.

Kafr Kassem Israeli Arab village in the center of the country in which 49 villagers were killed on October 29, 1956, on the eve of the *Sinai Campaign, by Israeli forces from the Border Police. The villagers were shot when they returned to Kafr Kassem from work, unaware of the fact that a curfew had been imposed. The commanding officer of the force had given his men instructions to shoot rather than detain anyone.

On November 1, 1956, a Commission of Inquiry, headed by District Court Judge Binyamin Zohar, was appointed to investigate the circumstances of the events at Kafr Kassem;

to establish the extent of responsiblity for these events of the various members of the Border Police force and whether they should be prosecuted; and to determine the compensation which the government should pay the families of those killed as a result of the conduct of these men. The commission recommended that 11 men be brought to trial. Eight of them were found guilty of murder and sentenced to a lengthy period of imprisonment. However, despite the fact that Prime Minister David *Ben Gurion expressed deep shock that such an act which "struck at the holiest principles of human morality" should have been committed, and promised that such an act "would never again take place in Israel," the sentences of all the persons found guilty were reduced, and the last of them was freed in 1960.

Kahan Commission A Commission of Inquiry set up, under the 1968 Commissions of Inquiry Law, on October 1, 1982, "to investigate all the facts and factors connected to the atrocities committed by a unit of the Lebanese forces against the civilian population in the camps at *Sabra and Shatilla." The commission, chaired by the President of the Supreme Court Yitzḥak Kahan, with the participation of ex-*Attorney-General Aharon Barak and reserve Brigadier General Yonah Ephrati, was set up following a mass demonstration in Tel Aviv organized by the *Peace Now movement and the *Israel Labor Party. It was set up to investigate why Israeli personnel had failed to stop the attack, despite the opposition of several members of the government who felt it was superfluous to investigate a massacre for which Israel was not responsible, and Prime Minister Menaḥem *Begin's preference for a less binding investigating committee. The Kahan Commission published its report on February 7, 1983, after hearing 48 witnesses.

The commission concluded that the direct responsibility for the massacre lay with the Lebanese Phalange forces, and that no direct responsibility lay with the State of Israel or those acting on its behalf. However, the commission found fault with the conduct of both the political and military leaders. Though the commission felt that had Prime Minister Begin shown greater interest in what was happening after the Phalange had entered the camps the alertness of the Minister of Defense and the Chief of Staff would have been enhanced, it did not criticize him severely for not taking interest in the details of the operation.

Minister of Defense Ariel *Sharon was found responsible "for disregarding the danger of acts of revenge and bloodshed by the Phalange against the population in the refugee camps" following the assassination of President-elect Bashir Jemayel; "for not taking this danger into consideration when he decided to let the Phalange into the camps" and "for not taking appropriate measures to prevent or limit this danger." Thus, the commission declared that the Defense Minister had not fulfilled his duty and recommended that he "draw personal conclusions." Sharon was finally replaced at the Ministry of Defense by Moshe *Arens but remained in the government as Minister without Portfolio.

Minister for Foreign Affairs Yitzḥak *Shamir was found to have made no real effort to check the accuracy of information given him on the massacres soon after they had begun, and was reproved for making light of the warnings. Chief of Staff Rafael *Eitan was found guilty of breach of duty for not giving appropriate instructions to avert the danger of acts of revenge and bloodshed by the Phalange and for not stopping the Phalange after they had entered the camps and had started the killing. However, since Eitan was about to end his term of service the commission did not recommend his removal. The Head of **Aman* (*IDF Intelligence), Yehoshua Saguy, was found guilty of "indifference, marked carelessness, and closing his eyes and ears" with regard to a matter on which it was his duty to be alert and to warn the decision makers, in his capacity as Head of Intelligence. The commission found him in breach of his duty and recommended his removal, which was carried out.

The Head of the **Mossad* did not fare badly even though it was found that due to the *Mossad*'s connection with the Phalange he should have considered the possibility of acts of revenge after Jemayel's assassination. Two commanding officers — the commander of the Northern Command and the Chief Officer of the Paratroopers and Infantry — were also found guilty of negligence and breach of duty. The former left his command soon thereafter to pursue studies abroad while the latter was switched to a non-command position in the army.

The commission also criticized the decision-making process, including the absence of proper reporting and recording procedures, and recommended the continued nurturing in the IDF of basic moral duties which must be upheld during fighting.

During Sharon's libel suit against *Time Magazine* the defense argued that the unpublished annexes of the Kahan Commission Report contained information which supported the Magazine's claim that Sharon had actually encouraged the Jemayels to take revenge for Bashir's assassination. However, those who were allowed to look at the secret annexes did not find any proof for this allegation.

Kahane, Meir (Martin David) Pseudonym: Michael King. Rabbi, founder of the Jewish Defense League (JDL) in the United States and the **Kach* Party in Israel, Member of *Knesset. Born 1932, New York. Kahane was a member of **Betar* from 1946–51 and of **Bnei Akivah* in 1953–54. In 1957 he was ordained Rabbi at the Mir Yeshiva and served in that capacity for the Howard Beach Community, Queens from 1957–59. He was a journalist for the *Brooklyn Daily*, and for the nationalist, Orthodox *Jewish Press*, and received an MA degree in International Law from New York University. Little is known of Kahane's activities in the sixties.

In 1968 he founded the JDL, an organization committed to fight anti-Semitism and help Jews protect themselves from physical attacks. In 1971 he was imprisoned for illegal possession of weapons and was bailed out by Mafia boss Joseph Colombo. He then immigrated to Israel and founded *Kach*, a small but active movement on the extreme right fringe of Israeli politics. Kahane apparently travelled back and forth between Israel and the US. In 1972, the JDL was held responsible for blowing up the offices of the Jewish impressario Sol Hurok, who brought Soviet performers to the US. A secretary was killed in the blast.

That year, too, he was involved in an unsuccessful attempt to smuggle arms out of Israel to attack the Libyan Embassy in Rome.

In 1972–73 Kahane began a campaign to convince Arabs to leave the *West Bank. In the 1973 and 1981 elections *Kach* failed to pass the one percent qualifying threshold, but in 1984, despite efforts to disqualify *Kach* on the grounds of its racist platform, Kahane was elected to the 11th Knesset. An amendment to the Basic Law: the Knesset (See *Basic Laws) was passed in 1985 which would prevent lists with racist platforms from running for election.

Kahane advocates the payment of compensation to all Arabs in Israel, the West Bank and *Gaza Strip in return for emigration. Alternatively, for those who choose to remain, he proposes a status of *Ger Toshav* (alien resident) with restricted privileges and no voting rights. Those Arabs who refuse either solution would be expelled. Kahane calls for total segregation of Jews and Arabs. He has attempted to introduce in the Knesset several racist bills. Knesset Speaker Shlomo *Hillel refused to table them. When the High Court of Justice ruled that the Speaker had no legal right to act in this way, the Knesset House Committee amended the Knesset's regulations to enable the Knesset presidium to refuse to table bills that either incite racism or reject the Jewish nature of the state. Although Kahane's freedom of movement has been legally restricted and the Minister of Education refused to allow him to address public school pupils, polls indicate that he gains in popularity after every terrorist attack on Jews. In August 1986 the Knesset passed an amendment to the Penal Code which makes racial incitement a punishable offense. The initiative for this amendment came in order to stop Kahane from inciting the public against the Arabs in his public appearances.

Kahanism A popular term which refers to the racist, anti-Arab ideology which Rabbi Meir *Kahane preaches, based on a selective interpretation of the Old Testament and the *Halacha* (Jewish law).

The entry of Kahane into the 11th *Knesset in 1984 at the head of the **Kach* list, and his growing popularity (some opinion polls in the course of 1985 showed his electoral popularity to have risen as high as 7 Knesset seats) caused concern to the Israeli authorities which have proceeded to combat the phenomenon by legal and educational means.

Kalanterism A term used to describe the phenomenon of politicians — on the national or local levels — who once voted into office as members of a certain party change their party affiliation in return for benefits to themselves or to interest groups which they represent.

Kalanterism is named after Raḥamin Kalanter

of Jerusalem who in 1955 was elected to the Jerusalem Municipal Council on the *National Religious Party (NRP) list. In mid-1956 the NRP left the municipal coalition over the question of approval for the construction of a school of archaeology in a building where a Reform synagogue was to be constructed. The NRP withdrawal left the coalition short of one member for a majority in the council. In return for various benefits and promises Kalanter crossed lines and remained in the municipal coalition as an independent member.

Karp Report A report prepared by a committee of jurists headed by Judith Karp of the *Attorney General's office, which examined irregularities in the conduct of police investigations of charges brought against Israeli settlers in the *West Bank and their repercussions on relations between the settlers and the Arab inhabitants of the area. The panel was appointed by Attorney General Yitzḥak Zamir on April 29, 1981 in answer to a letter from a group of Hebrew University and Tel Aviv University law professors expressing concern for the rule of law in the *occupied territories and the issue of "private vigilante activities by settlers in Judea and Samaria." The committee included a representative of the police, the Chief Army Prosecutor and the Regional Prosecutor. The report was completed on May 23, 1982 but its findings were not published until February 7, 1984.

The Karp Report looked into the activity of the investigating branch of the military police and advised a reassessment of the instructions given to soldiers on the conditions for opening fire. It also criticized the separation between regular and military police examinations as being detrimental to the inquiry process — the first for civilians and the military police for soldiers.

The committee examined police investigations of 70 cases, 53 of which had not been solved. In 15 files chosen at random the panel found police investigations were inadequate. The cases included complaints by Arabs in *Hebron of harassment by Jewish settlers, and complaints by Arab inhabitants of Kafr Kaddum about settlers having uprooted 300 olive trees. The committee found that a large number of similar unsolved cases pointed to a failure on the part of the police to investigate incidents in Judea and Samaria (See: **Yosh*), in which Jewish settlers had been accused of harassing and intimidating the local populace, thus justifying the concern expressed in the professors' letter.

The report caused a political uproar, with the Left arguing that the continued occupation was responsible for this state of affairs and calling for far-reaching reforms, and the Right accusing the committee of being one-sided and failing to deal with the problem of Arabs going unpunished for attacks on Jews. (M.B.-S.H.R.)

Kasztner Affair Israel (Rezsö Rudolf) Kasztner (1906–1957) was a Hungarian-born Jew, a senior official in the Ministry of Industry and Trade and a **Mapai* candidate for the 2nd *Knesset. In 1953 he was accused by Malkiel Grunwald of having collaborated with the Nazis during World War II in the extermination of Hungarian Jewry; having kept the danger of the extermination secret from the Hungarian Jews in order to save some 1,700 "important" Jews, including his relatives and friends, who were allowed to leave Budapest for Switzerland; and of helping save Nazi criminal Kurt Becker by giving evidence in his favor at the Nuremberg trials.

Kasztner sued Grunwald for libel. Grunwald was defended by the attorney Shmuel *Tamir. In June 1955 District Court Justice Binyamin Halevi stated in his verdict that the accusations made by Grunwald regarding Kasztner's collaboration with the Nazis had been proven, and that "Kasztner had sold his soul to the devil." He also found that Kasztner had given a false affidavit on behalf of the *Jewish Agency in the trial of Kurt Becker at Nuremberg. Kasztner's protagonists argued that he was, in fact, a hero who against all odds and despite the emotional difficulty of dealing with Nazis such as Adolf *Eichmann, had done his best to save as many Jews as possible.

Since the verdict in the trial was a reflection upon *Mapai* as well, the government decided to appeal to the Supreme Court. On June 28, 1955 a motion of no-confidence was brought to the Knesset by **Maki* and **Ḥerut* regarding the manner in which the affair had been dealt with. When the *General Zionists abstained on this motion the Prime Minister, Moshe *Sharett resigned.

On March 4, 1957, Kasztner was shot by a young nationalist extremist, and died of his wounds. This was considered the first political assassination in the history of the State of Israel

(See also: *De Haan assassination). In January 1958 the Supreme Court decided, by a majority of three of five judges, that Kasztner had not collaborated with the Nazis and that in certain circumstances a leader may keep the facts secret from the public. All five judges found that Kasztner had given a false affidavit in 1947, and had thus saved a senior SS officer from punishment.

The whole episode is still the subject of controversy in Israel, and in 1985 was dramatized in the Hebrew theater.

Katznelson, Berl (1887–1944). Labor Zionist leader and educator. Katznelson was born in White Russia where he studied at a *ḥeder* and with private tutors. He was later active in **Po'alei Zion* and the party of Zionist Socialists. He immigrated to Palestine in 1909, worked as a farm laborer and became friendly with the writers and thinkers A.D. *Gordon and Y.H. Brenner. Katznelson was an ardent supporter of both the *kibbutz and *moshav forms of settlement, and was responsible for organizing the famous 1911 strike at Kinneret. At first he did not join any of the existing parties in Palestine since he fought to unite all the workers' forces in the country into a single party. During World War I he volunteered for the Jewish *Legion where, together with David *Ben Gurion and Yitzḥak *Ben Zvi he worked toward the unification of the labor movement. Katznelson was one of the founders of **Aḥdut Ha'avodah* in 1919, the **Histadrut* in 1920 and its various institutions such as the cooperative sales organization Hamashbir Hamerkazi, Kupat Ḥolim (Sick Fund) and Bank Hapo'alim in the following years, as well as being one of the founders of **Mapai* in 1930. In 1925 he founded the *Histadrut*'s daily *Davar*, which he edited until 1944, and its publishing house Am Oved. Katznelson opposed the idea of the *partition of Palestine. Toward the end of his life, influenced by the *Holocaust, he changed his previously rigid attitude to Jewish-Arab relations and was inclined to compromise and understanding. During his last years Katznelson concentrated on educational and cultural activities. Beit Berl, the educational center of *Mapai* (today the *Israel Labor Party) is named after him.

Katz, Shmuel Publicist and political activist. Born 1914, Johannesburg. Katz studied at the University of Witwetsrand and joined **Betar* in 1930, immigrating to Palestine in 1936 where he became the Bureau Director of the South African Honorary Consul. Katz joined the **IZL* in 1937 and edited its English publications. At the outbreak of World War II, *Jabotinsky called Katz to London to edit the *Jewish Standard*, where he also became a correspondent for the *Daily Express*. He returned to Palestine in 1946 and was appointed a member of the *IZL* High Command. After *IZL*'s disbandment in June 1948 he became the commander of its remaining Jerusalem unit.

Katz was elected to the first *Knesset as a member of the **Ḥerut* Movement and edited its daily newspaper. In 1952 he left politics and established the Karni publication house. Following the *Six-Day War Katz was among the founders of the *Land of Israel Movement and travelled abroad on its behalf. The day after the **Likud*'s 1977 election victory he was appointed Information Advisor to the Prime Minister. He resigned in January 1978 severely criticizing Menaḥem *Begin's *Autonomy Plan, the proposed terms of the peace with *Egypt and the influence of Moshe *Dayan and Ezer *Weizman. He became a columnist for *Ma'ariv* and the *Jerusalem Post*.

(I.M.)

Kessar, Israel Trade Union leader and Knesset member, born 1931 in Yemen. Kessar immigrated to Palestine in 1933 where he attended elementary and secondary school in Jerusalem. Before and after the *War of Independence Kessar attended teachers' seminaries after which he instructed and worked in a youth center and with new immigrants.

In 1956 he completed a BA in Sociology and Economics at the Hebrew University of Jerusalem. In 1960–61 he worked as an Assistant and Advisor to the Minister of Labor, Giora Josephtal. From 1961–66, Kessar was Director of Vocational Guidance and the Rehabilitation Division of the Ministry of Labor. He became a member of the **Histadrut* Executive Bureau in 1966. He was Chairman of the *Histadrut* Youth and Sports Department between 1966–71 during which time he became Chairman of the Manpower Department. He continued his studies at Tel Aviv University and earned his MA degree in Labor Studies in 1972 after which he became *Histadrut* Treasurer until 1977. He joined the *Israel Labor Party Bureau in 1977 and until 1984 was Chairman of the Trade Union Department and

Deputy Secretary-General of the *Histadrut*. Kessar became Secretary-General of the *Histadrut* and Chairman of the *Histadrut* holding company, *Ḥevrat Ovdim* in 1984. He was the first non-Ashkenazi to be chosen for these posts. And, in 1984, like all previous Secretaries-General of the *Histadrut*, Kessar was elected to the Knesset. Kessar's full cooperation with the government on its economic policy is said to have been the determining factor in its success. At the same time Kessar has been mindful not to allow real wages to fall too steeply and has fought against the implementation of the policy leading to excessive unemployment.

kibbutz A collective settlement originating in the years of the Second **Aliya*. The first organizations were not actual settlements but groups which got together to obtain jobs in manual labor for their members who lived as collectives. The first collective settlements were called *kvutzot* (groups) and were small units (30–40 members) which concentrated on agriculture and were influenced by the doctrines of A.D. *Gordon. The first *kvutzah* was Degania, established in 1910. The early *kvutzot* did not belong to general settlement movements. Until the mid-40s a debate ensued between those who favored the *kvutzah* and those who favored the *kibbutz*, which was larger and had more diversified economy which included, in addition to agriculture, industry, work outside the settlement, tourist enterprises, etc. The first kibbutz was Ein Ḥarod established in 1921. To all intents and purposes, all the fully collective settlements are now kibbutzim. The *moshav shitufi* and the *moshav ovdim* (see: **moshav*) are forms of semi-collectives. But both the *kvutzah* and the kibbutz were based on the principles of communal ownership of all means of production and consumption; communal organization for the supply of the material and spiritual needs of the members; communal education influenced by the particular ideology of the movement to which the settlement belongs; and self-labor. Each member contributes to the collective in accordance with his ability and talents. Kibbutzim differ with regard to whether or not children live in separate children's houses or with their parents, as well as what personal possessions members may own.

Each kibbutz has a General Assembly which chooses a secretariat (larger kibbutzim have a council as an intermediary organization) and committees which deal with specific issues.

All the kibbutzim belong to settlement movements which are politically affiliated, except for two which are directly affiliated to **Po'alei Agudat Yisrael*. Individual members are, however, free to vote in general elections as they please. The kibbutzim are divided between the **Takam*, which is affiliated with the **Israel Labor Party;* **Hakibbutz Ha'artzi*, affiliated with **Mapam*; and **Hakibbutz Hadati*, affiliated with the *National Religious Party. The *kvutzot* and the kibbutzim were the leaders in the early pioneering of the country and in the revival of the principle of Jewish labor to rebuild a homeland for the Jewish people. They were responsible for the settlement of the Galilee and other rural areas (See: *Land Policy), draining swamps, building roads and defending Jewish settlers.

About three percent of the population live in kibbutzim but their influence on Israel's political, cultural, military and social life has been far greater. There are 9 kibbutz members in the 11th Knesset. Hundreds of thousands of foreign (mostly non-Jewish) volunteers have spent periods of at least several months working in kibbutzim, some out of ideological motives, some as an experience and an inexpensive way of living abroad; others have viewed it as a temporary solution to unemployment in their home countries.

In the past the kibbutz youth was famous for volunteering for fighting units in the *IDF. Especially since the *Lebanese War there has been a decline in this trend, associated with the slogan "*rosh kattan*" (small head, or "do as you're told and don't ask questions or volunteer!").

The kibbutzim played an important role in the education of immigrant children in the early years of the state, but only a small percentage stayed on in kibbutzim, which have remained predominantly Ashkenazi. In the elections to the 10th and 11th Knessets there was a good deal of tension between the kibbutzim affiliated with the *Alignment and the development towns, in which a high percentage of the population are **Edot Mizraḥ* and supporters of the **Likud*. The background to this tension has been socio-economic — the development towns accusing the kibbutzim of being elitist, well-to-do and pampered economically. The fact that the kibbutzim are the owners and managers of numerous regional industries which employ workers from the development towns is a further cause of resentment. In recent years the kibbutzim have made an effort to improve these relations.

kibbutz movements See: *Hakibbutz Ha'artzi; *Hakibbutz Hadati, *Hakibbutz Hame'uḥad; *Iḥud Hakvutzot Vehakibbutzim; *Takam.

Kiryat-Arba See: *Hebron.

Kissinger shuttle diplomacy A term phrased by Under-secretary of State for Political Affairs Joseph Sisco in January 1974 to describe the flying back and forth of Secretary of State Henry Kissinger between Jerusalem and various Arab capitals after the *Yom Kippur War in an effort to get *Disengagement Agreements signed between Israel and its neighbors. The shuttle was carried out by a US Air Force Boeing 707 called SAM 86970.

The first shuttle led to the signing of the Egyptian-Israeli Disengagement Agreement on January 18, 1974. The second shuttle led to the signing of the Syrian-Israeli Disengagement Agreement on May 31, 1974. Though the term "shuttle" is used only in connection with these two agreements, Kissinger started to travel between Moscow, the various Arab capitals and Jerusalem toward the end of the Yom Kippur War, trips which continued through November and December of 1973, the goal of which was first to bring about a cease-fire and then get the peace process off the ground.

"Kitchen" Cabinet The name used for the informal inner cabinet of Prime Minister Golda *Meir, rumored to meet in her kitchen. It had no official status but wielded much influence. Of the ministers in Meir's governments the only permanent members in the "kitchen" were Israel *Galili and Moshe *Dayan.

Knesset Hebrew word meaning assembly. The Knesset is the parliament of Israel, a unicameral legislature, with 120 members whose seat is *Jerusalem.

HISTORY: In order to emphasize the renewal of the Jewish sovereign existence the name Knesset was chosen, derived from the name of the first representative assembly in Jewish history *Haknesset Hag'dolah* (the Great Assembly) which had been convened in Jerusalem following the return of the Jews from Babylonia in the 5th century BCE. The number of Knesset members was also adopted from its ancient predecessor.

The Knesset was preceded by *Mo'etzet Ha'am* (the People's Council) which became the Provisional Council of the State on May 14, 1948 upon the *Proclamation of Independence, in accordance with the constitutional provisions of the UN partition resolution. The tasks of the Council of State were to appoint and supervise the executive organ of the new state, as well a prepare elections for a constituent assembly before October 30, 1948. Owing to the exigencies of war these eventually took place on January 25, 1949, while the war was still being waged.

The Provisional Council of State was made up of 40 members, appointed on a party basis from among the members of the two democratically elected bodies of pre-state times — **Assefat Hanivḥarim*, the elected assembly of the **Yishuv* and the *Jewish Agency for Palestine, which represented the *World Zionist Organization. Th electoral, political, parliamentary and procedural practices of both parent bodies were to have decisive influence on the character of th Knesset.

The Constituent Assembly did not accomplish its principal task — the adoption of a *constitution. In view of basic differences of opinion concerning the need for, and the substance of, a written constitution, the asssembly adopted compromise resolution under which the constitution would be enacted chapter by chapter. The assembly thereupon changed its name to the First Knesset after adopting the Transition Law, popularly known as the "Little Constitution."

Even though Israel does not have a written constitution, constitutional provisions were laid down in the *Basic Laws which are neither entrenched nor superior to ordinary laws, except for a few of their features.

Article 4 of the basic Law: the Knesset, passed in 1958, lays down that the Knesset is to be elected by universal, secret vote according to a system of proportional representation. This article can only be changed by an absolute majority of the Knesset members. The system of proportional representation was adopted because it had been the system used in *Assefat Hanivḥarim* and because the delimitation of constituencies was impossible in a state whose borders were still undefined. Even though it was adopted on a strictly ad hoc basis it has become entrenched in Israel's constitutional and political reality (See

*Electoral System). Voting rights are granted to all citizens aged 18 and above — the age of obligatory military service. Eligible for election to the Knesset are all citizens above the age of 21, except those holding public office (such as the President, judges — both secular and religious — army officers and senior civil servants). Originally no qualifications were required for candidates. Only in recent years have persons found guilty of crimes against the security of the state been disqualified under certain circumstances. In 1985 an amendment was adopted banning lists which negate the Jewish or democratic character of the state.

The Knesset is elected for a period of four years, but may dissolve itself before the expiration of its term by enacting a dissolution law which also fixes the new election date. In fact, out of the eleven elections between 1949 and 1984, only six took place on the date fixed by the law. Four were advanced and the 1973 elections were postponed by several months because of the *Yom Kippur War.

FUNCTIONS: The Knesset is the legislature of Israel. The laws enacted by it are not subject to judicial review, except with regard to points of procedure which the Supreme Court has on several occasions adjudicated. The Knesset elects the President of the State. During the President's temporary absence the speaker of the Knesset assumes his functions. A new government requires a vote of confidence by the Knesset before assuming its duties. According to the Basic Law: the Government (See *Government) the Prime Minister must be a member of Knesset, while other ministers may come from outside the Knesset. In fact, rarely have there been more than two cabinet members at any one time who were not members of Knesset as well (See: *Norwegian Law).

Through a vote of no-confidence the Knesset may bring a government down. Such a government will continue to serve until a successor government is duly sworn in. Motions of no-confidence are frequently proposed to draw attention to a subject of interest to the proposer, even though his chances of getting such a motion adopted are extremely small. So far no government in Israel has fallen as a result of such a motion.

The Knesset is sovereign and its powers are unlimited. The government is constitutionally subject to its supervision and control. This is achieved in plenary debates, especially when budgets are being discussed; motions for the agenda; questions — written and oral, ordinary and urgent; and in committees, where ministers or their representatives may be summoned to report on their activities.

The *State Comptroller, who also acts as Ombudsman, is elected by the Knesset, and his reports, as Comptroller and Ombudsman, are presented to the Committee on State Control. Their conclusions are debated and voted upon in plenary. Since the government of the day, by definition, controls a majority in the Knesset, and its members are drawn from the coalition party leaders, it can generally achieve its objectives in the Knesset. This applies to committees as well, since traditionally the coalition enjoys a majority in all committees — a situation which has frequently given rise to the charge that the Knesset is subservient to the government, or little more than "rubber stamp."

Because of Israel's peculiar circumstances an unusually large proportion of the Knesset's time is devoted to general debates on the political and security situation, or specific issues related to it. Among the most memorable debates were those which dealt with German restitution payments (1952) — the only debate interrupted by a physical assault on the Knesset by opponents of the agreement (See: *Restitution Agreement); the occupation of the Sinai (November 7, 1956); the decision to withdraw from the Sinai (March 1957) (See: *Sinai Campaign); the unification of Jerusalem (June 1967); the counterattack in the *Yom Kippur War (October 14, 1973); the *Camp David Accords (September 1978).

The Knesset has ceremonial functions, including administering the oath to a new President. It has been addressed by foreign heads of state and of international parliamentary institutions. The most memorable occasion was President Sadat's visit in November 1977, and the speech in which he proclaimed "no more war" to be his policy.

PROCEDURE: The Knesset debates and approves its own rules of procedure. These are supplemented by various precedents, rulings and decisions by the Speaker or his deputies and interpreted by a special committee. Any amendments must be approved by the House Committee. Following the formulation of the principal rules by the 1970s, amendments have been relatively few, dealing with such questions as the disciplinary powers of the Speaker, his deputies and committee chairmen, timing of no-confidence motions, and arrangements for question time.

Unlike most democratically elected parliaments, the Knesset does not require a quorum, and all decisions (except those concerning Article 4 of the Basic Law: the Knesset, and several others, concerning the suspension of the provisions of that law by means of emergency regulations and the impeachment of the President, neither of which have been invoked) are adopted by a simple majority of those present and voting. Abstentions are not counted. A draw equals a negative vote. The Speaker has the right to vote. Votes are taken by a raising of hands, except for certain personal issues such as election of the President of the State and representatives of the Knesset on committees for the selection of judges, or a decision to lift the immunity of a member of Knesset as a result of criminal charges brought against him. Such votes are carried out by secret ballot. Twenty members of the Knesset may at any time request a roll call vote.

The Knesset holds two sessions a year, one in the winter and one in the summer, which together must last for at least eight months. The government may call an extraordinary session of the Knesset during recess, as may any 30 members of the Knesset. In 1985, due to the fact that there were only 23 Knesset members in opposition, that number was reduced to 20.

Members must draw a salary as provided by law and, in order to preserve their independence, may not draw a salary from any other source. They may, however, receive additional income from work, provided it is in the form of a fee.

The Knesset building and its immediate vicinity enjoy immunity. Order is maintained by the Knesset Guard. There is a special area facing the entrance where demonstrations may be held.

OPENING SESSION: A new Knesset is opened by the President of the State. He yields the chair to the oldest member of the Knesset who administers the oath of office. It is a non-religious pledge of allegiance and a promise to perform faithfully the duties of a member of Knesset.

SPEAKER: The first task performed on the first day of a new Knesset is usually the election of a Speaker from among the Knesset members. The Speaker's main duties are to direct the affairs of the Knesset, preserve its dignity, represent the Knesset to outside bodies and enforce the rules of procedure, primarily through the moral authority vested in his office. Except for one Speaker elected from the Opposition to conclude the term of the first Speaker, Joseph Sprinzak, who died in midterm, all others have been elected from among members of the major coalition party. Deputy Speakers, whose number is decided ad hoc for each Knesset, are also elected at the opening session, or shortly thereafter. The Speaker has special powers of arrest and control within the Knesset precincts. The Knesset Guard, under command of the Sergeant at Arms, acts at the Speaker's direction to preserve order and discipline. The Knesset Secretariat, under the Secretary-General, is responsible to the Speaker for making all necessary arrangements connected with the work of the Knesset, as well as budget and administration.

LANGUAGE: Knesset proceedings are conducted in Hebrew. Arab members have the right to speak Arabic, and their speeches are translated into Hebrew. They are also entitled to an interpreter, a privilege rarely sought in recent years. No other language may be used except by special permission of the respective committee.

COMMITTEES: The Knesset works through ten standing committees: Foreign Affairs and Security; Constitution, Law and Justice; Education and Culture; Economics; House; Finance; Labor and Welfare; Interior Affairs and Environment; State Control; Immigration and Absorption. Originally the number of members of each committee was set at 19. Over the years it came to vary from 10 to 25, depending on the relative importance and interest of the committee as well as the party make-up of the Knesset. Committee Chairmen are selected from the major parties, both coalition and opposition, proportionally to their relative strength. Chairmen of committees which must work closely with the government are selected from the coalition benches.

The Foreign Affairs and Security Committee is the Knesset's most prestigious committee, and one of its sub-committees reviews the most secret of security related issues. In March 1987 this subcommittee was appointed as one of two committees to inquire into the *Pollard affair. However, the Finance Committee, with statutory power

›ncerning approval of subsidiary legislation .volving expenditure, government budgets and ıarantees, etc., is by far the most influential ›mmittee. These powers are based on no less ıan 150 legal instruments. With time, the ·actice of conditioning subsidiary legislation on ›nsultation with or approval of a standing com-ittee has also been adopted regarding non-fiscal ·eas of legislation. The functions of the standing ›mmittee are: to examine, amend and report on lls referred to them by the Knesset, following ıe first reading, which are then transmitted to ıe House Committee for the second and third, : final reading; to inquire into the working of ıe Executive Branch and report their findings; › discuss any subject introduced in a motion for ıe agenda, and transmitted to the respective ›mmittee, and formulate its recommendations. /hile such recommendations are not binding on ıe minister concerned, he is obliged to report ithin six months from the time such recom-ıendations have been put on the table of the [ouse on the measures he has taken pursuantly. 'he Knesset may appoint committees of inquiry › study problems warranting more than a rou-ne investigation, but has in fact never employed ıis authority. The House Committee may, and equently does, institute joint committees and ıbcommittees, some of a semipermanent nature. .mong the committees set up in this way have een committees dealing with energy, traffic :cidents, and prison affairs.

AGENDA: The agenda of Knesset sessions is pro-osed by the government and set by the speaker ıd his deputies, except for one session each week evoted to the motions introduced by members r to private members' bills. At the beginning of ıch week the Speaker and his deputies confer 'ith a representative of the government to draw p the agenda for the following week. The Knes-:t meets three days a week — Mondays, Tues-ays and Wednesdays. The total time allotted to ıch debate is decided in advance by the House :ommittee. This is then divided proportionally etween the different factions, in accordance /ith their numerical strength. No group will ave less than eight minutes in each debate. In onpartisan debates, such as the first reading of ills, the time limit for each individual speech is redetermined. The possibility for filibusters is lmost completely eliminated.

INTERPARLIAMENTARY RELATIONS: The Knesset is a member of the Interparliamentary Union and regularly sends observers to the sessions of the Parliamentary Assembly of the Council of Europe. Regular meetings are held by its delegates with those of the European Parliament, alternatively in Europe and Israel. A number of parliamentary friendship associations with other countries have been established by the Knesset on the basis of reciprocity. The Secretary-General of the Knesset is a member of the Association of Secretaries-General of Parliaments.

CRITICISM OF THE KNESSET: The Knesset has frequently been criticized — by the media, the public and even by its own members and officers — for the low attendance of its members. A proposal to institute a quorum has been introduced several times by the incumbent oppositon only to be rejected by the current majority.

Another frequently-voiced criticism relates to the conduct of some members of Knesset and their inappropriate use of language. In the same context the exceptionally far-reaching immunity granted to members has been faulted as being liable to infringe on the principle of equality before the law. In addition, there are complaints concerning the relative impotence of the Knesset vis-à-vis the government, which becomes more acute the larger the size of the coalition. Different remedies — first and foremost *electoral reform and direct accountability of the individual member of Knesset to a definite constituency — have been proposed.

Nevertheless, despite the low esteem in which the Knesset seems to be held, candidates for each election number some 3,000, and turnout of the electorate at election time averages close to 80 percent. (N.L.)

KNESSET SPEAKERS:

1949–59	Joseph Sprinzak (1887–1959)
1959–59	Naḥum Nir (1884–1968)
1959–69	Kadish Luz (1895–1972)
1969–72	Reuven Barket (1905–1972)
1972–77	Yisrael Yeshayahu (1908–1979)
1977–80	Yitzḥak *Shamir (b. 1915)
1980–81	Yitzḥak Berman (b. 1913)
1981–84	Menaḥem Savidor (b. 1917)
1984–	Shlomo *Hillel (b. 1923)

Knessets of Israel

1st Knesset (elected January 25, 1949)

	Seats after elections	Seats at end of term
*_Mapai_	46	46
*_Mapam_	19	20
*United Religious Front	16	16
*_Herut_ Movement	14	12
*General Zionists	7	7
*Progressive Party	5	5
*Sephardi List	4	4
*_Maki_	4	3
Nazareth Region Democratic List[1]	2	2
*Fighters List	1	1
*WIZO	1	1
*Yemenite Association	1	1
MKs A. Jabotinsky and H. Kook	0	2

2nd Knesset (elected July 30,1951)

	Seats after elections	Seats at end of term
Mapai	45	47
General Zionists	20	23
Mapam	15	10
*_Hapo'el Hamizrahi_	8	8
Herut Movement	8	8
Maki	5	8
Progressive Party	4	4
Democratic Arab List [1]	3	3
*_Agudat Yisrael_	3	3
Sephardi List	2	0
*_Po'alei Agudat Yisrael_	2	2
*_Hamizrahi_	2	2
Progress and Labor[1]	1	1
Yemenite Association	1	0
Farm and Development List[1]	1	1

3rd Knesset (elected July 26,1955)

	Seats after elections	Seats at end of term
Mapai	40	40
Herut Movement	15	15
General Zionists	13	13
*National Religious Front later *National Religious Party	11	11
*_Ahdut Ha'avodah-Po'alei Zion_	10	10
Mapam	9	9
*Torah Front	6	6
Maki	6	6
Progressive Party	5	5
Democratic Arab List	2	2
Progress and Labor[1]	2	2
Farm and Development List[1]	1	1

4th Knesset (elected November 3, 1959)

	Seats after elections	Seats at end of term
Mapai	47	47
Herut Movement	17	17
National Religious Party (NRP)	12	12
Mapam	9	9
General Zionists	8	0
Ahdut Ha'avodah-Po'alei Zion	7	7
*Religious Torah Front	6	0
Progressive Party	6	0
Maki	3	3
Progress and Development[1]	2	2
Cooperation and Fraternity	2	2
Farm and Development List[1]	1	1
Agudat Yisrael	0	3
Po'alei Agudat Yisrael	0	3
*Liberal Party of Israel	0	14

5th Knesset (elected August 15, 1961)

	Seats after elections	Seats at end of term
Mapai	42	35
Herut Movement	17	17
Liberal Party of Israel	17	17
National Religious Party	12	12
Mapam	9	9
Ahdut Ha'avodah-Po'alei Zion	8	8
Maki	5	5
Agudat Yisrael	4	4
Po'alei Agudat Yisrael	2	2
Cooperation and Fraternity	2	2
Progress and Development[1]	2	2
*_Rafi_	0	6
Min Hayesod	0	1

6th Knesset (elected November 2, 1965)

	Seats after elections	Seats at end of term
*Alignment	45	63
*_Gahal_	26	22
National Religious Party	11	11
Rafi	10	1
Mapam	8	0
*Independent Liberals	5	4
Agudat Yisrael	4	4
*_Rakah_	3	3
Po'alei Agudat Yisrael	2	2
Progress and Development[1]	2	1
Cooperation and Fraternity	2	1
*_Ha'olam Hazeh-Ko'ah Hadash_	1	1
Maki	1	1
*_Hamerkaz Hahofshi_	0	4
Arab-Jewish Fraternity[1]	0	1
Israeli Druze Faction[1]	0	1

[1] *Minority List

7th Knesset (elected October 28, 1969)

	Seats after elections	Seats at end of term
Alignment	56	57
Gahal	26	26
National Religious Party	12	11
Agudat Yisrael	4	4
Independent Liberals	4	4
*State List	4	3
Rakah.	3	3
Progress and Development	2	2
Po'alei Agudat Yisrael	2	2
Cooperation and Fraternity	2	2
Ha'olam Hazeh-Ko'ah Hadash	2	0
Hamerkaz Hahofshi	2	2
Maki	1	1
Independent Members	0	2
**Meri*	0	1

8th Knesset (elected December 31, 1973)

	Seats after elections	Seats at end of term
Alignment	51	49
**Likud*	39	39
National Religious Party	10	10
Religious Torah Front	5	0
Independent Liberals	4	3
Rakah (changed name to **Hadash*)	4	4
*Civil Rights Movement	3	2
Progress and Development	2	0
**Moked*	1	1
Bedouin and Arab Village List[1]	1	0
United Arab List[1]	0	3
*Social-Democratic Faction	0	2
Independent Members	0	2
Agudat Yisrael	0	3
Po'alei Agudat Yisrael	0	2

9th Knesset (elected May 17, 1977)

	Seats after elections	Seats at end of term
Likud	43	40
Alignment	32	33
*Democratic Movement for Change	15	0
National Religious Party	12	12
Hadash	5	5
Agudat Yisrael	4	4
**Shlomzion*	2	0
**Mahaneh Sheli*	2	1
*Flatto-Sharon (later *Pituah Veshalom*)	1	1
United Arab List[1]	1	1
Po'alei Agudat Yisrael	1	1
Civil Rights Movement	1	1
Independent Liberals	1	1
**Shinui*	0	5
**Telem*	0	4
**Tehiyah*	0	2
**Ha'ihud*	0	2
**Ahva*	0	1
One Israel	0	1
Independent Members	0	4

10th Knesset (elected June 30, 1981)

	Seats after elections	Seats at end of term
Likud	48	46
Alignment	47	49
National Religious Party	6	5
Agudat Yisrael	4	4
Hadash	4	4
Tehiyah	3	3
**Tami*	3	3
Telem	2	0
Shinui	2	2
Civil Rights Movement[2]	1	1
**Matzad*	0	1
State List	0	1
Movement for Renewal	0	1

11th Knesset (elected July 23, 1984)

	Seats after elections	Seats in Jan. 1987
Alignment	44	40
Likud	41	41
Tehiyah*-Tzomet*	5	5
National Religious Party	4	4
Hadash	4	4
**Shass*	4	4
Shinui	3	3
Civil Rights Movement	3	4
**Yahad*	3	0
**Progressive List for Peace*	2	2
Agudat Yisrael	2	2
**Morasha*	2	2
Tami	1	1
**Kach*	1	1
**Ometz*	1	1
Mapam	0	6

Knesset Yisrael In mandatory times, the general term used to describe the organizational framework of the **Yishuv*.

Kollek, Teddy Mayor of Jerusalem. Born 1911, in Vienna. Kollek immigrated to Palestine in 1934 and joined Kibbutz Ein-Gev in 1936. He was **Hehalutz* representative in Britain, and in 1939 succeeded in getting exit permits for 3,000 Jewish Austrian youngsters from Adolf Eichmann (See: *Eichmann Trial). During World War II Kollek worked in the Political Department of the *Jewish Agency in Istanbul and Cairo where he served as liaison with British and American Intelligence. In 1947 he was head of the **Haganah* mission to the US where he led an operation to illictly gather military supplies. In 1951–52 he was Israel's minister plenipotentiary in Washington and Director-General of Prime

[2] The Civil Rights Movement joined the Alignment immediately after the 1981 elections and left it soon before the 1984 elections.

Minister David *Ben Gurion's Office until 1964 (within the framework of which he established the Government Tourist Corporation), was in charge of Israel's 10th anniversary celebrations and instrumental in raising funds for the Israel Museum in Jerusalem, of which he is founder and chairman.

After the split in *Mapai* in 1965 he joined **Rafi*. While President of the commercial Africa-Israel Investment Company, in 1965, he was persuaded to run against the *Mapai* candidate for Mayor of Jerusalem. Kollek won that election and has been Mayor of Jerusalem since 1966, at first establishing a coalition with **Ḥerut* and the religious parties. Two years later, in June 1967, Kollek became Mayor of reunited Jerusalem. In the other municipal elections Kollek has run on his own list but has had the full support of the *Israel Labor Party. Kollek has left his imprint on reunited Jerusalem, trying to reach a modus vivendi with all its communities — Jewish and Arab, religious and secular, Ashkenazi and Sephardi. Under his mayorship Jerusalem has flourished, developed and expanded. He established the Jerusalem Foundation to channel funds from foreign philanthropists, both Jewish and non-Jewish, for the improvement of the city. He also instituted the Jerusalem Committee, composed of foreign scholars, planners and dignitaries, to serve as an advisory council. He has established good relations with the heads of all the various churches. Kollek considered running for the 11th Knesset in 1984 but finally decided against the idea, preferring to concentrate on the affairs of Jerusalem.

Kook, Rabbi Avraham Yitzḥak Hacohen (1865–1935) Rabbi and thinker. First Ashkenazi Chief Rabbi during the British mandate. Born in Latvia. Rabbi Kook identified with the Zionist idea, believing that the return to **Eretz Yisrael* would hasten divine redemption. He immigrated to Palestine in 1904. Unlike most other Orthodox Rabbis he welcomed the *Balfour Declaration.

In 1921 he was appointed Chief Ashkenazi Rabbi, hoping that the office of the *Chief Rabbinate would evolve into a Sanhedrin (the assembly of 71 ordained scholars which served both as legislature and Supreme Court during the period of the Second Temple). In 1924 he set up a yeshiva in Jerusalem, which later came to be known as Merkaz Ha-Rav (the Rabbi's center which encouraged a positive attitude towar Zionism among its students. Rabbi Kook's atti tude toward **Hamizraḥi* was ambivalent due t what he regarded as the religious party's exces sive dabbling in politics, but he objected to th anti-Zionist line of **Agudat Yisrael* and **Netur Karta*. The latter attacked him incessantly. I 1933 Rabbi Kook adopted the controversial posi tion of defending Avraham Stavsky, who ha been accused of murdering Labor leader Ḥair *Arlosoroff and was acquitted for lack of evi dence.

Rabbi Kook, who advocated a more uni versal view of the world than most of his col leagues, was highly respected by secular Jews fo his practical approach to solving problems. H himself believed that secularism was a passin phenomenon.

Kook, Rabbi Zvi Yehuda (1891–1982 Yeshiva head and mentor of **Gush Emunim* Rabbi Kook was born in Lithuania, and wa educated in the traditional religious school sys tem as well as at the University of Halberstadt i Germany. In 1904 he immigrated to Palestin with his parents when his father Avrahan Yitzḥak Hacohen *Kook, later to become Chie Rabbi, assumed the position of Rabbi of Jaffa an the Jewish colonies.

He left Palestine to study in Europe prior t World War I and returned from Switzerland i 1919. Kook became head of the Merkaz Hara Yeshiva, edited his father's philosophical an theological works and himself published reli gious and political commentaries.

Kook participated in the first *Gush Emunin* settlement effort in June 1974 at Hawara an remained a source of inspiration and guidance t the *Gush*, with whom the leaders of various par ties conferred. Like his father, Kook taught tha *Zionism is possessed by a dynamism based on a unfolding process of redemption. Inherent in thi theory is the conviction that Zionism is undergo ing a transformation: ultimately religious legiti macy will replace the secular political leadership The relationship between the Jewish people an its land is part of a divine scheme and the Land o Israel is endowed, as is the people of Israel, wit an immanent holiness. Rabbi Kook was childles and left no heirs to assume his leadership.

(I.M.

L

La'am Hebrew word for "to the people." A bloc within the *Likud* established in 1976, made up of members from the *State List, the *Land of Israel Movement and **Hamerkaz Ha'atzma'i*. Within the *Likud*, *La'am* had eight seats in the 9th Knesset (1977), four in the 10th Knesset (1981) and three in the 11th Knesset (1984). In 1985 *La'am* merged with **Herut*.

Labor Party See: *Israel Labor Party.

Land Day A day celebrated every year by the *Arabs of Israel to commemorate the bloodshed which took place on March 30, 1976, when six persons were killed when the Israeli army and police intervened in the strike held in protest against the confiscation of Arab lands in the Galilee.

Though it was felt that undue force had been used, and that only in Nazareth was there really any reason to fear violent clashes between Arabs and Jews, Prime Minister Yitzḥak *Rabin justified the use of force, and the confiscation of land for purposes of regional development, the aim of which was to bring economic welfare to the inhabitants of the Galilee. He added that efforts were being made to ensure that as little as possible agricultural land be confiscated and that the owners of confiscated land be properly compensated. He also accused **Rakaḥ* and other factors of using violent means to force people to participate in the strike.

In recent years Arabs in the *West Bank have demonstrated their sympathy with their Arab-Israeli brethren by joining the annual Land Day strike.

Land of Israel Movement (LIM) Hebrew: *Hatnu'ah Lema'an Eretz Yisrael Hashlemah*. A political lobby, made up primarily of intellectuals, which advocated the retention of all the territories occupied by Israel in the *Six-Day War. The movement was established in August 1967 when a manifesto was published in the major Israeli dailies, signed by over 70 well-known political and literary personalities.

The initiators of the movement came from the Labor Zionist stream (such as Moshe Shamir), but included members of the *Revisionist camp (such as Israel *Eldad), religious personalities, a wide variety of poets, writers, intellectuals and academics, as well as personalities with a military background (such as Avraham Yoffe). A bi-weekly, *Zot Ha'aretz* (this is the land) was published from April 1968 until January 1981, and served as the movement's organ.

The movement's first public activity was a demonstration against the return to the *United Nations of its former headquarters in no-man's land in Jerusalem. During the resettlement attempt of Hebron in early 1968 by Rabbi Moshe *Levinger's group, the LIM extended crucial moral and financial help and interceded with central government figures.

In the 1969 elections to the 7th Knesset, an appeal was made by some LIM leaders not to vote for Labor. Others supported the *Ken* (yes) list headed by Israel Eldad and Oved Ben Ami which did not pass the 1 percent qualifying threshold. Several members of the LIM were elected to the Knesset on other lists: Isar Harel (who had been the head of the **Mossad* at the time of the *Eichmann affair) was elected in *Ben Gurion's *State List, Binyamin Halevi was returned as a **Gaḥal* member, Moshe Zvi Neriah and Avner Shaki were members of the *National Religious Party, and all propagated the movement's ideas within the framework of their parties.

Partially in response to the adoption in 1973 by the *Israel Labor Party of the *territorial compromise formula in its platform, as well as to increased international pressure for Israeli territorial concessions, LIM activists from the Labor Party set up an independent faction, *Tnu'at Ha'avodah Lema'an Eretz Yisrael Hashlemah* (Labor Movement for the Integral Land of Israel) which eventually joined the **Likud*. After the 1973 elections Avraham Yoffe represented it in the 8th Knesset, and Moshe Shamir after the 1977 elections in the 9th Knesset within the framework of **La'am*. However, following the *Camp David Accords Shamir broke off from the *Likud*, together with Ge'ula *Cohen, to form the **Bana'i* faction — the forerunner of the **Teḥiyah*.

With the rise and success of *Gush Emunim* and later on the *Teḥiyah*, the LIM lost its uniqueness and attraction to the younger generation, especially since it never was an activist group, and only seldom engaged in field work, remaining an intellectual circle trying to exert pressure behind the scenes.

To all intents and purposes both *Hatnu'ah Lema'an Eretz Yisrael Hashlemah* and *Tnu'at Ha'avodah Lema'an Eretz Yisrael Hashlemah* have ceased to exist. (I.M.)

land policy Israel's land policy goes back to the year 1901 when the Jewish National Fund (JNF — in Hebrew: *Keren Kayemet Leyisrael*) was founded to purchase and develop land in Palestine and Syria on behalf of the *World Zionist Organization for Jewish settlement. The JNF's policy, and that followed by the State of Israel since 1948 and the Israel Land Administration since it was founded in 1961, has been that all land purchased on behalf of the Jewish people is inalienable and in so far as possible should remain under national ownership. Thus, national land is rarely sold. It is usually leased for 49 years with an option for prolongation by the lessee or his heirs.

The idea of setting up a national fund, and the ideal of national ownership of land were first propagated in the 19th century by Hermann Schapira (1840–1898) who presented a proposal in that spirit to the first Zionist Congress in 1897.

The JNF purchased the first plots of land in 1904 in Kfar Hittin in the Lower Galilee. In 1908 the Palestine Land Development Corporation (*Haḥevrah Lehachsharat Hayishuv*) was established by Arthur Ruppin (1876–1942) to do the actual purchasing of land — both for the JNF and for private individuals and groups.

In 1920, when the Foundation Fund (*Keren Hayesod*) was founded by the WZO as the main financial instrument of the Zionist movement, the JNF was declared "the instrument of the urban and rural land policy of the Jewish people, devoted exclusively to land acquisition and improvement." In 1921 one of the JNF's most famous land purchases took place — that of the Valley of Jezreel. During mandatory times most of the land was purchased from absentee Arab landowners and occasionally involved the removal, with compensation, of the Arab tenants who had worked the land for the absentee landowners. This resulted in the myth that massive dispossession was taking place, and in the publication of the Hope-Simpson Report of 1930, which stated that very little additional cultivable land was left for Jewish settlement.

By 1947 about 936,000 dunams (234,000 acres) had been purchased by the JNF — over half the total Jewish holdings in Palestine at the time. About 70 percent of all the Jewish-owned land had been purchased by the Palestine Land Development Corporation.

One of the large private landowners in Palestine before the establishment of the State was the Baron Edmond de Rothschild who leased his land to farmers, and whose lands were run from 1900 until 1924 by the Jewish Colonization Association (ICA) and from 1924 until 1957, when the lands were transferred to the State of Israel, by the Palestine Jewish Colonization Association (PICA). Since the land in Palestine had been neglected for centuries under Turkish rule, both PICA and the JNF were actively involved in land improvement. The JNF started its first tree-planting experiments in 1908, and rapidly became involved in major afforestation activities. Another activity was the draining of swamps, both to get rid of the scourge of malaria and to uncover cultivable land. The largest drainage project carried out by the JNF was the draining of the marshes of the Huleh in the years 1952–56, which produced some of Israel's most fertile land. A further improvement activity involved the terracing and stoning of mountain slopes for purposes of cultivation. Finally, especially after land was purchased in the Negev, the JNF was involved in preparing the desert land for cultivation.

After the establishment of the state, Israel took over the state lands which it inherited from the mandatory government and which Britain had inherited from the Turkish Empire. Over 90 percent of the land in Israel is state land, though in the Coastal Plain two-thirds of the land is privately-owned while in the Negev there is very little private ownership.

After 1948 the JNF almost completely ceased purchasing land from non-Jews, and dealt primarily in land improvement and afforestation and the opening of new areas for settlement. The Palestine Land Development Corporation makes land in and close to the principal Israeli cities available for purposes of residential, commercial, industrial and recreational development, and in partnership with other companies is involved in various profit-yielding investments, including several resort hotels.

In 1950 the Absentee Property Law was passed y the *Knesset, dealing with all Arab-owned roperty, including land, abandoned after November 29, 1947, for which a custodian was ppointed. Israel refuses to recognize the auto-natic right of those who fled the country in 947–49 to return and reclaim their property, ut has at various times expressed willingness to each a settlement based on compensation on ondition that the Jews who left the Moslem ountries, leaving all their property behind, will lso be compensated (See: *World Organization f Jews from Arab Countries).

In 1960 the Basic Law: Israel Lands was passed See: *Basic Laws) together with the Israel Land aw and the Israel Land Administration Law. The Israel Land Administration (*Minhal Mekar-e'ai Yisrael*) was founded in 1961 through the nitiative of Yosef Weitz, in order to concentrate he management of national lands in the hands of single authority. Upon its foundation a cove-nant was signed between the Government of srael and the WZO which settled relations and he distribution of functions between the Israel and Administration and the JNF.

The function of the Israel Land Administra-ion is to manage the national lands and make and available for various purposes if and when equired for economic and social development projects as determined by the Government of srael — including population dispersal, housing, ndustrial, agricultural and service development, ecurity needs, welfare, cultural, recreational and nvironmental requirements.

The Israel Land Administration is a branch of he Israeli government, and its employees are civil servants. However, the policy followed by he Administration is decided by the council of he Administration which also supervises its activities, rather than directly by the govern-ment. Two ministeries have joint responsibility for implementing the Israel Land Law and the Israel Land Administration Law — the Ministry of Finance and the Ministry of Agriculture. The Israel Land Administration is not the owner of land. The owners of national lands are the state, the Development Authority, which owns land purchased from the custodian of abandoned property and the custodian of enemy property, and the JNF. The Administration gathers and records all information regarding national land, controls the price of land, allocates land, and is in charge of making sure that the national land is not misused or occupied illegally. In addition it is responsible for offering tenders for land development.

The confiscation of land is the responsibility of the Ministry of Finance. The registration of land, land evaluation and the management of aban-doned land is in the hands of the Ministry of Justice.

Of the lands occupied during the *Six-Day War those in *Jerusalem and the *Golan Heights are treated as Israeli territory. The land in the *West Bank and the *Gaza Strip is under control and responsibility of the Ministry of Defense and the Civil Administration. The law applicable to these territories is the Jordanian law with regard to the West Bank and Palestine mandatory law with regard to the Gaza Strip, while the provi-sions of international law regarding occupied ter-ritories applies to both. All Jewish settlement in these areas is carried out on state lands which are run by the "commissioners for government prop-erty" in the West Bank and Gaza Strip, respec-tively, and are leased to the settlers, or on land purchased privately from Arab owners. Land is confiscated (with compensation) in the occupied territories only for military purposes or for the construction of infrastructure. In 1978 the Gov-ernment of Israel decided that private property should not be used for the establishment of Jew-ish settlements in the territories unless voluntar-ily sold by its owners, so that Israeli settlement activities in the territories would not dispossess the local inhabitants.

The 1973 *Galili Document dealt favorably with private land purchases in the territories, though it advocated full cooperation between private purchasers and the Israel Land Adminis-tration to ensure that the purchasing was done for development purposes and not speculation. However, private land deals became widespread after 1977 when the **Likud* government took over. In recent years several Arabs have been con-victed of selling land which did not belong to them to over-eager Jews who did not thoroughly check whether the sellers were indeed the lands' legal owners. Investigations were made into alle-gations that *Likud* Member of Knesset Michael Dekel in the 10th Knesset, had been involved in illegal deals while he was Deputy Minister of

Agriculture, but insufficient cause was found to press charges against him.

One of the problems regarding land in the West Bank is that ownership of over two-thirds of this land has not been finally settled and recorded. The Israeli political parties which advocate eventual annexation of the territories to Israel favor maximal purchases of land from Arab owners. The parties which favor the *territorial compromise or the return of all the territories to Arab sovereignty do not favor land purchases in areas from which Israel might some day withdraw.

Within Israel, though the *Likud* advocates a policy of denationalization of land, little was done in this direction in the years 1977–84. In 1985 the possibility of selling state lands as one temporary means for closing the state budget deficit was mentioned, but was not adopted by the government.

Latin America and Israel In 1947, when the Palestine question was debated in the UN General Assembly, the Latin American countries were called upon, for the first time, to take a stand regarding the question of the establishment of a Jewish state. Their reaction was not uniform. In countries with democratic and liberal regimes there was great sympathy for the Jewish cause, while the attitude of the conservative-Catholic governments was reserved, *inter alia* because of the negative attitude of the Vatican to *Zionism in this period. On the other hand, the Jewish communities in these countries played a positive role. Under their inspiration committees "for a Hebrew Palestine" made up of famous personalities were established in most of the countries of the region. However, in some countries, such as Chile and Honduras, the local Arab communities managed to exert effective pressure on the governments. In the *United Nations deliberations, Guatemala and Uruguay took pro-Zionist positions. These small, liberal countries, together with Peru, had participated in the UN Special Committee on Palestine (UNSCOP) and were instrumental in its accepting the principle of the establishment of a Jewish state and the adoption of the *Partition Plan. Two conservative Latin American countries, Colombia and El Salvador, opposed the plan when it was discussed by the Second Assembly of the UN in the autumn of 1947.

In the last stages of the deliberations the *United States exerted its full influence in favor of the Partition Plan, and acted energetically in an effort to persuade hesitant Latin American states, such as Haiti and Paraguay.

In the historic vote of November 29, 1947, 13 of the 20 Latin American states voted in favor (Bolivia, Brazil, Costa Rica, the Dominican Republic, Ecuador, Guatemala, Haiti, Nicaragua, Panama, Paraguay, Peru, Uruguay and Venezuela), one voted against (Cuba) and six abstained (*Argentina, Chile, Colombia, El Salvador, Honduras and Mexico).

Even those states which had reservations about the plan to establish a Jewish state soon acquiesced to the existence of Israel. The Latin American support of Israel reached its peak in the vote for Israel's acceptance for membership in the UN on May 11, 1949. Eighteen Latin American states voted in favor, and only two (El Salvador and Brazil) abstained.

Almost all of the first Latin American states to recognize Israel belonged to the liberal camp. Guatemala recognized Israel on May 17, 1948, and Costa Rica, Nicaragua, Panama, Uruguay and Venezuela followed in the months May, June and July. The remainder announced their recognition between September 1948 and April 1949.

In January 1949 Israel opened a consulate in Montevideo, Uruguay. It was the first Israeli diplomatic representation in Latin America and its fourth in the world. Later, under the initiative of the Argentinian President Juan Perón, Israel and Argentina decided to exchange diplomatic representations, and in the summer of 1949 an Israeli consulate was set up in Buenos Aires and an Argentinian consulate was opened in Tel Aviv. In 1952 Israel opened a representation in Brazil, and in 1953 in Mexico. In 1952–55 Brazil, Uruguay and Guatemala established representation in Israel — the latter in *Jerusalem.

Bilateral relations between Israel and the Latin American states flourished in the 1960s. By that time Israel had earned a name for itself due to its rapid economic, technological and social development, and had established a technical aid program, primarily in the agricultural sphere (See: *Foreign Aid from Israel). In the meantime, far-reaching political and social changes had taken place in Latin America. In several states, including Argentina and Brazil, democratic governments were elected. In others, military regimes imbued with a consciousness regarding economic development, came to power. All these wished to benefit from Israel's experience and know-how and technological cooperation ties were formed, even with Cuba after the assumption of power by Fidel Castro. The number of Latin American representations in Israel rose to 15, of which ten were in Jerusalem, constituting an overwhelming majority of the diplomatic corps in Israel's capital. Only the representations of Argentina, Brazil, Colombia (which moved its embassy to Jerusalem in 1965), Mexico and Peru remained in Tel Aviv.

The closer relations between Israel and the Latin American states also manifested themselves in the UN and other international organizations. Most of the Latin American states voted in this period against resolutions viewed as being contrary to Israel's security and in favor of Israel-Arab negotiations. In 1956–57, following the *Sinai Campaign, the issue of Israel's control of territories occupied during the war arose. The Latin American states adhered to the principle of opposition to territorial conquests, and supported a series of resolutions which called for the withdrawal of Israeli forces from the *Sinai Peninsula. However, in 1967, after the *Six-Day War, 22 Latin American states voted against a draft resolution by the non- aligned states which called for immediate and unconditional Israeli withdrawal from all the occupied territories. In the same debate 20 Latin American states proposed an alternative resolution (which was also defeated) laying down the link between the principle of withdrawal and the principles of ending the state of warfare and of "coexistence based on good neighborliness." The position of the Latin American bloc was a decisive factor in the formulation of *Security Council Resolution 242.

The rate of support for Israel in the Latin American bloc (which had increased numerically through the independence of four new Caribbean states: Barbados, Guyana, Jamaica and Trinidad Tobago) was much higher in 1960–67 than that of the other blocs, including the Western Bloc.

In the late 1960s Latin America underwent political changes. In 1968 a left-wing military regime was established in Peru. In 1969 a Communist-Socialist coalition headed by Salvador Allende came to power in Chile. In 1973 Juan Perón was reelected President in Argentina. All of these states joined the non-aligned movement to which Cuba already belonged, and which was later joined by additional Latin American countries. Furthermore, the number of increasingly radical Caribbean states grew by the mid-1980s to 15. These developments contributed to a broad radical Latin American alignment following a strong anti-American and anti-Israeli line. This alignment also existed in the "group of 77," the organization of Latin American, African and Asian countries established in 1964 in order to attain preferential trade terms from the wealthy and industrialized states. Even though the group of 77 had originally been established as an economic organization, it became active in the political sphere and started to adopt anti-Israeli resolutions as of the conference held in 1971 in Lima, Peru. In the 1980s the number of non-aligned states reached 95 and the number of states who were members of the 77 grew to 126 — both organizations turning into factors of decisive weight in the multilateral arena.

A further development was the oil crisis which had a devastating effect on the economies of most of the Latin American states. The soaring oil prices in the years 1973–74 and 1979 created a dependence on the mostly Arab oil producers. Brazil turned pro-Arab, and the oil-producing Latin American states, such as Venezuela and Ecuador, strengthened their relations with the Arab oil producers, due to their joint interests.

In several Latin American states there was also an awakening of ethnic and political consciousness among the population of Arab origin, which numbered over 2.5 million persons (compared to less than a half-million Jews).

The seizing of power in such countries as Argentina and Chile by military juntas did not lead to a change in the pro-Arab policy introduced by previous governments with a leftist orientation.

The side effects of all these developments were the rapid growth of diplomatic relations between the Latin American and Arab states, and the opening of *Palestine Liberation Organization (PLO) offices in Cuba, Peru, Mexico, Brazil, Bolivia and in Nicaragua after the Sandinist revolution in 1979.

At the UN a significant change occurred in the Latin American position on the Palestinian question. In 1974 seven Latin American states voted for General Assembly Resolution 3236 which recognized the PLO as the representative of the Palestinian people and the right of the Palestinian people to national independence and sovereignty. In 1982 the number of Latin American states supporting these demands increased to 20. At the same time the Latin American support for resolutions condemning Israel on such issues as Israel's continued control of the *occupied territories and violations of the rights of the Arab population increased. In 1975 five Latin American states (Brazil, Cuba, Guyana, Granada and Mexico) voted in favor of General Assembly Resolution 3379 which equated *Zionism with racism (See: *Anti-Zionism), while ten voted against and ten abstained (including Chile which had voted in favor in Committee). In the early 1980s the voting patterns of the Latin American bloc closely resembled those of the African and Asian states. Some states, such as Mexico, and to a lesser extent Argentina, Brazil and Peru, adopted the line of supporting all anti-Israeli resolutions. The remainder of the Latin American states have supported most of the resolutions against Israel and have abstained only on the most extreme ones. There remains a small number of states, such as Costa Rica, the Dominican Republic, El Salvador, Granada (since the change of government there in 1983), Guatemala and Haiti, which have been willing from time to time to adopt a pro-Israel position, either by voting against or by abstaining when anti-Israeli resolutions have come up for a vote.

Cuba, which chaired the non-aligned bloc during the years 1979–83 contributed to the more extremist line of this group. The positions which the Latin American states have adopted in the UN have affected their bilateral relations with Israel. For example, in 1980, after the Knesset had approved the Basic Law: Jerusalem (See: *Basic Laws) and the Security Council called for the removal of all the foreign representatives from Jerusalem in retaliation, the 11 Latin American states which held embassies in Jerusalem (as well as the Netherlands) complied and moved them to Tel Aviv. Nevertheless, Costa Rica returned its embassy to Jerusalem in 1982, and El Salvador followed suit in 1984. Three Latin American states broke relations with Israel: Cuba in 1973, Guyana in 1974 and Nicaragua in 1982. Despite these developments the Israeli diplomatic representation network in Latin America has continued to grow as a result of the establishment of Israeli representations in the Caribbean and Central America (El Salvador, Haiti and Jamaica in the 1970s and Honduras in 1986). In 1986 Israel had 19 embassies in Latin America and hosted 17.

Israeli technical aid in the 1980s included long-term projects in Colombia, Costa Rica, the Dominican Republic and Honduras, in the spheres of agriculture, rural development, community development and public health. Seven hundred trainees participate annually in these projects — some of them in Israel and some in their own countries.

Trade relations have always been of secondary importance in Israel-Latin America relations. In 1974 trade in each direction was valued at less than $50 million. In 1980 Israeli exports reached $150 million while imports were $140 million. The economic crisis in several Latin American countries caused a drop in trade in 1983–84. In 1985 Israeli exports were $149 million and imports $124 million. Most of Israel's exports are chemicals, agricultural produce, equipment and electronics. A major item not included in these statistics is military exports (See: *Arms Sales). According to the Stockholm International Peace Research Institute (SIPRI) yearbooks, between the years 1970 and 1983 Israel has sold arms to Argentina, Bolivia, Brazil, Chile, Colombia, Ecuador, Paraguay, Peru and Venezuela in South America and Costa Rica, the Dominican Republic, El Salvador, Guatemala, Haiti, Honduras, Mexico, Nicaragua and Panama in Central America. Imports include meat, grain, corn, cocoa, coffee, sugar and metals and an item not included in the import statistics is oil from Mexico. Israel began to import Mexican oil in 1975 at an annual value estimated at $400 million. Israeli banks, companies involved in agricultural planning and development, and construction firms are active in Latin America.

(Y.B.R.)

Lavon affair The cause célèbre of Israeli politics since independence, the Lavon Affair, the first stage of which was known as the **essek bish*, began in 1954 as a result of an Israeli intelligence fiasco. An Israeli spy ring was captured in Egypt, during Pinḥas *Lavon's tenure as Israel's Minister of Defense. Eleven Egyptian Jews were arrested on suspicion of having planted bombs in movie-houses, a post-office and on the premises of the US Information Centers in Cairo and Alexandria. The suspects were accused of working for the Israeli secret service in an effort to sabotage relations between the West and Egypt, at that time negotiating with the British on withdrawal from Suez. Two received the death sentence and six long prison terms. Two Israeli agents were tried *in absentia*.

Prime Minister Moshe *Sharett, it seems, had not been informed about the operation. Defense Minister Lavon also claimed no knowledge, but the Head of the **Aman*, Col. B. Gibli, stated that he had received oral instructions to carry out the operation from Lavon. Chief of Staff Moshe *Dayan also held the Minister of Defense responsible. The Prime Minister appointed a two-man investigation committee which was unable to verify Gibli's claims. As a result of this affair and differences of opinion regarding Israel's defense policy Lavon resigned in February 1955 and David *Ben Gurion was appointed Minister of Defense. Shortly thereafter he assumed the post of Prime Minister as well.

The question of Lavon's guilt or innocence was opened again in 1958 during the course of a secret trial of "the third man," a double agent operating out of Germany who had allegedly been involved in the Egyptian operation. At the end of the 1960s Lavon's appeal to Ben Gurion for rehabilitation was rejected. A committee consisting of seven Ministers concluded that Lavon had not given the order to Gibli and had not known of the operation in Egypt. This affirmation of Lavon's innocence was endorsed by the government. As a result, Ben Gurion resigned, stating that political inter-party affiliations rendered the government incompetent to judge. New Knesset elections were called in 1961, after which Lavon was dismissed from his post as Secretary-General of the **Histadrut* in order to facilitate Ben Gurion's return as Prime Minister/Defense Minister.

Nearly two years later, in 1963, Ben Gurion resigned and returned to Kibbutz Sde Boker. He was replaced by Levi *Eshkol. The following year Ben Gurion demanded that Eshkol appoint an independent commission of inquiry to determine whether the 1961 "committee of seven" had acted correctly. Eshkol refused. A struggle on the issue in the 1965 *Mapai conference ended with 60 percent of the participants supporting Eshkol and 40 percent Ben Gurion. Ben Gurion and some of his followers then seceded from the party and established **Rafi*. Lavon, in the meantime, disappeared from the political scene.

Law of Return A law passed by the *Knesset on July 5, 1950, which states the principle that "every Jew has the right to immigrate to the country" and which was described by the then Prime Minister David *Ben Gurion as expressing one of Israel's central goals — that of "the ingathering of the dispersions." Ben Gurion added that the law "states that it is not the State which grants the right to settle in the State to the Jews abroad, but that this right is ingrained in him insofar as he is a Jew."

The law gives legal validity to the declaration in the *Proclamation of Independence that "the State of Israel will be open to the immigration of Jews from all countries of their dispersion." Several days after the establishment of the state all the regulations of the Mandatory Immigration Ordinance, which had limited Jewish immigration to Palestine, were cancelled, and the immigration of Jews who had entered Palestine "illegally" in mandatory times was retroactively made legal.

The 1952 Citizenship Law grants automatic citizenship to any Jew who immigrates to the country on the basis of the Law of Return, unless he opts out of such citizenship.

A proposal to prohibit the expulsion of any Jew from the country was rejected as discrimination against non-Jewish citizens. According to the 1977 Extradition Law an Israeli cannot be extradited to another country except for an offense committed before he was an Israeli citizen. However, the Minister of Justice may use his discretion and decide not to extradite an Israeli who has committed an offense before becoming an Israeli citizen, as he did in December 1986 in the case of William Nakash, who a French court found guilty in absentia of murder. Minister of Justice Avraham Sharir decided not to extradite him to France because, it was argued, his life would be in danger. Sharir's decision was strongly criticized. Originally the Law of Return did not include a definition of a Jew to whom the right of immigration applies. It was added only in 1970.

According to the *Halacha* (Jewish law) a Jew is anyone born to a Jewish mother or who has converted to Judaism. The subjective secular approach regards as a Jew anyone who considers himself to be a Jew. Until 1970 the Supreme Court, in a series of judgments, decided that the term Jew in the Law of Return should be understood in its secular meaning. However, in the case of Brother Daniel, a Jew who had converted and become a Carmelite monk, it held that for the purpose of the Law of Return a Jew who has converted to another religion is not to be considered a Jew, though according to the *Halacha* a Jew who changes religion is still considered a Jew.

On March 19, 1970, the Law of Return was amended to define a Jew as anyone born to a Jewish mother or who has converted to Judaism, and is not a member of another religion. The *halachic* part of this definition, that a Jew is anyone born to a Jewish mother or who was converted to Judaism, was based on the opinion of scholars in Israel and abroad who had been approached by Ben Gurion on October 27, 1958. The addition which diverges from the *Halacha* definition is the exclusion of anyone who is a member of another religion.

Since the amendment was passed a controversy has raged over the meaning of the word "conversion" — if it applies to any conversion, whether or not it is recognized by the *Chief Rabbinate in Israel, only to conversions carried out according to the *Halacha*, or only to conversions carried out by Orthodox Rabbis. The question arises in connection with conversions carried out by Reform and Conservative Rabbis abroad, whose conversions are not recognized by the Rabbinate (See: *Conservative Movement and *Progressive Judaism). The issue was never settled in an Israeli civilian court.

In recent years an amendment to the Law of Return, calling for the addition of the word "*kahalacha*" (according to the *Halacha*) after the words "who has converted," has several times been brought to the Knesset by the religious parties. However, the proposed amendment has been repeatedly defeated, mostly by a narrow majority. Voting in favor of the amendment in the 11th Knesset have been the four religious parties, the **Teḥiyah*, Rabbi Meir *Kahane, most of the **Likud* and Rabbi Menaḥem Hacohen from the *Israel Labor Party. Some Liberals from the *Likud*, the *Alignment and the remaining parties from the Center and Left voted against.

The 1970 amendment also recognized the right of non-Jewish spouses, children and grandchildren of Jews to immigrate to Israel on the basis of the Law Return. This amendment was introduced in order to avoid the breakup of mixed families, in the event the Jewish member wants to immigrate to Israel, and to encourage all Jews, even those whose families are not Jewish, to immigrate to Israel.

The Law of Return is based on the recognition of the natural and historic right of the Jewish people to be a nation like all the nations, and to enjoy independence in its sovereign state — a right recognized by the *United Nations. According to the Proclamation of Independence Israel is a Jewish state, into which Jews have a right to immigrate and in which they have the right to settle and live. Though only a Jew is eligible to enjoy the natural and historic right of immigration to Israel, all of its citizens, both Jewish and non-Jewish are ensured equal rights within the state. However, the granting of citizenship and residence rights by the state is not subject to the principle of equality, since in this sphere all states have the right to control their population make-up and nature. This right was explicitly recognized by the 1965 International Convention on Racial Discrimination provided that "provisions. . . concerning nationality, citizenship or naturalization. . . do not discriminate against any particular nationality."

The practical provisions of the Law of Return call for the issuing of immigration visas "to any Jews expressing a desire to settle in Israel, unless the Minister of the Interior is satisfied that the applicant: (i) acts against the Jewish nation; (ii) may threaten the public health or State security; or (iii) has a criminal past and is liable to endanger the public's peace." The latter clause, added in 1954, was used to prevent the immigration to Israel of American gangster Meyer Lansky in 1971. These reservations were included, despite the objection of those who called for recognition of the unconditional right of any Jew to enter and settle in the Jewish state, in order to prevent Israel from turning into a refuge from justice and an asylum for the mentally infirm.

The law recognized that Jews who had immigrated to the country before the law was passed, and Jews born in the country, enjoy the same status as do those who immigrate to Israel on the basis of the Law of Return. Similarly according to the Citizenship Law, citizenship can be obtained on the basis of the Law of Return by anyone who immigrated to the country or was born in it before the establishment of the state, anyone who immigrated to Israel or was born there after the establishment of the state, and anyone who became an immigrant after having arrived in the country as a non-immigrant. In 1971 the Citizenship Law was amended to enable the Minister of the Interior to grant Israeli citizenship on the basis of the Law of Return to anyone who received, or is entitled to receive an immigration visa, even before his immigration. This amendment was enacted in particular for immigrants from the USSR who have given up or lost their Soviet citizenship before leaving the *Soviet Union. (J.K.)

Lebanese War Also known as "Operation Peace for the Galilee," the Lebanese War began on June 6, 1982 and terminated when the *IDF (Israel Defense Forces) officially withdrew to behind the international border in June, 1985.

The background to Israel's invasion of Lebanon was the continuous buildup of *Palestine Liberation Organization (PLO) bases in southern Lebanon from which Russian-made Katyusha rockets were launched against Israel's northern settlements, and terrorist infiltrations into Israel's territory were initiated. Minister of Defense Ariel *Sharon believed that a sweeping operation could both clear southern Lebanon from PLO presence and liquidate the organization's operative capabilities by destroying its headquarters and infrastructure in Beirut.

The operation was to have been implemented in full cooperation with the Phalange forces of Bashir Jemayel which Israel had been assisting since the mid-1970s; it was understood that after Bashir would be installed as President of Lebanon he would sign a peace treaty with Israel. Another expected side effect was to have been the withdrawal of Syria from Lebanese territory.

(S.H.R.)

The invasion of Lebanon began on June 6, with Israeli forces advancing northward along three axes: the Mediterranean coast, the central

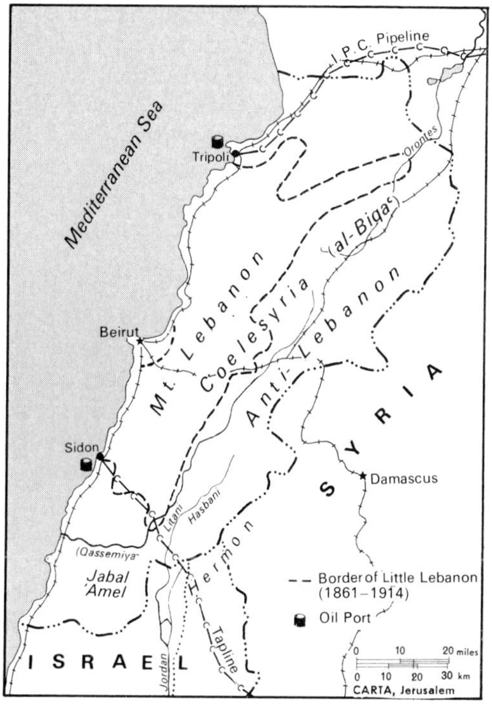

Map of Lebanon.

mountain region and the eastern sector, near the Lebanese-Syrian border. A fourth important axis which developed later was in the Beka valley. The operational instructions to the forces were to destroy PLO positions while avoiding a confrontation with Syrian forces in the Beka valley. At the end of the first day, Israeli tanks and mechanized forces reached the Kuseima Bridge on the Litani River, some 17 miles north of the border, while some infantry units advanced further north toward Sidon. Along the central axis Israeli forces carried out a flanking movement toward the PLO-held town of Nabatiya, some six miles north of the border. By nightfall an IDF infantry unit had taken the Beaufort fortress, a PLO hilltop artillery stronghold. Along the eastern axis the IDF moved toward Hasbaya, a town seven miles north of Metullah, Israel's northernmost town.

On June 7 the IDF continued its advance along the coastal axis reaching the outskirts of Damour, some 14 miles south of Beirut. In the meantime, the Israeli navy conducted a vertical flanking operation, landing tank and infantry forces at the mouth of the Awali River. On the central axis,

Israel's forces took Nabatiya and continued their advance to areas east of Lake Kar'un. In the eastern sector IDF forces took positions along the Hasbaya-Kaukaba line, seven miles northeast of Metullah. The Syrians moved their First Armored Division into the Beka, to an area north of Hasbaya and southeast of Lake Kar'un. A number of limited encounters with Syrian forces had already taken place on the second day of the war, including some artillery exchanges in the eastern and central sectors, a short air battle over Beirut, and an exchange of tank fire west of Jezin.

After two days of advance the IDF was halted on June 8, along the coast, at the outskirts of Damour. South of that area, other units fought a difficult battle with PLO guerrillas entrenched in Tyre, Sidon and a number of refugee camps. The IDF's advance was also slow in the eastern sector, from Hasbaya to Ein Eita. The IDF continued its advance in the central sector, moving north of Jezin and west of Lake Kar'un, reaching Ramlaya and Ein Zahalta, four miles south of the Beirut-Damascus highway.

On June 9 the invasion of Lebanon turned into a full-scale confrontation with Syria, particularly in the air and in the suppression of air-defense. In a preemptive strike the Israeli Air Force destroyed 17 of the 19 SAM batteries which Syria had installed in the Beka. An unprecedented air battle also took place, with the participation of 150 fighter aircraft. Twenty-nine Syrian Mig-21's and Mig-23's were shot down. Armored warfare took place in the Kar'un Lake area, both south of Jezin and in areas southeast of Kar'un, and heavy fighting in the vicinity of Ein Zahalta, south of the Beirut-Damascus highway, with very slow Israeli progress. On the coastal axis the IDF conquered Damour and reached Khalde, south of Beirut airport. The Syrians meanwhile moved some forces out of Beirut to strengthen their defenses along the highway.

On the following day the confrontation with Syria continued, moving to the ground as well. In the early morning the largest tank battle of the war began north and northeast of Lake Kar'un, between an Israeli armored corps and the Syrian First Armored Division. The IDF prevailed, its forces moving north toward Jub Jenin. In another large-scale airbattle some 25 Syrian Migs were shot down. The IDF continued its slow advance along the coastal axis, meeting Syrian and PLO resistance north of Khalde, two miles south of Beirut airport. On the central front Israel's tank forces were halted by heavy Syrian resistance in the mountain passes of the Ein Zahalta region.

Thus, when a cease-fire came into effect at noon on June 11, Israeli forces were positioned about two miles south of Beirut airport on the coastal front; a few miles south of the Beirut-Damascus highway in the Ein Zahalta area; in the vicinity of Jub-Jenin — well below the highway — in the Beka, and in Kafr Kuk on the eastern axis near the Lebanese-Syrian border.

THE "CRAWLING" STAGE: The cease-fire declared by Israel and Syria on June 11 did not bring a halt to Israel's operations against the PLO. There was now a "crawling" stage, initially meaning Israeli movement to cut off the PLO in West Beirut from its Syrian suppliers. At first this involved artillery exchanges between the IDF and PLO forces south of Beirut. On June 13–14 Israeli tank and paratroop units completed the encirclement of Beirut by linking up with the Christian Phalangist forces in East Beirut. They also won control of Beirut's exit to the Beirut-Damascus highway and reached the proximity of the presidential palace at Ba'abde and the outskirts of Beirut airport. This was achieved in heavy battle, involving Syrian tank and anti-tank commando forces. On June 15 IDF forces began to "crawl" five miles east of Beirut, to the Jamhour region, in an effort to extend their control over the Beirut-Damascus highway eastward. Syria had meanwhile reinforced its positions along an axis south of the highway, especially in the Aley Bahamdun-Shtura region. On June 17 Israeli forces continued their movement east and southeast toward Aley, and on June 19 artillery duels took place between IDF and PLO forces in Beirut, while IDF and Syrian artillery exchanged fire in Kafr Kuk, near the Lebanese-Syrian border. On June 20 the PLO and Syria withdrew their forces from Beirut airport, and Israeli forces gained control of the airport without a battle.

The second part of the "crawling" stage began on June 21 with a major battle initiated by the IDF against Syria's reinforced tank and commando units in an effort to gain control of the Beirut-Damascus highway in the Aley-Bahamdun area. The battle raged for almost a week and when it ended Israel had gained control

›f the highway to a point just east of Bahamdun.

THE SIEGE OF BEIRUT: The siege of Beirut, aimed at forcing the PLO and the Syrian forces to evacuate the city, took place throughout July and most of August, with artillery, naval and air bombardment of PLO positions in Beirut, and incremental advances into the western parts of the city. On July 23 Israel forces intensified their air and naval bombardment. On August 3, IDF infantry entered the Hayal-Salum neighborhood in southwest Beirut. The following day it encircled Burj al-Baraj'neh. After a 20-hour battle Israel forces, advancing a little more than a mile, gained control of the al-Uazai quarter and the museum area. On August 11–12 the Air Force conducted a massive bombardment of Beirut. The following day the PLO agreed to withdraw under the protection of a multi-national force beginning August 25. PLO chairman Yasser Arafat left Beirut on August 30, as did the Syrian brigade positioned in the city. By September 4 the evacuation of all PLO and Syrian forces from Beirut was completed and the multi-national force was withdrawn.

THE "HOLDING" STAGE: The expulsion of the PLO and the Syrians from Beirut was followed by a "holding" stage. On September 14 Israel's ally, President-elect Bashir Jemayel, was assassinated. Israel's reaction was to order the IDF into West Beirut, officially to keep order. On September 17 Phalange forces entered the *Sabra and Shatilla refugee camps and massacred several hundred Palestinians. Under heavy US pressure Israel began to withdraw its forces from Beirut on September 19, and the multi-national force — including some 1,800 US Marines — returned to take their place.

Up until September 1983 the IDF's main task was to hold its positions pending the outcome of the negotiations. Militarily and politically it still had to cope with three types of threats — first, Syria's entrenched military forces in Lebanon, which now included some three divisions (two armored, one mechanized), and a number of independent brigades and commando units, totalling the equivalent of over four divisions. From a total of 350 tanks in Lebanon before the war, Syria had increased the number to some 1,200 tanks positioned in the Beka, both north and south of the Beirut-Damascus highway. Although this force still lacked air and air-defense cover, its inferiority in these realms was allevaited to some degree by the introduction of Soviet SAM 5 systems into Syria in late 1982. Overall, the Syrians enjoyed an impressive defensive capability against the IDF in the Beka.

The second problem the IDF had to face was the intense conflict in the Shouf Mountains between the Maronite Christians and the Leftist *Druze, led by Walid Junblatt. Since the area was under Israeli control from late June 1982 for over a year, the IDF often found itself in cross-fire between the warring factions.

Finally, the IDF had to cope with an escalation of resistance or terrorist activity in Lebanon. Small but armed terrorist squads remained in Israeli-held territories of Lebanon, while others infiltrated through the areas held by the Syrians, the Christians and the multi-national force. Moreover the squads were increasingly made up of Shi'ites. The result was that while the war relieved the towns of northern Israel (at least temporarily) from the danger of terrorist attack, the IDF was under attack by terrorist resistance in Lebanon. One account noted 256 terrorist incidents against the IDF in Lebanon between September 1982 and April 1983. Resistance continued after Israel's unilateral withdrawal to the Awali River in September 1983. On November 4 a suicide-terrorist operation conducted by Syrian-backed Shi'ites destroyed the IDF's headquarters in Sidon, killing 36 Israelis. Terrorist operations intensified as Israel implemented a staged withdrawal from South Lebanon in late 1984 and early 1985. They diminished only after April 1985, when the IDF completed its withdrawal from all of Lebanon except for a narrow security zone north of the Israeli-Lebanese border. The IDF officially withdrew to the international border in early June 1985, but claimed freedom to patrol and carry out security operations in that zone where it continued to support a local, mostly Christian South Lebanese Army.

POLITICAL CONSEQUENCES: In the international arena the result of the Lebanese War was a further worsening of Israel's international standing, with only the US government offering reserved support. Most international reporting of the war was openly biased against Israel and its activities were sometimes viciously compared to those of the Germans in World War II.

Inside Israel the Lebanese War intensified the internal political rift. Many Israelis from the Center and the Left felt that for the first time in its history Israel was fighting a war because it had chosen to do so (a war of "*yesh breira*," there is a choice) and not because others had forced it to fight. They also argued that most of the war's aims were not achievable: the PLO could not be physically destroyed; Israel could not impose an unpopular government on the Lebanese; it could not resolve overnight all the internal conflicts in Lebanon; the Syrians would not leave Lebanon. It should be pointed out that the *Israel Labor Party supported the initial stages of the war, involving the occupation of 40 kilometers north of the Israeli border, but objected to Israel's further advance. Though most soldiers, regular and reserve, served despite the objections of some to the war, a few soldiers refused to serve in Lebanon. However, many Israelis, mostly from the Center and Right, felt the war was just and correct and that the Left was sabotaging the war effort through its criticism. The Phalange massacre of Palestinians in Sabra and Shatilla brought the public debate to a climax, leading to the establishment of a Commission of Inquiry (See: *Kahan Commission) and the resignation of Ariel Sharon from the Ministry of Defense.

The turning of Amin Jemayel (Bashir's brother and successor as President) away from Israel, the growing number of Israeli casualties from terrorist (primarily Shi'ite) attacks, budgetary constraints and the formation of the *National Unity Government led to Israel's withdrawal from Lebanon.

The security of Israel's northern settlements, the renewed shooting of Katyushas from Lebanese territory and the constant infiltration attempts by terrorists from the north remain sensitive political issues in Israel.

(See also: *Arab-Israel Conflict, *Lebanon and Israel).

Lebanon and Israel In the 1930s and 1940s a close relationship existed between the **Yishuv* in *mandatory Palestine and some of the religious and political leaders of the Christian Maronites in mandatory Lebanon. The Maronites saw the Jews in Palestine as sharing a community of fate against the pressures of Islam and Pan-Arab nationalism, and subsequently supported the establishment of the State of Israel.

The *Jewish Agency had cultivated relation also with non-Maronite politicians, but the rela tions with the Maronites corresponded with th prevalent concept, later adopted by the Govern ment of Israel, regarding the natural allianc between the non-Arab minorities in the Middl East.

In 1946 the relationship with the Maronit community of Lebanon was formalized by a agreement between the Jewish Agency and th Maronite Church, but was kept secret upon th latter's insistence. The limited value of the agree ment was demonstrated during the *War c Independence when the Maronite-led Lebanes government bowed to domestic and extern Arab pressure and joined the Arab war effo against Israel, fighting in the Galilee.

Following the War of Independence th Israeli government was not averse to a Christia takeover in Lebanon, though it was dubious as t the prospects of such a takeover. In 1950–51 th Israeli government considered backing the Pha ange financially in its bid to win several seats i the Lebanese parliament. As late as 1954–5 David *Ben Gurion and Moshe *Dayan believe that Israel could take advantage of separati Maronite sentiments to bring about a pro-Isra change in Lebanon, even though such sentimen were marginal. Moshe *Sharett, on the oth hand, believed that Israel ought to accept a plu alistic Lebanon as an established fact.

From 1949–70 the Israeli-Lebanese bord was quiet, and Lebanon stayed out of subseque Arab-Israel wars. In Israel it was general believed that if it were up to the Christians, Leb non would be the first Arab state to sign a pea treaty with Israel. But the Maronite community standing in Lebanon continued to erode, and th most Israel could do was to offer discreet aid to i friends.

After the *Palestine Liberation Organizatio (PLO) was ousted from Jordan in 1970, Lebano became the organization's principal base, thoug a PLO presence had existed in Lebanon befor The PLO now expanded its autonomy and acti ity in Lebanon, taking advantage of the state inherent weakness, while at the same time co tributing to its gradual disintegration. Israel preemptive and punitive raids across the nort ern border, and such raids as that on Beirut international airport in December 1968 after

PLO attack on an El Al plane in Athens, while educing PLO pressure, also inadvertently weakned the Lebanese state to Israel's own lisadvantage.

In November 1969, *Egypt's President Gamal Abdel Nasser hosted a meeting of the Supreme Commanders of the Lebanese army and a PLO lelegation, which resulted in the signing of the Cairo Agreement. The agreement defined the round rules of the relationship between the Lebnese government and the PLO, while purporting to regulate the PLO's activities in and from ebanon. In fact the agreement legitimized PLO reedom of action and did little to protect ebanon's interests.

In the winter of 1975–76 the outbreak of civil war in Lebanon, the ascendancy of the PLO and s Lebanese allies, and the specter of Syrian interention persuaded the government of Yitzḥak Rabin that since the old status quo was no longer enable, it must adapt its policy to the new reality. he policy chosen was to accept the Syrian interention but within limitations. The so-called Red Line Agreement" – an informal and indiect understanding negotiated in 1976 by the US etween Syria and Israel – defined the Syrian ntervention in Lebanon within limits acceptable o Israel, i.e., Syria would not dispatch forces outh of the Litani River, would not use its air orce, and would not deploy ground-to-air misiles on Lebanon's territory. At the same time srael continued and intensified its relationship vith the status quo militias in Lebanon, in the orm of arms sales. In 1976 the "Good Fence" vas first opened on the border between Israel and ebanon near the Israeli northern town of Metullah, to enable villagers from southern Lebnon to receive Israeli medical care. The opening n the border was gradually to develop into an nstitution with hundreds of South Lebanese rossing into Israel every day, *inter alia* to follow conomic pursuits.

At one stage of the Christian attack between une and August 1976 on the fortified refugee amp of Tel el-Za'atar when several thousand alestinians were killed, an Israeli observer was resent, but Israel was not involved in the fighting, its policy being "to help the Christians help hemselves."

During the first two years of the first *Begin overnment Israel's preoccupation with the Palestinians in southern Lebanon overshadowed its active interest in the Lebanese crisis as a whole. The improvement in the PLO's relations with Syria facilitated its activities there. In response Israel constructed an elaborate defense system along its northern border, supported by three enclaves of Major Sa'ad Haddad's militias, while striking at PLO targets in Lebanon.

Nevertheless, Palestinian terrorists occasionally managed to penetrate into Israel. In March 1978 a Palestinian force, originating from Lebanon, infiltrated into Israel from the sea, landing near the Haifa-Tel Aviv highway, and taking over a busload of passengers, many of whom were eventually killed. Israel retaliated with the *Litani Operation later in March, which was based on the assumption that the problem of southern Lebanon could be solved, or at least neutralized, by destroying the PLO's military strength south of the Litani without attempting to resolve the broader Lebanese crisis.

Though the operation did not solve the problem, it did result in the expansion of the Haddad-controlled territory all along the Israeli border, adding a Shi'ite element to Haddad's militias, and bringing a *United Nations force – UNIFIL – into the area. In the conflict which developed at this time between Syria and the Lebanese Front (a status quo coalition of the Christian leaders, formed in 1976) Israel supported the Front with arms and military training, with the Israeli Air Force flying warning and reconnaissance missions over Beirut. However, it was determined not to be drawn into a war with Syria over Lebanon's future.

The policy started to change late in 1980 when relations with Bashir Jemayel, the newly-emerged leader of the Front, were strengthened. This occurred after the resignation of Moshe Dayan and Ezer *Weizman from the government, and the rise in influence of the new Chief of Staff, Rafael *Eitan.

In addition, the weakening of President Assad's regime in Syria, and his apparent difficulties in maintaining Syria's position in Lebanon, the continued attacks from Lebanese territory by the PLO, which was not fully supported by Syria, as well as the attitude of the new Reagan Administration in the *United States, induced the Israeli government to reconsider its tacit agreement for the continued presence of Syria in Lebanon. Furthermore, by 1980 the **Mossad* and some of Israel's leaders started to view Bashir not only as a charming if volatile younger son of the veteran political leader Pierre Jemayel, but as the mature head of the most powerful political and military force in Lebanon, and a true ally of Israel. This tendency was strengthened after Ariel *Sharon became Minister of Defense in Begin's June 1981 government when the relationship between the Phalange and Israel became largely a personal one between Sharon and Bashir.

In the aftermath of the Syrian "missile crisis" (involving the Syrian introduction of ground-to-air missiles into the Zahle area in the spring of 1981 after Israel had shot down two Syrian helicopters sent to aid the PLO against the Phalange), and the intensified fighting between Israel and Palestinian forces along the Israeli-Lebanese border (which resulted in a US-Saudi arranged cease-fire in July 1981), as well as Bashir Jemayel's disappointment by the end of 1981 with the results of Saudi-initiated efforts to solve the Lebanese crisis through "traditional patterns of Lebanese and Arab politics," concrete plans for a joint Israeli-Phalange operation started to develop.

Sharon's plan (the "great plan") which was eventually implemented in the *Lebanese War, was based on the premise that a large-scale operation in southern Lebanon was inevitable; that Israel could afford to act only once on a large scale; that the problem in the South could not be solved without solving the wider Lebanese crisis; that a solution to the crisis was possible; and that it could be the key to a significant change in the political situation in the region. Consequently, there was no sense in an operation seeking to create just a security zone of some 40 kilometers, the range of the PLO artillery north of the Israeli border; instead, the goal should be to destroy the PLO base in Lebanon. Furthermore, Syria should be forced out of Lebanon, while the Lebanese Front should be helped to take over the whole of Beirut and Bashir Jemayel to be elected president.

However, the Lebanese Front, whose cooperation in the war (which began on June 6, 1982) was essential for the success of the Israeli plan, failed to "deliver," keeping its participation to a minimum and even obstructing the plan's implementation. The Front's failure to act as expected resulted in Israel's entry into Beirut and a ten-week siege of West Beirut, none of which wa part of Sharon's original plan. Finally, the massacre by Phalange forces in the Palestinian refuge camps of *Sabra and Shatilla following Bashir' assassination in September 1982, further complicated Israel's precarious situation.

After his election President Bashir Jemaye began to consider other options besides the Israel one, while his older brother Amin, who becam President after his assassination was not in favo of the Israeli alliance at all.

By December 1982 Israel discovered that th Jemayels did not fully represent the Phalange that the Phalange did not represent the whol Maronite community, that the Maronite community did not speak for all Lebanese Christian and that Lebanon's Christians were no longe assured of their ascendancy.

The evolution of the Israeli-Maronite and th broader Israeli-Lebanese relations must not b seen in purely political terms. For six years th connection had been clandestine, limited to small number of participants on each side. Th 1982 War brought a large number of Lebanes and Israelis into contact, and the enthusiasm wit which many Maronites, and other Lebanese happy to be rid of the PLO, welcomed the Israel troops dissipated. By December 1982 the libera tors of June had become a force of occupation.

At this stage the Lebanese governmen adopted a two-pronged strategy. On the on hand it agreed to formal negotiations with Israe under American auspices, and on the other han members of Amin Jemayel's entourage hel secret negotiations with Ariel Sharon, in whic the principles of a Lebanese-Israeli agreemen were hammered out, which would lead not onl to an Israeli withdrawal from Lebanon but to th withdrawal of Syrian and Palestinian forces a well. However, when on December 14 Sharo disclosed that an agreement had been reached – apparently seeking to force the Lebanese govern ment's hand and to strengthen his own positio within the Israeli government – the Lebanes government denied its existence. The forma negotiations nevertheless continued.

For Israel the interest in a Lebanese-Israel agreement lay in its justification of the war. Fo Lebanon the agreement was a means for achiev ing an Israeli withdrawal. With American medi ation an agreement was finally reached on Ma

17, 1983 — two months after Ariel Sharon had been forced to resign as Minister of Defense following the publication of the *Kahan Commission Report. The Agreement declared an end to the state of war between Israel and Lebanon, and provided for a complete Israeli withdrawal from Lebanese soil. Implicitly it included a Lebanese promise to prevent acts of terror being carried out from its territory against Israel, and to bring about a withdrawal of Syrian forces — promises which the Lebanese government had no power to implement. The Agreement also provided for the presence of international peace-keeping forces in Lebanon, made up of troops from countries which maintain diplomatic relations with both sides, and for the integration of the South Lebanese forces in the Lebanese army. A normalization of relations between the two states was to follow the Israeli withdrawal and the end of the state of war. However, it was almost at once vehemently denounced by Syria, and on March 5, 1984, was abrogated by Amin Jemayel on Syria's demand.

Following the signing of the stillborn Agreement, Israel ended its exclusive relationship with the Maronite community and sought to develop dialogues with other communities as well — especially the *Druze and the Shi'ites. The initiative taken with regard to the Druze was successful in the short run, facilitating Israel's withdrawal from the Shouf Mountains, helping to prevent Palestinian operations against Israel and reduce tensions inside Israel with the Israeli Druze. However, when Israel continued its withdrawal the Druze leader, Walid Junblatt practically severed his relations with it and turned to Syria. The effort to develop a comparable dialogue with the Shi'ites failed — and gradually part of the Shi'ite community became as vicious an enemy as the PLO, carrying out terrorist activities against Israeli targets.

By the end of 1983 three schools of thought had developed in Israel regarding the desirable policy in Lebanon. The government's policy, as represented by Prime Minister Yitzḥak *Shamir and Defense Minister Moshe *Arens, was to bring the *IDF back to the international border only after providing adequate security arrangements in southern Lebanon. Another school of thought, represented by opposition leader Shimon *Peres argued that the quest for such arrangements was futile and counterproductive, and that Israel's security interests would best be served by a quick withdrawal from Lebanon. A third school reached the opposite conclusion from the same premise: since Israel's security could not be ensured by proxy, Israel should stay inside Lebanon along a line running some 30 kilometers north of the border.

The Lebanese debate was one of the major issues in the 1984 election campaign to the 11th Knesset. Following the establishment of the *National Unity Government in September, Israel tried to reach a tacit agreement with Syria which would facilitate Israel's withdrawal from Lebanon. However, by December 1984 these efforts floundered, and in January 1985 the Israeli government decided on a three-phase withdrawal to the international border — a decision supported only grudgingly by the **Likud* after one of its Ministers, David *Levy decided to support the *Alignment position.

Following the withdrawal a security zone was established, controlled by the South Lebanese Army, now headed by Brigadier General Antoine Lahad following the death of Major Haddad in January 1984. The IDF was deployed on the Israeli side of the border, as it had been before June 1982, ready to operate north of the border if the South Lebanese Army proved unable to cope with its PLO or Shi'ite adversaries. In mid-1986 the arrangement, though far from ideal, was assessed to be working satisfactorily. (I.R.)

"Left-Wing Mafia" A term used by politicians of the Right in Israel in reference to the predominance of persons of Leftist-Liberal political leanings in the media, especially radio and TV.

Legal Advisor to the Government See: *Attorney-General.

leheitiv im ha'am Hebrew for "benefit the people." An expression associated with the **Likud*'s populist *economic policy. The *Likud* had argued that until 1977 successive Labor governments had kept standards of living unnecessarily low. The policy of *leheitiv im ha'am* manifested itself primarily in the lifting of constraints on consumption, travel abroad and the access to easy capital gains. The *Alignment argued that it was this policy which was largely responsible for the uncontrollable growth of inflation in the years 1977–84.

Leḥi Hebrew acronym of *Loḥamei Ḥerut Yisrael*

(fighters for the freedom of Israel). Underground resistance group in pre-state Israel. Referred to as the "Stern Gang," after its founder Avraham *Stern who assumed the *nom de guerre* Ya'ir.

Leḥi was formed by breakaway **IZL* members in 1940 in the aftermath of the *IZL* decision to cease its attacks against the British administration. The *Leḥi* manifesto was contained in a document entitled "The 18 Principles of Renaissance." In it Stern defined the mandatory authority as an alien ruler who must be expelled from the Jewish homeland, characterizing *Zionism as the movement for the redemption of the Jewish people. *Leḥi*, in a revolutionary posture, adopted the tactics of personal terror and direct action, committing acts of political assassination, most notably that of Lord Moyne in Cairo in 1944.

Leḥi viewed the Arab problem as being exacerbated by British imperialist intrigues and advocated a solution to the Arab-Jewish conflict based on a population *transfer. *Leḥi*'s diplomatic efforts during 1940–41 were directed at Italy and Germany in the belief that anti-British aid would be forthcoming. In addition, it was hoped that these contacts would ease the situation of European Jewry. A *Leḥi* emissary did meet with a German Foreign Office representative in Beirut but was informed that Germany supported Arab nationalism. In mid-June 1941, Stern met **Haganah* leader Yitzḥak Sadeh (1890–1952) who was seeking recruits for the **Palmaḥ*, but declined since he saw no *quid pro quo* in this cooperation.

Stern was shot dead by the Central Investigation Department (CID) officers in Tel Aviv in February 1942 and a replacement triumverate command was eventually organized comprising Nathan *Yellin-Mor, Israel *Eldad and Yitzḥak *Shamir. One of *Leḥi*'s prominent members, and its clandestine radio announcer, was Ge'ula *Cohen.

Leḥi escaped the anti-dissident "Saison" campaign and in 1946 cooperated with the *Haganah* and *IZL* in the *T'nuat Hameri Ha'ivri* (Hebrew Resistance Movement). It carried its attacks abroad and struck at targets in London. Three of its members were sentenced to hanging. Two were executed in Cairo in 1945 and another blew himself up in the Jerusalem prison in 1947.

A fundamental political orientation promoted by *Leḥi* was the neutralization of the Middle East. After World War II approaches were made to the *Soviet Union and other Eastern bloc countries and a Bulgarian Communist delegation met with *Leḥi* in Tel Aviv in 1947.

Leḥi disbanded in May 1948 and most of its members enlisted in the *IDF. In Jerusalem it preserved a separate status until it was outlawed after the assassination of *UN Mediator Count Bernadotte in September 1948.

Like the *IZL*, *Leḥi* too ran a list in the 1st *Knesset, the *Fighters' List, which obtained a single seat.

Service in *Leḥi* was eventually granted official recognition which entitled its members to army service pensions.

(I.M.)

Levinger, Rabbi Moshe **Gush Emunim* leader and prominent settlement activist. Born 1935, Jerusalem.

Levinger was a sickly child who spent time abroad for health reasons. His early education was the **B'nei Akivah* Yeshiva at Kfar Haro'eh followed by the Kfar Hadarom Yeshiva at Reḥovot. He served in the **Naḥal* and continued his studies at the Merkaz Harav Yeshiva in Jerusalem. Levinger was the Rabbi of Kibbutz Lavie between 1962 and 1966 and then moved to Moshav Naḥalim. Following the *Six-Day War Levinger devoted himself to Jewish settlement beyond the *Green Line.

Levinger planned and initiated the return to *Hebron on Passover eve, 1968. He played a central role in the establishment of *Gush Emunim* and was present during the negotiations with Minister of Defense Shimon *Peres over the Elon Moreh settlement group at Sebastia in December 1975. His name was linked to the *Jewish Underground as one of the group's mentors. Levinger conducted a three-month vigil at the entrance of the Deheishe refugee camp to protest against stone-throwing, and has been highly visible at hunger strikes, protests, negotiations with government figures and rallies and funerals of Jewish victims of Arab terror.

Today he lives in the center of Hebron in a neighborhood reestablished in 1979 through the actions of his wife and 20 other women who slipped into the building of the pre-1929 Hadassah clinic and remained there until they received legal status and army protection. (I.M.)

Levy, David Union leader and politician. Born 1937, Morocco.

Levy studied in Rabat at the Alliance school and immigrated to Israel in 1957, at first living in a *ma'abarah* (new immigrant camp) and later settling in the development town of Beit She'an.

In 1964 Levy became the representative of the construction workers union in the Beit She'an Workers' Council and the following year was a member of the Beit She'an Municipal Council and Deputy Mayor as a representative of the **Ḥerut* Movement. In 1966 he became a member of the *Ḥerut* Central Committee and Executive. Levy was first elected to the Knesset in 1969 and gradually improved his position of leadership in *Ḥerut* — he is one of the first authentic leaders to emerge in a major Israeli political party from **Edot Mizraḥ*. He became Chairman of the *Tchelet-Lavan* (Blue-White) *Ḥerut* faction in the **Histadrut* in 1971.

In Menaḥem *Begin's first government, Levy was appointed Minister of Immigrant Absorption. Since 1981 he has been Deputy Prime Minister and Minister of Construction and Housing.

During the *Lebanese War he objected to Ariel *Sharon's defense policy and to allowing the Phalange to enter the refugee camps of *Sabra and Shatilla after Bashir Jemayel's assassination. On the issue of the withdrawal of the *IDF from *Lebanon he supported the *Alignment position in the *National Unity Government.

David Levy is a potential contestant for the leadership of the *Ḥerut* Movement, and it was largely due to the conduct of his supporters at the *Ḥerut* conference in March 1986, in protest against what they regarded as manipulations by the *Shamir camp, that the conference broke up.

Liberal Center Party officially founded on May 18, 1986, by a group of breakaways from the *Liberal Party because, they claimed, the Liberal Party had betrayed the principles of liberalism and had sold themselves to the **Ḥerut* Movement for Knesset seats.

Among the founders of the new party, hoping to repeat the 1977 success of the *DMC, were Chairman of the *World Zionist Organization, Arie Dulzin, Tel Aviv Mayor Shlomo (Chich) Lahat (who was to head the party's list), Yitzḥak Berman, previous Knesset Speaker and Minister of Energy (who was later expelled from the new party), Yeḥezkel Flomin, previously Deputy-Minister of Finance under Simḥa *Ehrlich and Yosef (Tommy) Lapid, the Director-General of the Israel Broadcasting Authority during the **Likud* governments.

The new party advocates the reduction of government intervention in the economy, i.e., a policy of laissez faire while accepting the principle of *territorial compromise in a future peace settlement — "the country's peace frontiers shall be determined in negotiations between Israel and the neighboring states according to criteria of defense needs and the maintenance of the country's Jewish character."

Liberalim Atzma'im See: *Independent Liberal Party.

Liberal Judaism See: *Progressive Judaism.

Liberal Party of Israel Known in Hebrew as *Hamiflaga Haliberalit Hayisraelit*, the Liberal Party is a centrist party founded in 1961 through a merger between most of the *Progressive Party and the *General Zionists who had split off from the same party in 1948. The party is primarily middle class, with the private farmers playing a major role. The Liberal Party advocates the existence of a private economy with minimal government interference; a *constitution; the separation of the trade union and production sections in the **Histadrut*; obligatory arbitration in labor disputes and the nationalization of the health services. In its 1971 convention the party passed a resolution opposing the repartition of **Eretz Yisrael*, i.e., the return of areas west of the *Jordan River to Arab sovereignty.

The Farmers' Association, the middle-class settlements of the *Oved Hatzi'oni*, the Maccabi sports club, and the *No'ar Hatzi'oni* youth movement have all been associated with the Liberal Party. Until 1966 the party published a daily paper, *Haboker*, which closed down for financial reasons in that year.

In 1965 the Liberal Party of Israel set up a political bloc together with the **Ḥerut* Movement which was called **Gaḥal*, as a result of which most of the previous members of the Progressive Party broke away and established the *Independent Liberal Party. The Liberal Party continues to exist as an independent party within the *Likud*, and its current leader, Yitzḥak *Moda'i, wishes to bring about a complete merger between *Ḥerut* and the Liberals. Following the political *upheaval of 1977 a Liberal, Simḥa *Ehrlich was appointed Minister of Finance, implementing a policy of drastic economic liberalization called the "economic upheaval" (See: Economic Policy).

In the *National Unity Government a Liberal, Yitzḥak Moda'i, was once again appointed as Minister of Finance and replaced in April 1986 by another Liberal — Moshe Nissim. The Chairman of the *World Zionist Organization since 1978, Arie Dulzin, was also a member of the Liberal Party when elected to the post.

Knesset Seats: 5th Knesset (1961) — 17; 6th Knesset (1965) — 11 out of *Gaḥal*'s 26; 7th Knesset (1969) — 11 out of *Gaḥal*'s 26; 8th Knesset (1973) — 12 out of *Likud*'s 39; 9th Knesset (1977) — 15 out of *Likud*'s 43; 10th Knesset (1981) — 18 out of the *Likud*'s 48; 11th Knesset (1984) — 12 out of the *Likud*'s 41.

Lifta Group A group of three Israelis who attempted to smuggle explosives to the Temple Mount in Jerusalem in order to blow up the El Aqsa and Omar Mosques in the winter of 1984. The three had lived as drifters in the abandoned village of Lifta at the western entrance to *Jerusalem and called themselves "the Tribe of Judah." They succeeded in scaling the eastern wall of the Temple Mount and bringing a large quantity of explosives into the courtyard of the Mosques. They were discovered during the night by Moslem guards and fled. The explosives and equipment which they left behind led to their capture. Their motive was apparently mystical, and during their trial at the beginning of 1985 it was argued that they were mentally unstable.

(M.B.)

Likud Hebrew for "Union." A parliamentary bloc, the outgrowth of **Gaḥal*, formed in 1973 by two senior parties: the **Ḥerut* Movement and the *Liberal Party, and by several smaller groups: the *Free Center, the *State List, and part of the *Land of Israel Movement. The moving force in the *Likud*'s formation was Ariel *Sharon who in 1973 resigned his army appointment to join the Liberal Party.

The major elements of the *Likud* agreement were: insistence on the extension of Israel's sovereignty to the territory west of the Jordan River, while still asserting a claim to the entire former territory of mandatory Palestine; emphasis on the economic and social betterment of Israel's disadvantaged communities; increased Jewish content in the educational curriculum; full civil rights for all Arabs and other non-Jewish minorities; respect for traditional Jewish religious values.

Though the *Likud* gained impressive results in the 1973 elections to the 8th Knesset, it was nonetheless unable to bring down the *Alignment. However, in 1977, when it was made up of the *Ḥerut* Movement, the Liberal Party, **La'am* and the State List, it won sufficient seats and was able to find enough coalition partners for Menaḥem *Begin, Head of the *Ḥerut* Movement to form his first government. A *Likud*-led government was again formed after the elections to the 10th Knesset in 1981.

The *Likud* ran in the 1984 elections on a platform which *inter alia* called for the following: eventual Israeli sovereignty over Judea, Samaria (See: *Yosh) and the *Gaza Strip; rejection of any territorial compromise which undermines the Jewish right over the land, will inevitably lead to the establishment of a Palestinian state, undermine the security of the civilian population, endanger the existence of the State of Israel and frustrate the chances for peace; the implementation of the *autonomy plan, it being understood that autonomy was neither state, nor sovereignty nor self-determination; the establishment of additional settlements in all parts of **Eretz Yisrael* "without leading to the dispossession of anyone from his land, village or town." The platform also called for equal civil rights for all of Israel's citizens and stated that there would be no negotiations with murderous organizations, i.e., the *Palestine Liberation Organization (PLO). The largest part of the platform dealt with economic issues: ways of stabilizing the economy and encouraging economic growth. The platform also lauded the *Likud*'s "quiet social revolution" which had led to a large part of the population (i.e., **edot mizraḥ*) feeling like real partners in the regime and in Israeli society for the first time since the establishment of the state, while fully identifying with the state's national goals.

The *Likud* also promised to complete the enactment of Israel's *basic laws so that Israel would have a single *constitution. The stalemate resulting from the 1984 elections forced the *Likud* to join the Alignment in the formation of a *National Unity Government in which the premiership would be rotated from Shimon *Peres to Yitzḥak *Shamir halfway through the government's term of office.

The *Likud* partners maintain their separate workers' factions in the **Histadrut*. In 1986 moves were under way to unite the *Ḥerut* Movement and the Liberal Party into a single party, but the terms of the union and the disunity inside the *Ḥerut* Movement as manifested in its conference in March 1986, has prevented it thus far.

(I.M.)

Litani Operation Operation carried out by the *IDF in Lebanon in March 1978 at the time that Ezer *Weizman was Minister of Defense and Mordechai *Gur was Chief of Staff, following the attack along the Coastal Road by terrorists landing from the sea in which a large number of Israeli civilians were killed. The IDF occupied a ten-kilometer-wide strip north of the Israel-Lebanon border, reaching the Litani River, and cleared the area of *Palestine Liberation Organization (PLO) positions while avoiding an open clash with the Syrians. Israel pulled out in June 1978 after the formation of the UN Interim Force in Lebanon (UNIFIL).

local government The State of Israel adopted the local government system of *mandatory Palestine. The 1934 Municipal Corporations Ordinance and the 1941 Local Councils Ordinance, were adopted and modified by the 1948 Law and Administration Ordinance and subsequent legislation. The functions of the High Commissioner in this sphere are now assigned to the Minister of the Interior.

Israel is divided into six districts (Haifa, Tel Aviv, Jerusalem, Northern, Central and Southern), headed by commissioners (*memunim*), whose powers are much more limited than those of the district commissioners in mandatory times who had dealt with all spheres of government. Today's commissioners are responsible only for the business of the Ministry of Interior. There are also 15 subdistricts. Ministries other than the Ministry of Interior do not necessarily organize their operations within the same geographical divisions.

There are 40 municipalities in Israel, three of them Arab, with a population of over 20,000, with the exception of Eilat which was declared a city before its population reached that number, and 126 local councils, 60 of them Arab, in towns or villages with over 2,000 inhabitants.

The mayors and heads of local councils are elected, since 1978, by direct elections every four to five years. The councils are elected on the basis of proportional representation. Many mayors and heads of local councils run on local lists, rather than on national party tickets, though many local lists are affiliated to the national parties. Of the mayors elected in 1983, 17 were from the *Alignment (not including Teddy *Kollek of *Jerusalem), nine from the **Likud*, one from the *National Religious Party, one from **Tami* and one from **Ḥadash* (Nazareth). There are three mayors (two *Likud* and one *Ḥadash*) and two heads of local councils (both *Likud*) who are also members of the 11th Knesset.

Toward the end of the 10th Knesset the Alignment banned MKs from serving simultaneously as mayors or heads of local councils, resulting in the resignation of the Mayors of Dimona and Safad in 1983. Both towns were subsequently lost by the Alignment.

The Local Government Center (*merkaz hashilton hamekomi*) is a voluntary association which represents the municipalities and local councils. It acts as a lobby but is also an address for negotiations on local government affairs and is mentioned in several laws as a body which must be consulted on certain matters.

In addition to municipalities and local councils there are 45 regional councils, one of them *Druze, made up of several settlements — *kibbutzim, **moshavim* and villages. Thirty- two Arab villages are members of eight of the regional councils. Regional councils are not elected. There are several Arab villages which still have traditional *mukhtars* (village heads) and several Jewish settlements which are not part of the general local government system. In the *West Bank and *Gaza Strip there are nine Jewish local councils and seven regional councils which come under the jurisdiction of the Ministry of Interior even though they are located in *occupied territories.

As in other countries so the Israeli local authorities provide local services to citizens, such as water supply, drainage, roads, garbage collection, parks, social services, as well as sports, health, education and cultural facilities. The central government provides the education, health, welfare and religious services.

Municipal councils may pass by-laws which

are subject to the approval of the Minister of the Interior, while the by-laws of local councils are subject to the approval of the regional commissioners.

The income of the local authorities comes from local taxation and levies (an average 50 percent of the total); transferred income (such as from vehicle registration fees) which comes from the government budget, mostly on the basis of laws; designated income (such as for education) which comes from the budgets of the relevant ministries, part of which is distributed on the basis of laws and part on the basis of special arrangements; and balancing grants, from the Ministry of the Interior, to cover deficits. In recent years, in the general liberal atmosphere, many local authorities have not kept within the limits of their budgets and have gone into deep debt to the banks.

Due to the small size of the country, its political centralization and sectoral particularism, little room is left for local autonomy and initiative. The Zanbar Report on Local Government in Israel, published in 1981 by a national commission set up in 1976 under the chairmanship of Moshe Zanbar, proposed far-reaching reforms in the sphere of finances and the redistribution of functions between the local and central government. An interim recommendation that mayors and heads of local councils be elected directly was implemented in 1978.

Loḥamei Ḥerut Yisrael See: *Leḥi.

M

Ma'arach See: *Alignment

Mafdal Hebrew acronym for *Miflagah Datit Le'umit*. See: *National Religious Party.

Maḥal Hebrew acronym for *Mitnadvei Ḥutz-La'aretz* (volunteers from abroad). A heterogeneous group of some 3,000 volunteers from English-speaking countries, many non-Zionist and some non-Jewish who went to Israel to fight in the *War of Independence. The volunteers included pilots, naval captains and other highly qualified military personnel. The American volunteers were in breach of the American law and many arrived under assumed names. Most famous of the Maḥalniks was American Colonel David Marcus (1902–48), a legendary figure also known as Mickey Stone or Mickey Marcus.

Maḥaneh Sheli Hebrew for *Sheli* Camp. *Sheli* — acronym for *Smol Yisraeli* (Israeli Left), a socialist party established in 1976 before the elections for the 9th Knesset (1977). It was made up of Zionist groups to the left of the Alignment. These were **Moked*, **Meri, Brit Hasmol Hatzi'oni-Hasozi'alisti Ha'atzma'i* (The Independent Zionist-Socialist Left Alliance) and some of the *Black Panthers.

Maḥaneh Sheli ran for the elections on a platform which called for, among others, the withdrawal of the *IDF from all territories occupied during the *Six-Day War; granting the Arabs of the *occupied territories the right to self-determination; negotiations with any Palestinian factor recognizing the State of Israel and its right to exist as an independent state; ending all discrimination against the *Arabs of Israel involving the expropriation of lands and administrative detentions; strengthening the rule of law in the state and securing the rights of the individual; war against religious coercion; war against "black capital" and various untaxed capital gains; the encouragement of labor through the offering of a higher return on labor in the production process; the granting of a cost-of-living increment equaling the full rise in the cost-of-living index; opposition to obligatory arbitration in labor disputes in the public sector; assistance to weaker population groups in the sphere of housing and social benefits; improving the standard of education.

Maḥaneh Sheli gained only two seats in the 9th Knesset and Arie Lova *Eliav proposed a rotation agreement which would enable five members of the party to serve in turn as Knesset members. These were Eliav himself, Me'ir *Pa'il, Uri *Avneri, Se'adia Marziano and Walid Sadek. In 1979 Arie Lova Eliav left over ideological disputes. In the elections to the 10th Knesset (1981) the party did not pass the 1 percent threshold. Several of its members were among the founders of the *Progressive List for Peace. (D.B.M.)

Mahapach See: *Upheaval

Maimon (Fishman), **Judah Leib** (1875–1962) Rabbi and **Hamizraḥi* leader. Rabbi Maimon was born in Bessarabia where he, together with Rabbi Isaac Jacob Reines (1830–1915), founded *Hamizraḥi* at its first conference in Vilna in 1900.

Maimon participated in all the Zionist Congresses beginning with the second. In 1935 he became a member of the Zionist Executive under the leadership of David *Ben Gurion — the beginning of the *"historic coalition" between **Mapai* and *Hamizraḥi*. Maimon headed the Department for Artisans and Retail Business, as well as the Department for Religious Affairs. In 1913 he settled in Palestine, and was one of the founders of *Hamizraḥi* educational network. During World War I he was imprisoned and expelled by the Turkish authorities, spending the war years in the United States. After the war Rabbi Maimon became friendly with Rabbi Avraham Yitzḥak Hacohen *Kook. Together they established the *Chief Rabbinate of Palestine, with Rabbi Maimon preparing its constitution. In 1936 Maimon established the *Mossad Harav Kook* (a religious research and publishing institute). Although he maintained his adherence to the organized **Yishuv* Rabbi Maimon often expressed his sympathy with *IZL and **Leḥi*. On Black Saturday, June 29, 1946, when the British arrested the leadership of the *Yishuv*, Rabbi Maimon was interned as Acting Chairman of the *Jewish Agency Executive. In the first years after the establishment of the state Rabbi Maimon advocated the institution of a Sanhedrin (in ancient times the Sanhedrin was the supreme Jewish authority on all religious matters). In the Provisional Government and first Government of Israel, Rabbi Maimon was Minister of Religions and Minister in charge of war casualities. He was a member of the 1st Knesset. After 1951 he dedicated himself to literary work.

Maki Hebrew acronym for *Miflagah Kommonistit Yisraelit* (Israel Communist Party). The Communist Party in Israel has undergone many metamorphoses since its establishment in 1919 as *Mifleget Poa'alim Sozi'alistit* (Socialist Workers' Party). This party joined the Comintern in 1924 as the *Palaestinische Kommonistische Partei* (PKP).

In 1922 the party, which had been declared illegal by the British mandatory authorities, set up the Workers' Fraction within the **Histadrut*, which demanded continuous class warfare. However, in 1924 it was expelled from the *Histadrut* due to its anti-Zionist activities. Most of the original members of the PKP left Palestine in the 1920s, many of them going to the *Soviet Union to be later imprisoned and executed during the purges of the 1930s.

Under Comintern pressure an Arab was appointed as Secretary of the party, with the party demanding Arab rule and the termination of Jewish immigration. In the 1936 disturbances the party insisted that its Jewish members commit acts of terror in Jewish areas, expelling those who refused.

The events of the *Holocaust, the growing strength of the Jewish **Yishuv* and the participation of the Soviet Union in World War II as an ally of the western powers encouraged the Jewish members of the party to oppose the PKP's Arab nationalist line; it then split into two blocs.

In 1945 a Jewish section left the party and set up the Hebrew Communist Party which demanded an independent Jewish state within a Palestine federation. Most of the Arab members of the PKP broke off and established the League for National Liberation, which called for an independent Arab Palestine and opposed any Jewish immigration and settlement activities.

After the establishment of the state, and the Soviet support of the *partition plan, the various splinters reunited and established *Maki*. But in 1949 *Maki* once again split, and the Hebrew Communists joined **Mapam*.

In 1964 internal struggles intensified between the Arab bloc which emphasized anti-Israeli Arab nationalism and supported Pan-Arabism under the leadership of Gamal Abdel Nasser — and the Jewish bloc which adopted a more positive attitude to the state and immigration. A split occurred in 1965 with the Jewish bloc retaining the name *Maki* and the pro-Arab bloc, headed by Me'ir Vilner, Tawfiq *Toubi and others setting up **Rakaḥ* (Hebrew acronym for *Reshimah Kommonistit Ḥadashah* — New Communist List).

Maki did not manage to maintain its electoral power and was reduced to one Knesset seat after the split. Toward the elections to the 8th Knesset (1973) *Maki* split again, with a new party *Aki* (Hebrew acronym for *Oppositzia Kommonistit Yisraelit* — Israel Communist Opposition) led by Esther Vilenska arguing that *Maki* had moved too far to the right. *Maki* then set up a new list together with the Blue-Red Movement (a movement made up of various left-wing groups and led by Me'ir *Pa'il) which ran for the 8th Knesset (1973) as **Moked*. *Maki* published a daily *Kol Ha'am* in 1949 which was made into a periodical before ceasing to appear in 1970.

Knesset Seats: 1st Knesset (1949) — 4; 2nd Knesset (1951) — 5; 3rd Knesset (1955) — 6; 4th Knesset (1959) — 3; 5th Knesset (1961) — 5; 6th Knesset (1965) — 1; 7th Knesset (1969) — 1.

Mamlachtiut A Hebrew term meaning roughly "statism," used primarily in the context of the debate in the early years of the state's existence as to which took precedence, the overall national-state point of view or the sectarian-movement point of view.

The principle of *mamlachtiut* implied that the state existed as an abstract system independent of the movement or parties in government at any given time. On the other hand the movement orientation emphasized the intimate relationship between the Labor movement's hegemony in the government and the very legitimacy of the government. The state orientation regarded the legitimacy of the government as entirely independent of the groups constituting its political base of support, whereas the movement orientation may be interpreted as advocating conditional legitimacy. The disbandment of **IZL* and the **Palmaḥ* in 1948, and the decision to give up the Labor stream in education in 1953 were viewed as decisions in favor of the principle of *mamlachtiut*, while the decision to keep *Kupat Ḥolim* (the **Histadrut* health fund in which an overwhelming majority of the Israeli population is insured) within the Labor-dominated *Histadrut* was a movement decision.

Mandatory Palestine Under the League of Nations system of mandates Britain undertook, on July 24, 1922, the Mandate for Palestine, including the territories of western *Palestine and *Transjordan. It had been British and Empire armed forces which conquered the various territories which made up Palestine from the Ottoman Empire in 1917–18. While Britain's interest in Palestine was primarily strategic, its occupation and subsequent administration of the country must be seen against the background of two sets of promises made by it: one to the Arabs within the framework of the McMahon-Hussein correspondence of 1915–16, the other to the Jews in the *Balfour Declaration of November 2, 1917. In the McMahon-Hussein correspondence Britain undertook to support the establishment of an independent Arab state in return for an Arab revolt against the Ottoman Empire. McMahon, the British High Commissioner in Egypt excluded "the district of Mersina and Alexandretta and portions of Syria lying to the west of the districts of Damascus, Homs, Hama and Aleppo" from the Arab state, since these could not be said to be purely Arab. The Arabs claimed in later years that this definition did not exclude Palestine from the territory of the Arab state and eventually Britain conceded that, technically speaking, the Arabs had a case.

In the Balfour Declaration Britain promised to "view with favour the establishment in Palestine of a national home for the Jewish people," a promise which very few people in Britain took to mean the establishment of a Jewish state in the whole of Palestine. The Balfour Declaration was included in the text of the mandate, though Britain was given the authority not to apply the national home provisions to Transjordan. The mandate also called for "the development of self-governing institutions" and the safeguarding of the "civil and religious rights of all the inhabitants of Palestine, irrespective of race or religion." (S.H.R.)

GOVERNMENT AND COMMUNITIES Neither the Arab nor the Jewish community in Palestine was formally represented in the mandatory government, which was administered directly by British officials according to directives from the Colonial Office in London. Proposals were made in the 1920s and 1930s to create a legislative council in which representatives of both communities would participate with "official" members representing the government, but these were never put into effect because of the tangled web of suspicion and hostility that linked Jew and Arab in Palestine. Finding mutually acceptable criteria of representation was the major stumbling block. Proportional representation would have given the Arabs a decisive majority among the representatives of the local population. The Jews argued that this would contradict the manifest purpose of establishing a "Jewish national home in Palestine." The Arabs claimed, however, that if the Jews were over-represented this would not reflect the actual composition of the local population.

As a result, the mandatory government continued to the end to administer without any participation of the local population, contravening British policy in other colonial and mandate territories, which sought to replace direct with indirect rule. The Peel Commission of 1937 pointed out that this type of rule was inappropriate for the Jewish community in Palestine. "The form of government. . . which circumstances have imposed on the whole of Palestine is not a suitable or natural form for the Jewish section of its population." This conclusion was predicated on the commission's recognition that the "National Home is a highly educated, highly democratic, very politically-minded, and unusually young community." Therefore, the commission concluded, the Jewish community "can never be at ease under an alien bureaucracy."

Differences between the two communities were apparent in all areas of life. The Jewish sector was mainly urban while the vast majority of the Arab sector was rural. At the time of the 1931 census 83.2 percent of the Jewish population lived in urban settlements and 16.8 percent in rural settlements. Conversely, only 24.8 percent of the Muslim population lived in urban settlements while 75.2 percent lived in rural areas. The tendency of the Jewish population to concentrate in urban areas increased over the years, and by 1945, 84.6 percent of the Jews resided in urban areas, including 64.3 percent in full-fledged cities.

In the economic sphere, two levels of wages existed for the same occupations and even two levels of prices for the same agricultural produce. The daily wages of an Arab baker were 219 mills in 1939 and 500 mills in 1944, and carpenters earned 200 mills a day in 1939 and 658 mills in 1944. Their Jewish counterparts earned 511 mills in 1939 and 1105 mills in 1944, for the baker, and 370 mills in 1939 and 1010 mills in 1944, for the carpenter. An unskilled Arab laborer in the building industry earned 160 mills a day in 1939 and 500 mills a day in 1945, while the daily wage of an unskilled Jewish laborer was 300 mills a day in 1939 and 1350 in 1945.

Of course wages are only one component of economic activity. Estimates of national income per capita clearly show different levels of development for the Jewish and Arab economies. In 1936 the per-capita income for Jews was 47.5 Palestine Pounds while for the Arabs it was 16.3 LP. In 1947 the figure for Jews was 169.3 LP and for Arabs 67.7 LP.

No less significant were the differences between the two communities in the sphere of education and culture. A vivid description of the cultural differences between the Jewish and Arab populations appears in the Peel Commission report which reaches the conclusion that: "With every year that passes, the contrast between this intensely democratic and highly organized modern community and the old-fashioned Arab world around it grows sharper, and in nothing, perhaps, more markedly that on its cultural side."

It is only natural that these extensive differences would also be expressed in the political sphere. The Jewish community established elected representative institutions, while no elected institutions existed in the Arab community. Political activity in the Arab community was never fully institutionalized, and to the extent that a political center did exist, it lacked formal authority recognized by the mandatory government. The Supreme Muslim Council was exceptional in that it possessed considerable political influence, even though its formal functions were nonpolitical. Among other things, the Council controlled the vast properties of the Muslim religious endowments (Waqf) and supervised the network of Muslim religious courts (*sharia* courts). But the Supreme Muslim Council could not be considered representative, in national political terms, of the entire Arab population, in part, because 10 percent of this population was Christian.

There were repeated attempts to establish a representative authority for the entire Arab population. In 1920 an Arab congress convened in Haifa and elected a body from among its participants called the Arab Executive Committee. Even though this congress referred to itself as the "legal representative of all classes and groups of the Arab people in Palestine," in fact it was an assembly of notables most of whom were associated with one of the two influential rival families, the Husseinis and the Nashashibis.

After 1920 a number of Arab congresses convened to protest Jewish settlement in Palestine, but neither these nor the Arab Executive Committee elected by them received government recognition. In 1923 a British proposal to create an

"Arab agency" parallel to the Zionist Executive in Jerusalem was rejected. The later congresses were not basically different from the one of 1920, because they too reflected the elitist and particularistic nature of Arab politics, which was not based on permanent institutionalized mass participation. Political activity remained the province of a narrow elite, though sporadic attempts were made to mobilize the Arab masses for action against the Jewish community and at times against the mandatory government. A higher level of political mobilization was attained only in 1936–39 after the Arab parties established a new body, the Arab Higher Committee, which for all practical purposes succeeded the Arab Executive Committee. This body led the guerrilla movement of 1936–39 referred to in Jewish sources as the "disturbances" and in Arab sources as the "Arab revolt."

In the course of the revolt the Arab leadership resorted to terror and other forms of pressure in asserting its authority, and it may be assumed that without a considerable degree of consensus in the Arab community it would not have been possible to conduct a general strike and guerrilla operations over an extended period. Even so, without an organizational infrastructure, a cadre of political professionals, rules of the game for the resolution of internal conflicts, and other institutionalized patterns of action, Arab political organization returned to its previous state of weakness at the end of the revolt. This weakening was also caused by the expulsion of several leaders of the Arab Higher Committee to the Seychelles and the flight of the Mufti of Jerusalem, at first to Syria and Iraq and later to Nazi Germany. But even when the committee renewed its activities in the 1940s with some of its formerly exiled leaders, it did not regain the stature it had achieved during the revolt.

Among the factors which explain the low level of institutionalization of the Arab political center, the most prominent are related to the characteristics of the traditional Arab elite. Its position was based not so much on political activity per se as on its social and economic preeminence. The power of the traditional leadership rested on family status and ownership of land. Only on rare occasions did this elite have recourse to strictly political processes in order to secure political leadership. In addition, the basis of the leadership's power was local, which hampere the emergence of a countrywide nation leadership.

The character of the elite influenced its rel tions with the broader Arab society. The leade had little authority over the followers and we not accountable to them. As in other societi characterized by the "politics of notables," mo of the political activity among the Arabs in ma datory Palestine was not directly connected the mobilization of support based on articulatic and representation of demands. Only for sho periods in the years 1936–39 did the leadersh function as an elite capable of wielding influen and mobilizing public support. But even in th period the level of mutual dependence betwee leaders and followers was low.

The Jewish political elite, by contrast, reache a higher level of political professionalization an developed recruitment patterns based to a larg extent on achievement. The political organiz tion of the Jewish minority was institutionalize in frameworks operating more or less contin ously according to "rules of the game" accepte by the great majority of the *Yishuv*. The centr political institutions, referred to as the "nation institutions," operated through a permane organizational framework according to an estal lished division of labor and by means of form administrative procedures. The first and mo powerful of the two "national institutions" w the *Jewish Agency, which enjoyed a legal stat recognized by the mandatory government ar the League of Nations. Until the Jewish Agen was established in 1929, immigration and settl ment activities were conducted by the Jerusale office of the Executive of the *World Zioni Organization (WZO), which assumed the fun tions of the Zionist Commission formed imm diately after the British conquest.

Because the interest of world Jewry in the Jev ish national home was not limited to the WZO a fact noted in the mandate charter itself — it w decided to establish a more comprehensive inst tution than the Zionist Executive to represent th non-Zionist interest as well in the developme of the "national home." The executive of th institution, the Jewish Agency, consisted of th members of the WZO Executive and a few repre sentatives of the "non-Zionists."

The second national institution was **Kness*

'israel (Jewish Assembly), which was recognised y the mandatory government as the institu-onal system of the Jewish community. The roadest representative institution of the Knesset 'israel was **Assefat Hanivḥarim* (Elected Assem-ly) which was chosen through general elections ased on proportional representation. The elec-›rate was composed of Jews who did not reject iembership in the organized Jewish commu-ity. A smaller parliamentary body which con-ened more frequently, the **Va'ad Le'umi* National Council) was chosen by *Assefat Ianivḥarim*. The executive body of *Knesset Yisrael* 'as known as the Executive of the National :ouncil and was responsible to the plenary of the *'a'ad Le'umi*.

Differences between the Supreme Muslim :ouncil and the institutions of the Knesset 'israel reflected the differences between the two ommunities. The former was primarily a reli-ious institution operating according to tradi-onal patterns, but it did not abstain from politi-al activity, and made no distinction between olitical roles and religious roles. In contrast, the xecutive of the *Va'ad Le'umi* was composed of oliticians, not religious leaders, and functioned ı strictly secular fields. Supreme religious uthority was vested in another institution, the Chief Rabbinate, also a part of the institutional 'amework of Knesset Yisrael.

A striking difference between the national ıstitutions of the Jews and those of the Arabs 'as apparent in the scope of political participa-.on in decision making processes. The best xpression of widespread participation among he Jews was the elections to *Assefat Hanivḥarim* vhere voting ran between 56 and 70 percent. 'his was a relatively high rate of participation in lections within a nonsovereign framework, specially considering that the elections were oycotted at times by various groups due to con-licts over the electoral system.

Differences between the Arab and Jewish olitical systems were also manifested in the reg-lation of internal political conflicts. The con-licts themselves were indeed different. The most nportant political conflicts in Arab society were :ruggles between parties which were actually roups of notables divided along family and *amula* (extended family) lines.

The Palestine Arab party (founded in 1935), the dominant element in the Arab Higher Committee, was identified with the family of the Mufti of Jerusalem, Hadj Amin al-Husseini. The Husseini family attained its powerful position due to the decision of the first High Commissioner for Palestine, Sir Herbert Samuel, to appoint Hadj Amin to the Presidency of the Supreme Muslim Council. Despite the role the mandatory government played in securing this key position for the Husseini family, the family and the party associated with it tended to assume an extreme nationalist stance, opposing not only Zionism but the British as well.

The second most prominent family-based party was the National Defense party led by the Nashashibi family. The head of the Nashashibi family and leader of the party was a former Mayor of Jerusalem, Ragheb Bey Nashashibi. Another important leader of this party, who was later assassinated (probably by agents of the Husseini family), was Fakhri Nashashibi. The Nashashibi party was supported by several Arab mayors, the most prominent being Suleiman Ruqan of Nablus. Besides these two large parties there were several others led by members of other prominent families.

In addition to the disputes among family-based factions, there were conflicts between Christians and Muslims and, during the later years of the Mandate, conflicts between the traditional leadership and the young intelligentsia, who in many cases were not members of prominent families. Yet there was almost no political expression of conflicts rooted in the class structure of Arab society. The Arab peasant population lacked any sort of political articulation while the sector of urban workers was very small, and there were hardly any Arab trade unions until World War II.

The low level of political institutionalization among the Arabs was reflected in modes of conflict regulation. The Arab elite did not develop institutionalized "rules of the game" to provide a foundation of legitimacy to political processes. Consequently, Arab political groups sought the support of the mandatory government or of Arab political centers outside of Palestine in strengthening their position vis-à-vis other groups within Palestinian Arab society.

It was the very establishment of a governmental center, with key positions filled by British officials, which facilitated the political separation of Arabs and Jews. It relieved the need for Arab and Jewish political elites to cultivate direct relationships, since it was possible to conduct most of the political bargaining through the British authorities in Jerusalem and in London. This technical possibility of avoiding direct political contacts was exploited by both sides in ways which reflected their respective national aspirations.

Despite the general separation between the communities, there was at least one area where Jews and Arabs did establish direct relations in a common political framework: municipal government in the mixed cities. But even there, in the elected bodies, local representatives were chosen on a basis which implied a recognition of each community's distinct interests. The mandatory government set a fixed number of representatives from each community, usually according to their proportion of the population. Thus election results and rates of participation in different parts of the population had no effect on the balance of political forces between Arabs and Jews. (D.H.-M.L.)

ATTITUDES TOWARD THE MANDATE At least until 1937 Britain believed that it could fulfill all of its obligations under the mandate, and though an erosion clearly took place in its attitude regarding the Jewish National Home it allowed it to continue to develop (albeit with growing restrictions) while at the same time encouraging development in the fields of agriculture and education in the Arab sector, and constructing an infrastructure. Until the early 1930s attempts were also made to introduce a measure of self-government.

However, the 1937 Peel Commission Report concluded that the mandate was unworkable due to the contradictory demands and goals of the Jews and Arabs and the contradictory promises made by Britain. As a result of the international situation Britain continued to struggle with its impossible task for another 11 years. While the years 1933–39 saw the development of Arab violence against Britain, from 1944 until 1948 Jewish resistance developed into open violence as well and an ever-growing amount of the administration's attention had to be devoted to its own security. In March 1947 Britain brought the Palestine issue to the UN which, following a report by the Special Committee on Palestine (UNSCOP), adopted on November 29, 1947, a resolution in favor of the partition of Palestine. Britain completed its departure from Palestine on May 15, 1948.

Arab opposition to the Zionist enterprise took on a nationalist form after the Young Turk takeover in Turkey in 1908. The Arabs denied that the Jews had any rights in Palestine and rejected the mandate due to its inclusion of the Jewish National Home provisions. Throughout the mandatory period, they instigated outbursts of violence — first directed against the Jews only and after 1933 against the British as well.

The main consequence of the mandate for the Arab population of Palestine, besides bringing rapid development and the raising of standards of living, was to create a powerful Palestinian national consciousness which might never have developed otherwise. However, the militant, all-or-nothing policy initiated by the Higher Arab Committee and the Mufti of Jerusalem, proved in the long run to have been totally destructive since it led to the Palestinians losing everything despite the fact that under the UN partition plan they could have had a state in a much larger territory than the present-day West Bank and Gaza Strip, and the 500,000 Arabs who fled the territory of Israel in 1948–49 could have remained in their homes.

While many Jews were disappointed with the British policy in mandatory Palestine which after every successive commission of inquiry seemed to become more restrictive regarding the development of the Jewish National Home, and most became increasingly sceptical as to whether a *modus vivendi* could be found with the Arabs of Palestine, under the British administration the embryo of a Jewish state was allowed to develop. By 1948 the Jewish *Yishuv* had developed an independent economy with both public and private sectors, an education system running from kindergartens to universities, a nation-wide health system, a tradition and institutions of parliamentary government, and most important of all a highly disciplined army with some fighting experience and a good deal of resourcefulness. Without these the UN partition plan would never have translated into a Jewish state. (See also: *Yishuv; *Arab-Israel Conflict) (S.H.R.)

Mapai Acronym for *Mifleget Poa'alei Eretz Yisrael* (the Party of **Eretz Yisrael* Workers). A socialist Zionist party which existed from 1930 to 1968. It was founded in 1930 upon the merging of *Aḥdut Ha'avodah* and **Hapo'el Hatza'ir*, and constituted not only the central and dominant political force in the Jewish labor movement but in the whole Jewish **Yishuv*. *Mapai* led the Jewish labor movement in *Eretz Yisrael* on the course of "constructive socialism," seeking to attain both national and class goals at one and the same time, while maintaining the principles of democracy and active participation in class, national and international institutions and organizations. "Constructive socialism" was based on an active pioneering movement which viewed itself as a vanguard for achieving social and national goals. *Mapai* gave these ideals a pragmatic backbone which ensured their practical success. *Mapai* was one of the first social democratic parties in the world which understood that one cannot reach hegemony without the cooperation of non-socialist parties which accept some basic social-democratic premises. In the case of *Mapai* this led to the *"historic coalition" with the Zionist religious parties which lasted until 1976 as well as with the centrist General Zionists. These ideas were expressed by the spiritual leader of *Mapai*, Berl *Katznelson while their actual implementation was carried out by the party's long-time leader David *Ben Gurion. This pragmatic approach was not accepted by some elements of the party which, for example, refused to approve the *modus vivendi* agreement signed in 1935 between Ben Gurion and *Revisionist leader Ze'ev *Jabotinsky. Disagreement with this pragmatic approach also caused *Si'a Bet*, made up of members of **Hakibbutz Hame'uḥad* and several party members from Tel Aviv to break away from *Mapai* in 1944 to form the *Tnu'ah Le'aḥdut Ha'avodah* (See: **Aḥdut Ha'avodah-Po'alei Zion*) which presented itself as the protector of the interests of the individual worker and small man vis-à-vis the labor movement bureaucrats and managers.

Following the death of Katznelson in 1944 and in the course of the final struggle for the establishment of the state, Ben Gurion became the undisputed leader of the party, a status which he held until 1963 when he resigned the premiership against the background of the *Lavon Affair. In 1965 *Mapai* joined with *Aḥdut Ha'avodah-Po'alei Zion* to form the first *Alignment, and in 1968 the *Israel Labor Party was established by the merger between this Alignment and **Rafi*.

The organizational structure of the party was based on a conference, meeting every four years, a central committee meeting several times a year and a secretariat meeting two to three times a month. The party leadership formed an informal body called **Ḥavereinu* (our colleagues or friends) in which all the *Mapai* ministers, the Secretary-General of the **Histadrut*, the Party Secretary and frequently the Chairman of the coalition as well, took part.

As long as *Mapai* existed all the Prime Ministers of Israel, all the *Presidents but one, all the *Histadrut* Secretaries-General, and all the *Knesset Speakers but one were members of *Mapai*. Party membership was considered vital for advancement to the top echelons of the administration.

Mapai's regular media organ after 1930 was the weekly *Hapo'el Hatza'ir* (which continued to appear until 1970) and the *Histadrut* daily *Davar*. In 1949 *Mapai* set up an ideological center near Kfar Saba called *Beit Berl* (named after Berl Katznelson) which today serves the Israel Labor Party.

Knesset Seats: 1st Knesset (1949) — 46; 2nd Knesset (1951) — 45; 3rd Knesset (1955) — 40; 4th Knesset (1959) — 47; 5th Knesset (1961) — 42. In the elections to the 6th Knesset *Mapai* ran within the framework of the Alignment.

(D.B.M.)

Mapam Acronym for *Mifleget Po'alim Me'uḥedet* (United Workers' Party). Zionist Socialist party established in 1948 following the merger between **Mifleget Poa'lim-Hashomer Hatza'ir* and **Aḥdut Ha'avodah-Po'alei Zion*. In the early years *Mapam* followed a pro-Moscow policy which it disavowed after Stalin's death.

In 1954 a small pro-Moscow leftist group headed by Moshe *Sneh left *Mapam* (and joined **Maki*) over its growing criticism of Soviet policy, especially after the anti-Semitic doctors' trials in Moscow. In the same year *Aḥdut Ha'avodah-Po'alei Zion* also withdrew over foreign policy issues and *Mapam*'s decision to accept Arab members (*Mapam* was the first Zionist party to include an Arab in its Knesset list). In 1968 another leftist group withdrew to establish the Socialist Zionist Union of the Left. The stable majority in *Mapam* has alway been based on *Hakibbutz Ha'artzi* kibbutz movement and the members of the predominantly urban **Hashomer Hatza'ir* party.

The ideology of the party was for many years based on a Marxist interpretation of the Jewish national question, i.e., the territorial concentration of the Jewish People in **Eretz Yisrael* and the realization of the goals of Labor Zionism without dispossessing the Arabs, and in full cooperation with the Arab working class. The party never supported the concept of the dictatorship of the proletariat in Israel, and as a democratic party never supported the idea of world revolution. In the fifties and sixties it strongly criticized **Mapai*'s activist security policy, its gradual withdrawal from a policy of encouraging the development of a socialist economy and society in Israel, and David *Ben Gurion's concept of "from social class to nation" which expressed a shift away from class struggle to **mamlachtiut*.

Soon after the *Six-Day War *Mapam* started to advocate withdrawal from most of the territories occupied in 1967, objecting to the establishment of Jewish settlements in the *West Bank and *Gaza Strip and advocating a special regime for *Jerusalem which was to remain united under Israel sovereignty.

In 1974 *Mapam* Minister of Health Victor Shemtov proposed, together with Aharon *Yariv of the *Israel Labor Party the *Shemtov-Yariv Formula regarding negotiations with the Palestinians. However, the formula was never adopted by the government. In 1981 it officially recognized the Palestinian right to self-determination within the framework of a peace settlement. Though working closely with the Labor Party within the framework of the *Alignment in the years 1969–84, *Mapam*'s socio-economic program was much more socialist by nature; it advocated greater neutrality in foreign policy, complete equality for the Arabs in Israel and restraint in military retaliatory operations. *Mapam* objected to the *Lebanese War *ab initio*. It withdrew from the Alignment following the elections for the 11th Knesset (1984) against the background of the formation of the *National Unity Government since it felt that the Labor Party had given up too many principles. From the very beginning of the Alignment in 1969 there was a substantial minority in *Mapam* which opposed it. By the 10th Knesset opposition to the Alignment mounted, especially among the urban members who felt that *Mapam* was not being treated as an equal partner and its ideological platform was of little consequence within the Alignment framework. At the party's 1982 conference *Mapam*'s two veteran leaders — Me'ir *Ya'ari and Ya'acov *Ḥazan — put their full weight behind the continued existence of the partnership with the Labor Party, and by a majority of only 17 the conference voted in favor of remaining in the Alignment.

The supreme institution of *Mapam* is the conference. Between conferences a council which elects the central committee is the acting organ of the party. Between meetings of the central committee a political committee and secretariat run the party's affairs. Me'ir *Ya'ari was *Mapam*'s Secretary-General from 1948 to 1973. Me'ir Talmi was Secretary-General from 1973–80, followed by Victor Shemtov 1980–85 and Elazar Granot who took over in 1985.

The party publishes a daily paper *Al Hamishmar*, papers in Yiddish, Romanian, Bulgarian and Persian, and a bi-monthly in Arabic.

Mapam has been a member of the *Socialist International since 1983.

Knesset Seats: 1st Knesset (1949) — 19; 2nd Knesset (1951) — 15; 3rd Knesset (1955) — 9; 4th Knesset (1959) — 9; 5th Knesset (1961) — 9; 6th Knesset (1965) — 8; 7th Knesset (1969) — 9 (out of the Alignment's 56); 8th Knesset (1973) — 8 (out of the Alignment's 51); 9th Knesset (1977) — 5 (out of the Alignment's 32); 10th Knesset (1981) — 7 (out of the Alignment's 47); 11th Knesset (1984) — 6 (out of the Alignment's 44).

Masada Complex The conviction, said to play a role in Israeli political thinking, that it is preferable to fight to the end than to surrender and acquiesce to the loss of independent statehood. The term stems from the experience of 960 Jewish zealots who held the fortified castle of Masada (constructed above the Dead Sea by King Herod in the years 37–31 B.C.E.) from the year 66 to 73 C.E., and refused to surrender to the surrounding Roman forces despite the hopelessness of their situation. When the Romans finally broke through they discovered that all the zealots, except two women and five children, had committed suicide, preferring death to surrender.

Masorti Movement See: *Conservative Movement

Matzad Hebrew acronym for *Miflagah Zionit Datit* (religious Zionist party). Knesset faction set up by Rabbi Ḥaim Druckman who broke away from the *National Religious Party (NRP) in the course of the 10th Knesset (1981–84), because of the NRP's lack of militancy.

Matzad together with **Po'alei Agudat Yisrael* and several religious members who broke off from the **Teḥiyah* set up a new party **Morasha* prior to the elections to the 11th Knesset (1984). Rabbi Druckman and other *Matzad* members returned to the fold of the NRP in June 1986.

media and politics A salient expression of Israeli democracy is the freedom of expression in the country as reflected in the status of the media. The press is independent, and as the "fourth estate" is free to criticize the government, report objectively about the judiciary, and argue with the *Knesset. Since the government in Israel is an important source of information and a major "generator" of events, the press is unavoidably dependent on it. But due to the nature of the regime, the government is also dependent on the press in order to realize its publicity goals — both internal and external. Thus, the media and the government are interdependent.

The interdependence reaches its peak at election time. Coverage of the elections in the public media — radio and television — is subject to legal constraints which restrict the appearances of the personalities who are running for election. By contrast, the printed media, which are under no such constraints, have a free hand during election campaigns, covering the activities of the parties extensively.

Between campaigns, the press in its function of criticizing the government, often contributes to public protest movements, as happened after the *Yom Kippur War and during the *Lebanese War, when the press played an instrumental role in the process which led to the establishment of the *Kahan Commission on the *Sabra and Shatilla massacres.

The nature of the special relationship between the political system and the media is well reflected in the many debates devoted by the Knesset to television coverage of various subjects, not the least its reporting from the Knesset itself. The presence of TV cameras in the plenary encourages stormy debates, and in their absence, issues have actually been removed from the agenda. The electronic and printed media are the main source of information for parliamentary questions, motions for the agenda and other parliamentary initiatives which, in cyclical fashion, subsequently become themselves the subjects of news reports. The result is that the importance of news items is escalated to the satisfaction of both the journalists (who are the "real" source of news) and the politicans (who take political advantage of it).

Critical editorials in the press, as well as various reports and programs in the electronic media about the government, the Knesset and other state institutions occasionally create tension and result in pressure being exerted on the media. Governmental pressure on the media takes the form of complaints by officials to editors or the directors of news departments; veiled (and occasionally explicit) threats of economic sanctions; or legal action. Politicians at all levels do not hesitate to react by attacking the media, for undermining their credibility. On the other hand, a study of the media consumption habits of Israeli politicians and leaders reveals their growing appreciation for the media as an important source of information regarding moods and opinions.

Historically, press licensing in Israel has been regulated by the 1933 Press Ordinance. Newspapers may not be published without a license from the Ministry of the Interior. Publication of a newspaper without a license constitutes a felony under the Press Ordinance and the 1945 Defense (Emergency) Regulations (See: *Emergency Regulations).

The origin of this state of affairs may be found in the report of the Shaw Commission which investigated the 1929 disturbances in Palestine, and which determined that the Arab newspapers had played a role in inciting the population to attack the Jews. As a result the Press Ordinance was promulgated to give the administration the means to supervise the newspapers and other publications. The State of Israel adopted the system after 1948. Journalists in Israel are not licensed. On the basis of a gentleman's agreement between all the press institutions, journalists' associations and the Broadcasting Authority, the Government Press Office is authorized to issue press cards to working reporters.

The electronic media are centrally managed by force of the Broadcasting Authority Law. The Broadcasting Authority is in charge of educational, entertainment and information programs in Hebrew, Arabic and other languages.

The Authority serves the Israeli population and diaspora Jewry, as well as Israel's image abroad. The law requires the Authority to ensure that broadcasts will reflect the various points of view prevalent among the public, and that the information broadcast is credible.

The Director-General of the Authority is appointed by the government, i.e., by the political level. He acts according to the decisions and directives of the Board of Governors, which is also government-appointed, but which includes the representatives of the main political blocs.

Before the Broadcasting Authority was declared an independent body in 1965 radio broadcasts were the responsibility of a department in the Prime Minister's Office (TV broadcasts started only in 1968) which was able to give political directives. Today the government's ability to influence the content of broadcasts is limited. For many years from 1965, however, the Likud complained about the dominance of Labor-oriented personnel in the Authority, and after 1977 set out to redress what it felt to be an imbalance. Israel's radio, *Kol Yisrael* (The Voice of Israel) broadcasts 24 hours a day and operates six stations, each with a distinctive program. The second program, which concentrates on news, current events, special features and sports, is the most important station from the point of view of the politicians who use it to gain exposure for their positions and opinions. The fourth program broadcasts 18 hours a day in Arabic, its audience being the *Arabs of Israel and of the neighboring states. There are broadcasts in 16 additional languages for new immigrants and diaspora Jewry — including the Jews in the *Soviet Union and other East European countries, as well as *Iran.

Israel TV broadcasts 6½ hours a day, including 1½ hours in Arabic. The broadcasts in Arabic are under a separate administrative framework. The evening news broadcast is watched by the largest number of viewers and is thus a highly valued forum for politicians seeking exposure. In the absence of a second channel Israel TV competes with Jordanian TV, and several other stations. Educational TV broadcasts for 9½ hours a day on the same channel as Israel TV. The possibility of starting a second — commercial — TV channel is being examined. A law regarding local broadcast by cable TV has been passed by the Knesset and the educational TV and the Voice of Israel have began to broadcast the Teletext which *inter alia* brings information to the viewers on government services.

The radio station run by the *IDF (Israel Defense Forces) broadcasts, in addition to military programs, current events and popular music programs. The IDF radio tunes into the Voice of Israel for the hourly news broadcasts. On non-military subjects the broadcasts are subject to the supervision of the national broadcasting authority institutions. The Editors' Committee, founded by the editors of the daily newspapers on the eve of the establishment of the state to react to the British mandatory authorities, has a special position within the media-government relationship. Since its foundation the Editors' Committee has turned into the body which represents the newspapers vis-à-vis the government. By means of this committee the editors may receive classified information on matters of security, foreign policy, etc., on condition that they do not publish it.

Israel's security situation has, since the establishment of the state, necessitated arrangements for preventing the publication of information liable to harm the interests of the state. The prolonged conflict has meant that many temporary measures have been maintained for close to 40 years. The military censorship was initiated before the establishment of the state, on the basis of a voluntary agreement between the journalists of the Jewish press and the Jewish authorities, as part of the press's contribution to the struggle for national independence.

The first censorship agreement, between the General Staff and the Editors' Committee, was approved in January 1950, and withstood both legal and public criticism for 15 years. In 1966 a new agreement was drawn up by a joint committee representing the IDF and the Editors' Committee. This agreement stated that: "the purpose of the censorship is to prevent the publication of security-related information liable to benefit the enemy or harm Israel's defense. The censorship is based on cooperation between the military authorities and the press in order to attain this goal. . . the censorhip is not applicable to political matters, opinions, commentary or appraisals, or any issue other than information relating to security." The self-restraint of the press regarding security issues has been an important barrier to the use of military censorhip in political matters. There have been issues in which the narrow divide between security and politics has raised heated public debate, such as in the *Lavon Affair or the cease-fire agreement with Egypt in August 1970 which turned into a political issue resulting in **Gaḥal* leaving the *National Unity Government at the time. The press has criticized the politicians for occasionally stifling criticism on military-security grounds even more than does the censorship.

For security reasons military censorship applies to foreign correspondents and the international press as well. The East Jerusalem press, which for the most part is an Arab-Palestinian press (part of it actually financed by Palestinian organizations outside the country), is subject to strict censorship regulations. The most prominent of these papers are: the pro-Jordanian *Al Quds*, the pro-PLO *Al Fajr* and *Al-Shaab* and *Al Mithak*, which is affiliated with the Popular Front for the Liberation of Palestine (PFLP). In addition, nine weeklies and eight monthlies are published in Arabic, which, like the bulk of the Arabic dailies, are not strictly press publications, but political propaganda tools serving various Palestinian and other interests in their political struggle in the *administered territories. In November 1986 the authorities called for the expulsion of the editor of *Al-Shaab*, Akram Haniye, on grounds that he had allowed the paper's premises to serve as a meeting place for subversive factors.

By force of its moral-normative authority, the Press Council, established in 1963, is the supreme institution of the press in Israel. The Press Council, which is not a statutory body, protects the freedom of the press in Israel and the public's right to know; guards the standards of the Israeli press and its observance of professional ethics; watches out for trends likely to limit the supply of information of public interest and value; ensures free access to sources of information and defends the right of the journalist to maintain the secrecy of his sources of information.

The Press Council's constitution of professional ethics serves as a sort of normative code on how to report the news. It is also recognized by politicians and public figures, who refer to it whenever they consider that they have suffered some personal injury, or that an issue or a body which they serve has been wronged.

In addition to the Press Council's code of ethics, there are several legal limitations to the work of newsmen in Israel. Those that are relevant to the subject of the media in politics are: the law against libel; bans related to classified information as specified in Article 113 of the 1977 Penal Code and on the basis of which the cabinet declares the meetings of the Ministerial Committee on Defense to be secret; the ban on hidden listening devices and the publication of information attained in this way; the rule of sub judice; and the censorship, which functions under the 1945 Emergency Regulations, and is entitled to ban reports in newspapers which do not comply with the agreement between the defense authorities and the Editors' Committee.

The law protecting privacy and the proposed bill banning the publication of names of suspects, though on the face of it not a political issue, have led to a virtual crisis in the relations between the press and the government due to press concern regarding the legislators' intentions. The Association of Journalists, the Editors' Committee and the Press Council have called for maintaining the good-will arrangements rather than introducing legislation the enforcement of which could undermine the freedom of the press.

Some 350 foreign correspondents are permanently stationed in Jerusalem, and an additional 1,000 visit Israel annually for temporary assignments or the reporting of specific topics or events. They are all serviced by the Government Press Office. This office is the authorized institution for the distribution of information on the activities of the government, the Knesset and the IDF, both to the Israeli and foreign press. The Government Press Office is the official meeting place of the press and the authorities. While serving the needs of the press and playing by the "rules of the game" of the mass media, the Government Press Office watches over the government's interests, and functions in accordance with its policy.

There is a wide variety of newspapers in Israel.

The Hebrew dailies are: *Davar*, (which belongs to the **Histadrut*), *Ha'aretz* (independent), *Hatzofeh* (owned by the World Mizraḥi Movement-*NRP), *Ḥadashot, Ma'ariv* and *Yediot Aḥaronot* (all three independent evening papers), *Al Hamishmar* (published by **Mapam-Hakibbutz Ha'artzi*), *Hamodi'ah* (owned by **Agudat Yisrael*). There is one Arabic daily: *Al Ittihad* (the Communist Party).

Foreign language dailies include *The Jerusalem Post* (English), *Uj Kelet* (Hungarian), *Viata Noastra* (Romanian), *Israel Nachrichten* (German), *Letzte Neues* (Yiddish), *Nascha Strana* (Russian), *Nowiny Kurier* (Polish). All are Labor-oriented papers.

While the Labor movement and the religious bloc have been successful in maintaining their own press, the **Ḥerut* Movement's *Ḥerut* and the *General Zionist-Liberal Party *Haboker* ceased to appear in the 1960s. A recent attempt by the **Likud* to launch a weekly, *Yoman Hashavu'ah*, failed. Among the many weeklies published in Israel are *Omer* (for new immigrants), *She'arim (*Po'alei Agudat Yisrael), Bamaḥaneh* (*IDF), *Ha'olam Hazeh* (owned by Uri *Avneri), *Koteret Rashit* (close to Labor), *Ksafim* (financial).

In recent years a lively local press distributed free of charge has developed in Israel. In addition *Itim*, the Israeli news agency, supplies news to the media and acts as the sole Israeli distributor of news and photographic services to international agencies. (I.P.)

Meḥdal Hebrew word which translates into something like "culpable failure resulting from inadequate preparation and inaction," and in the Israeli political dictionary, refers to the state of surprised unpreparedness with which the Israeli government and military establishment responded to the outbreak of the *Yom Kippur War.

Meir (formerly Meyerson) **Golda** (1898–1978) Labor leader, fourth Prime Minister of Israel. Golda Meir was born in Russia and educated in the United States where she was trained as a teacher. She immigrated to Palestine in 1921 and lived in Kibbutz Merḥaviah from 1921–24. Golda Meir was active in the **Histadrut*, becoming Secretary of its Council for Women Workers in 1928, a member of the Executive Committee in 1934 and Head of its Political Department in 1936. Meir played an active role in **Mapai* and in the political struggle for immigration, self-defense and independence. In 1946 when Moshe *Sharett was arrested by the British Meir replaced him as Head of the Political Department of the *Jewish Agency. She met secretly with King Abdullah of Transjordan (See: *Jordan and Israel) in an effort to come to an agreement. In May 1949 she was appointed Israel's first Minister to Moscow.

Meir was a Member of *Knesset from its establishment in 1949 until 1974. She was Minister of Labor from 1949–56 and Minister for Foreign Affairs, 1956–66. She initiated Israel's policy of active cooperation with the newly independent countries of *Africa. In 1965 Meir was appointed Secretary-General of *Mapai*. In this capacity she succeeded in reuniting *Mapai* with the breakaway factions of **Aḥdut Ha'avodah-Po'alei Zion* and **Rafi* with together formed the *Israel Labor Party in 1968. When Levi *Eshkol died in March 1969 Meir became Prime Minister to head the ongoing *National Unity Government. In July 1970 the **Gaḥal* bloc left the government because of the latter's acceptance of the *Rogers Plan. Golda Meir formed an Alignment-led government after the elections to the 8th Knesset (1973) but resigned following the publication of the *Agranat Commission Report. Meir's views on the *Arab-Israel conflict and Israel's social problems were generally considered to be simplistic and rigid. Nevertheless, she was highly regarded and held in awe both in Israel and abroad. In 1972 Meir was elected Deputy Chairman of the *Socialist International. (See: *Women in Politics; *"Kitchen" Cabinet.)

(I.R.-S.H.R.)

Memorandum of Understanding Over the years several memoranda of understanding have been signed between the *US and Israel. However, the best known and most frequently quoted one is that signed in September 1975 as a corollary to the Interim Agreement between *Egypt and Israel, which included the following US commitments to Israel: 1) to be "fully responsive," subject to congressional approval and the availability of resources, to Israel's defense, energy and economic needs; 2) to hold consultations with Israel in the event of a "world power" (i.e., the Soviet Union) interfering militarily in the Middle East; 3) to accept the Israeli view that another Egyptian-Israeli agreement and any negotiations with Jordan should be within the framework of an overall Middle East peace settlement; 4) to coordinate policy with Israel regarding the timing and procedure of a reconvened *Geneva Peace Conference; and 5) not to "recognize or negotiate with" the *Palestine Liberation Organization so long as that organization "does not recognize Israel's right to exist and does not accept *Security Council Resolutions 242 and 338"; 6) to oppose any changes in Security Council Resolutions 242 and 338 which did not correspond "with their original purpose."

Meri Hebrew acronym for *Maḥaneh Radicali Yisraeli* (Israeli Radical Camp). The name assumed by Uri *Avneri's one-man Knesset faction after *Ha'olam Hazeh-Ko'aḥ Ḥadash* split in the course of the 7th Knesset. In 1973 *Meri* joined with a group from *Si'aḥ* (acronym for *Smol Yisraeli Ḥadash* — New Israeli Left) in a new list *Meri Veḥazit Hasmol* (Meri and the Left Front) which ran in the elections for the 8th Knesset (1973) but failed to pass the 1 percent qualifying threshold. The movement was active in demonstrations against administrative detention of Arabs and the fencing off of the *Rafa Salient, and supported the return of the refugees from Bir'am and Ikrit to their Galilee villages and lands.

Mifleget Ha'avodah See: *Israel Labor Party

Mifleget Po'alim-Hashomer Hatza'ir Hebrew for "Workers' Party — Young Guard." Zionist socialist party founded in Palestine, 1946.

**Hashomer Hatza'ir* began as a scouts youth movement in 1912 in Galicia. In 1913 it took on the name *Hashomer* and adopted a Zionist ideology. During World War I the movement united with the Austrian *Tze'irei Tzion* (young Zionists) students association and in 1918 they adopted the name *Hashomer Hatza'ir*. In 1919 the new movement adopted the "ten commandments" of *Hashomer* which included mutual assistance and sexual purity. In 1920 its first members immigrated to Palestine and organized themselves into labor brigades, and the first *kvutzah* (See: *Kibbutz) of the movement was set up. Later on *Hakibbutz Ha'artzi* was established as the roof organization of all movement's *kvutzot* and kibbutzim.

In 1936 *Hashomer Hatza'ir* was joined by an urban contingent "the Socialist League." The two united in 1946 into *Mifleget Po'alim-Hashomer Hatza'ir* which advocated class warfare as a factor which furthered the building of the country; an activist approach to the issue of coexistence with the Arabs (some members were active in the *bi-national movement); education and information based on Marxist socialism; participation in the *World Zionist Organization; the centrality of agricultural settlement, etc.

Hakibbutz Ha'artzi put at the disposal of the new party its daily *Mishmar* which had started to appear in 1943, which was now called *Al Hamishmar*. In 1948 the party united with **Aḥdut Ha'avodah-Po'alei Zion* to form **Mapam*.

Military Administration Hebrew: *Mimshal Tzva'i*. Established in 1948 under the *Emergency Regulations as the special administrative framework for the Arab (See: *Arabs of Israel) and *Druze minorities in Israel. The Military Administration applied to the minorities in the Galilee, the Triangle, the Negev, the towns of Ramleh, Lod, Jaffa, Ashkelon and Jerusalem. The first military governor was Dov (Bernard) *Yosef. The aim of the Military Administration was to prevent hostile activities against the state from within. The system was opposed both from the Left which felt it was anti-democratic and unnecessarily oppressive, and from the Right (especially Menaḥem *Begin) who objected to a system based on the Emergency Regulations taken over from mandatory times. While David *Ben Gurion favored the system as a necessary evil, Levi *Eshkol, when he became Prime Minister, was inclined to relax its restrictions. The main regulations implemented by the Administration were Regulation 109 which permitted the arrest of a person for being in a prohibited area; Regulation 110 which allowed police supervision over a person for up to one year; Regulation 111 which provided the legal basis for administrative detention by military commanders; Regulation 124 which provided for regional house arrest; and Regulation 125 which permitted military commanders to declare certain areas closed areas wherein persons entering or leaving must possess a special permit. Gradually the areas to which these regulations applied were limited. In 1962 the Druze were excluded, and in 1966 the Military Administration was lifted altogether though the Emergency Regulations may still be implemented by the heads of the various military commands.

military and politics Despite the constant state of war and military preparedness of the State of Israel and their heavy burden on the state budget; despite the extended periods of reserve duty served by most adult Israeli men (See: *IDF); and the employment of many persons in defense-related industries; and despite the centrality of security in Israeli affairs and the high prestige and status of the military — Israel has not turned into a Laswellian "Garrison State" in which the military leaders are also the political decision-makers.

Rather, Israel has evolved into a "nation in arms," which, while praising and idealizing its warriors, has maintained the undisputed supremacy of politics over the military. There are several reasons for this.

First, the IDF is primarily a citizens' army in which reserves constitute the majority of the fighting forces. Israel's second Chief of Staff Yiga'el *Yadin once said that the reservists are "soldiers on 11-month leave." Consequently, the IDF is a reflection of the society and not a separate caste, which is a solid barrier against militarism.

Second, the IDF was constructed on the basis of egalitarian values, in which members of all the Jewish communities within the society have an equal chance of rising to the top. Israel's 12th Chief of Staff is of Iraqi origin.

Third, the IDF, and the **Haganah* before it, played a central role in the nation-building process, as in the establishment of border settlements by the *Naḥal*, or the employment of women soldier-teachers to deal with the problem of illiteracy in the early years of the state's existence. The result has been a blurring of the boundaries between the society at large and the military insofar as the IDF's nonmilitary activities are concerned, without the military assuming exclusive control over these activities.

Fourth, there has been a deliberate policy of rapid and intensive turnover within the top echelons of the IDF, and the early retirement of senior officers, which has prevented the creation of a military clique with distinct interests and viewpoints.

Fifth, a situation has developed in which the society accepts certain rules-of-the-game in the security sphere which are different to those prevailing in other frameworks of organized social activity, and which by mutual and tacit agreement between the state and the citizens are not applied in the nonmilitary sphere.

Finally, Ben Gurion, as first Prime Minister and Minister of Defense of Israel, strictly applied the principle of the supremacy of the political leadership over the military — a principle which had been introduced in pre-state times in the relations between the *Haganah* and the *Jewish Agency. The consequence of this has been that Israeli society has not become militarized while the military in Israel has become "civilianized."

Nevertheless, there is a broad, and often unique, interaction between the military and political levels — some of it institutionalized. Thus, for example, the Chief of Military Intelligence is also the Prime Minister's advisor on intelligence, with all that this implies regarding the source of assessments on the state of national security. Again, the Chief of Staff and other top commanders of the IDF are frequently invited to cabinet meetings and are thus privy to the political decision-making process. There are cases in which the military leadership actually forces the hand of the political leaders — as when Chief of Staff Moshe *Dayan undermined Prime Minister Moshe *Sharett's efforts in the mid-50s to move toward conciliation with the Arab states and foster closer relations with the *United States. He did this by deliberately seeking to bring about a full-scale war between *Egypt and Israel in order to stop the infiltration of **Feda'iyin* from the *Gaza Strip since he felt that the policy of reprisal raids had been too mild.

The *Lavon Affair was another example of an action by the military level leading to far-reaching political consequences.

A common phenomenon in the relations between the political and military level has been the tacit coalitions formed between them. It has been common for generals to be promoted on advice of the political level when those generals show understanding of and cooperate with the politicians. Later, upon retirement, many of the generals were co-opted into the political parties of their benefactors.

In the early years of the state Ben Gurion had two kinds of military and political coalitions, one with veterans of the British army, such as Shlomo Shamir and Ḥaim Laskov whom he trusted professionally, the other with officers affiliated with the workers' movement, such as Assaf Shimoni, Yosef Avidar, and Moshe Dayan whom he trusted politically. At the same time he was disturbed by the *Mapam-Palmaḥ* coalition, and at the first opportunity put an end to it, *inter alia* cutting short the military career of Yigal *Allon.

Later coalitions included Ben Gurion-Moshe Dayan; Levi *Eshkol and the **Aḥdut Ha'avodah* leaders-Yitzḥak *Rabin; Golda *Meir-David Elazar; and the trio Menaḥem *Begin-Ariel *Sharon-Rafael *Eitan.

The phenomenon of generals entering politics after their retirement is not uncommon in Israel. Generals have frequently shed their military ways, become civilians and adapted to political life with great speed. At first most of the generals joined the Left, reflecting the fact that officers known to harbor right-wing views could not a priori reach the top military echelons. Currently ex-generals are to be found in most of the non-religious parties. The military leaders who joined parties of the labor movement (some of them had also originally emerged from the labor movement) were Israel *Galili, Moshe Carmel, Moshe Dayan, Yigal Allon, Yitzḥak Rabin, Ḥaim *Bar Lev, Ḥaim *Herzog, Aharon *Yariv, and Mordechai *Gur. There have been cases of generals joining the extreme Left. Moshe *Sneh joined the Communist Party, Me'ir *Pa'il joined **Moked* and later **Maḥaneh Sheli*, while Mattityahu *Peled is a member of the *Progressive List for Peace. Others have joined right-wing parties. Ezer *Weizman joined the **Herut* Movement, though in the late 1970s he moved to the Center. Ariel Sharon after flirting with various parties of various shades joined *Ḥerut* in 1977. Rafael Eitan formed his own party, **Tzomet*, within the framework of which he joined the **Teḥiyah* in 1984. The central political stream was represented by Yiga'el Yadin, who was one of the founders of the *Democratic Movement for Change, joined by another two ex-Generals: Me'ir *Amit and Me'ir Zore'a. Ezer Weizman, who had at first been a member of the *Ḥerut* Movement formed his own center party **Yaḥad* in 1984 which joined the *Israel Labor Party in October 1986. Shlomo Lahat (Chich) who was elected Mayor of Tel Aviv on behalf of the *Liberal Party, was one of the founders of the Liberal Center in 1986.

The duration between retirement from military service and the entrance to politics has also varied widely. Some, like Bar Lev, joined the government immediately after leaving the army. Others, like Yadin, entered the Knesset and government after many years of civilian-academic life. (Yadin left the army in 1952 and entered the Knesset in 1977.)

The *National Unity Government under Shimon *Peres included three ex-Chiefs of Staff (Rabin, Bar Lev and Gur) and another two generals (Sharon and Weizman). The existence of the phenomenon of a military-industrial complex in Israel similar to that in the US has yet to be proven, though there are allegations that the Lavi aircraft project is a case in point. Finally, due to the special security situation in Israel and the occupation of extensive territories in the *Six-Day War, the Israeli military has been involved in governing Arab civilians, first in the form of the *Military Administration in Israel proper until 1965, and then in the form of the *Military Government in the *administered territories since 1967. While the rule over civilians has meant another form of the "civilianization" of the military, it has also involved the ability of the military to influence the nonmilitary policies of Israel toward the areas in question, including the issue of Jewish settlements and the well-being of the Arab population. (U.D.)

Military Government The Israeli administration in the *West Bank and the *Gaza Strip since 1967, modified in 1981 by the introduction of the Civilian Administration. The legal basis for the operation of the Israeli administration was proclamations on Law and Administration issued soon after the occupation of the regions by the *IDF in June 1967. These proclamations granted the commanders of the IDF forces in these regions full appointive and administrative powers of government and legislation.

The Military Government was originally made-up of military personnel exclusively, both regular and reserve. It was responsible both for preserving security and for ensuring the smooth running of the civilian administration. The district military commanders were responsible to two parallel systems, one military and one civilian. In their military capacity they were subordinate to the regional military commanders and through them to the Chief of Staff. In their civilian capacity they were responsible to the *West

Bank and *Gaza Strip governors (who dealt with civilian matters) and through them to the coordinator of activities in the territories, who was himself directly responsible to the Minister of Defense.

These two chains of command united only in the office of the Minister of Defense to whom the Chief of Staff is responsible. The first phase of the Military Government was concurrent with Moshe *Dayan's term as Minister of Defense. It was notable for its complete centralization and the full coordination of the military and civilian arms of the administration. Until 1974 Dayan was personally involved in the decision-making on both levels. A civilian bureaucracy, nevertheless, began to emerge at the level of staff officers, who while theoretically subordinate to the governors in fact acted in tandem with the Israeli government ministries. Increased political agitation in the territories preceding the *Yom Kippur War, as well as Dayan's resignation as a result of the *Agranat Commission report, brought about structural changes in the Military Government.

The military arm was now subordinated to the regional commander who until then had dealt with civilian affairs only. This centralization at the local level was considered an appropriate response to political extremism in the territories, and an effective tool for opposing radical forces. The result was neglect of many matters in the civilian sphere, since the staff officers were left with no central coordinating authority now that the regional commanders dealt with military matters as well.

Following the election of radical mayors in the 1976 municipal elections held in the West Bank, and the **Likud* assumption of power in Israel in 1977, there began a period of open confrontation between the military and the municipalities. During Ezer *Weizman's term as Minister of Defense (1977–80) the degree of confrontation was relatively moderate. However, after his resignation when Prime Minister Menaḥem *Begin assumed the Defense portfolio, and gave the Chief of Staff, Rafael Eitan, full responsibility for the Military Government, the friction increased.

The Coordinator of Activities in the territories was made directly responsible to the Chief of Staff, making the civilian branch completely subordinate to the military branch. However, in November 1981, after Ariel *Sharon became Minister of Defense the setup was changed through the establishment of the Civilian Administration in the territories.

Order 947 established a complete separation between the two branches, each with its own separate bureaucracy — one military (on the local and regional level) and the other civilian. Civilians were appointed as Coordinator of Activities in the territories and Head of the Civilian Administration. The two systems, operating in an uncoordinated fashion, created duplication and generated personal disputes. In February 1982 Sharon approved a new definition of the system of Military Government in the territories with regard to its civilian functions.

a) The Coordinator of Activities in Judea, Samaria (See: *Yosh) and the Gaza Strip is directly responsible to the Minister of Defense.

b) His tasks are to instruct, guide, advise, coordinate and supervise the activities of all government ministries, the Civilian Administration, state institutions, the various public authorities and private bodies in all matters concerning their activities in Judea, Samaria and the Gaza Strip.

c) The coordination of civilian operations between the Israeli ministries and the Civilian Administration is carried out by the coordinator *inter alia* through a committee of Directors General of the ministries.

d) The chain of authority for dealing with the affairs of the Civilian Administration is as follows: the Head of the Civilian Administration is responsible to the Coordinator of Activities who is responsible to the Minister of Defense. The Minister of Defense approves all decisions regarding civilian issues, which are submitted to him by the Coordinator of Activities, who deals with problems referred to him by the Head of the Civilian Administration. The direct links and working arrangements between the staff officers of the various government ministries and the ministries themselves remain in effect. (M.B.)

Ministers for Foreign Affairs

1948–58 Moshe *Sharett (**Mapai*)
1958–66 Golda *Meir (*Mapai*)
1966–74 Abba *Eban (*Mapai*-*Israel Labor Party)
1974–77 Yigal *Allon (Israel Labor Party)
1977–79 Moshe *Dayan (Independent)

1979–80 Menaḥem *Begin (**Ḥerut*)
1980–86 Yitzḥak *Shamir (*Ḥerut*)
1986– Shimon *Peres (Israel Labor Party)

Ministers of Defense

1948–54 David *Ben Gurion (**Mapai*)
1954–55 Pinḥas *Lavon (*Mapai*)
1955–63 David Ben Gurion (*Mapai*)
1963–67 Levi *Eshkol (*Mapai*)
1967–74 Moshe *Dayan (**Rafi*, after 1968 *Israel Labor Party)
1974–77 Shimon *Peres (Israel Labor Party)
1977–80 Ezer *Weizmann (**Ḥerut*)
1980–81 Menaḥem *Begin (*Ḥerut*)
1981–83 Ariel *Sharon (*Ḥerut*)
1983–84 Moshe *Arens (*Ḥerut*)
1984– Yitzḥak *Rabin (Israel Labor Party)

Ministers of Finance

1948–52 Eliezer Kaplan (**Mapai*)
1952–63 Levi *Eshkol (*Mapai*)
1963–68 Pinḥas *Sapir (*Mapai*)
1968–69 Ze'ev *Sherf (*Mapai*)
1969–74 Pinḥas Sapir (*Israel Labor Party)
1974–77 Yehoshua Rabinowitz (Israel Labor Party)
1977–80 Simḥa *Ehrlich (*Liberal Party)
1980–81 Yiga'el *Hurwitz (**La'am*)
1981–83 Yoram *Aridor (**Ḥerut*)
1983–84 Yigal Cohen-Orgad (*Ḥerut*)
1984–86 Yitzḥak *Moda'i (Liberal Party)
1986– Moshe Nissim (Liberal Party)

minority lists Also known as associated parties. Lists made up of Arabs and *Druze, based on family groups (*ḥamulot*) and Bedouin tribes, which were closely linked to **Mapai* and later the Israel Labor Party, but ran separately in all elections until the elections to the 10th Knesset (1981) when they failed to pass the one percent threshold. The minority lists supported all the Labor governments until 1977 except the 17th (March 10 – June 3, 1974), but never had ministerial representation. Due to changes which took place within Israeli Arab society in the seventies, the Labor Party decided to stop supporting separate lists and integrated Arab members into its ranks. Following the elections to the 10th Knesset Ḥamad Khaleila entered the Knesset as a Labor Party member and in the 11th Knesset he was replaced by Abdel Wahab Darawsha.

Knesset Seats: 1st Knesset (1949) — 2; 2nd Knesset (1951) — 5; 3rd Knesset (1955) — 5; 4th Knesset (1959) — 5; 5th Knesset (1961) — 4; 6th Knesset (1965) — 4; 7th Knesset (1969) — 3; 8th Knesset (1973) — 3; 9th Knesset (1977) — 1.

Distribution of Seats: Nazareth Region Democratic List: 1st Knesset — 2. Democratic Arab List: 2nd Knesset — 3; 3rd Knesset — 2. Farm and Development List: 2nd Knesset — 1; 3rd Knesset — 1; 4th Knesset — 1. Progress and Labor: 2nd Knesset — 1; 3rd Knesset — 2. Progress and Development: 4th Knesset — 2; 5th Knesset — 2; 6th Knesset — 2; 7th Knesset — 2; 8th Knesset — 2. Cooperation and Fraternity: 4th Knesset — 2; 5th Knesset — 2; 6th Knesset — 2; 7th Knesset — 2. Bedouin and Arab Village List: 8th Knesset — 1. United Arab List: 9th Knesset — 1.

Mizraḥi See: **Hamizraḥi*

Moda'i (formerly Madzowitch), **Yitzḥak** Politician and business manager, former Minister of Finance. Born 1926, Tel Aviv. Moda'i graduated as a chemical engineer from the Technion in 1957 and as a lawyer from the Hebrew University in 1959.

He joined the *Haganah while still a high school student in 1941 and served in the Palestine police from 1943. Between 1948–50 he served in the *IDF both as a field and staff officer with the rank of Lieutenant Colonel and was Military Attaché in London between 1951–53. Moda'i headed the Israel-Syria and Israel-Lebanon Armistice Agreement Commissions in 1953 after which he became involved in various industrial ventures, becoming Managing Director of Revlon (Israel) in 1961 in which capacity he served until 1977.

Moda'i joined the *Liberal Party in 1961, becoming Chairman of its Young Guard in 1962. Three years later he strongly supported the formation of **Gaḥal*, and in 1965–68 served in the Liberal Party executive, constantly calling for full unity with the **Ḥerut* Movement.

During the *Six-Day War Moda'i was appointed Military Governor of Gaza. In 1969–73 he was a member of the Municipal Council of Herzliya. He entered the Knesset in 1974 and in 1975 was one of the members who influenced the Liberal Party to adopt a resolution against Israeli withdrawal from the *West Bank and *Gaza Strip, even though he had expressed willingness to accept some compromise in an interim agreement as long as it did not involve the repartition of western **Eretz Yisrael*.

Moda'i set up the Ministry of Energy and Infrastructure in the first *Begin government in 1977, and served as its Minister in 1977–81 and again in 1982–84. He was Minister of Communications 1979–80 and Minister without Portfolio 1981–82. In 1980 Moda'i became Chairman of the Liberal Party Presidium.

In the *National Unity Government formed in September 1984, Moda'i was appointed Minister of Finance, at first working closely with Prime Minister Shimon *Peres in the preparation and introduction of the economic stabilization plan.

Though his economic policy was generally viewed as a success, professional and personal friction developed between himself and other ministers. In addition, the Labor ministers felt that Moda'i was deliberately trying to damage the *Histadrut economic sector and its health fund — *Kupat Ḥolim*. In April 1986 Peres decided to remove Moda'i from the Ministry of Finance after he had spoken out against the government's policy and disrespectfully of the Prime Minister. Moda'i exchanged portfolios with Minister of Justice Moshe Nissim and soon after taking office had to deal with the **Shabak* Affair.

In July 1986 he was forced to resign from the government after again speaking disrespectfully of the Prime Minister.

After the *rotation Moda'i returned to the government as Minister without Portfolio. At the same time differences arose in the Liberal Party between Moda'i and the other Liberal leaders regarding his chairmanship of the party.

Moked Hebrew for "focus", *Moked* was a political bloc set up in 1973 when **Maki* and the Blue-Red Movement united. The bloc advocated Israeli withdrawal to the 1949 borders; acceptance of a Palestinian state in the *West Bank and *Gaza Strip after the establishment of peace; the limitation of the influence and rights of private capital; reduction of the dependence on the US; direction of the state's major resources to combat poverty and close social gaps. In 1976 *Moked* united with **Ha'olam Hazeh-Ko'aḥ Ḥadash* to set up **Maḥaneh Sheli*.

Knesset Seats: 8th Knesset (1973) — 1.

(D.B.M.)

Morasha Zionist religious party formed in 1983 by former members of the *National Religious Party (NRP) who objected to the policy line of the veteran leadership and wanted to rejuvenate religious political life and by members of **Po'alei Agudat Yisrael* which had failed to elect any members to the 10th Knesset (1981).

The Party was headed by MK Yosef Shapira, Rabbi Ḥaim Druckman (who had broken away from the NRP during the 10th Knesset), Ḥanan Porat (one of the leaders of the religious kibbutz movement and a Member of Knesset for the **Teḥiyah* in the 10th Knesset who resigned his seat after the withdrawal from Yamit to concentrate on religious matters) and MK Avraham Verdiger (from *Po'alei Agudat Yisrael*). The new party won two seats in the 11th Knesset and Shapira was appointed Minister without Portfolio in the *National Unity Government. The party's political line favored settlement in *occupied territories and its religious positions were rigid. In June 1986 Rabbi Druckman returned to the NRP and *Morasha* remained with a single Knesset seat. (Sh.M.)

Morocco and Israel In 1948, when Israel gained independence, Morocco was still under a French protectorate. At that time there were over one quarter of a million Jews living in Morocco, and as in other Arab countries they were subject to attacks by the local population, resulting in at least 43 deaths and much destruction of property. However, partly due to the geographical distance of Morocco from the central arena of the *Arab-Israel conflict, anti-Zionism and hatred for the Jews never assumed the same extreme dimensions as in other parts of the Moslem world. In the years 1948–55 close to 70,000 Jews left Morocco for Israel — over half of them in 1954–55, around the time that Morocco gained independence. There was also a large migration of Jews to France which included the wealthier and more educated classes.

Anti-Jewish riots resumed on the eve of Moroccan independence in 1954. In 1958 Morocco joined the Arab League, and even though it avoided taking any extreme measures against the Jews during the *Sinai Campaign and subsequent Arab-Israel wars, it fully adopted all the Arab League resolutions regarding Israel. Thus, the exit of Jews to Israel was formally prohibited, and Jews could not obtain passports in order to leave Morocco. Zionist activity within the Jewish community was also prohibited, and all the offices which dealt with the organization f *aliyah* (immigration) to Israel were closed own. Nevertheless, in the years 1956–60, 7,000 Jews left clandestinely for Israel. During ne latter part of the reign of King Muhammad V 1927–61) the conditions of the Jews in Iorocco improved, and they were formally ranted equal rights. A Jew was even appointed Iinister of Posts.

In 1961 Hassan II assumed the throne, improvng relations with the Jews and legalizing emiration to Israel. Several Jews were also ppointed to high positions. Though anti-Jewish ropaganda was prevalent, it was not initiated by ne Court but by the Istiqlal Party which also ncouraged an economic boycott of the Jews folowing the *Six-Day War. After 1967 wealthier nd more educated Jews started to migrate from Iorocco to Israel, and by 1970 the Jewish comnunity there had dwindled to 35,000. By the nid-1980s it was down to about 15,000.

Unlike most of the other Arab states, Morocco id not break its diplomatic relations with the Federal Republic of Germany when Bonn estabshed relations with Israel in 1965. King Iassan's position was similar to that of President ourguiba of Tunis who sought a realistic policy nd a political settlement.

When the *Palestine Liberation Organization PLO) renewed its activities after the Six-Day Var, Hassan condemned the terror, but after 970, when the PLO started to promote the stablishment of an Arab-Jewish Palestine in hich Moslems, Christians and Jews would live n peace together, he granted it his recognition nd contributed an annual $14 million to its udget.

Morocco sent troops to fight in the *Six-Day Var, but they arrived too late to participate. In he *Yom Kippur War a Moroccan unit did take art in the fighting in the *Golan Heights.

A major change in Moroccan policy occurred n the mid-seventies. In 1975, according to forign reports, Israel assisted the King in his war ver the western Sahara. It was reported that sraeli military advisors trained Moroccan troops n anti-guerrilla warfare but these reports were ever officially confirmed in Israel. In October 976 Prime Minister *Yitzḥak Rabin paid a visit o Morocco incognito. Hassan, who was conerned about the growing extremism in the Arab vorld, hoped that as a result of this meeting with Rabin *Egypt and Saudi Arabia would become involved in a direct political process with Israel.

The relationship between Hassan and Rabin was cut short by the 1977 political *upheaval in Israel, but a slow process of normalization was initiated by Morocco, with the mediation of French diplomatic factors. A semiofficial visit to Morocco by the Chairman of the World Organization of North African Immigrants in Israel — Sha'ul Ben Simḥon — took place in the beginning of 1977. After the change of government in Israel, Foreign Minister Moshe *Dayan met, in September 1977, first with King Hassan, and then with Mohammad Hassan al-Tuheimi, the Deputy Prime Minister of Egypt — a meeting which began the Egyptian-Israeli peace process.

A visit by Prime Minister Menaḥem *Begin to Morocco, which was to have taken place in December 1977, did not materialize because Begin refused to come incognito. However, Shimon *Peres, as leader of the Opposition, met Hassan twice — once in the summer of 1978 after meeting Sadat in Vienna, and again in the summer of 1981.

As President of the Arab League, and as Chairman of the Quds (Jerusalem) Committee of the Islamic Organization of States, Hassan hosted many Arab summit conferences, including the 1974 *Rabat Conference and the one in 1982 which came up with the *Fez Plan. Under his auspices many meetings between Israeli and Arab personalities have taken place. In May 1984 the first delegation of Israeli Knesset members left for Morocco to participate in the first congress of Moroccan Jews, and as a result, *Syria broke off its relations with Morocco. One of the purposes of the moderate Moroccan policy was to obtain the support of the American Congress and public opinion, and influence the policy of the administration both with regard to the Sahara and economic aid. Since the mid-seventies Morocco has suffered from a serious economic crisis, resulting from the slump in the price of phosphates and the high cost of the war in western Sahara. In July 1986 Prime Minister Peres paid an official visit to Morocco, nine months after King Hassan had first expressed his willingness to meet with Peres officially. The purpose of the visit was to exchange views — not to negotiate. At the meeting King Hassan raised the Fez Plan, and the need for Israel to recognize the Palestinian right to self-determination, while Peres presented a ten-point document regarding Israel's conditions for a peace settlement. The meeting itself did not bring any major progress to the peace process, and was viewed in some Israeli circles as superfluous. The *Alignment presented the meeting as an important step in the establishment of an ongoing open dialogue between Israel and the more moderate Arab states.

moshav A form of agricultural settlement of which there are two types: the *moshav ovdim* — workers' settlement — and the *moshav shitufi* — cooperative settlement.

All *moshavim* combine elements of private and collective settlement. The idea was first developed during World War I. The *moshav ovdim* was based on the following principles: national land (See: *Land Policy); self-labor; mutual assistance; cooperative purchases and marketing. The family is the basic production unit in the *moshav ovdim* and each family works its own plot of land. From the beginning, the *moshav* was based on the idea of mixed farming. The first two *moshavim*, Nahalal and Kfar Yeḥezkel, were established in the Valley of Jezreel in 1921. By 1948 there were 58 *moshavei ovdim*. Many of the new immigrants who arrived in Israel during the 1950s were directed to new *moshavim* and by 1961 there were 346 *moshavim* with a total population of 120,000.

The idea of the *moshav shitufi* was developed to find a synthesis between the *kibbutz and the *moshav ovdim*. From the kibbutz the *moshav shitufi* adopted the principle of common production, but retained family life in separate units. The first two *moshavim shitufiyim* were established in 1936–37 — Kfar Ḥittin in the Lower Galilee and Moledet in the Ramat Issaschar region. In 1961 there were 20 *moshavim shitufiyim* with a population of 4,000.

The *moshav* movement, which is organized within the framework of the **Histadrut*, established a large number of organizations to serve the common needs of their members, as well as industrial enterprises to process their products. Since 1967 most *moshavim* have started to employ cheap Arab labor in the high season. The economic instability of the first half of the 1980s led to financial difficulties for many *moshavim* and their institutions. A further problem of many *moshavim* in recent years has been their inability to absorb all their sons and daughters into the community set-up. Today many *moshav* members are not engaged in agriculture and work outside the settlement.

In 1986 there were 405 *moshavei ovdim* with a population of 140,500 and 43 *moshavim shitufiyim* with a population of 9,000.

Mossad Short for *Hamossad Lemodi'in Vetafkidim Meyuḥadim*, the institution for intelligence and special tasks. Formerly *Hamossad Hamerkazi Lemodi'in Ulebitaḥon*, the central institution for intelligence and security. The body responsible for secret national activities outside the borders of the state, *Mossad*'s main spheres of responsibility are information collection on political, military and security issues; special operations, including intelligence warfare; research. According to the *Agranat Commission, the *Mossad* should also deal with intelligence evaluation based on the information which it collects.

The *Mossad* was founded in 1951, assuming the tasks of the Political Department in the Ministry for Foreign Affairs. The Head of the *Mossad* is directly subject to the Prime Minister. Among the *Mossad*'s best-known operations were the abduction of Adolf *Eichmann from *Argentina and liquidating all the persons responsible for the murder of the 11 Israeli athletes at the 1972 Olympic games in Munich. The *Mossad* was also responsible for the strong ties established with the Phalange in *Lebanon as of the mid-seventies. *Mossad*'s personnel and Heads are secret, and only after the term of service has ended is the name published. The *Mossad* was headed by Reuven Shilo'aḥ 1951–52, Isar Harel, 1952–63, Meir *Amit 1963–68, Zvi Zamir, 1968–74, and Yitzḥak Ḥofi, 1974–80.

N

Na'amat — Pioneer Women Voluntary women's organization. Na'amat is the women's section of the **Histadrut* which supplanted *Mo'etzet Hapo'alot* (the women's council) in 1976. Pioneer Women was established in New York in 1925, to provide social welfare services for women, young people and children in Palestine. Its original socialist-feminist ideology has since been much diluted, and in 1965 after decades of practical experience Pioneer Women became associated with Na'amat. Today the organization also has branches in several Latin American countries, Great Britain, France, Belgium, Canada, Australia, etc., and is associated with the *World Labor Zionist Movement. (See also: *Women in Politics).

National Committee of Arab Local Council Heads A committee established in 1974 by the Heads of the Arab local councils (See: *Local Government) in Israel to fight for equal treatment of Arab and Jewish settlements. As a result of the government's decision to confiscate lands in the Galilee for military purposes, in February 1976 the committee found itself in the status of representative of all the Arabs of Israel vis-à-vis the authorities. Following the first *Land Day of March 31, 1976, the committee adopted a line of protest and opposition on many issues, and became a lobby for Arab causes on the national level. The current head of the committee, Mayor of Shfar'am Ibrahim Nimr Hussein, has tried to steer the committee toward greater moderation.

The Arab settlements suffer from several special problems such as the absence of approved town planning schemes, the paucity of industrial enterprises, welfare services, and sources of employment and the inadequacy of public services. These problems create feelings of alienation and frustration, and have led the Arab MKs to join the committee (See: *Arabs of Israel).

(R.C.)

Nationalist Camp Slogan used by the **Likud* in the 1984 elections to the 11th Knesset to distinguish itself and all those opposed to any *territorial compromise in **Eretz Yisrael* from those parties advocating such compromise in return for true peace or on moral grounds.

National Religious Front The original name adopted by **Hamizraḥi* and **Hapo'el Hamizraḥi* when they united in 1956. In the course of the 3rd Knesset (1955–59) the party's name was changed to the *National Religious Party (NRP).

National Religious Party (NRP) Zionist-religious party established in 1956 when **Hamizraḥi* and **Hapo'el Hamizraḥi* united. The party is an inseparable part of the world federation of the two parties which strives for the revival of the Torah as a basis for the existence of the Jewish people. It recognizes the unity of the people of Israel and sees as its goal the continued cooperation of religious Zionism with all parts of the nation; the party promotes legislation which is based on the Torah and its laws; the party acts to preserve the religious character of the state in all aspects of its life, ensuring that religious services for the public and the individual are supplied as needed by state and local institutions.

Since its establishment the NRP has been a coalition partner in all the governments, traditionally holding the Ministries of the Interior and Religions. The NRP was responsible for much of the religious legislation in Israel and has caused numerous government crises over religious issues. For example, at the end of 1976 the NRP refused to vote with the government on a motion of no-confidence brought by **Agudat Yisrael* when an official ceremony connected with the arrival of new aircraft from the United States caused the desecration of the Sabbath. As a result, early elections were called for May 1977. After these elections the NRP joined the new **Likud*-led government thus breaking the *"historic coalition" which it had had first with **Mapai* and after with the *Alignment. In the *Likud*-led government of 1977–84 the NRP received the Ministry of Education as well as its traditionally held Ministries, but in the *National Unity Government, established in September 1984, it held only the portfolio of the Ministry of Religions.

The NRP is composed of a number of factions. Until 1970 the leading faction was headed by Ḥaim Moshe Shapira; after his death the leadership was taken over by Yosef *Burg and Yitzḥak Raphael, each of whom headed his own faction (*Lamifneh* and *Likud Utmurah*, respectively). Prior to the 1977 elections the faction of the younger generation (headed by Zvulun *Hammer and Yehuda Ben Me'ir) united with Burg's faction to depose Raphael. The internal upheaval which accompanied the end of the historic coalition with the Alignment caused major changes in the political position of the NRP in the direction of support for *Greater Israel and for **Gush Emunim*, as well as a more right-wing socio-economic position. Since the elections to the 9th Knesset (1977) the NRP party has become greatly weakened, partly because it has lost much of its uniqueness: the *Likud* and the **Teḥiyah* are much more right wing than the NRP, and *Agudat Yisrael* has become active in initiating religious legislation and changes in the *status quo for which the NRP and its predecessors had been previously largely responsible. Another reason for the weakening of the NRP was the establishment of **Tami* before the elections to the 10th Knesset (1981) by former NRP member Aharon *Abuḥatzeira who appealed to the Sephardi supporters of the NRP. The NRP also lost forces to **Morasha* which ran for election to the 11th Knesset (1984). In 1985 a committee was set up within the NRP to consider ways to rehabilitate the party. In June 1986 Rabbi Druckman and other members of *Morasha* who had left the NRP returned to its fold. In October 1986 Burg was replaced by Zvulun *Hammer as the NRP representative in the National Unity Government.

Knesset Seats: 3rd Knesset (1955) (under the title *National Religious Front) — 11; 4th Knesset (1959) — 12; 5th Knesset (1961) — 12; 6th Knesset (1965) — 11; 7th Knesset (1969) — 12; 8th Knesset (1973) — 10; 9th Knesset (1977) — 12; 10th Knesset (1981) — 6; 11th Knesset (1984) — 4. (Sh.M.)

National Unity Government A name for coalition governments in which both major political blocs, the *Alignment and the **Likud,* are members. By 1986 Israel had had four such governments (See: *Governments of Israel). In 1967, due to the crisis which erupted on the eve of the *Six-Day War **Gaḥal,* led by Menaḥem *Begin, joined Levi *Eshkol's Labor-led coalition. This coalition continued after the 1969 general election, and broke up in 1970 when *Gaḥal* left the government because the latter had accepted the *Rogers Plan which called for a withdrawal from territories occupied by Israel in June 1967. Following the 1984 elections to the 11th Knesset a National Unity Government was once again formed since neither of the two major political blocs were able to form a coalition without the other.

This government is based on parity between the two blocs, each of which has several smaller partners in the coalition. Parity in this context means that the government can act only if there is full consensus, or, in the absence of consensus, if one or more members of one bloc vote with the other. In 1984 it was agreed that the primary goals of the new government were to solve the economic crisis — especially the high rate of inflation and the balance of payments deficit — and to withdraw the *IDF from Lebanon.

The coalition agreement stipulated a rotation of the premiership, with Labor leader Shimon *Peres serving the first two years and **Ḥerut* leader Yitzḥak *Shamir serving for the second two years. The rotation agreement was effected in October 1986. The main issues on which the government is divided are Jewish settlement in Judea and Samaria (See: **Yosh*), and the manner in which the peace process with *Jordan and the *Palestinians should proceed.

While there is little disagreement about the fact that in 1984 the establishment of a National Unity Government was both desirable and unavoidable, many observers view its prolonged existence as endangering the Israeli parliamentary system, since the coalition is based on 97 out of the 120 Members of Knesset and the official opposition numbers only 23 Members (See *Knesset). In addition the principle of collective responsibility is greatly weakened in a national unity government and ministers have been known to criticize publicly the government's policy without being forced to resign as would normally be required under the principle of collective responsibility.

A third problem is that in addition to the two major blocs, which together command 81 Members of Knesset, there are five additional coalition partners (including the four religious parties) and thus one of the main advantages of a coalition between the two major blocs, namely, the ability to govern without giving in to small-party pressure, was lost.

Navon, Yitzḥak Labor politician, fifth President of Israel, born 1921 in Jerusalem.

Navon belongs to an established Sephardi family of prominent rabbinical lineage. He was educated in religious schools and at the Hebrew University secondary school and studied literature, Arabic, Islamic culture and education at the Hebrew University. In 1946–49 he headed the Arabic Department of the **Haganah* in Jerusalem and in 1949–51 served as a diplomat in Uruguay and *Argentina. Navon was Political Secretary to Foreign Minister Moshe *Sharett in 1951 and Chef de Cabinet in the Prime Minister's office nder David *Ben Gurion and Moshe *Sharett rom 1952–63. As Head of the Department of Culture in the Ministry of Education and Culture 1963–65), he directed the campaign to eradicate literacy, mobilizing hundreds of women soliers to teach adults in new settlements and evelopment towns. Elected to the Knesset on ne *Rafi list in 1965, he entered the *Israel Labor arty in 1968 when *Rafi* united with **Mapai* and *Aḥdut Ha'avodah-Po'alei Zion*. Navon was chairnan of the Foreign Affairs and Security Committe of the Knesset from 1974–77 and Chairman f the World Zionist Council from 1972–77. In pril 1978 Navon was elected President of the tate of Israel. He completed one term in 1983, nd considered contending for the Labor Party adership before the elections to the 11th Knesset (1984). Dissuaded from such a move, he was resented as the *Alignment's candidate for Minter for Foreign Affairs during the election camaign but upon the formation of the National Jnity Government Navon was appointed Deputy-Prime Minister and Minister of Education and Culture. In this capacity he has placed pecial emphasis on education for democracy, nd against racism and finding a synthesis etween Jewish and universal principles and alues.

Ne'eman, Yuval Member of Knesset and scientist. Born 1925, Tel Aviv. Ne'eman was a student at the Herzliya Gymnasium in Tel Aviv, tudied mechanical engineering at the Technion n Haifa and physics at the Imperial College in London. He completed his studies at the War College in Paris and received a PhD from the Jniversity of London.

Ne'eman joined the **Haganah* in 1940 and erved in the *War of Independence. From 952–54 he headed the Planning Department in he *IDF, and was Military Attaché in London, 958–60. He was a member of the Israeli Committee for Atomic Energy (1960–61) and in 961–63 served as scientific director of the tomic reactor in Dimona (See: *Nuclear Policy).

At the Technical Institute of the University of California, he was Research Fellow in 1963–64 nd Visiting Professor in Theoretical Physics in 964–65. During the following year he was a ellow at the International Institute of Theoretical Physics in Trieste. Ne'eman was Professor in he Department of Physics and Astronomy at the University of Tel Aviv in 1965–72, served as Deputy President of the University in 1965–66, and as President, 1971–75.

In 1975 he served as Senior Advisor at the Ministry of Defense, but resigned after the *Interim Agreement was signed with *Egypt because it required Israeli withdrawal from the Abu-Rudeis oil fields. In 1976–79 Ne'eman was involved in various research projects in the spheres of quantum gravity and the mathematical theory of supergroups and super algebras. He was chairman of the committee which investigated the various alternative courses for the Mediterranean-Dead Sea canal in 1978–80. In December 1980 he was appointed Chairman of the Mediterranean-Dead Sea canal project, which was dropped in 1985 for financial reasons.

Ne'eman has been Chairman of the **Teḥiyah* party since 1979, and a Member of Knesset since 1981. He served as Minister of Science and Development 1981–84, and at the same time served as Deputy Chairman of the joint Government-*World Zionist Organization Settlement Committee. Ne'eman is one of the most outspoken proponents of massive Jewish settlement in the *West Bank and *Gaza Strip and is strongly opposed to Israeli withdrawal from any territories occupied since 1967.

neo-Zionism A term used by several writers and political scientists in Israel and the US, but not by the alleged neo-Zionists themselves, to describe the new territorialist ideology which developed in Israel after the *Six-Day War when Israel occupied, *inter alia*, Judea, Samaria (See: **Yosh*) and the *Gaza Strip. Neo-Zionism is identified primarily with the *Land of Israel Movement, and **Gush Emunim*. While neo-Zionism has drawn from both right-wing and left-wing anti-partitionist ideologies (See: *Jabotinsky and *Tabenkin), it includes a religious element previously absent in these ideologies, and involves a reversal of the cultural identification with universal, liberal-humanistic principles.

The territorialism of neo-Zionism is closely connected with the idea of redemption, and those who profess the neo-Zionist ideology argue that Israel's rights to Judea and Samaria and to Jewish settlement in them are *sui generis* and cannot be judged by conventional political standards. Normal relations with other states, security issues and the striving for peace are subordinated to the mission of securing the Jewish state within its biblical borders. The notion of *territorial compromise, even in return for a peace settlement, is viewed as treasonous.

Unlike Rabbi Meir *Kahane, the neo-Zionists envision the full integration of the Arab population in the greater Israeli state provided they accept its predominantly Jewish character. The Jewish population will grow substantially through massive *aliyah* (immigration).

While the non-Zionist Orthodox establishment rejects the religious dogma of neo-Zionism, despite its Orthodox interpretation of Judaism, all the Zionist parties from the *Alignment and **Shinui* leftward reject its territorialism on both *Realpolitik* and moral grounds. Though some **Likud* members may be viewed as neo-Zionists the bloc as such, though strongly nationalistic and opposed to territorial compromise, cannot be understood in neo-Zionist terms.

neo-Zionists Unrelated to territorial **neo-Zionism*. In the last decade an increasing number of American Jewish leaders have insisted on calling themselves neo-Zionists (or new Zionists) by which they mean that they are fervent supporters of Israel and accept the principles of the *World Zionist Organization 1968 Jerusalem Program but do not feel it necessary to belong to a Zionist Federation. This trend has grown more evident since the Caesarea process was launched in 1981 (See: **Jewish Agency*).

Netivot Shalom Hebrew for Paths of Peace, *Netivot Shalom* is a moderate religious movement which emerged in the course of the *Lebanese War. Its founders included soldier-students from *Yeshivot Hesder*, as well as some prominent rabbinical figures. The assertion by *Netivot Shalom* regarding the primacy of peace and its critique of the messianic determinism of **Gush Emunim* and the fanatic chauvinism of Rabbi Me'ir *Kahane, derive from a religious rather than pragmatic perspective. The most widely publicized activities of *Netivot Shalom* have been its call for a commission of inquiry following the *Sabra and Shatilla massacres and its denunciation of the *Jewish Underground.

Netivot Shalom merged with **Oz Veshalom* in 1984. (M.B.)

Neturei Karta (Aramaic for Guardians of the City). A small group (centered in Jerusalem and in Brooklyn, New York) of extremely anti-Zionist ultra-orthodox Jews, who oppose th State of Israel and refuse to recognize its laws an to obey its authorities, their doctrine being tha only God can bring about the redemption of th Jewish people, and therefore any human effort i heretical. Thus *Neturei Karta* denounce religiou leaders, bodies or parties who are Zionists o cooperate with the state, and do not recognize th authority of the *Chief Rabbinate.

Regarding the *War of Independence as "godless" battle, *Neturei Karta* appealed to th British mandatory government to remain in Pal estine. They also attempted to contact the Arabs to surrender to their rule. *Neturei Karta* isolat themselves completely from the general commu nity; they maintain their own lawcourt, boycot all local and national elections, and refuse to pa taxes to the Israeli government; their sons an daughters refuse military service, taking advan tage of the general exemption granted to reli gious scholars. The Israeli government tolerate their activities — except when they disturb th public peace for example, attempting to preven Sabbath traffic by force.

New Zionist Organization A Zionist orga nization established by the *Revisionist Move ment, after it had broken away from the *Worl Zionist Organization (WZO) in 1935 followin the approval of a disciplinary clause by the Zion ist General Council which precluded indepen dent political activities by Zionist parties con trary to the official policy of the Zionis Organization.

Ze'ev *Jabotinsky was elected President of th new organization. The goals of the New Zionis Organization were declared at its first meeting i Vienna in September 1935, to be: "the redemp tion of the Jewish people and its land, the reviva of its state and language, and the implanting o the sacred treasures of Jewish tradition in Jewis life. These objectives to be attained by the cre ation of a Jewish majority in Palestine on bot sides of the Jordan, the upbuilding of a Jewis state on the basis of civil liberty and social justic in the spirit of Jewish tradition, the return t Zion of all who seek Zion, and the liquidation o the Jewish Dispersions. This aim transcends th interests of individuals, groups or classes."

The New Zionist Organization opposed th Peel Commission partition plan. Foreseeing tha a major catastrophe might befall the Jews i

Europe the organization called for a rapid evacuation of the Jews of Central and Eastern Europe in full and formal coordination with the governments concerned. Though this plan was not implemented, the New Zionist Organization played an active role in the "illegal" immigration movement to Palestine before and after the outbreak of World War II: (See: **Aliyah*).

In 1939 Jabotinsky called for a suspension of the struggle against the British for the duration of the war, the concentration of all efforts an defeating Nazi Germany, the creation of a Jewish army to fight alongside the Allies, and the creation of a Jewish World Council to represent the entire Jewish people at the peace conference which would follow the war. After the oubreak of war the New Zionist Organization continued to function in Jerusalem, London and New York, but upon Jabotinsky's death in August 1940 it lost its main driving force and no-one was elected to replace him. After the war the organization disbanded when the Revisionists rejoined the WZO.

Nili Hebrew acronym for *Netzaḥ Yisrael lo Yeshaker* ("the eternity of Israel will not lie"), *Nili* was a Jewish spy ring formed in Palestine in 1915 by the agronomist Aaron Aaronsohn (1876–1919) and Avraham Feinberg (1889–1917) to assist the British war effort by providing them with information on the Turkish and German troops in Palestine and other information of strategic value. *Nili* remained a small group made up predominantly of the sons of founders of the early Jewish settlements, and was vehemently opposed by **Hashomer* both ideologically and on personal grounds. The main reason for oppositon to *Nili* was fear of Turkish reprisals against the Jewish community should the ring be caught. Nevertheless, the official Jewish organizations used *Nili* to smuggle money into Palestine for the Jewish community. The ring was discovered toward the end of 1917. Two of its members, Na'aman Belkind (1889–1917) and Joseph Lishansky (1890–1917), were hanged by the Turks in Damascus. The legendary Sarah Aaronsohn (1890–1917), sister of Aaron, was tortured by the Turks and committed suicide without disclosing any secrets. Aaron Aaronsohn was killed in a plane crash during a flight from London to Paris in May 1919. The remains of Feinberg, who was shot near El-Arish in January 1917 by Bedouins while on the way to Egypt, were found buried under a palm tree in Rafa after the *Six-Day War and brought for final burial on Mount Herzl in Jerusalem.

non-Zionists Within the Israeli political system there are parties which are considered non-Zionist, i.e., parties which do not share the Zionist ideal and do not support its goals. In the 11th Knesset there are four such parties — two ultra-religious Jewish parties and two left-wing predominantly Arab parties. The two religious parties, **Agudat Yisrael* and **Shass*, object to Zionism as a secular movement, but give de facto recognition to the State of Israel. There is a minority within the ultra-religious Jewish community which does not even recognize the state (See: **Neturei Karta* and *Anti-Zionism). The two predominantly Arab non-Zionist parties are **Ḥadash* and the *Progressive List for Peace (PLP), both of which accept the Jewish reality of Israel but reject Zionism as a reactionary, imperialist ideology which obstructs the attainment of peace. There are Israeli Jews who support *Ḥadash* and the PLP, who view Israel as their home but reject Zionism as an ideology.

Until 1986 within the *Jewish Agency the "fund-raisers" who were not members of the *World Zionist Organization were referred to as non-Zionists. However, the 1986 Jewish Agency Assembly passed a resolution to enable the "fund-raisers" to be considered Zionists.

Norwegian Law In the 1950s and 1960s it was customary among members of Knesset appointed to ministerial posts to resign their Knesset seats upon entering the cabinet, thus enabling the next member on their party list to enter the Knesset in their place. This arrangement was especially common among the smaller parties which in this way increased their representation in the national institutions. One of the most persistent opponents of this custom in those years was the leader of the **Ḥerut* Movement, Menaḥem *Begin. Article 21(6) in the Basic Law: the Government (See: Basic Laws) which was proposed by Begin and adopted in 1968, stipulated that an MK who is also a minister would lose his seat in the cabinet if he resigned his Knesset seat. Begin's main argument in favor of this article was that the existing practice was a slight to the Knesset's honor since in a parliamentary democracy the Knesset is supposed to be above the government. Even though this provision could easily be circumvented (for example, by having the member resign his Knesset seat before being appointed to the government) since 1968 the practice has been discontinued. It should, however, be pointed out that except for the prime minister and deputy ministers, ministers do not have to be members of Knesset.

Since 1968 there have been proposals to revert to the pre-1968 system, and it has also been proposed that MKs who have resigned their Knesset seats when entering the cabinet should be allowed to regain their seats should they resign from the cabinet. The latter proposal has been supported by members from both the **Likud* and the *Alignment and is referred to as "the Norwegian Law" even though the arrangement in Norway is different from that proposed in Israel.

Following the elections to the 11th Knesset (1984) MK Michael Ḥarish (Alignment) has been at the head of the lobby to introduce the Norwegian Law in Israel. (A.D.)

nuclear policy Since 1965 Israel has adopted the cautious formula declaring that "it does not possess nuclear weapons and that it will not be the first to introduce them into the Middle East." This policy of deliberate ambiguity has survived various governments, suggesting a consensus on this issue between the *Alignment and the **Likud*.

While it is evident that Israel maintains a highly advanced scientific and technological nuclear infrastructure which could enable it to produce a nuclear military capability, there is no proof that it ever decided to do so. Periodically, the international media spread speculations regarding Israel's possession of nuclear weapons, but no solid and unequivocal evidence has ever been produced.

There are two nuclear reactors in Israel: one in Naḥal Sorek, an American-made 5MWth constructed in 1960, which is subject to international inspection; and a second in Dimona, constructed in 1957 with French assistance (See: *France and Israel) which is not subject to international inspection, and is reported to have, since 1964, the capability of producing sufficient plutonium for a military capacity. However, it is not verified whether Israel has a plutonium reproduction plant. In June 1974, following the signing of the *Disengagement Agreement with Egypt, President Nixon agreed to provide 600 MWth nuclear power reactors to both countries. The agreement was not implemented because of Israel's continued refusal to sign the Nuclear Non-Proliferation Treaty (NPT). In the course of 1985 Israel negotiated the purchase of a nuclear reactor from France for the production of electricity (See: *Energy Policy), but decided against the purchase for financial reasons.

Being in a permanent state of war with most of the Arab world, Israel maintains that it cannot afford to rely on NPT and the International Atomic Agency safeguards for its national security. The NPT does not provide for the possibility of carrying out special inspections on the basis of accusations or suspicion, and it allows each party, at any time, to openly declare its withdrawal from the treaty on three months' notice.

Israel declared at the *United Nations its willigness to negotiate a multilateral treaty, encompassing all nations of the Middle East, to establish a nuclear weapon-free zone in the region. The Israeli proposal called for the provision of "a contractual assurance of others' compliance with the commitment to abstain from introducing nuclear weapons into the region." However, the Israeli initiative was rejected by the Arab states. (See also: *Osiraq.)

In October 1986 an ex-employee of the Dimona nuclear reactor, Mordechai Vanunu divulged information and supplied photograph to the *Sunday Times* of London, which claimed that Israel was producing nuclear arms. Israel reacted by repeating its declared policy that it would not be the first state to introduce nuclear weapons into the Middle East.

Vanunu was brought back to Israel to face charges of espionage and other offences against the security of the state. (A.B.

O

occupied territories One of the terms used to refer to the territories occupied by Israel in the course of the *Six-Day War, and from which it has not, as yet, withdrawn. Israel, which ha applied its laws to the whole of *Jerusalem and the *Golan Heights no longer regards these territories as occupied.

Israel maintains that despite the fact that it has not annexed the occupied territories, the fourth Geneva Convention on occupied territories is not applicable to the territories occupied by Israel because of unresolved questions about their status from 1948 to 1967. Only *Great Britain and Pakistan recognized the Jordanian annexation of the *West Bank and *Egypt never annexed the *Gaza Strip. Nevertheless, Israel claims that it voluntarily undertakes to maintain the humanitarian rules included in the Geneva Convention. (See also: *Administered Territories).

Oded A movement established in 1962 in Paris by Moroccan Jewish students to reduce the social imbalance within the Moroccan Jewish community in Israel by encouraging the **aliyah* of students, intellectuals and professionals of Moroccan origin. The first group of 120 students came to Israel in 1964. In 1968 the movement's center was moved from Paris to Jerusalem and the next year there was an increase in the number of scholarships granted by *Oded* to students.

Among *Oded*'s early activities was the organization of voluntary help with school work to children of distressed neighborhoods — a pilot project later adopted by the relevant official authorities. Other projects included summer camps for underprivileged children, and vacations for mothers of large families.

A debate soon developed within *Oded* as to whether or not to enter politics. A few individual members joined **Mapam*, and a large group joined Yiga'el *Yadin's *Democratic Movement for Change which placed social problems high on the priorities scale. *Oded* objected to **Shinui*'s membership in the DMC because it viewed it as a liberal party too deeply concerned with civil rights and not sufficiently involved in social issues. In the 9th Knesset *Oded* was represented in the DMC by Mordechai Elgrabli. Following the party's disintegration Elgrabli tried unsuccessfully to be recognized as a separate faction so as to be able to obtain official funding to run in the elections to the 10th Knesset. He subsequently ran with Se'adiah Marziano, a member of the *Black Panthers, but they failed to pass the qualifying threshold.

Many members of *Oded*, including some who had earlier joined *Mapam*, were among the founders of **Tami* in 1981, though most of them were no longer active by the 1984 elections.

In the mid-seventies, *Oded* encouraged students of Moroccan origin who had grown up in Israel, to join the movement. One of its members, Eli Dayan, was elected Mayor of Ashkelon in 1978.

Altogether some 1,000 students came to Israel within the framework of *Oded*. It has not existed as on organized body since 1981.

Ometz Hebrew for "courage." A political group organized in 1984 before the 11th Knesset elections, around Yiga'el *Hurwitz, which called for its leader's appointment as Minister of Finance and a policy of economic austerity. *Ometz* gained a single seat and Hurwitz joined the *National Unity Government as Minister without Portfolio.

One Israel Knesset faction established by Yitzḥak Yitzḥaky who had been elected to the 9th Knesset (1977) as a member for Ariel *Sharon's party **Shlomzion*, after Sharon entered **Ḥerut*. Yitzḥaky ran in the elections to the 10th Knesset (1981) but did not pass the one percent qualifying threshold.

open bridges The term used for the network of ties which developed between *Jordan, the *West Bank and Israel by way of two bridges over the Jordan River — Allenby and Damia — when Moshe *Dayan was Minister of Defense. The system grew out of the circumstances created when hostilities ceased following the *Six-Day War. It started with Israel's tacit consent to agricultural produce being dispatched over the bridges. Over the years this became institutionalized, and is now the major factor permitting the continuation of a quasi-normal life on the West Bank. The possibility of crossing the Jordan River and returning, prevented the Palestinian community in the West Bank, and to a certain extent in the *Gaza Strip, from being cut off from Jordan and the rest of the Arab world.

The number of people crossing the bridges was approximately 300,000 per annum in 1976–78, and reached 380,000 in 1982. In addition, more than 100,000 visitors cross the bridges into the West Bank every year. The number of visitors inceases during the summer months, with the arrival of tens of thousands of West Bankers who work abroad.

The economic ties between the West Bank and the Arab world are important to the territories but have made no real contribution to the growth of the Palestinian sector of the West Bank, since the Isreli policy has been to maintain the economic status quo in this region and not to encourage development. The Israeli and Jordanian authorities, which have collaborated in institutionalizing the open bridges, have changed the terms of their relationship from time to time. The Israeli administration, aware of the importance of the ties to the Palestinians, has frequently prohibited the transfer of goods and people over the bridges as a means of collective punishment, involving various population groups.

The *Military Government has ruled that persons in their twenties and thirties who depart by way of the bridges may not return until nine months from their date of departure. This ruling is based both on security considerations and the unofficial policy of encouraging the emigration of Palestinians. A person who does not return within three years of departure loses his right to reside in the West Bank. A blacklist prevents the entry of "undesirables." The importation of packaged goods is prohibited for security reasons. Jordan also forbids the entry of "undesirables" to its territory, and in 1983–85 restricted young West Bank residents to visits of one month to discourage emigration. Jordan also restricts agricultural and industrial imports from the West Bank, though it is known that Israeli products do reach the Arab world through this avenue despite the *Arab boycott.

From time to time the closing of the bridges has been advocated on both sides, but the advantages of keeping them open have always outweighed the disadvantages. (M.B.)

Operation Jonathan See: *Entebbe Operation.

Operation Moses See: *Ethiopian Jews.

Operation Peace for the Galilee See: *Lebanese War.

"Oriental" Jews See: **Edot Mizraḥ*.

Osiraq Operation On Sunday, June 7, 1981, the Israel Air force attacked the nearly completed nuclear reactor Osiraq constructed by the French near Baghdad, and destroyed it. According to the Iraqis the reactor was to have been used for purely scientific purposes. Israel argued that even though Iraq had signed the non-proliferation treaty the Iraqis were intending to use the ne reactor for military purposes, and Israel would b the obvious target for Iraqi constructed nucle weapons. Israel had made several abortiv attempts to dissuade *France from selling th reactor to Iraq, and other states from selling i nuclear knowhow and materials.

The operation was deliberately carried out o Sunday when all the foreigners working on th site were away. The Israeli Government claime that since the reactor was to become operative i July or September, June was the last chance t destroy the installation without causing radioac tive fallout.

The *Alignment, which approved of the oper ation in principle, claimed that Menaḥem *Begi had decided to carry it out in the beginning c June as an election ploy (elections to the 10t Knesset were to take place that month) Begi claimed that he had chosen to carry out the opera tion before the elections because he did nc believe that Shimon *Peres, if elected, woul carry it out, and Begin viewed the reactor as a rea and immediate threat to Israel.

While officially Israel's operation wa strongly condemned and criticized internation ally as an irresponsible act, unofficially man states sympathized with the Israeli move, agree ing that a nuclear capability in the hands of a extremist regime like Iraq was a danger not onl to Israel but to the entire world.

Oz Veshalom Hebrew for "Strength an Peace." A moderate, anti-territorialist ideologica forum which was founded in 1971 within th *National Religious Party and which becam autonomous in 1975.

Oz Veshalom advocates a tolerant, moderate an pluralistic attitude on questions related to reli gion and state, religious - secular relations, gen eral culture, science, humanistic values and th status of women. Regarding the *Arab-Israe conflict it advocates a peace settlement based o territorial compromise, to prevent Israeli rul over an Arab population which would ultimatel entail a moral decline in Israeli society. Contrar to **Gush Emunim* it denies that a contradictio exists between the *Halacha* and *territorial com promise.

Through publishing articles and organizin public meetings the movement has sought t spread its credo in opposition to that of th national-religious extremists. The group, which is made up primarily of academics and intellectuals, joined forces in 1984 with the more broadly based *Netivot Shalom* movement.

P

Pa'il (formerly Pilavsky), **Me'ir** Military commander, historian and politician. Born 1926, Jerusalem.

Pa'il volunteered for the **Palmaḥ* in 1943 and served as Deputy Battalion Commander and Operations Officer in the Staff of the Negev Brigade during the *War of Independence. He remained in the *IDF on staff, training and instruction assignments until 1971 when he retired as Colonel. In 1974 he received a PhD in history from Tel Aviv University for a thesis on the emergence of the Israeli military system from the pre-state Zionist underground.

Pa'il became a member of **Mapam* in 1948 and left in 1969 when *Mapam* joined the *Alignment. After that he was active in the Movement for Peace and Security. He was elected to the 8th Knesset a the only member of **Moked* and the 9th Knesset as a member of **Maḥaneh Sheli*, resigning his seat in 1980 under the party's rotation agreement. Pa'il remained in *Sheli* until the party disintegrated at the beginning of 1983. Since 1984 he has been the Academic Director of the Defense Forces' Historical Research Center at Efal — the United Kibbutz Movement's Seminar. Among other associations, he is a member of the *Israeli Council for Israeli-Palestinian Peace.

Palestine Name of geographical area along the Mediterranean in the Middle East bordered by *Lebanon in the north and the *Sinai in the south, whose eastern boundary is in dispute. There has never been an independent state by the name of Palestine. The name *Palaestina* was first used by the Romans, replacing the name *Judea* after the suppression of the last Jewish rebellion of 132–135 CE.

Under Roman-Byzantine rule the area was divided into three administrative units: *Palaestina Prima*, which included Judea, Samaria and the southern part of the eastern Jordan Valley; *Palaestina Secunda*, embracing the Valley of Jezreel, central and eastern Galilee, the *Golan Heights and the northern part of the eastern Jordan Valley; and *Palestina Tertia* — southern *Transjordan, the Negev, and the Sinai Desert.

Under Arab Muslim rule, this administrative division was basically preserved. *Palaestina Prima* became, more or less, *Jund Filastin, Palaestina Secunda* and the western Galilee became *Jund Urdun. Jund Filastin* existed until the Mongol invasion, although in the tenth century its territory increased, extending to Amman in the east and the Gulf of Aqaba in the south. In the course of the 12th and 13th centuries the term *Filastin* went out of use. The term Palestine was used, however, in the 19th century in Europe in reference to the Holy Land, and applied to both the west and east banks of the *Jordan River.

The Mandate of Palestine, which Britain started to administer in 1920, included not only the territories of present-day Israel, the *West Bank and the *Gaza Strip, but that of the Kingdom of Jordan as well. Since Transjordan was broken off administratively from Palestine west of the *Jordan River in 1922 the term Palestine has been used to refer to western Palestine only.

In Israel it is customary to equate the name Palestine with the Hebrew name **Eretz Yisrael*, which historically included both the West Bank and the East Bank of the Jordan River.

In 1950 King Abdullah of Jordan considered calling his kingdom, including the annexed West Bank, Palestine, but finally refrained from doing so for political reasons.

In the *Palestine National Covenant it is not clear whether the term Palestine is restricted to Western Palestine only or whether it includes Jordan as well. The *Palestine Liberation Organization (PLO) itself is vague on the issue, though the emblems of some of its component organizations include maps showing Palestine to include the whole territory of *mandatory Palestine.

Palestine Liberation Organization (PLO) The PLO is an umbrella organization, established in 1964, which claims to represent the Palestinian people (See: *Palestinians) both under Israeli rule and in exile, and has set as its main goal the liberation of Palestine from Israeli occupation. According to the charter of the PLO (See:

*Palestine National Covenant) the lands to be liberated include those of pre-*Six-Day War Israel as well, though at various times and under certain conditions, some elements within the PLO have implied that they would be content to retrieve the *West Bank and the *Gaza Strip only. The predominant view within the PLO is, however, that in the long run Palestine, as a "secular, democratic state" should include the territory of Israel, and that the mini-state in the West Bank and Gaza is but a first step in that direction.

BACKGROUND: Organized Palestinian opposition to the Jewish National Home began to crystallize in the early 1920s. The Arab Executive Committee, and then the British-inspired Supreme Muslim Council, headed by the Mufti of Jerusalem Hadj Amin al-Husseini, were, in a sense, the precursors of the PLO. In 1936 the Muslim Council was replaced by the Higher Arab Committee, a step which united the urban-merchant notables with the rural farmers. During the late 1930s, the Palestinian Arabs stepped up their violence against the Jewish presence and development in Palestine, though after 1937 when the Mufti was expelled from Palestine by the British the local leadership of the Palestinians was much weakened. The establishment of the State of Israel in 1948 resulted in the exile, voluntary or enforced, of over 500,000 Arabs from the territory of Israel, most of whom went to neighboring Arab countries where they were lodged in refugee camps, becoming recipients of *United Nations aid through UNRWA (See: *Refugees). In most Arab countries they were not allowed to integrate into the local population or gain local citizenship. Perpetuation of their refugee status was adopted by the Arab governments as a major policy decision in their conflict with Israel. Thus, the *Arab-Israel conflict, which had originated as an Arab protest against Jewish immigration and settlement in Palestine, and later developed into an effort to prevent the establishment of a Jewish State there and, once established, to destroy it, turned into a self-perpetuating conflict in which the plight of the Palestinian refugees became a pawn.

The loss of part of Palestine to the Jews on the one hand, and the dispersion of the Palestinians and their leadership on the other, undermined the authority of the traditional Palestinian leaders, including Hadj Amin al-Husseini. In th 1950s President of Egypt Gamal Abdel Nasse helped organize groups of *Feda'iyin (Arabic fc "suicide squads") in the *Gaza Strip which bega launching attacks on Israel. These *Feda'iyin* wer soon joined by *West Bank Palestinians. Afte the *Sinai Campaign, however, there followed period of relative tranquility.

1964–69: The formation of the PLO wa approved in 1964 by the first Arab Summit. It wa meant to be a tame instrument of Arab foreig policy, insofar as it was to organize the Palestini ans militarily and politically in the service of th Arab struggle against Israel. Aḥmed Shukeiri, veteran mercenary-diplomat of Palestinian ori gins, was appointed as the head of the new orga nization, but since the recruiting for the Palestin ian Liberation Army (PLA) among th Palestinian refugees at this time was subject t special approval by the government involved, n authentic link existed between Shuqeiri and th masses of Palestinians.

The Six-Day War and resulting occupation b Israel of the West Bank and Gaza Strip resulted i over 1.5 million Palestinians (including th 500,000 *Arabs of Israel) living under Israel' effective control. The new situation gave th PLO a new lease on life, also changing its basi *modus operandi*. Yasser Arafat, an El-Arish bor student of engineering at Cairo University o Palestinian origin, took the lead of the *Fatah*, new major component of the PLO founded i 1965, which advocated armed struggle. Arafa went to the masses in the camps and called o them to take their destiny into their own hands Following the battle of Karameh of March 1968 in which *Fatah* claimed a victory over invadin Israeli troops which had crossed into Jordan t clear terrorist bases, Arafat consolidated hi power and assured the *Fatah*'s predominanc within the PLO, of which he becam Chairman.

However, the *Fatah*'s central position did nc remain unchallenged. In 1966 a radical revolu tionary group, the Popular Front for the Libera tion of Palestine (PFLP) headed by Georg Habash, was founded. In 1969 Nayif Hawatme broke off from the PFLP and established an eve more radical group — the Democratic Front fo the Liberation of Palestine.

Disillusioned by the defeat of the Arab armie

in 1967, these various groups launched attacks on Israel independently, trying to keep the revolutionary zeal alive. Their main base was *Jordan where they established in effect a state-within-a-state, jeopardizing the authority of the Hashemite crown. The *Fatah* launched a *War of Attrition along the Jordan Valley, which took a heavy toll both in Israel and, following massive Israeli relatiatory acts, among the Jordanian-Palestinian population as well. The other groups, supported by the *Fatah*, specialized in pure terrorist acts such hijackings, taking of hostages, and bombing of civilian targets.

The differences between the *Fatah* and the more radical organizations were not only in their respective modes of struggle, but involved their long-term strategies as well. The radicals viewed the attainment of a socio-political revolution in the entire Arab world as a prerequisite for the liberation of Palestine. They stressed the need to interfere in the military and political affairs of the reactionary monarchies of the Arab world, such as those in Jordan, Morocco, Kuwait and Saudi Arabia, so as to hasten the onset of revolution there. Furthermore, they viewed armed struggle as the only means of attaining these goals, by arousing the masses of the Palestinian people, though this did not preclude the development of political cadres in order to educate and indoctrinate them in preparation for the revolution. The more moderate *Fatah*, on the other hand, did not rule out political means to achieve the revolutionary goals of the movement, though not as a substitute for the armed struggle. *Fatah* also stressed the need for national independence as a solid base for launching the struggle for Arab unity. By cultivating a policy of noninterference in the internal affairs of Arab countries it obtained diplomatic and financial support from some of the Arab oil-producing countries, as well as wide support among the Palestinians in exile, many of whom were employed by the Arab reactionary monarchies. In 1971 the radical splinter groups were taken into the PLO, thus justifying the PLO leadership's claim that it represented a broad Palestinian consensus.

1970–82: By the end of the 1960s the PLO had built numerous military and political bases in the refugee camps in Jordan from which it conducted both its guerrilla activities against Israel and its world-wide terrorist acts against Israeli institutions, individuals and interests. Israel's open bridges policy, which allowed a loosely controlled to-and-fro movement between the West Bank and Jordan, facilitated the PLO's strengthening its grip on the West Bank Palestinians both on a voluntary basis and by means of coercion. During 1970 Hussein faced serious internal problems resulting in clashes with the Palestinians. After a second assassination attempt, the King moved against the PLO in September 1970. His armies vanquished many PLO fighters, while most of the rest escaped to *Lebanon via Syria whose armies had invaded Jordan on September 19th. Ironically there were some who crossed over to the West Bank for protection. "Black September," as it became known, engendered a terrorist organization by the name, which became a major *Fatah* arm both against Israel (it was responsible for the murder of the 11 Israeli athletes in Munich in 1972) and the Jordanian regime (it was responsible for gunning down Jordanian premier Wasfi Tal).

Though the *Yom Kippur War was viewed by the Arabs as an Israeli setback, the *Disengagement Agreement and *Interim Agreement signed between Israel and Egypt, led to the PLO's being cast aside together with the other members of the "Rejectionist Front."

Nevertheless, the PLO achieved some prominence in the Arab and international arenas as a result of the Rabat Arab Summit of October 1974 which recognized it as the sole legitimate representative of the Palestinians, and of Arafat's invitation to speak at the UN General Assembly in November. The PLO's diplomatic offensive, which was regarded by the Arab rejectionists as a sign of weakness, was coupled with a sustained effort of the PLO to rebuild its bases in Lebanon and to prepare a new military, social and political infrastructure. Already in the late 1960s, when the *Fatah* became predominant in the PLO paramilitary training, political propaganda, mass mobilization and arms stockpiling took place in the Palestinian refugee camps in Lebanon. In face of the weakness of the Lebanese government and its inability to arrest the development of Palestinian power, by the early 1970s the PLO had built a state-within-a-state in Lebanon, with its own military and administrative services. The PLO had, in effect, taken control of large tracts of Lebanese territory, especially in and around refugee camps and in the southern part of the country, called "Fatahland," at the foot of Mount Hermon. The Cairo Agreement of 1969 had attempted to resolve the early clashes between the Lebanese Army and the Palestinian guerrilla groups by legitimizing the latter's presence in southern Lebanon and their activities against Israel from that territory. But the PLO was also aware of the necessity to build a strong military force, in order to maintain its hegemony in southern Lebanon, and to be prepared to fight official and unofficial Lebanese armies in order to retain its position there.

A long string of skirmishes, negotiations and compromises occurred during the years 1970–77, but the situation remained unstable. When open clashes broke out in Sidon in April 1975 between the PLO and Christian Lebanese forces, it soon spread to the rest of Lebanon. The Christians launched a counterattack against the PLO, and in August 1976 conquered Tel al-Zaatar, the PLO stronghold in Beirut, killing a large number of Palestinians in the process. However, the PLO, supported by the Muslims in Lebanon, continued to rule West Beirut and most of South Lebanon. In September 1976, the Syrians entered Lebanon on the side of the Christians and together they launched an operation against the PLO which resulted in Palestinian military collapse. However, in October 1976 the Riyadh Summit decreed another cease-fire which restored the 1975 status quo while invoking the Cairo Agreement to curtail PLO activities inside Lebanon and permitting them to channel their terrorist activities against Israel. In 1977 the level of violence again escalated into a full-fledged war between the PLO and the Christians, only by this time Syria had switched sides and aligned itself with the PLO. After 1977 the PLO had a free hand to reinforce its bases and forces in southern Lebanon without incurring any risk or restriction on the part of the now non-existent Lebanese army. Indeed, after Tel al-Zaatar the PLO shifted its attention from Beirut to the South again, with the active aid of the Lebanese Muslims and some leftist elements such as the local Communist party and the pro-Iraqi Ba'ath Party, both of which were strongly entrenched in Tyre, Sidon and Shi'ite villages. PLO activities from Lebanon against Israel mounted, reaching a climax on March 11, 1978 when an Israeli civilian bus driving along the Coastal Road, was intercepted and most of its passengers murdered by PLO terrorists who had arrived from the sea. In retaliation the Israeli Army launched its *Litani Operation four days later with the intention of destroying PLO bases in southern Lebanon and occupying territory up to the Litani River.

Upon Israel's withdrawal the UN Interim Forces in Lebanon (UNIFIL) were posted in southern Lebanon with the task of, *inter alia*, stopping a renewed PLO takeover, but soon proved unable to perform this task. Consequently, in 1979, Israel adopted a policy of bombing PLO bases in southern Lebanon — a policy which had little effect upon PLO activities against Israel. Furthermore, the PLO consolidated its hold on large areas of Beirut and other coastal cities in Lebanon which became logistic centers, equipment and ammunition depots, training bases for infantry and naval forces, supply ports and launching grounds for terrorist missions against Israel and Israeli and Jewish targets abroad. In the South alone some 6,000 PLO members were encamped in dozens of different locations, 700 of them within UNIFIL territory. They openly operated jeeps, mortars and artillery, including 130mm Russian-made guns, 155mm French-made guns and Katyusha rockets of all calibers.

At the beginning of 1980 the PLO sent its elite Ein Jalut Brigade to southern Lebanon, and introduced large quantities of tanks, thus posing a direct challenge to Israel's northern settlements, PLO acts of terror against Israel continued unabated, including heavy shelling of some Israeli villages and towns, and attempts to land in Israel from the sea. Israel reacted by bombing, strafing and mounting commando attacks on selected targets within PLO-held territory. In July, 1981, following a particularly intensive exchange of fire between the PLO and Israel, a cease-fire was arranged under UN auspices. However, while the cease-fire was more or less kept along the Lebanese-Israeli border the PLO pursued its terrorist activity against Israeli targets elsewhere. Israel reacted with a series of air raids in April-June 1982, and following the attempt on the life of Israeli Ambassador to London, Shlomo Argov, launched its Operation Peace for the Galilee (See: *Lebanese War) on June 6, which inaugurated a new phase in the destiny of the PLO. In the first stage of the war the Palestinian troops were pushed by the Israeli thrust into their strongly defended bases in West Beirut, from whence their 15,000 troops were finally forced out and scattered in several Arab countries in the Middle East and North Africa.

SINCE 1982: When the PLO's main base was transferred to Lebanon in 1970, the organization struggled to improve the military cooperation between its various groups so as to circumvent the political and ideological differences which had plagued its unity. In 1971 the PLO formed a new Executive Committee numbering 15 representatives from the major guerrilla groups, though the *Fatah* retained the lead. By incorporating the radical organizations, Arafat was forced to adopt more radical views as far as its terrorist activities were concerned, but he scored a huge success in asmuch as he could present a united front of all PLO organizations under one command, and he did in effect even exercise some restraint on the splinter groups: the PFLP, the PFLP General Command (headed by Ahmed Jibril), the DFLP, the Palestinian Liberation Front (headed by Tala'at Yacoub), and Abu Nidal's *Fatah* Revolutionary Council. However, from 1977 onward, following President Sadat's peace initiative and the ensuing *Camp David Accords and *Egyptian-Israeli Peace Treaty both of which left the Palestinian question unresolved, the PLO turned to the radical rejectionist Arab states. This was, at least in part, the background for the escalation of PLO activities which had climaxed in the 1981–82 events, and Israel's incursion into Lebanon.

Israel's policy, under Minister of Defense Ariel *Sharon, was not only to destroy the PLO's infrastructure in southern Lebanon, but also to expel the PLO from Lebanon altogether. This, it was believed, would weaken the PLO's Muslim allies and enhance the Christian militias and their hold over the country. Sharon hoped that the destruction of the PLO in Lebanon would convince the Palestinians in the West Bank and Gaza Strip to come to terms with Israel on a permanent settlement along the lines of the *Autonomy Plan and the *Jordan is Palestine idea (i.e., that a national homeland for the Palestinians could exist within the territory of Jordan). The Lebanese War was the first time that the whole array of PLO forces faced Israel in battle. The siege of Beirut which led to the exodus of the PLO from the Lebanese capital, lasted for over two months. However, though Arafat presented the safe exit of his men as a victory of sorts, he soon found himself once again at the mercy of Arab leaders. As he stepped up his relations with Egypt and Jordan, even though both had expressed support for the *Reagan Plan of September 1982 which called for a Palestinian entity associated with Jordan, the pro-Syrian groups within the PLO revolted. Bolstered by Syria, a PLO faction headed by Abu Musa broke away from Arafat's majority and set out to dislodge his supporters from their strongholds in Northern Lebanon. The battles, which culminated in Tripoli (Lebanon) in 1983, resulted in Arafat's second exodus from Lebanon, this time at the hands of the Syrians. He has since been banned from *Syria. Arafat then subscribed to the February 17, 1986, Amman Declaration which implied his acceptance of *Security Council Resolutions 242 and 338 and also renounced terror (he was later to argue that this applied to areas outside Israel and the occupied territories). However, unwilling or unable to enforce this policy within the PLO, Arafat did nothing until King Hussein announced in the spring of 1986 the invalidation of that declaration.

In the meantime the PLO continued its terrorist activities against Israel and other western states, despite Arafat's public denial of his sponsorship of or connection to most of them. In addition to Abu Musa's group, which numbered some 5,000 fighters, all based in Syria, new terrorist groups sprang up following the Lebanese debacle: the Popular Struggle Front (headed by Dr. Ghousha) and the Palestine Liberation Front (headed by Abu Abbas) which split from the anti-Arafat Tala'at Yacoub faction. Larger anti-Arafat coalitions also came into being: the Democratic Alliance (1983) which is critical of the PLO Chairman on a personal level although it renounces terrorism outside Israel and the occupied territories, and the Palestine National Salvation Front (1985), an anti-Arafat umbrella organization based in Damascus. The latter rejects any talks with Israel, but would accept a reduced Palestinian state in the West Bank and Gaza Strip as a first step toward full Palestinian self-determination.

In retaliation to PLO-inspired acts of terrorism, especially the murder of three Israeli tourists on their yacht in Larnaca, Cyprus, Israel bombed the PLO headquarters in Tunisia in October, 1985. American efforts to get talks going between Israel and King Hussein and non-PLO Palestinians with the PLO's tacit consent, led nowhere, principally due to Arafat's inability to publicly accept the Security Council Resolutions 242 and 338. This has resulted in a new impasse. Abu Za'im, one of Arafat's lieutenants in Jordan, rebelled in the spring of 1986 and declared his loyalty to King Hussein and his support for Jordan's more moderate position. Thus, Arafat finds himself overtaken on the Left by Abu Musa and Syria, and on the Right by Abu Za'im and Jordan, while he himself is no longer able to hold the middle ground and finds himself increasingly isolated, with very little ability to maneuver.

(R.I.)

ISRAEL'S OFFICIAL POLICY VIS-À-VIS THE PLO: While Israel recognized in the Camp David Accords the Palestinians' legitimate rights (which are viewed by some political parties as the right to self-government in the form of an autonomy, by some as the right to self-determination within a Jordanian-Palestinian State, and by others as the right to self-determination in a separate state) no Israeli government has ever been willing to recognize the PLO as the legitimate spokesman of the Palestinian people, or to negotiate with it. Among the Israeli parties from the Liberal Party and toward the Right there is an unwillingness even to recognize the nationhood of the Palestinians, as opposed to their being part of the Arab nation. The *Alignment which recognized the Palestinians as a people (Shimon *Peres made a declaration to that effect at the Labor Party Conference in April 1986), will not deal with the PLO because of its refusal to amend its charter, to accept Security Council Resolutions 242 and 338, to openly recognize Israel, and to give up terrorism.

Israel's policy vis-à-vis the wave of terror which began at the end of the 1960s, was to refrain from any contact or the carrying out of any sort of negotiations with the organizations or individuals responsible for it. The official policy has been to try to release hostages held by the terrorists without any negotiations — direct or indirect. However, on several occasions contacts have been made with representatives of the PLO and other Palestinian organizations, as over the release of the three Israeli soldiers held by Jibril's organization from 1982 to 1985, after Israel was convinced of the danger to them and of its inability to bring about their release by force or diplomacy.

Israel has carried out, with various degrees of intensity, a policy of hitting at the organizations and individuals responsible for specific acts of terror. Thus for example, all the individuals responsible for the murder of 11 Israeli sportsmen at the Munich Olympics in 1972 were eventually eliminated, and in 1985 the Israel Air Force attacked the headquarters of the PLO's Force 17 in Tunis for its involvement in the murder of the three Israelis in Larnaca.

Israel's policy has been to convince countries friendly to it not to recognize the PLO, not to meet with its leaders and to refrain from accepting the demand for the establishment of a separate Palestinian state in the West Bank and Gaza. While many Israeli political leaders realize that acts of terror will continue as long as the Palestinian problem is not satisfactorily resolved, and are thus concerned with finding a solution to the problem simultaneously with the fight against the terror, some believe that it can be dealt with on a purely military basis.

As long as acts of terror continue, Israel's alertness to the possibility of such acts taking place in Israel and abroad is extremely high, with extensive precautionary measures being constantly taken. Israel's intelligence services, which have reached a high level of proficiency in preventing acts of terror or catching those responsible in the event of their taking place, closely cooperate with the services of other countries dealing with the problem of terror who are willing to cooperate with them.

Both **Ḥadash* and the *Progressive List for Peace (whose leaders have met Arafat) call for Israel's recognition of the PLO as the sole spokesman of the Palestinian people. The Arab members of Knesset from **Mapam* and the *Israel Labor Party call for direct negotiations with the PLO (Abdel Wahab Darawsha from the Israel Labor Party had tried to visit Amman at the end of November 1984 to participate in the Palestinian National Council meeting there). Until August 1986 some Jewish members of *Mapam* and the Civil Rights Movement, as well as Labor

Party moderates met with prominent members of the PLO believed to be willing to recognize Israel.

In August 1986 the Knesset passed an amendment to the "Prevention of Terror" law which prohibits meetings between Israelis and members of the PLO, unless authorized by the government. The amendment was passed as part of a deal between the Alignment and the *Likud* under which the *Likud* supported the amendment to the Penal Code regarding racial incitement in return for the Alignment's support of this amendment. Though a majority in Israel objects to contacts with the PLO as currently constituted, many have criticized the new law for interfering with individual freedom. It has been argued that harmful meetings with members of the PLO could have been dealt with within the framework of the law even before the new amendment was passed.

(S.H.R.)

Palestine National Covenant Also known as the "Palestine Charter." The first version of the covenant was adopted by the *Palestine Liberation Organization (PLO) in its first conference in 1964, its basic principle being the elimination of Israel and the establishment of an Arab-Palestinian state in the whole of Palestine.

The covenant was redrafted as a more articulate and clear document by the Palestine National Council at its conference in Cairo in July 1968. The 1968 version of the covenant rejects the partition of Palestine which "with the boundaries it had during the British mandate (it is not clear whether this definition of Palestine does or does not include Transjordan — See: *Palestine) is an indivisible territorial unit" (Article 2) and "the homeland of the Arab Palestinian people" (Article 1). Only the Jews who "resided in Palestine until the beginning of the Zionist invasion" (Article 6) are to be recognized as Palestinians (the date of the "invasion," too, is unclear). Palestine will be liberated by armed struggle (Article 9) with "commando action" (i.e., terror) constituting "the nucleus of the Palestinian popular liberation war" (Article 10), the aim of which is "the elimination of *Zionism in Palestine" (Article 15) — Zionism being defined as "an illegitimate movement" the existence of which should be outlawed and the operations of which banned (Article 23).

Article 20 of the covenant rejects any Jewish rights in Palestine: "The *Balfour Declaration, the Mandate for Palestine and everything that has been based upon them, are deemed null and void. Claims of historical or religious ties of Jews with Palestine are incompatible with the facts of history and the true conception of what constitutes statehood. Judaism, being a religion, is not an independent nationality. Nor do Jews constitute a single nation with an identity of its own; they are citizens of the states to which they belong." Article 21 rejects any compromise: "The Arab Palestinian people, expressing themselves by the armed Palestinian revolution, reject all solutions which are substitutes for the total liberation of Palestine and reject all proposals aiming at the liquidation of the Palestinian problem, or its internationalization." Israel has argued that the Palestine National Covenant reflects the true intentions of the PLO and therefore the organization is not acceptable as a negotiating partner. While some PLO spokesmen have argued in return that the covenant is nothing but "a piece of paper," the organization has refused to change a single word in it.

Palestinians Arabs who resided in the territory of *mandatory Palestine until the end of the British mandate in 1948. Following the first Arab-Israel war (1948–49) the Palestinians became dispersed primarily throughout the Middle East. As of 1986 the Palestinian people numbered over 4 million, of whom close to 1.5 million lived in the *West Bank and *Gaza Strip, which have been under Israeli control since the *Six-Day War. There are 700,000 Palestinians who constitute a national minority living within the State of Israel (See *Arabs of Israel). The remainder live in various Arab countries, with the largest concentrations being in *Jordan (over 1 million), *Lebanon (about 200,000) and the Gulf States (about 300,000). Smaller Palestinian communities are to be found in other Arab states. Tens of thousands of Palestinians have emigrated, on an individual basis, to countries outside the region, especially in North and Latin America and western Europe, and in several western countries there is a beginning of Palestinian communal development. The overwhelming majority of Palestinians are Moslems, the remainder Christians. The ancestors of some of them came to Palestine over the ages from North

Africa, Sudan and Yemen, though the majority are probably indigenous.

The growth of a national consciousness within the intellectual elite of the Arabs in Palestine was part of the Arab national awakening in the Fertile Crescent districts of the Ottoman Empire toward the end of the 19th century and the beginning of the 20th. Palestine was a desolate and backward territory within the larger region, and its place within the awakening Arab national movement was, consequently, only marginal at first. The members of the political elite of *Jerusalem, which enjoyed a certain amount of self-government within the Ottoman Empire, were inclined to support the Osmanic (pro-Ottoman) stream among the Arabs. However, in the course of World War I, and especially after the defeat and dismemberment of the Ottoman Empire, the Arab national stream gained the upper hand over its Osmanic and traditional Islamic rivals, and won wide-scale public support. At the same time the Arab political elite in Palestine became worried by the inflow of a new type of Jewish immigrant and the development of the Zionist enterprise which it suspected of harboring political ambitions which could undermine the Arab character of the country. As early as 1891 the Moslem and Christian communal leaders in the Jerusalem district demanded that the central Ottoman government prohibit the Jews from immigrating to Palestine and from purchasing land. Until World War I several Arab organizations were formed in Palestine in order to organize the public to an anti-Zionist awareness. Indeed, the Zionist challenge to the "Arabness" of Palestine made a strong impact on the national movement of the Palestinian Arabs.

After the conquest of Palestine by the British forces in 1917–18, the Zionist danger assumed even greater proportions in the eyes of the Palestinian Arab community, especially since the *Balfour Declaration was understood by Arabs and Jews alike as a promise to establish a Jewish state in Palestine immediately. In the course of 1918 the Palestinian Arabs expressed their fears through the formation of various associations to struggle against the establishment of a Jewish state.

At the end of 1918 the Palestinian Arabs confronted a major dilemma, to be repeated periodically over the coming decades: whether to view themselves as a separate and unique national entity, or as an integral part of a more comprehensive Arab national framework. In November 1918 the governments of *Great Britain and *France announced their recognition of the right of the people of *Syria and Iraq to establish governments which would draw their authority from popular support. Palestine was deliberately left out of the announcement, and in January 1919 the Palestinian Arabs convened their first congress which declared that Palestine was Southern Syria, and that the only way to push Zionism out of Palestine was by means of a union with the Feisal regime in Damascus.

The feelings of anger and frustration of the Palestinian Arabs in face of the determination of the British government in Palestine to base its policy on the Balfour Declaration, manifested themselves in mass demonstrations and violent attacks by Arabs on Jews in Jerusalem and other places in April 1920. However, after a British civilian government was established in Palestine in the middle of 1920, and a French mandate was imposed in Syria following the expulsion of Feisal and his men from Damascus, the dream of Greater Syrian unity collapsed, and the Palestinian Arabs, whose sense of uniqueness grew, started to concentrate their efforts on stultifying the Zionist policy of the British government.

Part of this struggle involved the refusal to participate in Arab administrative bodies proposed by the British authorities in 1922–23, even though several dignitaries, especially the then Mayor of Jerusalem Ragheb al-Nashashibi, were inclined to cooperate with the British mandatory authorities. Against this background a radical nationalist stream started to develop under the leadership of the al-Husseini family, the most prominent member of which was Hadj Amin al-Husseini, Mufti of Jerualem and President of the Supreme Moslem Council. Under the inspiration of Hadj Amin the religious confrontation around the status of the Western (Wailing) Wall and Jewish rights there turned in 1928–29 into an active national confrontation, accompanied by attacks on Jewish settlements and communities and, after 1934, clashes with the British security forces as well. These clashes escalated into a general Arab revolt which broke out in the spring of 1936, inspired by the impressive political achievements of the Arab national movements in

Egypt, Iraq and Syria; the accelerated development of the *Yishuv in Palestine; and the rejection by the British Parliament of the idea of establishing a Legislative Council in Palestine in which the numerical superiority of the Palestinian Arabs would be given expression.

A general strike was declared with the demand to stop Jewish immigration, to prohibit the sale of land to Jews and to establish a national government. The strike was accompanied by violent acts against isolated Jewish neighborhoods and settlements, gradually assuming a more daring character with attacks on British army units and police stations throughout the country. The revolt lasted for three years, but even in its early stages cracks appeared in the united Palestinian Arab front regarding the partition recommendations of the Peel Commission. To the violence against the Jews and British was added internal violence among Arabs which greatly weakened the effectiveness of the revolt and general strike. The banishment of Hadj Amin and some of his colleagues in 1937 also contributed to the revolt's failure, and the intervention of the Arab governments was required to bring it to an honorable end. From then on the involvement of the neighboring Arab states in the affairs of Palestine and the fate of the Palestinians progressively increased.

The May 1939 White Paper issued on the eve of the outbreak of World War II, put an end to the previous pro-Zionist policy of Britain by limiting Jewish immigration and land purchases. It was a significant achievement for the Palestinians, but the Higher Arab Committee in exile rejected it, insisting on an "all or nothing" policy which was to prove catastrophic for the Palestinians while strengthening the Zionists.

The decision of Hadj Amin and his colleagues to support the Axis during World War II, especially in the sphere of propaganda and the mobilization of Moslem support, further increased the involvement of the Arab states in the struggle of the Palestinian Arabs. The main task of the Higher Arab Committee, reconstituted in Palestine in the summer of 1946 by the Arab League, was to ensure that the Arab states did not make any concessions on the Palestine question, and immediately after the UN General Assembly voted in favor of the *partition plan in November 1947 it rejected the proposal for an Arab state in part of Palestine, declaring war against the *Yishuv*. The Arab League put money, arms and volunteers at the disposal of the Palestinians, placed political and economic pressure on the western powers not to support the Jews, and deployed the regular armies of the Arab states along the borders of Palestine. However, in the course of February and March 1948, the irregular Palestinian forces were defeated by the Jewish forces, resulting in the collapse of the Palestinian political community, the mass exodus of Palestinian Arabs and the direct involvement of the Arab armies in the war immediately following the British withdrawal in May 1948. The intervention of the Arab states in the war failed to tip the balance in favor of the Arabs and even increased the perceived dimensions of the defeat. (See also: *War of Independence and *Arab-Israel Conflict.) The total collapse of the Arab political community in Palestine led to the transfer of the Palestinian issue to the custody of the Arab states — especially Egypt and Jordan where it was dealt with primarily as a refugee problem.

While Egypt viewed the Gaza Strip which it now controlled but did not annex, as a temporary guardianship which, under suitable circumstances, must be returned to the Palestinian Arabs, Jordan sought to permanently integrate the *West Bank which the Arab Legion and Iraqi forces had occupied, into the Hashemite Kingdom of Jordan. In reaction to the establishment in Gaza of the Egyptian-inspired but short-lived "all-Palestine Government," the Jordanians called a Palestinian convention in Jerusalem in December 1948 which granted legitimization to the absorption of the West Bank into the Kingdom of Jordan. "The unity of the two banks" (of the Jordan River) was officially announced after a unanimous vote by the two houses of the Jordanian Parliament on April 24, 1950.

Throughout the 1950s and 1960s Jordan served, to all intents and purposes, as an alternative to the Palestinian state which had failed to emerge in 1948. The Palestinian Arabs who had remained in Israel became Israeli citizens, though until 1965 they were subject to a special *Military Administration. The Palestinian people as a whole ceased to function as a unified political community, and many of its members remained without any citizenship or national status symbols.

The Palestinian Arabs, dispersed and separated, set all their hopes in those years on a military victory by the Arab states over the State of Israel, which would give them back their country and rights.

Many young Palestinians were drawn to the banner of Pan-Arabism which was popular at that time in the Arab world. However, the decline of Pan-Arabism in the early 1960s restored a separate Palestinian consciousness among groups and individuals in the diaspora, and led to the establishment of the underground *Fatah* movement under the leadership of Yasser Arafat. This movement strove, *inter alia*, to put an end to the custodianship of the Arab states over the Palestine issue, and to attain "independent decision."

The first Arab summit conference in Cairo, in January 1964, decided to establish the *Palestine Liberation Organization (PLO) as a tangible expression of the Palestinian entity, though the resolution under which the new organization was established was so drafted as to leave control and supervision over it in the hands of the Arab governments. The selection of the lawyer Ahmed Shukeiri, who more than any other Palestinian personality represented Palestinian submissiveness to the Arab custodianship, fortified this resolution, as did the exclusion of the *Fatah* organization. Israel's crushing victory in the *Six-Day War led not only to the military collapse of the Arab armies and the Israeli occupation of areas which had previously been under Egyptian, Jordanian or Syrian control, but also to the collapse of the PLO establishment under Shukeiri. A new focus on the Palestinian problem resulted from Israel's control over more than a million Palestinians in the West Bank and Gaza Strip.

A renewed PLO, different in organization, structure, personnel, social makeup and political content, was established in 1968 under the leadership of *Fatah* Chairman Yasser Arafat, with a covenant which was stronger and more uncompromising than the covenant drawn up in 1964 (See: *Palestine National Covenant). The organization mounted a campaign of terrorist attacks against Israel and Israeli targets abroad, and concentrated its efforts on gaining international recognition for itself and drawing attention to the Palestinian problem as a national rather than a refugee problem. It reached the peak of its success in 1974 when Yasser Arafat was invited to address the UN General Assembly and the PLO was granted observer status in the UN. In recent years the PLO, which was established to carry out an armed struggle for the liberation of Palestine and which had rejected the concept of conciliation and compromise with Israel, has started to consider a political course of action, such as attempts to cooperate with Jordan, to establish a dialogue with Israelis associated with the *peace camp. The former did not prove durable, the latter has very little support in Israel. However, due to the increased influence of the more radical elements within the organization all the opening moves of the PLO political initiatives have been ambivalent and indecisive. (Yo.A.

While the Palestinians have started to inch their way toward a political solution of their problem, Israel's refusal to negotiate with the PLO, or to accept the Palestinians' right to establish a separate state in the West Bank and Gaza Strip, has remained absolute. Though Israel has rejected the PLO it has not given any other Palestinian elements in the occupied territories — whether pro-Jordanian or independent — a chance to develop an alternative leadership, and has prohibited all political organization in the West Bank and Gaza Strip. There are several Palestinian Organizations which have withdrawn from the PLO or have developed outside of it which continue to reject any means other than the armed struggle. These organizations are part of what is known as the rejectionist front and are supported by the Arab governments, especially those of Syria and Libya, which reject the peace process.

Though it is impossible to tell just how much support the PLO has among the Palestinians inside the occupied territories and elsewhere (a public opinion poll published in *El Fajr* in September 1986 suggests that the PLO enjoys overwhelming support, but it is difficult to evaluate the poll's accuracy) there is no doubt that a majority of the Palestinians view it as the sole representative of the Palestinian people and a symbol of the Palestinian national struggle, even though they are not members of the organization and do not plan an active role in the struggle.

The PLO's main achievement has been to bring back to the world's attention the existence of a Palestinian people seeking self-determination. Its main failures have been in achiev ing a unified policy line, both regarding goals and means, and in setting realistic short-term goals and sticking to them, failures which the PLO holds in common with previous leaders of the Palestinians.

ISRAEL'S POLICY TOWARD THE PALESTINIANS: Throughout the mandatory period the Zionist organization and since 1948 the Israeli government, have usually regarded the Palestinians as part of the Arab nation rather than a separate nation or people. This position enabled Israel to claim that the Palestinians are not entitled to national self-determination since the Arab nation already has a large number of states (in 1986, 23 states were members of the Arab League), while the Jews have only one state and that in only part of their historical homeland in which Palestinian Arabs can live as a minority. On the other hand an approach developed which stated that Palestine embraces the whole of mandatory Palestine, including Transjordan, and that the Palestinians are the Arabs living both on the West and East banks of the *Jordan River. This positon enables those who believe in the *Jordanian option and the *"Jordan is Palestine" concept to argue that Palestinian self-determination is realized in Transjordan, or should be realized in a Jordanian-Palestinian state embracing the East Bank and parts of the West Bank and Gaza Strip. In fact, the *Jewish Agency recognized the right of the Palestinian Arabs to an independent state when it accepted the 1947 partition plan. However, the Israeli government argued after the War of Independence that the Palestinians had not taken advantage of the opportunity offered them, and through their own policy of "all or nothing" had lost their chance to establish a state west of the Jordan River. In the *Camp David Accords Israel recognized the "legitimate rights of the Palestinians," which each party in Israel interpreted in accordance with its own ideology.

Menaḥem *Begin viewed the *autonomy plan which he proposed as satisfying these rights. Today four Israeli parties — **Ḥadash*, the *Progressive List for Peace, **Mapam* and the *Civil Rights Movement — recognize the Palestinian right to self-determination, though only the first two interpret this right to mean a separate Palestinian state in the West Bank and Gaza Strip. Shimon *Peres announced in March 1979 that the *Israel Labor Party recognized the legitimate rights of the Palestinians and in April 1986 announced that the "Palestinians are a people," a fact denied by Golda *Meir when she was Prime Minister. In August 1986 an effort by the left-wing members of the Labor party to achieve formal party recognition of the Palestinian right to national self-determination failed to pass the party's central committee. Of the Israeli parties only **Kach* advocates the expulsion of the Palestinian Arabs from Israel, while the **Teḥiyah* advocates encouraging them to leave. (S.H.R.)

Palmaḥ "Striking force" of the **Haganah*, the *Palmaḥ* was established in 1941 under the command of Yitzḥak Sadeh (1890–1952) as a full-time military force of volunteers, to meet the danger of a German and Italian invasion. In the spring of 1942, a joint Jewish-British program was adopted to form sabotage and guerrilla units partly with the help of British instructors. Nevertheless, for want of funds, only six companies were formed in the first year; volunteers stayed in their homes and trained only a few days a month. In 1945, when Sadeh was promoted to Acting Chief of the *Haganah* Yigal *Allon replaced him as Commander of the *Palmaḥ*.

With the passing of the danger, the *Palmaḥ* became the principal force of the *Haganah*, in the struggle against the mandatory government. The financial problem was solved by an arrangement, under which the enlisted lived in *kibbutz settlements where they financed a fortnight of training by a fortnight of work. This combination became the *Palmaḥ* symbol — two sheaves and a sword.

Prior to the *War of Independence, the *Palmaḥ* numbered 3,000 men in 15 companies forming four battalions. One of the battalions comprised special units: naval, air and reconnaissance. The *Palmaḥ* was the elite unit of the *Haganah*, with a high level of training and operational capability. In the first, local guerrilla stage of the war, the *Palmaḥ* was the force that provided protection for the Jewish community while it was gearing itself for full-scale war. But afterward also, when organized into three brigades, it played a decisive role in the Israeli victory.

The *Palmaḥ* was disbanded in October 1948, following a decision of David *Ben Gurion that no unit in the new state's army would retain its separate command. Opponents of the disbandment claimed that this was done in order to wipe off the influence of the *_Mapam_ party and its leftist kibbutz movement. The values of the _Palmaḥ_ and the principles on which it was based served as an example to _Naḥal_ (Pioneering and Fighting Youth), which still forms a part of the *IDF (Israel Defense Forces).

Parties in Israel The parties in Israel are an extremely heterogeneous group of political entities. Their multiplicity derives from the *electoral system, and Israel's highly complicated social and historical background.

Several of Israel's parties and political blocs have roots in the pre-state *_Yishuv_ or Zionist organization (See: *World Zionist Organization). This is reflected in their ideology and historic frame of reference. One cannot, for example, understand the complicated relations which exist today between the *Alignment and the *_Likud_ without going back to the pre-state relations between *_Mapai_ and the *IZL and *_Leḥi_ (from which *_Ḥerut_ emerged). The various metamorphoses of the *National Religious Party (NRP) and *_Agudat Yisrael_ must also be taken into account in order to understand their political positions today.

There are also parties whose emergence is recent, reflecting current developments in Israeli society and politics. For example, the *Democratic Movement for Change (DMC) came into being in 1977 against the background of Labor's decline and the public's discontent with the existing system. *_Tami_ emerged in 1981 and *_Shass_ in 1984 because of the feelings of discrimination of the Jews who came from Moslem countries, particularly the Moroccan community. On the whole, these types of parties, some of which have had a meteoric success, vanished from the Israel political map after only one or two *Knesset terms.

Among the parties there are some which have a complete ideology and _Weltanschauung_ with platforms which deal with several issues — political, security, social and economic. These include parties such as the *Israel Labor Party, *_Mapam_, _Ḥerut_ and *_Ḥadash_. Others are one-issue parties, such as _Agudat Yisrael_ whose concerns are mainly religious (though its Knesset members are highly involved in financial issues) and the *_Teḥiyah_ whose _raison d'être_ is to hasten new and to prevent evacuation of existing Jewish settlements in Judea, Samaria (See: *_Yosh_) and the *Gaza Strip. Many one-issue lists run for each Knesset election but fail to pass the one percent qualifying threshold.

Another typological division is between heterogenous "catchall" parties, which appeal to voters from all walks of life and communities, as has been the case with _Mapai_ and later the Israel Labor Party, and homogeneous sectarian parties which appeal to a very specific public, such as _Agudat Yisrael_.

Though powerful personalities have dominated most Israeli parties at one time or another (for example, David *Ben Gurion in _Mapai_, and Menaḥem *Begin in _Ḥerut_ and the _Likud_) the more established parties have survived without these personalities. On the other hand there have been many one-member parties, or parties whose main appeal was the personality of their leader, such as Uri *Avneri's *_Ha'olam Hazeh — Ko'aḥ Ḥadash_ in 1965, Ben Gurion *State List in 1969, Ariel *Sharon's *_Shlomzion_ in 1977, Moshe *Dayan's *_Telem_ in 1981, Ezer *Weizman's *_Yaḥad_ and Yiga'el *Hurwitz's *_Ometz_ in 1984. Despite the popularity and charisma of some of these personalities these lists have never gained more than a handful of Knesset seats.

A division can also be made between Zionist and non-Zionist parties. Despite wide ideological differences the Zionist parties all maintain that Israel offers the only solution to the Jewish problem and that Jews from the Diaspora should be continuously encouraged to immigrate to the Jewish state which is the homeland of all Jews. The non-Zionist parties include *_Ḥadash_ and the *Progressive List for Peace, both of them mixed Arab-Jewish lists which accept the Jewish state as a _fait accompli_ but do not accept the Zionist ideology, and _Agudat Yisrael_ and _Shass_ which are both ultra-Orthodox religious parties. Unlike *_Neturei Karta_, the latter accept the State of Israel as a fact and benefit from cooperation with it; they nevertheless reject the secularism of mainstream Zionism and the activist nationalism of such religious parties as the *National Religious Party and *_Morasha_.

Some Israeli parties have split from existing parties due to ideological and personal differences. Thus *_Aḥdut Ha'avodah — Po'alei Zion_ broke from _Mapam_ in 1954 and *_Rafi_ from _Mapai_ in 1965.

While the general trend in Israeli politics has been toward fragmentation, there have been several attempts to group into larger blocs. The two successful efforts were the establishment of *Gahal in 1965 which became *Likud* in 1973, and the incremental construction of the *Alignment starting in 1965. Efforts to get the four religious parties to run as a single list in the 1984 elections were unsuccessful. Attempts are being made to unite the left-wing Zionist parties, groups and individuals into a single list before the elections to the 12th Knesset, and similar efforts are being made in the political Center.

One of the goals of those who call for *electoral reform in Israel is to encourage the establishment of larger political blocs, though the prospects of reaching a two-party system are dim due to the nature of Israeli society.

partition One of the solutions proposed in mandatory times to the contradictory claims made by the Jews and Arabs over Palestine, was that of partition.

The first *de facto* partition of *mandatory Palestine occurred in 1922 when the area of *Transjordan, constituting 74 percent of the territory of the mandate, was separated administratively from the rest of Palestine and handed over to the Emir Abdullah.

The first partition plan for western Palestine was proposed in 1932 by the Zionist representative in Geneva, Victor Jacobson, but was never seriously discussed.

In 1937 the Peel Commisssion proposed the partition of Palestine into a Jewish state, an Arab state and a British mandatory zone as a practical solution to the Palestinian problem. The small Jewish state was to have included the coastal region from a point south of Jaffa northward, and the Galilee. The British zone was to have included the holy cities of *Jerusalem and Bethlehem, an enclave connecting them to Jaffa and to the port of Haifa, and the Arab towns of Lydda and Ramleh. The rest of Palestine, together with Transjordan, was to have constituted an Arab state. This proposal was rejected by the Arabs but accepted by the 1937 Zionist Congress as a basis for discussions.

However, the Woodhead Commission, sent to Palestine in 1938 to further investigate partition, suggested three possible alternative plans, each of which would have further decreased the territories of the Jewish and Arab states to the benefit of the British zone. The British government finally rejected the whole idea as impracticable.

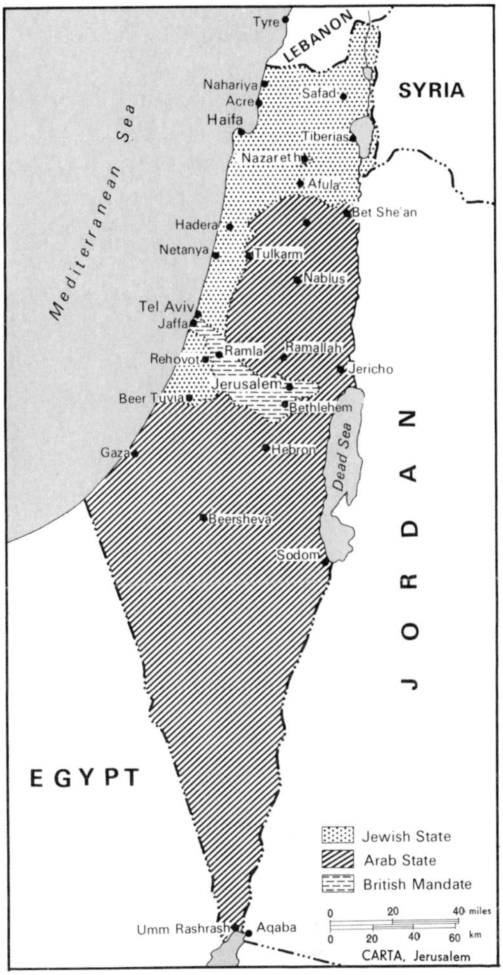

The Peel Commission partition plan, 1937.

Partition was again proposed by the 1947 United Nations Special Committee on Palestine (UNSCOP). This plan, approved by the UN General Assembly on November 29, 1947, advocated the establishment of a Jewish state which included the coastal plane from near Ashkelon to Acre, the eastern Galilee and a certain area to its south and much of the Negev. The Arab state was to include the rest, except for Jerusalem, which was to be internationalized. While the plan was welcomed with mixed feelings by the Jews, it was rejected out of hand by the Palestinians and

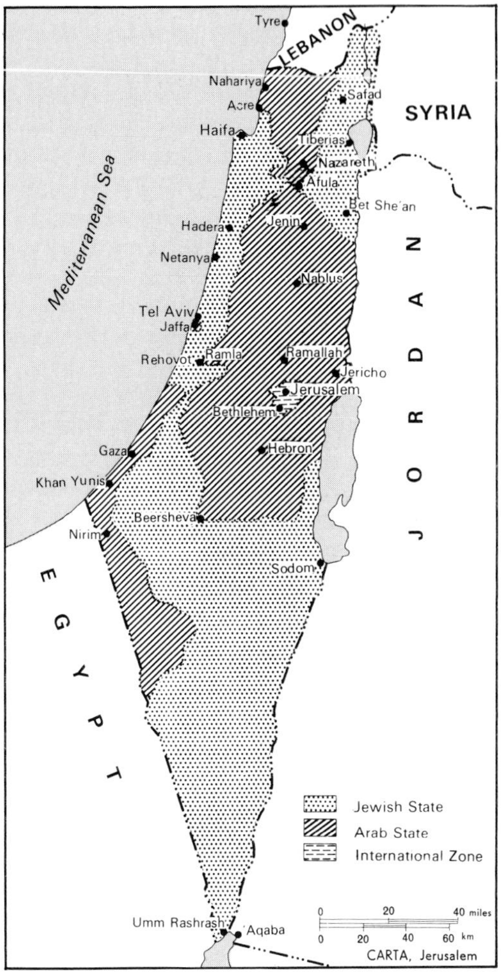

Palestine: the Jewish and Arab states according to the 1947 UN resolution.

the Arab states. When the British mandate ended on May 15, 1948 and the Jewish state was proclaimed on the basis of the UN resolution, the Arab armies invaded the Jewish state (See: *War of Independence). When the armistice lines were finally drawn in the 1949 *Armistice Agreements the Jewish state was somewhat larger than foreseen by the UN, while what remained of the Arab territory was divided between *Jordan and *Egypt and no Palestinian state was set up. In the *Six-Day War Israel gained control over the remainder of western Palestine. The political parties in Israel from the Center to the Right have rejected any repartition of the country even in return for peace, arguing that the only acceptable partition was that of 1922. The remainder of the parties, from the *Alignment leftward, are all in favor of returning occupied territories in return for peace and security. Some, like **Ḥadash* and the *Progressive List for Peace, advocate complete Israeli withdrawal to the Green Line and the establishment of a Palestinian state abutting both Israel and Jordan. Others, like the *Israel Labor Party call for certain changes in the old border (See: *Allon Plan) and the establishment of a single Jordanian-Palestinian state.

It is claimed that moderates in the *Palestine Liberation Organization (PLO) would now be willing to accept the principle of partition — i.e., a Jewish state and a Palestinian state adjacent to one another in western Palestine. This, however, has never been officially declared by the PLO.

party key The distribution of benefits and resources among parties on the basis of a certain agreed scale. In the **Yishuv* in mandatory times the party key served as a yardstick for the activities of the political bodies in all spheres: for the distribution of immigration certificates, for determining the order by which pioneering core groups (*garinim*) would be assigned land for settlement, for the allocation of funding to the various streams of education and to the housing budgets, for determining the composition of *Youth Aliyah groups, and even in forming the queue for "illegal" immigration. This arrangement contributed to peaceful coexistence among most of the political forces within the *Yishuv* at a time when there was no national coercive force in existence. The only group which felt it was discriminated against under this system was the *Revisionists. This system continued to exist after the establishment of the state, ensuring that the distribution of political forces in the country remained relatively stable for many years despite the demographic changes brought about by the mass immigration of the fifties. It also helped to preserve the predominance of the various sections of the Labor movement — a predominance which was lost only in 1977 with the political *upheaval. (D.B.M.)

Pathways to Peace See: *Netivot Shalom.

peace camp A loose term used to describe all the individuals, groups and parties in Israel, Zionist and non-Zionist, who since 1967 have advocated Israel's placing the furtherance of peace at the top of its national agenda, and have favored giving up territories in return for peace.

The camp includes Marxists, democratic socialists and liberal intellectuals. Unlike its European couterpart, the Israeli peace camp, strongly rooted in the realities of the *Arab-Israel conflict, is not pacifist, and is not a priori concerned with disarmament and nuclear weapons.

All sections of the peace camp reject the exclusivity of both Jewish and Arab claims to **Eretz Yisrael*, believing that Palestinians and Jews can coexist in the area as long as the national rights of both are mutually recognized and arguing that rigidity in both camps has so far prevented a peaceful solution.

Only a handful of individuals in the peace camp advocates *bi-nationalism (one state with two nations), and only the Communists and *Progressive List for Peace advocate the establishment of a "third state" — i.e., a Palestinian state composed of the *West Bank and the *Gaza Strip. The others propose a solution to the Palestinian problem based on a system of ties between Jordan, the West Bank and the Gaza Strip. Some advocate complete Israeli withdrawal from the territories occupied by Israel in 1967 while others would accept minor modifications in the pre-Six-Day War Israeli borders.

While all sections of the camp reject the official Israeli attitude that the *Palestine Liberation Organization (PLO) cannot be a partner to negotiations, some recognize the PLO as the only legitimate representative of the Palestinian people, while others recognize it as one of the Palestinian spokesmen. While some are willing to have contacts with the PLO unconditionally others are willing to have contacts only with members of the PLO who explicitly recognize Israel's right to exist.

The peace camp unanimously rejects the amendment to the "Prevention of Terror" law passed by the *Knesset in August 1986 which makes unauthorized meetings with membes of the PLO a punishable offence.

Peace Now Hebrew name: *Shalom Achshav*. Extra-parliamentary, non-partisan, peace movement established in the spring of 1978 when 350 army reserve officers addressed a letter to Prime Minister Menaḥem *Begin urging him to pursue the road to peace. The movement was extremely active and constituted a strong interest group pressuring the government toward peace negotiations with rallies, demonstrations, letters and meetings.

After the peace treaty with Egypt was signed, Peace Now concentrated its activities on keeping the peace process at the forefront of the public agenda, and urging the government not to miss any opportunity to try to further it. Peace Now considers the continued occupation of the *West Bank and *Gaza Strip as inconsistent with the objective of peace. It proposes five basic guidelines for negotiations, which include the principles of territorial partition in which each side will compromise on its historic rights; recognition of Israel's right to a sovereign existence within secure and mutually recognized boundaries; Isrel's recognition of the right of the Palestinian people to a national existence; the need for arrangements which will cater for Israel's security needs without major territorial adjustments; the indivisibility of Jerusalem as the capital of Israel with provisions for all the various religious and national interests in the city.

Peace Now was in the forefront of the protest against the *Lebanese War and was the central force behind the mass demonstration in Tel Aviv on September 25, 1982, following the massacre in *Sabra and Shatilla. The movement advocates a redefinition of Israel's priorities and is involved in the campaign for democracy and tolerance.

Though it is not a pacifist movement and is patriotic in its outlook, Peace Now is a target for animosity by the Israeli Right which accuses it of defeatism — even treason. The predominantly Ashkenazi and university-educated active membership of the movement has been unsuccessful in rallying the masses to its cause. On February 10, 1983, during a demonstration which called on the government to implement the recommendations of the *Kahan Commission, Peace Now activist Emil Grunzweig was killed by a grenade thrown into the crowd. The murder, which shook most sections of the political spectrum, drew attention to the growing danger of violence in Israeli society.

Peace Now decided against independent participation in the 1984 election. Most of its members voted for the *Alignment, **Shinui* and the *Civil Rights Movement.

Pe'ilei Eretz Yisrael Hashlemah Hebrew for Activists for the Greater Land of Israel. The name was adopted by **Tnu'at Ha'avodah Lema'an*

Eretz Yisrael Hashlemah after joining the *Likud* and receiving one seat in the 8th Knesset (1973). In 1976 the movement was one of the founding members of *La'am.*

Peled (formerly Hifland), **Mattitiyahu** Military commander and politician, born 1923, Haifa. After finishing school in Jerusalem Peled joined the *Palmaḥ* in 1941 and in 1946–47 went to London to study law. Returning to Israel at the outbreak of the *War of Independence, Peled commanded the convoys to the besieged settlements in the Jerusalem area and was severely wounded in the Yo'av operation to liberate the Negev, almost losing his eyesight. He served in the General Staff in 1949 and was subsequently sent to a course for staff officers in Great Britain and in 1953 was among the founders of the IDF Staff and Command College in which he served as Chief Instructor. At the end of the *Sinai Campaign Peled served as Commander of the Shlomo region, and Military Governor of Gaza. He became Commander of the Jerusalem district in 1957, returning to the General Staff in 1959. Following his studies for a BA in Oriental Studies at the Hebrew University, he was appointed assistant to the Deputy Minister of Defense on rearmament. In 1964 Peled, now a Brigadier General, headed the supplies branch within the General Staff and introduced far-reaching reforms. He became increasingly critical of the fact that the gains of the *Six-Day War had not been utilized to start a peace process and he resigned from active service in 1969. In 1971 he completed a PhD in Arabic literature at UCLA, subsequently becoming a lecturer in Arabic literature at Tel Aviv University. Moving progressively to the Left, he declined to join the *Alignment or Uri *Avneri's list. In 1975 Peled joined *Ya'ad* and was one of the founders of the *Israel Council for Israeli-Palestinian Peace. He was one of the founders of *Maḥaneh Sheli* in 1977 and partially responsible for its breaking up over the *Lebanese War. One of the leaders of "Alternative" which joined in the foundation of the *Progressive List for Peace in 1984, Peled was elected to serve on its behalf in the 11th Knesset. Peled is highly critical of the *IDF and believes that its deterioration began when Ḥaim *Bar Lev was Chief of Staff. He has met *Palestine Liberation Organization (PLO) Chairman Yasser Arafat and other PLO leaders, and believes that Israel has not been forthcoming even though the PLO made some conciliatory moves. While Yitzḥak *Rabin was Prime Minster he reported to him on these meetings. He does not distinguish between guerrilla warfare and conventional warfare. He views himself as a "peace-camp Zionist." In the 11th Knesset, Peled has been more active than any other member in the plenary.

Peres (formerly Perski), **Shimon** *Israel Labor Party leader and 9th Prime Minister of Israel. Born 1923, Poland. Peres immigrated to Palestine with his family in 1934 and was educated at the Geula school in Tel Aviv and the Ben Shemen agricultural school. One of the founders of kibbutz Alumot in 1940, he was elected Secretary of the *Hano'ar Ha'oved* youth movement in 1943.

Peres started working with David *Ben Gurion and Levi *Eshkol at *Haganah* headquarters in 1947 and continued to serve them after the establishment of the state. In 1949 he was appointed Head of the Defense Ministry delegation sent to the United States for the purpose of arms procurement.

He became Deputy Director-General of the Ministry of Defense in 1952 and Director-General the following year, in which capacity he established close ties with *France and promoted the development of Israel's aircraft industry. He was first elected to the *Knesset in 1959 and was appointed Deputy Minister of Defense, a post which he held for six years.

In 1965 Peres left *Mapai* with Ben Gurion and became Secretary-General of *Rafi*. In 1968 he was instrumental in bringing *Rafi* back into *Mapai*, to form the Israel Labor Party.

In 1969 Peres became Minister of Immigrant Absorption, with responsibilities for the economic develoment of the *administered territories. The following year he was Minister of Transport and Communications.

In 1974 Peres was appointed Minister of Information in Golda *Meir's government, and Minister of Defense in Yitzḥak *Rabin's government, in which post he had the task of remodeling the *IDF (Israel Defense Force) following the *Yom Kippur War. During his tenure of office as Minister of Defense the 1975 *Interim Agreement was signed with *Egypt, the *Entebbe Operation took place and the Good Fence between Israel and Lebanon was opened. At the Labor party conference of February 23, 1977 Peres contested the party leadership and lost to Rabin by 41 votes. However, he gained the leadership after Rabin's resignation on April 7th, 1977.

Peres headed the *Alignment list in the 1977 elections to the 9th Knesset, and led the Alignment in opposition until 1984. In the course of this period he made great efforts to reconstruct the Israel Labor Party.

In 1978 Peres was elected Vice-President of the *Socialist International, an organization in which he played an active role during the years in opposition. Peres led the Alignment for the third time in the 1984 elections to the 11th Knesset. Though the Alignment gained only 44 seats, Peres, as leader of the largest political bloc, was called upon by President Ḥaim *Herzog, to try to form a government. After it became apparent that the Alignment would be unable to form a narrow government, the *National Unity Government was formed September 13, 1984. According to the coalition agreement Peres would be Prime Minister for two years, and **Likud* leader Yitzḥak *Shamir would be Prime Minister for the remaining two years of the government's term.

During the two years that Peres was Prime Minister, his popularity rose considerably due to his success in managing the complicated coalition which he headed and his efforts not to allow past differences with the *Likud* and with Yitzḥak Rabin to disturb the smooth running of the government. Peres was instrumental in bringing about the withdrawal of the IDF from Lebanon. Despite differences of opinon with the *Likud* concerning the continuation of the peace process Peres made a major effort to improve Israel's relations with *Egypt and promoted negotiations with *Jordan. He also played an active role in the economic stabilization plan and its successful implementation. In October 1986, following the *rotation, he became Deputy Prime Minister and Minister for Foreign Affairs.

When the second stage of the economic plan was presented by Minister of Finance Moshe Nissim in December 1986 Peres again played a major role in getting the plan modified and accepted and in securing the *Histadrut's cooperation.

Pe'ulah Shemit See: *Semitic Action.

Pit'ḥat Rafi'aḥ See: *Rafa Salient.

Pitu'aḥ Veshalom See: *Development and Peace, *Flatto-Sharon, Shmuel.

PLO See: *Palestine Liberation Organization.

PLP See: *Progressive List for Peace.

Po'alei Agudat Yisrael (Pai) Hebrew for "Workers of the Association of Israel," a religious labor movement which broke away from the world movement of **Agudat Yisrael*, while remaining ideologically close to it. *Pai* advocates a partnership with the secular population on national questions and does not object to service in the Israel Defense Forces (*IDF). Unlike the other religious groups, its workers are organized within the framework of the **Histadrut*. *Pai* was set up in 1922 in Poland and started its activities in Palestine in 1925. Its declared goal is to set up a state based on the Torah. The members of the party developed a model agricultural settlement which follows all the Torah laws, among them the prohibition to work the land on the fallow seventh year during which they concentrate on hydroponic crops.

Pai and *Agudat Yisrael* split up in 1937 because of the establishment of the youth movement *Ezra*, to which *Agudat Yisrael* objected, despite the fact that boys and girls participated separately. *Pai*'s cooperation with the secular population aggravated the split, the climax of which came in 1960 when *Pai* joined the government coalition against the ruling of *Mo'etzet Gdolei Hatorah* (the Council of Great Torah Scholars). The two parties nevertheless ran together in a common list — the *Religious Torah Front — for the 3rd, 4th and 8th Knessets. In the elections to the 10th Knesset (1981) *Pai* failed to pass the one percent qualifying threshold. Prior to the elections to the 11th Knesset (1984) *Pai* set up a joint list with **Morasha*, a group which had left the *National Religious Party, led by Yosef Shapiro and Rabbi Ḥaim Druckman. The list gained two Knesset seats, one of which is held by *Pai* representative Rabbi Avraham Verdiger. This partnership lacks, however, a solid ideological basis and serious differences of opinion between the two component groups in the new party finally led to Druckman's return to the NRP fold. (Sh.M.)

Po'alei Zion Hebrew for Workers of Zion. Jewish socialist-nationalist workers' party which first emerged in 1901 when widespread associations of Jewish Zionist workers met in Minsk. Three major parties emerged from *Po'alei Zion* of which only one remained attached to **Eretz Yisrael* and survived as an independent political movement.

In 1906 the Zionist section of *Po'alei Zion* organized into *Mifleget Hapo'alim Hayehudit Hasozial Demokratit — Po'alei Zion* (Social-Democratic Jewish Workers' Party — Workers of Zion), initiated by Ber *Borochov. In 1907 a world-wide movement was established with a platform drafted by Borochov on the basis of his doctrine. The first *Po'alei Zion* groups were established in Palestine by several members of the Second **Aliyah* (second wave of immigration) who had belonged to the movement in Eastern Europe. They were joined in 1906 by David Green (*Ben Gurion), Yitzḥak *Tabenkin and others. The platform of the Palestine party was based on that of the world movement, and from the very beginning called for political independence for the Jewish people in *Eretz Yisrael. Po'alei Zion* called for a Hebrew state based on socialist foundations to be established by means of class-warfare. Over the years the movement in Palestine developed independently under the leadership of Ben Gurion. It fought for *avodah ivrit* (Jewish labor) and was among the founders of **Hashomer*.

At the second conference of the movement in 1909 the Palestine branch of *Po'alei Zion* supported the plan of Shlomo Kaplansky (1884–1950) for cooperative settlement as advocated by Franz Oppenheimer (1864–1943). In 1919 *Po'alei Zion* in Palestine together with non-partisan groups set up **Aḥdut Ha'avodah*. One left-wing group did not join the new party and instead set up the Socialist Workers' Party (see: **Maki*).

At the fifth conference of *Po'alei Zion* in 1920 the movement split — one part becoming *Po'alei Zion Smol* (Left), the other the World Alliance of *Po'alei Zion Yamin* (Right). (*Po'alei Zion Smol* in Palestine united in 1946 with *Hatnu'ah Le'aḥdut Ha'avodah* to establish *Aḥdut Ha'avodah — Po'alei Zion.*) In 1930 *Aḥdut Ha'avodah* and **Hapo'el Hatza'ir* united to set up **Mapai*.

Various sections of the world movement of *Po'alei Zion* continue to exist and are affiliated to the *World Labor Zionist Movement.

(D.B.M.)

Pollard Affair An affair involving espionage for Israel, carried out by an American Jew, Jonathan Pollard, employed in the American Navy Intelligence. Pollard was apprehended in November 1985 by the FBI and accused of selling to Israel highly classified documents connected with military installations of foreign states including the *PLO headquarters in Tunis. Pollard was operated by the Bureau for Scientific Relations in the Ministry of Defense, headed by Raphael (Rafi) Eitan who had been Prime Minister Yitzḥak *Shamir's advisor on terrorism in 1983–84. Israel claimed this operation was exceptional, carried out independently without authorization, and agreed to cooperate with the Americans in the investigation of the affair. In December 1985 Israel disbanded the Bureau for Scientific Relations, returned documents received from Pollard and allowed the American authorities to interview Israelis involved.

However, as Pollard's trial progressed in June 1986 the US Department of Justice sought to bring charges against an Israeli Air Force officer, Avi'em Selah, who was alleged to have established the contact between Pollard and Eitan. There were American allegations that the Israeli government had not been absoutely candid in its treatment of the issue, and insinuations that Israel ran a wide espionage network in the US. Pollard pleaded guilty and was sentenced in March 1987 to life imprisonment. His wife received a five year prison sentence as an accomplice. Pollard claimed that his motives had been ideological — to help Israel — and that he had not intended to harm the US.

The US administration expressed great displeasure that instead of being punished, Eitan was appointed chairman of a major government-owned company while Selah was to be promoted to the rank of General.

On March 11 the inner cabinet of the Israeli government decided that the affair would be examined by an investigating committee (rather than a commission of inquiry) and by the subcommittee on Intelligence of the Knesset Foreign Affairs and Security Committee.

Israeli government circles and public opinion were deeply concerned about the possibility that the Pollard affair would have a long-term negative effect on Israel-US relations and on the relations between American Jewry and the Jewish State. Israel's moral obligations to the Pollards and the engagement in espionage of a unit not subject to the professional standards and supervision of the *Mossad* were additional questions which caused a heated public debate in Israel.

population exchange See: *Transfer 1.

populism (economic) See: *Leheitiv im Ha'am, *Aridor, Yoram.

President of Israel In Hebrew: *Nassi*, ancient title of the head of the *Sanhedrin*, the assembly of the ordained scholars which was both supreme court and legislature from the 1st century BCE, to the 5th century CE. The President of the state has very little real power. He is elected by secret vote of the *Knesset for a five-year term, and may serve for two terms. The Basic Law: the President, passed by the Knesset in 1964, deals with the election of the President, his qualifications, authority and the procedures of his office. The President's tasks include: ceremonial functions, such as the signing of all laws and international conventions to which Israel has acceeded, accrediting Israel's diplomatic representatives to other states, receiving the credentials of foreign diplomats accredited to Israel, and opening the first session of a new Knesset; formal functions, such as receiving reports of the government's meetings; representing Israel in visits to foreign countries; and some substantive functions, such as the summoning the leader of the lists elected to a new Knesset to form a new government, or recommending a pardon or commutation of sentence for prisoners.

Until now all except the first President, Chaim *Weizmann, have been candidates of *Mapai* or the *Israel Labor Party. Until the 1977 political *upheaval the president elected was always the man proposed by the Prime Minister, while during the **Likud* governments in 1978 and 1983, neither of the Prime Minister's presidential candidates was elected by the Knesset.

All of Israel's Presidents, except Professor Ephraim Katzir, were active politicians before being elected. One, Yitzḥak *Navon, returned to active politics six months after his term ended.

There have been proposals to increase the President's powers, or eliminate some of the anomalies and weaknesses of the existing system by changing it to resemble the American or French presidential system. However, there seems to be little possibility of any drastic reforms being made.

Presidents of Israel

1948–52	Chaim *Weizmann (1874–1952)
1952–63	Yitzḥak *Ben Zvi (1884–1963)
1963–73	Shne'or Zalman Shazar (1889–1974)
1973–78	Ephraim Katzir (b. 1916)
1978–83	Yitzḥak *Navon (b. 1921)
1983–	Ḥaim *Herzog (b. 1918)

Prime Ministers of Israel

1948–54	David *Ben Gurion (1886–1973)
1954–55	Moshe *Sharett (1894–1965)
1955–63	David Ben Gurion
1963–69	Levi *Eshkol (1895–1969)
1969–74	Golda *Meir (1898–1978)
1974–77	Yitzḥak *Rabin (b. 1922)
1977–83	Menaḥem *Begin (b. 1913)
1983–84	Yitzḥak *Shamir (b. 1915)
1984–86	Shimon *Peres (b. 1923)
1986–	Yitzḥak Shamir

Prisoners of Zion In Hebrew: *Assirei Zion*. The term originally implied the Jewish exiles' longing for Zion. Since the establishment of the State of Israel, the name has been applied to persons imprisoned for their professed Zionism. Today the term is used primarily with regard to Jews imprisoned in the *Soviet Union because of their desire to emigrate to Israel and their Zionist activism. The *United States has helped free some of the Prisoners of Zion by exchanging them for Soviet spies. The most well-known Prisoner of Zion Anatoly (Natan) Scharansky, was released from the Soviet Union in the winter of 1986. Israel makes the renewal of diplomatic relations with the Soviet Union conditional on the release of all the Prisoners of Zion and a more lenient policy regarding emigration of Jews from the Soviet Union.

Proclamation of Independence The declaration of the State of Israel made on May 14, 1948, by the members of the People's Council — the parliamentary body of the "state on the way." The proclamation is made up of four parts: one which deals with the history of the Jewish people, its struggle to renew its national life and the international recognition of its right to do so; the second, the operative part, which declares the establishment of the state; the third which proclaims the principles which will guide the State of Israel; and the fourth which is an appeal to the *United Nations, the Arab inhabitants of the state, the Arab states and Diaspora Jewry.

The first and fourth parts do not serve any legal purpose nor are they normative instruments, although they first served the courts for purposes of interpretation (for example, with regard to the word Jew in the *Law of Return).

The second part gives normative instructions regarding the establishment of the state and its name, government authorities and their identity; the holding of elections to the Constituent Assembly which was to prepare a *Constitution; and the setting up of duly elected bodies in accordance with the constitution.

These declarations are the first source of authority in Israeli law, a basic norm which characterizes the beginning of a new political system, and may be treated not merely as a proclamation but as an actual act of legislation. Later on there was a divergence from the instructions of the second part of the proclamation in that the elections did not take place on the decreed date, the membership in the State Council was not identical to that of the National Council and the Provisional State Council did not continue to serve after the Constituent Assembly convened. These divergences were settled in subsequent laws. However, the noncompliance with the provisions regarding a constitution and the Harari resolution regarding the preparation of *Basic Laws were never given the force of law.

The third part is a policy declaration regarding the nature of the state: a democratic, national Jewish state, open to Jewish immigration, in which equal rights and the principles of civilized society included in the United Nations Charters are guaranteed for all citizens regardless of religion or race. This part of the proclamation was given restrictive legal significance by the courts which turned it into a mirror of the spirit of Israel's domestic law, and a basis for interpretation. The courts laid down the rules that the administrative branch must view the principles of the proclamation as instructions from which it must not diverge except by an explicit law, and that the legislature should not pass legislation which is contrary to these principles unless it explicitly states that it intends to do so. Thus, though the proclamation is not a law or ordinary legal document, it does have legal validity.

There were those who were inclined to view the Proclamation of Independence, especially its declaratory part, as a constitution. However, in a succession of decisions, the Supreme Court stated that the proclamation does not have the force of constitutional law and is not a supreme law which can cancel laws and regulations which contradict it. (J.K.)

Progressive Judaism Progressive Judaism, known also as Reform and Liberal, with some 1.25 million adherents in 26 countries, is the most liberal of the streams of Judaism. It has been guided over the past 200 years by the conviction that Judaism must interact with the modern environment and be open to empirical knowledge. Reform Judaism, as it evolved in late 18th century Germany, emphasized the universalist aspects of Judaism, especially as enunciated by the prophets, and tended to see Judaism primarily as a religious faith. At first, the Reform movement rejected *Zionism because of its insistence that Jews were also a nation, though within the Zionist leadership of the *United States in the late 19th and early 20th centuries there were a number of prominent Reform rabbis.

The rise of National Socialism in Germany changed the basic attitude of the Reform movement, and the 1937 Columbus Platform of Reform Judaism affirmed the obligation of all Jewry to aid in the upbuilding of Palestine as a Jewish homeland, as a refuge for the oppressed, and a center of Jewish culture and spiritual life.

The most recent articulation of North American Reform's position on Israel was presented in the Centenary Perspective in 1976: "We are bound ... to the newly reborn State of Israel by innumerable religious and ethnic ties... We have both a stake and a responsibility in building the State of Israel, assuring its security and defining its Jewish character. We encourage *aliyah* (immigration) for those who wish to find maximum personal fulfilment in the cause of Zion. We demand that Reform Judaism be unconditionally legitimized in the State of Israel.

"At the same time ... we reaffirm the mandate of our tradition to create strong Jewish communities wherever we live . . ."

The first Progressive congregations were established in Palestine in 1936, in Haifa, Tel Aviv and Jerusalem. The Leo Baeck School in Haifa, the first non-Orthodox religious school in the country, was founded in 1939. The Har-El congregation in Jerusalem, founded in 1958, is the oldest Israeli Progressive synagogue.

Subsequently, many more Progressive congre-;ations emerged. In 1984 a woman rabbi was ppointed for the first time to serve a Progressive ongregation in Israel.

The Progressive rabbis in Israel are federated nto the Israel Council of Progressive Rabbis, vhich, among other functions, sponsors a Rab-inic Court for conversion and prepares the novement's prayerbooks. The Progressive rabbis n Israel do not accept the definition of a Jew dopted by the Reform movement of North merica in 1976 which recognizes as Jewish per-ons whose father or mother is Jewish. (The defi-ition according to Orthodox sources is that a hild born to a Jewish mother is deemed Jewish).

Among the institutions of Progressive Judaism n Israel are the Jerusalem branch of the Hebrew Jnion College — Jewish Institute of Religion, vhere all North American Reform rabbinic, antorial and education students are required to pend their first academic year, and which, since 975, has been training rabbis in Israel; the head-uarters of the World Union for Progressive udaism which moved to Jerusalem in 1972, oining the *World Zionist Organization WZO) in 1976; *Arzenu* the International Asso-iation of Reform Zionists, which has six ational constituencies and has been affiliated as a Zionist party within the WZO since 1982.

In 1959, the Union of American Hebrew Con-;regations began sponsoring educational pro-;rams in Israel for North American Reform outh, while in 1980, *Netzer Olami*, the Interna-ional Reform Zionist Youth Movement, was ounded in Jerusalem with some ten national ranches. The Israeli branch, *Tsofei *Telem*, is ffiliated to the Israeli scout movement.

In 1977 Kibbutz Yahel was set up in the Arava y native-born Israelis and immigrants from a lozen countries. A Progressive ideological semi-ar center for youth was established at Yahel. Kibbutz Lotan, also in the Arava, was set up in 1983.

In 1985 a Progressive *mitzpeh*, Har Ḥalutz, was ounded in the Carmiel area, and in the same ear, an educational center was constructed at Kibbutz Tzor'ah to house work-study university rograms for North American Reform students.

Because of the monopoly which the Orthodox ewish establishment has had in Israel since its stablishment regarding matters of personal status, the religious *status quo which evolved since the 1930s and the politicization of religion in Israel through religious parties, Progressive and other non-Orthodox religious Jews do not enjoy equality. Unlike the Orthodox, none of their rabbis are salaried by the state, their synagogues are neither built nor maintained by the state, and their rabbis are neither permitted to perform marriages, divorces or conversions, nor to sit on religious councils or serve as military chaplains. In addition, Progressive Jews are frequently subjected to covert and arbitrary harassment and discrimination such as annual advertisements in the national press warning the public not to attend their high holiday services and schools.

On several occasions the movement has initiated and supported suits to redress grievances before the High Court of Justice. In November 1986 the Court instructed the Ministry of the Interior to register as a Jew, in accordance with the *Law of Return, Shoshana-Susan Miller who had undergone Reform conversion several years prior to her arrival in Israel. In another case dealing with the licensing of Reform rabbis to perform marriages in Israel the decision is still pending. Other cases are being prepared.

The Law of Return, which grants the right of every Jew to settle in Israel, defines a Jew for the purpose of the law as "anyone born to a Jewish mother or has converted and is not a member of another religion." Thus Reform Jewish converts whose conversion took place abroad prior to their immigration were to be recognized as Jews by the State of Israel for the purpose of *aliyah* and citizenship. Several times the Orthodox parties have tried to insert after the words "has converted," the phrase "according to the *Halacha*" (the Orthodox Jewish law), which would in effect have disenfranchised Reform Jewish converts wishing to settle in Israel as Jews according to the Law of Return, as well as registering doubt as to the Jewishness of people in the Diaspora who had been converted to Judaism abroad under non-Orthodox auspices.

While the Center to Left parties in Israel oppose the amendment of the Law of Return and advocate equality for all streams in Judaism, since the number of Progressive Jews in Israel is still small, since the movement has no Knesset representation, and due to the current distribution of political power in Israel which results in the dependence of the *Aligment and the **Likud* on the Orthodox parties in the formation of narrow coalitions, the prospects for change in the situation in the foreseeable future are small.

(H.F.S.)

Progressive List for Peace (PLP) A *non-Zionist party set up on May 30, 1984, before the elections to the 11th Knesset, which united the Jewish movement "Alternative" and the Arab Progressive Movement of Nazareth, as well as several other radical groups and individuals. The goals of the party are: full equality for Jewish and Arab citizens within the State of Israel as defined by its borders on June 4, 1967; recognition of the right of the two peoples — the Jewish Israeli and the Arab Palestinian — to national self-determinaton; Israeli withdrawal from all territories occupied in the *Six-Day War, including *Jerusalem; mutual recognition by the State of Israel and a Palestinian state to be established in the territories to be evacuated by Israel. In its platform for the 1984 elections the PLP also called for Israel's immediate withdrawal from *Lebanon.

Attempts were made to disqualify the party from running in the elections, under the pretext that it was anti-Zionist and that its real goal was the elimination of the Jewish state. Furthermore, it was argued that the party must be disqualified because one of its Arab leaders, Mohammad Mi'ari had been involved in the **al-Ard* Movement which was declared illegal in 1965, and because its Jewish leaders — Mattityahu *Peled, Uri *Avneri and Ya'acov Arnon had met in 1984 with Yasser Arafat of the *Palestine Liberation Organization. After the Central Elections Committee had decided to disqualify the PLP, as well as **Kach*, the Supreme Court approved the participation of both lists in the elections.

Miari and Peled, the two PLP members of Knesset, met again with Arafat in January 1985, and as a result of this meeting an amendment to the 1948 Prevention of Terror Ordinance was brought to the Knesset by Minister of Justice Moshe Nissim to restrict meetings between Israelis and members of the PLO. Amendment No. 9 to the Basic Law: the Knesset (See: Appendix III) which states, inter alia, that a list which rejects the existence of "the State of Israel as the state of the Jews" cannot participate in Knesset elections, was introduced by those who continue to believe that the PLP does not really recognize the legitimacy of the state. The PLP is viewed as a major political threat by *Ḥadash* which accuses it of being a tool of "Western imperialism."

Progressive Party of Israel A party established in 1949 by three political groups: *Aliyah Ḥadashah* (New Immigration), set up in 1942 by mostly German-speaking immigrants from Central Europe with progressive-liberal leanings which had one member, Pinḥas Rosen (1887–1978), in the Provisional Government from May 14, 1948 to March 9, 1949; *Ha'oved Hatzi'oni* (the Zionist Worker) established in 1936 as the labor section of the General Zionist Federation with membership in the **Histadrut* and a group of individuals who had left the General Zionist Federation. The party adopted a social-liberal platform. The Progressive Party closely cooperated with the labor camp and participated in most of the Labor-led governments until 1961 when it merged with the General Zionists to form the *Liberal Party. In 1965 most of the ex-Progressives broke off from the Liberal Party and established the *Independent Liberal Party.

Knesset Seats: 1st Knesset (1949) — 5; 2nd Knesset (1951) — 4; 3rd Knesset (1955) — 5; 4th Knesset (1959) — 6.

Property Transfer See: *Transfer 2.

R

Rabat Conference Arab summit meeting which convened on October 25, 1974 in *Morocco. The conference adopted a resolution, with only *Jordan voting against, which a) confirmed the right of the Palestinian people to return to their country and determine their own future; b) recommended the return of any liberated Palestinian territory to the Palestinian people under "the leadership of the PLO" — in effect the establishment of a Palestinian state in the *West Bank and the *Gaza Strip once Israel withdrew its troops from all or part of them, with all Arab "confrontation forces" supporting any independent Palestinian authority.

The Rabat Conference paved the way for Yasser Arafat's appearance before the UN General Assembly in November 1974, and was partially responsible for the *Jericho Plan coming to naught.

Rabin, Yitzḥak Military commander, diplomat, sixth Prime Minister of Israel and Minister of Defense. Born 1922, in Jerusalem. Rabin studied at the Kedourie Agricultural School. He joined the **Palmaḥ* in 1940, in which he served until the end of the *War of Independence and was Commander of the Harel Brigade on the Jerusalem front. Rabin was a member of the Israeli negotiating team which signed the *Armistice Agreement with Egypt at Rhodes. Following the war he remained in the *IDF and served as Head of the Northern Command in 1956–59; Head of Operations Branch of General Headquarters in 1959–63; Deputy Chief of Staff in 1963 and from 1964–68 Chief of Staff, commanding the IDF during the *Six-Day War.

Soon after his retirement from the IDF Rabin was appointed Ambassador to the *United States where he remained until December 1973 when he joined Golda *Meir's government as Minister of Labor. In June 1974, following Golda Meir's resignation Rabin was elected by the Central Committee of the *Israel Labor Party as its candidate for the premiership, defeating Shimon Peres by a few votes.

During Rabin's premiership *disengagement agreements were signed with *Egypt and *Syria in 1974 and an *interim agreement was signed with Egypt in 1975. The first *Memorandum of Understanding was signed between Israel and the United States in September 1975 and in June 1976 the cabinet decided to carry out the Entebbe Operation.

Toward the end of 1976 Rabin broke up the coalition with the *National Religious Party, which had abstained in a vote of no-confidence over the desecration of the Sabbath resulting from an official ceremony at an air base. A second contest with Peres for the Labor party leadership took place in February 1977, with Rabin once again winning by a narrow margin. However, due to a minor scandal involving his wife's illegal bank account in the US Rabin resigned and Peres stood at the head of the *Alignment list during the elections to the 9th Knesset (1977), in which the Alignment suffered a major electoral defeat.

Rabin contested the Labor party leadership again in December 1980 but gained only 29 percent of the votes. In September 1984 he joined the *National Unity Government as Minister of Defense in which capacity he acted to withdraw the IDF from *Lebanon and was responsible for the Israel Air Force attack on the PLO headquarters in Tunis in October 1985.

Rafa Salient Territory in the northeast corner of the *Sinai Peninsula bordering on the *Gaza Strip, occupied by Israel in June 1967. After the *Six-Day War several Jewish settlements were established in the area, including the town of Yamit, as a barrier between the Sinai and Gaza Strip. The intention was to ensure that in a peace settlement both the Gaza Strip and Rafa Salient would not be returned to Egypt. Within the framework of the *Allon Plan the Salient was to have remained in Israeli hands.

Even after President Sadat's visit to Jerusalem it was hoped that Egypt would forego the area, however, the 1978 *Camp David Accords called for Israeli withdrawal from the whole of the Sinai, including the Rafa Salient. It was because of this provision of the Camp David Accords that several members of the *Alignment, including Yigal *Allon, joined several central members of the **Likud* including Yitzḥak *Shamir in abstaining in the Knesset vote for the approval of the accords. Even after the Camp David Accords and *Egyptian-Israeli Peace Treaty were signed the opponents of the withdrawal continued to hope that Israel would somehow manage to get out of its obligation to leave the area, or at least obtain Egyptian consent for the Jewish settlements to continue to exist under Egyptian sovereignty.

However, as the final date of Israel's evacuation approached it became apparent that Egypt would make no concessions and that the Israeli government, though not happy about evacuating the Rafa Salient and the dismantlement of Jewish settlements, would go through with it.

In 1979 the League for the Prevention of the Withdrawal from the Sinai also known as *Ma'oz*, was established, with members of **Gush Emunim* and the **Teḥiyah* at its core. In the years 1979–82 *Ma'oz* established several new unauthorized settlements and resisted every stage of the evacuation. The final act of resistance was to the evacuation of Yamit, when some settlers with outside reinforcements confronted the *IDF. When several supporters of Rabbi Meir *Kahane threatened to commit suicide Kahane was called back from New York to talk them out of it. Between April 23 and 25, 1982, the whole of Yamit was razed to the ground, and the Rafa Salient was returned to the Egyptians on April 26.

Rafi Abbreviation for *Reshimat Po'alei Yisrael Ubilti Miflagtiyim* (the List of Israel Workers and Non-Partisans), the *Rafi* party was founded in June 1965 by a group who left *Mapai* under the leadership of David *Ben Gurion, against the background of the *Lavon Affair and in opposition to the establishment of the *Alignment. The new party, which was established during the 5th Knesset took seven seats from *Mapai*'s 42. In the elections to the 6th Knesset — *Rafi*'s platform called for a legal commission of inquiry for the Lavon Affair; regional elections; unemployment insurance; national health insurance; free compulsory education for ages 3–16; computerization of the state's information systems; the financing of elections from the government budget and personal elections for mayors. The new party won ten seats.

On the eve of the *Six-Day War *Rafi* member Moshe *Dayan joined the *National Unity Government of Levi *Eshkol as Minister of Defense. In 1968 *Rafi* reunited with *Mapai* and together with **Ahdut Ha'avodah-Po'alei Zion* formed the *Israel Labor Party, but without Ben Gurion, who established a new party — the *State List (*Hareshimah Hamamlachtit*). (D.B.M.)

Rakaḥ Acronym for *Reshimah Kommonistit Ḥadashah* (New Communist List) established in 1965 when **Maki* split in two — one part which was predominantly Jewish and continued to use the name *Maki*, and the other, predominantly Arab, called *Rakaḥ*.

The split took place against the background of the deterioration of relations between Israel and the Arab states when the *Soviet Union openly sided with the Arabs.

Rakaḥ viewed Zionism as a bourgeois-chauvinist movement serving imperialism while harming the true interests of the Arab and Jewish masses. It defined the *Six-Day War as an act of Israeli aggression and demanded complete Israeli withdrawal to the June 5, 1967, borders without prior negotiations to ensure a peace treaty. It demanded recognition of the Palestinian entity and the right of the Palestinians to establish a state while recognizing *Palestine Liberatio Organization terrorist activities, and that o other Palestinian organizations, as legitimat means in a national guerrilla war.

Rakaḥ acted in complete coordination wit Moscow both on domestic and internation issues. Domestically it advocated radical soci positions, objecting to all the government's an **Histadrut*'s economic, welfare and trade unio activities. Many of the party's Arab supporter were not necessarily Communists but supporte its national positions.

Rakaḥ published two papers, *al Ittihad* in Arabic and *Zu Haderech* in Hebrew. Prior to the elections to the 9th Knesset (1977) *Rakaḥ* unite with some of the *Black Panthers and establishe **Ḥadash* in which a greater balance between Ara and Jewish forces was reinstated.

Knesset Seats: 6th Knesset (1965) — 3 7th Knesset (1969) — 3; 8th Knesset (1973) — (D.B.M.

Ratz See: *Civil Rights Movement (CRM).

Reagan Plan On September 1, 1982, two day after the evacuation of West Beirut by the *Palestine Liberation Organization (PLO), Presiden Ronald Reagan enunciated the principles for a Arab-Israel settlement. The statement put the U clearly on record as favoring Israeli withdrawa and the association of an autonomous *Wes Bank and *Gaza Strip with Jordan. The Presiden stated that "the United States will not suppor the establishment of an independent Palestinia state in the West Bank and Gaza, and we will no support annexation or permanent control b Israel."

The plan repeated the American commitmen not to recognize or negotiate with the PLO unless it accepted *Security Council Resolution 242 and 338. It called for a freeze of all Israeli settlement activities in the territories, the status c existing Israeli settlements to be determined i the course of negotiations on the final status c the territories. The *Palestinians, including thos residing in East *Jerusalem, would be allowed t play a leading role in determining their ow future through the provisions of the *Cam David Accords. During the transitional period self-governing authority would be elected t assume real powers over the population, the lan and its resources. It would assume progressiv responsibility over internal security subject to i performance and the degree of its control over the situation. The status of East Jerusalem would be determined through negotiations.

The second *Begin government rejected the initiative in total the day after it was made public. The opposition *Alignment criticized the outright rejection, arguing that the plan contained many positive features.

The Arabs responded with the *Fez Plan of September 8, 1982. The Palestine National Council meeting in Algeria in February 1983 rejected the Reagan Plan for not fulfilling "the inalienable national rights of the Palestinian people." In the spring of 1985 an American attempt failed to reactivate the initiative.

Rechtman Affair A corruption scandal involving the Mayor of Rehovot, Shmuel Rechtman, when he was about to be elected to the 9th Knesset as a Liberal candidate for the **Likud*. Before the elections Rechtman was accused of taking personal bribes. Actual charges were brought against him in June 1978, after he had been a Member of Knesset for a year. He was found guilty and sentenced to imprisonment, serving 26 months. Afterward he was received as a hero in his home town and tried to return to public life.

Rechtman was the first MK to be sentenced to imprisonment on criminal charges. He was also the first Mayor to be found guilty of taking bribes. Since there was no legal way of dismissing him from the Knesset several factions initiated a bill which would allow the dismissal of an MK found guilty of a felony. However, this bill, which was referred to as the Rechtman Law, was never passed. Rechtman was persuaded to tender his resignation from the Knesset, which he did on June 13, 1979. Formally, Rechtman continued to serve as the Chairman of the *Liberal Party Council until the party's conference in 1980 when the heads of all the party's institutions were replaced.

Reform Judaism See: *Progressive Judaism.

Refugees The 1951 UN definition of a refugee is as follows: "A person who owing to well-founded fear of being persecuted for reasons of race, religion, nationality, membership in a particular social group or political opinion, is outside the country of his nationality and is unable, or owing to such fear, is unwilling to avail himself of the protection of that country."

After World War II close to 200,000 Jewish survivors of the *Holocaust or persons who had managed to find temporary asylum, arrived in Israel. Following the *War of Independence 586,000 Jews from the Arab countries of North Africa and the Middle East, who could no longer remain in their homes, poured into Israel (an additional 200,000 Jewish refugees from these countries settled elsewhere).

Some 700,000 Arabs had lived in mandatory times in the territory which became Israel on the basis of the 1949 *armistice agreements. In 1950 only 156,000 remained in this territory as Israeli citizens. About 90 percent of the remainder had fled their homes in the course of the war, and 10 percent were expelled (most of them from Lydda — today Lod — and Ramleh). Israel estimates the number of refugees at that time to have been 400,000, but according to UNRWA, which undertook to feed the refugees and care for their health, education and vocational training, there were 960,021 registered refugees receiving UNRWA rations in 1950. These included 127,600 refugees in *Lebanon, 82,194 in *Syria, 506,200 in *Jordan (including the West Bank), 198,227 in the *Gaza Strip and 45,800 in Israel (after 1952 Israel assumed responsibility for the "refugees" who remained in the country). The difference between UNRWA figures and Israeli estimates is at least partially due to false registrations by refugees in order to obtain extra ration cards.

Most of the refugees lived in dire conditions in refugee camps, with no Arab state (except Jordan, to a limited extent) being willing to resettle and integrate them. The Arab states argued that if the refugees were resettled, they would be giving up their claim to return to their homes.

Until 1967 the Palestinians did not object to their problem being referred to as a refugee problem. However, after the *Six- Day War and the emergence of the *Palestine Liberation Organization (PLO) they demanded that their problem be dealt with in terms of national self-determination. The PLO's main reason for rejecting *Security Council Resolution 242 as presently worded, and their main argument for its amendment has been that it deals with the Palestinians merely as refugees and not as a nation.

In 1984 the approximate number of refugees according to UNRWA was 2,125,200, distributed as follows: 263,600 in Lebanon (48 percent in camps), 276,900 in Syria (12 percent of them refugees from the *Golan Heights from the Six-Day War, 26 percent living in camps, 799,700 in Jordan (31 percent in camps), 357,000 in the *West Bank (34 percent in camps) and 428,000 in the Gaza Strip (56 percent in camps).

Israel allowed some family reunions after 1949, but refuses to permit a general return of the Arab refugees to their previous homes, viewing this as national suicide for Israel as a Jewish state. It is argued that since Israel absorbed close to 600,000 Jewish refugees from Arab countries a de facto population exchange (See: *Transfer) had taken place. Israeli spokesmen have expressed willingness to compensate the refugees for the property they left behind in Israel if a reciprocal agreement can be arranged for the Jewish refugees from Arab countries.

religious pluralism While the State of Israel was proclaimed to be "the Jewish state" in its *Proclamation of Independence, the proclamation guarantees "freedom of religion, conscience, education and culture" and undertakes to safeguard the *Holy Places of all religions.

It is the state which provides the public's basic religious needs. A provision to this effect has been included in the basic guidelines of all the Governments of Israel and approved by the *Knesset.

Since there are no civil marriages or divorces in Israel it is the various communities in Israel which are in charge of these matters, through their respective religious institutions. The religious communities in Israel are Jewish, Muslim (predominantly Shi'ite, but also Sunni and Achmadian), *Druze, Christian (there are about 30 different Christian sects affiliated to the Orthodox, Catholic and Protestant churches), and *Baha'i. Though most of the education system is state-run, there exist independent religious schools as well. Each religious community enjoys its own day of rest — Friday for the Muslims, Saturday for the Jews and Sunday for the Christians — plus its own religious holidays.

While pluralism among the various religions is satisfactorily implemented, there exists a problem with pluralism within the Jewish community. The only Jewish religious institutions which are officially recognized in Israel are Orthodox institutions, while the *Conservative movement and *Progressive (Reform) movement have no official status. The *Chief Rabbinate is headed by two Orthodox rabbis, one Ashkenazi and the other Sephardi, and there are no Reform or Conservative rabbis represented on the Rabbinical Council.

The small number of Conservative and Reform Jews in Israel, the determination of the Orthodox establishment, which totally rejects the Conservative and Reform movements as legitimate streams in Judaism, to maintain the full control which it has had on Jewish religious matters since mandatory times, and the ambivalence of most secular Israelis on the issue, have so far prevented any change in the religious *status quo in favor of the Conservative and Reform movements.

The *Israel Labor Party, **Shinui*, the *Civil Rights Movement and **Mapam* have all committed themselves in recent years to Jewish pluralism in Israel but do not have the power to bring about a legislative change. The Orthodox parties are determined to amend the *Law of Return so that only the Orthodox definition of "Who is a Jew?" will be legally recognized in Israel.

Religious Torah Front The name of the list under which **Agudat Yisrael* and **Po'alei Agudat Yisrael* ran for the 4th and 8th Knessets. The two parties ran together under the name Torah Front in the elections to the 3rd Knesset.

Knesset Seats: 3rd Knesset (1955) — 6; 4th Knesset (1959) — 6; 8th Knesset (1973) — 5.

Reshimah Sotzialistit See: *Socialist List.

Reshimat Haloḥamim See: *Fighters List.

Reshimat Hasephardim See: *Sephardi List.

Restitution Agreement An agreement signed on September 10, 1952, between the *Federal Republic of Germany and the State of Israel under which West Germany undertook to pay DM 3,000 million in goods and services, to help the resettling of "destitute Jewish refugees uprooted from Germany and from territories formerly under German rule" in recognition of the fact that "unspeakable criminal acts were perpetrated against the Jewish people during the National-Socialist regime of terror"

West Germany undertook to pay also a sum of DM 450 million for the benefit of the Conference on Jewish Material Claims Against Germany, as compensation for the persecution of Jews, deprivation of liberty, compulsory labor damage to health and to economic prospects. In addition, by 1971, restitution had been paid to individual Jews totaling $8,000 million, of which $1,500 million was to Israelis.

Germany made all the agreed 11 annual installments and implemented the agreement in 1965 through an Israeli company specially established for the purpose (the Israel Mission, also called Restitution Company). Goods to the net value of $741 million were imported into Israel (approximately 9 percent of total imports in that period), mainly: ships and equipment for electricity supply and transmission, railway, telephone and mining equipment, and oil.

During the period of the agreement, there were no diplomatic relations between the two countries, but the Mission — while being officially a German jurist — enjoyed a de facto diplomatic status.

The Restitution Agreement was the outcome of negotiations which commenced with contacts made by Nahum *Goldmann and the World Jewish Congress. Later, they were taken up by official Israeli representatives headed by the then Foreign Minister Moshe *Sharett.

The signing of the agreement was preceded by opposition of unprecedented intensity in Israel, sometimes in the form of violent demonstration inspired by the nationalist *Ḥerut* party, headed by Menaḥem *Begin. He claimed — and had much support in Israel and from world Jewry — that because of the Jewish people's somber historical account with Germany, there should be no contact whatsoever with the Germans, and that it was necessary to refrain from any act (such as the signing of a Restitution Agreement) which could be interpreted as rehabilitating the German people. Even after the signing of the agreement, the boycott — sometimes official — on contacts with Germany continued, apart from those required for the implementation of the agreement. Yet, the agreement was a definite step toward normalization of relations between the two countries and the subsequent establishment of diplomatic relations between them in 1965. (E.L.)

Revisionist Movement Zionist political party promoting the views of Ze'ev *Jabotinsky, founded in 1925 in Paris. The name originated in a demand that the Zionist Executive (from which Jabotinsky resigned in early 1923), and Chaim *Weizmann in particular, adopt a revision in their policies toward the British mandatory regime and the system of Zionist settlement in Palestine.

Revisionism considered Zionism primarily a political movement (as opposed to practical Zionism which sought to concentrate on settlement and development activities) and throughout the pre-state period was in sharp opposition to Labor Zionism. Revisionism demanded that the territory of the future Jewish state encompass the original mandate borders stretching over both banks of the *Jordan River. It stressed the military aspects of Zionism and the necessity to reestablish the *Jewish Legion.

In the economic and social sphere Revisionism favored industrial development, private enterprise and the middle-class, unlike its Labor rivals. It opposed the **Histadrut* monopoly in labor relations and employment opportunities. A fierce competition developed and led to deep feelings of animosity and outbreaks of sporadic violence between the two camps. In 1933 the Revisionists were blamed for the murder of Ḥaim *Arlosoroff and a major split came about leading to the Revisionist withdrawal from the *World Zionist Organization (WZO) in 1935. The Revisionists established the New Zionist Organization including a financial arm (*Keren Tel Ḥai*), a workers' federation (**Histadrut Ha'ovdim Hale'umiyim*), a health network (*Kupat Ḥolim Le'umit*) and sports clubs. It supported a youth wing (**Betar*) and surreptitiously aided **IZL*. The New Zionist Organization negotiated with Poland and Romania for the evacuation of their Jewish populations to Palestine. "Illegal" immigration, to overcome British mandatory restrictions, was promoted. Revisionists also played a leading role in the armed Jewish resistance in Nazi-occupied Europe in the ghettoes and the forests.

In 1946 the Revisionists returned to the fold of the WZO at the 22nd Congress and two Revisionists were among the signers of Israel's *Proclamation of Independence. Unwilling to come to terms with the *IZL*-based **Ḥerut* and considering itself the true standard-bearer of Jabotinskian thought, it ran a separate list in the elections for the 1st Knesset (1949) but failed to gain representation. Unity was achieved a year later when the world union *Brit Ḥerut-Hatzohar*, was formed. A Revisionist has been elected to the World Zionist Executive since 1963. (I.M.)

Rogers Plan On December 9, 1969, in the midst of the *War of Attrition, US Secretary of State William Rogers initiated a plan for breaking the deadlock of the *Arab-Israel conflict. The plan called for Israel to withdraw to the international boundary with *Egypt. The status of the *Gaza Strip and Sharm-e-Sheikh would be negotiated, but they would not remain under Israeli control. Jerusalem would remain united but under the administration of the three religious communities. And freedom of navigation for Israeli shipping would be ensured in the Suez Canal. This plan was rejected by Egypt as being excessively pro- Israel, and by Israel for not ensuring its security; not calling for direct negotiations to a formal peace treaty; and not ensuring that *Jerusalem remain under Israeli control. On December 18, a proposal by the US Representative to the *United Nations, Charles Woodruff Yost, expanded the Rogers Plan to the Jordanian front, proposing that Israel would withdraw to the 1949 Armistice lines, with slight border revisions. The Arab refugees were to be accorded the choice between returning to Israel or accepting compensation. And repeating the already rejected proposals on Jerusalem, the Yost Document called for Israel and Jordan to enjoy an equal status in Jerusalem in the religious, economic and civil spheres. Freedom of navigation in the Gulf of Aqaba would be ensured. This proposal was accepted by Jordan and rejected by Israel on December 22.

In June 1970 Rogers initiated a second plan, which proposed negotiations between Egypt and Israel under the auspices of Ambassador Gunnar Jarring, the Swedish United Nations emissary, who had previously attempted to get discussions going between Israel and its neighbors on a peace settlement (See: *Jarring Mission). The new negotiations were aimed at reaching an agreement on a just and lasting peace, to be based on mutual recognition of each country's sovereignty, territorial integrity and political independence, and on an Israeli withdrawal from territories occupied in 1967 in accordance with *Security Council Resolution 242. As a first step Rogers proposed that the cease- fire between Israel and Egypt be renewed. On June 21 Israel's Cabinet rejected the new plan. On July 22, Egypt, apparently worried by the possibility of further escalation of the War of Attrition, suddenly accepted the proposals. US pressure then intensified on Israel and after President Nixon sent clarifications to Prime Minister Golda *Meir saying that Israel's withdrawal would be to secure and agreed borders, not the pre-June 1967 borders; that no withdrawal would be demanded until a contractual binding peace had been signed; that the Arab refugee problem would be solved in a way which would not impair the Jewish character of the State of Israel; that the US would ensure the integrity, sovereignty and security of Israel; and that the balance of arms would be preserved, Israel accepted the plan on July 31 1970. This acceptance by the Israeli government led to *Gaḥal*'s withdrawal from the *National Unity Government. The cease fire between Egypt and Israel came into force on August 7 1970. However, since Egypt broke the terms of the agreement by moving anti-aircraft missiles along the Suez Canal, Israel suspended the Jarring talks which resumed again only in the beginning of February 1971.

A third Rogers Plan for an interim agreement along the Suez Canal was rejected by Israel on October 4, 1971, several hours after being delivered, since it did not ensure that such an agreement would be followed by peace moves.

The Rogers plans did not deal with the Syrian Israeli border.

Romania and Israel Like the rest of the Communist bloc Romania voted for the 1947 UN partition plan and established diplomatic relations with Israel soon after the foundation of the state, though not at ambassadorial level. Israel's first representative to Bucharest, in September 1948, was the Israeli artist Reuven Rubin.

Until the mid-sixties relations between the two states were correct but cool, with an occasional diplomatic incident. There were no cultural relations and trade was modest.

A change began to be manifested in 1964 when the first group of Israeli tourists was allowed to visit Romania and a Romanian dance troop visited Tel Aviv. Then, in August 1965, the Romanian government allowed a Hebrew language paper to appear — the first in any Communist country.

Another major change occurred in the beginning of 1967. In March a Romanian trade delegation visited Israel, and the following month the Israel Minister of Finance Pinḥas *Sapir visited

Bucharest and signed a trade agreement. At the same time the Romanian government made the gesture of allowing Romanian Jews to join the World Jewish Congress.

Following the *Six-Day War Romania was the only Eastern bloc state not to sign an anti-Israeli declaration on June 11, 1967, and not to sever diplomatic relations with Israel. This was partly, due to Romania's improved relations with the *United States at this time, and partly to Romanian assertiveness in the sphere of foreign policy, which the *Soviet Union tolerated as long as it did not manifest itself internally. (The Soviet intervention in Czechoslovakia the following year made this distinction between internal and external independence among its satellites quite clear.) It is also possible that the Soviet Union found the presence of an East European Embassy in Tel Aviv to be useful.

Romania, under President Nicolai Ceausescu, became one of the main proponents of direct negotiations between Israel and its neighbors, and though refusing the role of mediator, has on occasion acted as a go-between. The Romanian interest in a Middle East settlement has been primarily to reduce the direct Soviet military involvement in the region and to reduce tension.

In December 1967, following a visit by the Romanian Minister of Finance and Trade, direct flights began between Tel Aviv and Bucharest.

In June 1968, the first of several visits by George Macovescu, at the time acting Romanian Minister of Foreign Affairs, took place, followed by the visit to Romania of Ze'ev Sherf, Israel's Minister of Commerce and Industry, who undertook to help Romania with an irrigation project and reached an agreement regarding a joint scientific program.

The following year, in August 1969, the diplomatic missions of the two states were upgraded to Embassies, and many Arab states reacted by recalling their envoys from Bucharest, or breaking diplomatic relations with Romania. Throughout its contacts with Israel, Romania has insisted that Israel must agree to total withdrawal from the *occupied territories and recognition of the Palestinian right to self-determination, arguing that the Israeli position is too rigid. In April 1972 Egypt requested Ceausescu to pass on a message to Prime Minister Golda *Meir who was to visit Bucharest the following month, but there was no sequel to this initiative.

Romania supported both the *Rogers Plan and the *Jarring Mission, and though it constantly maintained direct ties with Israel at the highest level, its standpoint was much closer to that of Egypt than of Israel.

Following the *Yom Kippur War, in November 1973, Israel's Minister for Foreign Affairs Abba *Eban visited Bucharest. Speculation was rife about his meetings with Soviet and Arab representatives there.

Though relations between Israel and Romania continued smoothly, there was some tension over difficulties imposed by the Romanian government on Jewish emigration to Israel and its support of the *Palestine Liberation Organization (PLO).

Nevertheless, Romania attempted to keep a balance in its relations with Israel and the Arab states, and a visit by Ceausescu to Syria and Egypt in April 1975 was balanced by Israeli Minister for Foreign Affairs Yigal *Allon's visit to Bucharest.

In June 1976 a Romanian delegation participated in the **Mapam* party conference — the first delegation from a Communist country to do so. It was only in November 1979, however, that a non-Communist Israeli delegation, from the **Alignment*, was invited to attend the Congress of the Romanian Communist Party.

Soon after the 1977 *upheaval in Israel, Prime Minister Menaḥem *Begin visited Bucharest. The following month Minister of Industry, Trade and Tourism, Yigael *Hurwitz did so, and in April 1978 Foreign Minister Moshe *Dayan followed. All of these visits gave rise to speculations as to the direct role which Ceausescu was playing in the peace process. Romania was the only Communist country which did not condemn the *Camp David Accords. Several months after the *Egyptian-Israeli Peace Treaty was signed, the Chairman of the *World Zionist Organization, Arie Dulzin, visited Bucharest — the first Zionist leader to be invited to a Communist country. Just before the *Lebanese War Ariel *Sharon caused the Romanians some embarrassment by paying a private visit, which was rumored to be not completely private.

In 1983 tension rose due to renewed difficulties in the exit of Jews from Romania, and in

April 1983 Begin declined an invitation to visit Bucharest — though personal reasons were also involved. Nevertheless, Foreign Minister Yitzḥak *Shamir visited Bucharest in August 1983, *inter alia* trying to get Romanian assistance in locating and releasing Israeli prisoners of war in the Lebanese War.

In February 1985 Prime Minister Shimon *Peres visited Bucharest, among other things, asking the Romanians to help bring about a change in the positions of both the Soviet Union and China on the Middle East.

Throughout 1985 and the beginning of 1986 Romania was among the states propagating the convening of an international conference on the Middle East.

In 1984 Israeli exports to Romania amounted to $25.4 million while imports reached $26.3 million. Since the establishment of the state 260,215 immigrants arrived in Israel from Romania — 150,412 of them in the years 1948–60.

rotation Arrangement adopted by **Maḥaneh Sheli* in the 9th Knesset whereby the first five candidates on the party's list in the elections took turns filling the two seats received by the party in the *Knesset.

The rotation principle was also included in the *coalition agreement signed between the *Alignment and the **Likud* in September 1984. Article 1.5 of the coalition agreement stated: "During the first 25 months of the government's office it will be headed by Mr. Shimon *Peres. Mr. Yitzḥak *Shamir will be Deputy Prime Minister and Minister for Foreign Affairs.

"During the remaining 25 months the government will be headed by Mr. Yitzḥak Shamir and Mr. Shimon Peres will be Deputy Prime Minister and Minister for Foreign Affairs.

"For this purpose the Basic Law: the Government [See: *Basic Laws] will be amended to lay down the status and authority of the Deputy Prime Minister," (Amendement 4 to Article 19 of the Basic Law: the Government).

Despite forecasts that the Alignment would try to sabotage the rotation, it became effective in October 1986.

Rubinstein, Amnon Member of Knesset, Minister of Communications, Professor of Law, born 1931, Tel Aviv. Rubinstein studied economics, international relations and law at the Hebrew University of Jerusalem between 1952 and 1956. He received his PhD in Law at the University of London in 1966, having been admitted to the Israeli Bar in 1963. He was a member of the editorial board of the *Ha'aretz* daily newspaper and taught law at Tel Aviv University from 1961 to 1975, serving as Dean of the Law Faculty between 1969–74. In 1974 Rubinstein founded **Shinui*, a centrist political protest movement and in 1976 he, with other members of *Shinui*, joined the *Democratic Movement for Change (DMC).

In the 9th Knesset (1977–81) Rubinstein was a member of the Foreign Affairs and Security Committee. *Shinui* broke away from the DMC due to its objection to the party's role in the **Likud*-led coalition. Rubinstein led *Shinui* in the elections to the 10th Knesset (1981), in which it gained two seats. It was Rubinstein's eloquent speech on democracy during the debate leading to the early dissolution of the Knesset in March 1984 which convinced the Knesset Speaker, Menaḥem Savidor, to refrain from holding a secret vote. In the elections for the 11th Knesset Rubinstein once again led *Shinui*, using the slogan "This time — a government with *Shinui* (change)," thus hoping that the *Alignment would be able to establish a narrow government in which *Shinui* could play a decisive role, with Rubinstein appointed Minister of Justice.

Shinui joined the *National Unity Government and Rubinstein was appointed Minister of Communications.

S

Sabra and Shatilla Two Palestinian refugee camps near Beirut in which the Phalange militia forces carried out a massacre on September 16, 1982, in retaliation for the assassination of the new Lebanese President Bashir Jemayel. While Israel troops were not involved in the massacre the Phalange forces had entered the camps with the Israeli army's knowledge and approval, and it was later argued that the Israeli authorities should have foreseen and forestalled it.

The affair created an international furore. In Israel all those who had opposed the *Lebanese War from the outset or objected to its being carried beyond the first 40 kilometers of Lebanese territory, raised an outcry. On September 25, 1982, a mass demonstration in Tel Aviv, in which 400,000 participants were reported, was organized by the *Alignment, *Peace Now, **Shinui*, the *Civil Rights Movement and other groups. It called for a commission of inquiry into the affair; there were also demands that the government resign.

On September 29, the government decided, after some resistance, to set up such a commission under Supreme Court Justice Yitzḥak Kahan. The *Kahan Commission report was published on February 8, 1983, and led to the resignation of Minister of Defense Ariel *Sharon who was held responsible for failing to give suitable instructions to prevent or reduce the danger of a massacre as a condition for allowing the Phalange to enter the Palestinian camps. A second outcome was the resignation of Head of **Aman*, Yehoshua Saguy.

Even though the massacres were not carried out by Israeli troops, Israel's image abroad, which had suffered considerably as a result of the Lebanese War, reached a new low following the Sabra and Shatilla episode. It also further sharpened the differences between the two major political camps in Israel — between those who supported the war and viewed Ariel Sharon as not only a great soldier but a great statesman, and those who opposed the war and saw Sharon as a dangerous adventurer whom they accused of indirect responsibility for the massacres.

Time Magazine, which claimed in an article that Sharon had advised the Jemayel family to take revenge for Bashir's murder, was sued by him. Even though Sharon did not win the enormous damages which he claimed from the American magazine for libel, the Federal Court in New York accepted his claim that there was no evidence to substantiate what *Time* had published.

Sapir (formerly Koslovsky), **Pinḥas** (1907–1975). **Mapai* and *Israel Labor Party leader.

Sapir was born in Poland and studied at the religious Taḥkemoni school. He was active in the leadership of **Heḥalutz* movement in Poland, and served as its treasurer. Sapir immigrated to Palestine in 1929, settling in Kfar Saba and working in orange groves where he was responsible for organizing several strikes. Later he worked as a bookkeper. Sapir acted as Levi *Eshkol's deputy when he was General Manager of the Mekorot Water Company and served in that position from 1937–47.

From 1948–53 Sapir was Director-General of the Ministry of Defense, traveling to Europe during the *War of Independence to coordinate arms purchasing activities. He was Director-General of the Ministry of Finance from 1953–55 and was Minister of Commerce and Industry from 1955 to 1964 and from 1970 to 1972. From 1963–68 and 1969–74 he was Minister of Finance, thus serving as Minister of both Finance and Commerce and Industry in 1963–64 and 1970–72. While acting as first Secretary-General of the *Israel Labor Party in 1968–69 Sapir remained in the cabinet as Minister without Portfolio.

Sapir played an active role in uncovering the details of the **Essek Bish* and in the *Lavon Affair which finally led to *Ben Gurion's resignation. He was personally involved in obtaining financing for the development of the new towns, some of Israel's major industries, both private and public, the National Water Carrier, the Eilat-Ashkelon oil pipeline, and various universities and religious institutions. His ideological opponents accused him of being excessively pragmatic and of having betrayed the party's socialist ideals. He had the image of an invincible strongman, and the little black book in which he jotted down notes became a symbol of his manipulative powers. Sapir was not happy about Israel's territorial expansion in 1967 for economic reasons, and because of its demographic implications and the polarization it brought into Israeli society. He had reservations about Jewish settlement activities beyond the *Green Line and to a large extent held Moshe *Dayan responsible for them.

Sapir was instrumental in blocking Ariel *Sharon's appointment as Chief of Staff. It was suggested that Sapir be a candidate for the premiership after Golda *Meir's resignation in 1974, but he declined. Furthermore, he chose not to be a member of the last *Alignment-led government under Yitzḥak *Rabin, instead serving as Chairman of the Jewish Agency Executive in 1974, in which capacity he visited numerous

Jewish communities in the Diaspora. He died the following year. (A.A. — S.H.R.)

Sareinu Hebrew for "our ministers," which, until 1969, was a forum of all the cabinet ministers belonging to *Mapai, and from 1969 to 1977 and again since 1984, belonging to the *Israel Labor Party. In Labor-led coalitions *Sareinu* were responsible for determining much of the government's policy. In the *National Unity Government since 1984 they tried to coordinate the positions of the Labor ministers in the coalition. Formally, *Sareinu* have not imposed positions on individual ministers.

Sarid (formerly Schneider), **Yossi (Yosef)** Member of Knesset and publicist. Born 1940, Reḥovot, Israel. Sarid received his BA in philosophy and literature from the Hebrew University in 1964, and an MA in political science and sociology from the New School for Social Research in New York in 1969.

He served in the *IDF in the artillery and as a military correspondent. Between 1961–64, while studying, he worked as a reporter and editor of the daily newsreels in the Israel Broadcasting Service thereafter serving as **Mapai* spokesman until 1965. Later he was advisor to Prime Minister Levi *Eshkol. Sarid was one of Pinḥas *Sapir's confidants, and was viewed as one of Eshkol's and Sapir's "boys."

Between 1970–73 he headed the section dealing with academics in the Ministry of Labor. Sarid headed the *Mapai*, *Israel Labor Party and *Alignment information headquarters in the 6th through 11th Knesset elections. He has been a member of the Knesset since 1974 and since 1977 a member of the Knesset Foreign Affairs and Security Committee.

In 1974, following the murderous terrorist attack on Kiryat Shmonah, Sarid moved to the northern town with his family where he remained for three years, volunteering as a teacher at a local high school. He was elected four times to the Knesset on the Alignment ticket, but upon the establishment of the *National Unity Government in September 1984 left the Labor party and joined the *Civil Rights Movement in opposition. Sarid's serious disagreements with the Labor party started with the *Lebanese War when he was the only member of the Knesset Foreign Affairs and Security Committee to vote against the war to which he was opposed from the very first day. In the Knesset plenary he abstained, together with Shulamit *Aloni *Mapam* and MK Mordechai Virshuvsky from **Shinui*, on a vote approving the first stage of the war (the Labor party supported the operation in *PLO-controlled Southern Lebanon).

Sarid did not object to the National Unity Government on principle but opposed the principle of the *rotation, the inclusion of Arie *Sharon in the government and the undertaking to continue to support existing Jewish settlements in Judea and Samaria (See: **Yosh*).

Even before the Lebanese War Sarid became the declared enemy of the Israeli right-wingers who view his willingness to compromise on territories as defeatist and traitorous. There have been occasional threats on his life. Sarid expresses his views in a regular column in *Ha'aretz* and frequently contributes articles to other Israeli dailies.

seamen's strike A strike against Zim, Israel's largest shipping company, in 1951, by members of the seamen's union over work and salary conditions against a background of political tension between supporters of **Mapai* and the pro-Soviet **Mapam*. Since Zim was owned jointly by the government, the *Jewish Agency and the **Histadrut*, the strike was viewed, to a certain extent, as a rebellion against state authority.

The first stage of the strike (or the "small strike") broke out on the *S.S. Negbah* in June 1951 when the ship was anchored in Marseille over the seamen's demand for a greater foreign currency allocation.

The strikers tried to get the Communist-controlled French seamen's union to intervene. When the ship finally returned to Haifa two of its crew were called up for military service, which once again brought the *Negbah*'s crew out on strike. The strikers were taken off the ship by the police and the strike spread to six more ships. The strikers were in touch with some of the leaders of *Mapam* and **Maki* and the stevedore's union published a broadsheet on July 22 accusing the seamen of sabotaging the state's economy and security and calling on them to return to work and "the way of the *Histadrut*." On July 25 the *Histadrut* reached an agreement with the seamen that they would return to work and the Supreme Court of the *Histadrut* would start investigating the legality and actions of the "temporary committee" which was behind the strike, and which was trying to take over from the legitimately elected union committee.

New elections to the third seamen's convention were held in October, and the "temporary committee" which had increased in strength demanded a complete revolution in the union's regulations and *modus operandi*.

Under the leadership of the "mutineers" the "great strike" broke out on November 12, 1951, but the merchant navy continued to operate, with the government's and *Histadrut*'s approval, using volunteer labor and a group of seamen who had not participated in the strike.

Some of the strikers were called up for military service, recognized *post factum* to have been a mistake which only increased the tension. The strike, which became increasingly violent, was supported by *Mapam* and several writers who spoke of the government's "dictatorial activities." On December 14, 1951, striking seamen were taken off the *S.S. Tel Aviv*, the last ship in the striker's control, by a police force after a violent struggle. The strike officially ended on December 23, after the *Histadrut* promised to return all the seamen to work and to prevent any retaliatory measures being taken against the strikers and seamen who had resigned.

The strike was dubbed by Yosef Almogi, head of the Haifa workers' council who had been one of the main negotiators on behalf of the *Histadrut*, the "**Altalena* of the Left," because it was believed to have been Marxist-inspired and that its real goal was to gain control over the Israel Merchant Navy.

Security Council Resolutions 242 and 338 Resolution 242 was passed by the UN Security Council in the aftermath of the *Six-Day War on November 22, 1967, and was based on a British-American initiative. The main provisions of the resolution were the affirmation of two basic principles for the establishment of a just and lasting peace in the Middle East, namely: "withdrawal of Israeli armed forces from territories occupied" in the Six-Day War; and the "termination of all claims or states of belligerency and respect for the acknowledgement of the sovereignty, territorial integrity and political independence of every state in the area and their right to live in peace within secure and recognized boundaries free from threats or acts of force." The resolution further affirmed the necessity "for guaranteeing freedom of navigation through international waterways in the area; for achieving a just settlement of the refugee problem; for guaranteeing the territorial inviolability and political independence of every state in the area, through measures including the establishment of demilitarized zones." Finally it requested "the Secretary-General of the UN to designate a special representative to proceed to the Middle East to establish and maintain contacts with the states concerned in order to promote agreement and assist efforts to achieve a peaceful and accepted settlement in accordance with the provisions and principles" of the resolution, which constituted the basis for the *Jarring Mission. The English text of the resolution mentioned Israeli withdrawal "from territories," implying that it would not have to withdraw from *all* the territories, while the French text spoke of withdrawal from "*les territoires*" (the territories), implying total withdrawal.

This resolution, which has since been mentioned by all the *European Economic Community (EEC) statements dealing with the *Arab-Israel conflict, as well as in the *Camp David Accords and the *Egyptian-Israeli peace treaty, was accepted almost immediately by *Egypt and *Jordan. Israel accepted the resolution in December 1967, a fact made known to Jarring by Israel Foreign Minister Abba *Eban on February 12, 1968, but at least two Ministers, Moshe *Dayan and Menaḥem *Begin, were not aware of such an acceptance and denied it in May 1968. It was only when Israel accepted the second *Rogers Plan in August 1970 that its acceptance of Security Council resolution 242 was made public, and **Gaḥal* left the government as a result.

The *Palestine Liberation Organization (PLO) has so far refused to accept Resolution 242 because it speaks of the Palestinian problem as a refugee problem rather than a national problem, and because acceptance would imply recognition of Israel. Efforts in the beginning of 1986 failed to get the PLO to accept the resolution in return for participation in the negotiations for peace.

Resolution 338 was passed on October 22, 1973 toward the end of the *Yom Kippur War. It called for a cease fire, "the implementation of Security Council Resolution 242 in all its parts, and the beginning of negotiations" between the parties concerned under appropriate auspices, aimed at establishing a just and durable peace in the Middle East.

Security Services, General (GSS) See: **Shabak.*

Semitic Action In Hebrew: *Hape'ulah Hashemit.* Political group established by Uri *Avneri in 1956 which advocated Israel's integration into the region through a confederation including the whole territory of *mandatory Palestine, and inclusion of this confederation in a Middle East federation. Among the group's members was also Natan *Yellin-Mor. The group broke up in 1965 when Uri Avneri established a party — **Ha'olam Hazeh — Ko'aḥ Ḥadash* which ran for the 6th Knesset.

Sephardi List An ethnic party, representing the traditional Sephardi elite. It ran for the 1st *Knesset (1949) as *Reshimat Ha'iḥud Ha'artzi shel Hasephardim U'vnei Edot Hamizraḥ* (List of the National Union of Sephardim and Members of the Oriental Communities) and for the 2nd Knesset (1951) as *Reshimat Sephardim Ve'edot Hamizraḥ Vatikim Ve'olim* (List of Sephardim and Oriental Communities Veterans and Immigrants).

The Sephardi List (commonly known as "the Sephardim") joined David *Ben Gurion's first two governments in the course of the 1st Knesset, and their representative Bechor Shalom Shitrit was appointed Minister of Police. Its most prominent Knesset Member was Eliahu Eliashar.

In their political leanings the Sephardim were close to the *General Zionists whose Knesset faction they joined in the course of the 2nd Knesset. Shitrit returned to the 2nd Knesset as a member of **Mapai* and continued to serve as Minister of Police until 1966, with only a 20-month break. A contributing factor to the list's disappearance was its failure to appeal to new immigrants from **Edot Mizraḥ.*

Knesset seats: 1st Knesset (1949) — 4; 2nd Knesset (1951) — 2.

Sephardim See: **Edot Mizraḥ.*

settlement policy One of the major goals of *Zionism and the State of Israel has been Jewish settlement in **Eretz Yisrael.* Much of this settlement has been officially planned and directed. Zionist settlement in Palestine began in 1882 with the arrival of the First *Aliyah* (See: **aliyah*) — a wave of immigration by members of *Bilu* and *Ḥovevei Zion* who established the first settlements of Rishon Letzion, Zichron Ya'acov and Rosh Pina. By 1897, when the first Zionist Congress convened, there were 19 new Jewish rural settlements in existence. Most of them received financial support from the Baron de Rothshchild who also owned the land on which they were built. Their main crop was grapes, from which wine was manufactured. However, these settlements had no legal base in the Ottoman system and there was no central Jewish body responsible for the settlement enterprise as a whole.

At the 4th Zionist Congress of 1901 the Jewish National Fund (See: *Land Policy) was established as an institution of the Zionist Movement with the task of purchasing land for settlement. In 1907 the *World Zionist Organization (WZO) established a Palestine office in Jaffa, headed by Arthur Ruppin (1876–1942), with the task of directing settlement activities in the country on the basis of a comprehensive, systematic plan. In 1904 a new wave of immigrants (known as the Second *Aliyah*) started to arrive in Palestine, which, unlike the First *Aliyah*, brought with them contemporary socialist ideas upon which the first collective settlements were based.

By the outbreak of World War I, 43 settlements had been established with a population of about 12,000. Of these settlements the WZO had established 14. After the war the Palestine office was replaced by the Zionist Commission which included several departments, one of them the Department of Rural Settlement which was responsible for settlement activities. When the *Jewish Agency was established in 1929 through the cooption of non-Zionists, the Department for Rural Settlement became one of its departments. Among the department's activities were the establishment of a settlement infrastructure, the financing of new settlements through the supply of equipment and means of production, the physical and agricultural planning of the settlements, agricultural instruction and research.

By 1948, 291 rural settlements were in existence in various parts of Palestine, though few settlements were established on the less fertile land in the Negev, the Galilee, Judea and Samaria due to restrictions on land purchases imposed by the mandatory authorities. In the course of the 1936–39 disturbances (or "Arab Revolt") many fortifications were hastily put up in newly-established settlements, known as *Ḥomah U'migdal* (consisting, literally, of a "wall and a tower"). On October 6, 1946 11 such settlements were established in a single night. It was believed that the settlement map of the country would determine the boundries of the Jewish state and indeed only the settlements of Gush Etzion and Kibbutz Beit Ha'aravah (near the Dead Sea) had to be abandoned during the *War of Independence. The concept that the boundaries of Israel are determined by the location of Jewish settlements has guided Israeli settlement plans ever since. Thus, until 1967 Israeli governments built dozens of settlements along the 1949 Armistice Lines (See: *Armistice Agreements) and from 1967–77 successive Labor-led governments established new settlements within the parameters of the *Allon Plan. The *Likud*-led governments of 1977–84, which openly declared that no territories west of the *Jordan River would be returned to Arab sovereignty, carried out intensive settlement activities in all parts of Judea, Samaria (See: **Yosh*) and the *West Bank.

The mass immigration in the first years of the state, the collapse of the Arab agricultural economy within the boundaries of Israel and the severance of all trade relations with the neighboring Arab states which had previously supplied much of Palestine's agricultural needs, resulted in an intensified rural settlement effort. In the years 1949–50 over 200 new settlements were established and an additional 100 by 1953. This activity was carried out at first along the coastal plains and the Judean Mountains leading up to *Jerusalem (the Jerusalem Corridor). When water supplies were brought to the northern Negev, settlements were established there as well. The rapid pace of settlement frequently resulted in slipshod planning, and new immigrants, themselves untrained, were frequently brought directly upon their arrival to the hastily-constructed new settlements. Many of the new settlers, who had previously engaged in trade, left, thereby impairing even further the economic consolidation of the settlements. In the mid-fifties the concept of regional planning was first implemented in the Lachish district. The new method advocated the establishment of regions composed of agricultural settlements in groups around each of several settlement centers in which schools, clinics, cultural and entertainment facilities were concentrated, with an urban settlement (known as a development town) in the region's center. The population of each rural settlement was to be more or less homogeneous in terms of country of origin. Two other regions were planned according to this method: the Ta'anach District east of the Valley of Jezreel and the Adulam Region near Beit Shemesh in the Judean Mountains. After the *Six-Day War Jewish settlement in the *Golan Heights followed the same pattern. Toward the mid-sixties many of the new settlements were freed from the close supervision and direction of the various settlement institutions. The Settlement Department of the Jewish Agency is responsible for settlements within the *Green Line, its budget being covered from funds raised in Jewish communities abroad. Since 1967 around 115 rural settlements have been established within the pre-1967 borders, most of them in the Upper Galilee, the Western Negev (Ḥevel Shalom) and the Aravah.

The Settlement Section of the World Zionist Organization is responsible for the more controversial settlement activities in the West Bank, the *Gaza Strip and the Golan Heights; its activities are financed by the government budget.

Since the Six-Day War 186 settlements have been established by the Settlement Section of the WZO and the Ministry of Housing. The Jewish Agency department and the WZO section are jointly headed by an *Alignment and a **Likud* representative.

The Jewish National Fund is in charge of preparing the infrastructure for new settlements, purchasing and preparing land, and cutting new roads to the settlement sites.

Since the establishment of the state all agricultural matters have been dealt with by the Ministry of Agriculture. There are several organizations which coordinate the work of the settlement bodies and the ministry. The Ministry of Housing and the various settlement movements (such as the kibbutz movements) are also involved in the process.

The common forms of publicly aided rural settlements are the *kibbutz, the **moshav ovdim* (workers' settlement) and *moshav shitufi* (cooperative settlement). All three types of settlement are based on the following principles: the settlement is built on state lands which are leased to it and not sold; they are based, as far as possible, on self-labor, with minimal hired labor; and on cooperative organization and mutual assistance arrangements.

The kibbutz is a totally collective settlement in which production, marketing, purchases and consumption are carried out in common, and members receive equal allocations irrespective of the work they do. There is a common dining room, and the children usually live in childrens' houses. The kibbutzim, which used to be based almost exclusively on agriculture are now engaged in industry and tourist-vacation facilities as well. The *moshav ovdim* is made up of family units associated as a cooperative for marketing, purchasing and the supply of services. Occasionally a certain branch is held and worked by all the member families in common. The *moshav shitufi* is a hybrid between the kibbutz and the *moshav ovdim* — all production is carried out in common, but each family runs its own household.

After the Six-Day War a new type of rural settlement was developed in areas outside the Green Line, known as *Yishuv Kehilati* (community settlement). These settlements are not collective in the sense that the three other types of settlement are. Many members work outside the settlement, though some small light industry, crafts and sophisticated intensive agriculture have been developed. Several such settlements house *yeshivot* (schools for the study of the Talmud).

In the aftermath of the Six-Day War the issue of settlement in the territories occupied during that war became one of deep political controversy in Israel. There was almost unanimity of opinion about the need to settle the Golan Heights, which had served the Syrians as a base for artillery shelling of Israeli settlements, and such regions as the *Rafa Salient (returned to Egypt in 1982 within the framework of the *Egyptian-Israeli Peace Treaty), Gush Etzion, the Jordan Valley Rift and the adjacent mountains. There are major differences of opinion regarding settlement in the densely populated areas of Judea, Samaria and the Gaza Strip, which the *Alignment and Zionist parties to its left are willing to return to Arab sovereignty in return for peace, and which the *Likud* and the Zionist parties to its Right are not willing to forsake under any circumstances. In the *National Unity Government coalition agreement it was decided that new settlements would be established only in such locations as approved by a majority of the cabinet, i.e., only in locations agreed upon by both major political blocs.

Since the mid 70s several settlements were established by **Gush Emunim* without the prior consent or approval of the authorities, but many of these were subsequently approved or moved to new locations.

Non-organized private settlement has been concentrated from the beginning of the Zionist immigration in cities and towns. The largest purely Jewish city developed was Tel Aviv, founded in 1909 as a suburb of Jaffa. Completely private farming has continuously existed in small towns known as *moshavot* (plural of *moshavah*) and on some individual farms.

Shabak Acronym of *Sherut Bitaḥon Klali* (General Security Service). Also known as the *Shin Bet*. The body responsible for the prevention of hostile secret activity within the state, such as foreign espionage, internal and external sabotage, and illicit acts of violence. It uses both defensive measures — carrying out security checks on candidates for sensitive posts and laying down rules for safeguarding information, installations and personalities — and offensive measures — neutralizing the activities of those involved in illicit hostile operations.

The founder of the *Shabak* in 1948 and its Head until 1954 was Isar Harel. The name of the current Head of *Shabak* is never revealed for security reasons, but in May 1986 the American ABC Network identified Avraham Shalom, who had served as Head since 1982, as the personality implicated by *Attorney General Yitzḥak Zamir in the **Shabak* Affair.

Shabak Affair On May 25, 1986, the Israeli media revealed that the *Attorney General Yitzḥak Zamir had recommended that a senior official be removed, but that the government had declined to follow his advice. Two days later the American TV network ABC announced that the "senior official" was Avraham Shalom, Head of the **Shabak* (General Security Service) and that Zamir's accusation was connected with the killing of two Palestinian terrorists who had been taken prisoner after hijacking bus number 300 on the Tel Aviv-Ashkelon route on April 12, 1984. (Two terrorists were killed during fighting and photographs showing two more terrorists alive had been published in the media.)

Two committees were appointed to investigate the incident. The first, headed by Me'ir Zore'a, investigated the cause of death of the two prisoner-terrorists. The second committee, headed by State Attorney Yonah Blattman, investigated the question of who was responsible. As a result, Yitzḥak Mordechai, the commander of the Paratroop Corps who had stormed the bus, was implicated in causing grievous bodily harm to the prisoners. Mordechai was subsequently brought to an army disciplinary court which found him innocent. In the meantime, information reached the Attorney General that it was the Head of the *Shabak* who had given the order to kill the two remaining terrorists. He was informed that relevant evidence had been destroyed and that the evidence given by various officers before the two investigating committees had been falsified. Zamir called for an official commission of inquiry to investigate the whole affair, but was willing to consider dropping the issue if Shalom were dismissed. The government, however, refused to dismiss the Head of the *Shabak* and Zamir requested the Inspector General of the Police to start an investigation of the allegations. The government was wary of any investigation because of the damage it would cause Israel's security services.

In the meantime personalities on the political Left called for an investigation of the responsibility on the political level, especially that of the Prime Minister at the time of the killing, Yitzḥak *Shamir. It was alleged that the political level was as much to blame as was the Head of the *Shabak* if it had been aware of a deliberate attempt to cover up the facts and to use Yitzḥak Mordechai as a scapegoat.

After Zamir ended his term of office in June 1986, the new Attorney General Yosef Ḥarish decided that he had no alternative but to press the charges against the Head of the *Shabak*, unless an official commission of inquiry were established to deal with the issue. On June 25, 1986, Avraham Shalom and three other Shabak officers requested and received a pardon from President Ḥaim Herzog. The *President believed that by doing so the whole affair would be closed and no further damage would be done to Israel's security services. However, six petitions were brought to the High Court of Justice regarding the legality of the President's decision to grant a pardon before any charges has been formally brought against the persons concerned. On August 6, the High Court of Justice upheld the President's actions (following which decision seven additional *Shabak* men requested a similar pardon), but also decided that an inquiry should be held.

After the government rejected a proposal that an official commission of inquiry be appointed to investigate the affair, the Attorney General instructed the police to open its investigation on July 14. Two days later the government appointed a three-man committee under Aharon *Yariv to investigate the working procedures of the *Shabak*. The Yariv Committee recommendations were not published, but were implemented.

On December 28, a report prepared by a team under the Attorney General was presented to the government. It found that Prime Minister Shamir had not given the instruction to kill the two terrorists and did not back the later attempt to cover up the facts. The report recommended that the 11 *Shabak* officers implicated in the affair should not be brought to trial since they had already received a pardon from the President. The leadership of both the *Alignment and the **Likud* stated that they now viewed the affair as closed.

Shalom Achshav See: *Peace Now.

Shamir (formerly Yzernitzky), **Yitzḥak** Underground and party leader, eighth and tenth Prime Minister of Israel. Born 1915 in Poland. Shamir studied at Hebrew secondary school in Bialystock and was a member of **Betar*. He interrupted his study of law in Warsaw to immigrate to Palestine in 1935 and completed his studies at the Hebrew University of Jerusalem. In 1937 Shamir joined *IZL and when it split in 1940 he joined **Leḥi* whose leadership he took over after Avraham (Ya'ir) *Stern was murdered in 1942.

He was twice arrested by the British mandatory authorities, in 1941 and 1946, and both times managed to escape — the second time from a detention camp in Eritrea.

From 1948–55 Shamir was engaged in various commercial ventures and during the following decade held a senior position in the **Mossad* after which he returned to private commercial activities and was active in the struggle for Soviet

Jewry. Shamir joined **Ḥerut* in 1970 and was elected to its executive committee, directing the Immigration Department and later the Organization Department and in 1975 was elected Chairman of the *Ḥerut* Executive Committee.

Shamir has been a Member of Knesset since 1974. On June 13, 1977, he was elected Speaker of the Knesset and in March 1980 was appointed Minister for Foreign Affairs, in which capacity he oversaw the implementation of the *Egyptian-Israel Peace Treaty, initiated contacts with several African states which led to their resumption of diplomatic relations with Israel, and directed the negotiations that culminated in the agreement with *Lebanon in May 1983.

Following Menaḥem *Begin's resignation from the premiership, Shamir became Prime Minister on October 10, 1983, keeping the post of Foreign Minister as well. While he was Prime Minister strategic cooperation was established with the *United States and a decision in principle was taken on the etablishment of a Free Trade Area between the US and Israel. Shamir led the *Likud* election campaign in 1984, calling for the establishment of a *National Unity Government.

In the government formed by Shimon *Peres on September 1984 Shamir was appointed Deputy Prime Minister and Foreign Minister. In October 1986 a rotation of posts took place between Peres and Shamir, as stipulated by the rotation agreement, which mentions both persons by name, and Shamir re-assumed the post of Prime Minister.

Sharett (formerly Shertok), **Moshe** (1894–1965). Zionist Labor leader, Israeli statesman and writer.

Born in Russia, Sharett immigrated to Palestine with his parents in 1906. He was an officer in the Turkish army during World War I. He was active in the Labor parties *Aḥdut Ha'avodah* and, after 1930, **Mapai* and was a member of the editorial board of *Davar*, the daily newspaper of the **Histadrut*. After the assassination of Ḥaim *Arlosoroff in 1933, Sharett was appointed Head of the Political Department of the Jewish Agency, becoming chief Zionist spokesman to the British and the Arabs, with whom he frequently met in an attempt to find an agreed solution to the Palestine problem. His stubborn struggle with the British led to the formation of the *Jewish Brigade in 1944, which participated under his guidance in saving the survivors of the *Holocaust and bringing them to Palestine. His arrest (with other members of the Jewish Agency Executive) in 1946 by the British marked the increasingly violent nature of the Jewish resistance. Sharett was Foreign Minister from the establishment of the State of Israel, 1948, until 1956 and also Prime Minister from 1954–55. His resignation in 1956 was connected with the incompatibility of his moderate policies and the activism of Prime Minister David *Ben Gurion (e.g., concerning the events leading to the *Sinai Campaign 1956, and the *Lavon Affair). From 1960 until his death he was Chairman of the Zionist and Jewish Agency Executive, and Chairman of *Am Oved*, the *Histadrut* publishing house, Israel's largest publisher.

Sharon (formerly Sheinerman), **Ariel** Military Commander and Member of Knesset. Born 1928, in Moshav Kfar Malal. Sharon attended high school in Tel Aviv and joined the **Haganah* in 1945. During the *War of Independence he was Platoon Commander in the Alexandroni Brigade and was wounded in the unsuccessful Battle of Latrun. From 1952–53 he studied history and oriental studies at the Hebrew University in Jerusalem and was then appointed leader of the special 101 Commando Unit set up to carry out retaliatory operations against attacks by **feda'iyin*. In January 1954 Unit 101 united with a paratroop regiment of which Sharon became Commander, and continued to carry out unconventional operations across enemy lines. In February of the following year he was in charge of the attack on the Egyptian army camp in Gaza which President Nasser later claimed had caused him to believe that no peace settlement between Israel and *Egypt was possible.

Sharon was appointed Commander of a Paratroop Corps in 1956 and fought in the *Sinai Campaign in which he was accused of insubordination to his superiors in the attack on the Mitla Pass. In 1957 he attended the Camberley Staff College in Great Britain. During the years 1958–62 Sharon served as Infantry Brigade Commander and then Infantry School Commander, and attended Law School at Tel Aviv University.

Yitzḥak *Rabin appointed him Head of the Northern Command Staff in 1964 and Head of the Army Training Department, with a promotion to Major General in 1966. He participated in the *Six-Day War as commander of the armored division in which his tactical brilliance was generally acclaimed. He was appointed Head of the Southern Command Staff in 1969, in which capacity he worked to fortify the *Bar Lev Line and actively participated in the *War of Attrition. After the cease-fire along the Suez Canal went into effect in August 1970, and throughout 1971, Sharon concentrated on eliminating terrorist cells from the *Gaza Strip and clearing the Bedouin from northern Sinai. He proposed enabling the Egyptians to establish a civil adminstration in Sinai while the *IDF would remain in military occupation for 15 years during which time the two countries would develop relations of trust.

Considering his chances slim of being appointed Chief of Staff, Sharon resigned from the army in June 1972 to run for the Knesset as a member of the *Liberal Party within the **Likud*, which he helped establish. In the *Yom Kippur War Sharon was recalled to active military service to command an armored division, and crossed the Suez Canal with his troops. Despite Sharon's tactical brilliance, his relationship with his senior officers caused his conduct during the war to be in dispute. In December 1973 he was elected to the 8th Knesset, and declared his willingness to negotiate with the *Palestine Liberation Organization (PLO) leadership on a solution to the Palestinian problem within the framework of his *"Jordan is Palestine" concept. In December 1974, disgusted with political life, Sharon resigned his Knesset seat and accepted an emergency senior appointment in the IDF. From June 1975 to March 1976 Sharon served as special advisor to Prime Minister Rabin and started to plan his return to politics, establishing his own party **Shlomzion* after investigating various possibilities with parties and personalities from the Right, Left and Center. *Shlomzion* gained two seats in the 9th Knesset (1977) but ceased to exist when Sharon decided to join **Ḥerut* soon after the election and was appointed Minister of Agriculture and Chairman of the Ministerial Committee for Settlement, in which capacity Sharon advocated the establishment of a dense network of Jewish urban and rural settlements in Judea and Samaria (See: **Yosh*), to mitigate against the return of these territories to Arab sovereignty. In this period Sharon was viewed as the patron of **Gush Emunim*. Sharon was ambivalent regarding the peace process with Egypt, but advised Prime Minister Menaḥem *Begin at Camp David to agree to give up the *Rafa Salient in return for peace. Relations between them become tense when Begin hesitated to appoint Sharon as Minister of Defense following the resignation of Ezer *Weizman in 1980.

After playing an active role in the 1981 *Likud* election campaign Sharon was finally appointed Minister of Defense in the second Begin government. In January 1982 the General Staff completed, at Sharon's request, a plan for Operation *Oranim*, which was later implemented as Operation Peace for the Galilee (See: *Lebanese War). Sharon defined the operation's goals as freeing Israel's northern settlements from terrorist attacks; liquidating the terrorists in Beirut both militarily and politically; establishing a legal government in *Lebanon which would sign a peace treaty with Israel; forcing the Syrians away from the Beirut area. In April 1982 Sharon was in charge of the delicate evacuation operation of the Rafa Salient which was resisted by members of *Gush Emunim*. Sharon was personally involved in all stages of the Lebanese War which began on June 4, and frequently concealed or reported his moves to the Prime Minister *post factum*. He personally approved the entrance of the Phalange into *Sabra and Shatilla on the day after Bashir Jemayel's assassination on September 15, 1982 to enable them to seek Palestinian terrorists. Following the massacre which occurred in the camps and the *Kahan Commission Report Sharon was forced to resign from his post as Minister of Defense but remained in the cabinet as Minister without Portfolio. Despite opposition in the ranks of the *Alignment, Sharon was appointed Minister of Industry and Trade in the *National Unity Government. Soon after his appointment Sharon travelled to the US to attend the hearings of the libel suit he had brought against *Time Magazine* for publishing an article claiming that a secret appendix of the Kahan Commission Report contained evidence that Sharon had encouraged the Jemayel family to take revenge against the Palestinians. Both Sharon's and the magazine's attorneys were allowed to examine the appendix and other secret documents. Although the jury found the accusation unfounded and the article defamatory, it decided it had been published without malicious intent, and Sharon was denied his $50 million compensation claim against *Time Magazine.*

Sharon is viewed as a possible contestant for the *Ḥerut* party leadership in future. The general public in Israel is inclined to take only extreme positions regarding Sharon, whether in favor or against. (Y.A. — S.H.R.)

Sharon Plan A plan advocated by Ariel *Sharon, which calls for the annexation of most of the *West Bank to Israel.

Sharon's plan views Jewish settlement in the mountain plateau as a prerequisite for Israel' security, in contrast to the emphasis placed in the *Allon Plan on the importance of settlement in the Jordan Valley Rift as a security belt.

Sharon therefore advocated hastening the settlement efforts on the mountain plateau before the end of negotiations on the *autonomy plan, and was instrumental in implementing such settlement activities as Minister of Agriculture and later as Minister of Defense. The enclaves which were, according to the Sharon Plan, to remain outside of Israeli control, comprised a large portion of the Samaria plateau (including Nablus and Jenin), the area to the north of Ramallah and a strip of heavily populated land some five kilometers wide close to the *green line (including Tulkarem and Qalqilya).

The Sharon Plan offers solutions to potential military threats from the East. Although it does not call for annexation of the whole of the West Bank, it rejects a solution based on *territorial compromise and advocates a unilateral Israeli-implemented administrative reorganization of those parts of the West Bank which will not be annexed by Israel. In a sense the Sharon Plan offers an answer to those who argue that an annexation of the *occupied territories would turn Israel into either a bi-national state or an undemocratic one. (M.B.)

Shass Acronym for *Shomrei Torah Sephardim* ("Sephardi Torah Guardians"). An ultra-religious non-Zionist Sephardi party established before the elections to the 11th Knesset (1984) in protest over the inappropriate representation of the Sephardi sector in the **Agudat Yisrael* list. Ex-Sephardi Chief Rabbi Ovadia Yosef, who is *Shass*'s spiritual leader and Head of the seven-member *Mo'etzet Ḥachmei Hatorah* (Council of Torah Sages) was joined by the Lithuanian Rabbi Eliezer Shach, one of the leaders of *Mo'etzet G'dolei Hatorah* (Council of Great Torah Scholars), and together they led Shass to the impressive achievement of four Knesset seats while *Agudat Yisrael* went down from four to only two. *Shass* also took voters away from the Moroccan party **Tami*, and gained the support of many *ba'alei tshuvah* (penitents) who view Rabbi Shach as their spiritual leader.

Shass has a fundamentalist approach to religion and state, wanting Israel to become a *Halacha* (Jewish law) state.

Its political leader, Rabbi Yitzḥak Peretz, was Minister of the Interior in the *National Unity Government until December 1986. He resigned over the issue of registering as a Jewess, as prescribed by the High Court of Justice, a woman who had been converted to Judaism by a Reform rabbi in the US. (Sh.M.)

Sheli See: **Maḥaneh Sheli.*

Shemtov — Yariv formula See: *Yariv — Shemtov formula.

Shin Bet See: **Shabak.*

Shinui — Mifleget Hamerkaz Hebrew for Change — Party of the Center, a liberal party formed in the aftermath of the *Yom Kippur War by Amnon *Rubinstein, Mordechai Virshubski and others. The party developed out of the movements which protested against the refusal of the political establishment to take responsibility for the blunders in the conduct of the war (See: **Meḥdal*).

The founders of the party believed that deep political, economic and social deficiencies in the Israeli system endangered its security, strength and ability to function and that public protest alone was insufficient to remedy the situation. They invited 40 persons to attend a preliminary meeting and when 120 came they decided to call *Shinui*'s first public meeting on March 26, 1974; the party was officially founded on July 16.

Shinui's ideological platform rests on eight principles which have remained the basis for its activities. *Shinui* favors entering negotiations with Israel's neighbors which would include *territorial compromise; *electoral reform to ensure the responsibility of the representatives to their voters, the democratization of the parties and national supervision over the regularity of their activities through appropriate legislation; a written *constitution to ensure the basic rights of the citizen; minimal government involvement in the state's economic life, for purposes stemming from national, and not sectoral needs, and for the preservation of the welfare state; basing national public administration on the principle of personal responsibility and appointing and advancing government employees exclusively in terms of their qualifications and performance; organizing the education system to offer equal opportunities to all, and to provide education befitting a democratic society with a developed technological and scientific base; closing social gaps through an appropriate change in the taxation system and in salary policy, demographic planning and re-organization of the national welfare services; a fundamental change in the public life style and in the services available to the citizen, through education, the implementation of the law and suitable legislation.

Since its establishment *Shinui* has sought to become a widely-based party. In 1975 negotiations took place with the *Civil Rights Movement for a formal partnership but it did not materialize. In December 1976 *Shinui* joined Professor Yiga'el *Yadin in the establishment of the *Democratic Movement for Change (DMC). The DMC adopted most of *Shinui*'s platform, though with a more moderate position on such issues as territorial compromise and religion and state.

Though the DMC gained 15 seats in the 9th Knesset and hoped to be a pivotal force in the formation of the next government, Menaḥem *Begin was able to form a government without it. However the DMC did join the Begin government on October 24, 1977, despite *Shinui*'s objections. Two days before the *Camp David Accords were signed the DMC disbanded and eight of its members, including the members of *Shinui*, went into the Opposition. It adopted the name *Hatnu'ah Leshinui Veyozmah* (the Movement for Change and Initiative). Its leadership changed when Meir *Amit returned to the *Israel Labor Party and in 1980 the name *Shinui — Mifleget Hamerkaz* was adopted. In the elections to the 10th Knesset *Shinui* gained only two seats, going up to three in the 11th Knesset (the third member being a *Druze). Following the 1984 elections *Shinui* joined the *National Unity Government on the side of the *Alignment and Rubinstein was appointed Minister of Communications. *Shinui* has taken part in elections to the **Histadrut* and workers' council, where it calls for extensive structural reforms. *Shinui* has also run in local elections and is well represented in the municipal councils of Haifa and Tel Aviv.

Knesset seats: 9th Knesset (1977) — 5 within the framework of the DMC and later independently; 10th Knesset (1981) — 2; 11th Knesset (1984) — 3. (P.O.)

Shlomzion A political party formed by Ariel *Sharon prior to the elections to the 9th Knesset (1977) after the failure of his efforts to rejoin the **Likud* on his own terms, or to run together with some of the founders of the *Democratic Movement for Change. Politically *Shlomzion* favored the solution of the Palestinian problem in Jordan after the Hashemite Royal House had been deposed (See: *"Jordan is Palestine"). To this end, it was argued Israel should be willing to negotiate with any Palestinian representative. (Sharon himself was willing to meet Yasser Arafat.) The State of Israel should encompass the area from the Mediterranean to the Jordan River. The Palestinians could have self-government in the *West Bank as long as Israel remained militarily in control and Jewish settlement continued.

The economic policy propagated by *Shlomzion* called for austerity and living within one's means and the prohibition of strikes.

Two months before the elections Sharon sought to reenter the *Likud* with *Shlomzion*, but his efforts were thwarted by Simḥa *Ehrlich. *Shlomzion* eventually ran independently and gained two Knesset seats. When it became apparent that Menaḥem *Begin would establish the new government Sharon decided to join the **Ḥerut* movement with several of his followers and was appointed Minister of Agriculture in Begin's first government. *Shlomzion*'s second Member of Knesset, Yizḥak Yitzḥaki, remained in the Knesset as a one-man faction named *One Israel.

Shurat Hamitnadvim Hebrew for "column of volunteers," *Shurat Hamitnadvim* was a body set up in 1951 by a group of students and intellectuals to provide social assistance to new immigrants and inhabitants of slum areas, and to assist their absorbtion in the country. Within two years the organization numbered 500 members, many of them members of *Mapai*. One of the central personalities in the organization was attorney Eliakim Ha'etzni, today a Kiryat Arba activist (See: *Hebron). Gradually the activities of the group extended to a struggle for public integrity, and, with the support of Minister Dov *Yosef a struggle against the black market.

In 1955 *Shurat Hamitnadvim* published a pamphlet *Sakanah Orevet Mibifnim* (Danger Lurks from Within) which warned that the lack of pesonal integrity in the regime was dangerous to Israeli society.

One of the examples cited in the pamphlet concerned accusations of corruption against Amos Ben Gurion, the Deputy Inspector-General of the Police and son of David *Ben Gurion. In 1956 Amos Ben Gurion sued *Shurat Hamitnadvim* and won his case at the District Court level. But Defense Attorney Shmuel *Tamir appealed to the Supreme Court which found that the Inspector-General of the Police had lied at the trial. The court criticized Amos Ben Gurion for the methods used in the trial and objected to the public campaign carried out in the press against *Shurat Hamitnadvim* and Shmuel Tamir in the course of the trial. As a result the Inspector-General of the Police, Yeḥezkel Saḥar, was forced to resign having being convicted of perjury, and soon thereafter Amos Ben Gurion resigned as well.

Despite the appeal's success *Shurat Hamitnadvim* gradually disintegrated, after public funds for its work among new immigrants were stopped and the establishment carried out a public campaign against it through the weekly *Rimon*. Many of its members also lost hope that any change could be brought about in the system by means of the sort of public struggle carried out by the organization.

Si'aḥ Acronym for *Smol Yisraeli Ḥadash* — New Israeli Left. An extra-parliamentary movement founded in 1969 following a letter sent to Prime Minister Levi *Eshkol by graduating high school students. *Si'aḥ*'s central argument was that a national liberation movement of the *Palestinians exists alongside *Zionism, with an equal right to assert itself within the territory of *mandatory Palestine; hence the necessity of reaching a peace agreement with the Arabs on the basis of the June 4, 1967 borders.

During the 1973 election campaign, some members wanted to limit themselves to extra-parliamentary activity while others favored taking part in the elections, and a split followed: some *Si'aḥ* activists formed the "Blue-Red Movement" seeking to establish a socialist alternative to the State of Israel; others joined *Ha'olam Hazeh — Ko'aḥ Ḥadash*. With these developments *Si'aḥ* effectively ceased to exist.

(M.B.)

Sinai Campaign (October 1956). The Czech arms deal concluded by *Egypt in 1955, and the Suez crisis of the summer of 1956 created growing tension in the Middle East. Israel felt itself especially threatened by the Egyptian blockade of Eilat and the Gulf of Aqaba, imposed since 1954, the continuous sabotage raids across the Egyptian Armistice lines, and the speeches and statements threatening another round of war and Israel's destruction — all amounting, in Israel's view, to the abrogation of the 1949 Armistice Agreement (See: *War of Independence). Israel's sense of encirclement and immediate mortal danger was deepened by Jordan's adherence to the Egyptian-Syrian military pact and the establishment, in

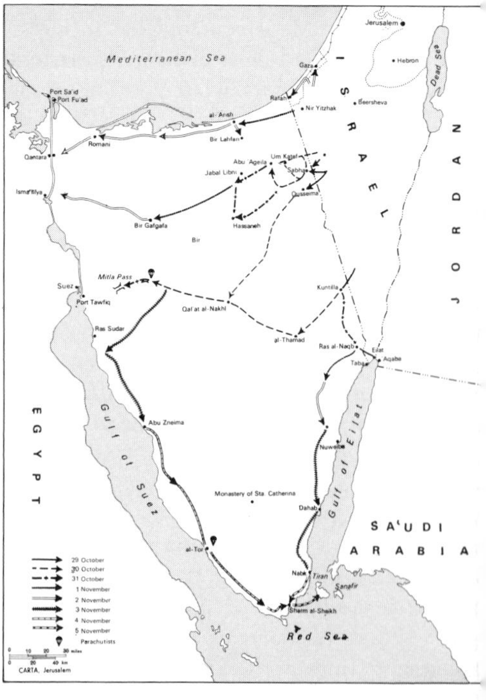

Map of the Sinai Campaign.

October 1956, of a Unified Military Command of these three countries' forces.

As a result Israel secretly coordinated an operation with *Great Britain and *France against the Egyptian nationalization of the Suez Canal on July 26, 1956. On October 29–30 Israel parachute battalions seized the Mitla Pass. Subsequently, three columns set out across the desert, tactically supported by the Air Force. One, striking south from Eilat along a road hitherto considered impassable, took Sharm-e-Sheikh, commanding the Straits of Tiran. Another column followed the central Sinai road in the direction of Ismailiya. The northernmost column outflanked the *Gaza Strip, then turned north to mop up enemy forces in the Strip, and southwest along the coastal road in the direction of Qantara. Within 100 hours the massive Egyptian forces in the *Sinai Peninsula had been completely routed. Heeding a predetermined Anglo-French ultimatum, Israel's forces halted 16 kilometers east of the Suez Canal. (Meanwhile the Israelis had captured an Egyptian destroyer off Haifa.) Other Arab countries — mutual defense treaties notwithstanding — did not take part in the conflict.

The Security Council was paralyzed because of the involvement of two of its permanent members, who had the right to veto any decision. On November 2, and again on November 7, the *UN General Assembly called — with rare unanimity of the *US and *Soviet Union — for the immediate withdrawal of Israel's forces to the Armistice Lines; the Soviets threatened to use force if the resolution were not heeded. The withdrawal of Anglo-French forces, which had in the meantime invaded the Suez Canal Zone, was also demanded. On November 4, the Assembly decided to create a UN Emergency Force (UNEF) to replace the withdrawing troops. On November 8, Israel agreed to withdraw upon the conclusion of arrangements with the UN concerning UNEF, after receipt of a letter from Premier Bulganin of the Soviet Union threatening Israel's existence as a state, advice from France, UN pressure and a threat of severe economic sanctions from the US. By January 22, 1957, it had evacuated all the occupied territory except for the Gaza Strip (occupied by Egypt since 1948, but not considered Egyptian territory) and the Sinai coast facing the Straits Tiran. Concerning these areas, Israel insisted on safeguards for free navigation and freedom from attack across its borders. In March 1957 the UNEF was stationed along the borders, including the Gaza Strip, and in Sharm-e-Sheikh, to provide such "safeguards," and Israel withdrew accordingly. Israel also received certain diplomatic assurances; but the precise extent of the UN and US commitment in that respect has remained controversial. The Gaza Strip was, contrary to Israel's expectations, immediately handed over to Egypt, and hostile incursions from the area were soon resumed. Freedom of navigation through the Straits of Tiran was maintained until May 1967 (See: *Six-Day War). (N.L.)

Sinai Peninsula Triangle-shaped desert area which forms the land bridge between Asia and Africa, bordered in the west by the *Suez Canal and the Gulf of Suez, and in the east by the Gulf of Aqaba. The rugged mountains in the southern part of Sinai are, according to some traditions, the site of Mount Sinai where Moses is said to have received the Ten Commandments. The area of the Sinai is 23,200 square miles and its population in 1948 was 38,000, mostly Bedouin. After 1948 the Egyptian army mounted a major military build-up in Sinai and its population grew to 126,000 by 1967. Sinai was the battleground for the *Sinai Campaign in 1956 and the *Six-Day War in 1967 and the canal zone for the *Yom Kippur War of 1973.

Along the western shore minerals were discovered and exploited: manganese at Um Bugma and oil at Ras Sudar, Abu Rudeis and the Alma Field on the Gulf of Suez (the latter discovered and first developed by Israel). Sinai was part of the Ottoman Empire from 1517. The Agreements of 1940–41, regulating the relations between the Sultan and his autonomous Viceroy of Egypt, left the administration of Sinai unclear and controversial. While Ottoman sovereignty was uncontested, sporadic Egyptian administration was maintained — at least since the late 1870s — and continued under the British occupation of Egypt in 1882. The Sultan claimed that Egyptian temporary rights of adminstration referred only to the northwestern part of the Peninsula and to a number of posts in the southern part, on the pilgrims' route to Mecca, while the central triangle — Suez-al Arish-Aqaba — was under direct Turkish rule. After 1882 the British, on their own initiative, claimed for Egypt — and tried to establish de facto — fuller rights of possession. British notes of 1892 and 1902 laid down the eastern boundary as a line drawn from al-Arish or Rafa to Aqaba. A tentative plan to develop the al-Arish area for Jewish settlement was briefly discussed in 1902–03 by Zionist Leader Theodor *Herzl and the British, but came to nothing. When the Turks set up a garrison in *Tab'a, south of Aqaba, in 1906, a sharp diplomatic clash with Britain ensued, and the Sultan, while not renouncing his claim, had to accept the Rafa-Aqaba line as a border. This line became the southern boundary of *mandatory Palestine in the years 1922–48. Israeli forces occupied part of the Sinai in 1949, toward the end of the *War of Independence, and the whole of the Sinai in the course of the Sinai Campaign — both times evacuating the territory thereafter. Except for the *Gaza Strip which Egyptian forces occupied in 1949, the international border between Israel and Egypt in the years 1949–67 was the boundary as it existed in mandatory times. The Sinai was again occupied by Israel in the course of the Six-Day War. After 1967 Jewish settlement activities took place in the *Rafa Salient (Pit'ḥat Rafiaḥ) where the town of Yamit and several other settlements were established, and along the coast of the Red Sea. Israel also constructed two major Air Force bases in the Sinai.

According to the original *Allon Plan Israel was to continue to occupy those areas in which the settlements and air bases were constructed, even after a peace settlement.

In the course of the *Yom Kippur War Egyptian troops crossed the Suez Canal into the Sinai Peninsula, and at the end of the fighting the Third Egyptian Army was surrounded on the eastern (Israeli) side of the Canal. According to the January 1974 *Disengagement Agreement and the September 1975 *Interim Agreement Israel started to withdraw in the Sinai along the canal and further inland, returning the Abu Rudeis oil fields to Egypt and enabling it to reopen the Suez Canal for navigation and rebuild the Egyptian towns along its bank. President Sadat's visit to Jerusalem in November 1977 was said to have been conditioned on prior Israeli agreement to evacuate the whole of Sinai in return for peace. Both the *Camp David Accords and the *Egyptian-Israeli Peace Treaty spoke of Israeli withdrawal from the Sinai in stages. The withdrawal was completed in April 1982, despite strong resistance by some settlers in the Rafa Salient, reinforced by members of **Gush Emunim* from outside the Salient who had to be removed by force.

None of the parties in Israel ever argued that the Sinai was part of "historic **Eretz Yisrael*," but some objected to Israeli withdrawal for security good faith. There is still a dispute between Israel and Egypt as to whether Israel must withdraw from Tab'a, a 600 square meter area bordering Eilat and Egyptian-held Sinai.

Six-Day War Arab-Israel tension rose steadily during the mid-1960s, because of the constant increase in Jewish casualties resulting from Arab sabotage and infiltration which had been actively encouraged by the Arab states. Sabotage and the shelling of Israeli border villages from Syrian territory, were particularly intensive in early 1967 with the active participation of the Syrian Army. On April 7, 1967, Israeli planes struck at Syrian artillery positions and brought down six Syrian MIGs sent to intercept them. Syria complained bitterly that Egypt had not rushed to help its ally

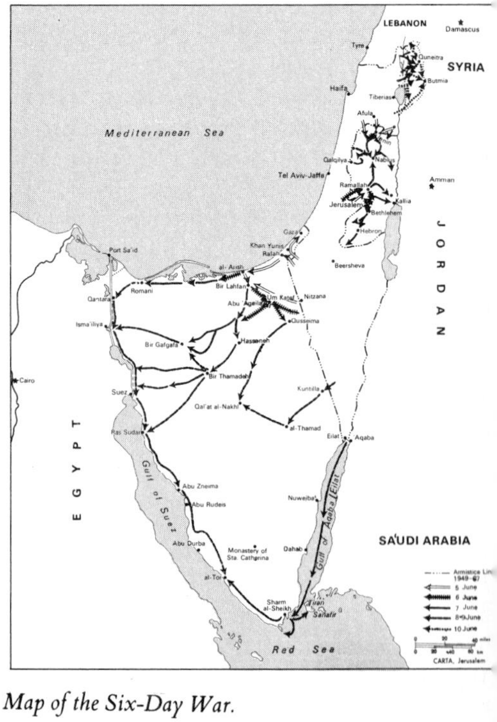

Map of the Six-Day War.

particularly in view of their defense pact of November 1966.

Egypt then announced that it would not tolerate any further Israeli action against Syria, and concentrate large numbers of tanks and infantry units in the *Sinai Peninsula close to the Israeli border. The Soviet Union encouraged Egypt in these war preparations, and warned it of Israeli troop concentrations against Syria (an allegation which was denied by the UN truce observers). Statements made by Israeli leaders in mid-May were interpreted by the Russians and Arabs as threats against Syria. On May 16, Egypt requested the immediate withdrawal of the UN Emergency Force (UNEF) from its position along the Egypt-Israel border and the Straits of Tiran and, on May 18, from the whole of Sinai. The UN Secretary-General U Thant, immediately complied with this request. While U Thant was on his way to Cairo for further talks, President Nasser, on May 21–22, reimposed a blockade in the Gulf of Aqaba (kept open since 1957 under the supervision of UNEF) by closing the Straits of Tiran to all shipping to and from Eilat. Israel had repeatedly stated that it would regard such a blockade as a *casus belli.*

The US and a number of other maritime nations while unprepared to take practical steps to make President Nasser change his decision nonetheless proclaimed that the Straits of Tiran were an international waterway open to free passage by ships of all nations. Egypt proclaimed that it would consider any attempt to break the blockade an act of war. President Nasser challenged Israel to war, announcing that Egypt was now strong enough to win and threatened Israel's destruction. Leaders of the other Arab states made equally bellicose speeches. In addition to the defense pact with Syria, Egypt concluded similar pacts with Jordan and Iraq on May 30 and June 4, 1967, resulting in Israel's complete encirclement and threatening its existence as a sovereign state. The Arab states were supported by huge supplies of Soviet military equipment.

After diplomatic attempts to calm the area and a plan for an international flotilla to break the blockade of the Straits failed, Israel, in the early hours of June 5, struck across the Sinai border while its Air Force set about destroying the Egyptian Air Force. That same morning the Jordanian forces began shelling and carrying out air

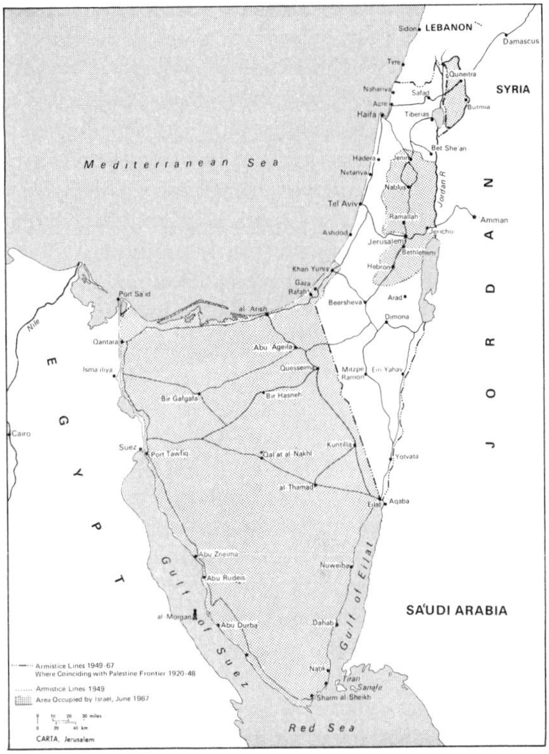

Cease-Fire lines, June 1967.

raids across the 1949 Armistice Line with Israel which sent a warning via the UN to King Hussein of Jordan to stay out of the war. The warning went unheeded: the Jordanian army attacked and captured UN headquarters south of Jerusalem. The Israel Air Force now took action and destroyed Jordan's Air Force. As Syria continued to shell Israeli villages, Syrian airfields were attacked, the same day, and its Air Force, too, was largely destroyed. During the first 16 hours of the war the Arab states lost well over 400 planes, as against the loss of 19 Israeli planes. On that first day of fighting Israel won complete aerial superiority while maintaining an almost total news blackout.

Simultaneously Israeli armored columns advanced into the Sinai Peninsula, in the direction of Rafa and al-Arish in the north, Abu Ageila, Bir Gafgafa in the center, and al-Qusseima in the south. A major battle took place on and around the elaborate fortifications of Abu Ageila. Bitter fighting occurred on the outskirts of Gaza. By the end of June 6, the Egyptian retreat had become a rout. Sharm-e-Sheikh, the Egyptian position from which the blockade of the Straits of Tiran had been enforced, was captured on June 6 from the sea; parachutists landed without opposition.

Israel reacted swiftly to Jordan's entry into the war. Reinforcements, rushed to Jerusalem, were able to retake, on June 5, the UN headquarters and to link up with the isolated outpost on Mount Scopus in the north, which had since 1949 constituted an Israel enclave behind Jordanian lines. Out of respect for the *Holy Places, strict orders were given to minimize damage to the Old City. On June 7, Israel forces took the Old City of Jerusalem.

By the end of the third day of fighting, Israeli forces had taken all of the Sinai Peninsula up to the Suez Canal, the *Gaza Strip and most of the *West Bank of Jordan. When the UN Security Council, after days of wrangling, called for a cease-fire, Israel was the first to accept it. Jordan's acceptance followed, and Egypt, after initially rejecting the cease-fire, acceded 24 hours later, on Thursday, June 8. Lebanon had played no significant part in the fighting. Syria, the most militant of the Arab states, was still intensively shelling border villages. An attempt to capture one of them had failed. Now Syria refused to accept the cease-fire, relying on the tremendous tactical advantage of its fortifications on the crest and slopes of the *Golan Heights. However, 20 hours of intensive up-hill fighting ended in the capture by Israel forces of the Golan Heights up to and including the town of Quneitra, and on June 10 the cease-fire came into effect also on the Syrian border.

In the course of less than six days, Israel had routed three of its neighbors who were supported by a number of other Arab countries. In addition to the Arab planes it had destroyed Israel destroyed or captured over 500 tanks. Arab military equipment lost included 70 percent of the heavy equipment of three Arab armies, valued at well over $1,000 million. Over 1,500 Egyptians were killed and 5,600 were taken prisoner; Jordan claimed to have lost about 6,000; Syria suffered about 1,000 casualties; over 700 Israelis were killed and 2,500 wounded.

The war left Israel in control of areas over three times its pre-1967 size, and of an Arab population of about one million (in addition to Israel's 400,000 Arab citizens). In the political struggle which followed, the Arab states demanded the complete evacuation of all *occupied territory as a precondition for any settlement; Israel, determined not to return to the strategic and tactical situation of a constant threat of war, decided to withdraw only to secure and recognized borders, to be established through a mutually agreed peace settlement. (N.L.)

POLITICAL CONSEQUENCES OF THE WAR: The immediate effect of the Six-Day War was a state of euphoria which embraced not only the State of Israel but the whole Jewish people. The Labor movement parties, which had led Israel to its great military victory, enjoyed increased popularity as manifested by the 1969 election results.

However, the entry of Menaḥem *Begin and *Gaḥal* into the government on the eve of the war gave the Israeli Right a new legitimization which opened the way for its gradual ascent thereafter, and its electoral victory in 1977. Israel's occupation of the West Bank, the Gaza Strip, the Golan Heights and the Sinai Peninsula opened a new front on the Israeli political scene. Whereas until 1967 few Israeli politicians ever spoke or thought of an extension of Israel's borders beyond the *Green Line after 1967 a growing number of political parties and movements started referring to the territories as having been "liberated" rather than "occupied," advocating their non-return to Arab sovereignty even in exchange for peace, and actively promoting Jewish settlement in all parts of these territories. (See: *Land of Israel Movement, **Gush Emunim*, **Likud*, **Teḥiyah*, **Morasha*, *territorial compromise). This development saw the progressive strengthening of a coalition between the "nationalist" and national-religious forces in Israel, and a significant increase in the public support which this coalition enjoyed.

Israel's military success and its occupation of territories containing a non-Jewish population of 1.2 million, resulted in its international image changing from that of the threatened little David to that of an oppressive Goliath. A growing number of states started viewing the Israeli position as intransigent regarding the *Palestinians and a permanent solution of the *Arab-Israel conflict.

One of the immediate effects of the war was that the *Soviet Union and its satellites as well as several Third World countries broke off diplomatic relations with Israel. Relations with *France, which had been particularly close in the 1950s, became demonstratively cool after de Gaulle decided to stop French arms deliveries to Israel and referred to the Jews as a "domineering people." (S.H.R.)

Sneh (formerly Kleinbaum), **Moshe** (1909–1972). Sneh was born in Poland and graduated from Warsaw University as a physician. He was active in the Zionist movement, becoming Chairman of the Polish Zionist Organization. He was a member of the left-wing of the *General-Zionists and a delegate to several Zionist Congresses. Sneh immigrated to Israel in 1940 and became a member of the *Haganah* High Command, 1940–46, and its chief, 1941–46. When, in July 1946, the *Haganah* stopped armed resistance against the British and the Zionist Congress failed in December to order its resumption, Sneh resigned his post as Chief of the High Command, becoming (1947–48) Head of the European Branch of the Political Department and Head of the "illegal" Immigration Department of the *Jewish Agency. Convinced that the future Jewish state should win Soviet friendship, Sneh resigned in 1948 from the Jewish Agency Executive to join the leftist **Mapam*. He led its left wing which broke away from *Mapam* in 1954 and merged with **Maki*.

When in 1965 the Communist Party split, Sneh stayed with *Maki*, the predominantly Jewish more moderate faction. After the *Six-Day War, Sneh severely criticized Soviet bloc policies. He regarded the Six-Day War as a justified campaign of Israeli self-defense. He was a member of the Knesset 1949–65, and again from 1969. He was editor of *Kol Ha'am* (Voice of the People), the daily newspaper of the Israel Communist Party, 1965–69.

Socialist International Organization established in 1951 in Frankfurt by 34 social-democrat parties, primarily from Europe. It believes that socialism should be achieved without diverging from democracy — through evolution, not revolution — and opposes the idea of the dictatorship of the proletariat. **Mapai* became a full member of the International in the mid-fifties and the *Israel Labor Party took its place in 1968.

**Po'alei Zion*, which had been a member of the Second (non-Communist) International from 1916 until its dissolution in 1939, also became a member of the Socialist International within the framework of the World Alliance of **Aḥdut Ha'avodah — Po'alei Zion*, and was replaced by the *World Labor Zionist Movement (WLZM) in 1968. However, as of the mid-seventies socialist groups which are not national political parties can no longer be full members of the International and the WLZM now has the status of associated organization.

**Mapam*, whose predecessor *Hashomer Hatza'ir* (See: **Mifleget Po'alim — Hashomer Hatza'ir*) had been a member of the Vienna International (the so-called "second and a half" International) in the early 1920s, became an observer of the Socialist International in 1981 and a full member in 1983. The Socialist International has always been an important forum for explaining Israel's position and gaining support for its policies. Golda *Meir was elected Deputy Chairman of the International in 1972 and held the post until 1978. In 1978 Shimon *Peres was elected to the same post (now called Deputy President). The Israel Labor Party was especially active in the International during its years in opposition (1977–84).

In July 1979 the two leading figures in the socialist International, Willy Brandt of the *Federal Republic of Germany and Bruno Kreisky of Austria, met with Yasser Arafat in Vienna. However, they did not meet with Arafat as representatives of the Socialist International and the meeting did not constitute official recognition of the *Palestine Liberation Organization (PLO).

The only representative of an Arab country in the Socialist International is Walid Junblatt's Progressive Socialist Party of Lebanon which became a member in 1980. During the *Lebanese War Kreisky initiated moves to expel the Israel Labor Party from the International due to its support of the initial stages of the war, but the initiative was thwarted.

The entry of many Third World parties (especially from *Latin America) has made the atmosphere in the International less congenial for the Israeli parties, though since 1983 Israel's status has been more or less stable. The Israel Labor Party and *Mapam* coordinate their positions before meetings of the Socialist International.

Socialist List In Hebrew *Reshimat Hasotzialistim*, it is a political list, most of whose members had belonged to **al-Ard* (outlawed in 1965), which was disqualified by the Central Elections

Committee from running in the elections to the 6th Knesset. The grounds for the disqualification were that the list's initiators reject not only the integrity of the State of Israel but also its very existence. The High Court of Justice rejected the appeal of the Socialist List, basing itself *inter alia* on the *Proclamation of Independence as the source of the normative principle that Israel is a Jewish state.

South Africa and Israel South Africa, under General J.M. Smuts' United Party, had been an ardent supporter of *Zionism since World War I when Smuts was a member of the British war cabinet and supported the issuing of the *Balfour Declaration. After the war Smuts was one of the statesmen who consistently fought for Britain's honoring of the Declaration and proclaimed his belief in its wisdom and justice.

South Africa voted for the 1947 partition plan in the UN General Assembly, and supported Israel's admission into the *United Nations in 1949. In the same month that Israel was established (May 1948) the Nationalist Party came to power in South Africa and introduced a series of laws which put apartheid, — racial segregation and discrimination against the non-white majority (over 85 percent of the population) in general and the Blacks in particular — on the statute books.

Despite their moral disapproval none of the western states broke diplomatic relations with South Africa. In 1950 Israel opened a legation in Pretoria which was maintained at ministerial level until 1960. During the 1960s most of the Black African states attained independence from colonial rule, and Israel established diplomatic relations with many of them (See: *Africa and Israel). At this stage the Black African states began to exert pressure on Israel regarding its relations with South Africa, as a result of which Israel reduced the status of the head of its diplomatic mission in Pretoria in 1963 to that of a chargé d'affaires. In the same year Israel made a small contribution to the outlawed Black South African African National Congress. South Africa reacted by temporarily suspending the transfer of funds from the South African Jewish community to Israel.

It should be noted that South Africa had no direct diplomatic representation in Israel when it was a member of the British Commonwealth and was represented by *Great Britain. Only afte[r] leaving the Commonwealth in 1961 did Sout[h] Africa send a Consul-General to Israel.

Israel's eagerness to maintain direct represen[-] tation in Pretoria, which persists to the presen[t] day, results among other things, from the exis[-] tence of a closely-knit Jewish community i[n] South Africa numbering 118,000. Before th[e] establishment of the state this community playe[d] an active role in the Zionist struggle and durin[g] the *War of Independence sent a higher percentage of volunteers to serve with the Israeli force[s] (especially in the fledgling Air Force) than an[y] other Jewish community in the Diaspora (See[:] *Maḥal*).

Since 1919 about 15,000 South African Jew[s] have immigrated to Israel and the South Africa[n] Jewish community has been a generous contributor. Israel feels closely involved in the welfare and safety of this community.

After the *Yom Kippur War in 1973, most o[f] the Black African states broke off relations, thu[s] joining other Third World and Communist bloc countries which had broken off relations with Israel in 1967. These same countries have been engaged, since 1969, in a campaign against South Africa in the *United Nations, and Israel voted with them in favor of the annual General Assembly resolutions condemning apartheid. In 1974 South Africa was suspended from participation in General Assembly sessions. In the same year *Palestine Liberation Organization (PLO) Chairman Yasser Arafat was invited to address the General Assembly, symbolizing Israel's precarious diplomatic situation in the aftermath of the war when the nations were deeply concerned about the world monetary crisis.

While Israel found itself increasingly isolated in the international arena, South Africa was one of the few states which was steadfast in its attitude toward Israel, allowing the Jewish community to continue to send as much financial assistance as could be raised — which far exceeded the annual quota for currency exports assigned to the community under South Africa's stringent foreign currency regulatoins.

As a result, relations between South Africa and Israel improved considerably and the Israeli diplomatic mission in Pretoria was raised to that of an Embassy in 1974. A South African ambassador was assigned to Tel Aviv in 1976, the year in which South African Prime Minister B.J. Vorster paid an official visit to Israel (in 1952 Prime Minister D.F. Malan had paid a private visit to Israel). In the course of this visit several economic and trade agreements were signed, and it was decided that economic missions from the two countries should meet annually to discuss and review the implementation of the agreements. These missions have met regularly, alternatively in South Africa and Israel.

In 1985 Israel exported $63.8 million worth of goods and imported $174.7 million. Israel has started, in recent years, to import South African coal at prices well below world market prices (See: *Energy Policy). The two countries also have exchange programs for scientific and professional know-how in several fields — mainly related to agriculture and medicine. Despite the cordiality of the relations, Israel has always openly and unequivocally condemned the racial discrimination practiced by the South African government. This criticism has been voiced not only by Israel's representatives at the UN but by its ambassadors to Pretoria as well. In his speech before the UN General Assembly on September 30, 1986, Israeli Deputy Prime Minister and Minister for Foreign Affairs Yitzḥak *Shamir stated that: "Israel, founded on basic moral and democratic values, cannot remain silent in the face of racial discrimination, wherever it may be. We reject and condemn apartheid as a political, social and economic system... Israel also believes that violence is not the path to reform in South Africa. We must urgently foster a climate to facilitate a political settlement if we are to avoid a further drifting into economic chaos, suffering and bloodshed. We hope responsible leaders on all sides will act to create such a climate, and that the government of South Africa will initiate negotiations which will satisfy the legitimate political aspirations of all South Africans, regardless of race or colour." Israel does not believe that economic sanctions are the correct means for changing the policy of the South African government, since such sanctions would hurt the South African Blacks and many Black African states (which purchase much of their food and basic commodities from South Africa) as much if not more than the white South Africans. It also doubts the value of breaking off diplomatic relations in order to bring about a change in a state's policies. However, Israel supports a policy of constructive engagement on the part of the western countries which would entail finding a solution to South Africa's problems by peaceful and evolutionary means, leading to the abrogation of apartheid and the granting of equal civil rights to all inhabitants of the country, without resort to revolutionary methods which would only result in bloodshed and human misery from which all sections of the South African population would suffer. Notwithstanding the fact that the trade relations between Israel and South Africa have remained modest in volume and value compared to that of many Western states (as well as the Arab oil-producing states), they have provided an excuse for anti-Israel propaganda on the part of the Communist bloc and the Arab states, which insist that these relations manifest an ideological partnership between the two countries. This distortion of reality reached the peak of absurdity in the establishment in 1974 of a special UN committee to examine the relations between Israel and South Africa and report to the Special Committee against apartheid. The reports published by the above-mentioned UN committee are distorted and frequently without any foundation.

Much has been written about Israel's military collaboration with South Africa. While Israel has admitted that such contacts exist, reports on their extent have been exaggerated. According to a report of the London-based Institute of Strategic Studies, South Africa receives most of its imported military supplies from *France, Great Britain, the *Federal Republic of Germany and the *United States. South Africa has established an armaments industry of its own with the help of mostly European and American industrialists, making it almost totally self-sufficient in arms. In January 1987 the Ministry for Foreign Affairs began a reevaluation of Israel's relations with South Africa in order to align Israel's policy with that of the rest of the free world, following the imposition of emergency regulations by Pretoria in June 1986.

On March 18, 1987, Minister for Foreign Affairs Shimon *Peres reiterated Israel's condemnation of the policy of apartheid, and announced its new policy which involves the reduction of Israeli contacts with South Africa, refraining from signing any new defense contracts with it and the reexamination of Israel's policy in light of developments in the policies of the other states of the free world

(El.L.)

Soviet Union and Israel Both Lenin and Stalin denied the existence of a Jewish nation, and the Bolshevik Party, both before and after the October 1917 Revolution which brought it to power, opposed Zionism in all its aspects (See: *Anti-Zionism). Yet, in 1947, the Soviet Union supported the establishment of a Jewish state in part of Palestine. As Deputy Foreign Minister Andrei Gromyko told the special session of the UN General Assembly in May 1947, the Jews had a historic right to Palestine just as did the Arabs; the West European countries had proven incapable of providing physical protection for their Jewish inhabitants, and those Jews living in Palestine, or wandering about Europe or in Displaced Persons camps had the right to have their own state.

Having reached the conclusion that Jews and Arabs were unable to live together in one federated bi-national state, the Soviet Union cooperated with the United States in October-November 1947 in working out the details and passing the partition resolution in the General Assembly.

In addition to political and moral support, the Soviet Union gave the **Yishuv* crucial military assistance in its *War of Independence in the form of arms from Czechoslovakia (See: *Arms Purchases). In order to strengthen the new state's military potential it also coordinated an effort for the emigration to Palestine from the East European Peoples' Democracies — though not from the Soviet Union itself — of Jews of military age (See: **Gaḥal*). The Soviet Union and Czechoslovakia were the first countries to grant the State of Israel de jure recognition in May 1948, and Soviet support continued from the War of Independence, which was perceived by the Soviets as a fight against British imperialism, until Israel became a member of the *United Nations in May 1949.

Once the aim of expelling Britain from Palestine had been achieved and Israel had become a viable state, the Soviet Union, which was well aware of the basic pro-West orientation of Israel's ruling party, **Mapai*, began to retreat from its pro-Israel position.

Even prior to this, discordant notes had appeared on the bilateral level as a result of the identification with the State of Israel of large sections of Soviet Jewry. Encouraged by the sympathetic attitude of the Soviet government to the Jewish state, many Jews believed that they too might be allowed to go to Israel and help in its War of Independence, and tens of thousands demonstrated their feelings by coming to Moscow's main synagogue upon the arrival there of Israel's first envoy to Moscow — Golda *Meir (then known as Meyerson). As of February 1949, when the Soviet Foreign Ministry first expressed its displeasure regarding Israel's contacts with Soviet Jews, the issue of Soviet Jewry began to complicate, and often dominate the Soviet-Israeli relationship. Although at the time the Soviet Union refused to acknowledge officially and publicly that this problem was in any way relevant to its relationship with Israel, the severance of diplomatic relations in February 1953 was the direct outcome of an increasingly severe anti-Jewish policy on the part of the Soviet leadership. This policy reached a climax in the Slansky Trial in Prague (November 1952) and the exposure of the "Doctors' Plot" (January 1953), in both of which Israel was accused of conducting anti-Soviet activities with the help of Czechoslovakian and Soviet Jewish figures. (A small bomb which had exploded on the premises of the Soviet Legation in Tel Aviv, was given as the official reason for the move.) Following Stalin' death (March 1953) and the denunciation of the "Doctors' Plot," the way was open for negotiations which led to the resumption of relations in July 1953, Israel promising at the time to refrain from joining any pro-Western military alliance directed against the Soviet Union.

In this period Stalin's successors were beginning to take interest in bringing the countries of Asia and Africa (which came to be known as the Third World) into the Soviet diplomatic orbit by exploiting their anti-Western feelings. It was in this context that Moscow approached those Arab countries which felt themselves particularly anti-Western and, in the process, adopted a pro-Arab position on issues related to the *Arab-Israel conflict. The first Soviet vetoes in the UN Security Council of Western-proposed resolutions which the Arabs considered to be directed against them were made in 1954.

In 1956 the *Sinai Campaign and Suez War

resulted in a Soviet diplomatic initiative which sought to demonstrate the Soviet Union's pro-Egyptian stance, which included the return to Moscow of the Soviet Ambassador to Israel, the unilateral abrogation of Soviet-Israel trade agreements for the supply to Israel of Soviet and Romanian oil, the cessation of a minor family reunification program by which a few elderly Soviet Jews were allowed to reunite with relatives in Israel, and the issuance of notes of warning threatening "the very existence of Israel as a state..." With the Israeli withdrawal from the *Sinai Peninsula and *Gaza Strip in March 1957, the Soviet Ambassador returned to Israel, but Soviet-Israel trade never again became significant, and family reunions took on meaningful proportions only as of 1964, until they were terminated again in the aftermath of the *Six-Day War.

Throughout this period the Soviet-Israel relationship remained strained, although officially declared "normal." On the one hand the Soviet Union became the major arms supplier of Egypt and Syria — Israel's two main adversaries — and on the other hand, Moscow accused Israel of interfering in its domestic affairs in demanding cultural and religious rights for Soviet Jews, as well as their right to emigrate to Israel.

In June 1967, at the end of the Six-Day War, the Soviet Union once again severed diplomatic relations with Israel, as did the other East European countries, except Romania. Officially, this time too, there was a pretext of Israel's "aggression" against the Arab states, but the underlying motive, as in 1953, might have been the desire to deprive Soviet Jews of moral encouragement, particularly that derived from the presence of an Israeli Embassy in Moscow.

Since June 1967 the Soviet Union has had no official relations with Israel. But Moscow has not withdrawn its recognition of Israel's right to exist within "secure borders," although it might be argued that the "de-Zionised" Israel which the Soviets advocate and which would absorb the Arab refugees of 1948/49 is unacceptable; even to those Israelis who call for an unequivocal withdrawal to the pre-Six-Day War boundaries. The Soviet Union has sought to persuade some of the more extremist Arab states and groupings, including the *Palestine Liberation Organization (PLO) to afford Israel at least de facto recognition. It has maintained sporadic contacts with Israelis — meeting in various places and at different levels — and has insisted that once Israel makes what the Soviet Union considers meaningful moves toward "eliminating the consequences of the [1967] aggression," it will reestablish relations. Israel has made it clear that it cannot conceive of relations which do not include measures to improve the lot of Soviet Jews, including the right of emigration for those who want to leave the Soviet Union. Moscow, however, insists that this is a Soviet domestic issue.

The Soviet Union continues to supply weapons to Israel's adversaries, especially Syria, with the full knowledge that this material is intended for use against Israel, thus in practice belying — in the view of many Israelis — its position of recognizing Israel's right to exist.

In October 1985 Prime Minister Shimon *Peres announced that Israel would agree to the Soviet Union's participation in an international conference on peace in the Middle East on condition that diplomatic relations were first resumed.

In August 1986 a low level formal meting took place in Helsinki between Soviet and Israeli diplomats. The Soviets wished to arrange for a mission to visit Israel to deal with Soviet church property. Israel insisted on raising the issue of Soviet Jewry which the Soviet delegation to Helsinki had no authority to discuss.

(Y.R.)

Spain and Israel Despite the fact that Franco's Spain, neutral during World War II, had helped save Jews, Israel decided not to establish diplomatic relations with it because of its association with the Axis powers. At that time, 1948–49, Spain had shown interest in such relations. Soon after it entered the *United Nations, Israel voted against Spanish membership, a move which Spain resented for many years. At a time when Spain was ostracized in the international community the Arab states drew closer to it, the first head of state to visit Spain after the war being King Abdullah of *Jordan.

By 1954, when Israel was considering the opening of a consulate in Barcelona, Spain indicated that it no longer sought a relationship. The Arab world had become and would remain an important target of Spanish foreign policy — and the refusal of Franco's Spain to establish relations with Israel, as well as its constant voting in favor of pro-Arab resolutions on the Middle East in international forums, was a reflection of this policy.

Subsequent Israeli efforts to raise the issue of the establishment of relations were rejected by Spain, though from time to time indications were given that the policy might change under suitable circumstances.

Toward the end of Franco's life and soon after his death in 1975 this change seemed imminent. In June 1975 Israeli Foreign Minister Yigal *Allon met in Madrid with the Spanish Prime Minister, and on November 22 King Juan Carlos announced that Spain would establish normal relations with all states. Indeed, in the beginning of 1976 efforts were made to achieve a normalization in relations between the two states. However, despite the intervention of several European personalities, Madrid finally backed down due to heavy Arab pressure, and, in December 1976, even cancelled the appearance of an official representative at a meeting of the World Jewish Congress in Madrid, as well as an audience which had been planned for Naḥum *Goldmann with the King. By the beginning of 1977 Spain stated that if Israel withdrew from the *occupied territories in accordance with *Security Council Resolutions 242 and 338 and recognized the right to self-determination of the *Palestinians, diplomatic relations would be established. In March Spain enabled the *Palestine Liberation Organization (PLO) to open an official office in Madrid. While various occasions were used to broach the issue of the establishment of relations, Spain's pro-Arab commitments gained the upper hand. This was again the case when Filipe Gonzales, leader of the Socialist Party, became Prime Minister in 1982. It had been no coincidence that in July 1977 Gonzales declared in Lisbon that his party supported the establishment of diplomatic relations with Israel. Special relations had existed between **Mapai*, and later the *Israel Labor Party, and the Spanish socialists. During the 1936–39 Spanish Civil War individuals from the labor movement in Palestine participated in the International Brigade, and later *Mapai* kept in touch with the Socialist Party in exile in Mexico. However, the older leadership of *Mapai* was sceptical about the chances for any change taking place in Spain, even after Franco's demise, and it was only the *Mapai* young guard which took the initiative in establishing close relations with their Spanish colleagues, providing some financial assistance and printing facilities. Relations were further strengthened in February 1967, at an underground meeting of the International Union of Socialist Youth in Bilbao, in which Michael Ḥarish, at the time Director of the *Mapai* International Department, took part. In 1971 Filipe Gonzales, who was soon to become the Chairman of the Spanish Socialist Party, paid a secret visit to Israel.

After Gonzales became Prime Minister the Israeli Ministry for Foreign Affairs decided to send a permanent representative to the International Tourist Organization in Madrid. Though Spain's entry into NATO in June 1982 seemed an appropriate opportunity to broach once again the question of diplomatic relations, the *Lebanese War served as a new excuse for the Spaniards to decline. The formation of the *National Unity Government in Israel under Shimon *Peres seemed to open new opportunities — especially due to the personal friendship between Peres and Gonzales, and Gonzales' promise that after Peres became Prime Minister relations would be established. However, since no progress was made by December 1984, the good offices of MK Micha Ḥarish were used by the Prime Minister to meet with Gonzales on the occasion of the Spanish Socialist Party Conference which Ḥarish attended. Between June 1985 and January 1986, when diplomatic relations were finally established, Ḥarish travelled frequently between Tel Aviv and Madrid, trying to overcome difficulties on the part of Spain, including its fear of Arab retaliation, and the influence of a pro-PLO faction in the Spanish Socialist Party. For Israel the establishment of relations with Spain was not only important for political and moral reasons but also for economic reasons. Though Spain's entry into the *European Economic Community caused Israel some difficulties in its citrus exports to the Community, the Spanish market, now open to Israeli industrial products by force of its 1975 Free Trade Agreements with the Community, is considered to have great potential. Israel could also benefit from Spain's close ties with *Latin America.

State Comptroller Since its inception in

1949 the office of the State Comptroller (*Mevaker Hamedinah*) has functioned as an inspection agency dealing not only with central government offices and agencies but also with the defense and security branches, local government and all bodies subsidized by the state and subject to inspection under any law or Knesset resolution, or under an agreement with the government. Inspection by the State Comptroller covers all aspects of the activities of bodies under review, except for legislative and judicial acts. While this office holds certain of the powers of an inquiry committee, the comptroller has no administrative authority to enforce compliance or impose sanctions on inspected bodies. The comptroller has, over the years, uncovered numerous cases of misconduct. His yearly report is made public and is formally presented to the Knesset State Control Committee. Since 1971 the comptroller has also acted as commissioner for complaints from the public (ombudsman) against any body or official whose activities are subject to the comptrollers' inspection. The State Comptroller is appointed by the President on recommendation of the Knesset's House Committee. Since the establishment of the state four persons have held this prestigious office.

State List Party established in 1968 by former Prime Minister David *Ben Gurion and members of **Rafi* who refused to unite with **Mapai* and **Aḥdut Ha'avodah — Po'alei Zion* in establishing the *Israel Labor Party.

The party's platform was very similar to that of **Rafi* but without its socialist bias. In the elections to the 7th Knesset (1969) the State List gained four seats. Running in the elections to the 8th Knesset (1973), the State List appeared as part of the **Likud*. In 1976 it was one of the founders of **La'am* within the *Likud*.

Statism See: **Mamlachtiut*.

status quo A term which defines the modus vivendi between the religious and non-religious parties in Israel regarding public religious observance, the interests of the religious establishments and the laws regarding matrimony and burial. The modus vivendi has been based on concessions made by the secular parties which have formed the coalition governments in return for the cooperation or non-obstruction of the religious parties. The specific agreements of the original status quo were: 1) recognition of the Sabbath as the day of rest of the Jewish population, and its public observance; 2) keeping the dietary laws in public institutions and government-run or subsidized bodies and services; 3) having all marital matters, including divorce, and those relating to burial, dealt with by the Rabbinate and Rabbinical Courts on the basis of the *Halacha* (the Jewish law); 4) enabling the existence of a religious stream in the national school system, and of an independent ultra-religious school system which is not supervised by the state; 5) public financing for religious services to various communities and for religious institutions.

The religious parties have constantly demanded changes in the status quo, particularly since 1977, relating to such issues as the Archaeology Law, the Autopsy Law, the Abortion Law and the *Law of Return.

The origins of the status quo go back to developments in the *World Zionist Organization (WZO) and the **Yishuv* in mandatory times. For example, the 1911 Zionist Congress agreed to support religious schools, even though the organization was predominantly secular. The 1920 Zionist Conference in London recognized the existence of two streams of Jewish education in Palestine — one general and the other of **Hamizraḥi*. In the mid-twenties when **Po'alei Agudat Yisrael* joined the **Histadrut*'s Health Fund (*Kupat Ḥolim*) the workers' kitchens were made kosher. Starting in the early thirties the Jewish National Fund (See: *Land Policy) included a clause in its contracts regarding the observance of the Sabbath on national lands, while **Assefat Hanivḥarim* passed a resolution regarding observance of the Sabbath in the organized Jewish community.

In 1934 the Zionist Executive passed a similar resolution, which was again adopted by the Zionist Congress of 1935, at which *Hamizraḥi* joined a **Mapai*-led coalition in the Zionist Executive (See: *Historic Coalition). However, it is the letter sent in the name of the *Jewish Agency by David *Ben Gurion, Rabbi *Maimon, and Yitzḥak Gruenbaum to **Agudat Yisrael* on June 19, 1947, which is regarded as the first status quo document. This letter, the goal of which was to convince the *Agudah* not to obstruct proposals for the establishment of the Jewish state, made the following promises on religious questions: a) the

Sabbath will be the legal day of rest in the Jewish state; b) steps will be taken to ensure that all national kitchens serving Jews will be kosher; c) everything will be done to satisfy the religious circles regarding laws of matrimony; d) the autonomy of the religious stream of education will be ensured. The Jewish Agency could not, however, promise that the *constitution of the Jewish state would be based on the *Halacha* as demanded by *Agudat Yisrael*.

Successive coalition agreements after the establishment of the state elaborated on these basic principles, adding, among other stipulations, that public religious needs would be supplied by the government without its intervening in religious matters; religious services would be conducted in the *IDF (Israel Defense Forces); religious girls and yeshivah students would be exempted from military service; the powers of the Rabbinical Courts over all the Jews in the country — including those who are not citizens — would be expanded on matters regarding matrimony and burial; a special branch in the Ministry of Education would be established to deal with the national religious education system.

Many political battles and cabinet crises developed around the status quo. These included the issue of education in the new immigrant camps (1950); the law regarding national service for girls exempt from military service for reasons of religion and conscience (1952); the "Who is a Jew?" debate regarding the Law of Return (1958, 1970 and several times since 1977); the non-kosher kitchen on the Zim ship the *S.S. Shalom* (1964); the *National Religious Party abstention on a vote of no-confidence against the *Rabin government because of the alleged desecration of the Sabbath on an Air Force base (1976); the stopping of El-Al flights on the Sabbath (1980).

While the religious parties, especially the non-Zionist ones, are constantly pushing to change the status quo to a more religious extreme, while more secular non-religious parties and groups complain about the religious coercion which the status quo agreements involve — the majority agree that life in Israel between the religious and secular publics would be unmanageable without it. (Sh.M. — S.H.R.)

Stern, Avraham (1907–1942) Underground leader. Stern was born in Poland, but spent his adolescent years in Russia. During the civil war which followed the Bolshevik Revolution he walked back the 1000 miles to Poland. In 1924 he immigrated to Palestine and attended the Reḥavia Gymnasium in Jerusalem, continuing his studies in Latin and Greek at the Hebrew University. Stern began his studies for a doctorate in Florence, Italy. In 1929 he served in the *Haganah*, and in 1931 broke off to join **IZL*. In 1934 Stern left his research to devote himself fully to underground work, personally smuggling weapons into Palestine. He established contacts with the Polish military and in 1939 arranged for 25 *IZL* members from Palestine to undergo a two-month course in guerrilla warfare given by Polish officers.

After the publication of the 1939 White Paper (See: *Mandatory Palestine) Stern returned to Palestine to organize resistance to the British, but was arrested on August 31, and held in detention for ten months. Upon his release, arranged by members of the *Revisionist Movement, Stern broke away from *IZL*, which he felt was not sufficiently militant in its struggle against Britain and too much under the influence of the Revisionist Movement. Assuming the *nom de guerre* "Ya'ir" he formed a new underground — *Loḥamei Ḥerut Yisrael* (**Leḥi*), commonly known as the "Stern Gang."

In his ideological manifesto, the "18 Principles of Renaissance," Stern expressed a new Zionist goal: the achievement of the age-old vision of Jewish redemption in the biblical borders of the Land of Israel, from the Nile to the Euphrates.

In an attempt to find allies in his anti-British activity, and unaware of the realities of the *Holocaust, Stern sought links with both Fascist Italy and Nazi Germany. Although these efforts had no results, they brought down on Stern the stigma of a fifth columnist. Stern, whose picture appeared on "wanted" posters, was discovered and shot dead in his hiding-place by British policemen on February 12, 1942. His followers argued that there had been no excuse for his being killed, and accused the British of cold-blooded murder. Avraham Stern himself, as well as his philosophy and political strategy, remain subjects of controversy. Stern was an accomplished poet. (I.M.)

Stern Gang See: **Leḥi*.

Suez Canal An artificial canal opened in 1869, connecting the Mediterranean and the Red Sea.

Its length is 101 miles (160 kilometers). Its northern outlet is at the city of Port Said and its southern outlet at the town of Suez. It passes through lakes, the largest of which is the Great Bitter Lake.

The French engineer Ferdinand de Lesseps conceived the idea of the canal and was the driving force behind its construction. *France gave him support, while *Great Britain, regarding the scheme as a French attempt to challenge British influence in the East, opposed it fiercely. Work on the canal finally began in 1859, and it was inaugurated on November 17, 1869. Egypt held 44 percent of the ordinary shares, in addition to preferred shares which entitled it to 15 percent of the profits, but the Egyptian Khedive (Viceroy), deep in debt, sold the Egyptian shares to the British in 1875. In 1882 Britain occupied Egypt and thereby gained control over the canal zone.

In 1888 the Maritime Powers signed a convention in Constantinople, in which they undertook to keep the Suez Canal "always free and open in time of war as in time of peace, to every vessel of commerce or of war, without distinction of flag." With regard to some clauses of the convention, priority was given to Egyptian security needs, but this did not apply to the freedom of passage which was established as an essential principle not limited by any conditions.

The Suez Canal started showing a profit several years after its opening. Until 1938 Egypt received no part of the Suez Canal Company's income or profits, because of having mortgaged its share to French banks in 1880. Under agreements signed in 1937 and 1949 Egypt began receiving 7 percent of the profits. In 1937 Egypt was also given representation on the company's Board of Directors.

When Britain granted Egypt nominal independence in 1922 it kept the right to station troops and bases in the canal zone, in order to defend it. In the Anglo-Egyptian treaty of 1936 Egypt recognized Britain's special interests with regard to the canal and agreed to the stationing of British forces in the canal area. The treaty stressed that this would not be interpreted as occupation or an infringement of Egyptian sovereignty.

After World War II, Egypt demanded the evacuation of all British forces and bases from her oil, including the canal zone. Under an October 1954 agreement Britain undertook to evacuate the canal zone within 20 months. The agreement reemphasized the freedom of passage, although for years Egypt had prevented the passage of ships sailing to and from Israel. The last British forces evacuated the canal zone in July 1956.

On July 26, 1956, Egypt nationalized the Suez Canal in retaliation for the discontinuation of promised Western aid. After various diplomatic moves had failed British and French troops moved into the canal zone in the beginning of November 1956, on the pretext of separating Egyptian and Isaeli forces in the *Sinai Campaign. In the course of the fighting the Egyptians blocked the canal by sinking 47 ships, thus causing a minor oil crisis as oil tankers were forced to sail around the Cape of Good Hope.

*United Nations intervention instigated by the *United States and the *Soviet Union forced Britain and France to withdraw their forces from Egypt. In January 1957 Egypt abrogated the Anglo-Egyptian Agreement of 1954, and in April the canal was reopened to navigation.

Ever since 1948 Egypt had prevented the passage of ships flying the Israeli flag, ships carrying Israeli cargo and ships which used the canal to call in Israeli ports. This was not only contrary to the Constantinople Convention of 1888 and other international agreements, including the Egyptian-Israel *Armistice Agreement of 1949, but was explicitly condemned by the UN Security Council on September 1, 1951. Subsequent Israeli attempts to get the Security Council to act were frustrated by a Soviet veto. The continued blockade of the Suez Canal was one of the causes of the Sinai Campaign and the *Six-Day War. The Suez Canal was closed a second time during the Six-Day War of June 1967, when Israeli troops reached the east bank of the canal. It remained closed until after the Israeli withdrawal from the canal within the framework of the *Disengagment Agreement between Egypt and Israel of January 1974.

In the course of the *Yom Kippur War Egypt crossed the Suez Canal and broke through the *Bar Lev Line of fortifications built along the canal by Israel during the *War of Attrition. Subsequently, Israeli forces under Ariel *Sharon crossed the Suez Canal and occupied Egyptian territory to its west. After the Israeli withdrawal from the canal Egypt cleared and dredged the accumulated sand, removing 15 ships trapped in the Great Bitter Lake since the Six-Day War. Egypt then deepened and widened the canal to enable the passage of super-tankers. Egypt also rebuilt and repopulated the towns along the canal which had been partly destroyed during the War of Attrition and consequently evacuated.

The Suez Canal was reopened for navigation on June 5, 1975. The 1974 Disengagement Agreement and the 1975 *Interim Agreement did not include provisions for the passage of Israeli ships and cargo through the Suez Canal. However, the 1978 framework for the conclusion of a peace treaty between Egypt and Israel which was included in the *Camp David Accords contained a provision regarding "the right of free passage by ships of Israel through the Gulf of Suez and the Suez Canal," a right reaffirmed by the 1979 *Egyptian-Israeli Peace Treaty in which Article V stated that "ships of Israel, and cargo destined for or coming from Israel, shall enjoy the right of free passage through the Suez Canal and its approaches through the Gulf of Suez and the Mediterranean Sea on the basis of the Constantinople convention of 1888."

Syria and Israel Conflicting trends existed in the relations between Syria and Israel even before the two states gained independence. Brief periods of contacts, talks and even agreements were interspersed with prolonged periods of hostility, confrontation and warfare.

In 1919 the Emir Feisal Ibn Hussein, who was in control of Syria in the years 1918–20, signed an historic agreement with Zionist leader Chaim *Weizmann, in which Feisal recognized the Jewish national rights in Palestine in return for Jewish support of Arab independence. However, the Syrian National Congress strongly objected to the Jewish national existence and supported the struggle of the Arabs of Palestine, called Southern Syria by the Syrian nationalists. Throughout the French mandate over Syria from 1920 until its independence in 1944, there were occasional contacts and talks between leaders of the **Yishuv* and senior members of the Arab national movement in Syria, who were searching for a political solution to the Palestine question. However, it proved impossible to bridge the polarized positions of the the two sides, and the Syrians continued to assist the Arabs of Palestine — both materially and politically — in their struggle against *Zionism and the Jewish national home in Palestine, especially during the disturbances (or Arab Revolt) of 1936–39.

Even before the UN General Assembly *partition plan was adopted on November 29, 1947 Syria stood at the head of the inter-Arab struggle against the establishment of a Jewish state in any part of Palestine. Syrian assistance included an economic boycott of the *Yishuv* within the framework of the Arab League (See: *Arab boycott), military preparations and the formation of voluntary units for the "Rescue Army," led by two Syrian commanders, Fawzi al-Qawuqji and Adib Shishakli, to participate in the war against the emerging Jewish state. The Rescue Army operated in various parts of Palestine under the direction of the Syrian General Staff. After May 15, 1948, the Syrian army proper invaded Palestine and fought in the region of the Sea of Galilee and the Upper Galilee (See: *War of Independence). Even though it was defeated in a battle for Semakh, the Syrian army managed to conquer the Jewish settlement of Mishmar Hayarden and the areas around the Sea of Galilee on the Palestinian side of the international border.

After at first obstinately refusing to sign an *armistice agreement with Israel, Syria, under Husni Za'im, who came to power following a military coup in March 1949, finally agreed. The agreement, within the framework of which the areas occupied by Syria west of the international border were evacuated and demilitarized, was signed on July 20, 1949. The new Syrian ruler had actually offered to sign a peace treaty with Israel on the basis of the ceasefire lines. This would have given Syria strategic advantages over Israel, including control of half of the Sea of Galilee. It was precisely for this reason that Prime Minister David *Ben Gurion rejected Za'im's offer, and insisted that the Syrian army withdraw across the international border before a peace agreement could be discussed. Za'im was deposed and executed in August 1949 by a group of officers under Colonel Sami Hinnawi. Four months later Hinnawi was deposed by Colonel Adib Shishakli who remained in power until 1954. Shishakli held secret talks with Israel regarding a settlement of the problem of the demilitarized zones, and a plan for developing the Huleh Valley north of the Sea of Galilee. However, when Israel started to drain the Huleh swamp without prior agreement with Syria in 1951, the Syrians opened fire all along the border, to which Israel reacted strongly by using its Air Force to attack Syrian targets close to the demilitarized zones. In response Syrian units occupied Tel-Mutillah, a strategically important hill within the territory of Israel north of the Sea of Galilee; the hill was reoccupied by the Israel Defense Forces (*IDF) following a long battle with heavy casualties, the first military confrontation since the end of the War of Independence.

After a brief period of calm, hostilities resumed over Syria's objection to sharing the *Jordan River waters among the three riparian states — Israel, Syria and *Jordan — and to Israel's construction of the Jordan-Negev national water carrier. Israel retaliated against Syria's attempt to sabotage its development plans, and the two states started an arms race, with Israel purchasing arms from France (See: *Arms Purchases) and Syria from Czechoslovakia with which it signed a major arms deal in September 1955. Following a Syrian attack on Israeli fishermen on the Sea of Galilee near the close of 1955, an IDF paratroop unit, aiming to deter further incursions, retaliated against Syrian positions northeast of the Sea of Galilee, causing heavy casualties.

It is possible that this operation, as well as the *Sinai Campaign at the end of 1956 contributed towards deterring the Syrians from additional attacks against Israel. However, these operations also encouraged Damascus to increase its military and political power in the face of what it viewed as an Israeli threat, as well as to unite with *Egypt in 1958, within the framework of the United Arab Republic (UAR).

The Syrian-Israeli conflict over the demilitarized zones intensified at the end of the 1950s. Once again there were shooting incidents initiated by Syria which led to a massive IDF retaliatory operation at Tawfiq in February 1960, to which Egypt reacted by sending military forces into the *Sinai Peninsula. These forces were withdrawn following Israeli threats.

In March 1962 Israel once again carried out a reprisal against Syrian positions at Nukeibi, east of the Sea of Galilee. In 1964, in reaction to attempts by the Ba'ath regime which had taken power in Syria in March 1963, to divert the sources of the Jordan River, the IDF attacked the Syrian earth-moving equipment and other targets. Syria then bombarded Israeli settlements and other Israeli targets and supported terrorist attacks by *Fatah* (See: *Palestine Liberation Organization — PLO). Syrian policy toward Israel became increasingly militant, particularly after a coup d'état by two Alawite officers, Salah Jadid and Hafez Assad, in February 1966.

At the bottom of the Syrian hostility was the belief that Zionism and Israel represented a foreign invasion of the Arab world and a threat to its territorial integrity, cultural values and national ambitions, especially in Southern Syria (i.e., Palestine). Syria considered itself to be the heart of the Arab national movement and was therefore duty-bound to serve the goals of Pan-Arab nationalism and to head the struggle against Zionism and Israel.

The Ba'ath regime was particularly unyielding in its advocacy of Arab unity and the liquidation of the State of Israel. The Syrians' resolute opposition to Israel was also a way to increase its status in the Arab world. Real fear of Israel's military power, fed by the massive retaliatory operations carried out by the IDF in the fifties and sixties, was also a factor in the Syrian position. The Alawite minority, seeking legitimization as an authentic Arab national regime, took special pains to appear as the true defender of the Syrian homeland and of the Arab world. In addition to the protection, aid and guidance which Jadid and Assad granted *Fatah* in its struggle against Israel after 1965, they also escalated their own military struggle against Israel in the summer of 1966. Twice they used the Syrian Air Force (under the command of Hafez Assad) against Israeli fishing vessels on the Sea of Galilee. Continued Syrian provocations against Israel led, in April 1967, to a major aerial battle between the two states in which six Syrian Mig aircraft were shot down. The *Six-Day War began shortly thereafter in June 1967.

Though Syria did not carry out a massive attack against Israel in June 1967, by the end of the war the IDF had occupied the *Golan Heights, adding a new and critical dimension to the Syrian-Israeli conflict. For the first time an integral part of Syrian territory was occupied by Israel, and the IDF was stationed only about 50 kilometers from Damascus.

Jadid and Assad disagreed on the nature of the struggle against Israel in the years 1966–70:

Jadid advocated a "popular liberation war" against Israel (i.e., guerrilla warfare), Assad preferred a classical military confrontation with regular forces. Following a coup in 1970 Assad started systematically to prepare the Syrian army for war against Israel, while trying to broaden the Pan-Arab political and military configuration. Nevertheless, Assad did not completely reject a political solution, at least in theory, and unlike his predecessor accepted *Security Council Resolution 242, though under conditions totally unacceptable to Israel.

In 1971 Assad joined the Federation of Arab Republics with Egypt and Libya and within its framework he strengthened his ties with Egyptian President Anwar Sadat. In October 1973 Egypt and Syria coordinated a surprise attack against Israel, which had been planned for almost a year. The Syrian army succeeded in penetrating deep into the Golan Heights before being pushed back by the IDF, which ocupied an additional enclave in the north of the Golan (the Bashan) within artillery range of Damascus (See: *Yom Kippur War).

In the *Disengagement Agreement negotiated with Israel through the mediation of the US Secretary of State Henry Kissinger (See: *Kissinger Shuttle), Syria regained the enclave occupied by the IDF, and the city of Quneitra, in return for a separation-of-forces agreement and an exchange of prisoners.

Despite the military defeat, Assad emerged from the Yom Kippur War as an Arab national hero. Though he did not hide his ambition to be likened to the legendary Moslem hero Saladin al-Ayyubi (who had united the Moslem world, defeated the Crusaders at the battle of the Horns of Hittin in 1187 and conquered Jerusalem), Assad understood that Arab unity was an unattainable dream and that he must settle for a strategic political-military alliance with neighboring Arab states, especially Egypt. However, to Assad's dismay, Egypt broke the alliance it had formed with Syria before the Yom Kippur War, and signed a separate cease-fire and disengagement agreement with Israel. While exerting pressure on Egpt to rescind its new policy, Syria started to seek alternative allies for an Eastern Front against Israel. Iraq, the second largest and strongest state in the region after Egypt, refused to join this Syrian initiative, arguing that Damascus' acceptance of *Security Council Resolution 338 and its disengagement agreement with Israel signed in 1974 committed Syria to a political process which Baghdad rejected. Assad then adopted the historic approach of a Greater Syria that included Lebanon and Jordan which would establish a line of confrontation with Israel running from Tyre in southern Lebanon to Aqaba in southern Jordan and which would improve his status in inter-Arab politics. Full union between the three states and the PLO being out of the question, Assad attempted instead to establish among them a political-military alignment under his leadership, attaining partial success. In the second half of the 1970s Assad significantly tightened Syria's military and political ties with Jordan, and gained control over most of Lebanon through his intervention in the Lebanese civil war of 1975, first on the side of the Christians and then on behalf of the Moslems. Paradoxically it was Israel which prevented Syria's striking at the PLO's autonomous hold in southern Lebanon when it warned Syria in 1976 not to cross the Jesin-Sidon line (the so-called "Red Line"), south of which, down to the border with Israel the "Fatah-land" had been established by the PLO.

After the *Likud* came to power in mid-1977, the Israeli government supported the Maronite Christian Lebanese forces in a guerrilla war against the Syrian forces in Lebanon.

Syria's strategic position in the conflict with Israel was weakened when Egypt signed the *Camp David Accords and the *Egyptian-Israeli Peace Treaty in 1978 and Jordan decided to break away from its strategic alliance with Damascus and strengthen its links with Baghdad in 1979. In 1980 Iraq's contribution to the conflict against Israel was neutralized through the outbreak of the Iran-Iraq war. In addition, Assad was forced to contend with a serious internal threat by the Moslem Brotherhood.

Againt this background Assad evolved the doctrine of "strategic balance" whereby Syria must be prepared to contend with Israel without the assistance of the other Arab states.

To achieve this goal, Syria must establish a large army capable of deterring Israel from attacking it, of defending itself effectively against possible Israeli attack, and of enabling Syria either to reoccupy the Golan Heghts or negotiate with Israel from a position of strength. In order to ttain this ambitious goal, Assad signed a friendhip and cooperation agreement with the *Soviet Jnion in 1980 and with its massive aid substanially enlarged and modernized the Syrian Army.

Though during the *Lebanese War in 1982 he Israeli Air Force shot down 90 Syrian aircraft nd the IDF pushed back Syrian land forces, the yrian armored and commando units demontrated improved fighting capability and caused he IDF significant losses.

Following the Lebanese War Syria increased ts army by three armored divisions, and at the eginning of 1987 the Syrian army numbered pproximately half a million regular soldiers, and quarter of a million reserves. Syria had about ten ighting divisions, most of them armored, parially equipped with modern Russian T-72 tanks, modern Air Force including Mig-29 fighters, nd a wide range of missiles, some of them capale of hitting any target in Israel. In addition, yria developed chemical weapons, apparently as a temporary response to the nuclear weapons which it believed Israel to have (See: *Nuclear Policy).

Simultaneously with its military build-up, Syria has since 1983 encouraged and assisted various groups to carry out guerrilla warfare against Israeli targets in Lebanon and to commit terrorist acts in Europe (such as attempts to attack El-Al flights in London and Madrid). This "war of attrition" contributed to Israel's decision in 1985 to withdraw from most of Southern Lebanon. Israel has also been relatively successful in its efforts to have Syria condemned in European capitals for international terrorist acts. It has been suggested but not proved that these activities are the precursors of an attack on the Golan Heights. However, it is more likely that they are an alternative to a military attack in which Syria, still far from achieving a strategic balance with Israel, is liable to suffer a crushing defeat.

(M.M.)

T

Tab'a A disputed area of several hundred quare meters on the Israeli-Egyptian border outh of Eilat. When Israel withdrew from the Sinai in accordance with its peace treaty with gypt, it refused to withdraw from Tab'a, claimng that it belonged to Israel while Egypt mainained it was on the Egyptian side of the border.

Tab'a contains a vacation village and hotel which was constructed after 1967. The Egyptian laim to the area is based on border markers datng back to 1949 when the *Armistice Agreenent between Israel and Egypt was signed, as well as a British map dated 1906 which indicates he border between British-held Sinai and Turkish-held Palestine. In 1906 Britain had orced Sultan Abdel Hamid to evacuate Tab'a when it sought to control all the natural springs long the west bank of the Gulf of Aqaba. The Turks, however, never recognized the new borler as an international border, referring to it as an 'administrative dividing line." Israel has claimed hat the 1949 Armistice Agreement referred to he 1906 border as a temporary dividing line only etween the armies of Israel and Egypt, but that he agreement does not constitute Israeli acceptnce of the validity of the 1906 border. It has also pointed out that the 1906 map also shows part of the disputed area on the Turkish side of the border.

However in Article II of the peace treaty, signed by Prime Minister Menaḥem *Begin and ratified by the Knesset, Israel appears to have accepted the 1906 map as showing the international border. Egypt has called for arbitration to decide the issue. Israel, basing itself on the peace treaty, which states that disputes should be solved through "negotiation, conciliation or arbitration," demanded that a process of negotiation and conciliation precede arbitration.

In the *National Unity Government formed in September 1984 the *Alignment called for Israeli flexibility on the Tab'a question provided that it is dealt with as one part of a complex of issues on which Israel and Egypt disagree. Believing that Israel has a good case, it was willing to go to arbitration. The **Likud* was less optimistic about Egypt's intentions, with many of its current leaders having opposed Israel's complete withdrawal from the Sinai in the first place, and therefore it was less willing to go to arbitration. However, under strong Alignment pressure the *Likud* agreed, on January 14, 1986, to arbitration provided that a conciliation process precedes it; the Egyptian Ambassador is returned to Tel Aviv; a timetable for the implementation of the agreements signed between Israel and Egypt on commerce, tourism, transportation, civilian aviation, culture and a political dialogue, is agreed upon; Egypt submits to Israel the report on the Ras Burka murder in 1985 of five Israelis; Egypt prevents the presence and activities of Palestinian terrorists on its territory and prevents hostile propaganda against Israel in the Egyptian media.

The Arbitration Compromise was signed on September 11, 1986, followed by a summit conference between Egyptian President Mubarak and Prime Minister *Peres. The Israeli government ratified the compromise on November 30 with one minister, Ariel *Sharon, objecting. The arbitration began in Geneva on December 8 with an international team of five arbitrators and will continue *in camera* until mid-1988.

Tabenkin, Yitzḥak (1887–1971) Labor leader and ideologist. Born in Russia, Tabenkin immigrated to Palestine in 1911.

He was one of the leaders of **Po'alei Zion* and advocated the enlarged *kibbutz and unity among the socialist parties. In 1919 Tabenkin was one of the founders of **Aḥdut Ha'avodah*. The next year he became one of the founders of the **Histadrut* and ten years later he was one of the founders of **Mapai*. Tabenkin was an activist in the settlement and Labor movements all his life.

He advocated total war against *Revisionist Zionism and objected to the partition of Palestine.

Tabenkin viewed **Hakibbutz Hame'uḥad* as the main tool for conquering the land through settlement and securing the borders of the future state. He was one of the initiators of the **Palmaḥ*. In 1944 he supported the splitting of the *Mapai* Party due to ideological differences and was among the founders of **Mapam*, but in 1954 his faction broke off from *Mapam* and reestablished *Aḥdut Ha'avodah-Po'alei Zion* as an independent party. After the *Six Day War Tabenkin opposed withdrawal and participated in the establishment of the *Land of Israel Movement. In the early sixties Tabenkin resigned from all offices and devoted himself to teaching.

Takam Acronym for *Hatnu'ah Hakibbutzit Hame'uḥedet* (the United Kibbutz Movement). Officially founded in 1979, largely through the initiative of Yigal *Allon, it reunited **Hakibbutz Hame'uḥad* and **Iḥud Hakvutzot Vehakibbuizim* which had split 28 years earlier. While the two movements had cooperated in many fields before 1979 it was only in 1980 that their separate institutions were actually merged.

Takam embraces 165 kibbutzim, including two each of the Reform (See: *Progressive Judaism) and *Conservative Movements. *Takam* is affiliated with the *Israel Labor Party and was represented by three members in the 11th Knesset.

Tami Acronym for **Tnu'at Massoret Yisrael* (Tradition of Israel Movement). A traditional Zionist party established in April 1981 by groups of activists from the **Edot Mizraḥ* (Oriental Jewish community), primarily of Moroccan origin, who had previously been members of other political parties or social protest groups.

The party was activated before the 1981 elections to the 10th Knesset following the first trial and acquittal of MK Aharon *Abuḥatzeira who had been a member of the cabinet on behalf of the *National Religious Party (NRP) in the first **Likud* led government.

The establishment of the new party under Abuḥatzeira, resulted from an awareness of the explosive problems in Israeli society brought about by social protest groups and activists in several parties, such as the *Black Panthers and *Yisrael Sheli* (My Israel), a group primarily concerned with the question of equality of opportunity for members of all ethnic groups in Israel, which broke away from the NRP because of alleged bias in favor of persons of Ashkenazi background.

Tami advocated equality for all citizens of the State of Israel irrespective of religion, ethnic group or nationality. It strove to achieve this equality by means of an active policy within the framework of the Establishment and governing institutions, such as the enactment of laws which would codify uniform criteria for the distribution of resources designated for social progress and education; the appointment of officials in the administration on an egalitarian basis according to the numerical ratio of various groups in the population (similar to affirmative action in the US); the adoption of an order of priorities which would give preference to the solution of socio-economic problems and the closing of social and economic gaps while paying special attention to wage-earners and the inhabitants of development towns and slum areas. *Tami* sought to prevent the development in Israel of a society of social classes based on ethnic origin.

It also emphasized the principles of Jewish tradition as a correct and representative basis for attaining the state's social goals.

In the elections to the 10th Knesset *Tami* received three seats, and as a member of the coalition in Begin's second government was represented by one Minister and one Deputy Minister. In the early elections to the 11th Knesset, held more than a year ahead of time due to an initiative by *Tami*, *Tami* received only one Knesset seat, losing many of its voters to **Shass*, an ultra-religious Sephardi party. *Tami* did not join the *National Unity Government. (D.A.)

Tamir (formerly Katznelson), **Shmuel** Politician and attorney. Born 1923 in Jerusalem. Tamir grew up in the atmosphere of the aftermath of the 1929 *Hebron massacre and at a time when persons associated with the *Revisionist Movement, whom he believed to be innocent, were accused by the Labor Party of the murder of Ḥaim *Arlosoroff. Tamir joined the **IZL* in 1938. He was a radio announcer on the Voice of Jerusalem but was dismissed in 1944 after his membership of the *IZL* became known. In 1946 he was appointed Deputy Commander of the *IZL* in Jerusalem and arrested in 1947 (his third arrest) and exiled to Kenya, where he was allowed to sit for the final law examinations of the Government School of Law. Tamir was returned to Israel in July 1948 but was not mobilized into the *IDF in the *War of Independence. He joined the **Ḥerut* Movement upon its establishment and belonged to the *Lamerhav* faction in the movement which favored uniting with the *General Zionists. Tamir left *Ḥerut* in 1952 and concentrated on his legal career.

Among his best known cases was the "Tzrifin case" in 1953 in which he defended an underground group known as *Loḥamei Malchut Yisrael* (the fighters for the Kingdom of Israel) which was responsible for an explosion in the Soviet Embassy in Tel Aviv in February 1953 (See: *Soviet Union). In 1954 Tamir defended Malkiel Grunwald in Kastzner's libel suit (See: *Kastzner Affair) and in 1956 defended **Shurat Hamitnadvim* in Amos Ben Gurion's libel suit, after promising not to involve David *Ben Gurion in the case. In 1962 he represented the Herzliya Film Studios in the appeal against the Film Censor's decision forbidding a newsreel showing a demonstration in the Arab village of Sumeil which had been broken up by force.

In 1957 Tamir was one of the founders of **Hamishtar Heḥadash*, a movement which sought to bring about a change in the Israeli political system. He was approached by Uri *Avneri in view of uniting his *Semitic Action and Tamir's movement but nothing came out of these contacts. Tamir returned to the *Ḥerut* Movement in 1964 and was instrumental in bringing about the formation of **Gaḥal*. Though he was viewed as a natural heir to Menaḥem *Begin Tamir was expelled from *Ḥerut* in 1966 after criticizing Begin's leadership which, he argued had led the movement from one defeat to another. In 1967 he was one of the founders of the *Free Cente. which joined the **Likud* in 1973, a move which Tamir was later to consider his greatest political mistake. In 1974 Tamir called upon the *Likud* to accept the principle of *territorial compromise, an initiative which led to the breakup of the Free Center in 1975.

In 1977 Tamir joined the *Democratic Movement for Change (DMC), though before doing so he held discussions with Ariel *Sharon, the *Independent Liberals and Shulamit *Aloni regarding other alternatives. In the first Begin government Tamir was appointed Minister of Justice. In this capacity he tried to hasten the enactment of the *Basic Laws and several months before his resignation in August 1980 he proposed to enable the Central Elections Committee to disqualify lists on the basis of their nature and not only for technical reasons (See: **Kach*). Tamir resigned from the government because he felt that the *Democratic Movement (one of the splinters of the DMC) which had remained loyal to Yiga'el *Yadin, with only four Knesset seats, did not deserve three ministerial posts. Tamir returned to his legal practice in 1981.

Teḥiyah Political party founded in October 1979 following the negotiations with Egypt and the *Camp David Accords when three major political groups — the Loyalist Circle in **Ḥerut*, the *Land of Israel Movement and **Gush Emunim*, held talks to establish a nationalist party in opposition to the *Begin government.

The founders of the *Teḥiyah* (Hebrew for Revival) labeled the policy of the government shameful and dangerous, and a divergence from fundamental Zionist precepts. They restated the Zionist-nationalist program as an uncompromising approach to the idea of the redemption of the Jewish people in the Land of Israel. The agreement to retreat from part of the homeland, which formed the basis of the Camp David Accords and the Peace Treaty with *Egypt, was anathema to them and they demanded its abrogation. *Teḥiyah* also rejected the explicit recognition of legitimate Palestinian rights in the Camp David Accords, as Zionist treason, claiming that the Palestinians have rights as individuals, not as a nation.

In an attempt to create an all-encompassing party, *Teḥiyah* called for the removal of the partitions which had separated the Jewish people into opposing camps: religious versus secular, doves versus hawks, nationalists versus socialists. These divisions were termed false and self-destructive. The slogan coined was "going it together."

One of the core groups in *Teḥiyah* had broken off from the **Likud*. The first signs of an ideological break within the *Likud* came with the resignation of Shmuel *Katz who had served as Prime Minister Begin's advisor on overseas information. This was followed by strong public criticism of the *Likud* government policy by two of its Knesset members, Moshe Shamir and Ge'ula *Cohen, whose stands in Knesset debates and votes on issues related to the peace process were often in opposition to the government. They formed **Bana'i* as a separate Knesset faction, which later took on the name *Teḥiyah*.

Early in 1979 when Yuval *Ne'eman issued the call for the opponents of the Camp David Accords to join forces, Rabbi Zvi Yehuda *Kook of the Merkaz Harav Yeshivah participated. He instructed his students to cooperate with the basically secular party, thus paving the way for most elements of the *Gush Emunim* leadership to join *Teḥiyah*.

A major parliamentary success of the *Teḥiyah* party in 1980 was the passage of the Basic Law: Jerusalem — the so-called Jerusalem Law — declaring the city to be Israel's capital. A second law proposed by *Teḥiyah*, calling for the application of Israeli law to the *Golan Heights, was adopted by the Knesset the following year.

In the elections to the 10th Knesset *Teḥiyah* gained three seats. In the spring of 1982, the three MKs led the campaign in Yamit in the *Rafa Salient to halt the withdrawal from Sinai

In the wake of the *Lebanese War *Teḥiyah* joined the coalition in September 1982. Ne'eman was appointed Minister of Science and Development, and Deputy Chairman of the Ministerial Committee on Settlement which subsequently authorized more than 40 new settlements, most of them in Judea and Samaria (See: **Yosh*).

Shortly before the 1984 elections one of the *Teḥiyah*'s MKs, Ḥanan Porat, resigned from the Knesset and joined **Matzad* which had just broken away from the *National Religious Party Prior to the 1984 elections former Chief of Staf Rafael *Eitan joined *Teḥiyah* with his party **Tzomet*.

In the elections to the 11th Knesset *Teḥiyah* gained five seats and remained outside the *National Unity Government primarily due to the clause in the coalition agreement limiting the establishment of new settlements and the furthe development of established ones in Judea Samaria and the *Gaza Strip.

In the 1985 **Histadrut* elections the *Teḥiyah* failed to gain the necessary 2 percent for representation, although *Teḥiyah* delegates were elected to several local labor councils. (I.M.

Telem

1. Acronym for *Hatnu'ah Hale'umit Hamitkademet* (the Progressive National Movement). *Telem* is an Arab students' union founded at the Hebrew University in Jerusalem in 1977 which demands national self-determination for all *Palestinians, including the *Arabs of Israel, recognition of the *Palestine Liberation Organization (PLO) as the only legitimate representative of the Palestinian people, rejection of *Security Council Resolution 242 and 338 and the establishment of "a national authority in any part of Palestine a an interim solution without peace." *Telem* view Jordan, Egypt and Saudi Arabia as reactionary and as much the enemies of the Palestinian people as *Zionism and imperialism. *Telem* ha remained a marginal phenomenon among the Arabs of Israel. (R.C.

2. Acronym for *Hatnu'ah Lehitḥadshut Mamlachtit* (the Movement for State Renewal), the *Telem* party was formed in April 1981 by Moshe *Dayan. In 1969, soon after the formation of the

*Israel Labor Party which Dayan had joined together with most members of *Rafi*, several of his colleagues tried to contest the party's leadership, attempting to replace Golda *Meir with Dayan as Prime Minister, but Dayan withdrew his candidacy. When Yizḥak *Rabin's government of 1974 did not include Dayan he considered running independently in the 1977 elections for the 9th Knesset, but was persuaded by Shimon *Peres to remain in the Labor Party.

Dayan left the Labor party soon after those elections to join the first government set up by Menaḥem *Begin as Minister for Foreign Affairs. Several supporters established a forum representing his political views — *Habamah Leberurim Mediniyim Ḥevratiyim* (Forum for the Clarification of Socio-Political Issues). It was only after he left the government and before the elections to the 10th Knesset in 1981 that Dayan and three other members of Knesset who had broken off from the *Likud* formed *Telem* as a parliamentary faction. The new movement called for a continuation of the peace process and for preventing its stalemate on the basis of the *Camp David Accords which had been concluded with Dayan's active participation; the rejection of the *territorial compromise advocated by the *Alignment, under which most of Judea, Samaria (See: **Yosh*) and the *Gaza Strip would be handed over to foreign sovereignty; the rejection of Israel's annexation of these territories; the immediate introduction of self-administration by the Arab inhabitants of the territories (See: *Autonomy Plan); the continued establishment of Jewish settlements in the territories on state-owned purchased lands without dispossessing any Arabs; the continued presence of the Israel Defense Forces (*IDF) along borders and in positions vital for the defense of Israel; the prevention of religious coercion and attacks on the freedom of conscience of the secular public, while preserving the values of Judaism and Jewish tradition; the development of suitable frameworks for national service for religious girls; the renewal of economic growth; the limitation of government expenditure and the achievement of a balanced budget by increasing efficiency and by redistributing some government functions to other authorities.

Telem did not express a preference for either the Alignment or the *Likud*, hoping to play a central role in the formation of the next government. However, despite findings of public opinion polls which showed that *Telem* could win up to 19 seats, it won only two. Dayan and Mordechai *Ben Porat entered the Knesset, but since *Telem* was not in a position to play the pivotal role it had hoped to play, they remained in Opposition. Nothing came of efforts by Shimon Peres to bring Dayan and Ben Porat back into the Alignment, and following Dayan's death in October 1981 and his replacement by Yigael *Hurwitz *Telem* decided to support the second Begin government. Ben Porat joined the government in 1982 as Minister without Portfolio responsible for Jews in distress (especially in Ethiopia and the Arab countries) and for devising a plan for the rehabilitation of the Arab refugees in the territories. However, on June 6, 1983, *Telem* broke up and its two MKs set up two separate factions in the Knesset — *Hatnu'ah Lehitḥadshut* (the Movement for Renewal) by Ben Porat, and the *State List by Hurwitz. Ben Porat left the government in January 1984, demanding the formation of a *National Unity Government. Both Ben Porat and Hurwitz ran for the 11th Knesset, but only Hurwitz's **Ometz* passed the qualifying threshold. (M.B.P.)

3. Acronym for *Hatnu'ah Leyahadut Mitkademet* (the Movement for Progressive Judaism), *Telem* was founded in 1965, setting forth as its primary aim "to strengthen the sense of belonging and loyalty of our people to the Jewish heritage and to base the State of Israel on the foundations of Jewish personal and social morality... to foster in Jewish society, both in the State and abroad, a Jewish way of life, a love of Israel and a cultural creativity drawing from the sources of Judaism."

The movement has been involved in various activities to improve the quality of life in Israel, including an annual summer camp for Jewish and Arab children (since 1981), the founding of *Ḥemdat*, an organization devoted to eliminating religious coercion, and the struggle for recognition by the religious authorities of the authenticity of *Ethiopian Jews. (H.F.S.)

4. Acronym for *Hatnu'ah Letzionut Magshimah* (the Movement for Zionist Fulfillment). *Telem* was established by Uri Gordon in Los Angeles in 1979 for the younger generation in the Diaspora seeking to change the Zionist movement.

Members of *Telem* must undertake to immigrate to Israel within three years. In the movement attempts to increase consciousness regarding *aliyah (immigration) and to change the order of priorities of the Zionist establishment which considers Zionist fulfillment (immigration to Israel) to be of lesser importance than fund-raising or strengthening Jewish communities outside of Israel. In Israel the movement helps in the absorption of new immigrants and strives to create a "Zionist atmosphere" which will strengthen links with the Diaspora and prevent *yeridah* (emigration). *Telem* has several thousand members in the *US, Canada, *Argentina and Israel. It is not affiliated to any political party in Israel.

territorial compromise The willingness in principle to give up some, perhaps most, but not *all* of the territories occupied by Israel during the *Six-Day War in return for peace. The principle of territorial compromise is included in the platforms of the *Israel Labor Party, **Mapam*, **Shinui* and the *Civil Rights Movement.

"third state" An expression used regarding the establishment of a Palestinian state in the *West Bank and *Gaza Strip adjacent to Israel and *Jordan. Except for **Ḥadash* and the *Progressive List for Peace all Israeli parties object to the third state on grounds that it would be too small to resolve the problem of the *Palestinian refugees; that it would be irredentist and that in terms of demography as well as territory, Jordan is already a Palestinian state (the majority of the population of the Kingdom of Jordan east of the *Jordan River is Palestinian and *mandatory Palestine covered both Cisjordan and *Transjordan) and there is no need for two Palestinian states.

TNT Acronym for *Terror Neged Terror* (terror against terror), TNT was a small, loosely organized Jewish underground group which operated in the early eighties. Most of its members were American-born and its objective was to strike at Arab supporters of the *Palestine Liberation Organization (PLO) and at non-Jewish places of worship. Operations attributed to it include planting explosives in a Baptist church in *Jerusalem, a church in Ein Karem and in various mosques around Jerusalem, and opening fire at an Arab bus. The members of TNT appear to have been supporters of **Kach*, Rabbi *Kahane's extreme right-wing political party.

(M.B.)

Tnu'at Ha'avodah Lema'an Eretz Yisrael Hashlemah See: *Land of Israel Movement.

Torah Front See: *Religious Torah Front.

Torah Va'avodah Hebrew for Torah and Labor, the motto of the Zionist religious labor movement after World War I, which advocated labor as a personal ideal to be realized within the context of a religious way of life. The name was adopted by the confederation of pioneer and youth groups of **Hamizraḥi*, established in Vienna in 1925.

Torah Va'avodah also became the slogan of **B'nei Akivah* (*Mizraḥi* youth). In the mid-1980s a group calling itself *Ne'emanei Torah Va'avodah* (the Faithful of Torah and Labor) started to function within the *National Religious Party to stop the radicalization of religious youth in the direction of ultra-Orthodox anti-Zionist piety and Kahanist (See: *Kahanism) fundamentalist chauvinism.

Toubi, Tawfiq Christian Arab politician, member of Knesset since 1949. Born 1922, Haifa.

Toubi studied at the Missionary High School on Mount Zion in Jerusalem and in 1941 joined the Communist Party of Palestine. In 1943 he was one of the founders of the League for National Liberation which fought, at first, against the *partition plan, but following the speech of Soviet Foreign Minister Andrei Gromyko in the UN in favor of partition, supported it as the only practical solution. Toubi and his colleagues blamed the imperialist forces and the reactionary Arab leadership as well as the Israeli government for the non-establishment of a Palestinian state in part of Palestine in 1948.

Between 1943-48 Toubi was employed by the Public Works Department of the Palestine government. After the establishment of the State of Israel he became a member of the Central Committee of **Maki*, and entered the 1st Knesset as its representative. The Israeli poet Natan Alterman wrote of him in 1949: "Who is Tawfiq Toubi? He is a Member of Knesset. He is an Arab Communist. He sits in the House of Representatives as of right — not by act of charity... Like all the other delegates in the House, so Toubi sits in it by force of the regime..."

Toubi became Deputy Secretary-General of **Ḥadash* in 1976. He has been a member of the Presidium of the National Committee for Peace since the 1950s, and is a member of the Presidium of the (Communist) World Peace Council.

He is the publisher and editor of *al-Ittihad*.

transfer

1. A term used to describe the idea that the conflict between Jews and Arabs over *Palestine, should be resolved by transferring the Arab population elsewhere, either voluntarily or by force.

The idea had first been mentioned by Theodor *Herzl and Arthur Ruppin before the First World War when Palestine and most of the other Arab-inhabited lands were still within the Ottoman Empire.

During the mandate period the idea was raised within the framework of plans to partition Palestine west of the *Jordan River into two states — one Arab and one Jewish — the more or less homogenous population of each to be ensured by a voluntary population exchange. Delegates to the 1937 Zionist Congress, and Zionists outside the Congress, addressed themselves to the subject after it was raised by the Peel Commission Report of that year. Those who favored it, including David *Ben Gurion, insisted that the voluntary transfer would have to be fully compensated. Those who opposed it, including Ze'ev *Jabotinsky, did so on moral grounds, arguing that Zionist development could take place without the dispossession of the Arabs.

The idea that a Jewish state should be established in the whole of Palestine, with the transfer of the Arab population to neighboring countries, was raised by the 1944 British Labor Party Conference as well as by President Franklin D. Roosevelt.

A de facto unorganized transfer took place during the *War of Independence when many of the Arabs who had previously lived in the territory which became the State of Israel fled to neighboring states and became *refugees. Meanwhile, however, there was a parallel transfer of an equal number of Jews from the Arab countries to Israel in the years which followed the establishment of the state.

Today Rabbi Me'ir *Kahane advocates the transfer of the Arab population from *Eretz Yisrael*, west of the Jordan River either voluntarily with compensation, for those willing to depart, or by force. The idea of a transfer by force is abhorrent to the overwhelming majority of Israelis and rejected out of hand by all political parties except *Kach*. The *Teḥiyah* supports the idea of encouraging Arabs to leave the country.

2. In Hebrew *ha'avarah*, a term used in the 1930s to describe the controversial agreement between the *Jewish Agency and the Nazi authorities in Germany by which Jews emigrating from Germany to Palestine were able to transfer some of their assets, largely in the form of equipment, to Palestine.

Transjordan Geographic term which refers to the area east of a line running from the *Jordan River to the *Dead Sea and continuing from there through the Aravah south to the Red Sea. It does not include the area north of the Yarmuk River as far as Mount Hermon.

The mandate for Palestine included Transjordan — with a territory of some 72,500 square kilometers (28,326 square miles) — though Article 25 allowed the mandatory power to exclude it from the mandate's provisions for a Jewish National Home. From 1921 to 1946 Transjordan was an Emirate within the Mandate for Palestine and was ruled by the Emir Abdullah. From 1946 to 1950 Transjordan was a Kingdom; then it annexed the *West Bank and became the Hashemite Kingdom of Jordan. Since Israeli occupation of the territory of the West Bank in June 1967 the Kingdom of Jordan controls the areas of Transjordan only.

At the beginning of the 20th century most of Transjordan's population was Bedouin. There was a migration of population into Transjordan after the British conquest of the entire area from the Ottoman Empire — largely Palestinians, who today make up the overwhelming majority of the population of Transjordan. The area west of the Jordan River is occasionally referred to as Cisjordan.

Tripartite Declaration A statement issued by the Foreign Ministers of the *US, *France and *Great Britain on May 25, 1950, recognizing the "need of the Arab states and Israel to maintain a certain level of armed forces for... their internal security and legitimate self-defense and to permit them to play their part in the defense of the area as a whole." Arms were to be supplied in accordance with these principles, and only to countries pledging themselves not to commit aggression against any other state. The three governments declared that such "assurances have been received from all the states in question" and pledged immediate action both within and outside the *UN, to prevent any violation of frontiers or armistice lines.

While primarily concerned with the Soviet threat to the region, the Tripartite Declaration came close to being a guarantee of the territorial status quo. Although issued without previous consultation with Israel or the Arab states, it was cautiously welcomed by the Government of Israel as a commitment to some Israel-Arab arms balance, a sign that discrimination in the supply of arms would henceforward be corrected, and a guarantee of sorts for the inviolability of its borders. The Arab states, in a joint statement, while "reaffirming their pacific intentions," expressed doubts concerning the Powers' intentions to intervene and stressed the sovereign right of each state to judge the level of arms it needed.

The Tripartite Declaration, originally interpreted as a coordinated Western guarantee of Middle East borders and Middle East defense, did not live up to such far-reaching expectations. Whatever influence it may have had ceased on the eve of the *Six- Day War in May 1967, when Britain and France announced that they no longer considered the Tripartite Declaration as binding. (N.L.)

Trumpeldor, Yosef (1880–1920) Zionist pioneer and military hero.

Born in Russia, Trumpeldor lost an arm while serving as an officer in the Russo-Japanese war of 1905. He settled in Palestine in 1912, worked in Kibbutz Deganya and took part in the defense of Jewish settlements in the Lower Galilee. During World War I Trumpeldor helped to organize the *Jewish Legion within the British army. He returned to Russia in 1917 and, after the October Revolution, formed a Jewish regiment which was disbanded in January 1918. He then devoted himself to organizing **Heḥalutz* in Russia, returning to Palestine in 1919. His heroic death in 1920 while defending Tel Ḥai against Arab attackers became legendary. Trumpeldor's words at that time: "*Tov lamut be'ad artzenu*" (It is good to die for our country) turned him into a symbol of the new fighting Jew among all political segments of the population. The *Revisionist youth movement and its sports club, **Betar* (acronym for *Brit Yosef Trumpeldor*), was named in Trumpeldor's honor.

Tzomet Political party founded by former Chief of Staff Rafael *Eitan in 1983 which, after protracted negotiations, united with **Teḥiyah* before the 1984 elections.

U

Underground Movements (Jewish) See: **Haganah; *Irgun Zva'i Le'umi; *Loḥamei Ḥerut Yisrael*; *Jewish Underground; *Lifta Group; **TNT*.

United Israel Appeal (UIA) Jewish fund-raising organization in the US. Established in 1925 as the United Palestine Appeal by Zionists who had withdrawn from a joint fund-rising campaign with the Joint Distribution Committee, which raised no money for Palestine. Joint campaigns were carried out again in 1930, 1934 and 1935, but it was only in 1939 that all the competing Jewish fund-raising groups joined together in the United Jewish Appeal (UJA). An overwhelming majority of UJA funds now was allocated for Palestine and, after 1948, for Israel.

The UIA receives over 90 percent of its funds from the UJA, and channels all its funds to the *Jewish Agency. Since the Jewish Agency was reconstructed in 1971 30 percent of the members of the Agency's Assembly have been representatives of the UIA. In the financial year 1985–86 the UIA covered 75 percent of Jewish Agency expenditure for immigration absorption, housing for new immigrants, secondary and higher education, rural settlements (inside the *Green Line), Project Renewal (the rehabilitation of slum areas), various social welfare programs and *Youth Aliyah. Since the establishment of the State the total income from all fund-raising activities abroad (primarily UIA and *Keren Hayesod* — Foundation Fund) has been $7,250 million. UPA/UIA funds in the years 1939–66 amounted to $1,925 million ($147 million during the *War of Independence). UIA funds in the years 1967–85 amounted to $4,300 million ($250 million right after the *Six-Day War and $438 million in the aftermath of the *Yom Kippur War). In 1984–85, $37 million were collected for Operation Moses (See: *Ethiopian

Jews). The funds channeled to Israel through the UIA are tax-exempt in the US and the uses to which they may be put are strictly controlled.

Fund-raising for Israel outside the US is carried out through the Foundation Fund, a financial arm of the *World Zionist Organization (WZO) which also channels funds to the Jewish Agency. Of the members of the Jewish Agency Assembly 20 percent represent the Foundation Fund.

United Kibbutz Movement See: **Takam*.

United Nations and Israel On November 29, 1947 the General Assembly of the United Nations adopted, by a majority of 33 to 13, and 10 abstentions, the recommendations of the UN Special Committee on Palestine (UNSCOP) to implement the *partition of Palestine into a Jewish state and an Arab state, and to internationalize *Jerusalem.

In the global constellation of that time, with the Cold War at its peak affecting the balance of forces within the UN, the joint support of the *United States and the *Soviet Union for the partition was exceptional, and played an important role in causing the departure of *Great Britain from Palestine.

The Arab states rejected the partition resolution and declared war in order to prevent its implementation; they gradually increased their influence in the UN, bringing about an erosion in the principle of negotiations between the parties to the conflict, and the omission of the principle of mutual recognition and peace between the Arabs and Israel from subsequent UN resolutions.

The UN was unable to bring about the implementation of the partition plan by peaceful means, and failed in its mediatory efforts and appeals to stop the armed conflict. The Palestine Conciliation Commission appointed by the General Assembly in December 1948, in which the US, *France and Turkey were members, failed to initiate talks between the parties to the conflict. This commission still formally exists and presents an annual report to the Assembly.

On the refugee issue also, the overwhelming majority in the UN accepted the Arab approach which rejected negotiations and attempts at resettlement which had been recommended in the UN. Instead a vast bureaucratic apparatus for dealing with the refugees, was established — the UN Relief and Works Agency (UNRWA), which built and ran refugee camps in the Arab countries bordering Israel.

In the first years of its existence, Israel's *foreign policy focused on the UN. Despite the reservations of Prime Minister David *Ben Gurion, he recognized the importance of the organization in international politics. Israel's acceptance as a member of the UN in May 1949 was viewed as an important achievement in the integration of the young state in the world arena. It may also be seen as a post factum legitimization of the changes in the borders of the Jewish state which occurred in the course of the *War of Independence and which were recorded in the *Armistice Agreements signed by Israel at the end of the war with its neighbors under the auspices of the UN. Upon the signing of the Armistice Agreements with the aid and mediation of UN Assistant Secretary-General Ralph Bunche, the active positive role of the UN in the Arab-Israel conflict came to an end. During the 1950s and 1960s there was an impressive strengthening of the Third World bloc in the UN and a consequent increase in the inclination of the majority in the organization toward the Arab positions on the issues in dispute with Israel.

Israel objected to the fact that the UN did not react when the Syrians shelled the Huleh Valley settlements and shot at fishermen in the Sea of Galilee, nor when saboteurs infiltrated from Jordan and Egypt and killed Israeli civilians. When Egypt in disregard of UN resolutions, prevented Israel from exercising its right under international law to use the Suez Canal for navigation, there was no UN response. Nevertheless, two important resolutions for Israel were adopted by the *Security Council, Resolutions 242 and 338, in 1967 and 1973, respectively, after Israel's military achievements in the *Six-Day War and the *Yom Kippur War. For the first time the principles of peace, security, mutual recognition and negotiations were introduced into UN resolutions on the conflict. They played, in later years, an important role in the Middle East peace process.

UN PEACE-KEEPING FORCES: in no other region in the world has there been such a varied, intensive and changing involvement of UN peacekeeping forces as in the Middle East. Beginning from the War of Independence, UN observer forces — the UN Truce Supervison Organization

(UNTSO) — supervised numerous cease-fires, and then the Armistice Agreement. UNTSO later joined the supervision of the thinning-out of forces and *disengagement agreements which were signed by Israel with Egypt and Syria after the Yom Kippur War.

Following the 1956 *Sinai Campaign, UN Emergency Forces (UNEF) were stationed in the *Sinai to secure the international border between Israel and Egypt. In May 1967 the then Secretary-General of the UN, U-Thant, hastened the advent of war by succumbing to pressure and threats by Egyptian President Gamal Abdel Nasser, and without consulting the Security Council instructed UNEF to evacuate the Sinai, leaving the border exposed to two armies at the height of military preparedness and escalation.

Following the Yom Kippur War the UN stationed UNEF-2 in the Sinai, which remained in the buffer zone between Israel and Egypt and moved with it in accordance with the Disengagement Agreements, until the establishment of peace between the two states.

The hostility of the UN General Assembly toward the *Camp David Accords and the oppositon of the Soviet Union in the Security Council led to the creation of a new framework outside the UN, the Multilateral Force, led by the United States, which was stationed in the Sinai after Israel's final withdrawal to the international border in April 1982.

The UN Disengagement Observer Force (UNDOF) has been stationed in the *Golan Heights since the signing of the 1974 disengagement agreement between Israel and Syria. The UN Interim Force in Lebanon (UNIFIL) has been stationed in southern Lebanon since the 1978 *Litani Operation. Though Israel does not view the UN forces as the guardian of its borders, it provides them with all required logistic and medical assistance and offers recreational facilities for their men, despite occasional outbreaks of suspicion, friction and misunderstanding.

THE POLITICAL STRUGGLE IN THE GENERAL ASSEMBLY AND SPECIAL AGENCIES: The Arab success in the use of oil as a weapon following the Yom Kippur War increased their strength in the Third World bloc in the General Assembly. The Third World was at first inclined to view the rise of oil prices as an example to be followed for other raw materials in the struggle for a new international economic order. This struggle became the central pivot in the deliberations of the UN until the late 1970s and lay at the root of the confrontation between North and South — between the Third World and the Western industrialized states. In 1974 Algeria, one of the most militant states in OPEC, and at that time Chairman of the nonaligned states and President of the UN General Assembly, succeeded in getting permanent observer status for the *Palestine Liberation Organization (PLO) in the General Assembly. On November 22, 1974, the General Assembly adopted Resolution 3236 regarding the Palestinian right to self-determination, national independence and sovereignty over Palestine, without mentioning, or even hinting at the existence of a Jewish people in Palestine — *Eretz Yisrael*, or at its right to exist and enjoy independent political sovereignty.

Calling into question the State of Israel's right to exist reached a climax in November 1975 when the General Assembly adopted by a majority of 72 to 35 with 35 abstentions, Resolution 3379 which declared that "Zionism is a form of racism and racial discrimination" (See: *Anti-Zionism). The voting exposed the ideological confrontation in the UN between the minority democratic pro-Israel camp and the totalitarian-dictatorial anti-Israel majority. Subsequently, the attacks on Israel and Zionism, replete with anti-Semitic nuances, spread to all the UN institutions and special agencies, and bore the nature of a campaign to delegitimize the right of the Jewish people to its own independent state. Every year, in every General Assembly, over 30 anti-Israel resolutions are adopted on various aspects of the *Arab-Israel conflict.

In the early 1980s the anti-Israeli campaign shifted to an effort to have the credientials of the Israeli delegation to the General Assembly disqualified, with the goal of having Israel suspended from the deliberations.

As a result of the determined American position, accompanied by US threats that it would withdraw if Israel were to be suspended, no deliberation on the disqualification of Israel's credentials has taken place. The decline in the power of the Arab oil-producing countries has also diminished their influence in the UN, and has been accompanied by a parallel process of erosion in the status of the PLO in the organization. Nevertheless, because of its make-up and internal balance of forces, the UN is unable to fulfill the role of an objective mediator in the Middle East conflict, and the diplomatic process which strives for a political settlement between Israel and the Arab states is carried on principally through other channels. (A.B.)

United Religious Front *Ḥazit Datit Me'uḥedet*, a religious list, made up of **Agudat Yisrael*, **Po'alei Agudat Yisrael*, **Hamizraḥi* and **Hapo'el Hamizraḥi*, which ran for election to the 1st Knesset and gained 16 seats. This was the only time that all the religious parties in Israel ran on a single list.

United States and Israel Eleven minutes after the State of Israel was proclaimed on May 14, 1948, the White House announced that President Harry Truman had extended diplomatic recognition to the new state. This act has come to symbolize the close and warm relationship which, in the main, has characterized contacts between the United States and Israel. This does not mean that there have never been differences between Washington and Jerusalem, still less that the US established the State of Israel. It does mean, however, that a special affinity has existed between the two countries from the very beginning. The United States supported the 1947 UN *partition plan but the State Department was opposed to it, and in the aftermath of the vote in the General Assembly on November 29, attempted to reverse the American position. This led to numerous and serious confrontations between the White House and the State Department. Thus, on March 19, 1948, the US Ambassador to the *United Nations, Warren Austin, announced that Washington was shelving the partition plan in favor of a temporary UN trusteeship for Palestine, and Secretary of State George Marshall later endorsed the plan of UN Mediator Count Bernadotte to detach the Negev from Israel and award it to *Jordan. Both these acts stunned and embarassed President Truman, who nevertheless succeeded in overcoming State Department machinations and reasserting the firm US commitment to the principles of partition. Likewise, in June 1948, Truman overrode State Department objections and appointed James G. McDonald as his Special Representative to the State of Israel.

Only in the matter of the embargo on the sale of arms to the Middle East, imposed by the State Department on December 5, 1947, did the President refrain from overturning State Department policy, even though the prohibition had a critical effect on Israel's prospects for survival (See: *Arms Purchases). Truman was dissuaded from lifting the embargo, largely because both the British Foreign Office and the State Department warned that such a move would jeopardize Anglo-American relations.

A flash crisis arose in US-Israel relations at the end of 1948. In December 1948, Israeli troops moved into the *Sinai Peninsula in an effort to land a final blow to the Egyptian forces which had invaded Israel at the outset of the *War of Independence. President Truman sent an urgent message to Prime Minister David *Ben Gurion on December 31, demanding the immediate withdrawal of all Israeli forces from the Sinai, and warning that unless Israel complied the United States would be compelled to reconsider its connection with Israel. This American move was dictated by the desire to head off an Anglo-Israeli clash which would have had incalculable consequences for America's Middle East policy.

Ben Gurion hastened to comply with the American demand and the brief crisis left no permanent scar on relations between the two states. In fact, in February 1949, following Israel's first Knesset elections, President Truman moved to accord de jure recognition to the Government of Israel, and to bring about Israel's admission to the *United Nations. Truman was also instrumental in arranging for a $100 million Export-Import Bank loan for the absorption of new immigrants in Israel (See: **Aliyah*).

Differences of opinion, nevertheless, arose between Washington and Jerusalem over such issues as the fate of the Arab *refugees and the future of *Jerusalem. The United States maintained that the refugees should be readmitted to Israel as a first step toward a comprehensive settlement, while Israel held that the refugee problem could be resolved, not before, but only within the framework of an overall peace settlement. Privately, Israeli leaders argued that a de facto exchange of populations had actually taken place when Israel admitted hundreds of thousands of Jews expelled by the Arab countries, and that it was now up to the Arab states to absorb the Palestinian refugees.

On the Jerusalem issue the US asserted that the UN resolutions on the internationalization of Jerusalem still had a bearing on the city's status. Notwithstanding the division of the city the United States insisted on treating Jerusalem as a separate unified entity to which a special American consul was posted who reported directly to Washington, not via the Embassy in either Amman or Tel Aviv. Israel, on the other hand, maintained that since the United Nations had not intervened to repel Arab aggression against the city, nor moved to institute an international regime for Jerusalem, internationalization was no longer to be considered and the city was effectively divided between Jordan and Israel. Israel maintained it was thus fully within its rights in incorporating West Jerusalem, with its Jewish population of some 100,000, into the State of Israel and declaring it its capital. Differences over Jerusalem have persisted, but have never constituted a serious obstacle in the relations between the two states. In fact, the US concentrated in the wake of the 1949 *armistice agreements on pressing all parties concerned to negotiate a peace agreement. The gap between the parties to the dispute proved, however, too wide to bridge.

The Arabs' refusal to reach a peace settlement with Israel, coupled with their search for arms and calls for a "second round" in which they would achieve what they had not achieved in the first — namely, the destruction of the Jewish state — prompted Israel to turn to the US to redress the arms imbalance. Washington responded by prevailing upon *Great Britain and *France to join it in a common annoucement that the three powers would act to forestall the development of any serious arms race in the Middle East.

The 1950 declaration was, in fact, essentially directed against Soviet penetration into the region, and anticipated that the states of the Middle East would assume a major role in Middle East security through the conclusion of a Middle East defense pact along the lines of NATO. From 1950–52 the Truman Administration canvassed the notion of such a security pact among Middle Eastern states, but made little headway. The Eisenhower Administration, with John Foster Dulles as Secretary of State, placed even higher priority on this plan. On more than one occasion Dulles suggested that Israel was hindering the formation of a regional security network.

The Eisenhower Administration's pursuit of Arab support for a Middle East security pact after 1952 foreshadowed a radical departure from the Truman Administration's partiality toward Israel, and reflected an approach which viewed the emergence of Israel as a stumbling block to the consolidation of Western defenses in the Middle East. This view characterized the approach of the Eisenhower-Dulles team for the better part of five years, resulting in the relations between Washington and Jerusalem reaching their lowest ebb ever. American efforts to enhance the military strength of certain Arab states caused consternation in Israel, but also antagonized *Egypt, which viewed the projected security network as an attempt to introduce Western imperial domination by the back door.

Colonel Gamal Abdel Nasser rejected American overtures to join the proposed Middle East network on the ground that Egypt was not fully sovereign as long as Britain continued to occupy part of its territory. This led Dulles to seek to obtain a British evacuation from the *Suez Canal zone in August 1954 to which Britain agreed. However, Nasser continued to oppose vehemently any regional defense pact, even after the British evacuation, and US efforts remained frustrated. Dulles now focused his attention on creating a northern defense network in the Middle East, one that would initially embrace only those states immediately bordering on the *Soviet Union, such as Turkey, Iran and Iraq — but the move to include Iraq, Egypt's rival, incensed Nasser.

Given the opposition of both Egypt and Israel, it was decided that the US would not, for the time being, become a full-fledged party to the Baghdad Pact, which was signed on March 30, 1955, but would furnish weapons and supplies. This would also help spare the adminstration a tough battle with the pro-Israel Senate whose advice and consent would be required to approve America's accession to a treaty.

Israel's concern over America's resolve to arm Iraq, a state which, alone among the Arab belligerents in the War of Independence, had refused to conclude an armistice agreement with it, was compounded by the news of the Egyptian-Czech arms deal announced in September 1955, which signalled the beginning of the Russian penetration into the Middle East.

Egypt's embroilment in 1956 in a dispute with Britain and France over ownership and control of the Suez Canal, opened the way for Israel to move, in cooperation with the two West European powers, against Nasser. In the *Sinai Campaign Israel attained the three primary goals it had set for itself: destroying the Egyptian military arsenal assembled for a war of annihilation against it; eliminating the *feda'iyin* camps in the Egyptian controlled *Gaza Strip; and lifting the blockade of Israeli-bound shipping in the Straits of Tiran.

However, the United States, still bent on courting Nasser, demanded an immediate and unconditional Israeli withdrawal from the Sinai. The confrontation which ensued between Washington and Jerusalem reflected the change in America's Middle East policy since the Eisenhower Dulles team had entered office and was one of the few instances in Cold War politics where both superpowers agreed on an international stand. This was well demonstrated in the American stand on the Straits of Tiran as an international waterway. The administration was unwilling to accede to the Israeli demand that beside the stationing of a UN force at Sharm-e-Sheikh to ensure that the Straits remain open, the US, in conjunction with other seafaring states, confirm the international character of the waterway. Nor was the administration prepared to offer assurances in return for an Israeli withdrawal.

By early 1957 an impasse was reached and the Eisenhower administration resolved to support a call by the UN Security Council for sanctions against Israel for its failure to withdraw from the Sinai. It was at this point that support for Israel in the US Senate induced a change of policy. The then Senate Majority leader Lyndon Johnson made it clear to the White House that Congress would balk at the imposition of sanctions against Israel. The crisis was finally resolved when President Eisenhower confirmed the freedom of passage through the Straits of Tiran in a letter to Israel, which was followed by an Israeli evacuation of the Sinai.

The final three years of the Eisenhower administration were characterised by deep disillusionment with Nasser and his policies, which was reflected in the Eisenhower Doctrine proclaimed on Janauary 5, 1957. The purpose of the doctrine was "to deal with the possibility of Communist aggression, direct and indirect," and the US gave notice that it would go so far as to employ its own armed forces, if need be, to limit the scope of Russian penetration.

Israel was an indirect beneficiary of the reorientation in American Midle East policy. Recognition by Washington that Nasser was committed to promoting Russian influence in the Middle East cast Israel in a new light within the framework of American policy interests in the region. This did not automatically turn Israel into an American ally in the campaign to forestall further Russian penetration, but it did raise new possibilities for closer coordination between Washington and Jerusalem.

By the time the Eisenhower administration ended its second term of office, relations between Washington and Jerusalem had become more cordial and were marked by a new spirit of cooperation. The death in 1958 of Secretary of State Dulles, and his replacement by Christian Herter, heralded a new era in US-Israel relations.

The improvement in ties went even further when President John F. Kennedy entered the White House in January 1961. Kennedy was the first US President to guarantee Israeli security. At a meeting with Israel's Minister for Foreign Affairs Golda *Meir in December 1962, the President assured her that "in case of an invasion the US would come to the support of Israel." This presidential commitment placed relations between the two countries on a new level of association, that is, an informal alliance.

In September 1962 the ties were given a practical boost when the administration announced that Washington would supply Israel with Hawk anti-aircraft missiles — the first US agreement to furnish Israel with a major weapons system — albeit for defensive purposes.

However, Kennedy also explored possibilities of building bridges to the Arab world, first and foremost to Nasser. Kennedy wrote letters to Nasser, attempting to open a direct line of contact with him, while increasing US aid and grants of wheat. However, these efforts were torpedoed by Egypt's embroilment in 1962 in the Yemen civil war on the side of the revolutionaries, which pitted Egypt against Saudi Arabia, a foremost American ally.

Lyndon Johnson, who succeeeded Kennedy,

did not make special efforts to court Nasser. As the US became increasingly involved in Vietnam, Middle East problems receded. As long as no immediate crisis enveloped the region, Washington felt it could safely ignore a dispute which had dragged on over one and a half decades.

The *Six-Day War forced the US out of its equanimity. Following Nasser's move in May 1967 to close the Straits of Tiran, coupled with his massing of troops in the Sinai, Israel turned to the US to restore the status quo ante and enforce freedom of passage through the Straits. However, the Johnson administration was reluctant to become militarily engaged in the Middle East, in view of its commitments in Vietnam, and chose to call upon other Western states to join it in forming an international flotilla of warships to affirm feedom of passage, a proposal which was never implemented.

Israel's successful lightning campaign spared the US any direct involvement in the conflict. Only when the Soviets hinted that they were contemplating intervention was Johnson compelled to react — by strategically placing the US Sixth Fleet in the Mediterranean. However, the war was over before any outside intervention could materialize. At the same time Washington was active in defending Israel's interests on the diplomatic front. In sharp contrast to 1956, the Johnson administration did not insist on the restoration of the status quo ante before the causes of the *Arab-Israel conflict had been eliminated. Therefore, both during and after the war it rejected every call at the UN for an unconditional return to the June 5 1967 lines. Return of the territories, Johnson stressed, must be accompanied by peace. Implicitly, Johnson was arguing that Israel was entitled to hold onto the territories it had occupied in June 1967 until the Arabs were prepared to accept the reality of Israel's existence and to sit down with Israeli representatives at the negotiating table to work out the terms of a peace settlement. The US repeatedly joined with the majority of UN members to reject Arab and Soviet demands for an immediate and unqualified Israeli withdrawal from territories. The only point of divergence was on the issue of Jerusalem which Israel had reunified in the aftermath of the conflict. The US abstained in the UN General Assembly resolution calling upon Israel to restore Jerusalem to its former status.

President Johnson's stand on a negotiated settlement was incorporated into *Security Council Resolution 242, adopted on November 22, 1967, which henceforth became the touchstone of American policy in the Middle East. "Withdrawal from territories" (rather than "the territories") was linked to termination of "all claims of belligerency." Despite considerable international efforts, there had been no direct negotiations between Israel and its neighbors by the time the Johnson administration ended its term of office in January 1969.

During the tenure of President Richard Nixon, US policy underwent a subtle but significant change. The US continued to advocate the principle of direct negotiations, but in practice, its policymakers began to outline the contours of a proposed settlement. Secretary of State William Rogers drew up a plan (See: *Rogers Plan) which called for an almost complete Israeli withdrawal from the territories it had occupied in 1967, in return for peace. Only "insubstantial" adjustments in the borders would be permitted. Israel, however, continued to insist on direct negotiations with its neighbors as the only guarantee for a settlement. Furthermore, Israel argued that a territorial settlement should also reflect the weight of past Arab belligerency, which had produced three wars in the space of 20 years. By the end of 1969, the US-Israel relations had seriously deteriorated as a result of the divergent approaches on the substance and procedure of peace negotiations. In December 1969 Prime Minister Golda Meir formally rejected the Rogers Plan. A crisis in American-Israeli relations was averted only by the then adamant Egyptian refusal to entertain the plan even as a starting point which prompted its dismissal by the Russians. Furthermore, the stationing of over 20,000 Russian troops in Egypt in early 1970 critically changed the regional power balance. During 1969 Israel had engaged in deep-penetration air raids into Egypt in response to the Egyptian-initiated *War of Attrition along the Suez Canal. Given Israel's mastery of the skies, Cairo called upon the Soviet Union to establish an effective air-defense network in Egypt. SAM ground-to-air missiles were introduced, manned by Russian troops, and Mig fighters, piloted by Soviets, were stationed at Egyptian air bases. The entrance of Soviet troops into a combat role represented a new and dangerous escalation in the Arab-Israel conflict, and portended the possibility of a major direct American-Soviet clash — possibly even a nuclear one.

American policymakers were determined to forestall any such development. Two moves were undertaken. The first was to bolster Israel's defenses by replenishing Israel's aircraft lost in the *War of Attrition. The second step was to secure a cease-fire along the canal which would make the Russian presence in Egypt unnecessary. The latter was achieved by Secretary Rogers at the beginning of August 1970, after both Israel and Egypt had agreed to the plan.

However, no sooner had the hostilities ceased than the Egyptians, with the active connivance of the Russians, deployed ground-to-air missiles along the entire length of the canal — notwithstanding the commitment they had made to maintain a military standstill within 50 kilometers of the waterways. This brazen violation of the terms of the ceasefire agreement dashed any hope for meaningful peace talks between the parties. The Americans felt the Russians were out to entrench themselves in Egypt, which would give them control of the Suez Canal.

Upon the outbreak of the Syrian-Jordanian border crisis in September 1970, against the background of clashes between the Jordanian authorities and the *Palestine Liberation Organization (PLO) ("Black September"), the US moved the Sixth Fleet into the eastern Mediterranean, while the 82nd Airborne Division in Germany and giant transport planes in Turkey were put on alert. Urgent consultations were also held between Washington and Jerusalem. Israel made it known that its Air Force stood ready to go into action against the Syrian advance into Jordan. This warning had the desired effect, and the Syrian forces were withdrawn. Thus, Israeli cooperation had added substance and credibility to the American deterrent. The result was that American aid to Israel increased in 1971 and 1972. For the first time it included not only defense systems but Phantom jets as well.

On July 18, 1972, President Anwar Sadat, who had succeeded Nasser in 1970, expelled the Russians from Egypt, thus restoring Egypt's freedom of action and allowing it to prepare for an all-out attack across the Suez Canal, timed to coincide with a Syrian attack from the north, on October 6, 1973. The American policy objectives after the *Yom Kippur War broke out were, according to Secretary of State Henry Kissinger: ensuring Israel's survival; producing a cease-fire which would facilitate negotiations between the parties; preventing unilateral Soviet gains, and avoiding a nuclear confrontation with the Soviet Union — all of which were achieved.

Thus, even though Washington rallied to Israel's aid with an enormous military airlift, the door to Cairo was kept open for the period following hostilities. Nuclear confrontation with the Soviet Union was avoided (although a crisis did arise in the final hours of the conflict) and the Soviet Union was unable to exploit the developments to reestablish itself in Egypt. One of the outcomes of the war was an American-Egyptian rapprochement. The new phase of American involvement in the Arab-Israel conflict was ushered in with the announcement, on November 7, 1973, at the conclusion of the Sadat-Kissinger talks in Cairo, that the US and Egypt were to resume diplomatic relations. This announcement paved the way for the US to assume an active diplomatic role in the peace process. Initially American diplomacy helped produce the 1974 *Disengagement Agreements between Israel and Egypt and between Israel and Syria, which aimed at stabilizing and extending the cease-fire, and ultimately it promoted the signing of the 1979 *Egyptian-Isreali peace treaty. In a real sense, the United States was able to institute a form of Pax Americana in the Middle East, while totally excluding the Soviet Union from the peacemaking process.

The key figure in this diplomatic initiative was Secretary of State Henry Kissinger who, in the course of the two years after November 1973, made some 11 trips to the Middle East (See: *Kissinger Shuttle Diplomacy). He won the confidence of both the Egyptian and Israeli leaders and gradually succeeded in extracting concessions from both sides in a series of step-by-step negotiations. There was one interlude in this process during which the parties met at Geneva under the joint auspices of the United States and the Soviet Union as was provided for in Security Council Resolution 338. But the *Geneva Conference turned out to be mere window-dressing since the parties themselves preferred to dispense with the international forum and rely on the direct services of the US in reaching an accommodation. By the time Kissinger left office in January 1977, substantial progress had been made in reducing tension in the Middle East and in moving the area from belligerency to actual peace — at least along the Egyptian-Israeli boundary.

A measure of the crucial role which the United States had come to play in the peace process is indicated by the special supervisory function America assumed in the Sinai, and by the secret supplementary agreements which it concluded with Israel in connection with the 1975 Interim Agreement. Thus, the US set up the Sinai Field Mission composed of 200 technicians to man three early-warning stations, and furnished Israel with the necessary assurances for its security. The Egyptian-Israeli peace process was consummated during the presidency of Jimmy Carter who had entered the White House in January 1977. In May 1977, Menaḥem *Begin, leader of the **Ḥerut* movement which had been in opposition since the establishment of the state, became Prime Minister of Israel. Thus concessions which would have met with fierce oppositon had they come from the *Alignment could now be made with only marginal opposition.

Sadat's announcement in the Egyptian parliament, on November 9, 1977, that he would be prepared to address the Knesset in Jerusalem if that would further peace made President Carter's earlier efforts to reconvene the Geneva conference purposeless. However, in the aftermath of Sadat's historic visit to Jerusalem at the end of November, US assistance was needed to enable Israel and Egypt to overcome several more problems before the peace treaty could be signed. The pivotal American role in the peacemaking process was highlighted by the shuttle mediation undertaken by Secretary of State Cyrus Vance and other State Department officials, and most notably by the convening of the Camp David Conference on September 5, 1978. The US played a major role in hammering out both the terms of the *Camp David Accords and the peace treaty itself. After much pressuring by the US government and extensive shuttle diplomacy, including a visit by President Carter to the Middle East, the peace agreement was signed on the White House lawn on March 26, 1979. The American achievement was largely due to US willingness to supplement the agreements leading up to the peace treaty with guarantees to both sides. The guarantees dealt not only with security matters, such as the creation of a multilateral force to supervise the peace in the Sinai (ultimately made up primarily of American forces) but also with economic matters, such as the promise (in 1975) to guarantee Israel's oil supplies for 15 years in return for Israeli surrender of the Sinai oil wells to Egypt. Without these guarantees, in the form of *Memoranda of Understanding, the negotiations might have failed.

By the time Carter was replaced in the White House by President Reagan on January 20, 1981 no recognizable progress had been made in the autonomy talks for the *West Bank and *Gaza Strip stipulated in the Camp David Accords. Furthermore, two major points of dispute had arisen between Washington and Jerusalem. The first was the decision of the Carter administration in March 1978 to sell 60 F15 planes to Saudi Arabia — presented as part of an arms package deal which also entailed the sale of arms and planes to Israel and Egypt. Due to the strenuous efforts of the Israel lobby in Washington the sale to Saudi Arabia was made subject to restrictions which would prevent use of the planes in an offensive capacity against Israel. The second bone of contention related to the establishment of Jewish settlements in the West Bank and Gaza Strip. The Carter administration had been sharply critical of the Begin government's policy of promoting such settlements. In contrast, the Reagan administration adopted a more tolerant attitude, and refused to condemn the Jewish settlement activities as illegal.

The *Reagan Plan elaborated by the President on September 1, 1982, envisaged some sort of permanent linkage between the West Bank, Gaza and *Jordan. The Israeli government objected to the Reagan Plan (even though it gave Israel almost exclusive control over Jerusalem), inter alia on the grounds that it preempted matters to be settled in direct negotiations between the parties thereby closing many of the options which might otherwise have been feasible.

The years 1982–85 were marked by heavy Israeli involvement in *Lebanon (See: *Lebanese War). Initially, Israel was led to believe that it had the implicit blessing of the US for the early stages of the war in June 1982. However, as the campaign dragged on, the American attitude became one of disillusionment, and ultimately, of sharp criticism. At one point the US assumed a peacekeeping role in Beirut, which enabled the PLO and its Chairman Yasser Arafat, to evacuate the city in safety. But after the headquarters of the US marines in Beirut was attacked by a terrorist car-bomb, with the loss of 241 American lives, President Reagan ordered an end to the US peacekeeping role, and the American forces were withdrawn. The differences between Washington and Israel over Lebanon were eventually resolved when Israel announced its withdrawal in May 1985.

Efforts were then made to bring about negotiations between Israel and a Jordanian-Palestinian delegation — without success. Prime Minister Shimon *Peres had attempted to revive them in 1986, but the Palestinians' refusal to recognize Security Council Resolutions 242 and 338 was accompanied by King Hussein's refusal to come to the negotiating table without the *Palestinians.

The period covered by the Reagan administration has been one of unprecedented cordiality between Israel and the US. In recent years Washington and Jerusalem have concluded several significant bilateral agreements such as the Memorandum of Strategic Understanding signed in 1982 and the unique Free Trade Agreement of 1985. At the same time the US has continued to extend to Israel vast economic and military aid (See: *Foreign Aid to Israel). The special relationship has proven its solidity by withstanding in recent years such events as the American sale of AWACS radar planes to Saudi Arabia mentioned above, and the *Pollard Affair. At the end of 1986 the relationship was tested by the affair involving the transfer of American arms by Israel to Iran — allegedly at the request of the US — and the alleged transfer of the proceeds to the Contra rebels in Nicaragua — an act denied by Israel.

The significance to Israel of the special relationship with the US is clear. From the establishment of the state but especiallly since 1973, the US has prevented Israel from being totally isolated in the international arena, and in recent years it has saved it from economic collapse, and is Israel's main source of arms and military know-how. An example of US sensitivity to Israel's special interests and concerns is the tax exemption allowed to contributors of money collected by the Jewish community for Israel (See: *United Israel Appeal). The US was also instrumental in getting the Soviets to allow close to one quarter of a million Jews to leave the Soviet Union since 1971 by such acts as the Jackson Amendment of 1972. Again, in 1976 and 1977, legislation was passed in the US making submission to *Arab boycott demands an offense.

From the American perspective the close relationship with Israel is the outgrowth of a combination of factors: the influence of the powerful American Jewish community; the American view of Israel as being a western outpost in the Middle East and a strategic asset; and a sharing by the US and Israel of basic human values and common perceptions of the international system.

(S.S.)

upheaval In Hebrew: *mahapach*. There have been two upheavals, one political, the second economic. The term political upheaval (*hamahapach hamedini*) is commonly used to refer to the change of government which took place following the elections to the 9th *Knesset (1977). Israel had been governed by **Mapai*, the dominant party from 1948 to 1968, and its successor, the *Israel Labor Party, from 1968 to 1977. The representatives of these parties held most of the top posts in the State of Israel and were predominant in determining the government's and *Knesset's policies and positions in all spheres, even though neither *Mapai* nor the Labor Party ever held an absolute majority in the Knesset.

The predominance of *Mapai*/Labor Party stemmed from two structural causes. First, even though the party did not hold an absolute majority, the number of its representatives was much larger — usually double or more — than that of the second largest faction in the Knesset. Furthermore, in the years 1965–77 the dominant party had a common bloc with other parties which gave it permanent control over at least 50 Knesset seats. Second, *Mapai*/Labor was pivotal as long as the parties to its Right (including the religious parties) could not achieve a majority in the Knesset. The parties to the Left of the dominant party were also far from being able to achieve such a majority. Since a functioning Israeli parliamentary regime requires a majority in the Knesset, and since the ideological gaps between the parties to the Right of *Mapai*/Labor and the parties to the Left excluded a coalition between them, until 1977 any coalition without *Mapai*/Labor was impossible.

The results of the elections which took place on May 17, 1977, brought about a drastic change even though the Israel Labor Party still held the largest number of Knesset seats (26 out of the *Alignment's 32) compared to **Ḥerut* with 19 seats (out of the **Likud*'s 43). The *Likud*, however, emerged as the largest bloc in the Knesset. Even before the elections it was predicted that the Labor party would lose its pivotal status and that the parties to its Right would, for the first time, gain a majority. Nevertheless, the extent of Labor's electoral defeat came as a shock. The expectation that Labor would be greatly weakened was based, *inter alia*, on the success forecast for the new party — the *Democratic Movement for Change (DMC) — in public opinion polls. The appearance of this party, which included many public figures previously identified with *Mapai*, and the Labor party acted as a catalyst for the process which led to the upheaval. The members of the DMC, who to a large extent represented the Israeli social-economic-academic elite, gave a sense of legitimization to the general feeling that the predominance of the Labor party had finally to be shaken. The results of the 1977 elections were surprising in that the parties to the Right of the DMC gained an absolute majority, and despite the DMC's impressive electoral success (15 seats) the new government could be formed without it.

The upheaval, which to a large extent changed the political character of the State of Israel, brought to a climax the process of legitimization of *Ḥerut* and its leader Menaḥem *Begin while faith in the leadership of the Labor movement had reached a low ebb. Some years before Begin was willing to pay a heavy political price to gain the legitimacy which had been denied him and his movement by David *Ben Gurion (See: *"Without *Ḥerut* and *Maki*"). In 1965 he gave up Knesset seats in favor of the *Liberal Party which had agreed to join *Ḥerut* to set up the **Gaḥal* bloc. In 1967 he agreed to enter the *National Unity Government in return for only two ministerial posts (both without portfolio).

The weakening of *Mapai*'s status began with the *Lavon Affair and continued with the replacement of the old leadership and the conflicts within the new leadership (especially between Yitzḥak *Rabin and Shimon *Peres). Finally, there came a succession of scandals involving the Labor leadership, including the *Yadlin Affair, which ended with *Histadrut* leader Asher Yadlin's conviction and imprisonment; Yitzḥak Rabin's resignation from the premiership after his wife's illegal bank account in the US was uncovered; vague suspicions being raised against Abba *Eban; and the Ofer Affair.

Support for the Alignment fell among all groups of the electorate by about 15 percent. While most of the Ashkenazi ("European") voters who left the Alignment voted for the DMC in 1977 (many of them returned to the Alignment in the 1981 elections) the voters from **Edot Mizraḥ* ("Oriental" Jews) shifted their votes to the *Likud* and did not return to the Alignment.

The "economic upheaval" (*hamahapach hakalkali*) refers to the dramatic economic liberalization measures introduced by Minister of Finance Simḥa *Ehrlich in 1977–78 (See: *Economic Policy).

(A.D. — S.H.R.)

V

Va'ad Le'umi National Council of the Palestine Jewish Community (**Knesset Yisrael*) elected by its Representative Assembly (**Assefat Hanivḥarim*). It was set up in 1920 (and recognized by the British in 1928) with rights of administration and taxation over the Jewish community, whose members were, however, entitled to opt out of community affiliation. The *Va'ad Le'umi* dealt with local government of Jewish settlements, education, health, welfare and religion. It represented (generally following policies set by the *Jewish Agency) the Jewish community before the mandatory government and the commissions of inquiry on Palestine. Upon the establishment of Israel, the Provisional Government took over the powers of the *Va'ad Le'umi*.

Village Leagues Association established in

the *West Bank after 1977 with the aim of furthering the economic and social development of the villages and creating a political framework which, while demanding Israeli withdrawal from the territories occupied in 1967, would seek peaceful coexistence with Israel and oppose the *Palestine Liberation Organization (PLO). The establishment of the leagues was encouraged by Professor Menaḥem Milson (See: *Way to Peace), who in 1977 was the Military Government's Advisor for Arab Affairs in Judea and Samaria and was appointed as Head of the Civil Administration in November 1981. Milson encouraged the leagues, believing that they could develop into an authentic Arab oppositon to the PLO, especially in rural areas.

The Village Leagues, one of whose central figures was Mustafa Dudein, thrived until 1983 when the new Civil Administrator, Shlomo Ilya, and the new Coordinator in the Territories, Binyamin Ben Eliezer (nicknamed Fuad, later a member of the 11th Knesset for *Yaḥad) not only stopped supporting them but also banned their political activities. Though the Village Leagues did not accept political dictates from the Israeli administration (for example, Dudein welcomed the *Reagan Plan which the Israel government had rejected) they were marked as quislings by both the PLO (who were responsible for the assassination of the Head of the Ramallah League in 1981) and the pro-Jordanian forces.

Members of the Village Leagues were allowed to carry arms for their own protection but their opponents were quick to accuse them of acting as a militia. The Israeli Left objected to the leagues, arguing that the PLO is the only authentic representative of the Palestinians. The Right, which seeks to annex the territories, felt threatened by the possible emergence of a moderate Palestinian political group which could justify coexistence.

Some cases of corruption and criminal charges in which several leaders of the Village Leagues were involved greatly damaged the leagues' reputation. One of the leaders of the leagues who continues to advocate a moderate line is Mohammad Nasser of the Hebron region.

Village Sons In Arabic *Abnaa el-Balad*. Groups of Arab youngsters, mostly nationalists, some having been previously connected to **al-Ard* circles, got together before the elections to the local authorities in December 1973, because of their disappointment with **Rakaḥ's* (the Communist party) moderation and lack of militancy. The movement was made up of different groups all of whom supported the following principles: non-recognition of the legitimacy of the State of Israel; non-participation in the elections to the *Knesset; the striving for a secular bi-national state (See: *Bi-nationalism) on a non-Zionist basis, which would include all the inhabitants of Palestine, and in which the Jews would no longer constitute a majority. The movement ran for local elections under various names.

In 1983 the movement split and some of its members established the *el-Ansar* list which before the elections for the 11th Knesset (1984), made contact with Uri *Avneri's Alternative Movement, resulting in the founding of the

voting statistics

Knesset	Date of elections	Number of registered voters	Number of voters (% of 3rd col.)	Number of invalid votes (% of 4th col.)	Number of voters per seat
1	Jan. 21,1949	506,567	440,095 (86.9)	5,511 (1.2)	3,592
2	July 30,1951	924,885	695,007 (75.1)	7,515 (1.1)	5,692
3	July 26,1955	1,057,795	876,085 (82.8)	22,866 (2.6)	6,938
4	Nov. 3,1959	1,218,483	994,306 (81.6)	24,969 (2.7)	7,800
5	Aug. 15,1961	1,271,285	1,037,030 (81.6)	30,066 (2.9)	8,332
6	Nov. 2,1965	1,499,709	1,244,706 (83.0)	37,978 (3.1)	9,881
7	Oct. 28,1969	1,748,710	1,427,981 (81.7)	60,239 (4.2)	11,274
8	Dec. 31,1973	2,037,478	1,601,098 (78.6)	34,243 (2.1)	12,424
9	May 17,1977	2,236,293	1,771,726 (79.2)	23,906 (1.3)	14,173
10	June 6,1981	2,490,014	1,954,609 (78.5)	17,243 (0.9)	15,312
11	July 23,1984	2,654,613	2,091,402 (78.8)	18,081 (0.9)	16,786

(A.D.)

*Progressive List for Peace. *El-Ansar* also tried to establish contact with nationalist factors among *Palestine Liberation Organization (PLO) supporters in the *West Bank, especially with deposed Nablus Mayor Bassam el-Shak'a.

(R.C.)

W

Wadi Salib A slum area in Haifa inhabited largely by Jewish immigrants of North African origin in which riots broke out on July 9, 1959 after false rumors were circulated that a policeman had shot and killed one of the inhabitants the previous day. Rioters moved toward Herzl Street, Haifa's main commercial street, breaking shop windows, damaging stores and overturning cars. A second outbreak of violence occurred in Haifa as a committee of inquiry was investigating the first event, when a group of youths from Wadi Salib tried to prevent the holding of a public meeting organized by **Mapai* which they considered to be the "Establishment" responsible for their problems. Sixty persons were subsequently arrested. Similar riots broke out in other towns as well.

The riots, the first of their kind in Israel, drew public attention to the sense of neglect felt by large sections of Israeli society who had immigrated from Moslem countries, and turned Wadi Salib into a symbol of the problem of the **Edot Mizraḥ* (Oriental Jewish communities) in Israel.

The riots were organized by a group called *Likud Olei Tzfon Africa* (Union of North African Immigrants), led by David Ben Ḥaroush, which rapidly developed into an extremist organization which professed a relatively new ideology of populist ethnic separatism, and was different from previous ethnic organizations which had tried to obtain improvements through the existing bodies. There were those who chose to see the Wadi Salib riots merely as the work of hoodlums incited by saboteurs and Ben Ḥaroush's extremism helped them to do so.

The *Likud Olei Tzfon Africa* ran in the 1961 elections while Ben Ḥaroush was serving a prison sentence for his role in the 1959 riots, but it did not obtain the 1 percent qualifying minimum of votes. The affair increased the awareness of the existing political parties of the ethnic problem and encouraged the inclusion of more members of *Edot Mizraḥ* in their Knesset lists. The government formed by David Ben *Gurion in 1961 included an additional Sephardi member. Several changes in the economy and education system were also introduced as a result of the riots.

War of Attrition Localized static fighting along all of Israel's post-*Six-Day War borders but especially in the south along the bank of the *Suez Canal, which continued from mid-1968 until August 1970. The name was first coined by Egyptian President Gamal Abdel Nasser who said on June 23, 1969: "I cannot conquer the Sinai but I can wear Israel out and break its spirit by attrition." Since Egypt had an advantage in fire power and believed it could depend on the *Soviet Union to continue to supply weaponry and to deter Israel from a massive retaliatory attack, Nasser felt that Israel would finally be forced to withdraw from the Suez Canal. As the War of Attrition escalated along the Egyptian front in October 1968 the *Bar Lev Line was constructed. This was the first time that the *IDF engaged in defensive planning on a large scale.

On October 31, 1968 Israel carried out its first attack in Upper Egypt, destroying a power station at Naj Hamadi, but a proposal to occupy stretches of land across the canal was rejected both because the IDF did not have appropriate equipment to cross the canal and for political reasons. Several months of tranquility followed until March 1969 when intense and sustained Egyptian artillery fire was directed at Israeli positions along the canal.

On July 20, 1969 the Israel Air Force started deep-penetration raids causing the almost total destruction of the Egyptian cities along the canal whose 750,000 inhabitants became refugees.

At the end of January and the beginning of February 1970 the Soviet Union supplied vast quantities of equipment to Egypt — including SAM-3 missiles, anti-aircraft guns and radar equipment — and large numbers of technicians to help man them and interception planes with Soviet pilots. In all 15,000 Soviet military personnel were sent to Egypt. On April 18, 1970 the first confrontation between Israeli planes and

Russian-flown Migs took place. On July 30, after Egypt had accepted the *Rogers Plan, five Russian-flown Migs were shot down by Israeli pilots, following which Moscow increased its pressure on Nasser to agree to a cease-fire.

Following the cease-fire on August 7, 1970 the Egyptians brought a missile formation forward to the waterfront in violation of the agreement, to which Israel reacted by temporarily suspending the *Jarring Mission. According to Ezer *Weizman and Mattitiahu *Peled Egypt had won the War of Attrition since it showed that Israel could not remain undisturbed along the canal. According to Moshe *Dayan and Haim *Bar Lev the Egyptians had lost, since they did not achieve any territorial gains and had to agree to a cease-fire.

The War of Attrition along the border with Jordan was carried out primarily by the *Palestine Liberation Organization (PLO) with tacit Jordanian support. It came to an end along Israel's eastern front after Black September in 1970, when King Hussein expelled the PLO from Jordan.

Israel's total losses along the various fronts were 721 killed of whom 594 were soldiers.

War of Independence The Resolution on the Partition of Palestine was adopted by the *UN General Assembly on November 29, 1947. It provided for the establishment of independent Jewish and Arab states and an international enclave comprising Jerusalem and its vicinity; all three were to constitute one economic unit. Although far from satisfying Zionist demands, the resolution was welcomed by the Jews. It was rejected by the Arab Higher Committee and by the Arab states, who threatened to use violence to prevent its implementation. (For maps, see *Arab-Israel Conflict.)

PHASE I: NOVEMBER 29, 1947 TO MARCH 31, 1948. Arab violence erupted the day after the adoption of the resolution. A Jewish bus was fired upon near Lod (Lydda) airport, a general strike called by the Arab Higher Committee led to the burning and looting of the Jewish commercial center near Jaffa Gate in Jerusalem. There were still about 100,000 British troops in the country, far superior to the fighting forces of either side. But, because of their opposition to partition, their general Middle East policy and their forthcoming evacuation, the British were unwilling to crush the riots at the outset. They intervened only sporadically, and primarily to safeguard the security of British forces and installations. These interventions were often directed against the Jews. During this period the main Arab military activity consisted of sniping and throwing bombs at Jewish traffic along major routes, all of which passed through Arab villages and towns, and at isolated Jewish quarters in mixed towns and outlying settlements.

At first, the **Haganah*, the underground military arm of the Jews, concentrated on defensive measures, limiting retaliation strictly to those directly guilty of assaults. The dissident **Irgun Zva'i Le'umi*, however, retaliated indiscriminately, for example, by planting a bomb in a market place. Between December 1947 and January 1948, the Arabs, with the help of volunteers from neighboring Arab countries, made several attempts to capture outlying Jewish settlements (Kfar Etzion, Tirat Tzvi, Kfar Szold) but were repulsed by their Jewish inhabitants. Terrorist-type attacks, sometimes assisted by British deserters, were more successful, especially in Jerusalem. They included the dynamiting of the Jewish Agency building, the editorial offices of *The Palestine Post,* and a number of houses in central Ben Yehuda Street.

In January 1948, an Arab volunteer force under Fawzi al-Qawuqji entered Palestine and took control of the Arab areas in the north; other volunteers, mainly from among the Moslem Brotherhood in Egypt, entered the Hebron-Bethlehem area in the south. Qawuqji's force, known as the Rescue Army, was about 2,000 strong in January and reached an estimated strength of 5–8,000 by April. It sent officers and small detachments to towns, such as Haifa and Jaffa, liable to Jewish conquest, and attacked Jewish settlements in the north (Tirat Tzvi, Mishmar Ha'emek, Ramat Yoḥanan), without any major success. It also attacked Jewish traffic along major routes, effectively isolating Jewish Jerusalem from the coastal plain, outlying settlements (including the Etzion bloc) from Jerusalem, the Negev from Tel Aviv, and Western Galilee from Haifa. These attacks almost achieved political success — late in March 1948 the United States proposed that Palestine become a UN Trusteeship rather than be partitioned into independent Jewish and Arab states, as decided.

PHASE II: APRIL 1 TO MAY 14, 1948. For political and military reasons the Jewish High Command decided to seize the initiative in order to gain effective control of the territories allotted to the Jewish state and to establish secure communications with Jewish settlements outside it. Operation *Nahshon* resulted in the reopening of the road to besieged Jewish Jerusalem, although only briefly. The *Haganah* captured the whole of Tiberias, where Jews had been besieged in the Old City (April 18); Haifa (April 22); the area connecting Tel Aviv with outlying quarters, and the Katamon and Sheikh Jarraḥ quarters in Jerusalem (this last had to be re-evacuated following a British ultimatum); Western Galilee; and all of Safad (there, too, the Jewish quarter had been besieged). British intervention prevented a Jewish takeover of Jaffa (the town later surrendered in May).

In spite of the irregular character of the fighting, the rights of the non-belligerent Arab population were generally respected. In Haifa, for example, the Jewish authorities did everything in their power to prevent an Arab exodus. The case of *Deir Yassin, captured by IZL and **Leḥi*, in which there was a relatively large number of civilian Arab casualties, was exploited by Arab propaganda and resulted in an increased flux of refugees. Some Arab attacks, such as the one against a convoy to the University Hospital on Mount Scopus, caused heavy loss of life, but did not achieve any strategic advantage. Qawuqji's Rescue Army was virtually beaten during this phase. The creation of a continuous strip of territory under effective Jewish control contributed to the decision of the President of the US to suspend the Trusteeship plan, and made possible the proclamation of the State of Israel on May 14, 1948.

PHASE III: MAY 15 TO JUNE 10, 1948. On May 15 Tel Aviv was attacked by Egyptian planes. This signalled the beginning of the invasion by the regular armies of the Arab states. The Arab states had originally decided to aid the Palestinian Arabs with volunteers, money, arms and logistic support, and to draw up their regular armies on the borders — but not to use them for a full invasion. This decision had been reversed in the first half of May — against military advice, and the decision to invade Palestine — in essence an Egyptian one — was reportedly imposed by King Farouq on an unwilling government and army. Undoubtedly Egypt also wished to foil King Abdullah's reported plans to annex Palestine (or, in rumored agreement with the Jews, only its Arab part). The invading armies' original plan, never properly coordinated, envisaged the Egyptian forces moving north toward Tel Aviv, the Syrian, Lebanese and Iraqi forces converging on Haifa, and Transjordan's Arab Legion occupying the *West Bank and Jerusalem.

The entry into battle of five regular armies against the war-weary *Haganah* which as yet possessed no artillery, Air Force or armor, created a critical situation. The Egyptian army moved along the coastal road, attacking nearby Jewish settlements, ultimately bypassing some (Nirim, Kfar Darom), and capturing others (Yad Mordechai, Nitzanim). It was halted only 35 kilometers from Tel Aviv, by a hastily mobilized blocking force, assisted by the first fighter planes which had arrived from Czechoslovakia.

The Arab Legion captured the Etzion bloc, Beit Ha'arava, and the Potash Works near the northern end of the Dead Sea; two other settlements north of Jerusalem were evacuated; and the Legion entered Jerusalem, where after bitter fighting it captured the isolated Jewish Quarter in the Old City, but failed, despite repeated attempts, to penetrate into the Jewish new city. *Haganah* was unable to dislodge the Legion from Latrun, which commanded the road to besieged Jerusalem. But an alternative route — the "Burma Road" — was built to bring in supplies and ammunition through which the city was saved from starvation or surrender.

The Syrian army occupied Masada and Sha'ar Hagolan, south of the Sea of Galilee, but was halted at the gates of Degania, with home-made Molotov cocktails and sightless artillery pieces which had just arrived from France. Subsequently the Syrians turned north and established a bridgehead west of the Jordan at Mishmar Hayarden. The Lebanese army captured Malkiya, but thereafter took little part in offensive operations.

By early June the Arab offensive had lost its momentum, and the confidently announced hopes of a swift victory, backed by much expert world opinion, had evaporated. Jewish forces, though, had suffered heavily. Thus it was with relief that both sides accepted the Security Council resolution calling for a truce of 28 days, which came into effect on 10 June 1948.

PHASE IV: JUNE 10 TO JULY 18, 1948. When fighting resumed on July 8, the situation had changed. Some heavy equipment, purchased before the proclamation of the state but imported only subsequently because of the British blockade, was incorporated into Israel's Defense Forces (*IDF) which had been formed out of the *Haganah*. Larger formations had been created enabling several brigades to be used for one mission. Israel now took the initiative in the north: Operation *Dekel* (Palm) resulted in the capture of Lower Galilee, including Nazareth, but Operation *Brosh* (Cypress) was only partially successful in reducing the Syrian bridgehead near Mishmar Hayarden.

On the central front, Operation *Dani* brought about the capture of Ramla and Lod (including the vital airport) from the Arab Legion; the operation's second phase was designed to capture Latrun and Ramallah and to secure a wide corridor to Jerusalem but there was no time to achieve this. In Jerusalem, an attempt to capture the Old City failed, and in spite of bitter fighting in various sectors the lines remained substantially unchanged.

In the south, the Egyptians again succeeded in closing the main road to the Negev and heavy fighting raged around Kibbutz Negba. An alternative route was used at night for Israeli north-south communications, while the intersecting east-west road to the Hebron mountains was used by Egyptian troops during the day. The initiative had passed to Israel, and it was probably as a result of an Arab request that the British representative on the Security Council proposed a truce of unlimited duration. This came into effect after ten days' fighting, on July 18.

PHASE V: JULY 19 TO JANUARY 5, 1949. The truce was uneasy. Efforts by Count Bernadotte, the UN Mediator, to achieve a political solution were unsuccessful. Meanwhile, the nascent State of Israel was maintaining an army of over 100,000, close to one-sixth of its entire population. Clearly this situation could not continue indefinitely.

Following Egyptian attempts to isolate the Negev, aggravated by Bernadotte's plan to exclude the Negev from the Jewish state, Israel on October 15 in a swift operation (*Yo'av*), succeeded in opening the road to the south, after bloody hand-to-hand fighting, capturing Beersheva on October 21. The Egyptian forces in the Hebron mountains and on the southern outskirts of Jerusalem were now isolated from their bases. Simultaneously, Operation *El Hahar* (To the Mountain) succeeded in widening southward the precarious, narrow corridor to Jerusalem.

Meanwhile Arab irregulars, who had never accepted the truce, continued to harass Jewish settlements and forces in the north. Israel's counterattack, Operation *Hiram* (October 29–31), resulted in the capture of Upper Galilee in a pincer movement from Safad in the east and the coast in the west; some Lebanese territory adjacent to Upper Galilee was also occupied. Operation *Horev* (named after Mount Horev, the Hebrew name for Mount Sinai) was designed to expel the remaining Egyptian forces from Palestine. Israeli forces advanced southward through the desert to the border village of Auja and into Sinai, capturing Abu Ageila and reaching the outskirts of el-Arish. Combined US-British pressure compelled Israel to withdraw from the *Sinai Peninsula, but its forces regrouped for attack east of the Gaza border. Now that Egyptian forces in the *Gaza Strip were in danger of isolation, and the roads into Egypt were undefended, Egypt agreed, on January 5, 1949, to negotiate an *Armistice Agreement — called for by the Security Council on November 16. A truce was reimposed on January 7. (An Egyptian brigade remained besieged and cut off in a small pocket around Faluja; one of its staff officers was a young major named Gamal Abdel Nasser.)

The War of 1948 — Israel's War of Independence — caused very heavy Israeli casualties; over 6,000 dead, almost 1 percent of its population, including over 4,000 soldiers. Arab casualties were estimated at about 2,000 dead for the invading regular armies, and an unknown number of Palestinian irregulars; but no reliable figures are available.

ARMISTICE. Negotiations with Egypt began on January 13, 1949 in Rhodes, under the chairmanship of Ralph Bunche, the acting UN Mediator. After six weeks of negotiations, and several crises over the evacuation of the besieged Egyptian brigade in Faluja, a "General Armistice Agreement" was signed on February 24, 1949. Its preamble states that negotiations had been undertaken in response to the Security Council's call and "in order to facilitate the transition... to permanent peace." This is followed by a non-aggression clause which forbids resort to miltary force; "no aggressive action shall be undertaken, planned or threatened against the people or armed forces of the other side;" "the right of each party to security and freedom from fear of attack shall be fully respected." The agreement emphasizes that it does not prejudice the rights, claims and positions of either party in the ultimate settlement of the Palestine question; "the provisions of this Agreement are dictated exclusively by military considerations and are valid only for the period of the Armistice." Similarly, "the Armistice Demarcation Line is not to be construed... as a political or territorial boundary, and is delineated without prejudice to rights, claims." Warlike or hostile acts by irregular forces and their advance beyond the armistice lines are prohibited; civilans are also barred from crossing the lines. The Israel-Egypt line was identical with the southern international boundary of Palestine, apart from the Gaza Strip, which was included in the territory under Egyptian control. The village of El-'Auja and its vicinity were demilitarized. A mixed armistice commission was set up — to ensure the proper execution of the agreement, and to deal with complaints presented by either side — under the chairmanship of an officer appointed by the UN, and with its seat in 'Auja.

The armistice agreement with Egypt served as a model for similar agreements with Israel's other three neighbors. The agreement with Lebanon was signed on March 23, 1949, at the border point of Rosh Hanikra (Ras al-Naqura) and that with *Transjordan on April 3, in Rhodes. The negotiations with Transjordan were complicated by the claims of both sides concerning communications with and water supply to Jerusalem, the Hebrew University enclave on Mt. Scopus, the disposition of the southern Negev, the reactivation of railway lines, etc. Some of these issues were resolved in secret direct contacts with King Abdullah, which took place simultaneously with the "official" negotiations held in Rhodes; others, enumerated in Article VIII and agreed in principle, were to be arranged by a special committee. These included free access to the *Holy Places of Old Jerualem and to the Jewish cultural and humanitarian institutions on Mount Scopus (which were to resume normal functioning) as well as "free movement of traffic on vital roads." This clause was never implemented and the free access, free traffic and normal functioning envisaged were not established until 1967. Iraq, whose forces had participated in the war, had authorized the Government of Jordan to negotiate "for the Iraqi forces" (which would be withdrawn) and the armistice covered them, although the declared state of war was never rescinded.

The most complicated negotiations were those with Syria, whose forces were the only ones to hold at the end of the war territory allotted to the Jewish state under the UN Partition Resolution. The deadlock was resolved by a complicated and deliberately vague formula establishing demilitarized zones in these areas, which were to be evacuated by Syrian forces. Israel regarded these demilitarized zones as part of its sovereign territory, with limitations only on military forces and installations, as specified, while Syria considered them as areas in which Syria had special rights and which did not fully and finally belong to Israel; there were frequent clashes and a state of almost permanent crisis. The armistice with Syria — with demarcation lines identical with the borders between Syria and mandatory Palestine, except for the demilitarized zones — was finally signed on July 20, 1949.

The armistice agreement with Egypt was the first to break down owing to constant attacks against Israel by irregular forces with the active encouragement of the Egyptian authorities. Israel considered these attacks a complete invalidation of the agreement and declared it null and void in 1956. The agreements with Syria and Jordan, although more often broken than kept, remained officially in force until rendered ineffective by the Six-Day War. However, since the 1950s Israel had stopped attending the Israel-Syrian Mixed Armistice Commission, as Syria insisted on discussing the demilitarized zones, which were, Israel held, within the competence of the Commission's UN-appointed Chairman but not of the Commission itself in which Syria had no standing. The agreement with Lebanon, though more scrupulously observed, was also, in Israel's view, terminated in June 1967, when it declared war on Israel. (N.L.-Y.S.)

"Wars of the Generals" The popular name given to the public debate which developed during the *Yom Kippur War among senior commanders in the *IDF, which began over complaints that Ariel *Sharon was disobeying orders and counter-accusations by Sharon that those who were running the war were incompetent. As a result Chief of Staff David Elazar decided, on January 21, 1974 to cancel Sharon's emergency appointment as a Group Commander.

The wars of the generals later continued in connection with the debate on the events of October 8, 1973 on the Egyptian front, when the IDF lost close to 190 tanks in battle after two attacks, carried out without intelligence data or effective artillery and air support, failed. The various commanding generals in the field — Sharon, Avraham Eden and Shmuel Gonen — accused each other of defective judgement and irresponsible operation.

Way to peace An association (in Hebrew, *Haderech Leshalom*) set up in 1983 by the inspiration of Menaḥem Milson who had held the position of Civil Administrator in the *occupied territories in 1981–82 and whose name was closely associated with the formation of the *Village Leagues in the *West Bank.

The Way to Peace advocates peace between Israel and its neighbors based on the *Camp David Accords and the five-year *autonomy plan; direct negotiations with any Palestinian agency recognizing Israel and rejecting terror; a major role for the *Palestinians in the West Bank and Gaza in the peace process; and the establishment of a Jordanian-Palestinian state and not a new Palestinian state in addition to Jordan. The association rejects unilateral annexation of territories by Israel; Jewish settlement in densely populated areas in Judea, Samaria (See: **Yosh*) and the *Gaza Strip; and terrorism by either Arabs or Jews.

Membership in the association is very small. It is in close touch with the Palestinian elements in the West Bank that are opposed to the *Palestine Liberation Organization (PLO). Most of its activities have been in the sphere of publications and efforts to convince the United Kibbutz Movement (See: **Takam*) to support the association's goals within the *Israel Labor Party.

Weizman, Ezer General and politician. Born 1924, Tel Aviv. The nephew of Chaim *Weizmann, first President of Israel, Ezer Weizman served in the Royal Air Force during World War II, stationed in Egypt and India. He was a member of the **Irgun Zva'i Le'umi* (IZL) from 1946–48 — one of his unaccomplished missions being the assassination in 1946 of General Evelyn Hugh Barker, commander of the British Forces in Palestine and *Transjordan, who was hated by the **Yishuv* for his infamous non-fraternization letter which followed the blowing up of the King David Hotel by IZL. He served in the Air Service which preceded the establishment of the Israel Air Force (IAF), flying ammunition and provisions to the Negev and Gush Etzion in 1948 and was sent to Czechoslovakia to learn to fly Messerschmidts and to fly one back to Israel. Weizman served in the IAF until 1966, the last eight years as its Commander, in which capacity he introduced electronic warfare.

Head of the *IDF Operations Branch and Deputy Chief of Staff from 1966–69, his political views were said to have prevented his being appointed Chief of Staff. In 1969 he served as Minister of Transport for **Gaḥal* in Levi *Eshkol's second *National Unity Government. From 1971–72 Weizman was Chairman of the **Ḥerut* Executive Committee, resigning in December 1972 over disagreement on the distribution of seats in the *Ḥerut* Central Committee. He returned to *Ḥerut* in May 1973 remaining in the party until 1980 and was in charge of the **Likud* election campaign for the 9th Knesset (1977). Serving as Minister of Defense from 1977–80, he played a major role in the peace process with *Egypt, launched the *Litani Operation in March 1978 and soon thereafter proposed the establishment of a "National Peace Government" to further the peace process — an idea which was rejected by the Prime Minister. While maintaining a low profile as Minister of Defense, Weizman's political views underwent a drastic change and he became increasingly critical of the rigid, uncompromising policy of his own party, frequently clashing with the Minister of Agriculture, Ariel *Sharon over settlement policy in the *West Bank. In May 1980 Weizman resigned from the cabinet, officially over cuts in the defense budget. He considered establishing a new party to be headed by Moshe *Dayan in November 1980 and as a result was ousted from *Ḥerut*. He kept his Knesset seat until the end of the 9th Knesset but from 1980–84 he was engaged in business activities. In March 1984

Weizman established a new party — **Yaḥad* — which ran on a dovish platform in the elections to the 11th Knesset, gaining three seats. On August 22, 1984 Weizman brought his party into the *Alignment and was appointed Minister without Portfolio and member of the inner cabinet in the National Unity Government. In January 1985 he was appointed Coordinator of Arab Affairs and abolished the office of Advisor to the Prime Minister on Arab Affairs. Weizman has tried to assist the Arab sector in Israel and has played an active role in the efforts to revitalize the process of normalization of relations with Egypt.

In the *National Unity Government under Yitzḥak *Shamir, Weizman is closely associated with the Ministry for Foreign Affairs. In October 1986 he joined the *Israel Labor Party with the rest of his party.

Weizmann, Chaim (1874–1952). Professor of chemistry and Zionist leader. First President of Israel. Born in Russia, Weizmann was active in the Zionist movement from its inception. In 1903 he was one of the founders of the "Democratic Fraction" which advocated "Practical Zionism" (See: *Zionism). In 1904 Weizmann migrated to Britain where he played an influential role in the discussions leading to the issuance of the *Balfour Declaration in 1917.

From 1920 to 1948, with only a short break (1931–35), Weizmann was President of the Zionist organization. His moderate policy of full cooperation with the British government was the main cause for his defeat at the 1931 Congress. Weizmann also advocated moderation with regard to the Arabs; until 1937, he propagated a political parity between the two peoples in Palestine irrespective of their relative numerical strength. From 1937, he supported partition and separate states — preferably within the framework of a Middle East federation.

Weizmann supported the *Biltmore Program instituted by David *Ben Gurion calling for a Jewish Commonwealth in Palestine; but Ben Gurion accused Weizmann of often acting too independently. Weizmann's moderate policies were not in accord with the violent struggle which was developing; his absence from Palestine aggravated his lack of contact with colleagues there. However, he retained considerable prestige and was in the forefront of the final struggle (1946–48) for the creation of the State of Israel. In May 1948 Weizmann became Israel's first President (sworn in on February 16, 1949), but due to the merely representative nature of the office (See: *President) and his poor health he did not play an active part in policy-making.

Weizmann's favorite projects were the Hebrew University of Jerusalem, opened in 1925, and the Weizmann Institute of Science in Reḥovot, opened in 1934. His autobiography, *Trial and Error* (1949) is an important Zionist document.

West Bank A geopolitical term referring to the territories west of the *Jordan River which had formed part of *mandatory Palestine and which were annexed by the Hashemite Kingdom of Jordan after the *War of Independence and occupied by Israel in the *Six-Day War. Since its occupation in 1967 Israel has officially referred to this area as Judea and Samaria (See: **Yosh*).

The West Bank covers 5878 square kilometers (2270 square miles) and was to have formed the rump of the territory allocated to the Arab state by the November 1947 UN partition plan. In 1948 the population of the territory was approximately 600,000 of whom 200,000 were Palestinian *refugees and the rest indigenous to the area. At the time of the Israeli occupation in 1967, the population was still only 600,000, since over 25 percent of the population had left the West Bank in the aftermath of the war. In late 1984 the West Bank population was 786,000. The number of Arabs who had left the West Bank surpassed the number entering it in the 1967–85 period by about 156,000. The Jewish population in the West Bank — all post-1967 settlers — was 44,250, not including *Jerusalem, in 1985. The Emir (after 1946, King) Abdullah of Jordan never concealed his intention of extending his control over Western Palestine, and was determined to expand his rule over as much as possible of the territory allotted to the Arab state by the partition plan. At the end of the War of Independence the Arab Legion was in control of the West Bank which the King began to integrate into his realm, officially annexing it by decree in April 1950, and declaring the two banks of the Jordan River the Hashemite Kingdom of Jordan. This annexation was never formally recognized by any Arab state, since the Jordanian occupation was regarded as a temporary situation until the final resolution of the *Arab-Israel conflict. In fact, the annexation was formally recognized only by *Great Britain and Pakistan.

The annexation changed the political composition of Jordan and upset its demographic balance. From a Beduin emirate the Kingdom became a predominantly Palestinian state in which the Hashemites did not enjoy automatic support.

Although West Bank *Palestinians formally shared in the administration on an equal footing with the East Bank residents, with an equal number of representatives in the Jordanian parliament and a visible presence in the cabinets of King Hussein (who assumed the throne in 1953), they were barred from influential positions. While on the one hand the Palestinians cooperated with the government in Amman in the 1950s, there were strong undercurrents of discontent and resentment which erupted periodically in the form of mass demonstrations and clashes with the police. The younger West Bank intelligentsia continued to seek ways to influence their people's fate, and though none of them came out publicly in favor of independence for the West Bank, many of them were able to identify with the *Palestine Liberation Organization (PLO), established in Jerusalem in 1964. Tensions between the Palestinians and the Jordanian authorities became progressively more acute, culminating in a new wave of unrest in the West Bank in 1966. In the period 1965–67 the West Bank was increasingly used by Palestinians to launch terrorist acts against Israel, similar to the pattern of the early fifties. In both instances these activities triggered off Israeli reprisals and Palestinian complaints that the Jordanian security forces did nothing to defend the West Bank. While the loss of the West Bank during the Six-Day War relieved the King of the need to deal with these problems, he nevertheless wished to regain control over the West Bank in general and Jerusalem in particular.

Though initially the Israeli policy was to sever the West Bank from Jordan subsequently Israel followed a policy of *open bridges, and Jordan continued its financial and political support and involvement in the West Bank.

Since 1967 developments on the West Bank may be divided into three major stages: the period of initial shock (1967–76), the emergence of a local leadership (1976–82) and Jordanian-Israeli coordination since 1982. Each of these periods may be characterized on two levels: first, the Israeli-Jordanian confrontation and dialogue over the fate of the West Bank and second, the political behavior of the local population.

A separate level of activity is the development of an Israeli settlement policy under which 150 Jewish towns and villages have been established. Recent studies suggest that this "creeping annexation" has created an irreversible situation (See: *Benvenisti Prognosis), though the *Alignment and other parties in the Center and Left still argue that most of the West Bank and Gaza Strip could be returned to Arab sovereignty within the framework of a negotiated peace settlement.

In the first period the Israeli authorities enabled Jordan to channel funds to the West Bank to pay Jordanian officials who continued their duties under Israeli rule. Simultaneously, Israel established a system of *military government responsible for all aspects of life in the territories, and using civilian experts, professionally subordinated to the Israeli ministries, to carry on nonmilitary activities. During the formative years of the first stage some measure of coexistence between the Jordanian and Israeli systems emerged. The most outstanding example of this was the West Bank mayors who resumed their activities after the war. Even though some of them publicly supported calls for rebellion against Israel (1967–69) and declared their support of the PLO position, for the most part they continued to cooperate both with Jordan and the Israeli military authorities who expedited the reelection in 1972 of most of the mayors. Though the mayors assumed a representative role for the local population they were only permitted to operate on the municipal level. The Israeli authorities prevented the emergence of any national leadership. An attempt, in July 1967, to establish a Supreme Moslem Council was sterilized by Israel of any political or national elements.

While the Six-Day War brought a halt to the process of integrating the West Bank into Jordan, Israel did not have a coherent policy vis-à-vis the area except for "keeping it quiet" and maintaining the elusive post-1967 status quo. The vague Israeli policy coupled with rising sentiments of Palestinian nationalism, provided the opportunity for the appearance of a new kind of leadership — young and middle-aged technocrats who viewed the PLO as their sole legitimate representative. Many of these new leaders were elected in the municipal elections of 1976, reflecting the rise in the authority and influence of the PLO after the October 1974 *Rabat Summit Conference, and the decline in the power of the traditional ledership.

Thus, in the second period the political power of the PLO was at its zenith, both in the international arena and in the West Bank. The pro-PLO positions taken by the new mayors were reinforced by the 1977 political *upheaval in Israel, and opposition to the Egyptian-Israeli peace process. The *Camp David Accords of March 1978, included clauses calling for the implementation of a five-year *autonomy plan for the Palestinian Arabs, which provided the West Bank mayors with an additional context within which to try and create a national leadership. The National Guidance Committee, which existed in the years 1978–82 under the leadership of Mayors Shak'a of Nablus, Khalaf of Ramallah and Qawasme of Hebron, became the national representatives of the West Bank Palestinians, with a potential of becoming the nucleus of a future Palestinian state. Its coordination with the PLO, which enjoyed wide-scale support in the West Bank, made this leadership more authentic than any previous leadership to have emerged in the West Bank. As the committee's leadership gained political influence, the supporters of Jordan declined in local political terms. Israel, on its part, tried to encourage the development of a local leadership which would cooperate in the implementation of the autonomy plan while condemning terrorism. In 1981 the *Village Leagues, which took advantage of the traditional conflict between the urban and rural population, began to operate within this framework.

The Israeli invasion of Lebanon and the developing conduct of the *Lebanese War, including the expulsion of the PLO from Beirut, which increased the PLO's dependence on Jordan, as well as the *Reagan Plan which recognized Jordan as the legitimate claimant to the West Bank, strongly influenced the West Bank Palestinians.

The 1985 Hussein-Arafat agreement was the first time since the Rabat Summit that the PLO, as the recognized representative of the Palestinians, and Jordan as the former sovereign of the West Bank, agreed on a coordinated policy. The West Bankers were now able to support the PLO without this interfering with the Jordanian desire to return to the West Bank. The precise nature of this solution was never fully explained, though it was understood to involve some loose union between the East and West Banks. In February 1986 the King announced his suspension of relations with the PLO allegedly because of the PLO's refusal to accept *Security Council Resolution 242, and started to pursue energetically a political line aimed at reconstituting a pro-Jordanian infrastructure in the West Bank, with Israel's tacit approval. In 1986 Israel also allowed a Jordanian bank to function in the West Bank for the first time since the Six-Day War.

Thus, a clear pattern of a condominium has emerged in which Israel is the de facto sovereign and Jordan maintains its own involvement in all spheres of life of the West Bank. (Al.B.)

Nevertheless, PLO influence is substantial and deep in the area, and the Palestinian organizations are not likely to resign themselves to such a condominium.

THE ISRAELI PARTIES AND THE WEST BANK: The incoherence of Israeli policy in the West Bank is largely due to differences of opinion among the parties in Israel regarding the future of the territory. While soon after the Six-Day War most of the Israeli parties agreed that the West Bank, and most of the other territories occupied during the war, should be given up in return for peace (with the exception of **Ḥerut* and a majority in **Aḥdut Ha'avodah — Po'alei Zion*) in the following years the national religious camp, as well as all the right-wing parties adopted policies rejecting withdrawal from the West Bank and Gaza Strip under any condition, arguing that these territories are part of **Eretz Yisrael* liberated from foreign rule. (The *Liberal Party adopted a resolution against withdrawal in 1971.)

The *Israel Labor Party adopted a policy of *territorial compromise in its 1973 platform, more or less on the basis of the *Allon Plan which called for Israel remaining in control of the Jordan Valley Rift (except for a corridor around Jericho) the Gush Etzion area and a few other minor areas such as Latrun. The densely populated areas of the West Bank are to be returned to Arab sovereignty, to form a Jordanian-Palestinian state, within the framework of a peace settlement. This policy was based on concern about the future Jewish democratic-egalitarian nature of the State of Israel.

The parties on the extreme Left have called for complete and unconditional Israeli withdrawal from the West Bank and Gaza Strip, and the establishment there of a Palestinian state — their policy being based on moral-ideological arguments.

While the parties of the Right advocate the complete integration of these territories into Israel (though preferably without their Arab inhabitants becoming Israeli citizens), those advocating territorial compromise or complete withdrawal have shown concern about creeping annexation and the growing economic dependence of the West Bank and Gaza Strip on Israel. However, projects to enable the independent economic development of these territories (Yigal *Allon advocated such a policy in June 1973 and on the eve of the 1984 elections the **Mashov* circle in the Labor party advocated its adoption as the official policy of the party) have come to very little, with the West Bank economy still largely dependent on agriculture (which has undergone extensive modernization since 1967), services, the income of tens of thousands of persons employed within the *Green Line, remittances from West Bank Palestinians working abroad, and money poured in from Jordan, the PLO and other Arab and non-Arab sources. None of this money has been invested in industry because of Israeli restrictions. In 1981 Moshe *Dayan suggested that since no progress seemed likely in the peace process Israel should introduce a unilteral autonomy plan in the West Bank and Gaza Strip. This proposal was raised again in 1985 and 1986 by Gad *Ya'acobi. (S.H.R.)

"Who's a Jew" See: *Law of Return.

"Without Ḥerut and Maki" An explicit statement made by David *Ben Gurion, repeated implicitly on several occasions, but especially after the elections to the 1st Knesset (1949) and the 2nd Knesset (1951) when he sought to establish a wall-to-wall coalition which would include "all the constructive forces from **Mapam* to the *General Zionists." Ben Gurion excluded **Ḥerut* and **Maki* because he believed both to be parties which sought to destroy democracy, one to form a right-wing dictatorship and the other a left-wing dictatorship. He argued that cooperation with them was impossible.

The boycott of *Ḥerut* ended only when Levi *Eshkol invited **Gaḥal* to join his coalition on the eve of the *Six-Day War. While the Communists were never invited to join the government (though after the election to the 11th Knesset in 1984 there was some talk about the *Alignment setting up a narrow government which **Ḥadash* would support), many viewed President Ḥaim *Herzog's attendance at the opening session of the *Ḥadash* conference in December 1985 as expressing an end to the boycott of *Maki*.

WIZO Acronym for Women's International Zionist Organization, a voluntary organization established in London in 1920. WIZO was set up to provide vocational and agricultural training for women and child welfare services in Palestine and to enlist support of women for *Keren Hayesod* (Foundation Fund) and *Keren Kayemet* (Jewish National Fund) activities. WIZO functions in all parts of the world except the US in accordance with an agreement with **Hadassah* of America. WIZO ran in the elections to the 1st Knesset and won one Knesset seat. It is a member of the *World Zionist Organization and the World Jewish Congress. It is also represented as a non-governmental body in the UN Economic and social Committee (ECOSOC) and UN Children's Fund (UNICEF). It runs nurseries for infants and small children, youth clubs, summer camps, vocational secondary schools and women's centers. In recent years it has been active in trying to increase women's consciousness regarding their status in Israeli society.

women in politics Despite the declaration by Theodor *Herzl in the First Zionist Congress regarding the equality of women in the *World Zionist Organization (WZO), the egalitarian ideology which characterized Israel society in the pre-state **Yishuv* and during the first decade of the state's existence, and the provisions of the *Proclamation of Independence that: "The State of Israel ... shall maintain complete social and political equality for all its citizens, without distinction of religion, race or sex," women have played a relatively small role in Israel's political system. Indeed, the number of women members of the first three Knessets exceeded that of the last three (9th — 11th).

In addition to the traditional problem facing women who wish to pursue a political career and also raise a family, which limits the number of women entering politics in all countries, there are several other factors to be considered with regard to Israel. Although women serve in the *IDF (for two years, in non-combat positions), the unending *Arab-Israel conflict has encouraged the development of a highly male-oriented society, in which all issues regarding security — the country's central concern — are looked upon as the domain of men. The army also serves as an "old boys' network" for the men who continue to serve in reserve duty up to the age of 50.

The fact that a large majority of the Israeli population is composed of **Edot Mizraḥ* (Oriental Jews) and Arabs whose culture and traditions do not recognize the equality of women, has also deterred large numbers of women from entering the political arena, even though some Oriental women have done so and have reached high positions. One of these is Shoshana Arbeli-Almoslino, a member of the *Alignment of Iraqi origin, who serves as Minister of Health in the *National Unity Government led by Yitzḥak *Shamir.

Under the *Halacha* (Jewish religious law) women do not enjoy equal status, and compared to other Western societies, religion plays a major role in Israel. Nonetheless, religious women have become Knesset members, and recently religious feminists have begun to speak out, demanding greater equality for women within the religious frameworks. At the end of 1986, a woman, Leah Shakdiel, was elected to the religious council (the body in charge of providing religious services) in the development town of Yeruḥam.

The method for nominating or selecting candidates for the party lists for election to the Knesset is biased against women. Only the *Israel Labor Party and **Mapam* maintain a quota for women in order to ensure minimum representation (20 percent of the list). Another party, **Shinui*, considered introducing the quota system but finally rejected it on principle.

Women's organizations, such as **Na'amat*, *WIZO and *Emunah* (the women's section of the *National Religious Party, NRP) have had a limited impact on women's advancement in "high politics." Despite the fact that these play a major role in Israeli society, and are geared to promoting women's interests and that in recent years they have encouraged greater women's participation in the political system, most of their energies have been invested in social and community affairs.

The largest number of women — 13 (of 120 Members of Knesset) — was elected to the 3rd Knesset (1955). The left-wing parties have always returned the most women to the Knesset and the decline in the number of women there coincides with the relative decline of these parties.

There has never been more than one women in the cabinet. Golda *Meir served in all the governments from 1949 to 1966, first as Minister of Labor, then as Minister for Foreign Affairs. In 1969–74 she attained the post of Prime Minister. Meir's non-feminist image was exemplified by the frequent assertion that she was "the only man in the cabinet." In 1974 Shulamit *Aloni of the *Civil Rights Movement (CRM) served for four months as Minister without Portfolio in the government of Yitzḥak *Rabin, but resigned when the NRP joined the government. Sarah Doron of the *Liberal Party served as Minister without Portfolio in the government of Yitzḥak Shamir (1983–84). Arbeli-Almoslino was Deputy Minister of Health in the National Unity Government under Shimon *Peres before becoming Minister of Health under Shamir.

In 1951 the Woman's Equal Rights Law was passed, which dealt with the equal status of women for the purpose of litigation, their right to purchase and possess assets even after marriage, and the equality of both parents as natural guardians of their children. However, as Member of Knesset Ḥannah Lamdan (*Mapam*) remarked when the law was debated in the Knesset, it is not a law for equality but for the reduction of inequality.

A feminist movement was initiated in Israel in 1972. One of its leaders, Marsha Friedman entered the 8th Knesset (1973) as the third candidate on the list of the CRM. In 1977 she ran for Knesset elections leading her own women's party, but failed to pass the qualifying threshold.

In the wake of the International Year for Women (1975) a commission on the status of women, chaired by MK Ora Namir (Alignment) was appointed by the Rabin government. The commission presented its report to the *Begin government in 1978. Most of its recommendations have not been realized. Most noteworthy among the few changes that the commission's report did bring about are: the appointment of an advisor to the Prime Minister on the status of women (in 1986, Niza Shapira Libai, a member of the Labor party, filled this position); the enactment in 1981 of the Equal Opportunities Law, which forbids discrimination against women in the hiring of workers; and the adoption of a resolution by the government in April 1985 regarding equal opportunities for women in ministries and offices subject to the ministries.

In 1984 the non-partisan Women's Network was established, with Alice Shalvi as Chairwoman, to improve the status of women. The Network functions as a lobby in the *Knesset and the *Chief Rabbinate and works at increasing women's awareness of their inferior status, so that more of them will become active.

Several of the women active in the promotion of more participation by women in the political system, advocate the establishment of separate lists for women in the various parties to run side by side with the regular lists and in this way increase women's representation in the Knesset. In the 1984 elections *Emunah* was prepared to present its own list of candidates for the Knesset when women were not included in realistic places in the NRP list, but, after opinion polls revealed that the party had lost most of its electoral support, *Emunah* cancelled its plan, placing its full support behind the party.

Within the Labor party there have been demands for the establishment of a separate women's "district" (*maḥoz*), which will inter alia, have a quota of places in the party list of candidates to the Knesset, as do all districts, in addition to the women who might enter the list as representatives of other sectarian or geographical districts. While the democratization of the Labor party institutions in 1986 has increased the number of women in the party's central committee and bureau, it is generally believed that *electoral reform, as currently proposed, will reduce the number of women in the Knesset since few women, if any, have sufficient local support to be elected directly.

The 1975 UN World Conference of the International Women's Year, which met in Mexico City, passed a resolution equating Zionism with racism (See: *Anti-Zionism). However, at the 1985 Nairobi Women's Conference the Israeli women delegates managed to thwart attempts to pass such a resolution again.

Women Members of Knesset:
1st Knesset (1949) — 12 (7 **Mapai*, 2 *Mapam*, 1 *General Zionists, 1 **Ḥerut*, 1 WIZO);
2nd Knesset (1951) — 12 (7 *Mapai*, 1 *Mapam*, 2 General Zionists, 1 *Ḥerut*, 1 **Maki*);
3rd Knesset (1955) — 13 (8 *Mapai*, 1 *Mapam*, 1 **Aḥdut Ha'avodah*, 1 General Zionists, 1 *Ḥerut*, 1 *Maki*);
4th Knesset (1959) — 10 (6 *Mapai*, 1 *Mapam*, 1 *Aḥdut Ha'avodah*, 1 *Ḥerut*, 1 NRP);
5th Knesset (1961) — 10 (5 *Mapai*, 1 *Mapam*, 1 *Aḥdut Ha'avodah*, 1 *Liberal Party, 1 *Ḥerut*, 1 *Maki*);
6th Knesset (1965) — 10 (6 Alignment, 1 *Mapam*, 1 **Rafi*, 1 *Ḥerut*, 1 *NRP*);
7th Knesset (1969) — 8 (6 Alignment, 1 *Ḥerut*, 1 NRP);
8th Knesset (1973) — 12 (8 Alignment, 2 **Likud*, 2 CRM);
9th Knesset (1977) — 10 (5 Alignment, 2 *Likud*, 1 CRM, 1 NRP, 1 *Democratic Movement for Change);
10th Knesset (1981) — 9 (5 Alignment, 2 *Likud*, 1 CRM, 1 **Teḥiyah*);
11th Knesset (1984) — 10 (4 Alignment, 2 *Mapam*, 2 *Likud*, 1 CRM, 1 *Teḥiyah*).

World Federation of Sephardi Communities Organization of Sephardi Jews the origins of which date back to 1925 when a conference of Sephardi communities was held during the World Zionist Congress in Vienna. At that time the organization did not get off the ground because some of the Sephardi leaders feared that the establishment of a separate organization would cause a split in world Jewry between Sephardi and Ashkenazi Jews. In 1947 an organization of Sephardi Jews was established in Palestine under the leadership of Eliahu Eliashar, who was later to represent the Sephardi communities in the 1st and 2nd *Knesset (See: *Sephardi List). The organization in **Erezt Yisrael* contacted Sephardi communities abroad and in 1951 convened a Sephardi World Congress in Paris. Subsequently the World Federation of Sephardi Jews was established with headquarters in London, but failed to become a world-wide organization.

The federation remained outside the *World Zionist Organization (WZO) until 1972 when the WZO established a special department to deal with Sephardi affairs. The establishment of this department must be seen against the background of a political awakening among **Edot Mizraḥ* (Oriental Jews) in Israel and their growing sense of political, social and economic deprivation within Israeli society.

Since 1973 the president of the federation has been Nissim David Ga'on, businessman and philanthropist, and Head of the Sephardi community in Switzerland. The World Federation of Sephardi Communities has remained a non-partisan organization. Since 1979 its 21-member presidium has included, besides the President, ten Israeli members (four from the **Likud*, three from the *Alignment, two from the religious parties — at first the National Religious Party [NRP] since 1981 **Tami* — one independent), and ten members from abroad (from the US, Canada, Latin America, France, Great Britain, Spain and the rest of Europe).

In Israel the federation concentrates its activities on the field of education (helping students from underprivileged backgrounds), welfare and immigration absorption. Abroad the federation helps in the provision of the religious requirements of Sephardi communities, Jewish education, the encouragement of ties with Israel and education for Zionism.

World Labor Zionist Movement Sister movement to the *Israel Labor Party in the *World Zionist Organization (WZO), established in 1968 when the World Union (the Diaspora party of **Mapai*) and the World Alliance of **Aḥdut Ha'avodah — Po'alei Zion* (the Diaspora party of *Aḥdut Ha'avodah — Po'alei Zion*), united. The movement has branches in North America, western Europe, Latin America, Australia, South Africa, and, until 1979, Iran.

The goals of the World Labor Zionist Movement are: to concentrate most of the Jewish people in the State of Israel by constant immigration (**aliyah*) and absorption; to strengthen the national identity of the Jewish people in the Diaspora and its ties with Israel through Jewish education and a systematic struggle against alienation and assimilation; to turn Israel into the national center of the Jewish People; to settle the frontier areas of Israel (see: *Allon Plan); to make Israeli society a free labor-society, based on social justice, productivity and progress; to nurture peace and cooperation with the neighboring states.

Since the Labor movement lost its predominance in the WZO in 1978, the World Labor Zionist Movement has worked together with other progressive forces in the Zionist organization like *Artza* (the *Reform movement in the Zionist organization) and **Hadassah* to further such joint causes as Jewish religious pluralism passed by the 1978 Zionist Congress.

In 1978 Yigal *Allon was elected Chairman of the World Labor Zionist Movement. Since 1982 Yeḥiel Leket has been Chairman. The World Labor Zionist Movement has associate status in the *Socialist International.

World Organization of Jews from Arab Countries (WOJAC) An organization founded in Paris in 1975 to disseminate information regarding the Jews who left Arab countries — most of them as refugees — after the establishment of the State of Israel, and to deal with claims for compensation for property left behind in the Arab states. Of over 800,000 Jews who lived in Arab countries in 1948 close to 600,000 immigrated to Israel — a number slightly larger than the number of Palestinian *refugees who fled Israel in 1948–49. Consequently, WOJAC argues, an exchange of populations has taken place (See also: *Transfer 1.)

The two Chairmen of the organization are Sir Leon Tamman of Great Britain and Mordechai *Ben Porat of Israel.

World Zionist Organization (WZO) The WZO was founded on the initiative of Theodor *Herzl, at the First Zionist Congress in Basle in August 1897, to realize the goals of *Zionism according to the Basle Program which sought "to create for the Jewish People a home in Palestine, secured by public law."

An annual congress (which later became biennial) was declared to be the "chief organ of the Zionist movement." In it were to be represented the national federations and transnational unions and parties. The number of delegates to be sent by each was determined by the number of its dues-paying members. The function of the congress was to take major policy decisions related to the diplomatic and practical work of the organization, to approve the organization's budget, elect its President and executive body — the Greater Actions Committee and the Inner Actions Committee (which came to be known as the Zionist Executive). The executive had the responsibility for carrying out the resolutions of the congress, and supervising the work being done between congresses. In 1907 a Palestine office was set up to represent the Zionist organization in Palestine. After World War I the Palestine office was replaced by the Zionist commission which in 1921 turned into the Palestine Zionist Executive. Besides carrying out the Zionist work in Palestine the Executive acted as the Jewish Agency which had been designated by the mandatory government to advise and cooperate with the administration of Palestine "in such matters as may affect the establishment of the Jewish National Home and the interests of the Jewish population in Palestine" and to "assist and participate in the development of the country."

The Zionist Executive was divided into departments such as: Political Affairs, Immigration and Labor, Colonization (i.e., settlement, which included a trade and industry section), Education and Health. The financial institutions of the WZO were the *Keren Kayemet* (the Jewish National Fund), founded in 1907, the main function of which was land improvement and afforestation (See: *Land Policy), the Palestine Land Development Company, established in 1909 to deal with land acquisition, and the *Keren Hayesod* (Foundation Fund) founded in 1920 to provide funds for immigration and settlement work, social welfare, public health and education.

In 1929 the *Jewish Agency was established to fulfill the functions of the WZO vis-à-vis the British government, Palestine Administration and League of Nations in cooperation with *non-Zionist Jewish groups and individuals who were willing to cooperate with the Zionist enterprise and further its development.

The whole system was unique in the annals of nations since it was totally voluntary and acted on behalf of a nation without a state to bring the members of this nation from the four corners of the earth back to its ancient homeland, and to establish therein a national home. In 1942 the goal of the WZO was officially declared to be "a Jewish Commonwealth" (See: *Biltmore Program), though all along it was generally accepted by most Zionists that the goal was the establishment of an independent sovereign state. The flag of the WZO (white background with two horizontal blue stripes and a blue Star of David in the center) and its anthem *Hatikvah* (the hope) were adopted in 1948 by the State of Israel.

(S.H.R.)

Upon the establishment of the State of Israel in 1948, the major goal of the WZO was achieved, and the question of whether it should continue to exist was raised. For a time Prime Minister David *Ben Gurion viewed the WZO as the scaffolding of the newly built Jewish state which had completed its function and should be dismantled. However, this view was not generally shared by the Zionist and Israeli leadership, and in 1951, at the 23rd Zionist Congress — the first to be held after the establishment of the state and the first to be held in *Jerusalem — the new tasks of Zionism were defined as being "to strengthen the State of Israel, to gather the exiles in the land of Israel, and to guarantee the unity of the Jewish People." The following year the *Knesset granted the WZO special status by law, recognizing the WZO and the Jewish Agency as "the authorized agencies which continue to operate in the State of Israel for the development and settlement of the country, the absorption of immigrants and the coordination of activities in Israel of Jewish institutions and organizations active in those fields." The law expressed the expectation that all the Jews would help in the building up of the state, that the WZO could work toward achieving the unity of all sections of world Jewry for this purpose.

However, these expectations were not fulfilled. During the following decade the Zionist movement lost much of its prestige and influence, and proved unable to become a force unifying all the Jewish communities around the State of Israel. The disappointment of the Israeli government with the WZO, especially in the fields of financial contributions and immigration (**aliyah*) from the western Jewish communities, resulted in efforts to develop alternative channels of connection with world Jewry, as through the *Merkaz Latfutsot* (Center for the Dispersions) set up in 1964, though this effort too lost its momentum the following year, when its initiator Moshe *Sharett died.

The reaction of world Jewry to the *Six-Day War in a sense saved the WZO. It gave a renewed impetus to the idea of direct involvement by the Israeli government in the Diaspora communities and renewed the interest and pride of world Jewry in Israel, thus creating conditions for the revival of the WZO. In 1968 the 27th Zionist Congress developed the Jerusalem Program which redefined the aims of Zionism as being: "The unity of the Jewish People and the centrality of Israel in its life; the ingathering of the Jewish People in its historical homeland, *Eretz Yisrael*, through *aliyah* from all lands; the strengthening of the State of Israel founded on the prophetic ideals of justice and peace; the preservation of the identity of the Jewish People through the fostering of Jewish and Hebrew education and of Jewish spiritual and cultural values; the protection of Jewish rights everywhere."

The 27th Congress also decided to open the membership of the WZO, which had been restricted since 1960 to Zionist Territorial Federations, to "Jewish national and international bodies," willing to accept the Jerusalem Program. Accordingly, five Jewish international organizations became members: the *World Federation of Sephardi Communities and the Maccabi World Union in 1972; the World Union for *Progressive Judaism in 1976; the World Council of Synagogues in 1977; and the World Conference of Synagogues and *Kehilot*, in 1978. Finally, a decision was taken to reorganize the Jewish Agency so as to involve major non-Zionist Jewish organizations in immigration and settlement work in Israel.

Thus, in 1971, the Jewish Agency was reconstituted as a partnership between the WZO (50 percent) and the fund-raising bodies in the Jewish communities (30 percent for the *United Israel Appeal which functions in North America, and 20 percent for all the other bodies — most of them connected with *Keren Hayesod*).

In principle, the WZO is and has been a democratic organization. Its Executive is elected by the Zionist Congress which convenes every four or five years. Each Israeli Zionist party is allocated a number of seats in the Congress proportionate to its strength in the Knesset. Most of the delegates (38 percent) come from Israel and the *United States (29 percent); 33 percent come from the rest of the world. In principle the delegates to the Zionist Congress are elected, but if all the Zionist groups in a given country agree they may distribute the seats among themselves according to an agreed formula. For the last two decades such agreements have been the prevalent method used.

The 1968 changes in the WZO and Jewish Agency enable the Zionist movement to maintain its status and autonomy while involving important sections of the Jewish communities abroad in ongoing and expanding Israel-oriented activities. In fact, since all participants in the Jewish Agency accept the Jerusalem Program, the distinction between non-Israeli Zionists and non-Zionists is almost impossible to make. However, the non-Zionists, who are involved in the work of the Jewish Agency but not of the WZO, are now seeking to change the rules in order to obtain a larger share in the partnership.

The WZO is once again seeking a way to maintain its uniqueness. The "Herzlya Process," named after the town of Herzlya where it was initiated in 1978, suggested two major directions of change: frequent visits to Israel by members of the Zionist movement who would become more active on Israel's behalf in the Jewish communities, learn Hebrew and provide a Zionist education for their children, and encourage youth from abroad to study in Israel. A resolution to this effect was adopted at the February 1986 meeting of the Zionist General Council. The council also decided in its June 1986 session to adopt a proposal of the *World Labor Zionist Movement granting priority to Zionist *Hagshamah* (fulfillment). The second proposed direction for change seeks the democratization of the movement which will revive interest in the Zionist movement among world Jewry, and turn the Zionist Congress into a parliament of the Jewish People.

(Y.M.)

Presidents of the WZO:

1897–1904	Theodor Herzl
1905–11	David Wolffsohn
1911–20	Otto Warburg
1921–31	Chaim *Weizmann
1931–35	Naḥum Sokolow
1935–46	Chaim Weizmann
1946–56	None
1956–68	Naḥum *Goldmann
1968–	None

Chairmen of the Zionist Executive:

1921–23	Menaḥem Ussishkin
1923–31	Frederick Kisch

1931–33	None
1933–35	Arthur Ruppin
1935–48	David *Ben Gurion
1948–60	Berl Locker
1948–56	(Co-chairman) Naḥum Goldmann
1960–65	Moshe *Sharett
1966–74	Louis Arieh Pincus
1974–78	Yosef Almogi
1978–	Leo Arieh Dulzin

WZO See: *World Zionist Organization.

Y

Ya'acobi, Gad Labor politician. Born 1935, Kfar Vitkin, Israel. Ya'acobi, a trained economist (MA, Tel Aviv University), was a member of *Rafi* and when the *Israel Labor Party was formed in 1968 he became a member of the Party Bureau. and has been a member of Knesset since 1969. Deputy Minister of Transport from 1969–74, Minister of Transport from 1974–77 and Chairman of the Knesset Economics Committee 1977–84, Ya'acobi was the *Alignment's main economic spokesman in the elections to the 11th Knesset (1984) and its candidate for Minister of Finance. However, in the *National Unity Government the two major economic ministries (Finance and Industry and Trade) were given to the *Likud* and Ya'acobi was asked by Prime Minister Shimon *Peres to serve as Minister of Economics and Planning in which capacity he prepared a five-year economic plan for Israel.

Over the years Ya'acobi was responsible for several private member bills on *electoral reform and was selected as Chairman of the Ministerial Committee on Electoral Reform which included an equal number of members from the Alignment and the *Likud*. He is also the active leader behind the task force set up with the cooperation of Jewish businessmen abroad to prepare the ground for renewed foreign investment in Israel, given a stabilized Israeli economy.

Since 1985 Ya'acobi has advocated Israel's unilateral implementation of the *autonomy plan.

Ya'ad Hebrew for "target."

1. Party formed in 1975 by the merger of the *Civil Rights Movement (CRM), a group led by Arie Lova *Eliav which broke off from the *Israel Labor Party, and several members of **Shinui* which had emerged against the background of the political fermentation following the *Yom Kippur War. In 1975 the party had four Members of Knesset (three from the CRM and Eliav). *Ya'ad* advocated *territorial compromise in return for peace; an Israeli peace initiative; an uncompromising struggle against poverty and social gaps; civil rights; and the separation of religion and state. The party split in 1976 over the question of recognition of the Palestinian national movement. Two of its Knesset members (one was Shulamit *Aloni) once more set up the CRM and another two (one was Eliav) set up the Independent Socialist Front which joined in the establishment of **Maḥaneh Sheli*. (D.B.M.)

2. Party formed in 1978. One of the splinter factions formed after the breakup of the *Democratic Movement for Change in 1978. *Ya'ad* had a single member — Assaf Yaguri — who ran for the 10th Knesset (1981) under the slogan "elect me as your Senator," but failed to pass the one percent qualifying threshold.

Ya'ari, (formerly Wald) **Me'ir** (1897–1987) **Hashomer Hatza'ir* and **Mapam* leader and ideologist. Born in Galicia, Ya'ari immigrated to Palestine in 1920 and with his colleagues formulated the basic principles of **Hakibbutz Ha'artzi*, which championed a far-reaching cooperative approach in all spheres of life. In 1910 he was one of the founders of Kibbutz Merḥaviah. He provided *Hashomer Hatza'ir* and *Mapam* with a Marxist-Leninist platform, which was translated into settlement activities and self-realization.

Only in the mid-fifties, following the Jewish doctors' trials in Moscow and the trial of Mordechai Oren in Prague did his admiration for the Communist world decline and he began to develop a positive approach to Israeli social-democracy.

After the *Six-Day War he supported the unification of the Labor camp, and was a staunch supporter of *Mapam*'s continued participation in the *Alignment until 1984.

Yadin (formerly Sukenik) **Yiga'el** (1917–1984) Professor of achaeology, second Chief of Staff of the Israel Defense Forces (*IDF), politician. Yadin was born in Jerusalem and began studying archaeology at the Hebrew University in 1935. After riots broke out in 1936 he left his studies for defense activities, first within the framework of field units and later in the *Haganah becoming Operations Officer in 1945.

During the *War of Independence Yadin was Acting Chief of Staff during Ya'acov Dori's illness. In the course of the war he had major disagreements with David *Ben Gurion, objecting to the attempt to conquer Latrun (which failed) and to the disbanding of the **Palmaḥ*. At the end of the war he headed the *armistice agreement negotiations at Rhodes and Lausanne. In 1949 Yadin was appointed Chief of Staff and formed the IDF into a regular and reserve army. He resigned in 1952 after objecting to cuts in the defense budget and returned to the university. In 1955 Yadin was appointed Lecturer in archaeology, conducting the digs at Tel Ḥatzor. In 1960 he discovered the archives of Bar Kochba's military commanders near Ein Gedi. He devoted many years to studying the Dead Sea Scrolls. In the years 1963/64 he conducted the archaeological digs at Masada.

Yadin acted as Military Advisor to Prime Minister Levi *Eshkol until the *Six-Day War, and supported the appointment of Moshe *Dayan as Minister of Defense during the crisis period which preceded the war. He was a member of the *Agranat Commission set up following the *Yom Kippur War.

In 1976 Yadin was one of the founders of the *Democratic Movement for Change (DMC) as a new centrist political force. The DMC gained 15 seats in the 9th Knesset (1977) and Yadin joined Menaḥem *Begin's first government as Deputy Prime Minister and Chairman of the Ministerial Committee on Welfare. He remained in the government until the 1981 elections even though the DMC disintegrated.

Notwithstanding the fact that Yadin did not run for Knesset elections, Begin offered him a seat in his second government, but Yadin preferred to return to his archaeological pursuits.

(Y.A.)

Yadlin Affair The first corruption scandal in Israel involving a major political figure. Asher Yadlin (born 1923), one of the leaders of the **Histadrut* and Chairman of its health fund *Kupat Ḥolim* from 1973–76, was to have been appointed Governor of the Bank of Israel in September 1976. Investigations regarding his activities were opened following the complaint of a reporter on the weekly *Ha'olam Hazeh*, that Yadlin was pocketing commissions for *Kupat Ḥolim* real-estate transactions, and taking bribes. Yadlin was arrested in October and the trial opened on December 13, 1976 when he admitted to five out of six charges brought against him, thus avoiding a prolonged trial. He claimed at the trial that he had transferred most of the funds which he had received to the *Israel Labor Party for election purposes. The claim was not examined in the Labor party because of a reluctance to stir up too much investigation into the grey area of party financing in Israel. Yadlin was sentenced to five years imprisonment and fined IL 250,000 ($28,100 at the rate of exchange at the end of December 1976). He was released in 1981. During his period in prison he wrote a book on the episode. After his release, feeling that he had been betrayed by his friends in the party, he moved to the United States. The affair caused the *Alignment great damage in the elections to the 9th Knesset (1977).

Yaḥad Hebrew for "together," *Yaḥad* is a party established at the end of March 1984 by Ezer *Weizman in preparation for the elections to the 11th Knesset. Weizman hoped to gather around him ex-military commanders and businessmen who had not previously been involved in politics, and who had refused to join with several members of the **Likud* who were planning to break off from the *Liberal Party. The party ran its election campaign under the slogan "together toward national unity, a lasting peace, a unified society and a stable economy."

Its platform called for flexibility in the peace process which would lead to Israel's full integration into the region; a speedy withdrawal from Lebanon; the full integration of all parts of Israeli society in the state's institutions and the eradication of social distress; cuts in the government budget; and the renewal of economic growth through the expansion of the country's production base. Opinion polls predicted that the party might get as many as six to ten seats in the 11th Knesset but it received only three. On August 22 1984, *Yaḥad* joined the *Alignment in order to block the *Likud* from forming a narrow government. Together with the Alignment *Yaḥad* joined the *National Unity Government in September 1984, with Weizman appointed Minister without Portfolio and a member of the inner cabinet.

Yariv, Aharon Military commander, politician and researcher. Born 1920, in Moscow.

Yariv immigrated to Palestine in 1935 and studied at the agricultural school in Pardes Ḥannah. He joined the **Haganah* in 1938 and the British Army in 1941, serving in the *Jewish Brigade at the rank of Captain. He took part in organizing "illegal" immigration to Palestine and was active in arms procurement for the *Haganah*. After his discharge from the British Army, Yariv studied at the training institute of the Jewish Agency's Political Department in preparation for diplomatic service.

In the *War of Independence Yariv commanded a battalion in the north. In 1950 he was sent to the Staff Officers College in Paris and was appointed Commander of the Operations Branch in the General Staff a year later. He was the first Commander of the Israel Defense Forces (*IDF) Command and Staff School in 1954 and was Head of the Central Command from 1956–57. He was appointed Military Attaché in Washington in 1957. From 1960–61 Yariv was Commander of the Golani Brigade. He served as Head of Military Intelligence (**Aman*) 1964–72. Retiring from active service in September 1972, Yariv served as Prime Minister Golda *Meir's Special Assistant for Combatting Terror and was active in the *Israel Labor Party election campaign of 1973. Serving as Special Assistant to the Chief of Staff during the *Yom Kippur War, Yariv headed the Israeli delegation to the Kilometer 101 talks in December 1973. He was elected to the 8th Knesset on behalf of the *Alignment and served as Minister of Transport in Golda Meir's second cabinet and as Minister of Information in Yitzḥak *Rabin's cabinet until he resigned in February 1975. He was the co-drafter of the *Yariv-Shemtov Formula.

In 1977 Yariv founded and became the Head of the Center for Strategic Studies at Tel Aviv University.

Yariv-Shemtov formula A formula drafted by the Minister of Transport Aharon *Yariv (*Alignment) and Minister of Health Victor *Shemtov (**Mapam*) defining an acceptable partner for peace negotiations with Israel. The formula was first presented to the government of Golda *Meir in 1974 and made public by Yariv during a visit to Washington. It stated: "Israel will carry out negotiations for peace with Jordan and with any Palestinian factor which will recognize its right to exist, will be willing to make peace with it and will not engage in terrorism."

Yariv resigned from the post of Minister of Information in the cabinet of Prime Minister Yitzḥak *Rabin in 1975 and the formula was presented once again to the government, but was not brought to a vote since it was supported only by two *Mapam* Ministers (Victor Shemtov and Shlomo Rosen), the two *Independent Liberal Ministers (Moshe Kol and Gideon *Hausner) and Labor Party Minister Avraham Ofer. Thus, the Yariv-Shemtov formula was neither adopted nor rejected by the government.

The US undertaking in its *Memorandum of Understanding with Israel signed in September 1975, which stated that "The United States... will not recognize or negotiate with the Palestine Liberation Organization so long as the Palestine Liberation Organization does not recognize Israel's right to exist and does not accept *Security Council Resolution 242 and 338," was viewed in Israel as a partial American adoption of the Yariv-Shemtov formula.

Yellin-Mor (formerly Friedman), **Natan** (1913–1980) Underground leader. Yellin-Mor was born in Poland and studied engineering in Warsaw. He joined the *Revisionist and **Betar* movements and in the late 1930s and supported the extreme activist approach in the **Irgun Zva'i Le'umi* (IZL). After the outbreak of World War II Yellin-Mor managed to reach Palestine and joined Avraham *Stern in his secession from IZL and the establishment of **Leḥi*. Yellin-Mor attempted to reach neutral Turkey in order to contact representatives of Nazi Germany to offer cooperation against Britain in exchange for the release of European Jewry, but he was arrested en route by the British in Syria. He escaped from prison and after Stern was murdered, became leader of *Leḥi*.

Yellin-Mor was arrested after the assassination of UN Mediator Count Folke Bernadotte in the fall of 1948. An Israeli military court found him guilty of contravening the provisional government's decree against membership in terrorist organizations, but acquitted him of complicity in

Bernadotte's assassination. Yellin-Mor was included in the general amnesty proclaimed by the provisional government. He was elected to the 1st Knesset (1949), the only member for the *Fighters List. Shortly thereafter, extreme socialist views became enmeshed in his ideology. Later he renounced Zionist ideology and in 1956 was associated with the political group *Semitic Action established by Uri *Avneri which supported the idea of a Jewish- Palestinian-Jordanian confederation within a Middle East Federation. After Avneri entered the Knesset in 1965 Yellin-Mor turned away from active political involvement.

Yemenite Association A Yemenite ethnic list with pre-state origins. In the 1920s Yemenite Jews were coopted to **Assefat Hanivḥarim* (Elected Assembly) and later were elected.

The Yemenite list ran in the elections to the 1st and 2nd Knesset (1949 and 1951), winning a single seat in each. In the course of the 2nd Knesset the Yemenite member, Shimon Garidi, joined the *General Zionist Knesset faction because of the Yemenite Association's financial difficulties. However, toward the end of the term Garidi announced his withdrawal from the General Zionists and his support for the coalition — apparently in an attempt to gain state support for the Yemenite Association before the elections to the 3rd Knesset.

Yishuv Hebrew word meaning "settlement" or "community." The word was used to refer to the Jewish community in pre-state Palestine. *Hayishuv Hayashan* (the old *Yishuv*) referred to the Jewish community composed mostly of pious non-Zionists or anti-Zionists living in Palestine before Zionist settlers started to arrive in the country. *Hayishuv Hame'urgan* (the organized *Yishuv*) referred to that part of the Jewish community which developed during mandatory times and which was organized within and accepted the authority of the Jewish national institutions. (S.H.R.)

HISTORY: Under the British mandate, Palestine was a state without a national identity which contained two national movements seeking statehood (See: *Mandatory Palestine). Moreover, there was never a time when the primary loyalty of either group was focused on the formal framework of the mandatory government. As early as the beginning of the mandate, the first indications of separate embryonic political systems appeared. These later developed into nearly autonomous political systems oriented symbolically and institutionally to wider frameworks: the Zionist movement in one case and the Arab national movement in the other. As a result, mandatory Palestine could not be considered a nucleus of a nation-state for two reasons: the population was divided into two separate ethnonational groups, and each group saw itself as part of a larger national entity whose borders extended beyond mandatory Palestine. Against this background, the concept of the *Yishuv* emerged. Perceived as an autonomous political system in embryo, the *Yishuv* was often defined as a "state in the making" or a "state within a state." The institutional framework was that of a quasi-state which in many spheres of political and social activity operated in a statelike manner.

Three traits distinguished the *Yishuv* as a political system from a full-fledged state.

First, the *Yishuv* was a minority in a dual social-political system. Moreover, not only was mandatory Palestine a bi-national political unit, but large sections of the country had a mixed population; there were almost no continuous areas of

Population of Palestine

Year	Total Population	Jews	Jews as % of Total Pop.
1922	752,048	83,790	11.1
1923	768,989	89,660	11.7
1924	804,962	94,945	11.8
1925	847,238	121,725	14.4
1926	898,362	149,500	16.6
1927	917,315	149,789	16.3
1928	935,951	151,656	16.2
1929	960,043	156,481	16.3
1930	992,559	164,796	16.6
1931	1,033,714	174,606	16.9
1932	1,073,827	192,137	17.9
1933	1,140,941	234,967	20.6
1934	1,210,554	282,975	23.4
1935	1,308,112	335,157	27.3
1936	1,366,692	384,078	28.1
1937	1,401,794	395,836	28.2
1938	1,435,285	411,222	28.7
1939	1,501,698	445,457	29.7
1940	1,544,530	463,535	30.0
1941	1,585,500	474,102	29.9
1942	1,620,005	484,408	29.9
1943	1,676,571	502,912	30.0
1944	1,739,624	528,702	30.4
1945	1,810,037	554,329	30.6

Jewish settlement without an Arab population.

Second, the system performed only some of the functions of a state. In particular, it lacked judicial functions, with no legal code or courts of its own. Other areas, such as postal and telegraph services, customs, and the maintenance of the transportation infrastructure, were a monopoly of the mandatory government. In the sphere of security the *Yishuv* had several paramilitary organizations, mainly the **Haganah*, but these organizations did not usually engage in enforcing law and order.

Finally, the *Yishuv* was dependent on the Diaspora. Without the latter's resources of manpower, funds and political support the *Yishuv* would not have been able to amass economic power or to maintain its political institutions.

The transformation of the *Yishuv* from a quasi-state into a state in 1948 involved demographic changes that made possible the creation of a society with an overwhelming Jewish majority and the acquisition of sovereign status entailing the three functions of a sovereign state: legislative, executive, and judicial. On the other hand, the special relationship between the *Yishuv* and the Diaspora persisted — along with the need for the Diaspora's resources. Nevertheless, the political implications of this connection were reduced by the separation of the functions of immigration and settlement — in which the Diaspora continued to take an active part through the institutions of the Zionist movement — from other spheres of policy-making that passed into the exclusive jurisdiction of the Israeli government.

Despite these changes, considerable continuity between the political system of the *Yishuv* and that of Israel can be discerned in the composition of the leadership, the political party structure, and the political culture — that is, the rules of the game and relations between political parties, ideological movements, and interest groups.

The evolution of a semi-autonomous Jewish community in Palestine was a gradual process which began with the wave of immigration to Palestine in 1882. This wave occurred in the wake of pogroms against the Jews in Russia and was part of the tide of Jewish immigration from eastern Europe to the west.

At this early stage, *Zionism was still an ideological and cultural movement rather than a political one. Its ideology called for settlement of Jews in Palestine to achieve a territorial concentration of Jews. The desire for a Jewish state became part of Zionist thought after the appearance of Theodor *Herzl and the convening of the First Zionist Congress in 1897.

In the last two decades of the 19th century, some of the Jews who came in the First **Aliyah* (i.e. the first wave of immigration) established settlements in Judea and the Galilee; others turned to *Jerusalem and Jaffa, which became the centers of the New *Yishuv*. The socio-economic pattern which evolved as a result of the dependence of the early settlers on hired Arab labor was challenged by the immigrants of the Second *Aliyah*, which began in 1904 and continued until 1914. Inspired by socialist ideas, they advocated the replacement of Arab workers by Jewish "self labor." As immigration to Palestine continued on a limited scale, the Zionist movement in the Diaspora developed its institutional framework in the form of the *World Zionist Organization (WZO), established in 1897. After Herzl's diplomatic endeavors to enlist international support for a Jewish commonwealth in Palestine failed, the Zionist movement concentrated its efforts on immigration and settlement in Palestine.

World War I ended the first phase in the development of the New *Yishuv*. The Ottoman Empire collapsed, the British occupied Palestine, and for the first time the Zionist movement had the support, albeit qualified, of the ruling power in Palestine. In the *Balfour Declaration of 1917, the British government stated its commitment to the establishment of a Jewish national home in Palestine. This commitment was confirmed by the League of Nations, which granted Britain the Mandate of Palestine. The British authorities recognized the WZO as the official agency to implement the establishment of a Jewish national home. This status enabled the Executive of the WZO in Jerusalem to become the authoritative representative of the Jewish community in Palestine. An institution whose functions were complementary to the WZO Executive in Jerusalem was the **Va'ad Le'umi* (National Council) of **Knesset Yisrael*, the central community organization of the Jewish population in Palestine which obtained official recognition in the mid-twenties.

The favorable conditions for the advancement of the Zionist cause created by the Balfour Declaration and the post-First World War climate supporting self-determination encouraged renewed Jewish immigration to Palestine. The Third *Aliyah*, which began in 1919, brought 37,000 immigrants to Palestine by 1923. As in the Second *Aliyah*, most of the newcomers were young pioneers who became the backbone of the Jewish Labor movement in Palestine.

The renewal of large-scale immigration provoked violent Arab reactions. The "Arab disturbances" of 1920 and 1921 were the first of a series of political riots which accompanied each stage of expansion of Zionist endeavor in Palestine. In 1922 the British made their first concession to Arab resistance to Zionism by creating the emirate of *Transjordan in the territory east of the *Jordan River, an area originally included in mandatory Palestine.

An even larger wave of immigration came during the Fourth *Aliyah*, 1924–30, which brought more than 60,000 Jews to Palestine, 35,000 in the year 1925 alone. Unlike previous immigrants from Russia, most of the Fourth *Aliyah* came from Poland. They brought some capital that was invested mainly in the building industry and triggered a boom. But there was not enough of the imported capital to create an infrastructure capable of allowing the economic absorption of these immigrants. Thus the prosperity was soon replaced by a severe recession which halted the expansion of the Jewish economy in Palestine. Immigration fell to its lowest point in the entire period of the mandate. At the end of twenties, a nascent economic recovery was accompanied by a new outburst of Arab riots. The riots led to a reevaluation of British policy in Palestine. But a white paper (the White Paper of Lord Passfield, 1930) stating the British intention to impose limitations on Jewish immigration and land purchases was not implemented due to vehement Jewish protests led by Chaim *Weizmann.

Another development in 1930 involved the internal politics of the Jewish community in Palestine, when the two largest labor parties merged. The unified party, **Mapai*, led by David *Ben Gurion, became the central political force in the *Yishuv*. At this stage of the *Yishuv*'s development, the Zionist Executive and the *Va'ad Le'umi* assumed control over the underground self-defense organization of the Jewish community, the **Haganah*.

Hitler's rise to power in Germany in 1933 gave new impetus to Jewish immigration to Palestine, which in 1935 reached a peak of 62,000 in one year. During the entire wave of immigration from 1932 to 1939, no less than 190,000 immigrants arrived in Palestine from Central and Eastern Europe. As a result, the Jewish population increased to 445,000 in 1939. While German immigrants made up only 20 to 25 percent of the total, they were the dominant group among these immigrants, and this wave is sometimes called the German *Aliyah*. More than any previous wave, this one — the Fifth *Aliyah* — was accompanied by extensive importation of investment capital, which laid the foundation for the economic revival of the Jewish community in Palestine.

The peak year of immigration, 1935, was followed by the most intense Arab reaction — the Arab revolt of 1936–39. This revolt left a strong impression on the attitudes and policies of the three parties involved in the determination of Palestine's fate — the Arabs, the Jews, and the British. The Arabs failed to achieve their military objectives, their guerrilla force was suppressed by the British army, and their political leadership obliged to leave the country. Yet they succeeded in demonstrating their ability to disrupt law and order, which induced the British government to reconsider its policy in Palestine.

The impact of the Arab revolt on the Jewish community was to call forth new approaches to the political struggle with the Arabs, particularly in the area of self-defense. The *Haganah* ceased to be a decentralized organization for the defense of life and property in a local context and became a centrally directed armed force. Its command supervised not only *Haganah* units armed with illegal weapons, but also, indirectly, the Jewish constabulary force which operated within the framework of the Palestine police. The central control of the Jewish self-defense forces was, however, incomplete. A splinter group, the armed **Irgun Zva'i Le'umi* (IZL) operated under the auspices of the nationalist right-wing *Revisionist party, which had seceded from the WZO in 1935 in protest against the moderate policies of the WZO President, Dr. Weizmann, and the Labor movement.

The British reaction to the Arab revolt was a reappraisal of the policy in Palestine. This led to the proposal, by a royal commission, to partition Palestine, a proposal which was rejected by the Arabs and became a controversial issue in the Zionist movement. In response to Arab opposition, the British government abandoned the idea of *partition and convened an Arab-Jewish "Round Table" in London to discuss the Palestine problem. As no agreement was reached, in 1939 the British government, in an effort to appease the Arabs, issued a white paper which recommended far-reaching restrictions on Jewish immigration and purchases of land, as well as the grant of Palestinian independence after an interim period in which the Arabs would remain the majority.

World War II and Hitler's European successes brought on a self-imposed suppression of most forms of resistance to this British policy — with the exception of illegal immigration, which continued on a reduced scale. The leadership of the *Yishuv* urged active participation in the war effort, and over 25,000 men and women volunteered to serve in the British armed forces out of a population of 500,000. In 1941–42, the danger of German invasion in the Middle East resulted in the resumption of cooperation by the Jewish leadership with the mandatory authorities, especially in promoting war effort. In 1942, under Ben Gurion's leadership, the Zionist movement officially adopted the demand for a Jewish state and tried to enlist the support of American Jewry and American public opinion. Aspirations for independence were enhanced when the first news of the *Holocaust in Europe reached the *Yishuv*. The official leadership of the Jewish community continued to hope for a change in the British policy when the war was over, but the splinter illegal military organization, the *IZL*, declared a revolt against British rule in Palestine. This act of defiance against both the British and the official Jewish leadership prompted the *Haganah* to resort to sanctions against *IZL*. However, when the war ended and the new Labor government in England continued the implementation of the 1939 White Paper, the official leadership of the *Yishuv* resumed the struggle against British policy.

The cumulative effect of American pressure, Jewish resistance in Palestine, and the Jewish refugee problem in Europe ultimately led the British government to submit the Palestine question to the *United Nations. An international commission of inquiry nominated by the UN General Assembly recommended the partition of Palestine into a Jewish state and an Arab state. This recommendation was adopted in the resolution of November 29, 1947, supported by more than two-thirds of the member nations, including the two superpowers, the *United States and the *Soviet Union. The British refused to implement the resolution and withdrew from Palestine, which became an arena of bitter fighting between Arabs and Jews. On May 14, 1948, a Jewish state was proclaimed in the territories controlled by the Jewish armed forces. On the same day, the regular armies of neighboring Arab states invaded Palestine in an unsuccessful attempt to eradicate the newly established state (See: *Arab-Israel Conflict).

POLITICAL PARTY MAP: The parties and political organizations that existed in the *Yishuv* immediately prior to the establishment of the State of Israel differed considerably from the array at the outset of the mandate. When steps were taken at the beginning of the mandate to create a comprehensive political organization for the Jews of Palestine, four major political groupings existed. The most articulate and organized was the Labor movement, which in the twenties included only **Aḥdut Ha'avodah* and **Hapo'el Hatza'ir*. In the early 1920s they were joined by smaller political groups formed by the pioneers of the Third *Aliyah*, such as **Hashomer Hatza'ir* and *Po'alei Zion Smol*. The bloc known as the *Ezraḥim* (Hebrew word for "civilians") was composed in part of quasi-political organizations, such as the Farmers Association and the Artisans Association, and in part of various political organizations that represented *General Zionist ideological sympathies. The third bloc, composed of the Sephardim and other Oriental ethnic groups, attracted 25 percent of the vote in the 1920 elections to **Assefat Hanivḥarim* (the Elected Assembly). The fourth bloc, the religious one, combined two separate movements, **Hamizraḥi* and non-Zionist ultra- orthodox groups. After the withdrawal of the ultra-orthodox from the organized *Yishuv*, *Hamizraḥi* joined the *Ezraḥim* bloc, while the Sephardim and other ethnic groups were unevenly divided between the *Ezraḥim* and the Labor bloc, most of them choosing the *Ezraḥim*.

Electoral strength of the main political Sectors in *Assefat Hanivḥarim* (percentages)

	Elections			
Sector	1920	1925	1931	1944
Labor parties	37.0	36.5	42.3	59.1
Center & right-wing parties	19.7	42.1	32.4	21.0
Religious parties	20.3	8.8	7.0	16.6
Ethnic groups	23.0	12.6	18.3	3.3
Total	100.0	100.0	100.0	100.0

From the mid-1920s, the organized *Yishuv* was composed of two major blocs, the Labor movement and the *Ezraḥim*. After the late 1920s a new political force emerged within the *Ezraḥim*, to gradually become the nucleus of a separate bloc — the *Revisionists. In the mid-1930s, when the Revisionists seceded from the WZO and established a rival movement, they were no longer considered part of the organized *Yishuv*, although they continued to participate in *Knesset Yisrael*.

One of the distinguishing features of the *Yishuv*'s political system was the constant change in the composition of the party map, reflecting numerous splits, mergers, and the rapid emergence and disappearance of new political groups. This trend applied to the Labor bloc and to the *Ezraḥim* bloc, though not to the same extent; there was more continuity among the parties and political groupings of the Labor movement.

Changes among the parties of the Labor movement were mirrored in the elections for the *Histadrut*, as it was the umbrella organization for these parties. Three major periods may be distinguished. The first period, the 1920s, was marked by numerous splits and the emergence of new groups, some of which later disappeared and some of which continued to exist until the 1940s; the largest and strongest parties of this period were **Aḥdut Ha'avodah* and **Hapo'el Hatza'ir*, which originated in the Second *Aliyah* and whose leaders arrived with this wave of immigration. In the early stages of the Third *Aliyah*, new political groups emerged which participated in the *Histadrut* elections but not in the elections for *Assefat Hanivḥarim*. The most important of these group in terms of its impact on the Labor movement in the 1920s was the Labor Brigade. This group underwent several transformations, until it was dissolved following a split between the right and left wings within the organization. This division resulted in the emigration of part of the brigade's left wing to the Soviet Union, and in the right wing's absorption into *Aḥdut Ha'avodah*.

Hashomer Hatza'ir was the second political group in the Labor movement that emerged during the Third *Aliyah*; it remained independent and to the left of **Mapai*. Until the mid-1930s, it saw itself as basically a settlement movement and possessed no formal party framework, but nevertheless took part in elections to the *Histadrut* and to the third *Assefat Hanivḥarim*. In the mid-1930s an urban-based offshoot of *Hashomer Hatzair* called the Socialist League was formed, and only ten years later did *Hashomer Hatza'ir* organize formally as a political party.

The third political group to emerge after World War I, *Po'alei Zion Smol*, was not exclusively composed of pioneers of the Third *Aliyah*. This party arose as a consequence of the split in the *Po'alei Zion* World Union; the right wing of the Union formed ties with *Aḥdut Ha'avodah*, the left wing with *Poalei Zion Smol*. The split was caused by *Po'alei Zion Smol*'s opposition to cooperating with the "bourgeois" parties in the WZO and its insistence on following a policy based on "class struggle."

The Palestine Communist party had a somewhat ambiguous status in the political system of the *Yishuv* and the Labor movement. This party went through numerous transformations, splits, and mergers, at times driven to an underground existence. As a result, it operated under different aliases. The party may be considered as part of the Labor movement since it ran in *Histadrut* elections. On the other hand, its exceptional status in the Labor movement resulted from its anti-Zionist stance, its bi-national composition, and its illegality under mandatory law.

The second period, the 1930s, may be described as a period of stability for the Labor movement. This stability was due mainly to the creation of *Mapai* in 1930 following the union of *Hapo'el Hatza'ir* and *Aḥdut Ha'avodah*. The new combined party won the support of between 70 percent and 80 percent of the electorate in the elections to the *Histadrut* conventions in 1933 and 1942.

The third period, covering World War II and the postwar struggle for independence, was again a time of divisions and mergers that altered the party map of the Labor movement. The most important change occurred in *Mapai* in 1944, when the left wing broke away to form a new party. The political base of this group was composed primarily of **Hakibbutz Hame'uḥad*, one of the two kibbutz federations affiliated with *Mapai*. The new party was called *Hatnu'ah Le'aḥdut Ha'avodah*, its name symbolizing the claim of the new party's leaders that they were returning to the path of "pure" socialism represented by *Aḥdut Ha'avodah* of the 1920s. Most of the leaders of the original *Aḥdut Ha'avodah*, however, remained in *Mapai* — particularly David Ben Gurion. The split was followed by a merger between *Po'alei Zion Smol* and *Hatnu'ah Le'aḥdut Ha'avodah* in 1946. Early in 1948 *Hatnu'ah Le'aḥdut Ha'avodah* joined the new party formed by *Hashomer Hatza'ir*, creating the United Workers Party or **Mapam*, which became the major left-wing force in the Zionist Labor movement.

While the various Labor parties were relatively well defined, stable, and institutionalized, the political parties of the Right and Center were different. In the Labor movement, the same parties or political groups created through alignments and mergers appeared consistently in elections for the *Histadrut*, *Assefat Hanivḥarim*, and the Zionist congresses. On the Right and Center, however, less institutionalized parties manifested a greater tendency to fragment, at times combining in ad hoc groupings for a particular election campaign. Other trends that characterized the parties of the *Ezraḥim* were wide divergences in the number and composition of the lists submitted in the various elections to *Assefat Hanivḥarim*, and the participation of organizations representing specific economic interests, such as the Farmers Association and the Artisans Association, in such elections.

The parties and political organizations of the Right and Center included General Zionists, "*Yishuvist*" parties without ties to sister parties in the Diaspora, Revisionists, the different elements of *Hamizraḥi* movement, and ethnic parties and *Landsmanschaften*.

The first group includes parties affiliated to the General Zionist trend within the Zionist movement. They included a relatively large number of leading figures who had been active in Zionist politics in the Diaspora. In the 1920s the General Zionist parties appeared under this name only in elections to the Zionist congresses. In the elections to the third *Assefat Hanivḥarim* in 1931, the parties appeared under the General Zionist label, but by this time and throughout the 1930s there were two separate General Zionist slates in the elections to the Zionist congresses. These two lists reunited only in 1945, in order to create a united front for the elections to the Zionist Congress in 1946. The two factions of the General Zionist movement differed mainly in their relations with the parties of the Labor movement. Led by Chaim Weizmann, the left wing of the General Zionists (the "A" General Zionists) collaborated with the Labor movement in the Zionist Executive, while the right wing (the "B" General Zionists) regarded the Labor movement as a bitter political opponent. The reluctance of the "B" General Zionists to cooperate with the Labor movement was seen in their refusal to participate in the Zionist Executive coalition in 1933–35 (the only period in which they were not represented); in their boycotting the 1944 elections to *Assefat Hanivḥarim* with the Farmers Association, the Association of Sephardim, and the Revisionists; and in their participation in the governing body of the dissident *Haganah* B group during the years 1931 to 1937. The close political and ideological ties of the "A" General Zionists with the Labor movement were exemplified, among other things, in the formation in 1936 of a General Zionist faction within the *Histadrut* called *Ha'oved Hatzioni* (Zionist Worker), which had its own settlement and youth movements. The "B" General Zionists maintained a labor organization independent of the *Histadrut*.

The major political base of the old guard of the *Ezraḥim* was composed of the local authorities of Tel Aviv and Petaḥ Tikva and the larger *moshavot* (small towns, most of which had been established by the First *Aliyah*). The leaders of these groups tended to view the local authorities of the *Yishuv* as a basis of independent Jewish rule parallel to the central national institutions. The oldest and strongest of these groups was the Farmers Association, which represented the farmers of the veteran *moshavot*. Other prominent organizations in this sector were the Landlords Association and the Merchants Association, which combined with other groups of the *Ezraḥim* to form ruling coalitions in the larger local authorities, primarily in Tel Aviv. In the early 1940s, an attempt was made to unite all *Ezraḥim* groups in a body called *Ha'iḥud Ha'ezraḥi* (the Citizen's Union), but this proved to be a short-lived venture.

Among the parties of the Right and Center, the group farthest to the Right was the Revisionist party, a bitter opponent of the Labor movement, which was active continuously in Palestine and the Diaspora from its inception in 1925 until the establishment of the state. They remained members of *Knesset Yisrael* throughout, although they boycotted the 1944 elections to *Assefat Hanivḥarim*. The Revisionists maintained their own labor and trade union organization, **Histadrut Ha'ovdim Hale'umiyim*, and their own health services. A split in the party occurred with the secession from the Zionist organization in 1935, when a minority faction called the Jewish State Party continued to participate. The Revisionist party and its youth movement **Betar* served as the political base and major recruiting ground for the *IZL* in the late 1930s and early 1940s; but relations between the *IZL* commanders and the Revisionist leaders became strained in the mid-forties after their leader's death, as the two groups of *Jabotinsky disciples struggled for primacy within the movement. Ultimately victory went to the commanders of the *IZL*.

Another set of parties in the Right and Center group was the religious Zionist bloc, affiliated to *Hamizraḥi* World Union. From the early 1920s, this bloc was divided into *Hamizraḥi* party and **Hapo'el Hamizraḥi*. The latter was nominally a labor organization, although it participated in the elections and institutions of *Knesset Yisrael* as a political party.

Also for various reasons belonging with the Right and Center bloc were the organizations of the various Oriental Jewish communities that participated in the elections to *Assefat Hanivḥarim* and the local authorities. The leaders and members of these groups did not necessarily hold views identical to those of the parties of the Right and Center, as there were some members of these groups that were ideologically closer to the Labor movement. Yet the patterns of political action that characterized some of these groups, especially the Association of Sephardim, were closer to the veteran groups of the *Ezraḥim*, such as the Farmers Association. These patterns may generally be described as the "politics of notables," since the political status of the leaders of these groups was based mostly on their social status in the *Yishuv* as it was before the changes caused by the Second and Third *Aliyah*. For example, the Sephardi leaders collaborated with the *Ezraḥim* on questions concerning the structure and electoral system of *Knesset Yisrael* and joined the Farmers Association, the "B" General Zionists, and the Revisionists in boycotting the elections to *Assefat Hanivḥarim* in 1944.

The Association of Sephardim represented a traditional elite whose status was undermined by the demographic changes produced by the waves of immigration from Europe. In contrast, a new political group arose in the late 1930s based on common countries of origin, but representing an entirely different trend. While the Sephardi elite was attempting to preserve its declining social status through political action, the newly arrived German Jewish elite formed the **Aliyah Ḥadashah* party to secure political, in addition to their social status. The transformation of this group into an established political party took place in the early 1940s. The German immigrants possessed a distinctive cultural background, economic assets, and professional and educational qualifications far above average, but when they arrived in Palestine they found the key positions in the political system occupied by Jews from Eastern Europe who formed the majority of the elite of the organized *Yishuv*. The German immigrants responded by organizing a political party that adopted a liberal outlook close to the "A" General Zionists but even more moderate on political issues such as relations with Britain and the Arab question.

At least one Jewish party did not participate in either the elections to the *Assefat Hanivḥarim* or the Zionist congresses. This party, **Agudat Yisrael*, comprised the relatively moderate wing of the non-Zionist ultra-orthodox groups and belonged to the *Agudat Yisrael* World Union. The more extreme elements among the ultra-Orthodox were not even organized into political party frameworks. (D.H. — M.L.)

ORIGINS OF THE HISTORIC FEUD AND THE *HISTORIC COALITION: Fundamental differences of opinion existed between the Labor movement and the Revisionists from the start. This difference concerned ideology, orientation, specific policies and style. The *Arlosoroff murder in

1933, of which the Labor movement accused persons close to the Revisionists, brought the feud to a boiling point. Efforts to bring about a reconciliation between David Ben Gurion and Jabotinsky in 1934 failed when the *Histadrut* refused to approve an agreement on a modus vivendi signed by the two. The Revisionists left the Zionist organization in 1935 when Ben Gurion became Chairman of the Zionist Executive. Menaḥem *Begin's declaration of revolt against Britain and *Leḥi*'s assassination of Lord Moyne in 1944, before the end of World War II, brought relations between the two camps to a new low. Though in 1946 the *Haganah* cooperated with the dissident organizations in a joint struggle against Britain — known as the Hebrew Resistance Movement — this broke up over *IZL*'s King David Hotel Operation on July 22, 1946, carried out despite *Haganah* orders that it be put off. There followed the *Saison* (the "hunting season") — a period in which part of the *Haganah* cooperated with the British authorities in rounding up members of *IZL*. The episodes of *Deir Yassin and the **Altalena* increased the emotional split between the two camps, though *IZL* and *Leḥi* ceased to exist soon thereafter. The bitterness continued between *Mapai* and **Ḥerut* in the first years of the state (See: *"Without *Ḥerut* and *Maki*"). The complexity of relations between the *Alignment and the **Likud* today cannot be understood without knowledge of the historical background.

Side by side with this historic feud there grew an historic coalition. This was the coalition between *Mapai* and *Hamizraḥi* which started in the Zionist Executive in 1935, and was based on Labor's acceptance of a religious *status quo in return for the cooperation by religious Zionists with Labor's moderate political line. Though the coalition was a marriage of convenience it lasted until 1976 when it broke up over a crisis which developed over the desecration of the Sabbath on an Air Force base. Growing nationalist militancy within the *National Religious Party (NRP) and the political *upheaval in 1977 pushed the NRP into the orbit of the *Likud*. (S.H.R.)

Yisrael Aḥat See: *One Israel.

Yom Kippur War In September 1973, Israeli intelligence noted indications of a build-up on both the Egyptian and Syrian fronts. These were regarded as routine major exercises which had been taking place at frequent intervals along the borders, and particularly along the *Suez Canal front. This assessment reconciled with an Israeli intelligence conception that *Egypt would not launch a war against Israel without superior air power and *Syria would not go to war alone. It was fortified by a highly effective deception plan mounted by the Egyptians and the Syrians parallel to their actual military preparations.

Early on Saturday, October 6, 1973, news was finally received confirming that war was about to break out on the same day. At 2 p.m. the Syrian and Egyptian armies attacked simultaneously with their total forces, and the Yom Kippur War began. Throughout the Jewish holy day of Yom Kippur, Israel mobilized its forces. One of the miscalculations made by the Arab leaders was to launch the war on this day, when the entire manpower of the country was available either at home or in synagogue, thus enabling the *IDF to save many valuable hours of mobilization, which were to prove vital at a later stage.

On the northern front the battle began with Syrian air attacks and a heavy artillery bombardment of the Israeli front line and headquarters. Three Syrian infantry divisions moved across the cease-fire line and hundreds of Syrian tanks deployed in an attack on Israeli positions in the *Golan Heights. Behind these three divisions, two Syrian armored divisions were ready to follow up. The Israeli line, a series of fortifications acting as outposts and observation points and supported in each case by a small force of tanks, was held and, apart from a position on Mount Hermon, not one fortification surrendered, though three were evacuated under orders.

The battle opened with an Israeli force of approximately 180 tanks holding the line against a major Syrian armored assault which developed into an attack by some 1,400 tanks. With the opening of the attack, Syrian helicopters brought infantry forces to attack the Israeli positions in the area of Mount Hermon. Within a matter of hours, the positions were overrun and taken.

The major battle was fought in the area of Nafah, where the Syrians developed a major thrust, reaching to within 10 kilometers of the confluence of the Jordan River into the Sea of Galilee. On the central axis, the Syrian forces reached the area of the Nafah camp. On Sunday, October 7, fighting continued all along the line

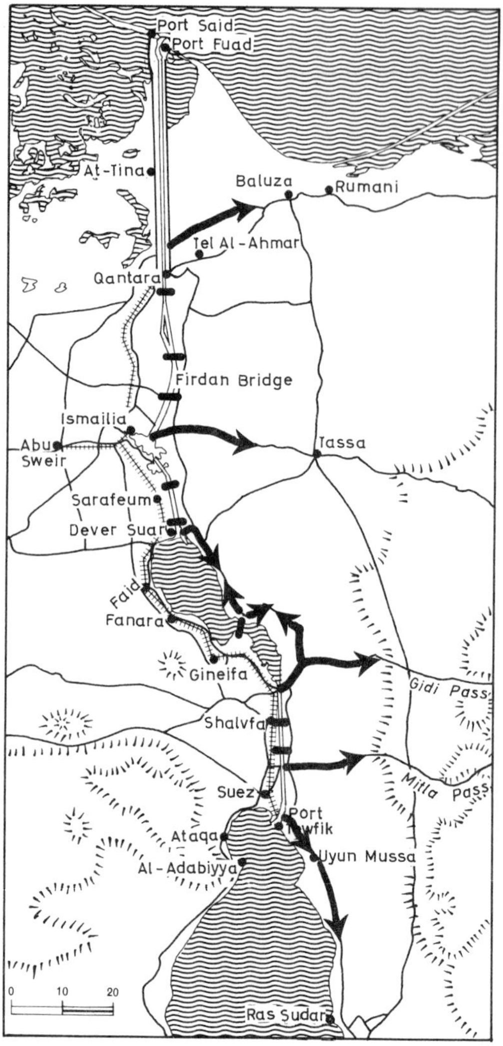

Phase 1 — Egyptian attack.

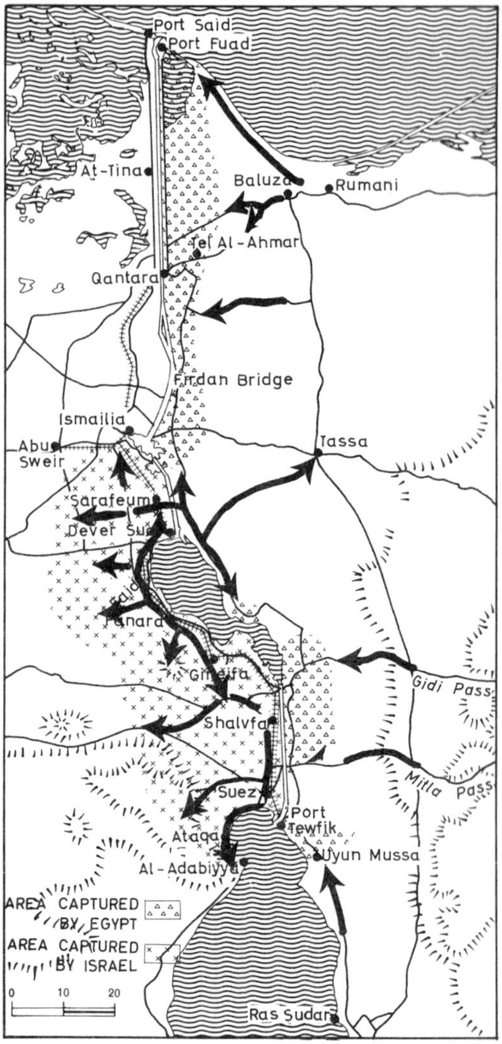

Phase 2 — Repulse of Egyptian army.

with heavy losses sustained by both sides. At this stage, the Israeli Northern Command received another division under its command, enabling it to counterattack on Monday, October 8. A heavy battle raged along the route between El Al and Rafid on Monday and Tuesday, October 8–9. By Wednesday, October 10, at 10 a.m., Israeli forces had driven the Syrians back to the 1967 cease-fire lines, after inflicting heavy casualties.

In the northern sector, both sides were wavering when one of the Israeli positions behind the Syrian lines reported that Syrian supply convoys were withdrawing. The Syrian attack had been broken, and in the area facing the Israeli Seventh Brigade, known as the Valley of Tears, north of Quneitra, some 300 Syrian tanks and armored personnel carriers were either abandoned or destroyed.

In the central sector, another Israeli division maintained the pressure around the area of Nafah and along the Tapline route, along which the major Syrian effort had advanced. Pushing in a southeasterly direction, this division gradually drove the Syrians back toward Hushniya. At this point, on Tuesday and Wednesday October 9–10, a two-division effort from the north and south boxed the Syrian forces in the general area of Hushniya, destroying a considerable number

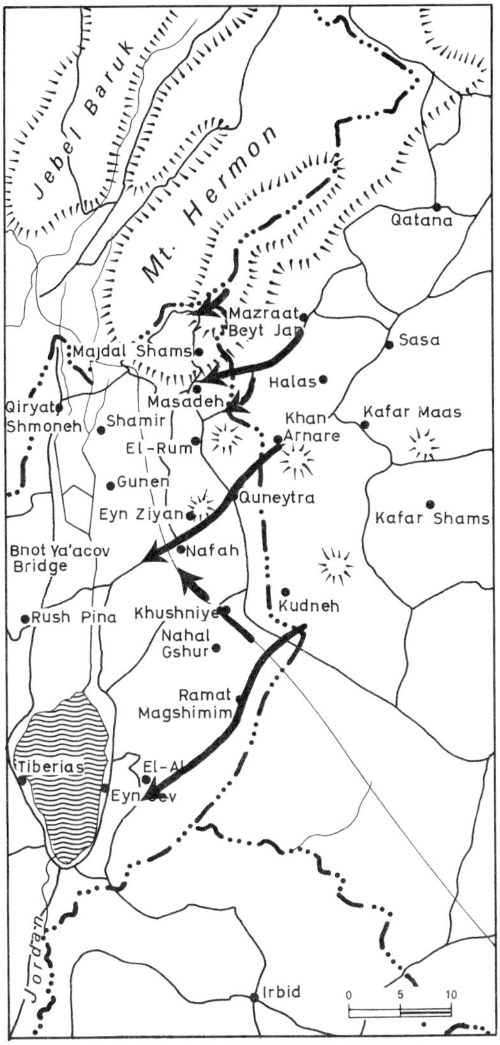

Phase 3 — Syrian attack.

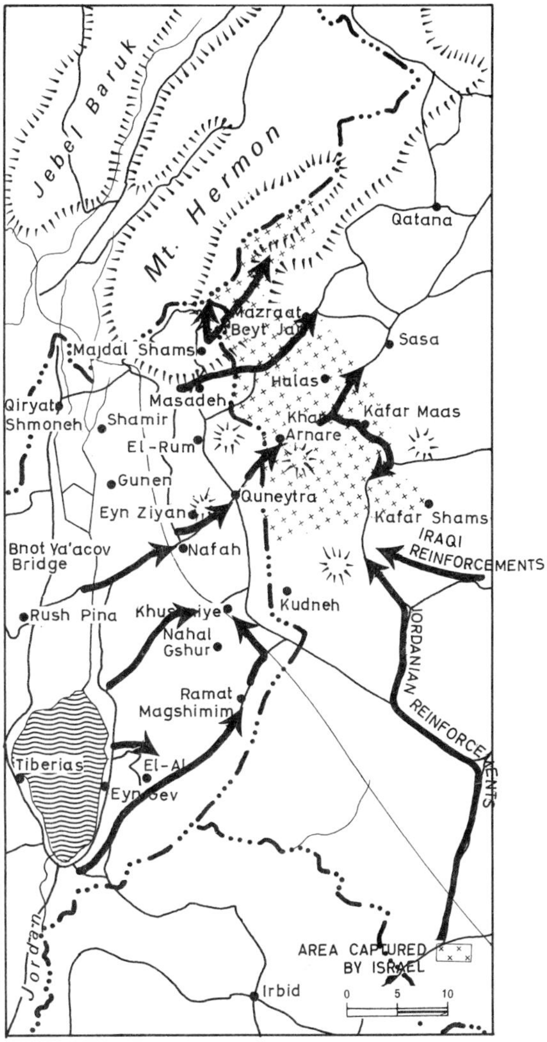

Phase 4 — Repulse of Syrian army.

of tanks in heavy fighting. By Wednesday, October 10, Israeli forces here, too, had regained the 1967 cease-fire line on the Golan Heights, and the attacking Syrian forces had been either destroyed or driven out of the area.

On Thursday, October 11, an Israeli counterattack was launched into Syria. One Israeli division broke into Syrian positions in the area of Jubata, while another attacked along the heavily fortified main Damascus route. On Friday, October 12, Israeli forces operating in the northern sector reached Mazraat Beit Jann and established defense positions. To the south, the other Israeli division widened its area of penetration, advancing toward Knaker; it was at this time that the Iraqi forces which had just entered Syria reached the area of battle. The first two Iraqi armored divisions advanced toward the flank of the advancing Israeli division, and a battle commenced at 3 a.m., which led to Iraqi withdrawal, leaving some 80 destroyed tanks on the field. The Israeli forces exploited their success and reached the area near Kafr Shams.

On Saturday, October 13, Israeli paratroopers captured the vital hill of Tel Shams. In the meantime, Jordanian forces had entered Syria to support the Iraqis on their left flank in the counterattack against the Israelis. These counterattacks by the combined Arab forces (Syrian, Iraqi and Jordanian) were of little avail, for the Israelis now held a very strong line.

On October 21–22, Israeli forces mounted an operation to recapture Mount Hermon, and on October 22 they succeeded in occupying all the Syrian positions.

In the battle for the Golan Heights and the attack into Syria, the Syrian army lost approximately 1,100 tanks; some 867 of these were in the Golan area, inside the 1967 cease-fire line, including a large number of the latest model T-62 Russian tanks. About 370 Syrian soldiers and 65 Israeli soldiers were taken prisoner by the opposing sides.

At all stages of the fighting, the Israel Air Force supported the ground forces, and at a later stage engaged strategic targets within Syria. By the end of the first week the Syrian Air Force, much of which had been destroyed, ceased to be a factor on the battlefield. Furthermore, the Syrian missile system was largely destroyed, freeing the Israel Air Force to deal with strategic targets deep in Syria, particularly in the Mediterranean ports, in the capital, Damascus, and in other cities.

On October 22, when the Syrian command agreed to a cease-fire, the Israeli forces were holding the strategic heights of Mount Hermon, dominating the entire area between the battlefield and Damascus, as well as positions as far eastward as Tel Shams, placing the outskirts of Damascus within Israeli artillery range.

Simultaneous with the Syrian attack, at 2 p.m. on Yom Kippur day, October 6, five Egyptian infantry divisions crossed the Suez Canal — some 70,000 troops against the less than 500 Israeli troops holding the *Bar Lev Line. The Israeli line was under intense shelling and air attack. Israeli armored forces rushed to occupy positions by 4 p.m., but by this time the Egyptian infantry had already crossed the Suez Canal, by-passing the widely dispersed Israeli fortifications of the Bar Lev Line. As Israeli armored forces approached their previously prepared positions, now occupied by Egyptian troops, they were met by hails of anti-tank Sagger-type missiles, causing heavy casualties to the tanks of the initial Israeli counter-assault.

The Egyptians set up three major bridgeheads across the canal: one in the north, basing on Qantara; one in the center, basing on Ismailia; and one in the south, in the area of the Great Bitter Lake and the town of Suez. The northern and central efforts were made by the Second Egyptian Army, and the southern one by the Third Egyptian Army. The entire Egyptian operation was carried out under cover of a dense anti-aircraft missile system which forced the Israeli aircraft to fly low, thus exposing themselves to the more effective conventional anti-aircraft guns which caused heavy casualties to the Israel Air Force. Efforts were made by Israeli forces to reach units besieged in fortifications of the Bar Lev Line, leading to very heavy casualties. Most of the Bar Lev Line had been either captured or abandoned by the third day of battle. The most northerly positions in the area of Baluza succeeded in holding out during the entire war. The most southerly position, at Port Tewfik, held out for most of the week, surrendering only after it had run out of ammunition and supplies.

On Monday October 14, the Egyptian army mounted a major tank offensive and throughout the day a heavy tank battle raged with the Egyptians endeavoring to break out at four different points. The major battle was waged on the central sector, where some 110 Egyptian tanks were destroyed. In the northern sector, as well as in the south, the Egyptian Third Army made a determined attempt to break out southward along the Gulf of Suez toward the oil fields at Abu Rudeis where the Israel Air Force knocked out the greater part of an Egyptian brigade and stopped the Egyptian thrust; they lost over 200 tanks in the assault and failed to advance.

On the night of October 15–16, Israeli paratroopers led General Ariel *Sharon's division across the Suez Canal, establishing themselves in Egypt proper on the west bank of the canal. The next day they were joined by elements of an armored brigade, which began to widen the perimeter. Egyptian forces on the west bank of the canal were taken by surprise, offering little opposition. In preparation for the crossing, Sharon's forces had launched an attack which brought them to the water's edge; however, the area had not been cleared of Egyptian forces, which were in a position to prevent any advance toward the canal. The northern Israeli division, which had been designated to follow through after bridges had been laid across the canal, was therefore obliged to postpone its operation and engage the Egyptians on the east bank, in the area of the Israeli breakthrough, to secure a corridor to the canal, widen it and mop up any Egyptian units there. At the same time an Egyptian armored brigade moved up from the Third Army area along the Great Bitter Lake, but it was soon destroyed. By this time Sharon's force was reinforced on the west bank of the canal, and it began pushing northward. One of the fiercest battles of the war, at the "Chinese Farm," was fought at the northern part of the corridor across to the canal. In the meantime, despite intense Egyptian bombardment, and artillery and air attacks, the Israelis brought up bridging equipment and two bridges were thrown across the canal.

On October 16–17, the northern Israeli division cleared the main routes to the bridging areas, as well as the corridor leading to them. This force then built bridges and crossed the canal on the night of October 17–18. Its first mission was to destroy as many anti-aircraft missile sites as possible and to advance southwards in the general direction of the Genifa Hills. On the same night Egyptian commando battalions unsuccessfully counterattacked from Ismailia southward against the paratrooper brigade which had crossed the canal initially. Large-scale air battles developed in the meantime, the Israel Air Force achieving the upper hand.

During the fighting at the end of the first week, Major General Mandler was killed, his command being taken over by Major General Magen. In the evening of October 19 this southern division crossed the bridges, bringing the total Israeli forces on the west bank of the Suez Canal to three divisions. Sharon's force drove through the cultivated area surrounding the Sweet Water Canal toward Ismailia, at the same time endeavoring to remain parallel to the Israeli forces on the east bank of the canal, which had encountered very heavy opposition from the Egyptian Second Army. The northern Israeli force was directed toward Genifa-Suez, clearing the area of the west bank of the Bitter Lakes and the west bank of the canal itself. The southern Israeli force, in a broad sweep to the west of the Genifa Hills, approached the port of Adabiya on the Gulf of Suez. Sharon's force, which at this stage had advanced some 6 kilometers north of the bridges, began to widen the Israeli bridgehead and push toward Ismailia. By October 22, they had pushed northward to the water purification plant of Ismailia. They also pushed northward on the east bank of the Suez Canal, in an endeavor to clear the area between the Great Bitter Lake and Lake Timsah, though they were not entirely successful.

The northern Israeli division continued southward along the Suez Canal between the Bitter Lakes and the town of Suez, maintaining constant contact with Egyptian forces on both banks of the canal. The southern Israeli division reached the Cairo- Suez road, cutting it early on October 22.

On October 21, the UN Security Council, hastily convened by Russia, called for an immediate cease-fire, to come into effect at 5:58 p.m. on October 22. By the time the cease-fire, as accepted by both Egypt and Israel, came into effect, the Egyptian Third Army was cut off and surrounded. Fighting continued after the cease-fire with units of the entrapped Egyptian Third Army trying to break out of the Israeli ring. The southern Israeli force consolidated its gains, closing the ring by taking Adabiya on the Gulf of Suez. Israeli forces moved into the town of Suez assuming that fighting was over, but came against Egyptian strongpoints and suffered casualties.

Fighting finally ceased on October 24, with Egyptian forces holding two major bridgeheads along the east bank of the Suez Canal, for a depth of some 10 kilometers, and with the Israeli forces occupying some 1,600 square kilometers inside Egypt proper, from the outskirts of Ismailia in the north to Mount Ataqa and Adabiya in the south, reaching a westerly point some 70 kilometers east of Cairo. The surrounded Egyptian Third Army had some 20,000 troops and approximately 300 tanks on the east bank of the canal, opposite the town of Suez and could have been destroyed within a matter of days by the Israeli forces.

Thus the war concluded on the Egyptian front, with the Egyptians celebrating their initial success in crossing the canal and their subsequent maintaining of the east bank of the canal. On the other hand, Israeli forces had effected a counterattack which gave them a good bargaining position for future negotiations. In the battle with Egypt, over 1,000 Egyptian tanks were destroyed and vast quantities of equipment were captured by the Israelis, and 8,000 prisoners taken. Some

240 Israeli prisoners were captured by the Egyptians. A prisoner-of- war exchange was effected following the cease-fire agreement.

In several naval battles during the war, including the first missile battles in naval history, Israeli naval forces destroyed most of the Syrian navy and part of the Egyptian navy, gaining complete control in the Mediterranean and the Red Sea.

On October 22, 1973, the UN Security Council passed Resolution 338 and on November 11, a Six-Point (cease-fire) Agreement was signed between Egypt and Israel at Kilometer 101 on the Suez-Cairo road. The *Geneva Peace Conference opened on December 18, 1973 with Egypt, Jordan and Israel participating, under the auspices of the *United States and the *Soviet Union. During January 1974 negotiations over an Egypt-Israel disengagement took place, with US Secretary of State Henry *Kissinger acting as the main mediator. On January 18, a *Disengagement Agreement was signed between Egypt and Israel. A similar agreement was signed between Syria and Israel on May 30 and implemented during June 1974.

The Yom Kippur War changed many concepts of modern warfare. Sophisticated anti-aircraft missiles, such as the SAM-6 Russian missile employed by the Egyptians and Syrians, proved to be very effective and had an important bearing on the air war.

From a purely military point of view, although the war began under the worst possible circumstances for Israel, and under the best possible circumstances for the Arab forces, the result was a military victory for Israel, but at great cost. Casualties on both sides were heavy, with an estimated 3,500 Syrians, 15,000 Egyptians and 2,700 Israelis killed (See: *Arab-Israel Conflict).

(H.H.)

POLITICAL CONSEQUENCES OF THE WAR. While from a strictly military point of view, Israel undoubtedly won an impressive military victory after it overcame the setback of the first few days, Egypt's initial success in breaking through the Bar Lev Line created the psychological breakthrough which led to an Egyptian-Israeli settlement. The 1974 *Disengagement Agreement and the 1975 *Interim Agreement were followed by Anwar *Sadat's historic visit to Jerusalem in November 1977, the September 1978 *Camp David Accords and the March 1979* Egyptian-Israeli Peace Treaty. Most analysts agree that none of these would have been possible had Egypt not felt that it had regained its honor in the Yom Kippur War. A second consequence of the war was Israel's growing dependence on the United States. This dependence manifested itself on the diplomatic front in terms of military supplies and economic aid which greatly increased during the Yom Kippur War and in its aftermath. Since the war cost Israel a year's GNP, Israel's external indebtedness reached such dimensions that it had to depend on vast amounts of American economic aid. A third consequence was that most Third World countries broke off diplomatic relations with Israel. And finally the war hastened the decline of the *Alignment. Though the Alignment was still able to form a coalition after the December 1973 election, the publication of the *Agranat Commission Report on the Yom Kippur War, followed by the resignation of Golda *Meir and Moshe *Dayan in March 1974, led to a further deterioration in the Alignment's popularity, preparing the ground for the 1977 political *upheaval.

The Yom Kippur War greatly shook the self-confidence of Israeli society. The result was the emergence of protest movements which for the first time since the establishment of the state questioned the entire Israeli political system.

(S.H.R.)

Yosef, Dov (1899–1980) Politician and attorney. Born in Montreal, Canada, as Bernard Joseph, Dov Yosef studied Arts and Economics at McGill University and received a PhD in Philosophy and Law in London. He was one of the founders of Young Judea in Canada. During World War I Yosef joined the *Jewish Legion in Canada. He reached Palestine in 1918 and remained there after the war, working as an attorney. In 1933 he joined *Mapai* and three years later became legal advisor to the *Jewish Agency Executive and Deputy Head of the Political Department, working closely with Moshe Shertok (*Sharett). During World War II Yosef coordinated the enlistment to the British army on behalf of the *Jewish Agency. He became a member of the Jewish Agency Executive in Jerusalem in 1945 and was arrested on "Black Saturday," June 29, 1946. Yosef was Military Governor of Jewish Jerusalem during the siege of the city in the course of the *War of Independence.

Yosef was elected to the Knesset in 1949 and remained there until 1959, occupying several ministerial posts: in 1949–50 he was Minister of Supply, Rationing and Agriculture, initiating the policy of austerity (*tzenah*); in 1950–51 he was Minister of Transport and in 1951–52 he was Minister of Trade and Industry. In 1953–55 he was Minister of Development, and in 1955, after the *General Zionists left the government, Yosef was also Minister of Health. In 1952 and again from 1961–66 Yosef served as Minister of Justice.

Yosh Acronym for "*Yehudah VeShomron*," (Judea and Samaria), the biblical, geographical and ancestral names for the territories west of the *Jordan River that were conquered by Jordanian forces in 1948 and occupied by Israel in June 1967. (Also referred to as the *West Bank.)

Judea and Samaria were respectively the southern and northern provinces around Jerusalem. The Romans used the terms in a geo-political sense. Judea first appears in the Old Testament in the Books of Ezra (Ch. 5) and Nehemiah (Ch. 11). Samaria, the capital of the Kingdom of Israel, is first mentioned in Kings I (Ch. 16).

Yosh entered common usage through the Israeli army practice of abbreviation. The term soon acquired ideological ramifications. Those who sought a solution to the *Arab-Israel conflict based on a *territorial compromise prefer to exclude from the contemporary political debate such emotive expressions as *Yosh*. Those who campaigned for the retention and full integration of the territories under Israeli rule insist on the exclusive use of the *Yosh* appellation.

In 1979 the Jewish inhabitants of *Yosh* established a Council of Jewish Communities in Judea, Samaria and the *Gaza Strip called in Hebrew "*Mo'etzet Yesha*" — the Council of *Yesha*. *Yesha*, which translates as "salvation," is also an acronym for *Yehudah, Shomron VeAzah* (Judea, Samaria and Gaza). (I.M.)

Youth Aliyah *Aliyat Hano'ar* (youth immigration), or Youth Aliyah, is an organization that began as a project started by Recha Freier on the eve of the rise of the Nazis to power in Germany to bring Jewish children to Palestine. It was subsequently organized in Palestine by Henrietta Szold (1860–1945) with the cooperation of the *Jewish Agency, the **Va'ad Le'umi* (National Council) and the *kibbutz movements. In 1941 Youth Aliyah cared for Jewish children already in Palestine, though even during the war groups of children were smuggled in, such as the group of Polish children, called the "Teheran children," which was brought to Palestine via the *Soviet Union and Teheran in 1943. In the years 1945–48 some 15,000 children, most of them orphaned *Holocaust survivors, were brought by Youth Aliyah to Palestine, many of them as "illegals" (See: **Aliyah*).

Following the establishment of the state, Youth Aliyah adapted itself to the absorption of waves of children of various origins and backgrounds, many of whom had arrived with their parents but whose families were unable to care for them at home. Most recently Youth Aliyah dealt with children from *Iran, following the overthrow of the Shah in 1979, and children from Ethiopia, following "Operation Moses" (See: *Ethiopian Jews).

Youth Aliyah developed its own education methods, primarily in children's villages, "youth communities" (*ḥevrot no'ar*), kibbutzim and boarding schools. Children from religious homes are provided with a religious environment, including education in *yeshivot*.

Whereas originally most Youth Aliyah activities could be described as rescue activities, today the emphasis is on education, primarily for Israeli children who come from disadvantaged families, or require special educational programs.

Close to one quarter of a million children have gone through Youth Aliyah programs since its establishment. Most of the financing for Youth Aliyah comes from the Jewish Agency.

youth movements See: **Betar*; **Bnei Akivah*; **Hamaḥanot Ha'olim*; **Hano'ar Ha'oved Vehalomed*; **Hashomer Hatza'ir*; **Hatnu'ah Hame'uḥedet*.

Z

Zahal See: *IDF: Israel Defense Forces.

Zionim Klaliyim See: *General Zionists.

Zionism The movement for national revival and independence of the Jewish people in **Eretz*

Yisrael. The name Zionism was coined by the Viennese Jewish writer Nathan Birnbaum (1864–1937) in 1885, and is derived from the word "Zion" — one of the biblical names for Jerusalem.

The religious yearning to return to *Eretz Yisrael* had existed ever since the final dispersion of the Jews following the unsuccessful revolt against the Romans at the end of the first and beginning of the second centuries C.E., and was closely associated with messianic beliefs. The new movement differed from the previous yearning for Zion in its predominantly secular content.

Modern Zionism developed in the atmosphere of fierce anti-Semitism in Europe, not only in the reactionary countries of Eastern Europe which saw successive waves of suppression and pogroms, but also in the enlightened countries of Western and Central Europe where the Jews had experienced emancipation and their thinkers were influenced by current nationalist and socialist doctrines and philosophies.

The Zionist thinkers were preceded by several pre-Zionist thinkers: the German Jewish socialist Moses Hess (1812–75) who in his book *Rome and Jerusalem* (1862) advocated the establishment by the Jews of an independent state based on socialist principles which would bring about the economic and social normalization of the Jewish people; Rabbi Hirsch Kalischer (1795–1874) who argued that the Messiah would come only after a large part of the Jewish people was reassembled in *Eretz Yisrael*; and Rabbi Judah ben Solomon Ḥai Alkalai (1798–1878) who, following the ritual murder charge against the Jews of Damascus in 1840, preached a return to Zion, first within the framework of traditional religious thought but later developing some elements of modern nationalist thought. The first Zionist thinkers were Yehuda Leib Pinsker (1821–1891), who in his book *Auto-Emancipation* (1882) argued that an emancipation granted by others could not solve the problems of the Jewish people and only its territorial concentration and sovereignty could create normal circumstances; and Dr. Theodor (Binyamin Ze'ev) *Herzl (1860–1904), who after considering various solutions to the Jewish problem concluded that the Jews must leave the lands of their dispersion and be concentrated in a sovereign state. In his famous book *Die Judenstaat*, *The Jewish State* (1896) Herzl explained that the Jewish problem could not be solved by assimilation because of the existence of anti-Semitism on the one hand and the Jewish will to survive on the other. The plight of the Jewish people could be transformed into a positive force only by means of a political solution — the establishment of an independent Jewish state — with the consent of the great powers. Herzl described the state which he envisioned in *Altneuland*, *Old-New Land* (1902).

Herzl made the first attempt to translate the theory of Zionism into political practice by establishing the *World Zionist Organization (WZO) which held its first Congress in Basle in 1897 and carried out diplomatic activities among the relevant powers (especially the Ottoman Empire and Germany). However, it was the settlement activities of *Ḥovevei Zion* (Lovers of Zion) in Palestine, starting in 1881, which heralded the beginning of "practical Zionism." Both the political and practical approach to Zionism continued to play an important role in the development of Zionism and the Zionist endeavor in Palestine. The combined approach was called "synthetic Zionism," and was associated with the name of Professor Chaim *Weizmann who played a major role in obtaining the *Balfour Declaration from *Great Britain in 1917, and in setting up a British mandate in Palestine under the auspices of the League of Nations. While for Labor Zionism the practical work was of predominant importance throughout the mandatory period, the *Revisionists argued that though 90 percent of Zionism was made up of tangible settlement work, it was the 10 percent of political work which was the precondition for success.

Though few Zionists believed that the majority of the Jewish people would actually move to Palestine, most believed that eventually through **Aliyah* (immigration) the Jews would constitute a majority. "Catastrophic Zionism," associated with the name of Max Nordau (1849–1923), argued that unless the Jews came to Palestine a catastrophe would befall them.

While most Zionists envisioned the movement's goal as being the eventual establishment of a Jewish state (even though for diplomatic reasons the terms "homestead," "national home" and "commonwealth" were used, rather than "state"), there were Zionists who believed that the establishment of a state was a pipe-dream and that the aim should therefore be the establishment of a "cultural-center" for the Jewish people in *Eretz Yisrael*. Cultural Zionism, which was associated with the name of the writer *Aḥad Ha'am (pseudonym of Asher Ginsberg, 1856–1927), thus viewed Zionism as a solution to the problem of Judaism rather than of the Jewish people. There were also Zionists who advocated the establishment of a bi-national (Jewish-Arab) state, since they did not believe there was any other moral solution possible to the confrontation between the national claims of the Jews and Arabs in Palestine (See: *bi-nationalism). However, both the cultural Zionists and bi-nationalists constituted a small minority in the Zionist movement.

In the early years the Zionist movement had to contend with the question whether the Jewish state must be established in *Eretz Yisrael* or whether other territories could be considered as an alternative. The issue was finally decided in favor of *Eretz Yisrael* when the "Uganda Plan," which proposed the establishment of a Jewish state in the British territory of Kenya was finally rejected by the Seventh Zionist Congress in 1905, one year after Herzl's death. Several Zionists, led by the British Jewish author and playwright Israel Zangwill subsequently left the Zionist Organization to establish the Jewish Territorial Organization (ITO). Some of the territorialists argued that the stateless Jewish people needed a "peopleless" territory, and that unfortunately Palestine did not fulfill this need, while others argued that the problem was urgent and the Jews should accept any available territory.

Throughout its history the Zionist movement had to decide among various options. The decisions taken by the majority were almost invariably preceded by fierce debates, though some were decided by events or the acts of individual Zionist leaders. When World War I broke out the Zionist offices were in Berlin, and in order to preserve the movement's neutrality they were moved to Copenhagen. However, Zionist leaders in Britain, most notably Weizmann, started as early as 1915 to pursue a moderate pro-British orientation with the intention of gaining British support for the Zionist cause. This infuriated the American Zionists, many of whom had pro-German sympathies, at least for as long as the *United States stayed out of the war, while the Zionists in the Central European states and the Jews in Palestine (who until the end of 1917 lived under the tutelage of the Ottoman Empire) were gravely concerned. But even among the pro-British Zionists there were fierce differences of opinion between the activists who wished Jewish troops to fight side by side with the British or otherwise assist the British war effort (these included Vladimir [Ze'ev] *Jabotinsky, Yosef *Trumpeldor and Aaron Aaronsohn) and those who feared that direct involvement would endanger the Jewish community in Palestine (See: *Nili).

Three years after the war, a major debate over Zionist policy erupted between the American Zionists and the predominantly Russian-born leadership of the Zionist organization. The Americans, led by Chief Justice Louis Brandeis (1856–1942), felt that with the attainment of international recognition and the expected approval of the British mandate by the League of Nations the political chapter of Zionism was closed and that future efforts should be concentrated on economic development based on private enterprise and sound business principles. This approach was rejected by Weizmann, backed by a majority in the organization and as a result Brandeis and his colleagues left the WZO.

Another major Zionist debate occurred in 1935 after the failure of an attempt to bring about a conciliation between **Mapai* under David *Ben Gurion and the *Revisionists under Vladimir *Jabotinsky. The Zionist General Council then voted a "discipline clause" intended to preclude independent political activities by individual Zionist parties, especially the Revisionists, who sought a more activist policy than that pursued by the official leadership. As a result the Revisionists decided to secede from the Zionist organization and established the *New Zionist Organization. Though the Revisionists returned to the WZO in 1946, its two offspring, **IZL* and **Leḥi*, did not accept the authority and discipline of the majority, as represented by the *Jewish Agency, the **Va'ad Le'umi* (National Council) and the **Haganah*, and there was no possibility of a reconciliation between them and the mainstream until the establishment of the state. It was largely due to Menaḥem *Begin, leader of *IZL* after 1943, that the rift concerning short-term goals and means did not deteriorate into civil war. It was only after the *Altalena* affair in June 1948 that the struggle became political and was fought out within the democratic framework of the state. In 1937, following the publication of the Peel Commission Report, the Zionist movement had to contend, for the first time, with the issue of whether to consider the establishment of a Jewish state in only part of western *Eretz Yisrael*. Though important Zionist forces opposed *partition, the 20th Zionist Congress in 1937 decided to enable the Executive to consider the possibility. At this stage partition was pigeon-holed by the British, but when the issue came up again, following the publication of the United Nations Special Committee on Palestine (UNSCOP) partition proposal in 1947, the Zionist movement once again reacted positively, and agreed to the establishment of a Jewish state in only part of Western Palestine.

During the Second World War the dilemma of the First, regarding neutrality, did not exist. Despite the disappointment with the 1939 White Paper issued by the British government which limited Jewish immigration and land purchases in Palestine, Ben Gurion could declare that the Jews would fight side by side with the British against Germany as if there were no White Paper, while continuing to struggle against the White Paper as if there were no war. However, as the war progressed, the magnitude of the *Holocaust became known, and the so-called dissidents (IZL and *Leḥi*) refused to refrain from an armed struggle against the British who continued to prevent the free entry of refugees into Palestine. As a result, Lord Moyne was assassinated by *Leḥi* and Begin declared a revolt against Britain in 1944. While the official Zionist and **Yishuv* institutions reacted sharply against these steps, its attitude was ambivalent except for a brief period in which *IZL* and *Leḥi* members were disclosed to the British authorities (a controversial episode in the history of the *Yishuv* known as the *Saison* — the hunting season).

There were several general issues which the Zionists had to contend with throughout the mandatory period. These included relations between Jews and Arabs; the extent to which the Zionists should cooperate with the British authorities in face of growing British animosity toward the Zionist endeavor; and the lines on which Zionist development in Palestine should take place. The various Zionist parties had different appraoches to these questions. The predominant line (which after 1935 was heavily tilted toward the positions of the Labor Zionists) was that a modus vivendi should be sought with the Arabs though not at the expense of immigration and land purchases; that the Zionists should officially continue to cooperate with the British but at the same time develop an independent defense force and continue settlement and immigration activities, even "illegally"; and that Zionist development should be mixed — national and private, socialist and capitalist, secular and religious. The emphasis was, however, on national, socialist and secular development. Following the establishment of the State of Israel there were many who felt that Zionism and the Zionist organization had completed their tasks. However, insofar as one of the tasks of Zionism is to bring as many Jews as possible to *Eretz Yisrael*, Zionism will continue to exist. Since 1948 Zionism has been broadened to imply the identification of world Jewry with Israel and it has assisted in bringing Jews to Israel from countries in which they are in distress; Zionism has also given financial, political and moral support to the Jewish state. There are those who argue that a distinction should be made between "Zionists" who intend to immigrate to Israel and "friends of Israel" who do not.

Since the 1970s a debate has developed in Israel as to whether it is possible to relinquish parts of *Eretz Yisrael* and still be consistent with the goals of Zionism. Throughout the history of Zionism the Zionists have cooperated with non-Zionists who were nevertheless in sympathy with the Zionist endeavor. Such cooperation manifested itself through joint involvement in specific projects and, since 1929, in the *Jewish Agency.

More difficult has been the Zionist confrontation with anti-Zionists, both from within the Jewish people and outside of it. Until World War II ultra-Orthodox Judaism, *Progressive Judaism, the *Bund, the Volkspartei and assimilated Jews, each for their own reasons, objected to Zionism: the Orthodox because Zionism was perceived as a secular movement and because they believed that the redemption will be brought by God — not man; the Reform movement because it had reinterpreted Judaism to exclude *Eretz Yisrael* from its frame of reference and objected to the definition of the Jews as a nation (it has since revised its position); the Bund and Volkspartei because they believed that the Jews, though a nation, should seek national autonomy in the countries of their abode — not in a separate state in *Eretz Yisrael*; the assimilated Jews because they felt that Jewish nationalism jeopardized their own status in their home countries. Among Jews, only the ultra-Orthodox may still be defined today as anti-Zionists, though wide Jewish circles are non-Zionist.

With very few exceptions the Arabs have always objected in principle to Zionism which they perceived as an effort to steal part of their land. *Anti-Zionism had the sympathy of most of the Moslem states after 1947, as well as that of several non-Moslem states, such as India. After 1973 the Arabs managed to spread anti-Zionism among the Third World countries, achieving a climax on November 10, 1975 when the *United Nations General Assembly passed a resolution equating Zionism with racism and racial discrimination. The anti-Zionist policy of the Soviet Union is directed against Zionists among Soviet Jewry, rather than against Israel's continued existence as a Jewish state, though the Soviet bloc did vote for the 1975 UN resolution. This anti-Zionism is accompanied by manifestations of traditional anti-Semitism.

In recent years there has been an effort to document an increased role in Zionist history for the Jews who came from Moslem countries and to reinterpret the role played by the Revisionists, *IZL* and *Leḥi*, reflecting the changing demographic and political balance within the State of Israel.

Zionut Aḥeret Hebrew for "A Different Zionism." A Jerusalem-based group which began to operate in 1977 and became one of the founding elements of *Peace Now. It emerged in protest against the Jewish settlements in the *occupied territories and the growing power of the extreme Right in Israel. The group publicized its reactions to events in the territories and fostered Jewish-Arab contacts, working through informal home meetings, activities among youth and contacts with other movements, such as **Oz Veshalom* and certain circles within the Labor movement. Its influence and support remained limited.

(M.B.)

SUPPLEMENT

FOREWORD

The first edition of the *Political Dictionary of the State of Israel* was published five years ago. Since then Israel has witnessed two elections, three governments, one war, one uprising and several peace initiatives. Its international status has improved significantly, and has undergone various political and constitutional changes. These issues, and some others, are dealt with in a new section of the dictionary, the Supplement, which follows the original text.

Most of the entries in the Supplement relate to developments since 1986-87. However, there are some new entries which go further back, in particular those regarding Israel's relations with states with which it had no diplomatic ties until recently. The information in the the Supplement was brought up to date to the end of December 1992. Several "old" entries have not been updated because there was very little of interest to add, and for lack of space.

In the new section entries which are a continuation of existing entries in the first edition are marked with an asterisk (*). Since the original text of the dictionary is reprinted without any changes, it was impossible to incorporate any corrections. Therefore a short list of corrections to the original text appears at the end of the book. A glossary appears on p.418.

In addition to the contributors whose initials appear at the end of some of the entries, a large number of experts and specialists were consulted, whom I would like to thank: Dr. Amazia Baram of Haifa University, who contributed the information relating to the policy of Iraq; Ms. Michal Cohen, Media Advisor to Minister of Tourism Uzi Baram; Dr. Dori Gold of the Jaffe Center for Strategic Studies at Tel Aviv University, who contributed the information relating to the policy of the United States; Uri Gordon, head of the Immigration Department of the Jewish Agency, on *aliyah*; Yeḥiel Leket, head of the Youth *Aliya* Department of the Jewish Agency, on settlement policy; Uriel Lynn, former *Likud* MK and Chairman of the Knesset Constitution, Law and Justice Committee, on new legislation; Reuven Merḥav, former Director General of the Ministry of Foreign Affairs and currently Director General of the Ministry of Absorption, on foreign policy; Dr. Yossi Olmert, former head of the Government Press Office and currently of the Dayan Center for Middle East Studies at Tel Aviv University, on Lebanon; Gideon Sagee, former head of the Organization Department and Workers Councils Section of the *Histadrut* and currently a Labor MK, on the *Histadrut*; Dr. Avraham Selah from the Hebrew University, Jerusalem, on the Arab-Israeli conflict; Professor Shimon Shamir, head of the Tami Steinmetz Center for Peace Research at Tel Aviv University, on Egypt; Muki Tsur, Secretary of the *Takam*, on the kibbutzim; Professor Shevah Weiss, Speaker of the Knesset, on the Knesset; Professor Dan Zaslavsky, of the Technion in Haifa, on water policy; Nissim Zvili, Secretary General of the Israel Labor Party, on the *moshavim*; Eliyahu Hassin, Journalist; Dr. Meron Medzini.

I should also like to thank the staff of the Knesset Library and Archive without whose assistance many of the entries in this dictionary could not have been written.

S.H.R.

CONTRIBUTORS TO THE SUPPLEMENT

A.B.	Dr. Avi Becker	Lecturer, Bar Ilan Unviersity; Dir. Jerusalem office of the World Jewish Congress.
A.D.	Prof. Avi Diskin	Chairman of the Political Science Department, Hebrew University, Jerusalem.
As.S.	Dr. Asher Susser	Director of the Dayan Center for Middle East Studies, Tel Aviv University.
B.N.	Prof. Binyamin Neuberger	Former director of the Open University, Tel Aviv.
D.R.	Danny Rubinstein	Correspondent on Arab affairs, *Ha'aretz.*
H.B.	Prof. Haim Barkai	Department of Economics, Hebrew University, Jerusalem.
I.M.	Israel Medad	Parliamentary assistant to MK Naomi Blumenthal of the *Likud.*
I.Z.	Dr. Ifrah Zilberman	Research fellow at the Truman Institute, Hebrew University, Jerusalem.
L.S.	Ms. Leslie Sachs	Spokeswoman of the Women's Network.
Mi.B.	Micha Bar	Expert on the IDF.
M.H.	Moshe Horowitz	Spokesman of *Meretz.*
S.M.	Dr. Sergio Minerbi	Scholar and retired diplomat.
Y.B.M.	Dr. Yehuda Ben-Meir	Lawyer and former National Religious Party MK.

All entries without initials at the end were written by the editor of the dictionary, Dr. Susan Hattis Rolef.

*** Abuḥatzeira, Aharon** Abuḥatzeira joined the *Likud* in August 1987, and was elected to the 12th Knesset. Before the 13th Knesset elections he advocated David *Levy's resignation from the *Likud* and the establishment of a new party. However, Levy decided to stay in the *Likud*. Abuhatzeira, who was 38th on the *Likud* list remained outside the 13th Knesset.

*** Africa and Israel** In June 1987 diplomatic relations were renewed with Togo during a visit by Prime Minister Yitzḥak *Shamir to Africa. Relations were established by the end of the 1980s with the Cameroons, the Central African Republic, Kenya and Ethiopia. The resumption of diplomatic relations with the Marxist regime in Ethiopia, in November 1989, was closely connected with the plan to bring the remaining *Ethiopian Jews to Israel.

As a result of the end of the cold war and the collapse of the Soviet Union, as well as the lack of unity in the Arab world and the beginning of direct Arab-Israeli negotiations following the *Madrid Conference, in the early 1990s relations were also resumed with Sierra Leone, Gambia, Ghana, Zambia and Nigeria, and for the first time relations were established with Angola. By the end of 1992 Israel had relations with 20 of the 40 African states which are not members of the Arab League, and it was expected that relations would soon be established with several others, including Mozambique and Mauritius. (B.N)

*** Agudat Yisrael** Towards the 12th Knesset elections the circles of the *Lita'im*, headed by Rabbi Elazar Menaḥem *Shach, left *Agudat Yisrael* and formed the **Degel Hatorah* list. The departure of Rabbi Shach led **Ḥabbad*, which had previously refrained from any partisan involvement, to support *Agudat Yisrael* in the elections. **Po'alei Agudat Yisrael*, joined the *Agudah* list. Following a stormy election campaign, *Agudat Yisrael* gained five Knesset seats, and joined the coalition.

Due to the disappointment of its leaders with Yitzḥak *Shamir, *Agudat Yisrael* supported the efforts of Shimon *Peres to form a government in March/April 1990. However, after Peres failed, *Agudat Yisrael* joined the government formed by Shamir.

In the 13th Knesset elections the party formed a single list with *Po'alei Agudat Yisrael*, its former rival *Degel Hatora* and Rabbi Yitzḥak *Peretz, which was called **Yahadut Hatorah Hame'uḥedet*. The new list did not have the support of *Ḥabbad*, and won only four seats, of which three were held by *Agudat Yisrael. Yahadut Hatorah* did not enter the government formed by Yitzḥak *Rabin because of the appointment of Shulamit *Aloni to the Ministry of Education. (M.H.)

*** Aliyah** In the 1980's immigration figures reached their lowest since the establishment of Israel, while emigration increased.

In the years 1980-89 there were altogether 153,833 immigrants of whom 29,754 arrived from the *Soviet Union and another 14,607 from *Romania. In 1990 the figure jumped to 199,516, of which 189,480 came from the Soviet Union.

While in the 1980s there was talk about "the end of Zionism" or the "post-Zionist era," from August 1989, when the monthly immigration from the Soviet Union first topped the 1,000, there was once again talk of "Israel's Zionist mission". The sudden flood of immigration resulted from the disintegration of the Communist bloc, followed by first signs of disintegration of the Soviet Union itself accompanied by economic hardships and uncertainties as well as manifestations of popular anti-Semitism.

The ongoing civil war in Ethiopia and the accompanying famine, together with the renewal of diplomatic relations between Israel and the Marxist regime of Colonel Haile Mariam Mengistu, resulted in a steep rise of immigrants from Ethiopia, which reached 4,137 in 1990. The peak of the immigration from the Soviet Union was in December 1990 when 35,625 immigrants arrived in Israel. In 1991 the immigration figures were still extremely high – 176,100 – made up of 147,292 immigrants from the Soviet Union and 20,014 from Ethiopia (See: *Ethiopian Jews).

However, in 1992 there was a steep fall in the number of immigrants from the Soviet Union, and in the first nine months of the year the number reached only 44,037 (compared to 118,423 in the corresponding period in 1991). In the course of 1992 small numbers of immigrants started to arrive from Yugoslavia, and especially war-stricken Sarajevo. The main reason for the drastic fall in the immigration figures from the former republics of the Soviet Union was the unemployment problem in Israel.

When the wave of immigration began towards the end of 1989 Israel had no clear absorption policy. However, very quickly it was decided that as opposed to the absorption policy in the 1950s, this time there would be minimal government intervention, and market forces would be allowed to do the job. This meant that immigrants would be able to decide themselves where to settle without going through absorption centers, and that after receiving an "absorption basket" to see them through their first year in the country, they would be left to fend for themselves. Since the Minister of Absorption in the years 1988-92 was the ultra religious Rabbi Yitzḥak *Peretz, besides immediate absorption arrangements the Ministry of

Absorption concentrated on providing the immigrants with religious services and education. Though tens of thousands of empty apartments were made available for rental to immigrants, there was a temporary housing shortage which led to rents rising steeply.

Soon after becoming Minister of Housing and Absorption in June 1990, Ariel *Sharon started to import and order in Israel thousands of caravans and other temporary housing, and to construct several hundred thousand housing units throughout the country. This hasty activity proved to be ill-planned, costly and at least partially superfluous. However, very soon it became apparent that the main absorption problem was not that of housing but of employment. Many immigrants were professionals, and a small country like Israel could not possibly offer them all suitable jobs. In addition, due to economic stagnation and the rejection of the option of government-initiated jobs, the Israeli economy was unable to increase the number of available jobs to offer employment to all the immigrants, unemployed old-time Israelis, and young Israelis entering the work force.

Talks about $10 billion of American loan guarantees for immigrant absorption began soon after the Gulf War, but were only approved by Congress on October 8, 1992, following the formation of the Labor-led government by Yitzḥak *Rabin. However, the loans contracted on the basis of these guarantees could not create jobs overnight. Immigration was expected to pick up again after the Israeli economy started to show signs of growth. The absorption of the immigrants from the former republics of the Soviet Union involved several surprises:

First, most of the immigrants chose to settle in the periphery, because jobs there were no less available than in the center, while the cost of living was lower.

Second, despite incentives only 0.8 percent of the immigrants chose to settle in the *West Bank and *Gaza Strip.

Third, tens of thousands of immigrants sought to try out life in the *kibbutzim even though it was initially believed that they would be deterred by the collective-socialist nature of this form of settlement.

Fourth, over 50 percent of the immigrants voted in the elections of June 1992 for the *Israel Labor Party and **Meretz*, despite the assumption that the majority would be inclined to vote for right-wing parties.

***Aloni, Shulamit** Aloni was one of the main proponents of the idea of forming a common dovish, human-rights oriented list for the elections to the 13th Knesset to be made up of the *Civil Rights Movement **Mapam*, **Shinui*. The new list - **Meretz*, which Aloni headed - won 12 Knesset seats, and joined the coalition formed by Yitzḥak *Rabin in July 1992. Aloni was appointed Minister of Education and Culture in the new government. (M.H.)

Arab boycott It was hoped that after the *Gulf War the Arab members of the anti-Iraq coalition would lift or ease their boycott of Israel as a gesture of goodwill to the Americans. However, little changed, and the linking of the boycott issue to that of continued Israeli settlement activities in the *West Bank and *Gaza Strip by the Group of Seven on July 17, 1991, dissuaded the Arab states to act. After July 1992, when the Labor-led government froze much of the settlement activities in the territories and started to show greater willingness to make concessions for the sake of advancing the peace process, the United States once again put pressure on the Arab states to respond in kind and cancel the boycott as a demonstration of goodwill.

On the level of the secondary and tertiary boycotts there were several positive developments in the aftermath of the Gulf War and the opening of the Middle East peace process. In July 1992 the German government passed legislation prohibiting German firms from including articles in commercial agreements expressing compliance with or acceptance of foreign boycotts. Germany, the Netherlands and France are today the most active proponents of the standardization of the laws and regulations within the *European Community on the boycott issue. Since the Gulf War there has been an easing in the application of the voluntary boycott by Japanese companies, especially with regards to exports to Israel, and in the beginning of December 1992, the Japanese government formally dissociated itself from the boycott. (G.F.)

Arab Democratic Party Arab party founded on the eve of the 1988 elections. Its founder, MK Abdel Wahab Darawshe, left the *Israel Labor Party in January 1988, in protest for the way Minister of Defense Yitzḥak *Rabin was handling the **intifada*.

The ADP recognizes the *PLO as the sole representative of the Palestinian people and supports the establishment of a Palestinian state in the *West Bank (including East *Jerusalem) and the *Gaza Strip. It also calls for complete equality for the *Arabs of Israel and the return of all land confiscated by the state to their Arab owners. The ADP, which was the first independent, purely Arab party to enter the Knesset, gained a single seat in the 12th Knesset. Unlike other nationalist Arab movements in Israel, the ADP never called for the boycotting of the government of Israel, and expressed willingness to join a Labor-led government. The ADP supported the "unification" of Kuwait with Iraq in August 1990, and before the outbreak of the

*Gulf War, Darawshe offered to mediate between Saddam Ḥussein and Israel.

Talks of the formation of a united Arab party before the elections to the 13th Knesset - which would include the ADP, the *Progressive List for Peace and independent members, with the full backing of the *Islamic Movement - failed to materialize. The ADP gained two seats in the 13th Knesset, and agreed to support the new government from outside after receiving a letter of principles from the Labor Party.

*Arab-Israeli conflict

1987-92 In May 1987 the prospect of peace talks between Israel and its neighbors seemed grim, as the *National Unity Government failed to approve the *London Agreement reached between Foreign Minister Shimon *Peres and King Ḥussein of Jordan regarding the convening of an international peace conference. However, this was but a temporary setback and did not disrupt the slow but visible changes in the basic attitude of the Arab world towards the conflict.

One of the causes for the change was the decline of Pan-Arabism in general and the united Arab position regarding the Palestinian cause in particular. By the 1980s it was clear that national particularism was gaining the upper hand in the Arab world. The Amman Arab Summit Conference of November 1987 reflected the new mood. The Conference decided that from now on individual Arab states would be able to determine their own policy towards Egypt, and as a result, within three months all the Arab states, except Syria, renewed their relations with Egypt which had been broken following the signing of the *Egyptian-Israeli peace treaty. This signified a collective Arab resignation to the fact that the largest Arab state had made peace with Israel, and legitimization of the peace treaty. After Syria finally renewed diplomatic relations with Egypt in 1989, the headquarters of the Arab League were returned to Cairo.

Another development at the Amman Summit Conference was that the Arab oil producing states decided to stop their institutionalized multi-annual financial aid to the Arab confrontation states and the *PLO. From now on aid was only to be forthcoming on a bilateral and quid pro quo basis. One of the immediate reasons for this decision was increased Iraqi pressure on these states for aid for its on-going war with Iran. Another effect of the Iran-Iraq war, which came to a formal end only in 1989, was that it made an Arab-initiated military confrontation with Israel highly improbable. Iraqi-Syrian tensions which persisted after the war was over, ensured that such a confrontation continued to be unlikely.

Even before 1987, a Palestinization of the Arab-Israeli conflict took place, involving increased emphasis on the Palestinian aspect of the conflict. It began during the *Lebanese War when Israeli troops were in direct confrontation with Palestinian forces, and was intensified following the outbreak of the **intifada* in December 1987. The *intifada* influenced the process in three ways. First of all, it drew massive international attention, which was extremely favorable to the Palestinians. Secondly, it emphasized the local, communal aspect of the Palestinian problem at the expense of the external, international aspect which had lost much of its momentum because the Arab world started losing interest in the conflict. Thirdly, within Israeli government circles (especially within the Labor half of the government) it was finally understood that the *Palestinians could not be ignored as direct participants in any attempt to resolve the conflict. This realization, accompanied by the declaration of King Ḥussein of Jordan in July 1988 that he was dissociating himself from the *West Bank (See: *Jordan and Israel), to all effects and purposes put an end to the so called *Jordanian option. An initial attempt by US Secretary of State George Shultz, in February 1988, to take advantage of the momentum created by the *intifada* for the purpose of opening peace negotiations between Israel and its neighbors, failed (See: *Shultz Plan).

However, in the course of 1989 and the first half of 1990, hopes for a breakthrough came from two directions. The first stemmed from the resolutions adopted by the Palestine National Council meeting in November 1988, and several declarations made by PLO chairman Yasser Arafat the following month, that the Palestinian organization was finally willing to recognize Israel and desist from its terrorist activities. The second stemmed from the *Shamir-Rabin peace initiative, adopted by the Israeli government on May 14, 1989. The hopes regarding the Israeli initiative were crushed when the *National Unity Government broke up in the middle of March 1990, as a result of the **Likud* procrastination over its implementation. The hopes regarding the PLO were dispelled after a PLO affiliated organization attempt to carry out a major terrorist attack along Israel's shores on June 1, 1989, and as a result of the PLO's expression of support for the invasion of Kuwait by Iraq in August 1990. The position of the PLO, which accurately reflected the Palestinian mood, was probably influenced to a larger extent by concern for the fate of the 400,000 Palestinians living in Kuwait than from hopes that Saddam Ḥussein would realize his aggressive threats against Israel. However, the reaction in Israel, even among certain left-wing circles, was extremely negative. Taken in conjunction with King Ḥussein's decision not to join the anti-Iraqi coalition or to comply fully with the economic embargo of Iraq, at least temporarily, the prospects of a breakthrough in the peace process seemed dim.

However, despite the Palestinian and Jordanian attitude during the Gulf crisis and *Gulf War which followed, the final outcome brought about a breakthrough in the peace process. Not only did Egypt, Saudi Arabia and the Gulf Emirates join the coalition created by the United States to confront Saddam Ḥussein, but Syria - which had only recently lost the support of its traditional patron, the Soviet Union, and was fearful of Iraq's military power following the end of the Iran-Iraq War in 1988 - joined in as well. The outcome of the war, and the complete disengagement of the Soviet Union from the Middle East, increased American leverage over the states which had participated in the anti-Iraqi coalition and the factors that had supported Saddam Ḥussein. Secretary of State James Baker was thus in a much better position to push through a new plan for opening Middle East peace talks, with the participation of all the parties concerned than his predecessor had been. Jordan, the Palestinians (formally not the PLO, but representatives of the inhabitants of the territories), Syria and Lebanon were all convinced to take part in peace talks which were to open by a regional conference under American and Soviet auspices and continue in direct talks with Israel. Most of the Arab states agreed to participate in multilateral talks, with Israeli participation, dealing with a series of regional problems.

The great importance of the *Madrid Conference, which opened the process at the end of October 1991, lay in the fact that for the first time in history all the Arab states, except for Iraq, were represented at the conference either by official delegations or observers. It was Israel which seemed the most reluctant among the parties concerned to enter the process. The government which came to power in Israel in June 1990 opposed any territorial compromise, was determined to enhance the Jewish settlement activities in the West Bank and Gaza Strip, and included a group of ministers who were highly suspicious of the American peace initiative. Nevertheless, Baker managed to fulfill all the conditions placed by this government for its participation in the Madrid Conference.

On July 13, 1992, a new Labor-led government came to power, and this government's attitude to the peace process was more positive, involving acceptance of the *territorial compromise principle, and in the first instance agreement to grant the Palestinians a real measure of self-government within the framework of an interim settlement. These positions were still far from those of the Arab participants in the peace talks, which called for an a priori Israeli commitment to withdraw from all the territories occupied in 1967, even before the essence of the permanent peace is discussed. However, the prospects seemed better than ever before.

Despite the peace process, the Middle East armaments race has not slowed down, and the prospects of non-conventional weapons entering the region have increased, while long range means of delivery are already present. Especially since 1988 countries such as Syria, Iraq, Libya, Egypt and Saudi Arabia either started developing or purchased long range missiles, while Iran, Iraq, Syria, Egypt and Libya are all involved in building a non-conventional capability (chemical and/or nuclear). It is believed that within the next five years Iran could have a nuclear capability, and it is today clear that before the Gulf War Iraq was even closer. While one can hardly conclude that the developing balance of terror helped advance the Middle East peace process, it is not surprising that arms limitations is one of the most urgent issues that must be dealt with in the multilateral talks.

One factor which is certainly an impediment to the peace process is the rise of the various Islamic movements in the Arab world. The Islamic movements would like a return to the extreme, Pan-Islamic, rigid position towards the conflict with Israel, which maintains that the whole of Palestine is Arab land. Within Israel there are also right-wing and religious forces which are acting against the peace process, though unlike their Muslim counterparts they favor an accommodation based on *Greater Israel.

*** Arabs of Israel** Following the outbreak of the **intifada* the dilemma between their identification as citizens of the State of Israel and their identification with the *Palestinians, grew more acute. In general the Israeli Arabs justified the *intifada* as a consequence of the frustrations of their brethren in the *occupied territories, and a legitimate means to bring about the establishment of a Palestinian state. In most cases their empathy with the *intifada* manifested itself in material aid to the Palestinians in the territories and in public demonstrations, but actual participation in *intifada* related activities was rare.

At the end of 1989 the Israeli Arabs showed their concern at the wave of immigrants from the Soviet Union. In February 1990 the *Village Sons started gathering signatures against the **aliyah*, while **Ḥadash* recommended to the Soviet Communist Party to resolve the problem of the Jews inside the Soviet Union. At the same time, efforts were made by the Arab leaders to prevent the annual *Land Day and "House Day" processions from turning violent. House Day was first proclaimed on November 15, 1988, formally to protest against the demolition of illegal structures in Arab settlements, but in fact to celebrate the proclamation of the Palestinian state in Algiers on that day. The Israeli Arabs were inclined to identify with Saddam Ḥussein's invasion of Kuwait, though following the Soviet line, **Ḥadash* opposed the move.

During this period the financial situation of the Arab local authorities deteriorated, and the issue of equating the government's financial allocations to the Arab local authorities with those of the Jewish local authorities was repeatedly raised. This led to numerous strikes by the local authorities. The government decided to equate the allocations in August 1991, but in fact inequalities persist. Among the most pressing problems of the Arab sector in this period were the poor conditions and achievements of the schools in the Muslim sector, and that of over 40 unrecognized Arab settlements in Israel. It was as a result of the financial distress of the Arab local authorities that the *Islamic Movement gained ground especially after 1988, by pouring funds into educational and social services.

In the beginning of 1988, two Arab Knesset members of Jewish parties - Abdel Wahab Darawshe of the *Israel Labor Party, and Moḥammed Wattad of **Mapam* - quit their parties against the background of the *intifada*. Though both Labor and *Mapam* filled their Arab slots in the following elections, these two departures were indicative of the mood among the Israeli Arabs at the time. Darawshe formed a new party - the *Arab Democratic Party - which won one seat in the 12th Knesset, and two in the 13th Knesset. What was new about the ADP was the fact that it was all-Arab and nationalist, and yet willing to enter an Israeli government under certain conditions.

Following the 1992 elections, *Ḥadash* and the ADP served as part of Labor's blocking majority in return for letters clarifying Labor's position on the issues of special concern to the Arab sector. In the 1988 elections the three predominantly Arab parties won 59 percent of the Arab vote. Only 41percent of the Arab vote was given to Jewish parties (Labor received 16.4 percent). Surprisingly, in the 1992 elections the three Arab parties received only 47.6 percent of the Arab vote, while the Jewish parties received 52.4 percent of the vote (Labor received 20.3 percent).

Altogether there were six Arab MKs in the 12th Knesset, and six in the 13th Knesset. The percentage of voters among the Arabs eligible to vote fell from 72.9 percent in 1988 to 65.7 percent in 1992, and in absolute numbers fewer Arabs voted despite the rise in the number of voters The main explanation for this was the failure in 1992 to create a united Arab party with the support of the Islamic Movement. In the government formed by Rabin in July 1992 two Arabs were appointed Deputy Ministers - Nawaf Massalha of the Labor Party in the Ministry of Health, and Ḥaj Yiḥia Walid Sadik of *Mapam* in the Ministry of Agriculture. The position of Advisor to the Prime Minister on Arab Affairs, which had existed since the establishment of the state, was abolished.

*** Arens, Moshe** Arens resigned from the *National Unity Government in September 1987 over the issue of the cancellation of the development of the Lavi aircraft, but was convinced to return the following January. In the government formed in December 1988 he was appointed Minister of Foreign Affairs, and supported Yitzḥak *Shamir in his struggle with the "constraint ministers" over the government's peace initiative of (See: *Shamir-Rabin peace initiative). He was in favor of giving Secretary of State James Baker a positive answer in February 1990 regarding the Palestinian participants in the proposed Cairo talks. In the government formed in June 1990 Arens was appointed Minister of Defense. Though he was placed in second place on the *Likud* list to the 13th Knesset, as a result of the in-fighting within the *Likud* and the defeat in the elections, Arens resigned his Knesset seat and retired from active politics.

*** Argentina** (See: *Latin America)

*** Aridor, Yoram** Aridor was appointed ambassador to the *United Nations in 1990. Following the formation of the *Labor government in July 1992 Aridor announced his resignation.

*** Arms Sales** The crisis in arms sales, which hit the military industries throughout the world in the early 1980s, and deepened in the 1990s, affected Israel as well.

The Israeli arms industries were forced to close down departments and plants and dismiss thousands of workers. The government-owned arms industries (*Ta'as*) lost $260 million in 1991 and about $100 million in 1992. In spite of this, Israel remained one of the ten largest arms exporters in the world, and has a clear superiority in specific areas, such as upgrading and improving old weapons systems and developing sophisticated sub-systems.

There is no accurate data regarding Israeli arms exports, but it is assumed that in the mid-1980s arms sales constituted about half of Israel's exports. In 1992 it is expected to reach $1.8 billion to some 60 countries (about 10 percent of the total exports) and, according to *Janes Defense Weekly* figures, just under 50 percent of Israel's total arms production. Of the $1.8 billion about $1.25 are from the aircraft industry.

In 1992 the United States purchased 25 percent of Israel's arms exports, and there are currently $1.7 billion worth of orders from the Pentagon for purchases of arms and services in Israel, including the refurbishing of 50 American F-15's stationed in Europe. The two countries are also cooperating in the development of the *Ḥetz* ("arrow") anti-missile missile and other systems. Sales to West European countries, which amount to $150-200 million per annum, are only half of what they used to be in the 1980s. Most of the decrease is due to cuts in German arms purchases. Arms sales to *South Africa have also been reduced. A great part of arms sales in recent years have been to 25-30 Third World countries - including countries with which Israel has or never had diplomatic relations. These sales are usually shrouded in secrecy. Among the deals which were published were those with Taiwan, Ethiopia and Columbia. Today Israel is attempting to expand its arms sales to the countries of *Eastern Europe and the former republics of the Soviet Union. It was reported in the press that Israel has sold $100 million worth of arms to these countries.

While the fact that many states have established or reestablished relations with Israel might well bring about an increase in Israeli arms sales. At the end of 1992 it was reported that the Ministry of Defense had laid down limitations on arms sales to areas of tension, such as Yugoslavia. Other restrictions on Israeli arms sales include the reluctance to reveal certain systems which were developed for the use of the *IDF, and the need to receive U.S. permission to sell arms with American components. To overcome the latter problem Israel might in future cooperate with countries like *China, *India, as well as several European countries, in arms development and production. (Mi.B.)

Atteret Cohanim ("Crown of the priests") Name of a yeshiva and one of the bodies involved in settling Jews in Muslim sections of *Jerusalem. It began as a yeshiva for advanced talmudic and rabbinic studies situated, since its establishment in 1979, in the Muslim quarter of the Old City of Jerusalem. It sought to revive a former yeshiva established by the first Chief Rabbi Rabbi Avraham Yitzḥak Hacohen *Kook, for the purpose of studying the laws of the Temple and ritual sacrifices in anticipation of the coming of the Messiah.

Atteret Cohanim functioned at first under the auspices of *Attara Leyoshna* ("former glory"), a group involved in the reclamation of former Jewish property within the Old City, and the purchase of Arab property. In 1984 it broke away from *Attara Leyoshna,* and embarked on a settlement project of its own. A third group involved in similar activities is *Ne'ot David* ("the pastures of David"), which rented the St. John's Hospice in a controversial move which at the end of 1992 was still being contested in the courts. A fourth group, *El'ad*, restricts itself to settling Jews in Kfar Shilo'aḥ (Silwan).

These activities enjoyed the moral support of Ariel *Sharon who as Minister of Construction and Housing was able to give them also material support. The Labor government which came to power in July 1992 did not view favorably the attempts to settle Jews in Muslim neighborhoods and used all legal means possible to curtail these activities. (I.M.)

*** Autonomy Plan** The debate in Israel on the merits of an autonomy plan for the *administered territories reopened following the outbreak of the **intifada*. The *Israel Labor Party viewed it as an interim arrangement involving a territorially based autonomy (of which the Arabs of East Jerusalem could be a part on a personal basis), while the **Likud* mainstream viewed it as a permanent arrangement involving a personally based autonomy (of which the Arabs of East Jerusalem would not be a part). The *Shamir-Rabin peace initiative of May 14, 1989, involving elections in the territories for an Administrative Council, did not mention the word "autonomy," but it was in fact implied.

The idea of an autonomy plan came up in the bilateral talks between Israel and the Palestinian delegation following the *Madrid Conference, and was the background to the decision of **Tzomet* and *Moledet to leave the *Shamir Government in January 1992. In the sixth round of the Washington talks which opened after Yitzḥak *Rabin had formed his government, talks on the substance of the autonomy plan began. The Israeli side offered a plan whereby the Palestinians would be in charge of all issues except security, foreign affairs and the Jewish settlements. Jordan would be involved, especially in the training of a strong local police force. The issue of water rights and state lands was left vague. Israel opposed the Administrative Council having the power to legislate, and was unwilling to discuss the nature of the permanent solution before the interim solution went into effect. The Palestinians, on the other hand, demanded that interim and permanent solutions be linked, that the autonomy be given much more extensive powers, including the right to legislate and full control over water rights and state lands.

Baker Initiative (See: *United States and Israel)

*** Bar Lev** (formerly Brazlavsky), **Ḥaim** Bar Lev continued to serve as Minister of Police until March

1990. He did not run in the Labor Party primaries in March 1992. Following the formation of the government by Yitzḥak *Rabin in July 1992 he was appointed ambassador to Russia.

*** Basic Laws** A new "Basic Law: the Government" was passed by the Knesset on March 18, 1992, replacing the law of 1968. The new law introduced the system of direct elections for the Prime Minister (See: *Prime Minister, direct election of). Its aim was to increase the power of the Prime Minister vis-à-vis the Knesset and the small parties, and thus increase the stability of the government system. It can only be amended by a majority of the Knesset members. The passing of this law was accompanied by appropriate amendments to the Basic Law: the Knesset, the Basic Law: the State Economy and several others.

While a Basic Law: Human Rights was not passed as a result of opposition by the religious parties, the 12th Knesset passed two basic laws which go some way to fulfill the same purpose. These are the Basic Law: Freedom of Occupation and the Basic Law: Human Dignity and Freedom.

THE BASIC LAW: HUMAN DIGNITY AND FREEDOM, passed on March 17, 1992, incorporates the core of a bill of rights and defines the basic human rights such as the right to life, body, property and dignity. It states that these rights are protected by the state. It defines the right to personal freedoms, to enter and leave the State of Israel, to individuality and privacy, the right to private property and protection against searches on one's body and through one's personal effects. An ordinary law cannot contravene the provisions of this basic law except for a worthy purpose involving public health, public peace and safety, state security and public morals, and in a manner conforming with the values of the State of Israel as a Jewish and democratic state.

THE BASIC LAW: FREEDOM OF OCCUPATION, passed on March 3, 1992, establishes the freedom of occupation as a basic right and imposes limitations on the restrictions which the authorities can impose on the licensing of an occupation or the conducting of a business. Such restrictions can only be imposed by means of a Knesset law - not subsidiary legislation - and must be for a worthy purpose.

One of the most important amendments to existing Basic Laws adopted by the 11th and 12th Knesset was Amendment No 12 to the Basic Law: the Knesset, passed on February 12, 1991, which greatly limits the ability of Knesset members to move from one Knesset faction to another in exchange of personal benefits (See: *Kalanterism). The Minister of Justice in the government formed by Yitzḥak *Rabin in July 1992, David Liba'i, is committed to passing the Basic Law: Human Rights.

*** Begin, Menaḥem** (1913-1992) In the last years of his life Begin lived in seclusion. He died on March 8, 1992, and in accordance with his wish, was buried in a simple religious ceremony. (I.M.)

*** Begin, Ze'ev Binyamin (Benny)** **Likud* politician. Born in Jerusalem in 1943, the son of Menaḥem *Begin. He studied geology, obtained BSc and MSc degrees from the Hebrew University, Jerusalem, and completed a doctorate at Colorado State University in 1978. From 1978-88 he was employed at the Geology Survey of Israel as head of its Environmental Division, and its Mapping and Marine Geology Division.

Encouraged by his father, Begin ran for a seat on the **Likud* list for the 12th Knesset. Since his election to the Knesset in 1988 he has been a member of the Foreign Affairs and Security Committee and of its Subcommittee for National Security Policy.

Begin's popularity stems largely from his father's. However, he has earned a reputation for his standing on matters of principle, as when he voted in the Knesset plenary against the appointment of Rehav'am * Ze'evi into the government in February 1991.

Begin is a contender in the *primaries for the *Likud* leadership to be held in March 1993. (I.M.)

Ben-Eliezer, Binyamin (Fuad) Military commander and Labor politician. Was born in Iraq in 1936 and immigrated to Israel in 1950. He served in the *IDF from 1950 to 1984, reaching the rank of Brigadier General. During the *Six Day War and the *War of Attrition he served as commander of the "Shaked" unit. In 1970 he was sent on a mission on behalf of the Ministry of Defense to Singapore. During the *Yom Kippur War he served as deputy commander of a brigade on the southern front. In 1974-76 he commanded a brigade along the Lebanese border and was one of the first Israeli commanders to enter Lebanon in 1976. He acted as coordinator with the Christian forces in Lebanon, was responsible for setting up the "Good Fence" (i.e., an open border for the residents of Southern Lebanon) and for the establishment of the Southern Lebanese Army. In 1978-81 Ben-Eliezer was commander of Judea and Samaria. After leaving the army for a year he returned in 1983 to serve as Coordinator of Operations in the Territories.

In 1982 Ben-Eliezer joined **Tami* and served for a year as its Secretary General. In 1984 he joined Ezer *Weizman in establishing **Yahad*, and was elected to the 11th Knesset. In 1986, together with Weizman, he joined the *Israel Labor Party, and was elected to the 12th Knesset on its behalf. In the 12th Knesset he was deputy chairman of the Knesset Foreign Affairs and Security Committee and chairman of its subcommittees on IDF preparedness and on the territories and *civil administration. He was also a member in the subcommittee on intelligence matters. In 1989 he headed Labor's organization staff for the **Histadrut* elections. In 1990 he was chosen to head the party's membership drive and was one of the strong proponents of the introduction of the *primaries system for the election of the party's representatives.

In the government formed by Yitzḥak *Rabin in July 1992 Ben-Eliezer was appointed Minister of Construction and Housing.

Betzelem ("In the image") Israeli human rights organization established at the end of 1988 at the initiative of MK Dedi Zucker (*Civil Rights Movement). It concentrates on breaches of human rights by the Israeli authorities in the *administered territories. The organization believes that the issue of human rights in the territories should not be exclusively the concern of foreign and Palestinian groups, frequently hostile to Israel, and radical Israeli groups. The immediate reaction to the establishment of *Betzelem* was the creation of a counter-organization called *Uvdah* (fact) by the Jewish settlers in the territories. At first the military authorities were not inclined to react to *Betzelem* reports. But after the foreign press started to rely on *Betzelem* information, the military authorities changed their attitude. Ehud Barak, the Chief of Staff from 1991 appointed a committee to examine allegations of torture in **Shabak* investigation facilities reported by *Betzelem*. The IDF also responded to another *Betzelem* report dealing with the activities of special units operating in the territories. The appointment of Dedi Zucker as chairman of the Knesset Constitution Law and Justice Committee in the 13th Knesset ensures that *Betzelem* reports will be reviewed in the Committee.

Burg, Avraham (Avrum) Labor politician. Burg was born in Jerusalem in 1955; the son of veteran National Religious Party leader Yosef *Burg. He was educated in a yeshiva, and then studied Sociology and African Studies at the Hebrew University in Jerusalem.

Following the *Lebanese War in which he was wounded, Burg founded a group called "Soldiers Against Remaining Silent" and was one of the speakers at a mass demonstration held in Tel Aviv in September, 1982, demanding a commission of inquiry on the *Sabra and Shatilla massacre and the resignation of Minister of Defense Ariel *Sharon. He was later involved in *Peace Now and was again wounded when a right-wing Jew threw a hand grenade during the Peace Now demonstration in February, 1983. As a result of the Lebanese War Burg joined the *Israel Labor Party and in 1984 was adviser on diaspora affairs to Prime Minister Shimon *Peres. In 1986-88 he headed the Center for Judaism and Tolerance, served as adviser to Minister of Foreign Affairs Peres and hosted a program on religious issues on Israeli TV.

Burg was one of a group of young "doves" elected on the Labor list to the 12th Knesset. Though he is religious, Burg advocates the separation of religion and state. In the primaries for Labor's Knesset list in March 1992, he came second after Shimon Peres. His surprising success was due to the clear positions he expressed on the issue of religion and state. In the 13th Knesset Burg was appointed chairman of the Education and Culture Committee.

*** Chiefs of Staff**

13. 1987–91	Dan Shomron
14. 1991–	Ehud Barak

China and Israel In the early 1950s the People's Republic of China was eager to establish relations with Israel, but Israel refused in order not to irritate the U.S. At the Bandung Conference of the Nonaligned States in 1958 China discovered the Arab world. In 1964 it was one of the few states to recognize the newly-established *PLO. After Mao Tse-tung's death in 1976 China's attitude changed. However, in 1978, Foreign Minister Moshe *Dayan did not show any interest in East Asia and even closed the Israeli consulate in Hong Kong for economic reasons. Nevertheless, a group of Israeli industrialists and a military delegation visited China. By the 1980s it was reported that Israel was selling China large quantities of arms.

In 1985 Reuven Merḥav, was appointed by Yitzḥak *Shamir as Consul General to Hong Kong, and one of his tasks was to prepare the ground for the establishment of relations with China. In the autumn of 1987 Foreign Minister Shimon *Peres met with the Chinese Foreign Minister at UN Headquarters in New York, and the following year Merḥav paid his first official visit to Beijin. At the beginning of 1990 a permanent Israeli delegation, officially representing the Israeli Academy for Sciences, opened an office in the Chinese capital, and the Chinese opened a delegation of their Ministry of Tourism in Tel Aviv. The two delegations were formally turned into consular offices half a year later. On January 24, 1992 full diplomatic relations were established during a visit by Foreign Minister David *Levy to China.

***Civil Rights Movement** The CRM won five seats in the elections to the 12th Knesset in 1988, and supported the efforts of Shimon *Peres to form a government in March/April 1990 after the fall of the *National Unity Government. The CRM was instrumental in forming the joint **Meretz* list with **Mapam* and **Shinui* before the 13th Knesset elections in 1992. The list won 12 seats of which six were held by the CRM, and joined the coalition formed by Yitzḥak *Rabin in July 1992. *Meretz* received at first three ministerial positions, and CRM leader Shulamit *Aloni was appointed Minister of Education and Culture, while another member of the CRM, Ran Cohen, was appointed Deputy Minister of Housing and Construction. In December 1992, Yossi *Sarid was appointed Minister of the Environment. (M.H.)

*** Cohen, Geula** In the 12th Knesset Cohen was a member of the Foreign Affairs and Security Committee, and became involved in the battle for the release of Jonathan Pollard (See: *Pollard Affair).

In the government formed by Yitzḥak *Shamir in June 1990 Cohen was appointed Deputy Minister for Science and Technology and an ex officio member of the Ministerial Committee for Immigration and Absorption, and was active over the issue of immigration and absorption of the Ethiopian Jews of Israel.

Cohen resigned her government post in November, 1991, in protest against the *Madrid Conference. Following the electoral failure of *Teḥiyah* in the 13th Knesset elections, Cohen found herself outside the Knesset. In November, 1992, she announced her return to the *Likud*, on whose list her son, Tzaḥi Hanegbi, has been a Knesset member since 1988. (I.M.)

*** Defense Policy** Following the trauma of the Lebanese War - an initiated war which failed to take the political constraints to the use of force into account - Israel returned to a more defensive political-strategic approach, combined with an offensive operational approach. The establishment of the Security Zone in Southern Lebanon on the basis of an "active defense" doctrine, was in full accord with this approach. (See: *Lebanon and Israel).

Though in 1990 Chief of Staff Dan Shomron returned to the formula of "preemptive counter-attack," which was first coined by Yigal *Allon, today the preemptive attack is not to be found in the declaratory level of Israel's security approach. Nevertheless, the IDF is called upon to maintain a capability to perform a preemptive attack if required to do so.

During the *Gulf War political constraints forced Israel to avoid retaliating after the Israeli hinterland had been attacked by Iraqi Scuds (and there were many who argued in Israel that the IDF was consequently in danger of losing its deterrence capability). Israel was also to forego the principle of self-reliance on the decision-taking level, when it accepted American manned PAC 2 Patriot batteries, and an undertaking by the United States that it would lift the missile threat on Israel in return for Israel abstaining from a reaction against Iraq. Nevertheless, the Gulf War did not shake Israel's basic political-strategic approach.

As a result of continuous publications regarding Israel's nuclear capability, and especially the Vanunu Affair at the end of 1986 (Mordechai Vanunu had worked as a technician at the nuclear reactor in Dimona, and divulged what were allegedly Israeli nuclear secrets to the *London Times*. He was kidnapped by the **Mossad* from Italy in November, and brought to trial in Israel), Israel continues to enjoy a credible nuclear deterrence without giving up its policy of vagueness regarding its true nuclear capability. It is not clear whether Israel has a clearly formulated approach regarding the integrated use of conventional with nuclear forces, or whether it has defined the existential threat which will justify the use of nuclear weapons.

Changes in Israel's overall security approach might soon be unavoidable, as a result of the rapid changes in the region, which have ramifications on the strategic, operative and even tactical levels. The changes in the international system following the collapse of the Soviet Union and their ramifications on the regional arena; the development of the political process which opened with the *Madrid Conference in October 1991, and its results; the non-conventional arms race, which could be accelerated should the political process fail or be curbed within the framework of an arms control agreement - all these will fundamentally change Israel's strategic environment, and will require suitable answers. Changes in the Israeli society, the undermining of the national consensus even in the security sphere, and the pressure to cut expenditures on defense, are also certain to have an effect. On the operative level of the approach, the nature of the future battlefield and the constraints which will be placed on movement and maneuverability in battle, will require a reconsideration of the relationship between defensive and offensive battles, with greater emphasis placed on the former which will have to be based on greater fire power. (Mi.B.)

Degel Hatorah An Ashkenazi *ḥaredi* party. On the eve of the elections to the 12th Knesset in 1988, as a result of the rapprochement between **Agudat Yisrael* and **Ḥabbad*, Rabbi Elazar Menaḥem *Shach, formed a new list. The list competed with *Agudat Yisrael* for the votes of the Ashkenazi *ḥaredi* population, in an extremely violent election campaign.

The *Degel Hatorah* Knesset list won two seats in the 12th Knesset. It joined the *National Unity Government formed by Yitzḥak *Shamir in December 1988 and the narrow government formed by him in June 1990, with both its Knesset members being appointed deputy ministers.

In the elections to the 13th Knesset *Degel Hatorah* ran within the framework of **Yahadut Hatorah Hame'uḥedet*, and received one Knesset seat only. Even though *Degel Hatorah* is now part of the **Yahadut Hatorah*, it continues to maintain its own *Mo'etzet Gdolei Hatorah* (Council of Torah Scholars) and institutions. (M.H.)

***Der'i, Arye** Political leader of **Shass*. Born in Morocco in 1959, Der'i immigrated to Israel with his family in 1968. He was educated at the Ashkenazi ultra-religious Porath Yosef yeshiva and later at the Hebron yeshiva in Jerusalem. Der'i was instrumental in getting his spiritual mentor Rabbi Ovadia *Yosef to form *Shass* in 1984 with the blessing of Rabbi Elazar Menaḥem *Shach.

The following year, as Secretary General of *Shass*, Der'i created the movement's education network, *El Hama'ayan*, which by 1992 had 6,000 pupils all over the country. In 1986 he was appointed by Minister of the Interior Rabbi Yitzḥak *Peretz to be Director General of his Ministry.

In the government formed in December 1988, the 29 year old Der'i was appointed Minister of the Interior. He soon impressed the public with his swift and decisive treatment of thorny issues. Der'i helped to bring down the *National Unity Government on March 15, 1990 by ensuring that five of the six *Shass* Knesset members would be absent from the plenary when the vote was taken. However, due to strong opposition on the part of Rabbi Shach and of *Shass's* constituency, *Shass* finally joined the narrow government led by Yitzḥak *Shamir on June 11.

It was at the time of the government crisis that a police investigation against Der'i was opened. The investigation involved alleged misallocations of funds - some concerning *Shass* institutions and public figures, and others personal. Since Der'i and the other persons involved chose to remain silent, by the end of 1992 the investigation was not yet completed. Der'i ran for the 13th Knesset at the head of the *Shass* list. He had declared before the elections that *Shass* would enter a coalition headed by the *Likud*. However, *Shass* was the only religious party to join Yitzḥak *Rabin's government on July 13, and Der'i remained Minister of the Interior. At Rabin's request he deposited a letter in which he promised to "suspend" himself from the government should the police decide to prosecute him.

***Druze** In 1987 the Israeli government declared the status of the Druze settlements equal to those of the development towns. However, the decision was never implemented, adding to the feelings of frustration felt by the Druze community due to the low standard of education, poor social services, and lack of economic enterprises within the Druze towns and villages. It is against this background that the "Druze Initiative Committee" - which is opposed to the enlistment of Druze youths to the *IDF, emphasizes the Arabness of the community, and maintains close contacts with Palestinian nationalist organizations in the territories - has increased its activities. Nevertheless, the majority of Israeli Druze still consider themselves an integral part of the State of Israel, and the "bond of blood," is not just an empty slogan.

The situation of the 16,000 Druze who live in the *Golan Heights is more ambivalent. Part of their population never accepted the annexation of the Golan Heights to Israel, and many are looking forward to it's return to Syrian sovereignty. However, following the occupation of Kuwait by Iraq and during the *Gulf War, there was widespread support among the Druze for Saddam Ḥussein.

No Druze was elected to the 12th Knesset, though by force of a rotation agreement in **Ḥadash*, the Druze poet, Moḥammed Naf'a, entered the Knesset in 1990, and another Druze, Salaḥ Tarif, joined the *Labor faction on the eve of the elections to the 13th Knesset. Two Druze were elected to the 13th Knesset: Tarif on the Labor list and Assad Assad on the **Likud* list. (G.F.)

Eastern Europe and Israel All the East European countries, except Albania, recognized Israel after its establishment in May 1948. During the 1948/9 *War of Independence, Israel's only official and substantial source of arms was Czechoslovakia. These arm supplies had the approval of the Soviet Union and continued well into the 1950s. In Poland the **Haganah* ran a military training camp for 1,500 young Jews before the *proclamation of independence, and after independence shipments of wheat were brought from that country.

Israel's main concern vis-à-vis the East European countries in the first years of its existence was to bring *Holocaust survivors to the country.

In general, the relations between Israel and the East European countries until 1967 - when all except *Romania broke off diplomatic relations following the *Six Day War - involved mostly economic relations. Relations with Yugoslavia, until the Bandung Conference of the Nonaligned states in 1955, were most cordial, and in 1951 Yugoslavia even voted in the Security Council in favor of a resolution calling for free navigation for all states through the *Suez Canal. But due to President Tito's close relations with Gamal Abdul Nasser of Egypt, the Yugoslav reaction to the *Sinai Campaign was extremely hostile to Israel.

In the case of Bulgaria there was the event involving an El-Al passenger plane which was shot down by the

Bulgarians in August 1955. All the passengers were killed. Relations with Czechoslovakia were strongly affected by the infamous trial in 1952 of Rudolf Slansky, the Jewish Secretary General of the Communist Party, who was accused with another 13 persons (10 of them Jews) of "conspiring against the state." Two Israelis were tried as well, and received long prison sentences, the Israeli chargé d'affaires was declared *persona non grata*, while Slansky himself was executed.

Relations with Poland were the most complicated, because of the cooperation (even if passive) of many Poles with the extermination of Jews during World War II. One of the first Israeli diplomatic missions abroad was established in Warsaw. Relations cooled down in the early 1950s, but the rise of Gomulka to power in 1956 led to a liberalization of the Polish attitude towards the Jews who for a certain period were allowed to leave Poland. However, nine months later diplomatic relations were severed. Following student riots in Warsaw and the attempt to oust Gomulka from power in March 1968, there was an outburst of anti-Semitism in Poland, which was encouraged by the Polish government. Nevertheless, those Jews who wished to depart for Israel were allowed to do so.

As a result of the political changes in the Soviet Union after 1986 the East European countries showed an interest in improving relations with Israel - not least of all because they hoped that with Israel's help it would be easier to have access to Washington. Poland was the first of the East European countries which exchanged interest offices with Israel at the end of 1986. In March 1988 the official paper of the Communist Party in Poland, the *Tribuna Ludo* published an article which reassessed the anti-Semitic outburst of 1968. The following month 350 Israeli youths marched from Auschwitz to Birkenau (the first of many such marches), accompanied by three Israeli ministers and several Knesset members in commemoration of the 45th anniversary of the uprising in the Warsaw Ghetto. Deputy Prime Minister and Minister of Education and Culture Yitzḥak *Navon was received by the Polish Minister of Culture, despite the protests of the *PLO representative in Warsaw.

The first East European country to renew full diplomatic relations with Israel was Hungary, in September 1989. Earlier that year direct air links were established between Israel with Hungary and Poland. At the end of December 1989 Israel sent a planeload of medical supplies to Romania, following the anti-Ceaucescu revolution in that country. Although Ceaucescu had maintained excellent relations with Israel throughout the period when the other Communist countries had broken theirs. Stories started to be told about the heavy financial price payed by Israel to Romania to enable Jews to continue to depart for Israel during Ceaucescu's regime.

Full relations were established with Poland and Czechoslovakia in February 1990, with Bulgaria in May, and with Yugoslavia in September 1991. Top level visits by East European leaders in Israel and Israeli leaders in Eastern Europe became commonplace. Of the visits which are most noteworthy was a visit to Israel in April, 1990 by the new Czech President Vaclav Havel - the first East European president to visit Israel. Polish President Lech Valesa visited Israel in May, 1991. During a speech in the Knesset, Valesa diverged from the written text and stated "Here I beg your pardon and forgiveness." During the campaign for the election of the Polish president, Valesa had made some statements which were regarded in Israel as anti-Semitic, and the issue came up during his visit to Israel. In general, the persistence of "anti-Semitism without Jews" in Poland is repeatedly raised in all formal talks between Poland and Israel, as does the issue of the Carmelite monastery which was established in 1984 by nuns in one of the buildings in the concentration camp of Auschwitz, and which the Jews find extremely offensive. Despite the intervention of the Pope and many Polish promises, at the end of 1992 the monastery had not yet been removed.

Since relations with Yugoslavia were reestablished at a time when it was disintegrating, the Yugoslav ambassador designate was not able to present his credentials to the President. Israel recognized Slovenian and Croatian independence, and supported the acceptance of Bosnia Herzegovina, to which it sent humanitarian aid, as a member of the United Nations. Due to Croatia's pro-Nazi past during World War II, the cooperation of Croatians in the extermination of Jews, and certain anti-Semitic remarks expressed by the Croatian president in a book published in 1989, Israel is averse to establishing relations with it unless a formal Croatian statement condemns these acts.

In addition to economic relations which have increased substantially since the end of the 1980s, it was reported in November 1992 that Israel had sold East European states $100 million worth of arms. (See separate entry for the *Soviet Union and Israel, and *Soviet Union, former republics of, and Israel.)

*** Eban, Abba** In 1988 Eban failed to be elected, in primaries held in the Labor Party Central Committee, to the Labor list to the 12th Knesset. He retired from politics and has been concentrating most of his time preparing and moderating a series of TV programs in the United States on the Jewish heritage and the history of the State of Israel.

* Economic Policy

1986-89 - LOW INFLATION AND ECONOMIC STAGNATION Though he had originally voted against the 1985 Economic Stabilization Plan (ESP), Moshe Nissim adopted it when he was Minister of Finance in April 1986. Following the appointment of Prof. Michael Bruno as *governor of the Bank of Israel in 1986, the Ministry of Finance and Bank of Israel cooperated to maintain the relatively low rate of inflation (around 20 percent) achieved by the ESP, while attempting to bring it down to a one digit figure. This required strict demand management, involving tight fiscal and restrictive monetary policies in order to maintain the exchange rate peg.

In 1986 government expenditure was cut by 2 percent, thanks to a 10 percent cut in domestic defense expenditure. However, what had been gained through restraint on government consumption expenditures, was cancelled out by a leap in transfer payments in 1986 and 1987. To avoid deficit financing, tax absorption was raised to an all-time high of 50 percent of GDP in these two years. The deficit remained within strict limits in 1988 as well, making it possible to maintain a highly restrictive monetary policy with high interest rates, which in turn maintained discipline in the markets for goods, services and foreign exchange.

The long spell of high real interest rates discouraged investment and stifled growth. A short-lived rise in the rate of growth to 5.9 percent in 1987 was driven by consumption. However, investment remained in the doldrums, and in 1987 didn't even recover its 1984, pre-ESP level. An agreement reached between the government, the employers and the **Histadrut* in 1985 for a real reduction in wages, greatly contributed to the decrease in the rate of inflation. However, as of the last quarter of 1986 the trend in wages - especially in the business sector - changed course and began rising again at a rapid pace. Since productivity did not rise at the same rate, this trend, which continued in 1987-88, resulted in a fall in profitability in the export industries. Thus, Shimon *Peres, who replaced Nissim in the government formed in December 1988, was forced to adjust the nominal rate of the exchange rate soon after becoming Minister of Finance. Though he and the Bank of Israel were more reluctant to accommodate the wage push by means of devaluations, the relatively low annual inflation rate of 20 percent in 1987 and 1988 still resulted in speculation and substantial loss in reserves.

The dramatic slowdown in the rate of inflation soon uncovered several structural imbalances in the economy. Among the sectors where this was most marked was the agricultural sector (especially the *kibbutzim and **moshavim*) which for decades had got used to subsidized inputs and price supports for many products. The construction industry which had enjoyed subsidized "directed" credit, had been in the doldrums for years due to the very low immigration rate in the 1980s, and in 1987 Solel Boneh, the *Histadrut's* flagship in the field of construction, collapsed. Many manufacturing industries, and especially Koor Industries - (the *Histadrut*'s industrial conglomerate) were affected by the slowdown in price inflation and the squeeze of rising wages. The structural weakness of these sectors was revealed when the government, under the restrictive monetary policies of the ESP, started to phase out subsidized inputs, price supports and subsidized directed credit, and changed the interest regime. Due to lopsided financial structures, involving excessive indebtedness and high equity ratios, Koor and Solel Boneh found themselves in deep financial trouble.

The construction industry picked up as a result of the crash building program following the wave of immigrants from the Soviet Union which began toward the end of 1989. However, the other two troubled sectors required the assistance of the government to reach financial arrangements with the banks, involving the cancellation of some debts, the recycling of the rest, the infusion of public sector finance to the agricultural sector, and the provision of government guaranteed collateral to Koor. In the case of Koor assistance was afforded only after the conglomerate had cut its labor force from 22,000 to 16,000, closed down unprofitable enterprises and sold several profitable ones. Despite ideological reservations, even Yitzḥak *Moda'i, who returned to the Ministry of Finance in June 1990, supported this move because he realized that the collapse of the Israeli agricultural settlements and of Koor would have a harmful effect on the economy as a whole.

Tackling the wages-productivity conundrum was a necessary condition for an attempt to push the inflation rate further down into the single digit range. Restructuring of the economy required placing it as a top priority item on the government agenda. However, while the Labor Party was not inclined to clash with the *Histadrut* over the wages-productivity issue, Yitzḥak *Shamir, as Prime Minister, gave all economic issues low priority. The result was that neither issue was dealt with by the successive National Unity Governments, while after the breakup of the last such government in March 1990, Shamir, now heading a narrow right-wing-religious government, was averse to introduce any measures which were liable to have a negative effect on the *Likud*'s prospects in the 1992 elections. Nevertheless, Shamir's two Ministers of Finance - Nissim and Moda'i - were given a free hand to implement the policies required to keep inflation down at their relatively low rate. In cooperation with the Bank of Israel the Ministry of Finance succeeded in holding the line through 1991, by continuing the tight fiscal policy for most of the time, and a highly restrictive monetary policy which kept interest rates at a very high plateau. In this way they managed to neutralize the effects of the wage push. The combination of high interest rates and a significant wage push raised unemployment to 8.9 percent in 1989 - the highest level in almost 25 years. A sustainable growth pattern failed to materialize.

1990–92 THE CHALLENGE OF IMMIGRANT ABSORPTION AND RENEWED GROWTH. The wave of mass immigration from the Soviet Union, (See: *aliyah*) created new challenges and incentives for the Israeli economy. The model adopted for the first stage of immigrant absorption was that of "direct absorption," which gave the newcomers the freedom to choose their place of residence upon arrival. Immigrants were provided with an initial monthly cash grant to see them through the first six months in the country. Free health and old age insurance, and basic tuition in Hebrew, Judaism and Zionism were also included in the absorption basket. The immediate housing requirements were filled by bringing tens of thousands of empty apartments into the rental market: with the help of tax incentives and a steep rise in rents, a crash building program for housing units was unavoidable. Such a program, involving massive direct government involvement in the housing market (but not in the actual building process), started to be implemented toward the end of 1990. Private and public contractors were encouraged to build. They were given government purchase guarantees for units that could not be sold. To encourage demand, immigrants and young Israeli couples were offered long-term mortgages at low real interest rates for Israeli residents, and zero real rates for the newcomers.

The immediate absorption of the immigrants required a major increase in the resources at the disposal of the economy. The only two sources available for this purpose were an inflow of real resources from abroad by means of a substantial increase of the import surplus, and the productive capacity of the economy. An increase of imports by 25 percent generated an increase of close to 100 percent in the import surplus, providing a significant fraction of the required resources. The second source was the rise in output in 1990–91. This was induced by the leap in aggregate demand generated by immigrant spending and the housing projects, and was made possible by underutilized capacity and the availability of labor. In the building industry this resulted from the crash building program.

GDP in 1990 and through 1992 grew at annual rates of over 5 percent, which were significantly above the average of the 1980s. In absolute terms employment grew rapidly as well, and by 1992 the number of persons employed rose by 10 percent compared to 1989. However, the unemployment rate rose to over 10 percent in 1991-92, as more and more immigrants were completing the six month initial absorption period and moved into the labor force. The increase in the demand for social and welfare services was financed through greater budgetary allocations by the central government and local authorities, and required a corresponding increase in tax revenues. A fraction of this increase was generated by growth itself. An additional increase in revenue was made possible by an "immigration surtax." However, with a tax burden of about 45 percent of GDP, there are limits to which higher tax rates can be resorted to. Since the budget deficit which resurfaced in 1989 had reached by 1992 a level which if further increased could endanger the hard-won relative price stability, the government had no other domestic option but to reconsider its priorities in budgetary allocations. Thus, economic priorities became a major issue in the June 1992 elections. The Labor-led government which came to power in July introduced at least one change in the priorities when it drastically reduced the expenditures for settlement activities in the *administered territories. Despite all efforts, the absorption feat could not be accomplished without resort to foreign resources. The leap in the import surplus to $7 billion (up by $3 billion) indicates the order of magnitude of the additional finance required. The Jewish communities abroad increased their contributions by 60 percent in the two years ending in 1991 to $1.4 billion, and the inflow of funds from the Independence Bond drive rose as well. But this still left a large deficit. Since there was no chance of getting the US Administration to increase its aid to Israel above the $3 billion already being provided, and since Israel's credit rating in the international capital markets was not sufficiently high to enable it to borrow at low interest rates approximating the relatively low rates available to the US government, the *Likud* government chose to request a $10 billion US loan guarantee for credits to be drawn over a five year period. However, the guarantees, first requested early in 1991, were finally approved by Congress on October 8, 1992, after the new Labor government froze most of the settlement activities in the administered territories (See: *United States and Israel)

The persistent increase in real wages was somewhat curtailed in 1989 as unemployment rose. This trend was accelerated in 1990 and 1991 and generated a trend of falling labor cost per unit of product, which in 1992 helped bring the rate of inflation down - after more than two decades -to a single digit figure. If maintained, the low inflation rate will enable a certain relaxation in the monetary policy and lower interest rates. This would increase profitability, thus generating a rise in private investment and economic growth.

However, in order to continue the downward trend in the inflation rate, a strict fiscal policy will have to be maintained, and the government will have to resist strong populist-inspired pressure to increase direct government expenditure on job creation and welfare. (H.B.)

*** Egypt and Israel** While Egypt continued to stress its adherence to the peace with Israel, it emphasized that normal relations could not develop as long as the Palestinian question remained unresolved. The peace between the two countries involved a one-way flow of tourists from Israel to Egypt and low-level agricultural and commercial cooperation.

Israeli Foreign Minister Shimon *Peres visited Cairo in February 1987, and in July again met President Ḥosni Mubarak in Geneva. Egyptian Foreign Minister Abd al-Majid visited Israel soon thereafter. The main subject discussed at these meetings was the convening of an *international conference. Egypt, favored Palestinian participation in such a conference within the framework of a Jordanian-Palestinian delegation. The rejection by the **Likud* half of the *National Unity Government of the *London Agreement reached between King Ḥussein and Peres in April 1987, was extremely disappointing to Egypt, and the outbreak of the *intifada* in December 1987 caused a further deterioration in Egyptian-Israeli relations.

In 1988 the Egyptian position in the Arab world improved dramatically, and Egypt was able to play a constructive role in the various peace proposals which followed each other in close succession, starting with a five-point proposal presented by Mubarak himself in January 1988 which was rejected by Israel. Mubarak viewed the peace plan of Secretary of State George Shultz (see: *Shultz Plan) favorably because it sidetracked the autonomy framework as proposed in the *Camp David Accords, which he considered outdated. The Egyptians tried to convince *PLO leader Yasser Arafat to enable a Palestinian delegation, made up of Palestinians not formally identified as PLO members, to meet with Shultz, but at this stage Arafat refused. The Egyptians were also urging the PLO to accept UN General Assembly Resolution 181 (the 1947 *partition plan), which the Palestinian organization did within the framework of its proclamation of Palestinian independence on November 15, 1988.

The return of *Tab'a to Egyptian sovereignty on March 15, 1989, rid Egyptian-Israeli relations of an irritant, as did the ruling by an Egyptian tribunal in January 1990 on the issue of compensation to the families of the Israeli victims shot by an Egyptian soldier at Ras Burqa in October 1985. In 1989 several Israeli ministers visited Egypt, but the relations remained cool, and Mubarak consistently refused to meet with Prime Minister Yitzḥak *Shamir, whom he viewed as an obstacle to peace. There were also several border incidents between the two countries in this period.

In May 1989 Egypt was readmitted to the Arab League, and soon not only did it renew diplomatic relations with Syria and Libya (it had renewed relations with the other Arab states the previous year), but the Arab League offices returned to Cairo. Though his initial reaction to the *Shamir-Rabin peace initiative of May 14 was reserved, Mubarak started to promote the idea of a meeting between Israeli and Palestinian delegations in Cairo to discuss Israel's plan. The Mubarak ten points, made public on September 19, one day after a brief visit by Minister of Defense Yitzḥak *Rabin to Cairo, were carefully drafted to take Israeli sensitivities into account. While the *Israel Labor Party welcomed Mubarak's initiative, the **Likud* reaction was negative. The National Unity Government fell over this issue, and its fall put an end to the Israeli plan and the initiatives connected with it.

Following the formation of the *Likud*-led government in June 1990, Egyptian-Israeli relations deteriorated to what has been termed an "angry peace." The wave of Jewish immigration from the Soviet Union, and a statement by Shamir to the effect that there was need for a large Israel to absorb the large number of immigrants, provoked Egyptian reactions. At the same time an attack by Palestinians on an Israeli tourist bus 62 kilometers east of Cairo, resulting in nine Israelis and two Egyptians killed, marred one of the few remaining positive features of the Egyptian-Israeli peace - namely Israeli tourism to Egypt. However, even though Egypt continued to react strongly to events in Jerusalem and the *occupied territories, its relations with the PLO deteriorated as well, following the decision of its leaders to side with Iraq in the *Gulf War.

The situation created by the Gulf War - namely the fact that Egypt and Israel found themselves politically on the same side of the conflict together with several other central Arab states, and Israel's restraint in face of numerous Scud attacks on her territory - relieved some of the tension in Egyptian-Israeli relations. However, there was no basic change in Egypt's attitude, and it continued to doubt whether Shamir was capable of participating in a real peace process. Egypt strongly supported the initiative of Secretary of State James Baker. However, within the context of Baker's shuttle diplomacy and the direct contacts which the Americans now had with most of the Arab parties concerned, Egypt was no longer at the center of the stage.

A strange affair, which erupted in February 1992, involving an Israeli Arab family and a Jewish furniture tradesman accused of spying for Israel, once again raised tensions, until the four persons involved were released by the Egyptians in May. The affair demonstrated the gullibility of the Egyptian public regarding Israeli spy stories spread by opposition elements in Egypt.

The formation of a new government in Israel on July 13, 1992, followed by a brief but high-profile visit by Prime Minister Yitzḥak Rabin to Cairo eight days later, significantly changed the atmosphere in Egyptian-Israeli relations. Mubarak, tried to convince him that President Ḥafez al-Assad of Syria was seeking peace and that Israel should not neglect Syria. The change in atmosphere in Egyptian-Israeli relations was demonstrated when during a visit to Cairo in November 1992 by Foreign Minister Peres, a group of mostly left-wing intellectuals, who had been opposed to the Egyptian-Israeli peace treaty and had previously refused to meet any Israeli personalities, met with him. A vast improvement was also noticeable in the way the Egyptian media dealt with Israel and the Jews. However, full normalization between the two countries can only be expected after a satisfactory conclusion of the peace talks.

*** Eitan, Rafael** Eitan broke away from the *Teḥiyah* in 1987 and ran at the head of **Tzomet* in the elections to the 12th Knesset. *Tzomet* won two Knesset seats. In the government formed in June 1990 he was appointed Minister of Agriculture gaining popularity by his simple ways. Eitan's popularity grew when he decided to leave the government in December 1991 after the **Likud* reneged on its undertaking to *Tzomet* to let its members vote freely on the law for direct election of the prime minister (See: *Prime Minister, direct election of).

In the elections to the 13th Knesset, *Tzomet* won eight seats, but Eitan preferred to stay out of Yitzḥak Rabin's government for both personal and ideological reasons. In the opposition Eitan became one of the most outspoken opponents of the government's settlement freeze and peace policies.

*** Elections to the Knesset** In the elections to the 12th Knesset in 1988, the power of the two large parties, the **Likud* and the *Israel Labor Party, continued to decline, after reaching a peak in 1981. The *Likud* emerged as the largest party, but received only 40 Knesset seats. Together with its satellite parties (the **Teḥiyah*, **Tzomet* and **Moledet*) it commanded 47. However, the religious parties managed to increase their representation from 13 in the previous two Knessets to 18 so that the right-wing parties and religious parties together commanded a majority of 65 seats.

The Israel Labor Party lost 5 seats and emerged with only 39. Together with its satellite parties (the *Civil Rights Movement, **Mapam* and **Shinui*) it had 49 seats only - down from 54 in the previous Knesset. The predominantly Arab parties (**Ḥadash*, *Progressive List for Peace and the *Arab Democratic Party) received 6 seats. Under the circumstances it seemed only natural that the *Likud* should form a narrow government, but instead a new *National Unity Government was formed, with the *Likud* enjoying preferential status. The *Likud* chose this course because Jewish circles from abroad exerted pressure on it not to give in to the demand of the religious parties to amend the *Law of Return, and because a narrow government would have created difficulties in the *Likud* regarding the distribution of certain portfolios. The *Likud* also sought to neutralize Labor's more dovish tendencies and in this way prevent a change in the American position toward the *Palestine Liberation Organization.

The National Unity Government survived until March 15, 1990, when it was brought down by a vote of no confidence, following which Yitzḥak *Shamir formed a narrow government with the right-wing and religious parties. In the 1988 elections five seats worth of votes moved from the left to the right - especially from Labor to the *Likud*, and a similar shift of votes occurred from the *Likud* to the ultra-religious parties which invested great efforts in reorganizing themselves. Although the *Likud* received less seats in 1988 than in 1984 its popularity increased due to the consolidation of Shamir's leadership, the renewed legitimization which the *Likud* gained in the course of its four years in government with Labor, and the relative lack of popularity of Labor leader Shimon *Peres. In the 1992 elections Labor managed, for the first time since the 1977 *upheaval, to regain the pivotal point and control the blocking majority with the support of Arab voters. Labor changed its image, its name (from the Israel Labor Party to Labor) and its leader. The number of seats increased back to 44 while its satellite parties, now united into a single list called **Meretz*, increased their strength from 10 to 12. Together with the predominantly Arab parties which received 5 seats Labor, under Yitzḥak *Rabin's leadership, now commanded 61 seats. However, Labor did not form a coalition with the Arab parties but with *Meretz* and the ultra-religious party *Shass*. The *Likud* was badly beaten, receiving only 32 seats. Of the *Likud*'s satellites the *Teḥiyah* vanished. While *Moledet* received 3 seats (only one seat more than in the 1988 elections), *Tzomet*, with a reputation for being a "clean" party, rose from 2 to 8. The religious camp went down from 18 to 16 seats, but didn't do as badly as expected due to internal rivalries, police investigations (in the case of **Shass*) and the decision of **Ḥabbad* not to support any of the parties. *Yaḥadut Ḥatorah Hameuḥedet* nevertheless won only 4 seats, compared to the 8 held by its four component *ḥaredi* parties in the 12th Knesset. Despite its inclination to join a *Likud* led government *Shass* joined Rabin's coalition immediately. The *National Religious Party, whose platform since 1969 has never been less hawkish than that of the *Likud*, further emphasized its right-wing tendency in the 1992 elections and gained an additional seat, largely at the expense of the *Teḥiyah*. The NRP, which has been a member of all the Israeli governments (except for a few months at the beginning of Rabin's first government in 1974), was left out of the new coalition.

The election results reflected the changes that had taken place in the electorate, and a shift of votes. Nine percent of the voters in the 1992 elections were new immigrants who had arrived in the country after the 1988 elections, and about 10 percent of the voters were young people voting for the first time. Together they amounted to more than 20 Knesset members worth of new voters. One of the consequences of these additional new voters and of the lower birth-rate in the Arab sector was that for the first time since the establishment of the state the proportion of Arabs in the electorate hardly grew at all (from 12 percent to 12.1 percent).

When the possibility of early elections was first considered at the beginning of 1992 *Likud's* popularity had reached a peak following the success of the *Madrid Conference. However, in the following months support for the *Likud* declined sharply. This was due to three main factors. The first concerned the internal changes which took place in Labor, and especially the election of Rabin as its leader. The second was the personal rivalries and squabbles within the *Likud*. The third was disappointment with the *Likud's* policies, especially in the sphere of economic growth and the absorption of the new immigrants. About half the newly arrived immigrants voted for Labor and *Meretz*, not because they were closer to its political positions than to those of the *Likud*, but because of frustrations due to lack of employment and other absorption difficulties.

The voting rate among the Arab voters was lower than expected, and surprisingly over 50 percent of them voted for Jewish parties. (A.D.)

*** Eliav** (formerly Lifshitz)**, Arie Lova** Eliav was elected to the 12th Knesset on the *Labor list. However, he became increasingly disillusioned with political life and concentrated his efforts on a youth educational community which he founded at Nitzana on the Egyptian border in 1987. At the end of 1992 Eliav was one of three Labor candidates for Israel's 7th president.

Emunim Extra-parliamentary political movement which advocates the extension of Israeli sovereignty over Judea, Samaria and the Gaza Strip and rejects Israeli withdrawal from these territories. Most of its leaders are Ashkenazi rabbis who grew up in **Gush Emunim*, but the movement aims at reaching non-religious and Sephardi circles as well.

The formal foundation of the movement in September 1992, followed talks which began several months before the elections to the 13th Knesset on the leadership crisis of the right, and ways of drawing the public out of its indifference and mobilize it on the issue of *Eretz Yisrael*. The electoral defeat of the right-wing parties and the establishment of a left-of-center government hastened the foundation of a new movement to replace the moribund **Gush Emunim*. At its head stands Rabbi Binyamin (Benny) Elon. The new movement does not include some of the more radical members of *Gush Emunim*.

*** Ethiopian Jews** In November 1989 Ethiopia renewed of diplomatic relations with Israel. The immediate benefit Israel derived from this was that in 1990 the number of Ethiopian immigrants to Israel was almost equal to that in the five previous years, reaching 4,137. With the intensification of the civil war and famine in Ethiopia, the Joint Distribution Committee (an American Jewish welfare organization), together with the *Jewish Agency and the Israeli Foreign Ministry, opened welfare centers in Addis Ababa for Ethiopian Jews who were encouraged to make their way to the capital. In the meantime negotiations were carried out by an Israeli emissary, Uri Loubrani, with the Ethiopian ruler, Colonel Haile Mariam Mengistu, about the price for getting some 15,000 Jews out of Ethiopia. Israel agreed to pay 30 million dollars. On Friday, May 24, 1991, not long before the Mengistu regime finally collapsed, Israel sent planes to Addis Ababa to "pick up" the 15,000 Jews. The operation, carried out with great success, was called "Operation Solomon".

It was believed that following the experience gained in the course of Operation Moses in 1984-85 it would be possible to absorb the new arrivals more smoothly. Although the initial absorption process was successful, the following stages proved much more difficult. The immigrants were at first housed in hotels requisitioned throughout the country for the purpose. But the immigrants were unhappy in the hotels and pressed to be moved to caravan centers, on occasion moving in before the caravans were connected to the water, sewage and electricity systems. There were problems in the supply of services and suitable education facilities for the children who were automatically sent to national religious schools which were not always ready to receive them; employment was difficult to find; there were occasional clashes between the Ethiopians and new immigrants from the former republics of the Soviet Union. More problems arose due to the fact that the Chief Rabbinate in Israel refused to accept automatically the immigrants as Jews (in fact, there were some Falash Mura - Jews who had converted to Christianity - among the immigrants). The Rabbinate also refused to enable the spiritual leaders of the Ethiopian Jews - the *Kessim* - to perform marriages and other religious ceremonies for members of their community, insisting that they be retrained despite the advanced age of most of them.

Despite all the difficulties, Israel is continuing to bring to Israel those Ethiopian Jews who were unable to join Operation Solomon. Immigration from Ethiopia reaches several hundred a month. A major difficulty has emerged concerning the Falash Mura, whose number in Ethiopia is estimated at between 30,000 to 500,000, many of whom want to come to Israel. Israel is inclined to bring those who have relatives in the country, but the Ethiopian authorities are opposed to this.

*** European Community and Israel** The decision of the European Community Commission, published on December 31, 1986,to grant unilaterally the same privileges enjoyed by Israeli products to Palestinian products originating in the *administered territories, gave rise to some tension between Israel and the European Community. After months of negotiations Israel accepted the European Community decision for direct export of agricultural products from the *West Bank and *Gaza Strip to the European Community, after which the Council of Ministers approved on December 15, 1987 three additional protocols with Israel, including one long-overdue on Israeli agricultural exports following the entry of Spain and Portugal to the European Community. However, in an unprecedented move the European Parliament, on March 9, 1988, refused to approve the ratification of the protocols because of the Israeli repression of the **intifada*, and alleged obstruction of Palestinian exports. The protocols were finally ratified on October 12.

On January 18, 1990 the European Parliament once again applied temporary sanctions when it called on the Commission to freeze all financial allocations to scientific cooperation with Israel, in reaction to the use of force by the Israeli police against a *Peace Now demonstration in *Jerusalem. The allocations were only renewed in 1991. As 1992 approached , Israel sought membership in the European Economic Space. However, the European Community, which sees membership in this space as a channel towards full membership in the Community, was visibly unenthusiastic about the idea. At the end of 1992 talks were to open between Israel and the European Community about updating the 1975 Industrial Free Trade Area Agreement between the two. This was especially important to Israel which still purchases close to 50 percent of its imports in Europe, while selling to it just over 35 percent of its exports, with an annual trade deficit of close to 4 billion dollars (which approximates Israel's total trade deficit). Following the temporary expulsion of 415 **Ḥammas* and *Islamic Jihad activists from the territories to Lebanon, the European Community announced that the talks would be held only after the deportees were allowed to return.

The European Community began granting financial aid to the Palestinians in 1982 with a small annual sum of 3 million ECU. Following the *Gulf War, emergency aid amounting to 60 million ECU was decided upon. However, the Commission insisted that the distribution of this aid would be carried out by a European Community representative to be stationed in Jerusalem, to which Israel strongly objected. By the end of 1992 the problem had not yet been resolved.

Foreign Minister Shimon *Peres presented his plan for holding an *international conference as a preamble to direct talks between Israel and its neighbors, to the Council of Cooperation in Brussels in January 1987. The following month the Twelve reiterated their position that a negotiated solution of the *Arab-Israeli conflict should be based on the 1980 Venice Declaration, and any peace conference should be held under the auspices of the United Nations. In June 1991, as plans for the convention of a regional conference on peace in the Middle East progressed, Israeli Foreign Minister David *Levy met in Paris with the three foreign ministers representing the Council of Ministers. The two sides agreed that the Community would be allowed to participate in the conference as an observer, and in return Israel would be admitted into the European Economic Space. Though no progress was made on the latter issue, the European Community was present as an observer at the *Madrid Conference. It was agreed that the European Community would participate in the *multilateral talks following the Madrid Conference and that Europe would play a major role in the talks on Middle East economic cooperation to be held in Brussels. The government formed by Yitzḥak *Rabin in July 1992 also agreed to European participation in the arms control talks. (S.M.)

Federal Republic of Germany and Israel The reaction in Israel to the first state visit by an Israeli President, Ḥaim *Herzog, to the Federal Republic of Germany (FDR) in April 1987, reflected the persisting ambivalent feelings towards Germany. But side-by-side with the call not to forget the past there was the ever-present practical side of the relationship, manifested by a visit of Minister of Defense, Yitzḥak *Rabin, to Germany in September, 1988, which involved talks about Israeli arms sales to the *Bundeswehr*, and the purchase of submarines by the Israeli navy from Germany. The growing military cooperation between the two countries finally led to a visit by Israeli Chief of Staff Ehud Barak to Germany in April 1992 and a return visit by German Chief of Staff Klaus Naumann, in November. At the same time, there was growing concern in Israel about reports in January 1989, of German involvement in the construction of a factory for the production of chemical weapons in Libya. Later reports implicated German companies in similar activities in Iraq.

In January 1988 the World Jewish Congress opened talks with the German Democratic Republic (GDR) about restitution payments for the Jewish victims of the Nazis. Formerly the GDR had refused to admit any obligation to pay reparations because it rejected on principle responsibility for the acts of the Third Reich. Now it was still unwilling to accept responsibility, but agreed in principle to pay, though it claimed that it was financially unable to do so. This change in the position of the GDR opened the way for talks about the establishment of relations between the two states - a development which was cut short by the unexpectedly rapid reunification of Germany in 1990. Following reunification, the FRG denied having any obligation to make restitution payments on behalf of the former GDR.

Despite efforts by the West German chancellor in April 1990 to reassure Israel that it had no reason to fear a united Germany, there was an extremely uneasy feeling in Israel. However, as the Gulf crisis broke out, attention shifted to reactions in Germany against the American intervention in Iraq, and the role of German companies and scientists in the building of the Iraqi war machine. During a visit to Germany in October 1990, Minister of Defense Moshe *Arens requested German military aid for Israel. The German Government responded by allocating $530 million for the construction of two submarines in Kiel for the Israeli navy. On January 24, 1991 Foreign Minister Hans Dietricht Genscher arrived in Israel for a brief visit, to express Germany's solidarity with Israel and offer immediate material aid to the cities of Tel Aviv and Ramat Gan which had been hit by Scuds, and about $166 million in compensation for the damage caused Israel during the war. During the war Germany sent military and medical equipment, much of it relative to the possibility of a chemical attack on Israel.

Minister of Foreign Affairs David *Levy, visiting Germany in March, 1991, raised the issue of German loan guarantees, and other forms of aid for the absorption of new immigrants. However, Germany followed the American example and conditioned the granting of any assistance on a freeze of all settlement activities in the territories, and added a condition of its own: progress in the peace process. The new government which came to power in Israel in July 1992 finally decided that it would rather receive German assistance in the form of investment in research and development and economic projects. The change of government in Israel led to several acts of goodwill on Germany's part. One of them was the introduction of new legislation making it illegal for German companies to include articles in commercial agreements expressing compliance with or acceptance of the *Arab boycott. Following the anti-Semitic and xenophobic outbursts of the extreme right in Germany, towards the end of November 1992, both the Israeli government and the Knesset expressed to Germany their serious concern.

*** Foreign Policy** From the mid-1980s the issue of plans for bringing about peace in the Middle East became prominent in Israel's contacts with foreign countries.

However, in the period of the *National Unity Government of 1984-88, and especially following the *rotation in 1986, Israel's foreign policy suffered from a certain duality resulting from differences of opinion between Prime Minister (later Foreign Minister) Shimon *Peres and Foreign Minister (later Prime Minister) Yitzḥak *Shamir. In addition to differences regarding the nature and parameters of the desired permanent peace, the two differed over the process itself. While Peres was in favor of convening an *international conference as an opening to direct talks with the Arab states, Shamir opposed the conference idea *ab initio*. Both were active in promoting their point of view abroad - especially in the west European capitals. In this period Israel was also actively seeking foreign assistance to get the Soviet Union to open its gates to Jewish emigration and to bring about the release of Israeli military personnel taken hostage in Lebanon.

The outbreak of the **intifada* at the end of 1987, at first placed Israel on the defensive in its efforts to explain the Israeli position abroad, especially in view of the worldwide hostile media coverage. However, by May 1989, with Peres now in the Ministry of Finance, Prime Minister Shamir and Minister of Defense Yitzḥak *Rabin managed to formulate a joint peace initiative for an interim solution which both could agree to, which included the holding of elections in the administered territories (See: *Shamir-Rabin peace initiative). Until March 1990, when the government fell over disagreements between the **Likud* and Labor on the issue of talks with the *Palestinians about the government's elections plan, intense diplomatic activity evolved around this initiative.

The rapid changes in the Communist bloc and in the Soviet Union itself after 1986, followed by the disintegration of both, had a profound effect on Israel's situation in the international arena. After years of isolation, positive contacts took place with many states which had either broken off relations with Israel in 1967 and 1973 (the Communist bloc and African states) or had never established relations with it in the first place (such as *China and *India).

In many cases the countries involved sought the Israeli connection because they believed that Israel had easier access to Washington. Israel's policy of restraint during the *Gulf War, the glaring Iraqi menace to neighboring Arab states, Western interests and world peace, in addition to the lack of unity within the Arab world, had positive effects on Israel's international status as well. On December 16, 1991 the *United States was even able to bring about the cancellation of the shameful 1975 UN General Assembly Resolution 3379 which equated *Zionism with racism - a resolution against which Israel had struggled for the better part of 15 years. The *Madrid Conference, and progress in the peace process, at least on the procedural level, served as a convenient background for many states to renew or establish diplomatic relations with Israel. By mid-1992, there were more than 30 new embassies in Tel Aviv. The new wave of immigration to Israel, which began in the summer of 1989, and the need to find the resources with which to absorb over 400,000 new arrivals (See: **aliyah*), forced Israel to concentrate great efforts to obtain loan guarantees from friendly countries (especially the US) in order to contract loans on the international money markets.

Simultaneously, major efforts were made to improve Israel's status vis-à-vis the *European Community towards "Europe 1992" with the aim of the integration of the Israeli economy in that of Europe, to increase Israel's economic relations with the Far East, and to bring an end to the *Arab boycott against Israel. The change of government in Israel in July 1992, which brought Peres back to the Ministry of Foreign Affairs, and resulted in a settlement freeze in the territories as well as greater flexibility in the Israeli positions presented in the Washington talks, brought an immediate improvement in Israel's bilateral relations with the United States and West European countries.

*** France and Israel** In 1987 there were renewed talks of Franco-Israeli cooperation. However, French support for the *international conference idea, rejected by Prime Minister Yitzḥak *Shamir, as well as its justification of Franco-Iraqi friendship, and its call for the association of the Soviet Union in the peace process and for self-determination for the Palestinians, prevented a real improvement in relations.

Though President Ḥaim *Herzog paid France a state visit in October 1988, and Shamir paid an official visit in February 1989, Arafat was received in Paris in April and was met by Mitterand. Israeli protests about the meeting, elicited negative French reactions. On October 1990 French Foreign Minister Roland Dumas met Arafat in Tunis, bringing back with him proposals from Iraqi President Saddam Ḥussein on the Gulf crisis. The French inclination to link the Gulf crisis with the Arab-Israeli conflict was expressed by Mitterand soon thereafter in a meeting with Israeli Foreign Minister David *Levy. At this meeting Mitterand also expressed his support for the establishment of a Palestinian state, but reiterated his friendship for Israel and the Jews. Although France sent a contingent to fight in the *Gulf War, Franco-Israeli relations further deteriorated in January and February 1991, when Israel accused France of having helped Iraq develop its non-conventional capability and improve its Scud missiles, and France claimed that Israel was exaggerating the damage caused to it by the Iraqi Scuds. To add insult to injury, in February Roland Dumas stated that he supported UN General Assembly Resolution 181 of 1947 concerning the establishment of two states in Palestine. After two more meetings with Arafat, Dumas declared that he understood the Palestinian leader's decision to support Saddam Ḥussein since Israel had rejected his peace offerings. An additional irritant was added at the end of January, 1992, when PFLP (Palestinian Front for the Liberation of Palestine) leader Dr. George Ḥabash arrived in Paris for medical treatment, apparently with the full cooperation of senior French officials.

Relations started to improve again in the first half of 1992, following the *Madrid Conference. A marked change occurred upon *Labor's return to power in Israel in July. France now made major efforts to assume an active role in the peace process. At the end of October, the mixed Franco-Israeli Economic Committee convened after having failed to meet for three years, and in November President Mitterand arrived in Israel for what was described as an historic visit. In the course of this visit a series of economic and cultural agreements were signed, but politically the position of the two states remains far removed.

Front of the Ten Group of ten Palestinian organizations formed in Damascus in september 1992 to oppose actively the Palestinian participation in the peace process and the *autonomy plan. The ten included the Popular Front for the Liberation of Palestine (PFLP) headed by George Ḥabash, the Democratic Front for the Liberation of Palestine headed by Na'if Ḥawatmeh, and the Palestine Liberation Front headed by Abu Abbas - all three members of the *Palestine Liberation Organization; the Muslim fundamentalist groups **Ḥammas* and the Islamic Jihad - Palestine; and the non-religious rejectionist groups; the Popular struggle Front headed by Samir Gousha, the Revolutionary Communist Party headed by Arbi Awad, the Popular Front-the General Command headed by Aḥmed Jibril, A-Zaika - the Popular Liberation War Pioneers Organization, and the Palestine National Liberation Movement (which revolted against *Fataḥ*) headed by Abu Mussa.

*** Golan Heights** The prospects of peace with Syria (See: *Syria and Israel) reopened the debate in Israel as to whether it should return the Golan after its annexation in 1981. While the **Likud* is ideologically committed not to return any more territories to Arab sovereignty, it was reported at the time of the *Madrid Conference, that some of its leaders (including Yitzḥak *Shamir, Moshe *Arens and David *Levy) were not opposed to withdrawing from part of the Golan in return for peace. Following a bitter debate between doves and hawks, the *Israel Labor Party declared in its 1992 electoral platform, that while it favored a territorial compromise and the application of *Security Council Resolution 242 to all fronts in return for peace, it would insist that Israel maintain a military and settlement presence on the Golan. This was the position outlined by Prime Minister Yitzḥak *Rabin and at the bilateral talks with Syria in the Washington talks.

While both the **Takam* and **Hakibbutz Ha'artzi*, which have *kibbutzim on the Golan Heights, agree with Rabin's policy, many members of the kibbutzim on the Golan have reservations, and find themselves in agreement with the position of the right-wing parties on this issue. Their main reason against withdrawal is security. Most of the National Religious rabbis argue that Israel should not withdraw from the Golan Heights for religious reasons. However, two important ultra-religious rabbis - Ovadia *Yosef and former Ashkenazi Chief Rabbi Shmuel Goren - announced that the Golan is not part of *Eretz Yisrael* and may be given up in return for peace with Syria.

Governments of Israel

TWENTY-FIRST GOVERNMENT (10TH KNESSET)

September 13, 1948 - October 20, 1986

Prime Minister: Shimon *Peres.

Coalition members: *Alignment, **Likud*, *National Religious Party, **Agudat Yisrael*, **Shass*, **Morasha*, **Shinui*, **Ometz*. Knesset majority of 97.

The government resigned upon the implementation of the *rotation agreement between the Alignment and the *Likud*.

TWENTY-SECOND GOVERNMENT (11TH KNESSET)

October 20, 1986 - December 22, 1988

Prime Minister: Yitzḥak Shamir .

Coalition members: same as the Twenty-First Government. *Shinui* resigned on May 26, 1987, over the issues of the *peace process, the *religious *status quo* and the paralysis of the government.

TWENTY-THIRD GOVERNMENT (12TH KNESSET)

December 22, 1988 - June 11, 1990

Prime Minister: Yitzḥak Shamir.

Coalition members: *Likud*, Alignment, NRP, *Shass*, *Agudat Yisrael*, **Degel Hatorah*, Knesset majority of 97.

The Alignment left the government on March 15. The government was brought down by a vote of no confidence on March 15 but continued to serve as a transitional government until Shamir formed his new government.

TWENTY-FOURTH GOVERNMENT (13TH KNESSET)

June 11, 1990 - 13 July, 1992

Prime Minister: Yitzḥak Shamir

Coalition members: *Likud*, NRP, *Shass*, *Degel Hatorah*, *Party for Advancing the Zionist Idea, **Teḥiyah*, **Tzomet*, Yitzḥak Peretz (formerly *Shass*), Eliezer Mizraḥi (formerly *Agudat Yisrael*) and Efraim Gur (formerly Israel Labor Party). Supported by 61 MKs, including Avraham Verdiger of *Agudat Yisrael*. *Agudat Yisrael* joined the government on November 16, 1990, and **Moledet* joined on February 5, 1991, increasing the government's majority to 66. *Tzomet* left the government on December 31, 1991 over the issue of the direct election of the Prime Minister (See: *Prime Minister, direct election of). The *Teḥiyah* and *Moledet* left the government on January 21, 1992 over the *autonomy issue, leaving the coalition with 59 MKs only.

TWENTY-FIFTH GOVERNMENT (13TH KNESSET)
July 13, 1992 -
Prime Minister: Yitzḥak Rabin
Coalition members: *Labor, **Meretz, Shass*, Knesset majority of 62 coalition members, with the support of an additional 5 from **Ḥadash* and the *Arab Democratic Party.

*** Great Britain and Israel** In 1987, relations between Israel and Great Britain were cordial, largely because of the rapport between Minister for Foreign Affairs Shimon *Peres and Prime Minister Margaret Thatcher. The good relations were symbolized by a state visit of President Ḥaim *Herzog to Great Britain in December 1987.

However, at the same time, there were tensions between the two countries over several incidents: the abduction by the **Mossad* in November 1986 of Mordechai Vanunu, a former technician in the Israeli nuclear reactor in Dimona who disclosed Israeli nuclear secrets to the *London Times*, and several other irritating incidents involving the Israeli secret service. The outbreak of the **intifada* and Israel's iron fist reaction to it, created tensions on yet another level. In the course of a visit to Israel and the *administered territories in January 1988 British Under-Secretary for Foreign Affairs, David Mellor, insulted an Israeli officer in the Gaza Strip and spoke of the conditions in the Jebalya refugee camp as "an insult to the values of civilization." A 15 billion dollar arms deal between Britain and Saudi Arabia of which Britain had not informed Israel in advance, and a meeting in February 1989 by the new Under-Secretary for Foreign Affairs, William Waldergrave, with Yasser Arafat in Tunis were additional irritants. A visit by Prime Minister Yitzḥak Shamir to Britain at the end of May, in which he presented the new Israeli *peace initiative (See: *Shamir-Rabin peace initiative), did not improve the atmosphere.

A month before the outbreak of the *Gulf War˙ during another visit by Shamir in London, Prime Minister John Major reiterated several points previously made by his Foreign Secretary, Douglas Hurd, to the effect that while there should be no linkage between attempts to resolve the Gulf crisis and the convention of an international conference, Britain favored the convention of such a conference. Like Hurd he admonished Israel for its policy in the territories and its attitude towards the Palestinians. Shamir replied that Israel would not agree that others decide its fate and future.

Israeli restraint in the Gulf War and progress towards the opening of peace talks between Israel and its neighbors which followed, finally reduced the tension in British-Israeli relations, and Hurd's relations with David *Levy were more cordial than with Levy's predecessor, Moshe *Arens. However, it was only after the change of government in Israel in July 1992, that a real improvement in the relations was felt. Major reacted positively to several requests brought to London by Foreign Minister Shimon Peres in September, including an end to the British embargo on arms sales to, and arms purchases from Israel imposed during the *Lebanese War, an end to the ban of the British oil companies to sell oil from the North Sea to Israel, action through the *European Community to bring an end to the *Arab boycott of Israel, and Israel's integration into the European Economic Space.

Gulf War Following the invasion of Kuwait by Iraq on August 2, 1990, which resulted in a strong American reaction and the imposition of economic sanctions by the UN Security Council, Iraqi President Saddam Ḥussein started threatening to attack Israel, and on August 31 announced that Israel would be attacked with missiles. As a reaction to the Iraqi threats Israel decided, on October 1 to distribute gas masks to the Israeli population.

From the very start of the crisis *Palestine Liberation Organization leaders, including Yasser Arafat, declared their unreserved support for Saddam Ḥussein. While the Palestinian leaders were undoubtedly concerned about the fate of the 400,000 strong Palestinian community in Kuwait, the feeling in Israel was that this support proved the real metal of the Palestinians who were trying to convince the world that they were willing to reach an accommodation with Israel, but as soon as they found a strong, authoritarian Arab leader who threatened to destroy Israel, they supported him wholeheartedly.

As the American preparations for a possible military confrontation with Iraq got under way, and Washington started to build up an anti-Iraqi coalition including the United States, some of its European allies and several Arab states (including Saudi Arabia, Egypt and Syria), it was made clear to Israel that it was expected to maintain a low profile and let others do the job. Nevertheless, on November 30, Israel declared that it would react with force if attacked by Iraq.

Throughout the crisis, in the course of negotiations with Iraq about a peaceful withdrawal from Kuwait, the Iraqis called for a linkage between a resolution of the Kuwaiti problem on the one hand, and a withdrawal of Syria and Israel from Lebanese territory and of Israel from the *occupied territories on the other. In the summit conference between Presidents George Bush and Mikhail Gorbachev in Helsinki on September 8, the Soviets were inclined to accept the linkage while the Americans were opposed.

Iraq was attacked by the coalition forces on January 17, 1991. The following day Iraq aimed 8 Scud missiles against Israel. By the time the war ended on February 28, about 40 missiles had been launched at Israel. They were conventional missiles, and caused much material damage; many persons remained homeless, one person was killed, several died of heart attacks, and several hundred were wounded. The Iraqi attack on Israel was designed primarily to elicit an Israeli reaction which would lead to the Arab states fighting with the United States to leave the coalition. However, the Iraqis decided not to use non-conventional warheads against Israel for fear of an Israeli reaction in kind.

While Israel declared that the red lines, as far as it was concerned, were a non-conventional attack by the Iraqis, an attack which would result in a large number of fatalities or an Iraqi movement of land forces towards Israel through Jordan, there was a broad consensus in the country that the American request that Israel remain passive so as not to endanger the participation of the Arab states in the war against Iraq, be respected. There were, however, voices within political circles in Israel which called for Israeli action (these included the hawkish Ariel *Sharon and the dovish Ezer *Weizman), arguing that by remaining passive Israel was neutralizing its own deterring capability, and that Israeli forces could deal more effectively than the Americans with the Scud launchers in western Iraq. On at least three occasions Israeli fighters were on the runways ready for sorties against Iraq. As it were, Israel remained passive until the end of the war.

This was the first war in which Israel was attacked but didn't retaliate, and in which the civilian hinterland was the front. This experience, together with the almost nightly alerts for civilians to remain in sealed rooms and put on gas masks, caused a major trauma in Israel. On January 20 the first American-manned Patriot PAC-2 anti-missiles and their launchers arrived in Israel. The Netherlands also sent several Patriot missiles to help defend Israel. The fall of the Scuds in Israel, and the Israeli restraint, elicited much international sympathy and offers for material aid. Israel, in turn, demanded that all the Western companies which had helped Iraq construct its war machines and especially its non-conventional capability (especially those in Germany) be dealt with severely by their respective governments.

*** Gur, Mordechai** In the *National Unity Government formed in 1988 Gur was appointed Minister Without Portfolio. Following the 1988 elections, he considered running for the Labor leadership, but in the primaries held in February 1992 supported Yitzḥak *Rabin. In the government formed by Rabin in July, Gur was given the post of Deputy Minister of Defense.

*** Gush Emunim** The uncovering of the *Jewish Underground in 1984 caused a split within *Gush Emunim* between the movement's radical and more moderate members. The crisis became more acute in the aftermath of a violent raid of retaliation on the Arab town of Kalkilya by a group of *Gush Emunim* activists headed by Daniela Weiss, following the killing of a Jewish pregnant woman in a car attacked by a firebomb. The moderates in *Gush Emunim* felt that the retaliatory attack, which resulted in a clash with the army, was contrary to the spirit of the movement and politically counter-productive. An attempt by the moderates, including Rabbi Yoel Ben-Nun, Rabbi Menachem Fruman and Hanan Porath, to dislodge the radicals, headed by Rabbi Moshe *Levinger and Benny Katzover, failed.

Gush Emunim was not at first impressed with the gravity of the **intifada*, but the Beita incident in May 1988, in which a group of settlers provocatively walked through the Arab village, with the result that a Jewish girl and an Arab teenager were killed, taught *Gush Emunim* that it could not defy the army (which had not been informed of the field trip) without a public backlash. Against this background tension in the movement mounted, leading to its gradual paralysis, which even the massive settlement activity in *Judea and Samaria after June 1990 could not overcome.

The political cohesiveness of *Gush Emunim* weakened to such an extent that the leading figures could not agree to run in a single list for the 13th Knesset. The two lists most closely identified with the movement - the **Tehiya* and Rabbi Levinger's "Land of Israel - Torah of Israel" - both failed to pass the qualifying threshold. In the wake of the Labor victory the second generation leadership of *Gush Emunim*, headed by Rabbi Binyamin (Benny) Elon, decided to establish a new movement, **Emunim*.

Ḥabbad Hebrew acronym for *ḥochmah, binah, da'at* ("wisdom, insight, knowledge"). A *ḥassidic* stream in the *ḥaredi* community, founded in1786 in Byelorussia, which is led today by Rabbi Menaḥem Mendel Schneerson (the Lubawitcher Rebbe, from Brooklyn New York). Rabbi Schneerson is a controversial figure in *ḥaredi* circles because of his views and the fact that his education included studies at a secular university. The *Ḥabbad* movement is different from the other *ḥassidic* movements in that its members engage in missionary work among both religious and non-religious Jews all over the world, since they believe that only by spreading the *Ḥabbad* doctrine will full redemption come. The *Ḥabbad ḥassidim* believe that their rabbi, who was born in 1902 and has never visited Israel, will reveal himself as the messiah.

In Israel, as elsewhere, *Ḥabbad* struggles against what it views as assimilation and alienation from true Jewish identity" but its approach is conciliatory - not confrontational. Until some years ago its representatives were allowed to enter *IDF military bases and lecture to soldiers. Since, unlike most of the other *ḥaredi* movements *Ḥabbad* is a strong proponent of the *Greater Israel doctrine, it is paradoxically frequently viewed as a *Zionist movement - or at least not an anti-Zionist one like the other *ḥaredi* "courts".

Since the 1970s *Ḥabbad* has borne the banner for the amendment in the *Law of Return of the definition of who is a Jew, so that only someone considered a Jew under the *halacha* will be considered a Jew under the law. The only Israeli elections in which *Ḥabbad* participated actively were those to the 12th Knesset in 1988, in which it supported **Agudat Yisrael*, one of whose candidates, Rabbi Eliezer Mizraḥi, is a member of the *Ḥabbad* movement. Mizraḥi was one of two *Agudat Yisrael* MKs who managed at the last moment to foil the efforts by Shimon *Peres to form a Labor-led government in April 1990. Due to the illness of Rabbi Schneerson during the electoral campaign to the 13th Knesset, *Ḥabbad* did not play an active role in the elections.

The greatest opponents of *Ḥabbad* among the *ḥaredim* are the *Lita'im*. The personal, ideological and scholarly rivalry between Rabbi Schneerson and Rabbi Menachem Elazar *Shach frequently reaches extremes.

*** Ḥadash** Towards the end of the 11th Knesset the number of seats held by *Ḥadash* rose to five as MK Moḥammed Wattad left **Mapam* and joined *Ḥadash* against the background of the outbreak of the **intifada*. In the elections to the 12th Knesset, in which it competed for the Arab vote against the *Progressive List for Peace and the *Arab Democratic party, *Ḥadash* gained four seats. In the course of the 12th Knesset the three veteran leaders of the party - Tawfiq *Toubi, Meir Vilner and Tawfiq Ziad - gave up their seats to make room for younger members (including one Druze and one Jewish woman). The one MK who was not a member of the **Rakaḥ* component of *Ḥadash* - Charlie Bitton - broke off from *Ḥadash* to form his own faction.

In addition to demanding full equality for the Arab citizens of the state, *Ḥadash* continued to maintain close relations with the *Palestine Liberation Organization, to advocate the establishment of a Palestinian state, and to demand the "right of return" of those Palestinian *refugees who might wish to exercise it. While *Ḥadash* supported the *intifada* it did not advocate the participation of the *Israeli Arabs. Following the line from Moscow, *Ḥadash* condemned the Iraqi invasion of Kuwait and favored the linkage between the resolution of the Gulf crisis and that of the *Arab-Israeli conflict.

Ḥadash refused to consider joining a united Arab list to run in the 13th Knesset elections because it continued to view itself as a joint Arab-Jewish party. However, for the first time in its history the *Ḥadash* Knesset list was headed by an Arab - Tawfiq Ziad. Despite ideological and financial problems caused as a result of the collapse of the Soviet Union and disintegration of the Communist bloc and internal squabbles, *Ḥadash* managed to win three seats in the 13th Knesset. *Ḥadash* agreed to support the government formed by Yitzḥak *Rabin in July 1992 from outside the coalition in return for a letter of "clarifications" from the *Israel Labor Party. One of the *Ḥadash* MKs - Ḥashem Mahmid - was given a seat on the Knesset State Control Committee at the expense of the Labor quota.

Ḥammas The military arm of the Muslim Brotherhood in the *Gaza Strip and *West Bank, founded on the eve of the *intifada*. In the course of the *intifada* the *Ḥammas* functioned parallel to the United National Command, issuing proclamations and declaring its own strike days, and despite ups and downs grew more powerful in the territories at the expense of the *Palestine Liberation Organization. Unlike the United National Command, the *Ḥamma*s has sought to minimize the disruption of commercial life (some of its backing comes from traders) and the smooth functioning of the schools (because of the importance which it attaches to education).

The *Ḥamma*s covenant, published in August 1988, includes the following basic points: implied rejection of the legitimacy of the PLO; rejection of the legitimacy of any permanent compromise with Israel (though in practice occasional tactical compromises are made); the whole of Palestine "from the sea to the river" is a Muslim *Waqf* (endowment); acceptance of the principle of Palestinian nationalism (the Palestinian Muslim Brothers were the first among the radical Islamic organizations to do so); the *Jihad* (holy war) is to be conducted not only against Israel but against corrupt and degenerate elements in the Palestinian society. The *Ḥamma*s has thus been responsible in recent years for killing Israelis and Palestinians. Especially in the Gaza Strip the *Ḥammas* has clashed openly with the armed groups of other Palestinian organizations. Recently, the *Ḥammas* started to create infrastructures abroad and to directly challenge the *PLO. It is linked in many ways to the Jordanian Muslim Brotherhood.

Following a rise in terrorist activities carried out by the Ḥammas and *Islamic Jihad, 415 leading figures from these two organizations were deported by Israel for a period of two years, on December 17, 1992. (I.Z.)

*** Hammer, Zvulun** Hammer was appointed Minister of Religious Affairs in the *National Unity Government formed in December 1988, and in the narrow government formed by Yitzḥak *Shamir in June 1990 he returned to the Ministry of Education and Culture. In the elections to the 12th Knesset the hawkish Prof. Avner Ḥai Shaki was placed at the head of the *National Religious Party Knesset list. In the 13th Knesset elections the relatively moderate Hammer once again headed the list, although the NRP shifted its positions towards the *radical right. In the 13th Knesset Hammer became one of the most outspoken critics of the new Minister of Education and Culture Shulamit *Aloni.

*** Hausner Gideon** Hausner died on November 15, 1990.

*** Hazan, Ya'acov** Hazan died on July 22, 1992, at the age of 93.

*** Herzog, Ḥaim** Herzog was criticized by the **Likud* and the right-wing parties, after the fall of the *National Unity Government in 1990, for first approaching Labor chairman Shimon *Peres to form a new government, despite the fact that Peres appeared to have the best chance of forming a government. Following the government crisis of March-June, 1990, Herzog strongly supported legislative moves for constitutional change. In November 1992, the *National Religious Party proposed that the law be changed to enable Herzog to serve a third term. Herzog had not been consulted and nothing came of the proposal.

Herzog's term as president will end in May 1993.

*** Hillel, Shlomo** Hillel was elected again to the 12th Knesset, but in March 1989, after failing to be chosen Chairman of the Knesset Finance Committee, he accepted the position of Chairman of *Keren Hayesod* (the "foundation fund" attached to the *Jewish Agency). At the end of 1992 Hillel was one of the three Labor candidates for Israel's 7th president.

*** Histadrut** In the 1980s, the *Histadrut* went through a series of crises for financial and organizational reasons, that raised basic ideological questions regarding its role in the future. The *Histadrut* leaders believe that its structure should remain more or less in tact, and any reforms should be to improve the performance of its various components. They argue that since the *Histadrut* serves a majority of the Israeli population, the government should give it moral and financial backing. The position of the **Likud* and the **Shinui* component of **Meretz* is that the *Histadrut* should be a federation of trade unions, that *Kupat Ḥolim* (its health fund) should be separated from it, and that the *Histadrut*-owned industries and financial institutions should be privatized. Within the *Israel Labor Party some support the position of the *Histadrut* leaders, and some advocate far-reaching reforms which would leave the *Histadrut* more or less intact, but greatly decentralized in its structure.

In 1986 *Kupat Ḥolim* suffered difficulties which were not seen at the time as a financial crisis. The outward symptoms included the practice of "black medicine" (specialists charging patients for services they should have received free of charge) and the departure from *Kupat Ḥolim* to the private health funds of young and better off members. The chairman of *Kupat Ḥolim* was replaced at the beginning of 1989 and some improvements were introduced in the services. However, by 1992 *Kupat Ḥolim* reached a state of financial bankruptcy, with debts of over 2 billion shekels. It argued that the government owed it large sums of money, including payment for services rendered to new immigrants and during the *Gulf War. The *Likud* government argued that it would not channel any funds to *Kupat Ḥolim* before it underwent major reforms, sold assets and used the full amount of the dues collected from members to pay for the health services instead of transferring 28 percent of these dues to the *Histadrut* apparatus. The Labor government in 1992 finally agreed to channel some funds after the *Histadrut* agreed to appoint a professional board of directors to run *Kupat Ḥolim* and introduce necessary reforms.

In the case of Koor, the Histadrut's industrial conglomerate, losses amounting to 759 million shekels in 1987 led to the appointment of a new director general, Benny Ga'on, to run it in May 1988. However, five months later Koor's American creditors appealed to the Tel Aviv district court to request its liquidation, and called for Ga'on's resignation. It was then revealed that Koor owed over one billion dollars to banks in Israel and abroad. A financial settlement was finally signed by Koor, the government and the banks in September 1991, after Koor had embarked on a painful recovery plan involving the sale of some profitable enterprises, the closing down of non-profitable ones, the decentralization of the system and laying off 6,000 of its 22,000 workers. The recovery plan led to a net profit of 203 million shekels in 1991. To all effects and purposes the *Histadrut* lost its full control over Koor and the future relationship between the two is unclear. The *Histadrut's* pension funds, and other parts of the system (including the sports association

"*Ḥa'poel*" and its daily paper *Davar*) are also in financial difficulties while in December 1992 the *Histadrut*-owned insurance company *Hasneh* was liquidated. By force of circumstances the *Histadrut* became active, in 1990, in immigrant absorption, and in the same year created an Institute for Eastern and Central Europe designed to establish contacts with trade unions and cooperative movements in the former Soviet bloc.

Before the *Histadrut* elections of November 1989 minor reforms were introduced under the slogan "the *Histadrut* in momentum," including structural changes in the Workers' Councils. However, these changes were largely cosmetic or aimed at improving Labor's chances in the elections.

Labor gained a major victory in the 1989 *Histadrut* elections when, under Israel *Kessar's leadership, it obtained 55.06 percent of the votes. The *Likud* received 27.38 percent, **Mapam* 9.00 percent, the *Civil Rights Movement 3.89 percent and the united Arab list 4.58 percent.

Secretary Generals of the *Histadrut*:

1984-92 Israel *Kessar
1992- Ḥaim Haberfeld

*** Hurwitz, Yigael** Hurwitz joined the **Likud* as head of **Ometz* before the elections to the 12th Knesset, in return for two reserved seats in the *Likud* list. He did not run for a place in the *Likud* list for the 13th Knesset.

*** IDF - Israel Defense Forces** In recent years the IDF has become increasingly professional, the level of education of its officers has risen, and its armament systems have become more sophisticated. Although the universal draft is still in force, the IDF prefers not to enlist problematic, marginal youths, and this in addition to 20,000 yeshiva students and girls who declare themselves to be religious (about 25 percent of the total number of eligible girls) who are not drafted annually. The new immigrants from the former Soviet Union, many of whom have a technical education, are expected to add qualitatively to the IDF (See: **aliyah*).

In organizational terms the IDF is based on armored brigades as the basic military formation, and in recent years larger frameworks - corps, of which, according to the British Royal Institute for Strategic Studies, there are apparently three - have been formed. In 1983 a combat-corps command was established to replace the separate existing combat forces, but at the end of 1992 the changes of authorities had not yet been completed. In 1992, following the *Gulf War, a fourth command was added to the three regional commands (Northern, Central and Southern) - the Hinterland Command.

In recent years the IDF has been subject to budgetary constraints, and in 1992 the budget for immigrant absorption was larger than the defense budget. While in 1973-74 the defense budget constituted about 30 percent of GNP, in 1990 it was down to 9 percent, though part of this cut was compensated by American military aid. In 1991 the budget was to have gone down to about 8.5 percent of GNP, but due to the Gulf War the budget was increased. The Gulf War also led to an increase in American and German military aid. In 1992 the defense budget was around $6.76 billion. No increase is expected in 1993.

In 1992 175,000 officers and men served in the IDF, of whom 140,000 are enlisted and the rest are professionals. In addition, there are about 430,000 officers and men in reserve. Of the 175,000 officers and men, 134,000 serve in the land forces, that are made up of three corps commands (including nine armored divisions), three armored divisions, two division commands engaged in the **intifada* (see below), four mechanized brigades, three regional divisions, one ground-to-ground missile ("Lance") battalion, and three artillery battalions. The main arms systems used by the land forces in 1992 included about 3,800 tanks (including 800 Merkava tanks, 1,080 improved Centurions, 750 M-60/A1, 650 M-60/A3 and M-48/A5, 100 (Soviet) T-54/55, 110 T-62), about 8,000 armored troop carriers, about 1,300 artillery barrels (155 mm.- L-33, M-50, M-109-A1/A2; 175 mm.- M-107; 203 mm.- M-110). 32,000 officers and men are in active service. In the air force, there are an additional 55,000 reservists. The air force is organized in squadrons, which are made up of planes of a single type, and wings, which may be made up of various types. In 1992 the IAF had 662 air craft, including about 112 F-4E (and 13 in storage), 63 F-15, F-16A/B/C/D, about 95 Israeli Kfirs (and another 75 in storage), about 121 A-4 Skyhawks (and 14 in storage). In addition it has six Boeing 707 aerial early warning aircraft, about 95 transport planes of which five are tanker (refueling) aircraft. The most important of these are 23 Hercules C-130H. The air force has also 233 helicopters of various types, including 18 AH-64A Apaches, 40 AH-1G/1S Cobras, 33 500-MG Defenders, as well as transport helicopters of various types. In the navy there are 10,000 officers and men in active service, and there is a similar number of reservists. There are three navy bases in Haifa, Ashdod and Eilat. The navy has three IKL/Vickers type 206 submarines armed with Harpoon missiles and is expected to receive another two submarines from Germany. It also has 19 Israeli manufactured missile vessels, using Israeli Gabriel and American Harpoon missiles, 40 small Israeli manufactured reconnaissance vessels, 13 landing craft, and two small missile-bearing hovercrafts.

The two main areas of IDF activity are Lebanon and the *administered territories. In the five years since the outbreak of the **intifada* 22 IDF soldiers were killed in *intifada* related activities and 4,200 were wounded. 804 Palestinians were killed from shooting (live, plastic and rubber ammunition), including 84 under the age of 14. In November 1992 there were 6,700 Palestinian detainees in army detention camps. Over 360 houses where perpetrators of violence lived, were blown up, and another 260 were sealed off. The role played by the IDF in the *intifada* has been primarily that of policing. Many army personnel have been tried for acting contrary to the standing rules and regulations.

The harm done to the IDF due to its involvement in the *intifada* is on four levels. Firstly, although the fighting units are as highly motivated as ever, and the number of volunteers to special units is high, the constant confrontation with a civilian population is demoralizing. Secondly, the IDF's training program is disrupted since the officers and men spend part of their service doing police duties in the territories. Thirdly, the credibility of IDF reporting has eroded. Fourthly, the IDF has been thrown into the heart of the political debate, and almost no matter what it does, one political camp or the other in Israel is dissatisfied (See: *military and politics).

Growing media exposure has resulted in the IDF becoming a subject of public criticism. The families of enlisted soldiers have also become more involved in the process of their sons' and daughters' integration and training, and this has increased the IDF's sensitivity to the way its men and women are treated. However, the IDF is finding it difficult to adapt to the reality of a more open and critical society. (Mi.B.)

India and Israel In the early 1940s David *Ben Gurion held a correspondence with Indian leader Mahatma Gandhi in which the future Israeli prime minister tried to gain the latter's support for the Zionist endeavor. But Gandhi objected in principle to Zionism within the context of the political reality in the Middle East.

Although India recognized Israel de facto in September 1950 it refused to establish full diplomatic relations or develop significant economic and cultural relations with the Jewish state, in deference to the sensitivities of its Muslim population. Later in the 1950s India's attitude towards Israel was affected by the close relations which India's first Prime Minister Jawaharlal Nehru, as one of the leaders of the Nonaligned states, maintained with Egyptian President Gamal Abdel Nasser. India's anti-Israeli rhetoric in the *United Nations and in other international forums intensified after the *Sinai Campaign, and various meetings by Israeli personalities with Nehru bore no positive results. Nevertheless, from 1953 Israel had a consulate in Bombey. The Israeli consul general was declared *persona non grata* in 1982, but in July 1988, under pressure of the US government and Jewish organizations, relations resumed as formerly.

Until the late 1980s official Israeli delegations were not welcome in India, but in July 1987 an Israeli tennis team was allowed to play against the Indian team. At the same time cooperation started to develop in the sphere of energy - some say in the nuclear field as well.

It was, however, the upheaval which followed the collapse of the East bloc and the Soviet Union that brought the real change in India's attitude. During his visit to India in June 1991, in order to help in the release of Israeli hostages captured by terrorists while traveling in Kashmir, Dr. Moshe Yegar, a deputy director general in the Ministry of Foreign Affairs, had conversations with senior Indian officials. Full diplomatic relations were established on January 29, 1992, on the eve of a visit by Indian Prime Minister Narasima Rao to the United States in search of economic and military aid. It has been reported that Israel and India are cooperating in military technology.

International Conference The traditional Israeli position has always been that bilateral negotiations with the Arab states, or talks through an intermediary are preferable to negotiations within the framework of an international conference. Israel believes that in an international conference it would be in an inferior position both tactically and strategically.

However, the 1973 *Geneva Conference proved that with proper coordination with the *United States and the appropriate terms of reference such a conference could be useful. In the *Memorandum of Understanding signed between Israel and the US in 1975 Israel received assurances regarding the conditions for reconvening the Geneva Conference: Israel would be consulted about the timing; the *PLO would not be invited unless it recognized Israel and *Security Council Resolutions 242 and 338; the US would coordinate its strategy regarding the conference with Israel; the US would make every effort to ensure that the talks on substance would be held on a bilateral basis; the US would oppose any attempt by the Security Council to change the powers of the conference to Israel's detriment; and the US would act together with Israel to ensure progress to attain "peace between Israel and its neighbors on the basis of negotiations."

In September 1977, Menaḥem *Begin expressed his agreement to an international conference, but the peace process with Egypt followed the "bilateral talks with the help of a mediator" model. The conference idea remained dormant until 1985, when King Ḥussein of Jordan raised the possibility of an international conference to act as an umbrella for direct talks with Israel. Prime Minister Shimon *Peres mentioned the idea in his speech at the *United Nations in October 1985, and expressed Israel's agreement that Palestinian representatives who are not members of the PLO be included in the Jordanian delegation.

The *London Agreement of April 11, 1987, reached between King Ḥussein and Peres (now acting as Minister of Foreign Affairs), concerned the convention of such a conference, but the *Likud*, under Yitzḥak *Shamir's leadership, rejected the idea, seeing it as disadvantageous to Israel. The international conference was the basis of both the 1988 *Shultz Plan and the 1991 Baker Initiative (See: *United States and Israel). On Israel's insistence, the *Madrid Confererence of October 1991, was merely a ceremonial opening to direct bilateral and multilateral negotiations which were to follow immediately. Although the Madrid Conference was not a continuation of the Geneva Conference, the US abided by the assurances it had given Israel in the 1975 Memorandum of Understanding.

Intifada From 1983 to 1987 there was a steep rise in what were termed "breaches of the order" against Israelis - but none involving firearms. Most of this activity was instigated by Arab nationalist circles connected with the PLO. The popular uprising in the territories, commonly known as the *intifada*, formally broke out on December 9, 1987 after four workers from the *Gaza Strip were run over and killed by an Israeli truck. Rumors spread that it was not an accident and during the funerals violent demonstrations broke out in the refugee camp of Jebalya and elsewhere in the Gaza Strip.

The more general background to the *intifada* was the growing frustration of the Palestinian population on political, economic and social grounds, further aggravated by the failure of the peace initiative of US Secretary of State George Shultz (See: *Shultz Plan).

During the first weeks the *intifada* was characterized by widespread, spontaneous demonstrations, and trade and school strikes throughout the *West Bank, Gaza Strip and East Jerusalem. In the first instance none of these were organized and there was no guiding hand. Every day pamphlets were distributed, and proclamations and slogans appeared on the walls, calling for a struggle against Israeli rule. Such occurrences had already taken place previously, but this was the first time that they did not subside after a while, and grew progressively more violent.

Minister of Defense Yitzḥak *Rabin, who was on a visit to the US at the time, underestimated its significance at first and did not curtail his visit. The *IDF, untrained to deal with this type of violence, reacted with force, and in clashes with Palestinian civilians during the first two months of the uprising, at least 51 persons were killed and hundreds were wounded. These events drew much attention from the international media which rapidly became extremely hostile towards Israel.

Hundreds of Palestinians were arrested and deportation orders were issued for nine activists, but these measures did not have a calming effect. On the contrary, the demonstrations intensified, while the deportation orders led to a condemnation of Israel by the Security Council and brought the *PLO into the picture. The PLO planned to send a "ship of return" with dozens of Palestinian deportees on board to Israeli territorial waters. But the ship was blown up in February 1988 while docking in the port of Limasol in Cyprus, and never set sail. Israeli intelligence was accused of being responsible for the explosion.

Encouraged by the international attention, aroused Palestinian leadership in the territories published a document in January 1988 with 14 conditions for ending the uprising, most of them dealing with an easing in the Military Government. Within the Palestinian population there was a growing sense of pride that finally they had taken their fate into their own hands.

In the following two months the uprising was gradually channeled into acts of organized civil disobedience. Proclamations signed by a body calling itself "the United Command of the *Intifada*" appeared with instructions to the population. The leaders were an anonymous body whose members kept changing and included representatives of various groups in the PLO and activists in the Islamic movements. In the winter of 1988 a radio station called *Al-Kuds* started broadcasting to the territories from the Syrian part of the *Golan Heights, and was extremely popular despite the fact that it expressed positions hostile to the PLO.

Civil disobedience was organized by active supporters of the PLO, and its goal was to sever contacts between the local Palestinian population and the Israeli authorities. In the middle of the school year (1988) most of the schools and universities were shut down by the military authorities because they were serving as foci of incitement to violence. Temporary teachers were laid off while the others were put on half-pay. This led to pressure on other local employees of the Israeli civil administration to resign, and those who refused were threatened. One of the results was that the territories were left with only a skeleton police force.

The United Command also proclaimed a boycott on Israeli goods except for essentials, and encouraged the local inhabitants not to approach the Israeli authorities, boycott the courts operated by the civil administration and avoid going out to work in Israel. Large weddings and celebrations were prohibited, as was the purchase of luxury goods, and people were discouraged from engaging in any public recreational activities. People were encouraged to grow vegetables, rabbits and chickens in backyards, house owners were requested to refrain from collecting rent from tenants without means and those considered wealthy were forced to help the needy.

Through the initiative of popular committees created by the political leadership of the PLO supporters in the territories, in the villages, refugee camps and urban neighborhoods in the territories, shops were only allowed to open for three hours in the morning, and only on days on which no general strike was declared. In the afternoons and on strike days all transportation was stopped and all public institutions were closed. The committees were also active in organizing stonethrowing on army patrols and on the cars of Jewish settlers. On several occasions settlers retaliated. In April 1988 there was a serious incident in the village of Beita near Nablus when a group of youngsters from the Jewish settlement of Eilon-Moreh were attacked while hiking through the village. A Jewish girl was killed and several were wounded. The IDF reacted by blowing up 13 houses and deporting some of those who had participated in the incident. On April 16, Arafat's deputy, Khalil al-Wazir (better known as Abu Jihad) who was considered the central operator of the *intifada* activists in the territories, was murdered in his home in Tunis. Israel never admitted responsibility, but the evidence seems to indicate that a special unit of the IDF was involved.

The IDF started to impose the closure of villages and refugee camps and carried out raids. Economic sanctions were introduced, such as not supplying petrol to gas stations and prolonged curfews. The civil administration also cut down the services (especially health and welfare) which it provided, alleging that the income of the administration had fallen. To force the inhabitants to renew their ties with the administration and pay taxes the administration demanded of anyone requiring a license of any sort to bring proof that he had paid all his dues. Property was confiscated from persons who had not paid their taxes.

Despite the difficulties and the number of casualties, by the summer of 1988 the Palestinians had a feeling of success. In May the US declared that it would consider opening a dialogue with the PLO on condition that the organization accept *Security Council Resolutions 242 and 338 and denounce the use of terror. At the end of July, King Ḥussein announced that his country had no claims over the West Bank and that he was in fact severing relations with the territories (See: *Jordan and Israel). This declaration was interpreted in the territories as a defensive measure on the part of the Jordanian regime which feared a spill-over of the *intifada* to the Palestinian population east of the River Jordan, but it was in fact a major political victory for the Palestinian national leadership in the territories and the PLO in Tunis, for this was an unequivocal declaration that Jordan no longer claimed to represent the population in the territories.

These developments, as well as efforts by the new leadership that had emerged in the territories (especially among the intellectuals and former security prisoners) and Western diplomats to get the PLO to adopt a more pragmatic approach, paved the way for the dramatic resolutions adopted by the Palestinian National Council that convened in Algiers in November 1988. On November 15, the PNC announced the establishment of an independent state and its acceptance of all the UN resolutions regarding the Arab-Israeli conflict, including Security Council Resolutions 242 and 338. Following this, PLO chairman Yasser Arafat (who had been declared by the PNC President of the Palestinian State) appeared at a special meeting of the UN General Assembly in Geneva in December, and in a press conference declared that the decisions of the PNC implied recognition of the State of Israel and expressed reservations regarding terrorist activities. Arafat's declaration was made in coordination with the U.S. which subsequently announced that it would open a dialogue with the PLO. This development was the peak of the political achievements of the *intifada*.

As the first year of the *intifada* came to a close the number of Palestinians killed rose to over 300, the number of those wounded to 20,000, and the number of Arab prisoners and detainees reached close to 12,000 - many of them held in detention camps in the Negev.

During the second year of the uprising (1989) cracks started to appear: there were acts of intimidation to discourage the population from cooperating with the Israeli authorities, and brutal murders of persons suspected of collaboration carried out by independent groups calling themselves "shock committees" or "internal security apparatuses" and assumed names such as "The Red Eagle" and "The Black Panther." In 1989 over 150 Palestinians suspected of collaboration were killed by their brethren. The number of Palestinians killed by the Israeli security forces (a few were also killed in clashes with Jewish settlers) was 300.

In 1990 and 1991 there was a sharp rise in the former figure and a decline in the latter. By the end of 1992 the total number of Palestinians killed during the *intifada* reached about 1,800, of whom over 800 were internal killings. At first the Palestinian population in the territories accepted the murder of alleged collaborators. But the cruelty of these executions, and the fact that many of those killed were not actually collaborators but persons from the fringe of society or those accused by extreme Muslim groups of propagating "the rotten Western culture," started to elicit reactions of anger and bitterness. In 1992 the number of such killings actually rose, despite the fact that special Israeli forces had managed to either arrest or kill many of the perpetrators.

In the beginning of 1989 the Israeli Defense Minister, Yitzḥak Rabin, who had come to realize in the course of the first year of the *intifada* that Israel no longer had a *Jordanian option, and would have to deal directly with the Palestinians proposed to hold elections in the territories as a first step towards the opening of talks with a recognized local Palestinian representation. This plan, later adopted by the Israeli government on May 14, 1989 (See: *Shamir Rabin peace initiative), was viewed by the more pragmatic inhabitants in the territories as a Palestinian success, since Israel had previously rejected similar proposal from the Palestinian side.

The Israeli authorities made several attempts to reopen the schools, but to no avail. An attempt to collect taxes by force raised negative international reactions. In July 1989 a young Arab from Gaza caused an Israeli bus travelling from Tel Aviv to Jerusalem to fall into a ravine, causing the death of 14 passengers. There followed numerous other attacks, mostly knifings in broad daylight.

At the beginning of 1990 some circles in the territories called for a return to the "armed struggle" against Israel, i.e., the resumption of terrorist acts and use of firearms which had been largely avoided in the first two years of the *intifada*. In May an Israeli youth retaliated to acts of terrorism by murdering seven Arab workmen, and on June 1, several terrorist bands from a pro-Iraqi organization connected with the PLO landed on Israel's southern coast with the intention of performing a major terrorist act. As the PLO did not condemn the attempt (which failed) the US broke off its dialogue with the PLO.

Despite the tensions caused by these and other events, including a serious incident on the Temple Mount in October 1990 which began when Muslim worshippers threw stones at Jewish worshippers at the Western Wall and 17 Arabs were killed by Israeli police forces, in the course of 1990 the *intifada* lost the popular enthusiasm which characterized it in its first two years.

The massive demonstrations and acts of civil disobedience ceased, though sporadic outbursts of violence and occasional knifings continued. The opening of direct talks between a Palestinian delegation from the territories and an Israeli delegation at the end of 1991, on the establishment of institutions of self-administration in the West Bank and Gaza Strip, also contributed to a change in the atmosphere. However, a bitter and at times violent debate erupted in the territories between PLO sympathizers who supported the participation in the peace process and members of the Islamic movements who opposed such a participation and the level of violence against Israeli civilians and armed forces rose sharply towards the end of 1992. (D.R.)

***Iran and Israel** Following the end of the Iran-Iraq war in August 1988 and the death of the Ayatollah Khomeini soon after, there was a lull in the anti-Western propaganda in Iran, but it did not mean an end to its hatred of Israel and *Zionism. Iran's antagonism to Israel was now concentrated on the military and the political level in the Middle East itself. Iran had two loyal partners to realize this policy the *Ḥizballah* in Lebanon, and extremist Palestinian organizations — both religious and secular — inside the *occupied territories. The disintegration of the Eastern bloc, which had previously supported the extremist organizations, and the willingness of most of the Arab states to give up the armed struggle to resolve the Palestinian question, were interpreted by Iran as an abandonment of the Palestinians, enabling it to present itself as their new patron.

In 1991-92 the leaders of the *Ḥizballah*, the **Ḥammas* and *Islamic Jihad were regular visitors to Teheran, which gave them generous financial and logistic assistance. According to Egyptian sources Iran also set up bases in Sudanese territory to train guerrilla fighters of extremist organizations - an allegation rejected by both Iran and Sudan.

In 1992 several secret conferences were held in Teheran with the participation of the leaders of anti-Israel organizations, to discuss means of increasing the **intifada* and guerrilla activities by the *Ḥizballah* in Lebanon. The results were soon felt in the field.

In order to strengthen his spiritual and political power in Iran and to justify the title "leader of the Muslims on earth" Khomeini's successor, the Ayattolah Hojatel-Eslam Seyyed Ali Khamenei, intensified his verbal attacks on Israel. This growing extremism blocked the way to the release of the Israeli prisoners held by the *Ḥizballah* in Lebanon at the time that all the Western hostages were released in 1991. At the end of 1992 the Iranian régime was viewed in Israel as the most serious danger to its welfare and to the stability of the region. During his visits to Europe in December 1992 Foreign Minister Shimon *Peres called for Western coordination in the struggle against Iranian extremism. (See also: *Irangate). (M.A.)

"Irangate" or "Iran-Contra Affair" Affair involving the sale of missiles and spare parts to Iran and the use of the proceeds to assist the Contras in Nicaragua in 1985-86 by the United States in collusion with Israel. The Iran side of the affair was first revealed on November 3, 1986 when a Beirut magazine published the fact that President Reagan's National Security Advisor Robert MacFarlane had visited Teheran. Twenty days later Nicaragua was linked to the story when a memorandum mentioning the use of profits from the arms sales to Iran to assist the Contras was uncovered.

In Israel the main actors were Amiram Nir (Prime Minister Shimon *Peres's advisor on terror, who was killed under mysterious circumstances in a plane crash in Mexico in December 1988) and Yaacov Nimrodi (a private businessman engaged in the arms trade). The affair was not regarded as a scandal in Israel, despite the controversial nature of the policies involved. Israel's leaders had decided to assist Iran because of its traditional policy towards the states peripheral to the Arab world, and to insure the welfare of the remaining Jewish community in Khomeini's Iran (numbering several thousand). In the case of Nicaragua, the Sandinistas had broken off relations with Israel in 1982 and were extremely hostile towards it. However, both in the case of Iran and Nicaragua, there were apparently private business interests involved as well.

At the end of 1992 there was still much which had not been revealed about this affair in Israel and in the United States.

Iraq and Israel Iraq was one of the most active proponents of intervention by the Arab states in Palestine, following the end of the British mandate on May 15, 1948. This was due to a combination of domestic difficulties and interests in the Arab arena. An Iraqi division was sent to fight Israel (See: *War of Independence), and operated in the area between *Kafr Kassem and Jenin, where it participated in very little actual fighting, and merely held the territory for King Abdallah of Jordan. Iraq did not take part in the talks with Israel after the war was over, but the *armistice agreement between Jordan and Israel included provisions for the withdrawal of the Iraqi troops.

In 1950-51 the Iraqi government allowed the 122,000 Iraqi Jews to depart for Israel (See: **aliyah*). This policy met with very little local opposition since all the vast Jewish property was taken over by the Iraqi government, while the Jewish businesses and positions, especially in private banking and trade, were taken over by educated Shi'ites.

On July 14, 1958 the Hashemite monarchy was brought down by General Abdul Karim Qassem. Qassem was not committed to Pan-Arabism, and in addition to clashing with Egyptian President Gamal Abdul Nasser, he was also less committed than his predecessors to the Palestinian issue. However, in order to prove his Arab patriotism, he was the first to form a Palestine Liberation Army manned by Palestinians, but commanded by Iraqi officers.

Qassem was overthrown in February, 1963, by a group of Nasserite officers headed by General Abdul Salem Aref and the Ba'th party. Aref managed to get rid of his Ba'th partners by November, and adopted a strongly pro-Nasserite policy on all issues including the conflict with Israel. Aref was killed in a helicopter crash in April 1966, and was replaced by his brother, General Abdul Rahman Aref who sent an Iraqi force to participate in the *Six Day War. The force never got close to the battlefield, but remained in Jordan until 1970-71. Aref was brought down by a Ba'th coup in July 1968, and General Ahmad Ḥassan al-Bakr became Iraq's new president. Even before coming to power the Ba'th party had rejected *Security Council Resolution 242, which Egypt had accepted, and even the cease-fire agreements which Syria had signed. It opted for a strategy of continued armed conflict with Israel, and this became Iraq's official policy after 1968. Iraq now became more involved in assisting the Palestinian organizations, and advocating the liberation of "Arab Palestine." The Palestinians, on their part, had hoped that the Iraqi forces stationed in Jordan would assist them during their clashes with the Jordanian army in September 1970, but the Iraqi forces remained neutral, Iraq fearing that any involvement in the fighting would result in American, British and even Israeli intervention.

Iraq, whose financial situation greatly improved following the imposition of the Arab oil embargo during the *Yom Kippur War and the artificial oil shortage which it caused, also managed to raise its military prestige by sending two armored and one infantry division to fight with the Syrians in the *Golan Heights. The Iraqi force fought poorly, but its arrival on the scene delayed the Israeli advance, and enabled the Syrians to regroup. In October 1974 the ailing Bakr made public a new Iraqi policy regarding Palestine, which was formulated at the *Rabat (Summit) Conference by his deputy, Saddam Ḥussein. The new policy did not reject political means, as long as these did not involve any Arab concessions to Israel or reciprocity. It also accepted the establishment of a Palestinian state in the *West Bank and the*Gaza Strip, as a first stage towards the liberation of the rest of Palestine. This new plan enabled Iraq to attack Egypt and Syria for accepting Security Council Resolution 338 and agreeing to sign *disengagement agreements with Israel, and to appear as the only true patriot in the Middle East.

From the mid-1960s until 1975 Israel assisted the Kurds in northern Iraq, under the leadership of Mullah Mustafa Barazani, in their revolt against Baghdad. Israel provided arms, military training and field hospitals and was instrumental in getting the Shah of Iran to assist them as well. However, in 1975 Iran stopped its assistance, and the Kurdish revolt was crushed.

Although after the signing of the *Camp David Agreements Iraq and Syria had a brief rapprochement, after Bakr resigned (or was deposed) in July 1979, Saddam Ḥussein, who was now president, once again distanced himself from Syria, while Syria formed close ties with Khomeini's Iran. Following the Iraqi attack on Iran on September 22, 1980, Saddam Ḥussein, being in need of spare parts for Soviet weapons and ammunition (because of his treatment of the communists in Iraq) approached Egyptian President Anwar Sadat.

After Sadat's assassination in 1981, the rapprochement between Iraq and Egypt developed more smoothly. At first it did not affect the Iraqi policy towards Israel and the *Arab-Israeli conflict, and the Israeli attack on *Osiraq in June 1981 did not at first encourage such a change. However, the realization that Iraq was within Israel's military reach started to affect Iraqi thinking. The first change was felt in September 1982 when Iraq accepted the *Fez Plan, and to all effects and purposes ceased to be a clearcut rejectionist state. Next, in January 1983, Iraqi Foreign Minister Tariq Aziz, stated in an interview to the French daily *Le Monde* that Iraq was encouraging Jordan and the *PLO to negotiate together with Israel. Towards the mid 1980s Iraq adopted a double attitude. On the one hand it declared that it would not object to an agreement accepted by the PLO. On the other hand, it was implied that Iraq would not be partner to any peace agreement with Israel.

In the beginning of 1984 Iraq was reported to have approached Israel indirectly in connection with an oil pipeline from Iraq to Aqaba. It sought a commitment from the US that Israel would not threaten the line, but Prime Minister Yitzḥak *Shamir refused. Shimon *Peres, who became prime minister in October 1984, was prepared to accept it, but soon afterwards the project fell through. Though relations between Iraq and the US were renewed in November 1984 and the US was essentially interested in the project, it was reluctant to become directly involved in it. Following the renewal of relations with the United States, the Iraqi ambassador to Washington, Nizar Ḥamdun, occasionally met with American Jewish leaders, and Peres received messages suggesting that new breezes were blowing in Iraq. President Ḥosni Mubarak was also instrumental in trying to convince the Israelis that Saddam Ḥussein had become moderate and was seeking peace.

Reports that Israel was asked by Iraq to sell it arms were never substantiated, though Israel did not stop arms for Iraq being unloaded in Aqaba. Some defensive Israeli equipment might have reached Iraq by indirect means, but the most important Israeli export item to reach the Iraqi army in this period were tomatoes. On the other hand, Israel was involved in 1985-86 in the sale of arms to Iran. The publication of the *Irangate affair at the end of 1986 opened a public debate in Israel on whether Israel's national interest was to support Iran, Iraq or remain neutral.

Though the Iraqi media attacked Israel, and the "Zionist-Khomeinist" alliance, Saddam Ḥussein (with American encouragement) gave King Ḥussein the green light to sign the *London Agreement with Peres in April 1987. In 1987 the Iraqi ambassador to Washington also met, for the first time, two senior Israeli officials on study vacations in the United States, (the meeting was arranged in such a way that he could deny that he knew whom he was meeting). Avraham Tamir, while acting as Director General at the Ministry of Foreign Affairs and after leaving the Ministry, admitted having four informal meetings in 1988 and 1989 with Nizar Ḥamdun, the Iraqi Minister of State for Foreign Affairs Sa'adun Ḥammadi, Tariq Aziz and a fourth person (believed to be Saddam Ḥussein's brother). While on the Iraqi side such meetings were undoubtedly approved by Saddam Ḥussein himself, they were never formally approved by any official Israeli forum, and were certainly not initiated either by the Israeli Ministry for Foreign Affairs or the government.

In June 1989 it was reported that Iraq had approached Israel to allow a shipment of arms for General Aoun who was still resisting the Syrians in Beirut, to pass through the Israeli port of Haifa and the south Lebanese port of Naqura. This report does not seem accurate, and while there were Iraqi-Israeli common interests on this issue, the Israeli contribution amounted to its refraining from stopping the freighters bearing the arms on the high seas.

The cease-fire between Iran and Iraq was signed on August 20, 1988. Israeli Minister of Defense Yitzḥak *Rabin frequently expressed Israel's mixed feelings regarding this event. On the one hand the end of the war meant that Iraq would now be free to concentrate on Israel; on the other hand there was a hope (a vain hope as it became apparent several years later) that Iraq would now stop developing and trying out non-conventional weapons. In September 1989 President Mubarak was still trying to convince a highly skeptical Rabin that Saddam Ḥussein was truly ready for peace with Israel. In December of the same year Iraq took a sharp turn and once again spoke of the liberation of Jerusalem and the whole of Palestine. One reason for the change were difficulties and frustration because the "victory" over Iran was not visible, and there were still about 70,000 Iraqi prisoners in Iran. In the meantime the Soviet bloc was disintegrating and there was a steep rise in the immigration of Jews to Israel.

After warning against an impending invasion of Iraq by the Americans and British, Saddam Ḥussein in April 1990 threatened that should Israel attack Iraq he would burn "half of Israel." He also warned that if Israel dared touch any Arab state Iraq would attack it. When Iraq invaded Kuwait in August 1990, one of the justifying arguments was that this was the first step towards the liberation of Palestine, since the money taken from Kuwait would be used to build an army for this purpose. When the Americans started landing in Saudi Arabia Saddam Ḥussein warned that any American attack on Iraq would lead to an Iraqi attack on Israel. Once the *Gulf War began Saddam Ḥussein did attack Israel, though the attack was with conventional missiles for fear of an Israeli retaliation with non-conventional means. Saddam Ḥussein had two reasons to launch Scud missiles against Israel. The first was to save his credibility: when the Americans attacked Iraq he had to retaliate as he had threatened to do. The second was his hope that Israel would respond and thus the Arab participants in the anti-Iraq coalition would find it difficult to remain in the coalition. Israel disappointed him.

Iraq did not even send observers to the *Madrid Conference, the Moscow Conference or the subsequent multilateral talks, because the economic sanctions against it were still in force and because of the American sponsorship. However, Saddam Ḥussein did not overtly object to the participation of the Jordanians (who did not join the anti-Iraqi coalition and did not abide by the embargo on Iraq) and the Palestinians (who publicly supported him) in the talks with Israel. He still refers to the Syrians (who had joined the anti-Iraq coalition) and their Lebanese puppets as traitors to the Arab cause.

Islamic Jihad (Palestinian branch) The name of several Muslim radical splinter groups. The Islamic Jihad first split off from the Gaza branch of the Muslim Brotherhood under Iranian inspiration, and the influence of the Islamic Jihad in Egypt. As opposed to the Muslim Brotherhood which believes in systematic institution building, the Islamic Jihad favors instant military action. In the course of the 80's the Islamic Jihad broke up into at least five groups. The first is still dependent on Iran, currently has its center in Lebanon and is close to the *Ḥizballah*. The second is headed by Sheikh a-Tamimi of Hebron, is known as the Islamic Jihad-Beit al-Makdas, is currently centered in Amman, and has contacts with both the *Fataḥ* and Iran. The third is a front organization for the *Fataḥ* which is involved in terrorist attacks. There are another two or three insignificant splinter groups, nowadays based mostly in Sudan.

Following a rise in terrorist activities carried out by the *Ḥammas* and Islamic Jihad, 415 leading figures from these two organizations were deported by Israel for a period of two years, on December 17, 1992. (I.Z)

Islamic Movement (in Israel) Front organization for the *Muslim Brotherhood in Israel since the late 1970s. After 30 years in which to all effects and purposes the Muslim Brotherhood was inactive in Israel, there was a religious reawakening inspired by a group of Israeli Arabs, some of whom had studied in religious colleges in the *West Bank, and by the general revival of Islam in the Middle East.

In 1981 the Israeli authorities apprehended a group of about 100 members, headed by Sheikh Abdullah Nimr Darwish of *Kafr Kassem, who had formed an organization, *Usrat al-Jihad* ("family of the holy war"), which had started to hoard arms, and to perpetrate terrorist attacks against Jews. Many of the members of the group were captured. While in prison they held debates on the future of their movement, and after their release (as of the mid-1980s) most of them presented (at least outwardly) a new pattern of activity. While still rejecting the existence of the State of Israel *de jure* they recognized it *de facto*, and they focused their activity on attempting to purify the Arab society and return it to the principles of Islam.

The activities of the Islamic Movement were based on the principles of reliance, grassroot activities, the building of independent institutions and the mobilization of funds - both abroad and locally. It managed to supersede partly the traditional kinship structures and loyalties and centered its activities around the mosques which turned into community centers which ran libraries, workshops for seamstresses, etc. The Islamic Movement rapidly began to appear as a practical and untainted alternative to all the existing political and social frameworks.

In the 1988 Israeli national elections the Islamic Movement instructed its members not to vote, but after its success in the 1989 municipal elections, in which its representatives managed to gain control of several important Arab towns and councils including Um-el-Fahm, their attitude changed. Towards the 1992 elections the Movement tried to get the *Arab Democratic Party, the *Progressive List for Peace and a group of independent Arab personalities to run for the Knesset in a single list which it would support. However, the effort failed. In future the Islamic Movement will have to decide whether to further recognize the state *de facto* by running its own candidates to the Knesset. Another problem which will have to be tackled concerns the inclination of individual members within the movement to emulate the **Ḥammas* in its attacks on Israeli soldiers and civilians. The murder of a group of Israeli soldiers in their sleep in a field camp in the Gil'ad in March 1992 by members of the Islamic Movement, was only half heartedly condemned by Darwish.

On November 9, Darwish stated that while the whole of Palestine belongs to the Palestinians, for the sake of peace he was willing to accept the principle of *partition. Such an acceptance, he said, was not political but in accordance with the laws of Islam. (I.Z.)

*** Israel Labor Party** Before the 12th Knesset elections the Israel Labor Party embarked on a campaign of democratization. The party's Knesset list was elected by the Central Committee instead of being selected by an appointment committee. The new system brought many younger members into the party's list.

However, as a result of four years in a *National Unity government which blurred the ideological differences between Labor and **Likud*, the lack of popularity of the party's chairman Shimon *Peres (despite his success as Prime Minister), the apathy of the party rank and file and a terrorist attack which occurred several days before the elections, the results of the elections were disappointing and Labor emerged with only 39 Knesset seats, while the left-wing - Arab bloc commanded only 55 seats (compared to 60 in the 11th Knesset). The Labor Party finally joined the new National Unity Government headed by the *Likud* in December 1988, under less favorable conditions than those under which the government had been formed in 1984.

The Labor Party wholeheartedly supported the government's *Shamir-Rabin peace initiative of May 14, 1989, but when the *Likud* started to obstruct progress it decided to support a motion of no-confidence in the government on March 15, 1990. Following the fall of the government Peres tried to form an alternative government but failed. Labor's popularity steeply declined as a result of the crisis. An attempt by Yitzḥak *Rabin to challenge Peres's leadership in July 1990 failed. The Labor Party Conference at the end of 1991 adopted a new system of *primaries for electing the party's leader and representatives. In February 1992 Rabin was elected in primaries as party chairman instead of Peres, and Labor's list for the 13th Knesset was also elected in primaries.

Labor won 44 seats in the 13th Knesset, and with a blocking majority of 61 MKs and a coalition numbering 62 (with the external support of another 5) Labor returned to power in July 1992, with a promise to the electorate to make progress in the peace process, stop financing Jewish settlement in the *administered territories and concentrate on immigrant absorption and the creation of jobs.

Knesset seats: 12th Knesset (1988) - 39; 13th Knesset (1992) - 44.

Chairmen: 1977-92 - Shimon Peres; 1992 - Yitzḥak Rabin.

Secretary Generals: 1984-89 - Uzi Baram; 1989-92 - Michael Ḥarish; 1992 - Nissim Zvili.

*** Jerusalem** In 1987-92 Jerusalem developed at an accelerated rate, while inner tensions in the population between Arabs and Jews, religious and secular, right and left intensified. There were also some frictions with the Christian authorities.

The population of the city rose from 482,700 at the end of 1987 of whom 71.7 percent were Jewish, to 544,200 at the end of 1991, of whom 72.2 percent were Jewish. Both the Jewish and non-Jewish population of the city grew through natural growth and immigration - both of Jewish immigrants and of Arabs from villages in the periphery of the city.

The cornerstone for the Mamila commercial and residential project, which was to fill the gap between West Jerusalem and the Old City where no-man's-land had been until 1967, was finally laid on May 30, 1989 and in 1992 was well advanced. After years of struggle with the religious population in the city the Teddy Stadium (named after Jerusalem mayor Teddy *Kollek) was finally constructed. As director general of the Ministry of the Interior and then as Minister, Arye *Der'i had done everything in his power to put off its construction. A third major architectural project was the High Court of Justice, built in the government compound at Givat Ram. In addition, tens of thousands of new apartments were constructed, especially in the new neighborhoods surrounding the city.

The **intifada* hit Jerusalem more severely than it did other parts of the country, and on January 22, 1988 a curfew was declared in an Arab neighborhood of

Jerusalem for the first time since 1967. The *intifada* manifested itself in violent demonstrations, stone-throwing, commercial strikes, and as it progressed, in a growing number of knifings - especially after the disturbances which erupted on the Temple Mount in October 1990. On that occasion Muslim worshippers, fearing that the *Temple Mount Faithful were planning to lay the cornerstone for the Third Temple on the Temple Mount, started throwing stones at Jewish worshippers at the Western Wall below. The Israeli border police, taken by surprise over-reacted, and the result was 17 Arabs killed and over 50 injured. Despite the disruptions and tensions, a semblance of normal life continued. One major Israeli institution - the **Histadrut* - expanded its activities and services in the Arab part of the city, and was kept from harm by the leaders of the *intifada*.

In this period the number of *ḥaredim* constantly grew, leading Kollek to express the fear that the Zionist (non-Arab and non-*ḥaredi*) majority in the city was endangered. Clashes between the secular and religious parts of the population occurred over the construction of the Stadium, the opening of places of entertainment on Friday night, the opening of a new road between the Jewish neighborhood of Sanhedria and the Arab neighborhood of Sheikh Jarach on Saturdays, and numerous cases in which *ḥaredim* tried to stop the activities of the Archeology Authority which saves archeological finds in areas where major construction works are in progress. The religious circles object to ancient Jewish burial grounds being dug up, and such sites have been uncovered in many parts of the city. Activist *ḥaredi* circles have frequently used violence on these occasions, and clashed with the police.

The tension between right and left has occasionally manifested itself in clashes between right-wing groups (especially Kahanists) and left-wing demonstrators. However, the main issue of contention in Jerusalem between right and left was over the activities of right-wing groups, such as **Atteret Cohanim* who were supported by right-wing Knesset members and ministers in settling Jews in the midsts of Arab neighborhoods. These groups argue that the presence of Jews in all parts of the city will increase security, and that Jews have the right to settle everywhere in the city. Kollek and left-wing circles objected to these activities on principle, believing that they increased tensions in the city. Kollek added that even if one has a right, it isn't always wise to realize it. The most noted cases of Jewish settlement in the midst of an Arab population were Sharon's acquisition of a house in the Muslim quarter of the Old City in December 1987, the entry of 150 settlers into the St. John Hospice in April 1990 (see below), and the entry of several Jewish families into houses purchased in Silwan (Kfar Shilo'aḥ) in October 1991. Following the formation of the Labor-led government in July 1992, all government funding for such activities was stopped, and the legality of some of the purchase and lease of Arab and Christian property was reexamined. The new government also abolished the superfluous Ministry for Jerusalem Affairs formed after the formation of the narrow right-wing-religious government in June 1990, and offered to Rabbi Avraham Verdiger of **Agudat Yisrael*.

Since 1967 Israel tried and usually managed to maintain correct and even cordial relations with the various churches. However, in April 1990, the entry of Jewish settlers into the St. John Hospice, which was purchased for a sum of $3.5 million (over half of this money allocated by the Ministry of Construction and Housing) elicited angry reactions from Christian circles because of its proximity to the Church of the Holy Sepulcher and the fact that the property belongs to the Greek Orthodox Church which had not approved the sale.

The reaction was that for the first time all the Christian churches decided to close the Holy Sepulcher for 24 hours in protest. At the end of 1992 the issue was still being dealt with by the courts. On June 3, 1990, the Latin Patriarch, Msgr. Sabaḥ, published a letter in which he justified the *intifada*. In the 1989 municipal elections "One Jerusalem" - Teddy Kollek's party - lost its majority in the city council and was forced to form a wall-to-wall coalition which greatly complicated the running of the city.

Mayor Teddy Kollek has announced that he will not run for another term in 1993. (S.M.)

*** Jordan and Israel** Though not part of a any formal negotiating process, Jordanian-Israeli contacts continued at the highest level in the late 1980s. On April 11, 1987, King Ḥussein and Israeli Foreign Minister Shimon *Peres reached an agreement in London outlining the procedure and basis for Jordanian-Israeli peace negotiations (See: *London Agreement). The agreement, which was made public in the Israeli media, failed to be ratified by the *National Unity Government, and it was denied by the Jordanians. The London agreement was soon overtaken by events. In December 1987 the **intifada* broke out, and forced Jordan to be cautious on the subject of relations with both Israel and the Palestinians. On July 31, 1988, King Ḥussein announced Jordan's disengagement from the West Bank, indicating to both Israel and the Palestinians that Jordan no longer intended to substitute for the Palestinians in any future peace process. It did not, however, exclude the option of coordinating with the Palestinians future negotiations with Israel, such as was in fact established at the *Madrid Conference in October 1991.

When Iraq invaded Kuwait in August, 1990, Jordan feared that it would become a battleground in the event of a regional conflagration involving Israel and Iraq. Well before the outbreak of the Gulf crisis Israel had warned Jordan against any military cooperation with Iraq. In August 1989, Israel had protested to Jordan, through the US, for permitting Iraqi aircraft to fly reconnaissance missions along Jordan's border with Israel. In February 1990, there were reports of the formation of a joint Jordanian-Iraqi air squadron, designed to overcome a cutback in the flying hours of the Jordanian air-force due to economic difficulties, by enabling Jordanian pilots to fly Iraqi aircraft. Israel protested again to Jordan through the US, but as neither Israel nor Jordan wished unnecessary tension, both downplayed the issue. Israeli Minister of Defense Yitzḥak *Rabin observed that the Jordanian-Iraqi cooperation was, at that stage, purely defensive, and that Israel would not be concerned by it unless it involved an Iraqi deployment of forces on Jordanian soil. It was against such a deployment of forces that Israel repeatedly warned, following the outbreak of the Gulf crisis, and threatened to use force to prevent it. As a result Jordan put its forces in a state of partial alert, while King Ḥussein declared that Jordan would not allow passage to anyone, in any direction, and that if threatened or attacked it would defend itself. Seeking to put Jordan at ease, Israel assured it that it had no intention of undermining its stability. Despite the Israeli assurances, and reported Jordanian counter-assurances that Jordan would not allow foreign forces on its territory, tension mounted along the Israeli-Jordanian border as January 15, 1991 (the date of the American ultimatum for Iraq to withdraw from Kuwait) approached. In late December 1990 and early January 1991, the Jordanian army held large-scale maneuvers close to the border with Israel. After both Iraq and Syria declared that they would regard an attack on Jordan as an attack on themselves, Jordan declared that it would seek their support if attacked. The official Jordanian reaction to the firing of Scud missiles from Iraq towards Israel over Jordanian territory during the Gulf War, which elicited reactions of popular enthusiasm in Jordan, was judiciously cautious. Jordanian leaders refused to condemn or condone the missile attacks.

In general, Israel has shown considerable restraint in its policy towards Jordan. From 1989 the security situation along the Israeli-Jordanian border took a turn for the worse. After many years of relative tranquility, there were frequent incidents of infiltration or clashes across the border involving Palestinian groups, radical Muslims and even individual Jordanian soldiers. The deterioration appeared to be related to the rise of Islamic fervor and the impact of the *intifada* in Jordan. Warnings were issued by Israel to Jordan after each incident, but as Israeli authorities believed that Jordan was making a genuine effort to prevent the incidents, there was no retaliation.

In the aftermath of the Gulf War, and Jordan once again assumed a central role in the planned peace process. The US now revived its "two track" approach, which called for Israeli-Palestinian negotiations simultaneously with inter-state ones, and Jordan had a keen interest in being involved. On October 30, 1991, the *Madrid Conference convened, with Jordan attending within the framework of a joint Jordanian-Palestinian delegation, where the Palestinian contingent included only Palestinians from the West Bank and *Gaza Strip who are not members of the *PLO. This arrangement coincided with the interests of both Jordan and Israel. Once the bilateral talks got underway the Jordanian-Palestinians split into two groups. When Jordanian issues were discussed nine Jordanians and two Palestinians took part, and when Palestinian issues were discussed the numbers reversed. Jordan chose to participate in the sessions of all five sets of *multilateral talks, although they were boycotted by Syria and Lebanon. This seemed to indicate a somewhat more urgent desire on the part of the Jordanians for an overall peaceful settlement with Israel. Jordan and Israel also held independent contacts outside the formal talks, on such current issues as the distribution and use of water between them (See: *water policy). In October 1992 it was reported that Israel had set up a removable bridge on that section of the Yarmuk River which serves as the border between itself and Jordan, in order to facilitate the frequent contacts between Israeli and Jordanian officials dealing with current problems regarding water exploitation. Jordan was the first Arab party to reach an agreement with Israel over the agenda for the talks between the two countries. The agenda included the issues of security and the abstention from the use of or the threat to use force, water, refugees, border and territorial issues, and bilateral cooperation in the spheres of natural resources, human resources, infrastructure and economics. While Jordan ostensibly no longer has any territorial claims over the West Bank, it has raised two minor ones: one over 350 square kilometers south of the Dead Sea in the Arava, the other over a very small area at the confluence of the Jordan and Yarmuk rivers. (As.S.)

*** Kach** The party was disqualified from running in the elections to the 12th Knesset on grounds that it incited to racism. Following the assassination of Meir *Kahane in November 1990, *Kach* split into two factions. One, *Od Kahane Hai* ("Kahane is still alive," or "another Kahane is alive") accepted the leadership of Meir Kahane's son Binyamin Ze'ev, and demanded a national referendum to choose a leader for the country with emergency powers. The second faction, assumed the name *Ko'aḥ* ("power") and was led by Baruch Marzel, a former aide of Meir Kahane. Both factions were involved in numerous attacks on Arabs and clashes with Jewish left-wing groups. The two lists were disqualified by the Central Elections Committee for the elections to the 13th Knesset. (I.M.)

*** Kahane, Meir** (1932-1990) In the fall of 1988 the Central Elections Committee disqualified *Kahane's party, **Kach*, from running in the elections, on grounds that it incited to racism. Kahane appealed to the High Court of Justice, but the disqualification was upheld. He continued to promote his policies in an extra-parliamentary fashion. On November 5, 1990 Kahane was assassinated while leaving a public gathering he had addressed in New York city. An Arab of Egyptian descent was apprehended, but was finally only convicted of illegal possession of a firearm. Kahane's funeral in Jerusalem was the occasion of anti-Arab and anti-leftist rioting. (I.M.)

*** Kalanterism** The worst manifestation of "Kalanterism" in Israel occurred following the fall of the *National Unity Government on March 15, 1991 and the attempts, first by *Israel Labor Party chairman Shimon *Peres and then by Prime Minister Yitzḥak *Shamir of the **Likud* to form narrow governments. While Labor managed to "buy" the support of a former minister of tourism from the *Likud* (Avraham Sharir) and tried to buy that of the *Party for Advancing the Zionist Idea, the *Likud* managed to buy the support of Labor MK Efraim Gur.

Following these events the Knesset passed an amendment to the "Basic Law: the Knesset" (See: *Basic Laws) which sets legal limitations to the practice. The amendment, passed by the Knesset on February 12, 1991, states that a Knesset member who has switched factions can continue to serve in the current Knesset, but cannot be made a minister or deputy minister, cannot be promised a seat in the next Knesset and is not entitled to party financing.

Katzav, Moshe **Likud* politician. Katzav was born in Iran in 1945 and immigrated to Israel with his parents in 1950. His family settled in the Kastina *ma'abarah* (transit camp) which later turned into the development town of Kiryat Mal'achi. After his demobilization from the IDF, Katzav worked for a while at Bank Hapo'alim, in the Vulcani Institute of Agriculture and as a reporter for *Yediot Aharonot* in the south. He later completed a BA in history and economics at the Hebrew University in Jerusalem, and was Chairman of the **Gahal* students' cell at the university.

In 1969, at the age of 24 Katzav was elected as head of the Kiryat Mal'achi local council. In 1977, he was elected to the Knesset on the *Likud* list, and became Deputy Minister of Housing and Construction in 1981, and was put in charge of *Project Renewal. In 1984, he was appointed Minister of Labor and Welfare, and in 1988 Minister of Transportation.

After the elections to the 13th Knesset, Katzav was chosen as chairman of the *Likud* Knesset faction. He is a candidate for the *Likud* leadership in the *primaries to be held in March 1993.

*** Kessar, Israel** Kessar was reelected as Secretary General of the **Histadrut* in November 1989 by a majority of over 55 percent. He ran in the primaries for the leadership of the Labor Party in February 1992 and received just under 20 percent of the votes. In the government formed by Yitzḥak *Rabin after the elections to the 13th Knesset Kessar was appointed Minister of Transportation and resigned as Secretary General of the *Histadrut.*

Kibbutzim In 1992 there were 278 kibbutzim, 176 affiliated to the **Takam*, 85 to **Hakibbutz Ha'artzi* and 17 to **Hakibbutz Hadati*. The population of the kibbutzim was around 140,000 (less than 3 percent of the total population) of whom about 12,000 were new immigrants but not members. The kibbutzim were responsible for about 40 percent of the agricultural produce of Israel and about 8 percent of its industrial production. By the second decade of the 1980s the kibbutzim were in a deep crisis resulting from a combination of causes. The first, with origins in the 1970s, was linked to the adaptation of the kibbutz to the capitalist society around it at a time when the kibbutz ceased to be a closed, self-sufficient community and its members started to seek more privacy and a higher standard of living. The second had its origins in the 1977 political *upheaval which left the kibbutz without government backing. The third was demographic by nature: veteran kibbutzim had to start contending with the problems of an aging population. The fourth factor was a serious financial crisis which hit most of the kibbutzim, and as a result of the system of mutual guarantees, the movement as a whole.

The financial crisis, which resulted from a combination of objective economic conditions, government policies and mismanagement of many kibbutzim, originated in the years of hyper-inflation in the early 1980s, and reached its climax in 1987-88. In 1989 negotiations took place for an overall settlement of the debts of the kibbutzim which had reached a sum of several billion shekels, involving cancellation of a part of the debts and a recycling of the rest. By 1992 only a third of the settlement was actually implemented and it was clear that complementary settlements would be required to complete the process. The crisis forced the kibbutzim to start undergoing major changes. Strict economic considerations began to play a central role in kibbutz life, and social changes followed. To many kibbutz industries professional boards of directors were appointed. Non-profitable economic branches were abolished. Many kibbutzim allowed their members to seek employment outside the kibbutz, and to sell a variety of services to non-members. Many kibbutzim considered charging members for the services they received and calculating the real income earned by individual members. The major ideological problem facing the kibbutz movements is how far it can change, economically and socially, without ceasing to be a kibbutz.

*** Knesset** Parliamentarism in Israel has eroded in recent years as a result of various distortions and malfunctions in the working of the Knesset. One major problem developed during the six years in which the *National Unity Governments ruled (1984-90), leaving an opposition of less than 30 Knesset members. Under these circumstances the opposition, from both extremes of the political spectrum, made itself heard, but was totally ineffective. Another problem was that the national unity governments was very large, which meant that about 25 percent of the Knesset members had government positions and were thus not involved in parliamentary work. In the two narrow governments which followed, that formed by Yitzḥak *Shamir in 1990 and that formed by Yitzḥak *Rabin in 1992, again the combined number of ministers and deputy ministers was excessive.

Another set of problems concerns a blurring of the separation of powers. On the one hand, the Knesset has been increasingly inclined to play an executive role and dictate policy through the way some of its committees have been functioning, and as a result of the percentage of private members' legislation growing from about 6 percent in the first 8 Knessets to 35 percent in the 12th. On the other hand, especially in the last two years of the 12th Knesset the High Court of Justice was approached on several occasions to decide in parliamentary disputes. In the same period, the Knesset also saw some of the most extraordinary cases of manipulation of the Knesset regulations and political bribery by the government in an attempt to prevent certain items of legislation getting through.

In structural terms only insignificant changes have taken place in the Knesset in recent years. One such change was the addition of a Drugs Committee to the original ten Knesset committees, following the 1992 elections. It was set up to resolve a dispute between *Labor and the **Likud*, and was handed over to **Tzomet*. Another change was the limitation of the number of permanent committee members to 17 in the case of the Finance Committee and Foreign Affairs and Security Committee, and to 15 in all other committees.

For the first time in the history of the State of Israel a government was brought down by a vote of no confidence by the Knesset on March 15, 1990. However, following this, the formation of a new government was accompanied by political horse-trading, which the Knesset tried to eliminate by means of three pieces of legislation. The first was the amendment to the Basic Law: the Knesset, passed on February 12, 1991, which limits *Kalanterism. The second was the amendment to the Knesset Elections Law passed on October 14, 1991, which raised the qualifying threshold from 1 to 1.5 percent, thus reducing the number of parties in the Knesset. The third was the new Basic Law: the Government passed on June 18, 1992, which introduced a system of direct elections of the Prime Minister which seeks to increase the power of the Prime Minister at the expense of the Knesset. This law will be applied for the first time in the general elections to the 14th Knesset (See: *Prime Minister, direct election of),

KNESSET SPEAKERS

1949 – 59	Joseph Sprinzak (1897–1959) -**Mapai*
1959 – 59	Naḥum Nir (1884–1968) - **Mapam*
1959 – 69	Kadish Luz (1895–1972) - *Mapai*
1969 – 72	Reuven Barkat (1905–1972) - Israel Labor Party
1972 – 77	Yisrael Yeshayahu (1908–1979) - Israel Labor Party
1977 – 80	Yitzḥak *Shamir (b. 1915) - *Likud*
1980 – 81	Yitzḥak Berman (b. 1913) - *Likud*
1981 – 84	Menaḥem Savidor (1917–1988) - *Likud*
1984 – 88	Shlomo Hillel (b. 1923) - ILP
1988 – 92	Dov Shilansky (b. 1924) - *Likud*
1992–	Shevah *Weiss (b. 1935) - ILP

*** Knessets of Israel**

11th Knesset (elected July 23, 1984)

	Seats after elections	Seats at end of term
* Alignment	44	40
Likud	41	43
* *Teḥiya*h-		
* *Tzomet*	5	4
(*Teḥiya*h)		
* National Religious Party	4	4
* *Ḥadash*	4	5
* *Shass*	4	3
* *Shinui*	3	2
* Civil Rights Movement	3	5
* *Yahad*	3	0
* Progressive List for Peace	2	2
* *Agudat Yisrael*	2	2
* *Morasha*	2	2
* *Tami*	1	0
* *Kach*	1	1
* *Ometz*	1	0
* *Mapam*	0	5
* *Tzomet*	0	1
Shimon Ben Shlomo	0	1

12th Knesset (elected November 1, 1988)

	Seats after elections	Seats at end of term
Likud	40	37
Alignment	39	38
Shass	6	5
Agudat Yisrael	5	4
Civil Rights Movement	5 }	
* *Mapam*	3 }	*Meretz* 10
Shinui	2 }	
National Religious Party	5	5
Ḥadash	4	3
*Teḥiya*h	3	3
Tzomet	2	2
* Moledet	2	2
* *Degel Hatorah*	2	2
Progressive List for Peace	1	1
* Arab Democratic Party	1	1
* Party for Advancing the Zionist Idea	0	3
* *Moriah* (Yitzḥak *Peretz)	0	1
* Black Panthers (Charlie Bitton)	0	1
* *Geulat Yisrael* (Eliezer Mizraḥi)	0	1
Ahdut Lema'an Hashalom Veha'aliya (Efraim Gur)	0	1

13th Knesset (elected June 23, 1992)

	Seats after elections	Seats at end of term
Labor	44	
Likud	32	
Meretz	12	
Tzomet	8	
National Religious Party	6	
Shass	6	
**Yahadut Hatorah Hame'uḥedet*	4	
Moledet	3	
Ḥadash	3	
Arab Democratic Party	2	

*** Kollek, Teddy** During the **intifada* Kollek saw his dream of a peaceful and united *Jerusalem, collapse. Nevertheless, he did not lose heart and continued to argue that he was optimistic about the future.

Kollek withstood pressures for a change in the religious *status quo in Jerusalem although he lost his absolute majority in the municipal council in the 1989 municipal elections, and became partially dependent on the religious factions. In November 1992 he announced that he would not run for a further term as mayor and that he would resign before his term was up.

Land for Peace A term used in connection with solving the *Arab-Israeli conflict. It implies that in return for full peace Israel would be willing to withdraw from all the territories which it occupied in June 1967. This principle was applied in the *Egyptian-Israeli peace treaty.

*** Latin America and Israel** The atmosphere in the relations between Israel and various Latin American states improved with the general improvement in Israel's status in the international arena after 1986. Israel has full diplomatic relations with 30 of the 33 Latin American countries. There are no relations with Cuba, Guyana and Nicaragua. In the late 1980s Cuba, which had broken relations with Israel in 1973, showed some interest in developing contacts with Israel. Towards the end of 1992 it was reported that relations would soon be established between Israel and Nicaragua. Relations had been broken in 1979, when the Sandinistas gained power, and officially severed by Nicaragua in 1982, during the *Lebanese War. Relations further deteriorated as Israel, in association with the US, supplied the anti-government rebels - the Contras - with arms in1985-86 (See: *Irangate).

Among the many official visits of Israeli leaders and leaders of Latin American states which took place in the years 1987-92, was one by Argentinian President Carlos Saul Menem, who was elected President in

May 1989. Menem, who is of Syrian origin, visited Israel in the beginning of October 1991, and in the course of an extremely friendly visit offered to host the Middle East peace conference in Buenos Aires. He addressed a mass pro-Israel demonstration on March 19, 1992, following the destruction of the Israeli Embassy in Buenos Aires by a terrorist bomb in which several Israeli diplomats were killed.

After 1988 the names of various retired Israeli officers came up in connection with scandals in various Latin American states. These involved the training of armed forces and sale of arms to various groups involved in drug cartels. Though there was no official Israeli involvement in any of these cases, the supervision over private Israeli arms sales was tightened, and the pseudo-military activities of former Israeli officers abroad were more closely watched.

Lebanon and Israel The relations between Israel and Lebanon since 1987 were a function of several factors: Israel's insistence on maintaining a security zone in Southern Lebanon in order to safeguard its northern settlements against terrorist attacks by Palestinian organizations (both *PLO and rejectionist) and Shi'ite organizations (*Amal* and the *Ḥizballah)*; efforts to free, or retrieve the bodies of the Israeli soldiers taken prisoner during the *Lebanese War; the political and communal instability inside Lebanon and growing Syrian control over Lebanon.

In the security zone Israel continued to maintain and train the Southern Lebanese Army (SLA), under general Antoine Laḥad. The force which was at first of about 2,500 men - most of them Christians - grew in 1990 to 3,000, and included Druze and Muslims as well. The security zone was never absolutely quiet. In addition to direct attacks on the SLA and Israeli forces and road bombs, from time to time Katyusha rockets were fired in the direction of Israel, and there were attempts (by Palestinian organizations) to cross the border to perform terrorist attacks inside Israel.

The year 1988 was much more eventful than 1987, largely because the Palestinian organizations competed with one another in showing their solidarity with the **intifada*, although after the Palestine National Council meeting in Algiers in November the *Fataḥ* held its fire as a result of Yasser Arafat's attempt to open a PLO-US dialogue. In 1989 and 1990 activities decreased again, but when the peace process seemed to be in motion following the *Gulf War, the acts of violence by the organizations opposed to the process, rose again. In addition to regular *IDF patrols in the security zone, Israel retaliated to every major attack upon itself or the SLA with artillery fire, occasional air strikes against the headquarters and training facilities of the various organizations, and rare major military operations, such as "Operation Law and Order" on May 2, 1988. In general, it was noted that the Shi'ite fundamentalist organization *Ḥizballah* - established in 1982, financed and supported by Iran and allowed to function more or less freely by Syria increased its power and activities in the south, while the implementation of the Ta'if Agreement of October 1989 (see below) more or less liquidated the more pragmatic Shi'ite organization *Amal*, while limiting the effective power of the Palestinians.

On July 27, 1989, Israel abducted Sheikh Obeid, one of the leaders of the *Ḥizballah*, with the express intention of exchanging him for Israel's soldiers believed to be held, by the Shi'ite organization, and western hostages. But the *Ḥizballah* would not make a move, and at the end of 1992 Obeid was still being held in Israel. At the end of the summer in 1991 there was talk that all the western hostages in Lebanon were to be freed. Israel contributed to their release by freeing numerous Lebanese terrorists held in Israel and by the SLA, hoping that this would encourage the release of the Israeli soldiers as well. But only the body of a *Druze soldier - Samir al-Assad who had been abducted in April 1983 - was returned to Israel in September 1991. On November 20, 1991 *Ḥizballah* leader Sheikh Abbas Musawi declared that all the western hostages would be freed, but that additional Israelis would be taken hostage. Partly as a result of this statement, and to activities inspired by Musawi to obstruct the peace talks, Israel attacked a convoy of cars in which Musawi was traveling on February 16, killing the *Ḥizballah* leader. In the middle of 1992 it was verified that the *Ḥizballah* was holding the bodies of two other Israeli soldiers known to have been caught alive, but continuous efforts to discover the fate of the navigator Ron Arad - the only Israeli believed to be still alive - came to nothing.

The presidency of the Christian, Amin Jemayel, came to an end in August 1988. For a period there was a presidential vacuum in Lebanon after Jemayel handed over power (and the Ba'abde presidential palace) to General Michel Aoun, and the Syrians tried to bring about the election of a pro-Syrian president. Israel had initially sought to help the Christian minority continue to rule in Lebanon, but its feelings toward Aoun were ambivalent. It was reported that Israel had allowed Saddam Ḥussein get arms to Aoun in June 1989 (See: *Iraq and Israel), but some observers argued that it was Israel which had deliberately leaked the information in order to foil them. When with tacit American approval the Syrians finally made a full scale attack on the Ba'abde palace on October 13, 1990, in order to oust Aoun, and contrary to their red-line understandings with Israel used their air force, Israel did not react. Now it was possible to start implementing the Ta'if Agreement of the previous year which called for constitutional reforms in Lebanon and the disarming of the various militias, to be followed by a Syrian withdrawal from most of Lebanon.. On the basis of the Ta'if Agreement, the Lebanese parliament chose Elias Harawi as president of Lebanon in November 1989 - 11 months before Aoun was ousted. Israel's feelings about the Ta'if Agreement were mixed. On the one hand it was in favor of a stable and strong Lebanese government capable of tasking charge of the whole of Lebanon and also of preventing attacks on Israel from its southern border. The prospect of the disarmament of the militias (though at this stage Israel would not consider the disarmament of the SLA) was also viewed favorably.

On the other hand, Israel was skeptical as to whether such a government could actually survive without continued Syrian involvement, which under certain circumstances could constitute a serious danger to Israel's security. Israel was thus not surprised when Syria and Lebanon signed a "fraternity, coordination and cooperation" agreement in May 1991, and the Syrian army did not redeploy in the Bek'a region at the end of 1991, as provided for in the Ta'if Agreement.

The bilateral talks between Israel and Lebanon which followed the *Madrid Conference, have been little more than a formality, with the Lebanese calling on Israel to abide by Security Council Resolution 425 (passed on March 19, 1978 during the *Litani Operation, which calls for Israeli withdrawal from Southern Lebanon), and Israel repeating that while it has no territorial claims in Lebanon, as long as there is no prospect of the Lebanese government preventing attacks on Israel from its territory, Israel will continue to hold on to the security zone and maintain the SLA.

*** Levinger, Rabbi Moshe** Prior to the outbreak of the *intifada* Levinger staged a one-man demonstration by the refugee camp of Deheishe from which Israeli cars were being regularly stoned, and was later involved in several incidents. In one he shot dead a bystander near a Hebron store, allegedly in self-defense. Levinger sentenced to a prison sentence for manslaughter in May 1990 and his standing as a leader of the settler movement greatly weakened. In the elections to the 13th Knesset he ran on his own list - the "Land of Israel-Torah of Israel" list - with Daniela Weiss as his number two, but got less than 10 percent of the minimum number of votes needed to pass the qualifying threshold.

*** Levy, David** Levy continued to serve as Minister of Housing and Construction in the *National Unity Government of 1988. Despite his moderate political views, for tactical reasons Levy joined Ariel *Sharon and Yitzḥak *Moda'i in their opposition to the*Shamir-Rabin peace initiative. In the government formed in June 1990, Levy insisted on being given the Ministry of Foreign Affairs. During his time at the Foreign Ministry diplomatic relations were renewed or established with over 30 states, including the *Soviet Union, *China and *India. Levy was favorable to the peace initiative of Secretary of State James Baker which followed the *Gulf War , but when the *Madrid Conference was convened in October 1991 Shamir insisted on heading the Israeli delegation, and Levy decided to stay away in protest.

In a contest to the *Likud* leadership in the *Likud* Central Committee on February 20, 1992, Levy came second with 32 percent, between Shamir and Sharon. However, the following week, when the *Likud*'s list to the 13th *Knesset was elected in the committee, Levy was placed in 18th place on the panel and in fourth place in the final list, while few members of his camp entered the list in realistic places. With a group of leaders from development towns Levy, who felt that Shamir, Sharon and the "*Likud* princes" had connived to humiliate him, planned to break away from the *Likud* and form a separate party. However, at the last moment Levy reached an agreement with Shamir.

Following the electoral defeat of the *Likud* in June 1992, Levy announced his intention to run in the primaries for the *Likud* leadership to be held in March 1993.

*** Likud** Though the *Likud* emerged from the elections to the 12th Knesset in 1988 with 40 Knesset seats compared to Labor's 39, and the right wing and religious parties together had a majority of 65 in the Knesset, Yitzḥak *Shamir decided to form another *National Unity Government with the *Israel Labor Party. In the latter part of 1989 there were growing signs of disunity within the *Likud* related to the *Shamir-Rabin peace initiative of May 14, 1989, which was openly opposed by the three *Likud* "constraints ministers" — Ariel *Sharon, David *Levy and Yitzḥak *Moda'i.

The National Unity Government was brought down by a vote of no confidence on March 15, 1990. On the day of the vote five members of the former Liberal Party, headed by Yitzḥak Moda'i, formally turned into an independent Knesset faction (See: *The Party for Advancing the Zionist Idea). The faction decided to enter the new government formed by Shamir on June 11, after the *Likud* Central Committee approved the coalition agreement with it, and two of the five returned to the *Likud*.

The period of grace enjoyed by the new government formed by Shamir - with the resumption of the mass **aliyah* from the *former republics of the Soviet Union, Operation Solomon (See: *Ethiopian Jews), the resumption or establishment of diplomatic relations with over 30 states, and the *Madrid Conference - did not, however, help the *Likud* put its house in order. On December 22, 1991, a proposed new constitution for the *Likud*, which was to institutionalize the formal union between the *Herut Movement and the *Liberal Party (which had been signed on August 5, 1988), was rejected by the Central Committee. This meant that the *Likud* was left without any legally valid institutions.

Though the *Likud*-led coalition started falling apart after *Tzomet* decided to leave the coalition, the *Likud* tried to avoid early elections. However, by the end of January 1992, after the *Teḥiyah* and **Moledet* left the coalition as well, Shamir gave in and agreed to hold early elections in June. On February 20, in a leadership contest within the Central Committee, Shamir managed to maintain his position, but received only 46 percent of the votes, with David Levy receiving 32 percent and Ariel *Sharon 22 percent .

The *Likud* ran an extremely aggressive campaign towards the elections in the 13th Knesset. In the elections its power fell from 40 Knesset seats to 32, while the right-wing - religious bloc fell from 65 to 59. Immediately after the elections Moshe *Arens resigned from the *Likud* Knesset list, and Shamir announced that he would resign after a new leader would be elected to replace him.

The *Likud* is to hold *primaries for its leadership in March 1993.

*** Local Government** In the late 1980s a growing number of local authorities were in grave financial difficulties. The financial problems of the local councils and municipalities led to frequent strikes, when they could not pay the salaries of their employees. The Ministry of the Interior was often forced to make special allocations to keep the local councils and municipalities above water. The problem resulted from a basic imbalance between the income of the local authorities and the cost of the services they are expected to provide, further aggravated by the financial burden of absorbing the new immigrants. Another problem was the frequent delays in the transfer of approved funds by the central government to the local authorities. Furthermore, there was gross financial mismanagement in many local councils, and no effective public control. At the end of 1992 the problem was still acute. The situation in the Arab local councils was worse than in the Jewish ones. The *Islamic Movement took advantage of this situation to gain support by funding education and various social services. On August 26, 1991 the government hurriedly took the decision to equate (at least on paper) the budgets of the Arab local councils to those of the Jewish ones, but in practical terms the inequalities remained.

Among the other issues which came up in this period was the so-called "authorization law" brought up by Minister of Religious Affairs Zvulun *Hammer in January 1988. This amendment to the Local Authorities Law, was designed to enable heads of local authorities to pass municipal laws on the issue of observance of the Sabbath and force places of amusement to remain shut on Saturday. The amendment, which came under heavy criticism from non-religious circles, was finally passed in December 1990, as part of the price paid by the **Likud* to the religious parties for joining the government it formed in June (See: *status quo, religious).

In the municipal elections held in February/March 1989, the *Israel Labor Party lost to the *Likud* 17 local authorities and won (in the second round) four. For the first time since the establishment of the state Labor lost to the *Likud* control over the Local Government Center. Municipal elections will be held again in November 1993.

London Agreement Secret agreement reached between King Ḥussein of Jordan and Israeli Foreign Minister Shimon *Peres in London on April 11, 1987. The first part of the agreement stipulated that the Secretary General of the UN would extend invitations to the five Permanent Members of the Security Council and to the parties involved in the Arab-Israeli conflict to negotiate a settlement based on *Security Council Resolutions 242 and 338 with the goal of achieving a comprehensive settlement that would ensure the security of the states in the region and the legitimate rights of the Palestinian people. The second part specified that the objective of the negotiations would be to solve the Palestinian problem in all its aspects, and the conference would invite the parties to form regional bilateral committees to negotiate common issues. In the third part of the agreement, it was agreed that the conference would not impose a settlement or veto any agreement reached by the parties; there would be direct negotiations in the bilateral committees; the Palestinian issue would be discussed in a committee composed of the Israeli delegation and a joint Jordanian-Palestinian delegation; and the participation of the Palestinians in the conference would be dependent on their acceptance of Resolutions 242 and 338 and their renunciation of violence and terrorism.

Jordan insisted that the agreement be treated with "great confidentiality," and be regarded as a set of commitments made by Jordan to the United States - not to Israel. The document was brought by Peres to the Israeli Cabinet for its approval in the beginning of May. The vote was a draw due to the *Likud*'s opposition, and it was rejected. King Ḥussein subsequently denied the existence of the agreement. (See also: *international conference, *Jordan and Israel, *Shultz Plan and *Madrid Conference). (As.S.)

Madrid Conference After seven months of intensive shuttle diplomacy in the Middle East which began in March 1991, Secretary of State James Baker obtained the agreement of all the parties directly involved in the Arab-Israeli conflict to participate in an *international conference, which at Israel's insistence would serve only as a preamble to direct bilateral and multilateral talks between Israel and its neighbors. The Israeli demand that the PLO should not be party to the negotiations, that Palestinians from the *administered territories (approved by Israel) should form part of a joint Jordanian-Palestinian delegation, and that there would be no pre-conditions to the talks, were also accepted.

The invitations to the conference were sent jointly by Baker and Soviet Foreign Minister Boris Pankin on October 18, 1991, twelve days before the opening session. The conference opened with speeches by Presidents George Bush and Mikhail Gorbachev, followed by Prime Minister Yitzḥak *Shamir (who insisted on heading the Israeli delegation although the other Arab states were represented by foreign ministers), the foreign ministers of Syria, Jordan, Lebanon and Egypt, the head of the Palestinians of the joint Jordanian-Palestinian delegation - Ḥaider Abd al-Shafi. Contrary to Israel's demand, Abd al-Shafi was given equal time with the other delegations to deliver opening and closing speeches. None of the speeches were conciliatory, and the Syrian Foreign Minister Farouk a-Sharaa was outright hostile, but the importance of the conference was that the parties directly involved in the Arab-Israeli conflict were present, and sat at the same table. Furthermore, all the other Arab states (except Iraq) were represented at the conference by observers. Immediately after the conference was over the first meetings between Israel's negotiating teams and three separate Syrian, Lebanese and Jordanian-Palestinian teams took place in Madrid, to be followed by bilateral talks which were to open without intermediaries in Washington on December 10, 1991.

The first five rounds of the Washington talks, held while the **Likud* was still in power in Israel, dealt almost exclusively with procedure. Israel, under the *Likud*, rejected any talk of territorial concessions and was only willing to discuss a limited *autonomy plan for the Palestinians. After Yitzḥak *Rabin formed his government in July 1992 the nature of the talks and the atmosphere changed, even though at first only the head of the negotiating team with Syria, Yossi Ben-Aharon, was replaced by Professor Ittamar Rabinowitz. The new Israeli policy was to agree in principle to the *territorial compromise formula. Its immediate goal was to reach interim agreements with the Syrians (possibly involving a token Israeli withdrawal on the *Golan Heights) and Palestinians (involving the establishment of extensive self-administration). As for Lebanon the problem was that it did not have a government able to ensure Israel security along its northern border in return for an Israeli withdrawal from Southern Lebanon, and that its government was totally dependent on Syria.The main problem with Jordan was that it did not want to reach an agreement with Israel before the others. However, the first real breakthrough in the talks occurred during the seventh round of talks which opened on October 21, 1992, when the Israeli and Jordanian teams agreed to an agenda for the talks, and Jordan conceded that the final goal was a peace treaty.

The first round of multilateral talks on regional issues opened in Moscow on January 28, 1992. The subjects on the agenda were water, the environment, economic cooperation and arms control, to which the subject of refugees was added. The Syrians and the Lebanese decided to boycott the Moscow meeting and the multilateral talks in general until progress was made in the bilateral talks. The Palestinians did not participate in the Moscow meeting because they insisted that the *PLO should formally participate - a demand Israel rejected. No real progress was made in the first two rounds of the multilateral talks held in the course of 1992 in various capitals, and little is expected before progress is made in the bilateral talks.

Mapam After running in the elections since 1969 within the framework of the *Alignment, *Mapam* ran on its own for the first time in 1988 and won three seats. Despite certain ideological doubts about running in a single list with *laissez faire* liberals, *Mapam* decided to run in the elections to the 13th Knesset in 1992 within the framework of **Meretz*. Four of the 12 *Meretz* MKs, and one of its three ministers in the government formed in July 1992 (Yair *Tzaban) are members of *Mapam*. One of the two Arab deputy ministers in the government formed by Yitzḥak *Rabin in July 1992, Ḥaj Yiḥia Walid Sadik, is also from *Mapam*. (M.H.)

Media and Politics Since the late 1980s and especially in the early 1990s, the growing number of local newspapers and the introduction of cable television on the one hand, and the introduction in the major parties of the system of *primaries, on the other, increased the significance of the inordinate close contacts between politicians and journalists. The phenomenon of leaks to the media, coming from politicians, police officers and even top military echelons reached worrying proportions.

Despite the fact that at the end of 1992 the National Broadcasting Authority still had an almost complete monopoly over news broadcasts on radio and television, the standard of news reporting remained high and the reporting itself highly credible. At the end of 1992 the problem of concessions for a second commercial television channel had not yet been ironed out.

Since 1965, when the Broadcasting Authority Law was passed, its governing bodies have been political. This became especially marked in the years of the *National Unity Government, when the coalition agreements included a provision that the chairman of the Authority would be from the *Israel Labor Party and the Director General from the *Likud. After the fall of the Unity Government in March 1990, a chairman was appointed from the *National Religious Party. The political balance in the plenary of the Broadcasting Authority ensured minimal political bias in the broadcasts of the national radio and television, despite complaints of the radical right regarding the "hostile media."

Between June 1990 and July 1992, attempts were made by some of the more extreme right-wing members of the Broadcasting Authority plenary to influence the news programs, by trying to bring about the removal of persons known to have left-wing views (e.g. the case of the *Druze reporter and news producer Rafiq Ḥalabi) or by other means (e.g. the attempt, temporarily successful, to move the weekly news magazine from Friday night - during peak viewing - to Saturday night).

At the start of the **intifada* the *IDF authorities tried to keep the media (especially the foreign media) away from trouble spots, but the networks started using local inhabitants equipped with video cameras. There is no doubt that the presence of the media occasionally helped create or prolong events, but after a while the extensive media coverage, which was highly damaging to Israel's image abroad, decreased, and by the end of 1992 the number of foreign reporters stationed in Israel fell. Throughout the *intifada* the East Jerusalem newspapers continued to appear under the usual censorship constraints, despite the direct involvement of many journalists in the *intifada*. Some central journalists such as Radwan Abu-Ayash, were detained for certain periods.

The role and effectiveness of military censorship, especially as applied to the foreign media, came up during the *intifada*, the *Gulf War and in November 1992, in connection with an accident during a military exercise at the Ze'elim base in southern Israel, in which five soldiers were killed.

Meimad A Zionist religious movement established just before the 1988 elections as a result of the shift of the *National Religious Party to the right. *Meimad*, adopted moderate positions on both political and religious issues, claiming to represent the traditional and authentic views and values of religious *Zionism. It supported the idea of a *territorial compromise in return for peace, and rejected changes in the *status quo by legislation on religious matters which do not enjoy wide public support. The movement was headed by Rabbi Yehuda Amital.

In the elections to the 12th Knesset *Meimad* failed to pass the 1 percent qualifying threshold. It did not run for 13th Knesset in 1992. Some of its former leaders and backers returned to the NRP, while others chose to support Yitzḥak *Rabin. Following the elections, several former members of *Meimad*, decided to form a lobby, by the name of *Meimad*, to act as a moderate counterpart to the official positions of the NRP on religious issues. The new lobby does not plan to become a political party. (Y.B.M.)

*** Meretz - Democratic Israel** Common list formed by the *Civil Rights Movement, **Mapam* and **Shinui* before the 13th Knesset elections in 1992. Soon after the elections to the 12th Knesset in 1988 the idea of forming a single front of all the parties of the Zionist *peace camp in Israel, took root among their leaders, as well as certain dovish groups within the *Israel Labor Party. Despite the differences between the three parties, especially on economic and social issues, their leaders decided to concentrate on what united them, namely support for a solution of the *Arab-Israeli conflict in general and the Israeli- Palestinian conflict in particular on the basis of Israeli withdrawal from most of the territories occupied by it in 1967, as well as concern for democracy and the rule of law in the State of Israel. The three parties decided to make do with a single Knesset list, but not to unite at this stage, and continue to maintain their separate party institutions and branches.

The *Meretz* list to the 13th Knesset was headed by Shulamit *Aloni. It gained 12 seats and became the third largest faction in the Knesset after Labor and the *Likud*. *Meretz* joined the coalition formed by Yitzḥak *Rabin in July 1992 and received three ministerial posts. In December it received a fourth one. Despite its commitment to human rights and its opposition in principle to deportations, *Meretz* supported the government decision of December 16, 1992 to deport for two years 415 leading figures of the **Ḥammas* and *Islamic Jihad in order to save the peace process and try to stop the serious deterioration in the security situation. (M.H.)

Meridor, Dan Lawyer and **Likud* politician. Meridor was born in Jerusalem in 1947 in a *Revisionist family. He was Government Secretary in 1982-84, and elected to the 11th Knesset on the *Likud* list. In the Government formed by Yitzḥak *Shamir in December 1988 Meridor was appointed Minister of Justice. As one of the prominent *Likud* "princes," he at first enjoyed great popularity in his party. However, as Minister of Justice he proved to be too liberal to the liking of many right-wingers as a result of his concern for human rights, especially in the *occupied territories, and the rule of law. As Minister of Justice Meridor also tried to make progress in passing the remaining *basic laws, but was only partially successful. With the support of Shamir Meridor was elected to the 16th place on the *Likud* list to the 13th Knesset. (M.H.)

*** Military and Politics** The **intifada* dragged the IDF into the bitter political controversy which divides the Israeli society. The IDF was accused by the left of frequently reacting too harshly to Palestinian violence, while the right accused it of being too soft, arguing that with greater determination the *intifada* could be crushed. As Minister of Defense, Yitzḥak *Rabin repeatedly stated that while the *intifada* could be contained by military means, it could only be brought to an end by political means.

Senior army officers have increasingly found themselves in the center of the political controversy after making strategic evaluations which seemed to verify the positions of one side or the other in the controversy. Thus, on the eve of his retirement from the IDF Chief of Staff Dan Shomron stated that in a peace situation the strategic importance of the territories would decline. This was immediately interpreted by the right as proof that Shomron supports a *territorial compromise. On the other hand, a statement by his successor, Ehud Barak, in August 1991 to the effect that "the Golan is a vital component in Israel's security and the ability to defend it (the state)" was interpreted as an attempt to influence the Israeli position in the approaching peace talks. The result of such incidents has been that the military has frequently refrained from expressing clear positions on certain issues, for fear that they would be given a political interpretation.

In December 1991, on the eve of his retirement from the IDF, the commander of the Air Force, Major General Avihu Bin-Nun, raised a major problem in the relations between the military and the political level. Bin-Nun (still in uniform) criticized the political level for failing, in recent years, to lay down the country's defense policy, and leaving it to the military. One might add that since the government has never succeeded in forming a permanent national security forum which is subject to the political rather than the military level, it is the IDF which is exclusively responsible for all strategic planning and intelligence evaluations. This has resulted in the military having an inordinate influence on the political system.

The process of former senior officers entering politics immediately or shortly after retiring from the IDF, continued in the 12th and 13th Knessets. In the 12th Knesset three former commanders joined the benches of the right wing parties - Major General (res.) Reḥav'am *Ze'evi as leader of **Moledet*, former head of Army Intelligence, Major General (res.) Yehoshua Saguy of the *Likud*, and Colonel (res.) Yo'ash Tzidon of **Tzomet*. Of the three only Ze'evi was reelected to the 13th Knesset. In the 13th Knesset three former generals joined the benches of the *Israel Labor Party - Major General (res.) Ori Orr, and Brigadier Generals (res.) Avigdor Kahalani and Ephraim Sneh. (Mi.B.)

***Ministers for Foreign Affairs**

1986-88	Shimon Peres (*Israel Labor Party)
1988-90	Moshe *Arens (**Likud*)
1990-92	David *Levy (*Likud*)
1992-	Shimon Peres (ILP)

***Ministers of Defense**

1984-90	Yitzḥak *Rabin (*Israel Labor Party)
1990-92	Moshe *Arens (**Likud*)
1992-	Yitzḥak Rabin (ILP)

***Ministers of Finance**

1986-88	Moshe Nissim (**Likud*)
1988-90	Shimon *Peres (*Israel Labor Party)
1990-92	Yitzḥak *Moda'i (*Party for Advancing the Zionist Idea)
1992-	Avraham Beiga *Shoḥat (ILP)

Moda'i, Yitzḥak In the government formed in December 1988 Moda'i was appointed Minister of Economics and Planning. Following the government's decision in favor of holding elections in the *administered territories on May 14, 1989 (See: *Shamir-Rabin peace initiative), Moda'i joined Ariel *Sharon and David *Levy in opposing the plan.

On the eve of the government crisis in March 1990 Moda'i and four other members of the former *Liberal Party broke away from the **Likud*. (See: *Party for Advancing the Zionist Idea). In return, for recognizing them as a separate faction, the five voted with the *Likud* against the motion. Following the fall of the *National Unity Government, Moda'i held talks with Shimon *Peres about the possibility of joining a Labor-led government, but opted for joining a government headed by Shamir in return for the Ministry of Finance. As Minister of Finance Moda'i had difficulty in getting any of his economic plans or budgets accepted because he lacked the backing of the other ministers. Though he held talks with the Americans about the $10 billion worth of loan guarantees for the absorption of immigrants, Moda'i was adamant that Israel should not give in to the US demand that in return Israel freeze its settlement activities in the *administrated territories. (See: *settlement policy).

Moda'i tried to return to the *Likud* in February 1992, but when he failed decided to run in the elections to the 13th Knesset with his own list, now called the *New Liberal Party. The new party, which concentrated on the need for a healthy market economy, did not pass the qualifying threshold.

Moledet ("homeland") *Party founded by Reḥav'am *Ze'evi on the eve of the 1988 elections. In these elections *Moledet* ran on a single issue platform calling for a voluntary *transfer of the Arabs who are unwilling to accept Jewish predominance in **Eretz Yisrael.* *Moledet* insists that its position has nothing to do with the transfer by force which was advocated by Rabbi Meir *Kahane. *Moledet* won two seats in the 12th Knesset.

In February 1991 *Moledet* joined the *Likud* government headed by Yitzḥak Shamir, despite the protests of several *Likud* ministers. It left the government in January, 1992, together with the **Teḥiyah*, in protest against the talks on an *autonomy plan for the Palestinians in the peace talks following the *Madrid Conference.

Negotiations concerning the possibility of *Moledet* running in a single list with the *Teḥiyah* in the elections to the 13th Knesset failed, as did an attempt to get *Moledet* disqualified on the grounds that it is a racist party. In its campaign, *Moledet*, once again emphasized the transfer idea and the need to deal with the problem of Arab terror harshly. *Moledet* won three seats in the 13th Knesset. Following the elections the party entered a major crisis as a result of Ze'evi's authoritarian methods.

Moriah Knesset faction formed by Rabbi Yitzḥak *Peretz when he left **Shass* in March 1990. *Moriah* ran in elections to the 13th Knesset, within the framework of the *Yahadut Hatorah Hame'uḥedet* list. Peretz was finally left out of the 13th Knesset, and *Moriah* ceased to exist as a political party.

*** Morocco and Israel** From the late 1980s visits by Israelis — including politicians from all political parties — to Morocco, became commonplace. Morocco was one of the major Arab supporters of the *Madrid Conference. Following the Israeli elections of 1992 King Ḥassan expressed his willingness to meet with Prime Minister Yitzḥak *Rabin whom he had hosted in Morocco in October 1976.

On December 2, 1992, the remains of 22 of the 43 Jews who had been on board the boat "Egoz" which smuggled them out of Morocco and drowned off the Straits of Gibraltar on January 11, 1961, arrived in Israel from Morocco. The graves of the 22 had been located in Al-Ḥassima in Morocco in 1983, and in February 1984 Shimon *Peres, as leader of the opposition, first approached King Ḥassan to enable the remains to be brought to Israel. Following protracted negotiations the remains were to have been brought in October, 1986, but it was only in 1992 that King Ḥassan gave his final consent, and as a humanitarian gesture, enabled the remains to be flown directly from Morocco to Israel.

Moshavim In 1987 the *moshav* movement suffered a major financial crisis, involving the collapse of most of the cooperative institutions and of many individual farm units. The reasons for the crisis were similar to those in the **kibbutzim*, involving a combination of objective economic conditions, the government's *economic policy and mismanagement by the *moshavim* themselves.

There were two formal settlements for the debts of the *moshavim* with the participation of the *moshav* movement, the government and the banks, the first in 1988 and the second in 1990. However, they were not realistic since they were based on the mutual responsibility of each *moshav* member for all the debts of his *moshav* - both individual and collective - even if he himself had incurred no personal debts. In point of fact, 80 percent of the debts were incurred by only 20 percent of the members.

As the situation worsened, with the banks seizing movable property and numerous cases of suicide of *moshav* members who had lost all hope, a law, initiated by Labor MK Gdalia Gal and dealing with the debts of the *moshavim*, was passed by the Knesset just before its pre-election recess in March 1992. The law, which was passed against the wishes of the government, laid down the principle that *moshav* members would be responsible for their personal debts and for debts based on mutual guarantees only up to a sum of about 12,000 shekels. It is believed that on the basis of the new arrangement the creditors will receive 45-50 percent of the debts due to them, and that about 10 percent of the *moshav* members will be unable to repay their debts.

The *moshav* movement is currently engaged in a structural and ideological reorganization of the *moshavim*. The reorganization is based on economic cooperation - on the level of the individual *moshav*, the regional or the branch - being voluntary, and communal level being mandatory, so that the *moshav* will remain a closed community which new members can join only if its existing members agree, but in which each member can run his economic affairs more or less as he sees fit.

Mubarak Ten Points (See: *Shamir - Rabin peace initiative).

Multilateral Talks (See: *Madrid Conference)

Namir, Ora Labor politician. Namir was born in Hadera in 1930. During the *War of Independence she served as an officer in the Upper Galilee. She was secretary of the **Mapai* Knesset faction and of the coalition executive. In 1954-57 she studied English literature at Hunter College, New York and worked as a secretary for the Israeli United Nations delegation. In 1959 Namir married Tel Aviv mayor Mordechai Namir and became involved in social work. She served as Secretary General of the Tel Aviv branch first of *Imahot Ovdot* and later of **Na'amat* 1969-79.

Namir has been a Knesset member since 1973. In 1975 she was appointed by Prime Minister Yitzḥak *Rabin as chairwoman of a Committee on the Status of Women in Israel. In the 9th and 10th Knesset she served as chairwoman of the Education and Culture Committee, and in the 11th and 12th Knessets as chairwoman of the Labor and Welfare Committee.

Namir hoped to be given a ministerial post in the *National Unity Government formed in 1988, but Labor did not nominate a single woman. She announced her candidature for the post of secretary general of the *Israel Labor Party at the beginning of 1989, but withdrew from the contest against Michael Ḥarish because she felt that it was an unfair contest. Namir ran in the primaries to the Labor leadership in February 1992 on a minute budget and the help of a handful of volunteers, and received less than 5 percent of the votes. In the government formed by Yitzḥak *Rabin after the elections to the 13th Knesset she was first appointed Minister of the Environment. In December 1992 she was appointed Minister of Labor and Welfare.

***National Religious Party** In 1988 the NRP moved further to the right, as the supporters of the *Greater Israel and **Gush Emunim* became the dominant forces in the party. Because of this shift to the right a group of moderates from within the NRP decided to break away and form their own party, **Meimad*. The NRP won five seats in the 12th Knesset, and in the *National Unity Government formed by Yitzḥak *Shamir in 1988, Zvulun *Hammer was appointed Minister of Religious Affairs and Professor Avner Shaki Minister Without Portfolio. In the narrow government formed by Shamir in June 1990 Hammer was appointed Minister of Education and Culture and Shaki Minister of Religious Affairs. Towards the elections to the 13 Knesset the NRP took a further step to the right, and its election slogan was "The NRP is to your right." The NRP increased its Knesset representation to six (mostly at the expense of the **Teḥiyah*). Despite its election declaration that it would only join a coalition headed by the **Likud*, after the elections it held talks with Yitzḥak *Rabin about the possibility of joining his government. However, the negotiations failed and the NRP found itself in the opposition for the first time since it had briefly remained out of Rabin's first government in 1974. (Y.B.M.)

*** National Unity Government** In the aftermath of the elections to the 12th Knesset in November 1988, Yitzḥak *Shamir decided in favor of another National Unity Government with the *Israel Labor Party. He had the option of forming a narrow government supported by 65 MKs, but he was also under great pressure from American Jewry not to give in to the demand of the *ḥaredi* parties to change the definition of "who is a Jew" in the *Law of Return which was their condition for joining a narrow government.

Labor joined the new unity government under worse conditions than it had joined the previous one, and after it joined there were pressures from within to quit. It was argued that the differences between Labor and the **Likud* were becoming blurred as a result of the prolonged participation in a single government, and that the Israeli democratic system was suffering. Those favoring the continued participation in the government argued that Labor could promote the peace process better from within and ensure government financial assistance for the settlement movements (See: *kibbutzim and **moshavim*) and Koor (the * *Histadrut* industrial conglomerate). However, by March 1990, when it appeared that the *Likud* had no intention of making any progress in the government's plan for holding elections in the territories (See: *Shamir-Rabin peace initiative), Labor decided to bring the government down by a vote of no-confidence.

*** Navon, Yitzḥak** Navon served as Minister of Education and Culture until March 1990. After leaving the government he became chairman of the Israeli Public Council for the Quincentennial Commemoration of the Expulsion of Jews from Spain and the Discovery of America.

*** Ne'eman, Yuval** Ne'eman was elected to the 12th Knesset but resigned in January 1990 to make place for Eliakim Ha'etzni.

In the government formed by Yitzḥak *Shamir in June 1990, which was joined by the **Teḥiyah*, Ne'eman was Minister of Energy and Infrastructure as well as Minister of Science and Technology. He was the first member of the Israeli government to meet with the then Soviet President, Mikhail Gorbachev, in Moscow. When the **Teḥiyah* left the Shamir government in February 1992 against the background of the *Madrid Conference, Ne'eman resigned. Following the *Teḥiyah*'s defeat in the elections to the 13th Knesset, Ne'eman returned to his academic post at the University of Tel Aviv. (I.M.)

Netanyahu, Binyamin (Bibi) *Likud* politician. Netanyahu was born in Israel in 1949. He served in the *IDF in an elitist fighting unit in 1967-72 reaching the rank of captain. He completed a Masters Degree in Business Administration at MIT in the United States in 1976. For several years after he was on the management of Rim Industries (a furniture enterprise) in Jerusalem. In 1980 Netanyahu founded and headed until 1987 the Jonathan Institute on terrorism, named in memory of his older brother Jonathan (Yonni) Netanyanu killed during the *Entebbe operation in 1976. He served as Consul General in Washington in 1982-84 and then as Israeli Ambassador to the *United Nations until 1988. He frequently appeared on the American media and was very popular in the American Jewish community. Netanyahu was instrumental in bringing about the opening of the UN archives on Nazi war crimes.

Netanyanu was elected to the Knesset on the *Likud* list in 1988 and was appointed Deputy Minister of Foreign Affairs when Moshe *Arens held the post of Minister. Several months after David *Levy replaced Arens in June 1990, he was appointed Deputy Minister in the Prime Minister's office, in which capacity he participated in the *Madrid Conference. In the 12th Knesset he was one of the few *Likud* Knesset members who openly and constantly supported the law for direct election of the Prime Minister (See: *Prime Minister, direct election of). Immediately after the elections of 1992 Netanyanu was one of the most active supporters of introducing the *primaries system in the *Likud*, and started an aggressive campaign to be elected as its leader.

New Liberal Party Party formed by Yitzḥak *Moda'i on the eve of the elections to the 13th Knesset with two other former Liberal MKs who had left the *Likud* with him in 1990 to form the *Party for Advancing the Zionist Idea.

Despite the fact that Moda'i had objected to the *Shamir-Rabin peace initiative in 1989, the New Liberal Party ran on a purely economic platform, calling for the introduction of a free market economy as the only cure for Israel's economic ills. In the elections, the NLP failed to pass the 1.5 percent qualifying threshold and ceased to exist.

*** Nuclear Policy** The *Gulf War vindicated the Israeli attitude regarding the Nuclear Non-Proliferation Treaty and inspections by the International Atomic Agency. The revelations, during and in the aftermath of the war, regarding the scope and advanced stage of the nuclear program of Iraq (which is a signatory of the NPT), and the extent of the transfer of technological components and knowhow by Western companies, highlighted not only the failure of Western intelligence, but the total bankruptcy of the NPT safeguards system. According to post-Gulf War IAEA estimations, the Iraqi program involved about 15,000 employees and a $10 billion budget.

On May 21, 1991 US President George Bush presented a Middle East arms control program which involved a nuclear dimension: the US proposed a freeze of the production of enriched uranium in the Middle East. In theory this would stop nuclear proliferation in the region, but in practice its immediate effect would only be on Israel. Israel saw the proposal as an American attempt to interfere in its nuclear program.

Following the October 1991 *Madrid Conference it was decided that arms control would be dealt with in the framework of the multilateral talks. In these talks, the Arab states demanded Israeli nuclear disarmament at the first stage of any disarmament process, while Israel (which does not formally admit having a nuclear capability) emphasized the need for a gradual process of confidence-building which would create the background for limiting the conventional arms race and advancing the political process.

While presenting his new government to the Knesset on July 13, 1992, Prime Minister Yitzḥak *Rabin emphasized that his government would "address itself to thwarting the possibility of any of Israel's enemies acquiring nuclear weapons." (A.B.)

Od Kahane Hai (See: *Kach)

*** Ometz** *Ometz* joined the **Likud* before the 1988 elections and received two reserved seats in the 12th Knesset. Following the formation of the narrow government in June 1990, one of the *Ometz* MKs, Zalman Shoval, was appointed Ambassador to Washington .

"One Israel" (Yisrael Aḥat) A movement founded in September 1992, with the participation of representatives of the right wing parties, **Emunim*, the **Yesha* council, right wing and religious youth movements and representatives of the settlements of the *Golan Heights, to oppose territorial concessions. MK Ariel *Sharon heads the movement, and MK Moshe Peled of **Tzomet* is his deputy.

Operation Solomon (See: *Ethiopian Jews)

Palestine Liberation Organization (PLO) Just before the outbreak of the **intifada*, the PLO seemed to be politically and financially at a dead end. At the opening of the Arab Summit Conference in Amman in November 1987, Yasser Arafat tried to generate disturbances in the *occupied territories in order to draw attention, but with little success. One of the outcomes of the Conference was that the Arab oil-producing states decided to stop the institutionalized multi-annual financial aid they had been granting the Arab confrontation states and the *PLO since 1979. From now on aid was only to be forthcoming on a bilateral and *quid pro quo* basis. The new era in the Soviet Union, heralded by Mikhail Gorbachev's accession to the presidency in 1986, was also affecting the Soviet willingness to back Israel's enemies.

The *intifada*, which broke out on December 9, 1987, took Israel and the PLO by surprise. The PLO managed to gain control over it through the United Arab Command, but the local pro-PLO leadership was showing a will and vitality of its own, while the Muslim Brotherhood became more active as an independent actor, frequently working at cross purposes with the PLO and trying to influence the development of the *intifada* through the **Ḥammas*. The PLO tried to draw even more attention from the media to the Palestinian cause by means of the "ship of return" which was to have sailed from Cyprus to Israeli territorial waters with Palestinian deportees and representatives of the world media on board. The ship never departed because it was blown up in Limasol on February 15, 1988, allegedly by Israeli agents. It was also assumed that Israeli agents were responsible for the assassination in Tunis on April 16, of Khalil al-Wazir (Abu-Jihad) - the man responsible for the military arm of the *Fataḥ*, who was regarded as the brain behind hundreds of terrorist attacks against Israel, and was known to be directly involved in planning the the *intifada*'s strategy.

Soon after the outbreak of the *intifada* the PLO leadership started to think of turning the psychological success of the uprising into tangible political gains. In January 1988 Arafat spoke of the establishment of a government in exile, but it was opposed by other senior members of the PLO, including Arafat's deputy Sallaḥ Ḥallaf (Abu-Iyad). The idea came up again at the beginning of August, after King Ḥussein of Jordan announced his legal detachment from the West Bank. *Fataḥ* supporters in the territories called on Arafat to take control of the institutions previously run by Jordan to prepare the infrastructure for the "state on the way". By the middle of 1988 a growing number of personalities within the PLO were talking of the possibility of establishing a Palestinian state. The pragmatic thinking within the PLO, was encouraged by the Palestinian leadership in the territories. In June Bassam Abu-Sharif, one of Arafat's advisors, published a paper stating that the Palestinians sought peace with the Israelis.

It was rumored that the document was actually penned by Arafat himself, and made public as a trial balloon. In August 1988 the drafting of the proclamation of a Palestinian state within the borders of the 1947 UN *partition plan were undertaken. Contacts were also being held with Washington on the opening of a US-PLO dialogue in return for a PLO acceptance of *Security Council Resolutions 242 and 338. On November 15, 1988 the Palestinian state was proclaimed by Arafat. The proclamation, was based on the 1947 UN partition plan which had called for the establishment of two states in the territory of *Mandatory Palestine, and implied recognition of Israel. It was accompanied by a long political statement. Both documents were drafted in the best tradition of PLO ambivalence. Nevertheless, it was generally viewed as a step forward on the part of the PLO, and a major departure from the *Palestine National Covenant, which was declared by Arafat at a press conference in Paris on May 2, 1989 as lapsed, null and void. The PLO's main diplomatic goal, at this stage, was to get the US to open a dialogue. However, the Americans demanded more from Arafat than what had been stated at the November PNC meeting in Algiers.

Following an address to a special UN General Assembly meeting in Geneva, Arafat stated on December 14 that the PLO would cease all terrorist activity. Although he declared that the *intifada* would continue until a Palestinian state was established, and did not explicitly recognize Israel's right to exist, the US agreed, in spite of strong Israeli protests, to open talks with the PLO through its ambassador to Tunis.

The PLO's reaction to the Israeli plan for holding elections in the territories, which began to crystallize in the beginning of 1989, (See: *Shamir-Rabin peace initiative) was negative. Arafat's deputy, Abu-Iyad called it "an act of deceit." The PLO objected to the fact that the Israeli plan did not mention an Israeli withdrawal from the territories, and proposed that the elections be held under the authority of the Israeli military administration. By accepting such elections, it was said, the PLO would be recognizing the legitimacy of Israeli occupation. The PLO was seeking an Israeli withdrawal from the territories according to a fixed timetable, and democratic elections to be held under international auspices and control. However, by the beginning of June Arafat was willing to appoint a team from the territories to hold talks with Israel on the essence of the elections, and in September he welcomed the Mubarak ten points concerning an Israeli-Palestinian meeting in Cairo. Israel rejected any direct PLO involvement in the proposed talks, but it became clear that there could be no Palestinian delegation whose members were not approved by the PLO, and whose positions were not closely coordinated with the PLO. However, on March 15, 1990 the Israeli government fell over the issue of elections in the territories, and while the political crisis dragged on the PLO grew increasingly worried by the prospect of a new wave of immigration to Israel from the Soviet Union (See: **aliyah*). Together with the Arab states it now concentrated great efforts to convince the Soviet Union to keep its gates closed to Jewish emigration, but to no avail.

The PLO's honeymoon with the West started going sour when the organization of Abu Abbas (a member of the PLO) attempted to carry out a mass terrorist attack on several beaches in Israel on May 30, 1990. Arafat refused to condemn the act (which was contrary to his undertaking in December 1988) or to expel Abu Abbas from the PLO. As a result, the US broke off its dialogue with the PLO. Arafat's decision to publicly support the Iraqi invasion of Kuwait on August 2, 1990, further aggravated his position. The PLO spokesman explained that the move was caused by the disappointment in the lack of response to the PLO's gestures of good will in the previous two years. However, the decision was probably closely linked with the concern for the welfare of 400,000 Palestinians who were living and working in Kuwait at the time. At the end of 1989 PLO policy was increasingly ambiguous, vascilating between pragmatism and radicalism. Two days before the outbreak of the *Gulf War Abu Iyad was murdered. This time Israel was not accused of the act since it was known that one of Abu-Nidal's men was responsible. By the time the war was over the PLO had lost much of its credit in the West, and because it had bet on the wrong horse also found itself in serious financial difficulties.

When Secretary of State James Baker embarked on his new peace initiative in March 1991 the PLO was not directly approached. It was, nevertheless, an open secret that it was the PLO which approved the Palestinian participation in the talks, that it was directly involved in selecting the members of the Palestinian delegation, and that once the talks began the delegation didn't make a move without prior consultation with the PLO. However, as the negotiations progressed, and the Palestinians started to discuss with Israel the modalities of the *autonomy plan, they became increasingly impatient with the inflexible positions the PLO tried to impose on it. In addition, three organizations within the PLO - the organizations of George Ḥabash, Naif Ḥawatmeh and Abu Abbas - joined the *Front of the Ten (established in Damascus), whose goal was to fight against the peace talks and autonomy plan, while inside the territories the *Ḥammas* (which was also a member of the Front), continued to grow stronger at the PLO's expense.

ISRAEL'S POLICY TOWARDS THE PLO: Both of Israel's two major parties, the **Likud* and the *Israel Labor Party, rejected direct contacts with the PLO which they argued had not really changed in essence, although certain MKs from both parties were known to have met with PLO personalities, with or without their leaders' approval. However, there were several differences in the approach of the two parties. The *Likud* continued to object to any change in the law prohibiting unauthorized meetings with PLO members, the Labor position was that it had been a mistake on Labor's part to agree to the law being passed back in August 1986 in return for *Likud* support of the law against racism. Following the formation of the Labor-led Government in July 1992, Minister of Justice David Libai undertook to amend the law to permit meetings with the PLO as long as this did not clash with the penal code. The amendment passed its first reading in the Knesset at the beginning of December. Another difference in the approach of the two parties concerned the negotiations with the Palestinians from the territories. The *Likud* at least formally insisted that the Palestinian delegation be totally detached from the PLO and that no Palestinians "from the diaspora" be allowed to participate in the negotiations, the Labor Party did not object to the Palestinian delegation holding consultations with the PLO in Tunis, and agreed that Palestinians from the diaspora should participate in the multilateral talks. Messages sent by Arafat to the Labor leaders towards the end of 1992 to the effect that he would be willing to meet them anywhere, were not answered.

Party for Advancing the Zionist Idea Party formed following the decision of five former Liberals in the **Likud* - Minister of Economics Yitzḥak *Moda'i and MKs Yossi Goldberg, Pinḥas Goldstein, Pesaḥ Grupper and Avraham Sharir - to break away from the *Likud* on February 19, 1990. The Party for Advancing the Zionist Idea was recognized as an independent Knesset faction on the day of the vote of no-confidence in the government on March 15, 1990, in return for a promise to vote against the motion.

Following the fall of the government the new party negotiated with Labor chairman Shimon *Peres about the possibility of its joining a government headed by him. However, it finally decided to join the government formed by Yitzḥak *Shamir in June 1990 after two of its members returned to the *Likud*, Moda'i was appointed Minister of Finance and Goldstein Deputy Minister of Education and Culture. The scandalous coalition agreement with the Party for Advancing the Zionist Idea included a provision that the *Likud* would pay it a large sum of money in the event of a breach of the terms of the agreement. When the agreement came to the *Likud* Central Committee for approval, only Ze'ev Binyamin *Begin spoke out against it. Towards the elections to the 13th Knesset the party's three MKs tried to rejoin the *Likud*, but were rejected. They formed the *New Liberal Party which failed to pass the 1.5 percent threshold.

*** Peled, Matityahu** In the elections to the 12th Knesset in 1988 the *Progressive List for Peace lost half its power and won only one seat. Peled remained outside the Knesset, and in fact stopped taking an active part in israel's political life, returning to his research work. At the third PLP Conference, in July 1990, he made a last effort to bring about the complete merging of the Arab and Jewish components of the party, but to no avail. (M.H.)

*** Peres, Shimon** As Foreign Minister from October 1986 to December 1988 Peres persisted in his efforts to give momentum to the peace process, first on the basis of the April 1987 *London Agreement with King Ḥussein and later on the basis of the *Shultz Plan. However, the **Likud* opposed both plans which involved convening an *international conference.

Following the 1988 elections, although the *Israel Labor Party received less seats than the *Likud*, Peres tried to get the religious parties to side with Labor, but failed. In the new *National Unity Government formed by Yitzḥak *Shamir Peres was appointed Minister of Finance. By the beginning of 1990, when the *Likud* once again seemed to be stalling over the peace process (See: *Shamir-Rabin peace initiative) and with the feeling that this time the religious parties would agree to enter an alternative government with Labor, Peres initiated a government crisis and a vote of no confidence in the Knesset. However, after the government fell Peres failed to form a new government.

Immediately after his failure Yitzḥak *Rabin decided to challenge Peres' leadership of the Labor Party. However, it was only when *primaries for the party's leadership were held in February 1992, did Rabin manage to beat Peres, by 41 to 34 percent of the vote. Peres came in first, far ahead of all the other candidates, in the primaries for Labor's Knesset list held in March. In the government formed by Rabin after the elections Peres was appointed Deputy Prime Minister and Minister for Foreign Affairs.

Peretz, Rabbi Yitzḥak Ḥaim Sephardi rabbi and *Shass* politician. Peretz was born in Casablanca, Morocco, in 1938. He immigrated to Israel in 1950 and was educated in ultra-religious yeshivot, completing his training as a rabbi and *dayan* at the Hazon Ovadia higher rabbinical academy in Jerusalem. At the age of 24 he was appointed Chief Rabbi of Ra'anana.When *Shass* was founded in 1984 he was chosen by Rabbi Ovadia *Yosef to stand at its head. Following the elections to the 11th Knesset Peretz was appointed Minister of the Interior. However, he resigned in order to avoid implementing a decision by the High Court of Justice to register as a Jewess a woman who had been converted to Judaism by a Reform rabbi (See: *Progressive Judaism).

Peretz was elected again to the Knesset at the head of *Shass* in 1988 and became Minister of Immigration Absorption. In March 1990 he resigned from *Shass* because he opposed its decision to help bring down the *National Unity Government by staying away during a vote of no confidence. He formed a one man faction, **Moriah*, and in the government formed by Yitzḥak *Shamir in June 1990 remained in the Ministry of Immigration Absorption.

Peretz is noted for his extreme religious views, and unlike Rabbi Ovadia *Yosef supports the *Greater Israel idea. As Minister of Immigration Absorption he objected to the non-religious *kibbutzim (whom he accused of forcing immigrant children in the 1950s to reject their religion) absorbing *Ethiopian Jews, and allocated large sums of money to "spiritual absorption."

Peretz was elected to the 13th Knesset in 1992 within the framework of **Yahadut Hatorah Hame'uḥedet* as its token Sephardi, but when this ultra-religious party failed to win at least five Knesset seats, was forced to give up his seat in favor of the representative of **Degel Hatorah*. (M.H)

*** Po'alei Agudat Yisrael** *Po'alei Agudat Yisrael* received one seat in the 12th Knesset within the framework of **Agudat Yisrael*. After *Agudat Yisrael* had reached an agreement to join the government which Shimon *Peres tried to form in March/April 1990, the representative of *Po'alei Agudat Yisrael*, Rabbi Avraham Verdiger, refused to support this government because of his support for *ideological reasons. The party was a part of the **Yahadut Hatorah Hame'uḥedet* list to the 13th Knesset, but its representative failed to be elected. (M.H.)

Political Settlements Term used by Yitzḥak *Rabin to distinguish between settlements established by the *Likud* in the *West Bank and the *Gaza Strip in the midst of a dense Arab population on land from which Israel will be willing to withdraw within the framework of a permanent settlement, and "strategic settlements" along the confrontation lines and other areas important for Israel's security. When he became prime minister on July 13, 1992, Rabin declared that investment would cease in the political settlements (See: *settlement policy).

*** Pollard Affair** The two Israeli committees which were appointed to examine the Pollard affair on March 11, 1987 reported on May 26. Both criticized the officials and military personnel involved.

Pollard appealed his conviction on grounds that the American authorities had reneged on pre-sentencing agreements, and that his case had been prejudiced by a secret memorandum on the alleged damage caused US security by Pollard, presented at the time to the judge by Secretary of Defense Caspar Weinberger. On October 13, 1992, the US Supreme Court of Justice rejected Pollard's request to withdraw his guilty plea and have his case retried.

The Israeli Government's policy was to avoid publicly intervening on Pollard's behalf until such time as he had exhausted all the legal means open to him. Following the ruling of the US Supreme Court the government decided once again to refrain from any intervention until after the Presidential elections in November 1992. A "Release Pollard" lobby was set up in Israel soon after Pollard was sent to prison, while MKs Geula *Cohen (*Teḥiyah*) and Edna Solodar (*Israel Labor Party) approached President Reagan and then President Bush to grant Pollard executive clemency. (I.M.)

Primaries A system of elections in which the leaders and candidates of a party are elected by the members or supporters of the party.

In Israel the system was first adopted by the *Israel Labor Party for the elections to the 13th Knesset in 1992. Labor's chairman and candidate for the premiership, and its candidates for the Knesset, mayors, local council heads, **Histadrut* and **Na'amat* secretary generals, and worker council and local Na'amat secretaries, are all elected by the registered, due-paying members of the party. In the election of the chairman and candidate for the premiership the nominee must receive at least 40 percent of the votes. Yitzḥak *Rabin won in February 1992 by a little less than 41 percent. In the first primaries held for Labor's Knesset list in March 1992, half the candidates were elected nationwide and the other half in 11 districts - eight of them geographical and three sectorial (*kibbutzim, **moshavim* and minorities).

In mid-November 1992 the **Likud* decided to nominate its chairman and candidate for the premiership by means of primaries. The nominees must receive at least 40 percent of the votes. The first primaries in the *Likud* are to be held in March 1993.

Prime Minister, direct election of As a result of the failure of the 11th Knesset to introduce electoral reform and the difficulties in forming a coalition following the 1988 elections, four Knesset members - Uriel Lynn (**Likud*), Prof. David Libai (*Israel Labor Party), Amnon *Rubinstein (**Shinui*) and Yo'ash Tzidon (**Tzomet*) - submitted to the Knesset four separate bills (amendments to the Basic Law: the Government - See: *basic laws) calling for a change in the Israeli system of government that would leave the parliamentary system intact while adding to it direct

Population of Israel
(in thousands)

	Total	Jews	***	Muslims	Christians	Druze and others
1948 (VI)	872.7	716.7	156.0			
1949 (XII)	173.9	1,013.9		111.5	34.0	14.5
1950	1,370.1	1,203.0		116.1	36.0	15.0
1960	2,150.4	1,981.7		174.9	51.3	23.3
1970*	3,022.1	2,582.0		328.6	75.5	35.9
1980	3,921.7	3,282.7		498.3	89.9	50.7
1990**	4,821.7	3,946.7		677.7	114.7	82.6
1991	5,058.8	4,144.6		701.4	128.0	84.8
1992 (VIII)	5,143.0	4,208.0	935.0			

* Including East *Jerusalem
** Including the *Golan Heights
*** All non-Jews

elections for the Prime Minister. The four bills passed their first reading on May 28, 1990. They were united into a single bill which was passed by the plenary on March 18, 1992, just before the 12th Knesset's pre-election recess, after it was agreed that the new system would only be applied in the elections to the 14th Knesset scheduled for 1996.

According to the new system the elections for the Knesset and the PM are to be held simultaneously. A vote of no-confidence in the government by 61 Knesset members, a decision by the PM to dissolve the Knesset or by the Knesset to dissolve itself, and failure by the Knesset to pass the budget law three months after the beginning of the fiscal year, will all result in new elections being held for both the Knesset and the PM. Though in the original proposal a new government did not require a vote of confidence by the Knesset plenary, as finally passed the law requires the PM to bring his government to the Knesset for its approval.

***Prime Ministers**

1986–92 Yitzḥak Shamir (**Likud*)

1992– Yitzḥak Rabin (*Israel Labor Party)

***Progressive List For Peace** The Progressive List for Peace concentrated its first efforts in strengthening its position within Arab circles in Israel, while securing *Palestine Liberation Organization support from the outside. However, the PLP had difficulties keeping its ranks united, and the appearance of the purely Arab *Arab Democratic Party on the political map further weakened it. In the 12th Knesset elections the PLP won only one seat. Moḥammed Miari, its leader, expressed increasingly radical positions. At the PLP Conference in July 1990 a proposal by Matityahu *Peled, head of the Jewish component of the PLP ("Alternative"), to effect a union between his movement and the Arab component of the list (the Progressive Movement) was rejected. Efforts to form a single Arab list for the elections to the 13th Knesset, to include the PLP, the ADP and independent members with the backing of the *Islamic Movement failed for personal and ideological reasons. The PLP did not pass the qualifying threshold.

***Rabin, Yitzḥak** Rabin remained Minister of Defense throughout the terms of the three *National Unity Governments from 1984 to 1990. During his term the **intifada* broke out in December 1987, and Rabin was directly associated with the iron fist policy adopted by the *IDF to confront it. At the same time he realized that a solution could not be brought about by force and that Israel would have to negotiate with the Palestinians. Against this background he proposed, in January 1989, a plan for holding elections in the *West Bank and the *Gaza Strip. This plan formed part of the *Rabin-Shamir peace initiative of May 14, 1989.

While Rabin favored the continuation existence of the coalition with the **Likud*, he was convinced in the middle of March 1990 that the *Likud* was stalling on the peace process and supported the initiative of Shimon *Peres to bring down the government by means of a vote of no confidence. However, when Peres failed to form an alternative Labor-led government, Rabin decided to challenge Peres's leadership. In *primaries for the leadership held by the Labor Party on February 19, 1992, Rabin received over 40 percent of the votes and won.

Labor's campaign towards the elections for the 13th Knesset was run under the slogan "Israel is waiting for Rabin". Following Labor's victory in the elections Rabin formed a coalition with **Meretz* and **Shass*. Rabin, who assumed both the posts of Prime Minister and Minister of Defense, committed himself to making peace, implementing an *autonomy plan for the Palestinians within a year, changing the national order of priorities, and improving Israel's relations with the *United States.

Ramon (formerly Vishnia), **Ḥaim** Labor politician. Ramon was born in a poor neighborhood in Jaffa in 1950. In 1968-73 he served in the Israel Air Force reaching the rank of captain. He studied law at Tel Aviv University in 1973-1977. In 1978-84 Ramon was Secretary of the *Israel Labor Party Young Guard, and first entered the Knesset in 1983. In the 11th Knesset he was coordinator of the Labor faction in the Finance Committee, and in the 12th Knesset he served as chairman of the Labor Knesset faction.

In 1985 Ramon founded, together with Nissim Zvili, the dovish "*Kfar Hayarok*" political circles into which he brought several young Labor activists several of whom became members of the 12th Knesset. In the 12th Knesset Ramon led a group of young Labor doves which worked in close cooperation and presented itself as Labor's future leadership. One of its widely reported acts was a visit to Egypt as guests of the Egyptian government at a time when Israeli-Egyptian relations were at low ebb.

Before the Labor Party's 5th Conference in November 1991 Ramon and a group of doves threatened to leave the party, and join the new dovish alignment between the *Civil Rights Movement, **Mapam* and **Shinui*, which was in the process of forming, unless their positions on various issues were adopted by the conference. Though on the economic and social issues Ramon and his group gained the support of just over 20 percent of the delegates, they managed to change the political platform to make it more dovish, and to get the conference to adopt a platform on religion and state which was much more radical than that originally proposed.

Following Rabin's victory in the *primaries Ramon joined the inner circle which worked closely with Labor's new leader during the election campaign. In the government formed by Rabin following the elections he was appointed Minister of Health. His immediate goals were to introduce a national health law, and to force the **Histadrut's* health fund, *Kupat Ḥolim*, to introduce major reforms.

***Romania and Israel** (See: *Eastern Europe)

***Rubenstein, Amnon** In the elections to the 12th Knesset, **Shinui* - headed by Rubinstein, won two seats. Rubenstein was one of the four MKs who tabled the bill for the direct election of the Prime Minister (See: *Prime Minister, direct election of). Contrary to many other members in his party he strongly supported *Shinui's* joining **Meretz*. In the government formed by Yitzḥak *Rabin in 1992 Rubenstein was appointed Minister of Energy and Infrastructure. (M.H.)

***Sarid, Yossi** Sarid entered the 12th Knesset on the list of the *Civil Rights Movement. He strongly supported the attempts of Shimon *Peres to form a government in March/April 1990 after the fall of the *National Unity Government. Towards the elections to the 13th Knesset in 1992, Sarid was one of the main proponents of the idea of forming a single dovish list, and was instrumental in bringing about the formation of **Meretz*. He was appointed Minister of the Environment in December 1992.

*** Settlement Policy** After coming to power in 1977 the **Likud* embarked on establishing as many new settlements as possible in **Yesha* where the driving force was Minister of Agriculture Ariel *Sharon who headed the Ministerial Committee on Settlement in the government and the Settlement Division of the *World Zionist Organization were represented. This activity slowed down significantly after the formation of the 1984 *National Unity Government. On the insistence of the *Israel Labor Party the coalition agreement specified that only six new settlements would be established beyond the Green Line - most of them within the parameters of the *Allon Plan - and the Ministry of Defense, under Yitzḥak *Rabin ensured a further slow-down. From 1984 to 1988 Yuval *Ne'eman headed the Ministerial Committee on Settlement. The coalition agreement of the National Unity Government formed in 1988, in which Labor's relative power fell, mentioned the establishment of an additional five to eight settlements, but the Ministerial Committee on Settlement was abolished and Labor had growing difficulties in containing unauthorized settlement activities in the *administered territories.

Following the break up of the National Unity Government in March 1990, and the formation of a narrow, *Likud*-led government in which Sharon was appointed Minister of Construction and Housing, the massive settlement and construction activity in the territories resumed. It was characterized by the almost total disregard for proper administrative procedures regarding formal approval of plans, appropriation of land and financial resources, and actual construction work performed by private contractors. The updated *Sharon Plan called for 11 "autonomous Arab districts" around the major Palestinian population centers to be surrounded by Jewish settlements. The timing of the foundation of some of the new settlements coincided with the visits of Secretary of State James Baker to Israel and was viewed as a deliberate provocation. Baker tried to link a stoppage of the settlement activities in the territories with the granting of American loan guarantees to Israel for the absorption of new immigrants, but the government rejected the linkage. Following the formation of the government by *Yitzḥak Rabin in July 1992, most of the settlement activities in the territories, beyond a certain state of construction, were frozen.

Within the Green Line the financial resources allocated to settlement activities by the *Jewish Agency Settlement Department, which until October 1992 was responsible for settlement activities in Israel proper, were greatly reduced as a result of the financial difficulties in the Jewish Agency. This development, together with the deep financial and ideological crises into which the kibbutz and *moshav* movements were going through in the late 1980s (See: *kibbutzim *(*moshavim*) led to major changes in the nature of settlement activities inside the Green Line. The inclination is now to develop communal settlements rather than collective and cooperative ones, and it is now the Ministry of Housing and Construction and the regional councils, rather than the Jewish Agency and settlement movements which are chiefly involved in settlement activities. In the course of the large immigration wave of 1989-92, which brought around 430,000 new immigrants to Israel (See: **aliyah*), the official policy was (contrary to the policy in the 1950s) to let the immigrants settle where they wished. A large proportion chose to settle in the periphery (but not in the territories) because of the lower cost of living.

Shach, Rabbi Elazar Menaḥem Spiritual leader of the *Lita'im*. Shach was born in Lithuania in 1898 to a family of traders. At the age of seven he left his parents' home to study in the most important yeshivot in Lithuania. In 1941 Shach immigrated with his family to *Eretz Yisrael*. He first settled in Jerusalem and then moved to Bnei Brak. He soon was noted for his diligence and genius. Shach taught in several yeshivot until he headed the famous leading Ponivezh Yeshiva in Bnei Brak, and joined the spiritual leadership of the *ḥaredi* community as co-president of *Mo'etzet Gdolei Hatorah* (the Council of Great Torah Scholars).

In *ḥaredi* circles Shach was well known as a scholar and teacher since the 1930s, the general public became acquainted with him after 1977, when the ultra-religious parties increased their activity in the political arena. Until the elections to the 11th Knesset Shach actively supported **Agudat Yisrael.* However, due to internal disagreements he left *Mo'etzet Gdolei Hatorah* in 1983 and before the elections to the 11th Knesset in 1984 encouraged the formation of the Sephardi ultra-religious party **Shass*, whose spiritual and political leaders had all studied in the yeshivot of the *Lita'im.* Towards the elections to the 12th Knesset in 1988 he formed an additional Ashkenazi ultra-religious party - **Degel Hatorah*, and an additional *Mo'etzet Gdolei Hatorah.* The fact that **Ḥabbad* supported *Agudat Yisrael* in the 1988 elections increased the tensions between Shach and the *Agudah*, due to his personal rivalry with the spiritual leader of *Ḥabbad*, Rabbi Menaḥem Mendel Schneerson. Towards the elections to the 13th Knesset in 1992 he participated in the formation of **Yahadut Hatorah Haméuḥedet*, in which *Degel Hatorah* participated.

Shach is a religious zealot and opposed to *Zionism. Politically he preaches in favor of compromise, and opposes the type of settlement activities carried out by **Gush Emunim* for *halachic* reasons, because it constitutes a provocation to the nations of the world. Nevertheless, due to his hostility towards the Labor Movement in general and the *kibbutzim in particular, which symbolize in his eyes the modern Israeli anti-religious secularism, Shach prefers the *ḥaredi* parties joining **Likud*-led coalitions. He believes that the future of the *administered territories will be determined by the United States.

In March/April 1990 Shach was largely responsible for the failure of Shimon *Peres to form a government after the fall of the *National Unity Government, and pushed *Shass* to join the government formed by Yitzḥak *Shamir in June. *Degel Hatorah* also joined that government. In July 1992 he stopped *Yahadut Hatorah* from joining the coalition formed by Yitzḥak *Rabin with **Meretz,* but was unsuccessful in preventing *Shass* from joining. As a result he strongly attacked Rabbi Ovadia *Yosef, and his followers clashed with members of *Shass*. (M.H.)

Shamir-Rabin peace initiative As the **intifada* entered its second year Minister of Defense Yitzḥak *Rabin proposed a plan for holding elections in the *West Bank and the *Gaza Strip for a self-administration authority which would also be responsible for negotiating a permanent peace settlement with Israel on behalf of the *Palestinians.

This idea, together with several others, was presented by Prime Minister Yitzḥak *Shamir in Washington in April 1989 (See: *United States and Israel) and was embodied in a formal peace initiative approved by the *National Unity Government on May 14. It dealt with four issues: strengthening the peace between *Egypt and Israel on the basis of the *Camp David Accords; establishing peace relations between Israel and the other Arab states; resolving the problem of the Arab *refugees; holding elections in the territories for nominating a representation that would conduct negotiations for a transitional period of self-rule, and later for a permanent settlement. A fifth point, dealing with arms control, was left out because Rabin objected to it.

The proposal stipulated that the political process would be by means of direct negotiations with the Arab representatives, that Israel opposes the establishment of "an additional Palestinian state in the Gaza district and in the area between Israel and Jordan." that Israel would not negotiate with the *PLO and that "there will be no change in the status of *Judea, Samaria and Gaza other than in accordance with the basic guidelines of the government" (i.e., no Israeli withdrawal from these territories).

In September 1989 President Ḥosni Mubarak of Egypt proposed that Israeli and Palestinian delegations meet in Cairo to start talks on the elections, and published his own ten point program for the implementation of the Israeli initiative.

The *Likud* objected to the mention in the ten points of the participation of Palestinians who are residents of East Jerusalem in the elections, and of the need for Israel to accept the principle of *land for peace. Rabin, on the other hand, stated after returning from a visit to Cairo, that the ten points took Israel's sensitivities into account, in that they did not mention the PLO, the Palestinian right to self-determination or a Palestinian state in the *West Bank and *Gaza Strip.

The Mubarak ten points were followed by a five-point document published by US Secretary of State James Baker on December 6, 1989 which dealt with certain technicalities for the opening of the Israeli-Palestinian dialogue to be held in Cairo. Of the five points one proved difficult to satisfy: the understanding that "Israel will attend the dialogue only after a satisfactory list of Palestinians has been worked out." After little progress on the issue Baker addressed the following question to the Israeli government in the beginning of March, 1990: "Will the government of Israel be ready to agree to sit with Palestinians on a name-by-name basis who are residents of the West

Bank and Gaza?" Though Foreign Minister Moshe *Arens was in favor of giving Baker a positive reply, Prime Minister Yitzḥak *Shamir objected. It was against this background that the *Israel Labor Party decided to bring down the government by means of a vote of no confidence.

*** Shamir, Yitzḥak** Following the 12th Knesset elections in 1988 Shamir preferred to form another *National Unity Government, despite the fact that he could form a narrow right-wing religious government supported by 65 Knesset members.

In the first few months of 1989, Shamir worked out, together with Defense Minister Yitzḥak Rabin, a four point peace initiative (see: *Shamir-Rabin peace initiative). However, growing opposition within the *Likud* forced him to adopt a more rigid position which finally led to the break-up of the government. On June 11, 1990, Shamir formed a narrow government with the right wing, and religious parties. Despite his compliance with American wishes that Israel stay out of the *Gulf War Shamir's relations with the American administration were tense due to disagreements and misunderstandings with President George Bush, especially on the issue of the continuation of Jewish settlement activities in the *administered territories. Despite his opposition to the *international conference idea, Shamir was unable to avoid Israeli participation in the *Madrid Conference, and decided to head the Israeli delegation himself, although the other delegations were headed by the foreign ministers of their countries.

Shamir's last government was rife with personal and ideological antagonisms, but he was not inclined to intervene. In the two years of this government Shamir visited the Knesset infrequently, usually to attend the meetings of the Foreign Affairs and Security Committee. He tried to avoid early elections, but after his government lost its majority he had no choice. Following the defeat of the *Likud* in the elections, Shamir announced that he would resign as chairman of the *Likud* after a new leader was elected.

*** Sharon, Ariel** As Minister of Industry and Trade, a post which he held until June 1990, Sharon continued to advocate his plan for *Judea, Samaria and the *Gaza Strip, involving massive Jewish settlement around 11 Palestinian autonomous areas which would make any *territorial compromise impossible (See also: *Sharon Plan).

Following the approval by the government of the plan for elections in the *administered territories on May 14, 1989 (See: *Shamir-Rabin peace initiative) Sharon, was one of the "constraint ministers" who fought against it, arguing that self-administration would lead to the establishment of a Palestinian state. In a stormy meeting of the *Likud* Central Committee on February 12, 1990, Sharon surprised everyone by announcing his resignation from the government.

In the government formed in June, 1990, Sharon was appointed Minister of Construction and Housing. In this capacity he was able to increase the pace of Jewish settlement in the territories (See: *settlement policy). It was also in this capacity that he provided public funds and administrative assistance to Jewish bodies engaged in gaining control over property in the Muslim quarter of the Old City of Jerusalem and in Kfar Hashilo'aḥ (Silwan). Sharon himself moved into an apartment in the Muslim quarter in December 1987.

Sharon was also responsible for the massive purchase of caravans and the construction of hundreds of thousands of housing units in order to solve the housing shortage for new immigrants. However, this massive construction activity was ill-planned and highly wasteful. Within the Shamir government Sharon joined the ministers from the **Teḥiyah*, **Tzomet* and **Moledet* in opposing the peace initiative of Secretary of State Baker and the *Madrid Conference. In February 1991, Sharon contested the *Likud* leadership in the *Likud* Central Committee and came in third (after Shamir and Levy) with a surprising 22 percent.

***Shass** In the 12th Knesset elections in 1988 *Shass* won six Knesset seats, and in the *National Unity Government formed after the elections Arye *Der'i (who was not an MK), was appointed Minister of the Interior, and the head of its Knesset list, Rabbi Yitzḥak *Peretz, Minister of Immigrant Absorption.

During the 12th Knesset the *Shass* leaders made moderate political statements, and Der'i cooperated with the *Israel Labor Party in bringing the government down in March 1990, which led the hawkish Peretz to leave *Shass* and form his own one man Knesset faction. Due to heavy pressure by *ḥaredi* circles, and especially Rabbi Elazar Menaḥem *Shach, *Shass* did not agree to join the government which Shimon *Peres tried to form in March/April 1990. *Shass* joined the government formed by Yitzḥak *Shamir in June 1990, with Der'i remaining Minister of the Interior and Rabbi Rafael Pinḥasi was appointed Minister of Communications.

In mid-1990 the police investigated several *Shass* MKs, including Der'i, on suspicion of misappropriation of funds. The 12th Knesset even lifted the immunity of one of the *Shass* MK, Ya'ir Levy, who was put on trial with his wife on charges of embezzling of funds. Despite the police investigations and attempts by **Yahadut Hatorah Hame'uḥedet* to attract religious Sephardi voters by placing Rabbi Peretz on its list,

Shass again won six seats in the 1992 elections to the 13th Knesset. It joined the coalition formed by Yitzḥak *Rabin in July 1992, with Der'i (now an MK) as Minister of the Interior, and two deputy ministers. The *Shass* decision to join the government, contrary to the directives of Rabbi Shach, led to a rift between the spiritual leader of *Shass* Rabbi Ovadia *Yossef, and Rabbi Shach. (M.H.)

***Shinui** In the 12th Knesset *Shinui* won two seats. It supported the effort of Labor chairman Shimon *Peres to form a government following the fall of the *National Unity Government in March 1990. Despite certain ideological doubts of running in a single list with socialists, Shinui ran for the 13th Knesset elections in 1992 within the framework of **Meretz.* Two of the 12 *Meretz* MKs and one of the four *Meretz* ministers (Amnon *Rubinstein) are members of *Shinui.* (M.H.)

Shoḥat, Avraham Beiga Labor politician. Shoḥat was born in Tel Aviv in 1936. He served in the IDF as a paratrooper in the Naḥal and in the years 1956-57 was a member of Kibbutz Naḥal Oz. Shoḥat studied construction engineering at the Technion in Haifa in 1957-61. In 1961-63 he was an engineer in the team, headed by Arie Lova *Eliav, which planned and established the southern town of Arad. In 1963-67 he was branch director of the **Histadrut's* construction company *Solel Boneh* in Arad and the *Dead Sea area, and from 1967 to 1989 was head of the local council of Arad.

In 1985 Shoḥat ran the Labor party's membership drive, and in the 1988 general elections headed the election staff. He was elected to the 12th Knesset, first serving as chairman of the Economics Committee, and then as chairman of the Finance Committee. In the Spring of 1989 until February 1991. Shoḥat was responsible for the drafting of Labor's economic and social platform advocating the privatization of government owned corporations and defined the spheres in which the government should be involved. In the *primaries for the Labor leadership held in February 1992 he acted as Rabin's campaign manager. Following the Labor victory in the elections to the 13th Knesset Shoḥat was appointed Minister of Finance.

Shultz Plan Peace plan proposed by US Secretary of State George Shultz in February 1988 - three months after the outbreak of the **intifada*. The plan called for convening an international "event" in April, 1988, with the participation of the parties to the conflict and the five Permanent Members of the UN Security Council. The opening event would be followed by direct negotiations between Israel, Jordan and the Palestinians in May on an interim settlement, involving *autonomy for the *West Bank and the *Gaza Strip, to be implemented in October for a period of three years. In December 1988, talks would begin on the permanent solution with the participation of the autonomy administration within the Jordanian-Palestinian delegation. The permanent solution would be based on the *land for peace formula. Palestinians from the outside (i.e., the *PLO) would be able to participate on condition that they accept *Security Council Resolutions 242 and 338 as the basis for negotiations.

In Israel the plan was welcomed by *Israel Labor Party chairman Shimon *Peres but turned down by Prime Minister Yitzḥak *Shamir because it included principles rejected by the *Likud*, did not condition the negotiations on the Palestinian uprising ending first, and because it ignored the *Camp David Accords. Jordan, Syria and the Palestinians also had serious reservations.

Shultz, who had hoped to get the peace process going before the end of President Ronald Reagan's second term, more or less gave up in despair in April, 1988.

*** South Africa and Israel** The decision of the US Congress in February 1987 to stop all aid to states which failed to abide by the embargo on the supply of arms and military assistance to South Africa, which was to go into force on April 1, created a dilemma for Israel. On March 18, Minister of Foreign Affairs Shimon *Peres formally announced that Israel would not sign any new defense contracts with South Africa. It was also decided to limit drastically the relations and commercial ties between the two countries. The relations were now referred to as "low profile." but there were persistent rumors about the scope of the relations between Jerusalem and Pretoria. While the formal relations were being played down, the **Histadrut* made great efforts to establish relations with part of the black trade-unions in South Africa.

In July 1988 Peres sent the imprisoned leader of the African National Congress, Nelson Mandela, greetings upon his 70th birthday. However, when Mandela was finally released in the beginning of 1990, his public statements included criticism of the way Israel was dealing with the **intifada*. Despite his open support for the *PLO Mandela also expressed his appreciation for *Zionism as a movement of national liberation, and praised the role of Jews in the anti-apartheid movement. In addition to releasing Mandela, at the beginning of 1990 the South African government also legalized the ANC and took the first steps towards the abolition of apartheid. In July 1991 the United States lifted its sanctions on South Africa, and soon thereafter Israel followed suit. South African Premier F. Wilhelm de Klerk visited Israel in November 1991.

Following the establishment of the Labor-led government in Israel in July 1992, the official Israeli policy was to draw closer to Mandela and to tighten relations with the ANC at the expense of those with Chief Buthelezi's Inkatha, which the previous *Likud*-led government had preferred. In the beginning of December 1992 Mandela was officially invited to visit Israel and responded favorably.

*** Soviet Union and Israel** The election of Mikhail Gorbachev as President of the Soviet Union in 1986 started to affect Soviet-Israeli relations positively the following year. For the first time since relations between the two countries had been severed at the time of the *Six Day War, an eight-man Soviet consular delegation arrived in Israel in July 1987. The delegation opened an office in the Finish Embassy in Tel Aviv which had represented Soviet interests in Israel for 20 years. *Prisoner of Zion Yuri Edelstein arrived in Israel with the delegation. The following month two Knesset members, Ora Namir (Labor) and Ḥaike Grossman (**Mapam*) participated in the World Women's Congress in Moscow, (previously only Communist MKs were welcome). At the opening of the winter session of the UN General Assembly in New York in September 1987, Israeli Foreign Minister Shimon *Peres and Soviet Foreign Minister Eduard Shevardnadze met to discuss the peace process, the bilateral relations between the two countries and opening the gates for the emigration of the Soviet Jews to Israel. The following month another famous prisoner of Zion, Ida Nudel, was allowed out of the Soviet Union.

In 1988 Soviet participation in the Middle East peace process (See: *Shultz Plan) was linked by Israel with the renewal of diplomatic relations between the two countries. The official position of the Soviet Union was at first that diplomatic relations would only be renewed after a comprehensive peace settlement was reached in the Middle East. But it conceded that normalization would be possible once the peace process got off the ground, and if the *PLO was allowed to participate in the peace conference. Simultaneously, in April Gorbachev called upon Yasser Arafat to recognize Israel. In January 1988 the Soviet Union finally allowed an Israeli consular delegation to come to Moscow, and in July the Israeli delegation opened an office in the Dutch Embassy in Moscow. The immediate return to the Soviet Union of a plane hijacked to Israel in December 1988 and generous Israeli aid to the victims of an earthquake in Armenia the same month, improved the atmosphere. The frequency of formal talks increased and the members of the Israeli consular delegation were received at the Soviet Foreign Ministry.

In January 1989 Foreign Minister Moshe *Arens met with Shevardnadze in Paris and it was agreed that the Israeli consular delegation would be allowed to move to the premises of the former Israeli Embassy in Moscow. The following month, during a visit to several Middle East states, Shevardnadze once again met with Arens in Cairo and the two foreign ministers agreed to formalize the contacts between the two countries, though the Soviet Union still conditioned the renewal of full diplomatic relations on the convention of an *international conference with the participation of the five Permanent Members of the UN Security Council and all the states involved in the Middle East conflict, and on Israel talking to the PLO. The Soviet reaction to the *Shamir-Rabin peace initiative of May 14, was ambivalent and vacillated between approval, to being referred to as "a satanic plot." Yet the impression was that the Soviet Union was less concerned with the content of the peace process than with finding a role for itself in it. Thus when Shevardnadze once again met Arens at UN Headquarters in New York in September 1989, in addition to the subject of the renewal of diplomatic relations and Jewish immigration by direct flights from the Soviet Union to Israel, the Soviet Foreign Minister offered to help bring about a meeting between Israeli and PLO representatives on Soviet soil - an offer turned down by Israel. However, the relations between the two countries in the second half of 1989 was dominated by economic ties, and at the end of July a Soviet trade mission arrived in Israel to purchase foodstuffs to the value of $30 million and to sign agreements for joint agricultural projects in the Soviet Union. Minister of Agriculture Avraham Katz-Oz was the first Israeli minister to visit the Soviet Union in over 22 years, officially to participate in the opening of a flower show in December. During his visit in the Soviet Union Katz-Oz arranged for 50 children from Chernobyl to come to Israel for medical treatment, and an Israeli army medical team was sent to provide medical treatment to the casualties of a train crash in the Ural Mountains in June, and brought back 61 casualties for further treatment in Israel.

The rapid rise in the number of Soviet immigrants to Israel from the end of 1989, led to pressure from the Arab states and the PLO on the Soviet Union to stop the flow. However, the Soviet Union was both unable and unwilling to comply with the Arab request, and although it warned Israel not to settle the immigrants in the *occupied territories, in December 1990 the number of Soviet immigrants reached a monthly peak of over 35,600. Soviet relations with its Arab allies also deteriorated as a result of a progressive slowdown in its supply of arms, especially to Syria.

On January 2, the first El-Al flight to the Soviet Union brought the Israel national theater *Habimah* to

Moscow, bringing back 125 immigrants to Israel. This was followed by visits to Moscow by several Israeli ministers. At the traditional meeting between the foreign ministers of the two countries at the UN in New York in September Shevardnadze and David *Levy announced the establishment of diplomatic relations at consular level. On May 1991 Soviet Foreign Minister Alexander Bessmertnykh visited Israel, and in August, just before the abortive coup in the Soviet Union, an agreement was finally reached on direct flights from the Soviet Union to Israel. The new Soviet Foreign Minister Boris Pankin arrived in Israel on October 24 - one week after the invitations were sent out by him and Secretary of State Baker for the *Madrid Conference - to sign an agreement with Israel concerning the reestablishment of full diplomatic relations between the two countries. The first Soviet ambassador to Israel in 24 years, Alexander Bovin, presented his credentials to President Ḥaim *Herzog on December 23, 1991, only one week before the dissolution of the Soviet Union. Within a week Bovin turned into the first Russian ambassador to Israel.

Soviet Union former republics and Israel Israel recognized the three Baltic republics of Lithuania, Latvia and Estonia, on September 4, 1991, soon after they became independent. Despite mixed feelings, because of the republics' anti-Semitic past, diplomatic ties were established with the three republics in January 1992. Israel recognized all the other former republics of the Soviet Union following its dissolution. The Soviet Ambassador, who had presented his credentials to the Israeli President only one week before - on December 23, 1991 - stayed on as the Ambassador of Russia.

Much thought was given in Israel to the issue of the predominantly Muslim republics, because of the fear that they might join an anti-Israel alignment with the Muslim states to their south. Therefore, the official visit to Israel in September, 1992, by the Prime Minister of Kazakhstan (on whose territory are to be found large quantities of nuclear weapons formerly belonging to the Soviet Union, as well as a nuclear testing ground and satellite launching base) and the establishment of full diplomatic relations with it, were of the utmost significance from an Israeli point of view. By the end of 1992 full diplomatic relations had also been established with Uzbekistan. Diplomatic relations without resident ambassadors were established with all the other former republics of the Soviet Union except Turkmenistan.

Spain and Israel In May, 1989, Prime Minister Yitzḥak *Shamir visited Spain. Prime Minister Felipe Gonzales tried to convince him that the *international conference idea was better than the government's plan for holding elections in the territories. Gonzales returned Shamir's visit in the beginning of December 1991 - one month after Spain, at very short notice but with noted success, hosted the *Madrid Conference. On this occasion Gonzales called upon Israel to freeze settlement activities in the territories and demonstrate flexibility on the territorial issue.

In February 1987 Minister of Education and Culture Yitzḥak *Navon met with King Carlos of Spain about the participation of Israel in the quincentennial commemoration of the discovery of America. Upon Navon's suggestion the king agreed that on the same occasion the expulsion of the Jews from Spain by King Ferdinand and Queen Isabella in 1492 should be commemorated as well. In March 1992 King Carlos and President Ḥaim *Herzog held a commemoration ceremony in the Madrid synagogue.

Status Quo (religious) The increase in the number of Knesset seats held by the ultra-religious parties from six in the 11th Knesset to 13 in the 12th, led to continuous attempts by the religious parties to change the status quo, and bitter debates between the religious and non-religious sections of the population.

In December 1988 a new *National Unity Government was formed at least partially because the ultra-religious parties were demanding an amendment in the definition of Who is a Jew in the *Law of Return as their price for joining the coalition, and American Jewry was up in arms. However, after the fall of the Unity Government in March 1990, the bargaining power of the ultra-religious parties once again rose. Both the *Israel Labor Party and the **Likud* were willing to increase the annual special allocation to the ultra-religious yeshivot to close to one quarter of a billion shekels and promise to pass "religious legislation," though not an amendment of the Law of Return.

Among the religious legislation passed following the formation of the narrow government in June 1990 was an amendment to the Authorization Law, which enables local authorities to rule that places of entertainment be closed on Saturdays (See: *local government) and an amendment to the penal code, which prohibits billboards with posters deemed offensive in religious circles (such as women in bathing suits). Amendments which did not go through dealt with limitations on the breeding of pigs and sale of pork, and on public transportation on Saturday. However, the existing law on the latter issue started to be more strictly implemented. At the same time Rabbi Menaḥem Porush, who became Deputy Minister of Labor and Welfare, started to apply more strictly the law prohibiting businesses and enterprises to work on Saturday. In December 1991 the *Likud* prevented the passing of a law to abolish the institution of special financial allocations outside the regular budget, of which the yeshivot were the main beneficiaries.

The atmosphere of an impeding *kulturkampf* was enhanced by a speech by Rabbi Elazar Menaḥem *Shach in March 1990, in which he accused the kibbutzniks of being totally ignorant of Judaism. In June 1991 Minister of Immigration Absorption Rabbi Yitzḥak *Peretz objected to new immigrants from Ethiopia (See: *Ethiopian Jews) being absorbed in kibbutzim which do not keep kosher kitchens and do not observe the Sabbath. Following the formation of the government by Yitzḥak *Rabin in 1992 the wrath of the religious parties was directed against Minister of Education and Culture Shulamit *Aloni who made some secularist statements - one of them about the fact that Darwinism is not taught in the religious schools. They demanded Aloni's dismissal, but Rabin refused to comply. At the end of 1992 attempts by *ḥaredi* circles to stop various development projects in *Jerusalem and archeological excavations on sites of ancient burial grounds raised tensions, accompanied by violence, to new heights.

The dilemmas regarding the status quo and the relations between religion and state were seriously dealt with at the 5th Labor Party Conference in November/December 1991. Labor adopted a platform which dealt with the separation of religion and politics and various necessary changes in the religious status quo. Of the parties which ran in the elections to the 13th Knesset in 1992 three - Labor, **Meretz* and **Tzomet* - called for the drafting of yeshiva students to the armed forces and other changes in the

***Syria and Israel** At the end of the 1980s Syria's policy regarding its conflict with Israel underwent a change caused by several developments. The first was related to the new Middle East policy of the Soviet Union after Mikhail Gorbachev became president. During a visit by President Hafez Assad to Moscow in April 1987, he was informed by Gorbachev that reliance on military force in settling the Arab-Israeli conflict had lost its credibility, and that Moscow would no longer support Syria's doctrine of strategic parity with Israel.

The end of the Iran-Iraq war exposed Syria, which had supported Iran, to a new Iraqi threat on several fronts. Since Syria was still at odds with Egypt following the latter's peace treaty with Israel in 1979, Syria's isolation in the Arab world grew, and it could no longer rely on military backing by any major Arab state.

The first manifestation of the change was an improvement in Syrian-Egyptian relations which were renewed in December 1989. During his first visit in thirteen years to Egypt, in July 1990, Assad declared: "We are ready to join the peace process... we accept *Security Council Resolutions 242 and 338 and we still call for a just and comprehensive peace." Assad had made similar statements earlier that year in meetings with American senators and former President Jimmy Carter. He also acted to improve Syria's relations with the United States, especially after George Bush became president. At first the two countries did not agree on the strategy for resolving the Arab-Israeli conflict. While the US advocated a step-by-step process to begin with negotiations between Israel and the Palestinians under its auspices, Syria insisted on the convention of a peace conference under UN auspices and with the Soviet Union playing a major role. However, following the Iraqi invasion of Kuwait in August 1990, Syria adopted a more flexible position.

Following Syria's decision to join the anti-Iraq coalition formed by the US towards the end of 1990, and the token participation of Syrian troops in the *Gulf War, Assad expected to be rewarded with American support for Syrian positions in the newly launched peace initiative after the war. Washington for its part was grateful to Syria not only for its support and legitimization of the American campaign against Iraq, but also for its contribution to a modicum of stability in Lebanon (achieved by Syria's consolidation of indirect control over Lebanon) and its potentially crucial role in the peace process.

By July 1991 Assad's position regarding the peace process fell more or less into line with the American terms. Syria now agreed to a regional conference under joint US-Soviet sponsorship, with only passive UN participation. While previously Syria had insisted on negotiations with Israel being indirect, it now agreed to hold direct talks following the ceremonial opening of the conference. It also dropped its previous demand that Israel commit itself to withdraw from all the occupied territories before negotiations opened, that the PLO should represent the Palestinians, and that the outcome of the negotiations should be the establishment of an independent Palestinian state.

Nevertheless, as reiterated at the *Madrid Conference by Syrian Foreign Minister Faruk a-Sharaa, Syria continued to demand complete Israeli withdrawal from all the territories it had occupied in 1967 and Southern Lebanon. In return the Syrian leaders offered a "peace agreement" which would avoid full recognition of Israel and in fact be more of a non-belligerency agreement than a peace treaty. Syrian officials continued to insist that peace with Israel would not include full diplomatic relations, or economic cooperation, cultural ties etc. In accordance with this position Syria did not participate in the early rounds of multilateral talks on specific fields of cooperation which took place alongside the bilateral talks following the Madrid Conference.

In the first stages of the peace process, the Syrians were not alone in taking a rigid stance. Generally speaking most Israelis are more reluctant, for strategic and psychological reasons, to give up the Golan than they were to give up the Sinai. Furthermore, the Israeli government which was in power until July 1992 was ideologically committed not to give up an inch of land. In addition, Prime Minister Yitzḥak *Shamir was inclined to try to maintain the status quo with Syria for as long as possible. This was reflected in the terms of reference of the Israeli team sent to negotiate with the Syrians in the Washington talks headed by the Director General of the Prime Minister's Office, Yossi Ben-Aharon.

However, Israel's attitude underwent a change after the Labor government was formed in July 1992. Labor's platform, adopted in November 1991, spoke of *territorial compromise on all fronts, including the Golan Heights, although it also stated that an Israeli military and settlement presence in the Golan would continue. Soon after forming his new government Prime Minister Yitzḥak *Rabin stated that he planned to give preference to a settlement with the Palestinians which implied that the issue of the Golan Heights would be deferred. However, following talks with President Ḥosni Mubarak and Secretary of State James Baker he started to speak of an interim agreement with Syria, although expressing at the same time concern about an experimental launching of a Scud-C missile by the Syrians.

Upon the renewal of the bilateral talks in Washington at the end of August Syria indicated that in return for an Israeli commitment to withdraw from the whole of the Golan Heights by the end of the process, and a solution of the Palestinian problem, it would be willing to reach interim agreements concerning demilitarized zones and early warning systems, and to reach a "total peace" with Israel.By the end of 1992 it was rumored that great progress had been made by Israel and Syria towards an interim agreement. (M.M.)

*** Tab'a** The arbitration tribunal on the Tab'a issue published its decision on September 29, 1988 to the effect that under international law the whole of the area in dispute was Egyptian territory. Tab'a was returned to Egyptian sovereignty on March 15, 1989.

Teḥiyah In 1987 **Tzomet* broke away from the *Teḥiyah*. In the 12th Knesset elections the *Teḥiyah* received three seats. It joined the government formed by Yitzḥak *Shamir in June 1990, with its chairman, Yuval *Ne'eman, assuming the post of Minister of Energy and Infrastructure and Minister of Science and Technology, and Geula *Cohen that of Deputy Minister of Science and Technology. Cohen left the government in November 1991 and Ne'eman left it in February 1992 against the background of the peace process which the *Teḥiyah* opposed, because it claimed that it would lead to Israeli territorial concessions and the eventual establishment of a Palestinian state.

The *Teḥiyah* refused to run in the elections to the 13th Knesset in a single list with **Moledet* because it rejected the latter's advocacy of a *transfer of the Palestinians. Due to internal frictions and the decision of Rabbi Moshe *Levinger to run in the elections to the 13th Knesset on his own list, the *Teḥiyah* expected to lose some of its strength, but it did not expect to fail to pass the qualifying threshold.

Temple Mount Faithful The most prominent group campaigning for the right of Jews to enter freely and worship on the Temple Mount and prepare for the construction of the Third Temple. Since 1970, under the leadership of Gershon Solomon, the Temple Mount Faithful have made attempts to demonstratively enter the compound of the Temple Mount in order to pray, and appealed to the High Court of Justice to permit Jews to worship on the Mount. However, while the Court stated that under the law for the protection of the holy places Jews had the right to worship on the Mount, due to the political and religious sensitivities of the Muslims, provocative activities of the nature carried out by the Temple Mount Faithful were forbidden and should be prevented by the police.

Since 1988 the Temple Mount Faithful have started planning to lay the cornerstone for the Third Temple. While few in number, their public relations success combined with violent Muslim responses have aroused much publicity. Other Jewish groups active on behalf of the Temple Mount Faithful include *El Har Hashem* ("to the Lord's Mount"), the Temple Mount Institute which maintains an exhibit of temple appurtenances, and the Movement for the Establishment of the Temple. (I.M.)

***Toubi, Tawfiq** In July 1990, after being an MK for 41 years, Toubi resigned his seat to enable a younger member of **Ḥadash*, Tamar Gozhansky, to enter the Knesset. Following his resignation he was appointed General Secretary of the Israel Communist party (**Maki*). (M.H.)

Tsaban, Yair **Mapam* leader. Tsaban was born in Jerusalem in 1930. He fought in the *War of Independence in the **Palmaḥ*, and was one of the founders in 1948 of kibbutz Zor'a. In the 1950s he was a teacher and educator. In 1948-52 Tsaban was active in *Mapam*, which he left in 1953, together with Moshe *Sneh (whose secretary he was in 1952-55), and joined **Maki*. In 1961-67 he served as Secretary General of *Maki*'s youth movement, and was one of the activists who gave *Maki* the national-democratic turn which led to the split between *Maki* and **Rakaḥ* in 1965. Following Sneh's death in 1972 he became chairman of the Political Bureau of *Maki*.

In 1973 Tsaban was one of the founders of **Moked*, and served as head of its faction in the **Histadrut* executive. Following the establishment of **Sheli* in 1977 (which *Moked* joined) he served as head of its faction in the *Histadrut*, and as representative of both *Moked* and *Sheli* in the World Jewish Congress Executive. In 1989 he headed the *Mapam* list in the elections to the *Histadrut*. In 1980 Tsaban rejoined *Mapam* and in the elections to the 10th Knesset in 1981 was elected on its list (within the framework of the *Alignment) to the Knesset. He headed the independent *Mapam* list in the elections to the 12th Knesset. Most of his legislative initiatives dealt with social and welfare issues. In the elections to the 13th Knesset Tsaban was placed second on the **Meretz* list, and following the establishment of the Labor-led government in July 1992 he was appointed Minister of Immigration Absorption, and chairman of the Absorption Cabinet.

Tsaban has played an active role in trying to create channels of communication with Palestinian leaders in the territories and abroad, in raising social issues and in the battle against religious coercion.

***Tzomet** ("crossroads") *Tzomet* broke away from the **Teḥiyah* in 1987. In the 1988 elections *Tzomet* received two seats. In addition to defending *greater Israel, and opposing the *autonomy plan, *Tzomet* concentrated in the 12th Knesset on issues of constitutional reforms (See: *Prime Minister, direct election of), against religious coercion and for the drafting of yeshiva students for military service, and on education - especially among underprivileged population groups.

Tzomet joined the government formed by Yitzḥak *Shamir in June 1990, and Rafael *Eitan became Minister of Agriculture. But the party left it in December 1991 against the background of the **Likud*'s position regarding the law for the direct election of the Prime Minister. It resisted attempts to form a radical right bloc for the elections to the 13th Knesset, and on its own it won eight seats.

Talks were held by *Labor with *Tzomet* after the 1992 elections, but the party decided to remain outside the coalition. The main reasons for this were the peace process and Labor's willingness to accept a *territorial compromise.

***United Nations and Israel** The collapse of the Soviet Union and the end of the cold war, as well as the significant weakening in the Arab position following the *Gulf War and the opening of peace talks following the *Madrid Conference, led to a dramatic change in Israel's standing in the United Nations. This manifested itself in the unprecedented repeal on December 15, 1991 of General Assembly Resolution 3379 passed in 1975 which had equated *Zionism with racism. The resolution which had been passed by a vote of 72 in favor, 35 against and 32 abstentions, was now repealed by a vote of 111 in favor, 25 against (including almost all the Arab and Muslim states) and 13 abstentions.

The change in the atmosphere at the UN improved Israel's chances of becoming a member of some of the UN bodies, such as the Security Council which were previously closed to it. At the end of 1992 Israel was approached by the Egyptian Secretary General of the UN, Butrus Butrus-Ghali, about sending professional personnel to participate in UN peacekeeping forces, and agreed.

After the Security Council condemned Israel for expelling 415 **Ḥammas* and *Islamic Jihad activists on December 17, 1992, representatives of the Secretary General were sent to Israel to try to work out a compromise. (A.B.)

***United States and Israel** While the US approved the *London Agreement reached by King Ḥussein and Shimon *Peres in April 1987, Secretary of State George Shultz became aware of the fact that this move was supported only by the Labor half of the *National Unity Government. However, in the pre-*intifada* period the US was more concerned with improving the quality of life in the *West Bank and *Gaza Strip than with a Middle East peace process. US-Israel relations were excellent. Israel had been invited in 1986 to join the SDI ("Star Wars") program, and legislation was passed in Congress in 1987 establishing Israel as a major non-NATO ally.

The **intifada* was a watershed, following which the US became directly involved again in the peace process. The *Shultz Plan, made known to the parties concerned on March 1, 1988, was more the result of the *intifada* scenes seen on American TV than of American national interests. Like the *Reagan Plan, so the new plan was issued without prior consultations with Israel. But what was especially disturbing to Israel about it was the fact that it did not coincide with the timetable outlined in the *Camp David Accords: talks about the final status of the territories were to begin within a certain period after talks began on the interim arrangement, irrespective of how much progress had been made in the latter. This procedure was termed "the interlock," and was favored by the Arab states.

Despite several visits by Shultz to the Middle East, the plan came to nothing. In the process of his shuttle trips Shultz was apparently convinced that no progress would be possible without the approval of the *PLO. The US-PLO dialogue, which opened after Arafat had clarified certain points in the course of a press conference in Geneva in December 1988, began between the end of the second administration of Ronald Reagan, and the beginning of the administration of George Bush. That the new administration would differ from the old one became apparent at the very warm reception Egyptian President Ḥosni Mubarak received in Washington in April 1989. It was on this occasion that Bush first referred to the *land for peace formula and expressed his support for the political rights of the Palestinians. In May Secretary of State James Baker added that Israel must forget its dream of *Greater Israel. However, an additional irritant to US-Israel relations resulted from a misunderstanding during a visit by Yitzḥak *Shamir to Washington in April. At a meeting of Bush and Shamir, the President was convinced that Shamir had implied that Israel would stop all settlement activities in the territories, while Shamir argued that he had never given such an undertaking. A second Bush-Shamir misunderstanding occurred just before the fall of the *National Unity Government in March 1990, when Shamir assured Bush that less than one percent of the new immigrants from the Soviet Union were settling in the territories, while American officials, including East Jerusalem in the definition of territories, informed the President that the figure was closer to 10 percent. The outcome was to place the settlements issue high on Bush's agenda.

The Administration's initial reaction to the *Shamir-Rabin peace initiative of May 14, 1989, was somewhat frosty. The section of the plan dealing with elections in the territories was based on the intention of creating an alternative Palestinian leadership to the PLO, and the Americans were skeptical as to whether the Israeli plan was feasible. Nevertheless, it finally received the approval of the Administration, and Baker became actively involved towards its implementation. This whole move collapsed in March 1990 upon the fall of the National Unity Government in Israel. But soon after, the US-PLO dialogue came to an end, as a result of the refusal of Arafat to condemn an attempted terrorist attack by one of the component organizations of the PLO on the shores of Israel in May. The US attitude towards Israel, in the course of the crisis which followed the Iraqi invasion of Kuwait in August 1990, was not just a function of Bush's feelings towards Israel, but of the fact that the US Middle East Command, established in January 1983, did not include Israel or any other Mediterranean state in its frame of reference. The Americans wanted Israel to maintain a low profile in this crisis and were extremely sensitive to any development which might jeopardize its efforts to build the anti-Iraq coalition. At the same time, however, Congress approved a $700 million "draw down" of surplus military equipment from the US forces in Europe which Israel could acquire and the prepositioning of additional American military equipment in Israel. However, neither of these provisions was implemented immediately. There was also a promise to provide Israel with anti-aircraft PAC-1 Patriot missiles, even though Israel had sought PAC-2 anti-missile Patriot missiles of which the US was short. When the PAC-2 anti-missiles were finally brought to Israel following the outbreak of the Gulf War, they were accompanied by American crews since Israeli crews had not been trained to use them.

In October 1990 Foreign Minister David *Levy met with Baker at the opening session of the UN General Assembly in New York. In connection with a 400 million dollar American loan guarantees for the absorption of new immigrants in Israel, Levy promised in a letter that Israel would report to the US about any new settlement activity in the territories as well as its expenditures in the territories. This letter was to create, later, additional tension in US-Israel relations, since Baker believed that he had received an implicit undertaking that Israel would not increase its settlement activities. Israel, on the other hand, was in the process of increasing its construction activities in Israel five-fold to house the immigrants, and construction in the territories increased proportionally. As the "Desert Shield" buildup advanced, there was a growing intimacy between the Administration and its Arab coalition partners - all of which was highly disturbing to Israel. Nevertheless, when Shamir went to Washington again in December 1990, he was received cordially. The US wanted a promise from Israel that it would not preempt any operation against Iraq, and that it would not respond to an Iraqi provocation.

In Israel there was a growing awareness that following the war the United States would make a major effort to get the peace process moving again, under circumstances less favorable to Israel. The U.S. now felt indebted to the Arab states, especially Saudi Arabia, Egypt and Syria. The immediate payoff to Saudi Arabia was a promise to sell that country $23 billion worth of military equipment, while Syria was allowed to strengthen its hold over Lebanon and Egypt had a $7 billion debt cancelled.

Israel's first disappointment came when Levy was refused the cancellation of part of Israel's debt to the

United States. Then in January during a visit to Washington, Finance Minister Yitzḥak Moda'i tried to cash in on the sympathy generated for Israel following the Scud attacks and Israel's restrained reactions, and mentioned an additional loan guarantee of $13 billion , and he too was turned down. In mid-February 1991 Israeli Ambassador to Washington, Zalman Shoval, in an interview to Reuters, complained that even over the $400 million loan guarantees the United States was giving Israel a hard time. Shoval became *persona non grata* in Washington. Nevertheless, these loan guarantees were approved on February 20, and in the beginning of March, through the intervention of Congress, Israel was accorded $650 million of supplementary aid (Israel had requested one billion) to cover its military expenses during the Gulf War. The issue of additional loan guarantees, to the amount of $10 billion, was put off for six months. In his victory speech to Congress, Bush spoke of taking advantage of the new situation to press for an Israeli-Palestinian settlement, and repeated the land for peace formula.

In March 1991 Baker paid his first of several visits to Israel and the region in an effort to get his peace initiative off the ground. During the talks leading up to the *Madrid Conference it became clear that Baker was making an effort to be receptive to the Israeli demands in the procedural sphere, such as over the non-participation of the PLO, a separate Palestinian delegation and Palestinians from East Jerusalem and the "diaspora" in the talks. Baker now agreed to the two-track negotiating procedure, whereby Israel would be talking simultaneously to the Palestinians and the Arab states - not just the Palestinians, as the Americans had previously advocated. However, with the progress in putting together the process for the peace talks, tension was growing between Israel and the US over the issue of further loan guarantees which the US insisted on linking with a freeze on all settlement activities in the territories, which it termed "an obstacle to peace." On September 12, 1991, the six month pause requested by the US before Israel renew its request for the $10 billion loan guarantees was up Moda'i submitted Israel's request even though the Administration sought a further delay because it didn't want to lose its leverage over Israel before the peace talks began. The pro-Israel lobby used its full power over Congress, which resulted in President Bush making a comment about the power of the Jews which was taken as derogatory. This incident resulted in a confidence crisis between the Administration and the Israeli government, and after the president announced that he would use his veto power in the event of Congress approving the loan guarantees. The whole issue was frozen until after the Israeli general elections in June 1992.

At the Madrid Conference it was noted by some Israeli observers that President Bush deliberately used the term *"territorial compromise" rather than "land for peace." This was regarded as an attempt by the president to placate the Israeli public. Although Israel was irritated by the reference to substance in the invitations sent out for the bilateral talks which caused its delegation to delay its arrival, the Washington talks proceeded with minimal US intervention.

Following the election of Yitzḥak *Rabin as leader of the Labor Party and its candidate for Prime Minister in February 1992, Shamir tried, through Shoval, to check with the Americans they would accept an agreement regarding the loan guarantees whereby Israel's annual investment in settlements in the territories would be deducted from the sum of the guarantees. Baker was willing to agree only to that whatever was under construction be completed, and then all such activities would have to stop. Soon after forming his new government, Rabin met Bush at Kennebunkport on August 10/11 1992. The meeting was influenced by the fact that Israel had a government whose positions were much closer to those of the United States by Bush's low popularity ratings three months before the presidential elections, and by the US determination to sell 72 advanced export model F-15's to Saudi Arabia. In return for Israel's acquiescence to the latter, the US was willing to supply to Israel a variety of used aircraft on account of the $700 million draw down promised in October 1990, and preposition $200 million worth of American equipment in Israel. Israel was also invited to join the US Global Protection System program, and the loan guarantees were approved by Congress on October 8. Following the expulsion by Israel of 415 **Ḥammas* and Islamic Jihad leaders on December 17, 1992, the US voted in favor of a Security Council Resolution condemning Israel and calling upon it to return the deportees.

The Vatican and Israel Since the establishment of the State of Israel in 1948, the Vatican has refrained from formally recognizing and establishing diplomatic relations with it. However, over the years official meetings were held on issues of immediate concern to the two parties, while two Israeli Prime Ministers (Golda *Meir in January 1973 and Shimon *Peres in February 1985) and three Foreign Ministers (Abba *Eban in October 1949, Moshe *Dayan in January 1978 and Yitzḥak *Shamir in January 1982) were received in private audience by the Pope.

The attitude of the Vatican towards Israel has been affected by theological considerations relating to the Jews, as well as by its concern for the status of the

Holy Places - especially those in *Jerusalem - for the safeguard of Catholic property, and for the welfare and needs of the Arab Catholic community in Israel. This ambivalent attitude was demonstrated when a visit by the Israel Philharmonic Orchestra to the Vatican in 1955 was described by the Vatican's daily *Osservatore Romano* as that of "Jewish musicians of fourteen different nationalities." An apparent change did occur, however, when the official Israeli representative to the coronation of Pope John XXIII in 1958, was described by the Vatican as a "special delegate of the State of Israel." However, during an historic visit to the Holy Land in January 1964, Pope Paul VI never once referred to the State of Israel by name, and a letter sent to Zalman Shazar after his departure failed to mention Shazar's title as *President of Israel, and was addressed to Tel Aviv - although the President's official residence is in Jerusalem.

One of the main obstacles to formal recognition by the Vatican of Israel as a Jewish state was of a theological nature, connected with the alleged guilt of the Jewish people for the crime of deicide. A major change occurred in 1965 when in his *Nostra Aetate* declaration, the Council Vatican II stated for the first time that it was only the Jews who had been directly involved in the crucifixion of Jesus who were to be held responsible for the act - not the Jewish people as a whole at all times. It was, however, only during a meeting with Jewish leaders in September 1987, that Pope John Paul II first stated that there was no theological obstacle to the establishment of full relations between the Vatican and Israel. This was apparently a sequel to the line adopted by the Church in June 1985 to the effect that there was no temporal link between the Jewish people and the State of Israel. In a statement issued on the 20th anniversary of the Vatican II declaration, Christians were invited to appreciate the religious attachment of Jews to the State of Israel, although it was added that the existence of the State of Israel and its political options should not be viewed within a religious context, but in reference to the principles of international law. While this approach helped the Vatican circumvent the theological obstacles, it denied the spiritual basis of *Zionism, and the link between the diaspora Jews and the State of Israel. On January 25, 1991, in the midst of the Gulf War, the Holy See published a document on the issue of diplomatic relations with Israel. It stated that the absence of such relations was not due to theological reasons, but to legal ones stemming from Israel's presence in the *occupied territories, its annexation of Jerusalem, and the status of the Catholic Church in Israel and the occupied territories.

Back in 1949 Pope Pius XII, who supported the idea that Jerusalem should be an international *Corpus Separatum*, stated in 1949, in the third of three encyclicals issued on the subject of the Holy Land, that Jerusalem and its environs be given "an internationally guaranteed judicial statute." Following the reunification of Jerusalem in June 1967 Pope Paul VI once again spoke of an internationally guaranteed statute for Jerusalem, though the idea of a *Corpus Separatum* was not repeated. The proposed statute was explained by the Holy See's observer to the UN, in a declaration published in December, 1979. It meant parity for the three religious communities in Jerusalem, with freedom of worship and access to the Holy Places, and equal rights with guarantees for the promotion of the spiritual, cultural, civil and social life of these communities. In all the meetings between the Pope and representatives of the Israeli government the importance of finding a just solution for the question of Jerusalem has constantly been emphasized.

A dispute over compensation for damages caused during the *War of Independence to Catholic churches and property in Israel, was resolved to the Holy See's satisfaction in 1955. In January 1972 an open clash between Israel and the Vatican was averted when the Israeli government cancelled the sale of Catholic Church property in Jerusalem to the Hebrew University - a sale which had not been authorized by the Vatican. The issue was already being dealt with by the Israeli courts, when the government decided to intervene.

The existence of an Arab Catholic community in Israel no doubt affects the attitude of the Vatican towards the Palestinian issue, beyond the humanitarian concern for the Palestinians expressed by the Holy See from time to time. Although Pope Paul VI in his annual message to the cardinals on December 21, 1973 (the day on which the *Geneva Conference convened), offered the Vatican's cooperation toward the attainment of an Arab-Israeli agreement "that may guarantee to all parties concerned a peaceful and secure existence and the recognition of their respective rights," Israel feels that the Catholic Church had a pro-Palestinian bias. This feeling intensified when on December 9, 1974, Hilarion Capucci, the Greek Catholic Archbishop of Jerusalem, was sentenced by an Israeli court to 12 years imprisonment for smuggling arms and explosives from Lebanon into Israel. Three years later the Pope approached President Efraim Katzir on Archbishop Capucci's behalf. Katzir commuted the sentence, and Capucci was released. However, a written promise by the Pope to the effect that Capucci would not "bring any harm to the State of Israel," was not respected as the prelate subsequently participated in numerous propaganda events organized by the *PLO. The audience given by Pope John Paul II to Yasser Arafat at the end of 1982, after the PLO leader had been forced to leave Beirut following the PLO's military defeat, was viewed in Israel as further proof of the Vatican's pro-Palestinian bias.

Following the *Madrid Conference, the Holy See finally agreed, in July 1992, to establish a bilateral permanent commission to discuss the outstanding issues toward the establishment of diplomatic relations. An official invitation was extended to the Pope to visit Israel, which he has accepted in principle. (S.M.)

*** Voting Statistics** (See Table below)

Washington talks (See: *Madrid Conference)

Water Policy At the 1919 Paris Peace Conference, when the boundaries of *Mandatory Palestine were being delineated, the Zionist Organization presented its own map, which included all the tributaries of the *Jordan River within the territory of Palestine. This proposal was not accepted but it demonstrated the awareness of the Zionist leaders to one of the country's most serious problems - water scarcity.

In the Middle East Israel and Jordan suffer most from this problem; it is therefore not surprising that over the years various proposals have been formulated for sharing the existing water sources and the creation of new ones. Best known of these was the Johnston Plan of 1955, named after President Eisenhower's advisor, Eric Johnston, sent to the region by the U.S. president in 1953 to prepare an agreement on a unified or coordinated regional water development plan for the exploitation of the Jordan River for the benefit of the riparian countries (Lebanon, Syria, Jordan and Israel). Johnston presented his plan for the distribution of the Jordan waters, which had been approved by the technical experts from the states concerned. However, the plan floundered as a result of the refusal of the Arab states to participate in a scheme in which Israel would be a party and beneficiary. Israel and Jordan then proceeded to implement independent projects while adhering more or less to the distribution as proposed by Johnston (38.5 percent and 46.7 percent of the water respectively). As of the early 1980s the two countries started to cooperate secretly over the water issue, and in 1985 regular meetings between Israeli and Jordanian professional teams took place. The Middle East water problem was dealt with as a separate issue in the multilateral talks between Israel and its neighbors following the *Madrid Conference. In the bilateral talks between Israel and the Palestinians on autonomy in the *administered territories (See: *autonomy plan), the issue of control over water resources was raised. While the Palestinians had concentrated on accusing Israel of robbing "their" water, Israel was seeking means of increasing the quantity of available water by means of desalination or by bringing water by pipe from abroad. The main obstacle to these projects is the high cost.

In 1964 Israel completed its National Carrier project designed to divert up to 320 million cubic meters of water annually to the coastal plain and the Negev. In an attempt to foil the Israeli plans Syria started work to divert the tributaries of the Jordan before they enter Israeli territory. However, Israel reacted by attacking the installations during retaliatory operations against raids into Israel. During the *Six-Day War Israel occupied the area on the *Golan Heights where the diversion works were being carried out. Despite the National Carrier, local projects in urban areas for purifying sewage water for agricultural use, a freeze in 1982 on the area devoted to irrigated agriculture, and great awareness regarding the need to economize in the use of water as a result of the growth in population and lack of systematic planning, there was overpumping of water, especially from the coastal aquifer. This has increased the danger of saline and polluted water entering the aquifer. In 1986 Israel suffered its first serious water crisis, followed by another in 1991. The authorities responsible for Israel's water economy - the Water Commission in the Ministry of Agriculture, *Tahal* (which is responsible for planning water projects) and *Mekorot* (which is responsibility for the actual supply of water) - were all blamed for the situation. It was argued that under the circumstances agriculture, which uses close to 70 percent of the water consumed in Israel, should be cut drastically. Agriculture, it was said, was supplied water at a much lower price than industry or private consumers, and this resulted in waste. The fact that the price of water was determined by a *Knesset subcommittee made up primarily of representatives of the agricultural lobby (mostly members of **kibbutzim* and **moshavim*), made changes impossible.

Knesset	Date elections	Number of registered voters	Number of voters (% of 3rd col.)	Number of invalid votes (% of 4th col.)	Number of voters per seat
12	Nov. 1, 1988	2,894,267	2,305,576 (79.7)	22,444 (0.9)	18,563
13	Jun 23, 1992	3,409,015	2,616,831 (77.4)	21,102 (0.8)	20,715

Though many plans and proposals were presented to the Government since 1986 little was changed in the water policy. In addition, no serious debate ever took place on whether the country's policy of encouraging agriculture at almost any cost (a policy with ideological roots in Mandatory times, and the determination after the establishment of the state that Israel should not only supply all its own food requirements but become a major exporter of agricultural goods) should be reconsidered.

*** Weizman, Ezer** In the *National Unity Government formed in 1988 Weizman was appointed Minister of Science and Technology. On the last day of 1989, a government crisis erupted about contacts which Weizman allegedly held with the *PLO, and Yitzḥak *Shamir threatened to fire him. Following the break up of the government in March 1990 Weizman became increasingly disenchanted with the *Israel Labor Party, and when his efforts to get Shimon *Peres and Yitzḥak *Rabin to step down and let a younger generation of leaders take over failed, he resigned his Knesset seat in February 1992. Weizman is one of three Labor candidates for the presidency after Ḥaim *Herzog concludes his term.

***Women in Politics** Seven women were elected to the 12th Knesset in 1988. Two years later another woman entered the Knesset as a result of a rotation agreement in **Ḥadash*, and two weeks before the elections to the 13th Knesset a woman of the **Likud* entered the Knesset, after the chairman of the Knesset House Committee resigned. There were no women in the two governments which served in the course of the 12th Knesset.

Eleven women were elected to the 13th Knesset - four of *Labor, three of **Meretz*, two of the *Likud*, one of **Tzomet* and one in *Ḥadash*. Two women were given ministerial posts: Shulamit *Aloni (*Meretz*) who was appointed Minister of Education and Culture and Ora *Namir (Labor) was first appointed Minister of the Environment and in December 1992, Minister of Labor and Welfare . A third woman, former *Na'amat Secretary General Masha Lubelsky, was appointed Deputy Minister of Industry and Trade. One of the Deputy Knesset Speakers is a woman (Esther Salmonowitz of *Tzomet*) and there are two women in the prestigious Foreign Affairs and Security Committee.

Toward the internal elections in the various parties before the 1992 election campaign there was great pressure, to ensure appropriate representation for women. Only Labor promised in advance four "safe" places for women in its Knesset list while **Mapam* (within *Meretz*) cancelled its own promised 20th representation (though one woman from *Mapam* was elected). The Women's Network (a lobby founded in 1974 as an independent non-partisan body to advance the status of women in Israel) was very active before the internal elections in the various parties to create a public atmosphere which would force them to elect women to realistic places. The Network also held seminars for political communications for women activists in all the parties in order to provide them with skill to help them succeed.

Toward the 1992 elections a women's party was established, accompanied by a debate in feminist circles as to whether women should contend within existing parties or establish a party of their own. The women's party received only 2,886 votes. At the same time many of the parties which ran in the elections appealed specifically to women by emphasizing their past records and future plans on women's issues.

The percentage of women in local councils never reached 19 percent and though in absolute terms the number of women serving in local councils has grown, so has the number of local councils. Until the 1989 elections there were no women in over half the local councils. In 1989 the number of local councils in which women serve went up to 64. In the 1983 municipal elections two women stood at the head of lists. In the 1989 elections there were 29, and one was actually elected to stand at the head of a local council. Over the years only six women served as heads of local councils. (L.S.)

***Ya'acobi Gad** Ya'acobi served as Minister of Communications in the *National Unity Government formed in 1988, until March 15, 1990. Though he had planned to run for the leadership of the *Israel Labor Party in the primaries held in February 1991, Ya'acobi finally decided to support Yitzḥak *Rabin. In the primaries to the Knesset list Ya'acobi was elected to the 45th place and remained outside the 13th Knesset. After the June 1992 elections he was appointed as Israel's Ambassador to the *United Nations.

Yahadut Hatorah Hame'uḥedet ("United Torah Judaism") An Ashkenazi *ḥaredi* list formed on the eve of the 1992 elections comprising **Agudat Yisrael*, **Degel Hatorah*, **Po'alei Agudat Yisrael* and Rabbi Yitzḥak *Peretz. These parties had together commanded eight seats in the 12th Knesset, but in the 13th they obtained only four. Of these seats *Agudat Yisrael* had three, and one was held by Peretz, who in accordance with a prior arrangement that in the event of the new list receiving less than five seats, was forced to resign to make room for the representative of *Degel Hatorah*. The representative of *Po'alei Agudat Yisrael* remained outside the Knesset. The list was eager to join the coalition, but because it objected to the appointment of Shulamit *Aloni to the Ministry of Education it remained outside. The head of the list, Avraham Shapira, was given a seat in the Knesset Finance Committee at the expense of the Labor quota. (M.H.)

Yesha Hebrew acronym for *Yehuda, Shomron Ve'aza* (Judea, Samaria and Gaza) which, as a metonym, translates as "salvation." The text of the entry **Yosh* (Hebrew acronym for *Yehuda Veshomron* (Judea and Samaria) applies to *Yesha.* (I.M.)

Yesh Gvul ("there are limits") A radical movement which supports refusal to serve in the *occupied territories. It was formed at the beginning of the *Lebanese War in 1982 by a group of reserve officers and soldiers who sent petitions to the Prime Minister demanding to do their military service exclusively within the territory of the State of Israel. The members of *Yesh Gvul* emphasize that their motive is not pacifism but objection to participate in the implementation of specific policies to which they are opposed. During the Lebanese War 165 of its members were imprisoned for refusing to serve in Lebanon. Following the withdrawal from Lebanon, after the outbreak of the **intifada*, 170 of its members were imprisoned for refusing to serve in the territories. The *IDF try to avoid clashes with the movement, and frequently respond to its members' requests to serve within the *Green Line. In November 1992 *Yesh Gvul* opened a campaign to convince highschool students not to volunteer for certain special units which serve in the territories. Other movements with a similar orientation are *Dai Lakibush* (enough with the occupation), *Hashana Ha'esrim Va'ahat* (the 21st year), and *Nashim Beshaḥor* (women in black). (M.H.)

Yosef, Ovadia Authority on *halachic* questions, and spiritual leader of **Shass*. Yosef was born in Baghdad in 1920, and was brought by his parents to *Eretz Yisrael* the following year. He was educated at the Sephardi yeshiva Porat Yosef in Jerusalem. From a young age he was noted for his diligence, phenomenal memory and intelligence. Towards the end of the 1940s he was appointed Chief Rabbi of Cairo and Egypt. After the foundation of the state he returned to Israel and became a rabbinical judge. In 1966 he was appointed Chief Rabbi of Tel Aviv, and in 1973-83 served as the Chief Sephardi Rabbi of Israel and President of the Supreme Rabbinical Court.

After his appointment as Chief Rabbi of Tel Aviv Yosef created a great stir in the Sephardi Torah world and rabbinate, encouraging and initiating the establishment of hundreds of yeshivo*t* and *kolelim* for youths of the **Edot Mizraḥ*. Several months after leaving the Chief Rabbinate, and with the encouragement and blessing of Rabbi Menaḥem Elazar *Shach, he founded *Shass* which received four seats in the 11th Knesset in 1984. Yosef was given much of the credit for *Shass's* electoral success.

Yosef preaches moderate and dovish political positions, based on the premise that in order to avoid bloodshed Israel should even be willing to give up territories. In 1990 he visited *Egypt, accompanied by his protegé, Minister of the Interior Arye *Der'i, and met with Egyptian President Ḥosni Mubarak. In March of that year he allowed Der'i to participate in the initiative of the *Israel Labor Party to bring down the government in a vote of no confidence and establish a Labor-led government. However, due to heavy pressure from Rabbi Shach, Yosef was forced to back down. This event was the beginning of a serious rift between the two rabbis, and following the June 1992 elections *Shass* joined the government formed by Yitzḥak *Rabin with Yosef's blessing and in spite of Shach's opposition. This move deepened the rift between the two rabbis and between the Ashkenazi and most of the Sephardi *ḥaredim*.

Yosef was awarded the Israel Prize for his multi-volume work *Yabiah Omer* which deals with *halachic* problems in daily life. In his teachings he emphasizes the importance of yeshiva students learning to deal with practical problems and not only engaging *halachic* dialectics. (M.H.)

Ze'evi, Rehav'am (Gandhi) Former IDF commander and leader of **Moledet*. Ze'evi was born in Jerusalem in 1926. He was active in the *Maḥanot Ha'olim* youth movement in the years 1936-44. He joined the **Palmaḥ* in 1944. His military career was always controversial. In 1964, with the rank of major general, Ze'evi was appointed commander of the Central Command. In 1968 he was appointed Head of the Operations Branch, resigning from the IDF in 1973, before the *Yom Kippur War. At the outbreak of the war he returned to active service as special aid to the chief of staff, later returning for a short period to the Operations Branch.

In the years 1974-77 Ze'evi served as advisor to Prime Minister Yitzḥak *Rabin on the war against terror. In the late 1970s several of Ze'evi's associates were cited as leaders of Israel's organized crime, but he himself was never directly implicated. In 1981 Ze'evi was appointed head of the Land of Israel Museum in Tel Aviv, holding the position for ten years. Here too his activities were the subject of controversy.

In 1985 Ze'evi started to advocate a "voluntary" *transfer of the Arabs from the *administered territories. Before the 1988 elections he formed the party *Moledet* ("homeland"). The party received two seats in the 12th Knesset. Despite his political success he remained a political pariah, and because he is Israeli-born and a former general, was regarded in mainstream political circles as more dangerous to the Israeli democratic system than Meir *Kahane ever was.

Ze'evi's entry into the government of Yitzḥak *Shamir in February 1991 was opposed by several senior **Likud* members, including Moshe *Arens, David *Levy, Dan *Meridor and Ehud Olmert. However, in the *Knesset only Ze'ev Binyamin *Begin voted against his appointment. Ze'evi was given the post of Minister Without Portfolio with a seat in the defense cabinet. He left the government in January 1992, with **Teḥiyah*, against the background of the peace talks which followed the *Madrid Conference.

Ze'evi tried to form a political bloc with *Teḥiyah* for the elections to the 13th Knesset, but the *Teḥiyah* leadership had serious reservations about collaborating with him. His party won three seats in the 13th Knesset and remained in opposition, but soon a crisis developed in *Moledet*; there were complaints about his authoritarian and non-democratic style of running the party.

GLOSSARY

aliyah: Immigration to *Eretz Yisrael.*

Ashkenazi (plural *Ashkenazim*): A Jew of Central or Eastern European ancestry; Most of those known today as *Ashkenazim* are of European or American origin.

Gadna: Acronym for *Gdudei No'ar* - youth battalions. Pre-army paramilitary youth training program.

Halacha: Jewish law. The legal part of the Jewish traditional literature.

ḥaredi (plural *ḥaredim*): Ultra-Orthodox non-Zionist or anti-Zionist Jews.

Ḥassidim Plural of *Ḥassid*; literally 'followers' or 'devotees': Followers of a popular Jewish religious movement which first developed in Eastern Europe in the 18th century, which emphasizes outward manifestations of happiness and joy; the *Ḥassidim* today constitute part of the *ḥaredi* community in Israel.

***Lita'im*:** (plural of *Lita'*i), Literally "Lithuanians": Members of an Eastern European Jewish religious community originally known as *Mitnagdim* (opponents), since they oppose the movement of the *Ḥassidik* movement on ideological ground; the *Lita'im* today constitute part of the *ḥaredi* community in Israel.

moshava (plural *moshavot*): Settlement. The villages or colonies established during the early years of Zionism before World War I.

Naḥal: Acronym for *No'ar Halutzi Loḥem* (fighting pioneering youth): A course of military service which combines military training and duties with work on a kibbutz.

Sephardi (plural *Sephardim*): Literally a Jew whose ancestors came from Spain and Portugal; most of those known today as *Sephardim* are of Moslem country origin.

Talmud: The commentaries on the Jewish oral laws.

Torah: The Pentateuch; the entire body of Jewish law as contained mainly in the Old Testament and the Talmud.

yeshiva: (plural yeshivot): Jewish religious seminary or talmudic college for men.

yeshivot hesder: Jewish religious academies whose students combine a program of religious studies with active military service in the IDF.

yishuv: Settlement or community; used also to descrbie the pre-State Jewish community in *Eretz Yisrael.*

CORRECTIONS TO THE FIRST EDITION

Aman - The head of Aman as of 1985 was Amnon Shahak.

Amana - Was founded in 1979.

Biltmore Program - Was adopted in May 1942, *before* the actual dimensions of the Holocaust became apparent.

Eliav, Arie Lova - In 1960-62 headed the Arad (a town in the Negev), Regional Development Project.

Eshkol, Levi - Was director general of the Ministry of Defense in 1948-51, head of the Jewish Agency Finance Department in 1949-52, and head of its Settlement Department in 1948-63.

Fahd Plan - Article (7) should read: "*acknowledgement* of the right of the states in the region to live in peace."

Holocaust - Adolf Eichmann was abducted from Argentina in 1960. Many scholars object to the word 'holocaust' being used as a translation for *sho'ah*, which means 'catastrophe' or 'utter ruin'.

Knessets of Israel - In the 2nd Knesset *Mapam* received 15 seats in the elections and went down to 11 (not 10) before the 1955 elections. The 11 member faction, which technically remained a single faction, no longer represented a united *Mapam*, but an association between seven members of *Mapam* and four of *Ahdut Ha'avodah-Po'alei Zion*. The two parties ran separately in the 1955 elections.
In the 9th Knesset *Ya'ad* was a one-man faction which broke off from the Democratic Movement for Change.

Land of Israel Movement - The *Ken* list was supported by Aharon Ben Ami.

Ministers for Foreign Affairs - Moshe Sharett served until 1956 when he was replaced by Golda Meir.

Rabin, Yitzhak - Rabin joined the *Palmaḥ* in 1941, returned to Israel from Washington before the outbreak of the Yom Kippur War, and joined the Government of Golda Meir in March 1974. The disengagement agreements with Egypt and Syria were signed while Meir was still Prime Minister.

religious pluralism - The Muslim community in Israel is predominantly Sunni.

United Nations and Israel - The vote on Resolution 3379 of the UN General Assembly in November 1975 was 72 in favor, 35 against and 32 abstentions.